Silver Judaica

from the Collection of the Jewish Museum in Prague

TEXT JAROSLAV KUNTOŠ
PHOTOGRAPHY
DANA CABANOVÁ

JEWISH
MUSEUM
IN PRAGUE

This publication has been supported by grants from
the **Rotschild Foundation (Hanadiv) Europe**
and the Jewish Museum in Prague Foundation.

CONTENTS

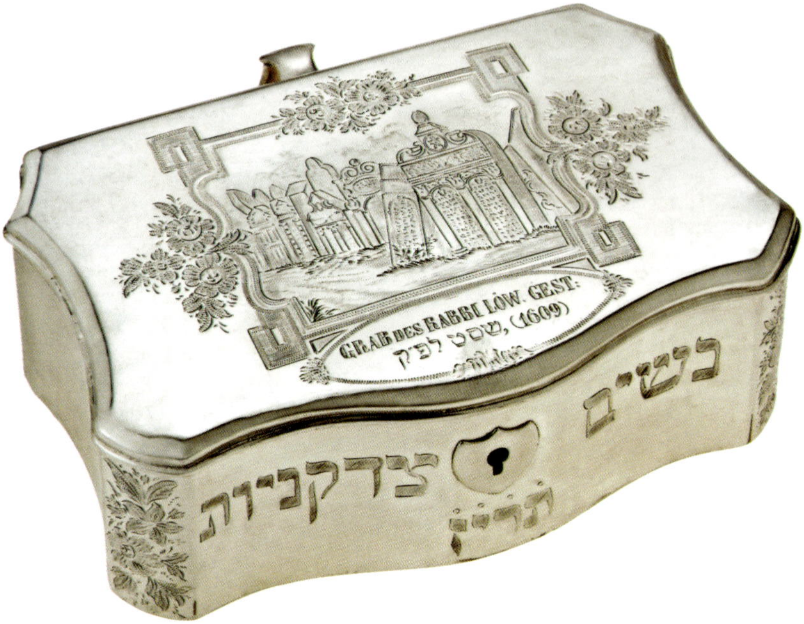

Cat. No. 300

INTRODUCTION

The Jewish Museum in Prague yearly welcomes hundreds of thousands of visitors to its sites. Most are attracted to the fame of Jewish Prague, the oldest functioning synagogue in Europe, and the Old Jewish Cemetery with the tomb of Rabbi Judah Loew ben Bezalel, generally considered the creator of the legendary Golem. Its wealth of preserved artifacts attests to the local Jewish community's centuries of cultural tradition, yet the average tourist sees only a fraction as the vast majority remain inaccessible. Custodian of the cultural legacy of Jews in the Czech lands, the Museum's exhibition spaces are of course limited, and this is the primary reason why only a small part of its unique, internationally renowned collection is available to the public. Part of the long-term mission of the Jewish Museum is to disseminate information about its collections as widely as possible, to specialists as well as to the public at large, and the present catalogue was compiled to help fulfill this mission by presenting a comprehensive overview of one of the most stunning parts of the Museum's holdings: the collection of silver ritual objects that were once the property of Jewish communities spanning the historical regions of Bohemia, Moravia, and Silesia.

The Jewish Museum's collection of silver ritual objects has never been published in detail. On those occasions when a few select objects have appeared in a publication, it usually has been to illustrate a general point or to illustrate what was typical for a given time and place. So the situation has persisted whereby the specialist community and the public are virtually unaware of the structure of a central pillar of the Museum's holdings. A detailed treatment of the full extent of the collection of silver ritual objects, including all aspects germane to such research, is, given the sheer number of objects and the complexity such a project would entail, a task too onerous and difficult for our limited personnel to undertake. Thus we decided to be selective in compiling the catalogue, which will present about 10% of the silver objects in the collection, with the proviso that the objects chosen will come from the entire spectrum of time represented in the collection and that the number and type chosen will correspond to the collection's overall typological make-up. The catalogue, therefore, not only includes objects of particular importance (in terms of their historical value and artistry), but also objects whose value is chiefly documentary. Though at first these might seem far less interesting, they do allow us to view the collection as a complex organism whose informative value is, in a manner of speaking, enhanced by its testifying to a certain non-homogeneity. In view of these aspects, I make no claim for the catalogue being exhaustive, and I should point out that as the author of this study and long-time curator of this collection I could not completely avoid being subjective in selecting which objects to include from the great number of those available.

The catalogue section was compiled and the objects were selected with an eye to what information this or that piece would provide, if its informative value was high compared to the wealth of material at our disposal. For this reason, the catalogue section devotes a good deal of space to identifying an object's maker's mark and hallmark, which have proven to be the most reliable data for determining an object's age and provenance. The donation inscription found on some of the objects are more often than not just a supplementary source of information on who the donor was or on life in the community where the silver object was in use. To rely on the inscriptions for completely accurate information in some cases would be a mistake. Given the idiosyncrasy of local Hebrew abbreviations and customary local usage, the donation inscriptions are given only in English translation and not in their original versions (in Hebrew or another language). To complete this work, archival sources were consulted, but these were largely limited to the 19th century, a period that saw the quantity of information grow significantly.

The sources from an older period (16th to 18th centuries) have been published only sporadically, and the main problem is that the fragmentary archival materials have never been adequately processed, not to mention that they are difficult to access, making it difficult, to say the least, if not outright impossible, to augment the information on extant objects in the collections.

A basic knowledge of Jewish culture and religion, particularly Ashkenazi culture, is requisite if one is to appreciate the significance and function of the silver ritual objects presented herein. Clarifying deep-rooted concepts, ritual practice, religious meanings or functions is not the purpose of this study. It is intended first and foremost as a comprehensive overview of a relatively specialized collection of objects within a closed territorial area. For those who are interested in this topic but are finding it difficult to navigate this material, perhaps it would be best to start with some basic literature of a more encyclopedic character.

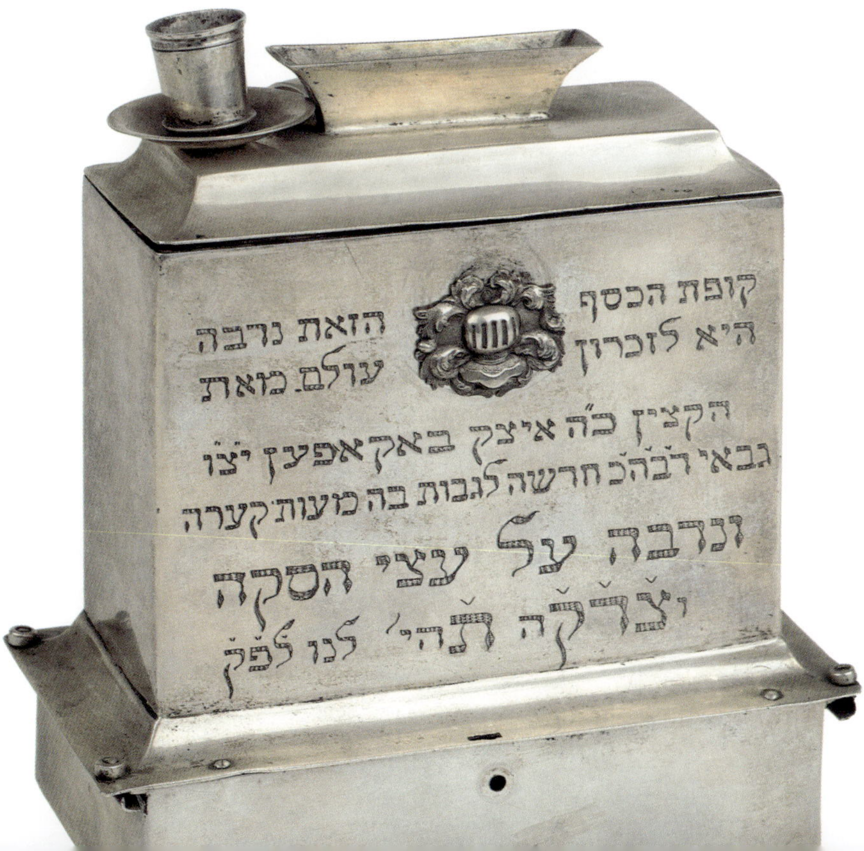

Cat. No. 298

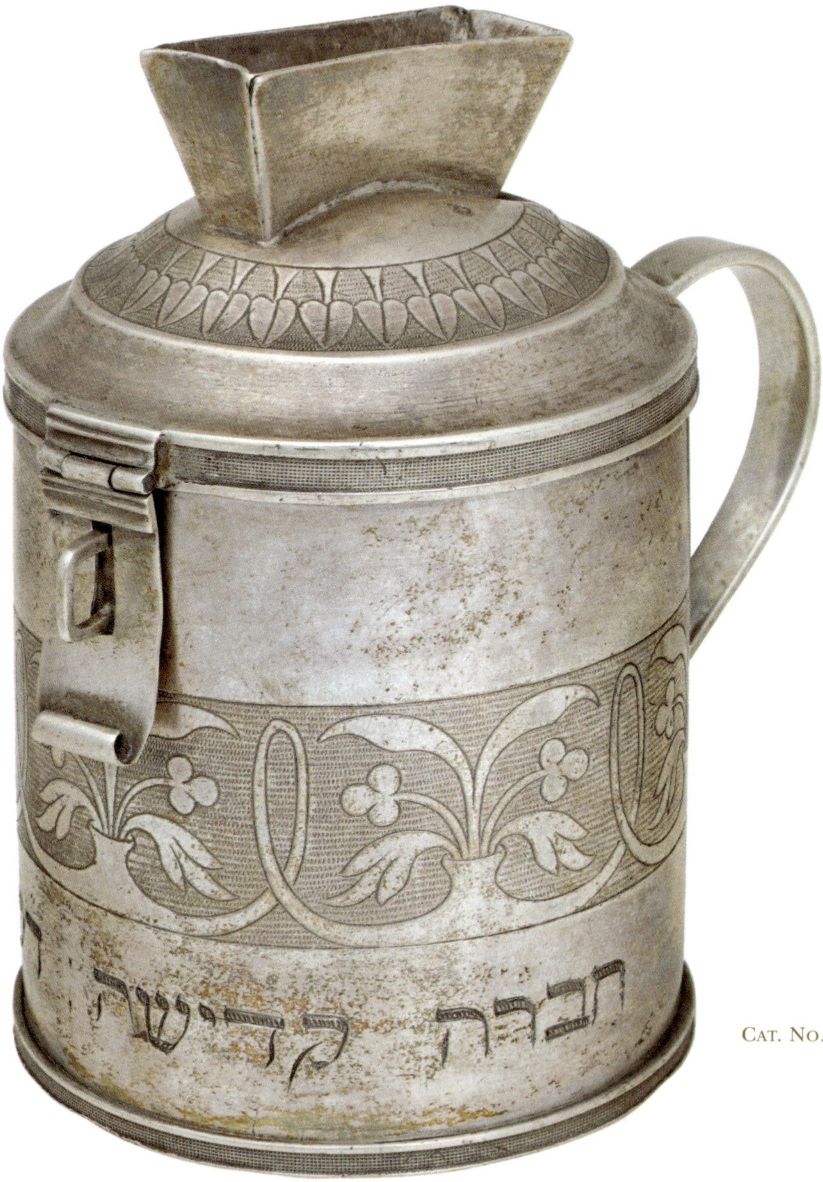

Cat. No. 291

CHAPTER 1

The Structure of the Collection, Chronology, and Regions of Production

The history of the Jewish Museum in Prague is starkly different from other similarly specialized institutions. The Museum's beginnings resembled other Jewish museums established in European cities, but the break came with Nazi Germany's occupation of Czechoslovakia and the creation of the Central Jewish Museum, to which Judaica was systematically transferred from the whole of the territory of the Protectorate of Bohemia and Moravia, as the Czech lands were then called under Nazi occupation. As a result of these tragic events, the composition of the Museum's collection was radically altered, both in the number and the types of objects it now housed.

The collections have a strong regional focus. From the very outset the Jewish Museum in Prague sought to delimit the regional scope of the collection to Prague and the territory of Bohemia. Yet for most of the present collection this was less a matter of intent than a result of how the objects had been acquired during the existence of the Central Jewish Museum in Prague (1942–45). For objects in the part of the collection that came to the Museum during the period of the Second World War, the catalogue of that time gives what is called the collection point, and despite some inconsistencies and lacunae it allows us to roughly match a given object with a place.[1] If the individual objects in the collection of silver were to be classified by place of origin (production), it is no great surprise that the majority are the work of local Prague silversmiths (or from Brno, Moravia), with the smaller part coming from other Moravian localities, followed by the work of master silversmiths from neighboring countries, in particular

[1] These objects were transferred to the former Central Jewish Museum (est. 1942) during the war. Listed on the catalogue cards from that time is the collection point, that is, the place from where the object was transported to the Museum. The collection point must not necessarily coincide with the place where the object was in use, but in the majority of cases it does point us to the general locale. One should bear in mind, however, that the collection point served a larger area where the object was used or stored at the beginning of the 1940s, so this information does not refer to an object's previous history. For a more detailed discussion of this problem see: A Note on the Catalogue.

a sizable group of Viennese origin. Objects from further afield represent only a fraction of the collection, the exception being the ritual objects of German origin, which are somewhat more numerous than the handful that have come from Poland, Russia, Slovakia, Silesia, and Palestine.

If the collection were to be arranged by number of particular object type, the most numerous would be those that are intended for adornment of the Torah scrolls. The collection contains hundreds of examples for each of these object types (with the exception of the Torah crowns). The proportion of preserved silver synagogue objects in relation to one another supports our view on the actual quantity and proportional representation of these objects in the individual Jewish communities or in specific synagogues.[2] Another prominent class of silver object found in the collection is the alms box and charity dish, which were used both in the synagogue and at the cemetery to collect donations of money.[3] Of the extant objects commemorating the activities of the Burial Society, there is a smaller set of beakers dedicated to their annual banquets as well as the combs and cleaner picks that were used to ritually cleanse the corpses of the deceased.[4] From synagogue furnishings there are eternal lights, Levite sets, dishes and containers for etrogs, and other types of objects preserved in far fewer number (except eternal lights). Kiddush cups should also be counted among the synagogue objects, even though where exactly each was used is difficult to determine,[5] as should the set of bells for the Torah curtain.[6] The ritual object most commonly connected with home use is the spice box.[7] Compared to the aforementioned sets of synagogue objects, the number of spice boxes might seem rather small, but the collection contains even fewer silver objects that almost certainly came from Jewish homes (for example, Havdalah candleholders or Hanukkah lamps).[8]

The silver collection comprises objects coming from different periods over a rather long stretch of time, unevenly distributed in number as some periods are more well represented than others. Those objects that have a traditional type of marking allow for a relatively precise determination of production date, even the exact year for the

[2] The collection of ornamentation for Torah scrolls numbers over 650 Torah shields, over 620 pairs of finials, almost 150 crowns, and nearly 1200 pointers. Included in the number for Torah pointers are also those made from base metals and wood; the number of pointers solely of silver represents about 75% of the total. For the other types of Torah objects, the number of those made from base metals is negligible. The numbers are further skewed by the fact that not all these objects are from the wartime transfer; a small number were acquired by the Museum before the war and in the standard manner. In the period following the war, before the Museum was nationalized, some of the ritual objects were given out to serve the needs of the reconstituted Jewish communities in Czechoslovakia. This took place between 1947 and 1948 and it mostly concerned those objects that adorned Torah scrolls. Over the subsequent years some of these silver synagogue objects came back into the Museum's collection as the Jewish communities again became defunct.

[3] The collection contains over 450 alms boxes and charity dishes, about 300 of which are made of silver.

[4] There are 36 beakers in the collection, but whether they all belonged to the Burial Society cannot be reliably determined, especially when no donation inscription exists. Combs and cleaner picks, or combinations thereof in a set, number about 150 pieces.

majority. The oldest of these types in the Museum's collection comes from the late 16th century.[9] In this instance, however, the object, as with the majority of the other 17th-century silver ritual objects in the collection, was made from an earlier silver object. The gradual increase in the number of objects can be traced to the beginning of the 18th century when there began to appear individual types that seem not to have been produced primarily for ritual use, and they become more numerous in the latter half of the century. A sharp spike in the number of silver ritual objects found in the collection coincides with the first two decades of the 19th century.[10] After this period, the growth in the number of new objects stagnates save a slight revival around mid-century, and the last third of the 19th century sees a steady shift to serial factory-produced objects. The end of the 1930s also marks the end of the collection's chronology, and the number of silver objects from this general period can again be counted in solitary pieces.

[5] From the data on the collection points we are not able to determine what percentage of the roughly 350 silver cups were for home use and what for the synagogue. The donation inscription might offer a clue, but on most of the extant cups an inscription does not exist.

[6] Unfortunately, the set of more than 400 bells was catalogued secondarily only after having been removed and separated from the Torah curtains that had been transported to the Museum. For the most part, which bells belong to which curtain is virtually impossible to determine today.

[7] Over 200 pieces.

[8] Why these object types are so few is not exactly known, but household items of deported persons were subject to a different process (going to the *Treuhandstelle*) and were not automatically transferred to the Museum.

[9] Burial Society Beaker, inv. no. JMP 002.925, cat. no. 335.

[10] This was a result of official decrees regulating the ownership of precious metal objects; the topic is taken up in more detail in the chapter on the compulsory purchase of silver.

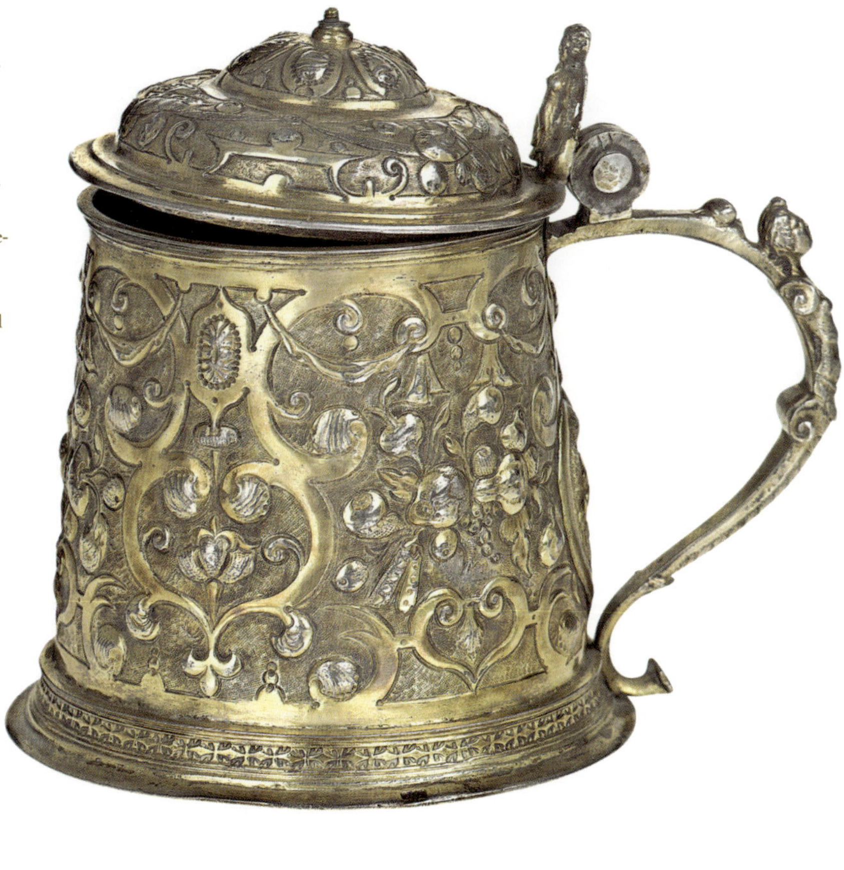

CAT. NO. 335

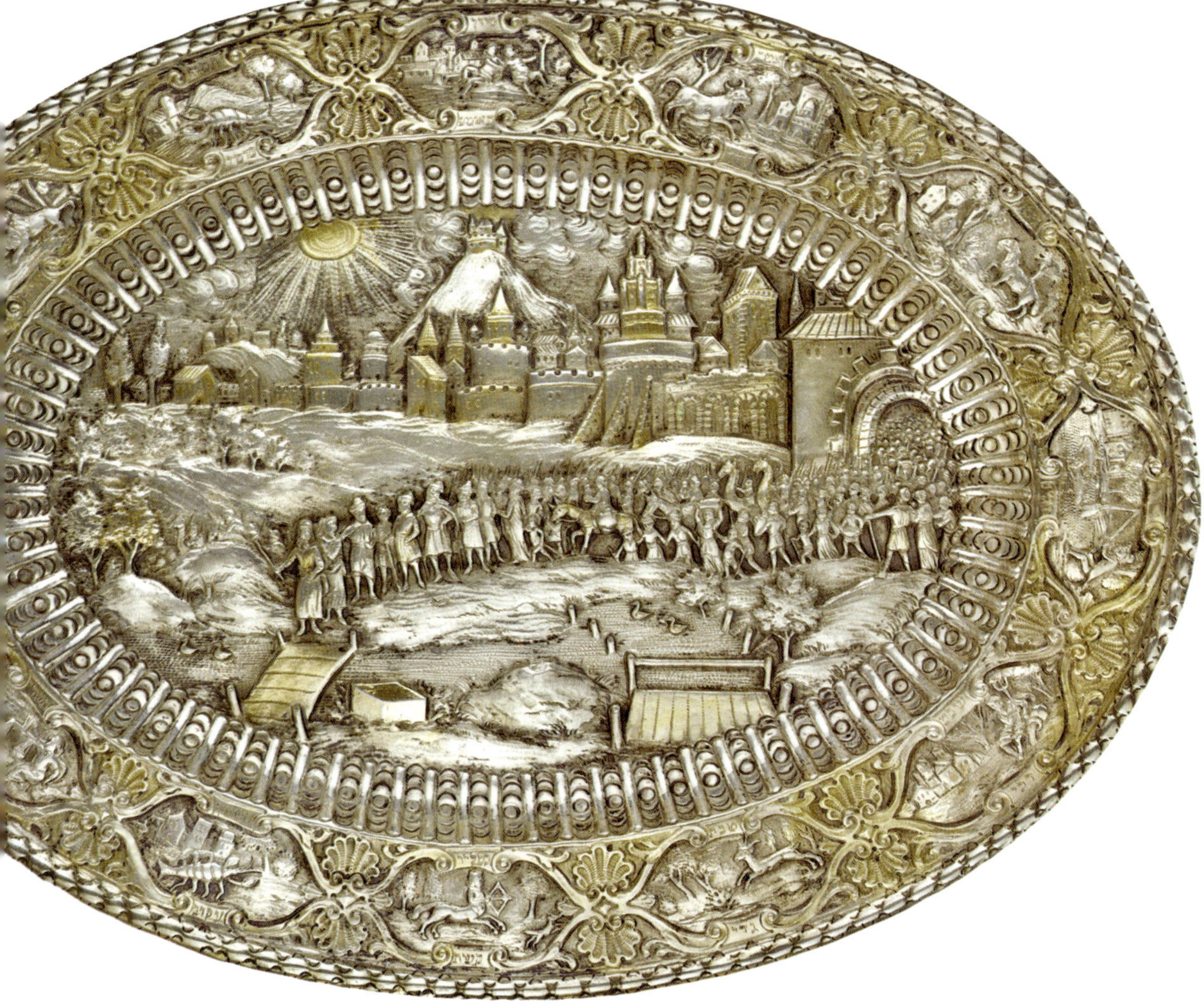

Cat. No. 459

CHAPTER 2

Silver Objects of Foreign Make in the Jewish Museum's Collection

In addition to the work of domestic production, both Christian and Jewish, the collection contains silver ritual objects of master craftsmen from neighboring lands. Yet this fact is not surprising given the personal and business contacts of members of the Jewish communities.[1] How and when an object came to the territory of Bohemia or Moravia is usually difficult to ascertain with any specificity. Often it was the case that between when an object was produced, relatively easy to determine by the maker's mark or hallmark, when there is one, and when it was donated as given in the inscription a great deal of time had elapsed, during which gap the object's exact fate is difficult to know.[2]

The majority of silver Judaica produced beyond the borders of Bohemia, Moravia, and Silesia comes from Vienna. This is understandable as the city was, until the last two decades of the time frame under discussion here, the capital of the Austro-Hungarian Empire, to which the historical Czech lands belonged, which means that inside the empire there were no territorial barriers inhibiting commerce and distribution. The oldest extant object in the collection with Viennese provenance is a beaker for the Burial Society. It dates to the mid-17th century and is probably the work of Hans Koller, Sr., though it likely did not come into the possession of the Society until the 19th century to replace one that had been relinquished or ruined.[3] The same could be said for another object from Vienna, a Kiddush cup dating to the beginning of the 18th century from the workshop of Zacharias Fayll.[4] In the time period that follows, a Torah pointer

[1] Leaving aside the objects of Viennese origin, which are rather well represented in the collection, the remainder of pieces from abroad is not that extensive. What is interesting is the type of piece concerned and its period of origin.

[2] This is primarily the case for the older objects of German origin that came from the two main centers of goldsmithing: Augsburg and Nuremberg.

[3] Burial Society beaker, inv. no. JMP 002.704, not included in catalogue.

[4] Kiddush cup, inv. no. JMP 003.597, not included in catalogue.

from 1784–1794 is undeniably a ritual object and evidently comes from the workshop of Ignaz Schubert.[5] From the beginning of the 19th century the number of silver ritual objects in the collection produced by Viennese silversmiths grew slowly before later experiencing a significant spike.[6] Of the Judaica largely produced by renowned Viennese silversmiths, ornaments for the Torah scrolls are the more numerous (predominantly Torah pointers) and Kiddush cups.[7] Another influx of Viennese silver Judaica can be approximately dated to the 1840–1860 period, in which Torah ornaments again predominate.[8] The objects from Vienna in the collection that date to the last third of the 19th century and the beginning of the 20th century were factory produced and for the most part come from the catalogues of Judaica offered by large Viennese companies, for whom manufacturing Jewish ritual objects was only a small part of their overall production. Typical examples of these producers are the Vincenz Czokally Company (later co-owner of the company Würbel&Czokally) and Hermann Südfeld (Südfeld H. & Co.).[9] The connection to Vienna was not entirely severed after the breakup of Austro-Hungary and the founding of an independent Czechoslovakia: one of the more recent pieces from Viennese, or Austrian, provenance in the collection is a filigree spice box bearing an Austrian hallmark from the period after 1922.[10]

A smaller set of objects come from the regions of Germany. Only a few of the silver objects in this set can be said for certain to have been originally intended for Jewish ritual use as the work is typical of items made for the general consumer market: small cups, beakers, dishes. This is clearly the case with one of the oldest, accurately dated silver objects of German origin in the JMP's collection, a beaker produced by the Augsburg silversmith Salomon II Spitzmacher between 1595 and 1600.[11] From the rare Hebrew donation inscription giving a much later date we can ascertain that objects of this

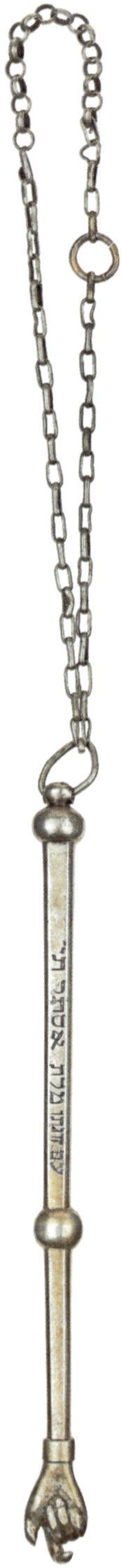

Cat. No. 229

[5] Torah pointer, inv. no. JMP 004.466, cat. no. 182; for the maker cf. Neuwirth (2002), p. 193. The donation inscription dates to 1848.

[6] The reason for this radical increase of newly produced objects was the desire to replace those objects lost to the compulsory purchase program after 1810 (see the chapter on this). Judging by the collection points from where these objects came to the Jewish Museum, those of Viennese origin were mostly utilized in the areas of Moravia that bordered Bohemia.

[7] Good examples are Torah pointer, inv. no. JMP 007.404, cat. no. 229, from the workshop of Johann Würth, 1814–1819, and Torah finials, inv. no. JMP 007.063/01, 02, cat. no. 118, evidently from the workshop of Wilhelm Streithof, 1807. On Johann Würth see Neuwirth, 2002, p. 196 and for Wilhelm Streithoff, p. 240, though the maker's attribution in this latter case is not entirely unambiguous.

[8] A typical example are Torah finials, inv. no. JMP 037.749/01, 02, cat. no. 140, from 1844 by an unknown master silversmith. The spike in imports of Viennese objects during this period might be explained by the stature of Vienna as the fashion center of the empire, and thus the desire to acquire an item characteristic of the work being done then, or at least an item that would have a high value. The same period saw a decline in local production in Bohemia and Moravia for this sector of the market, which in itself might be a reaction to the increase in deliveries from Vienna.

type were originally used by Christians and only later adapted for Jewish ritual use, often without any additional alterations, a practice in place through the first half of the 19th century, a period that saw an extreme shortage of silver Judaica.[12]

If we leave aside the oldest extant Torah shield in the JMP's collection, the German provenance of which is not certain, most of the German produced objects can be dated to the period after the mid-18th century.[13] A rare exception is the simple Torah pointer with the hand carved from red coral, which originated in the workshop of Nuremberg silversmith Johann Conrad Weiss during the first third of the 18th century.[14] Perhaps the most interesting extant objects in the collection of German production form a set comprising a Torah shield and finials, which were created some time before 1763 by the Nuremberg master silversmith Johann Samuel Beckensteiner.[15] From a Central European perspective, the finials are interesting for how they are constructed as they can be identified

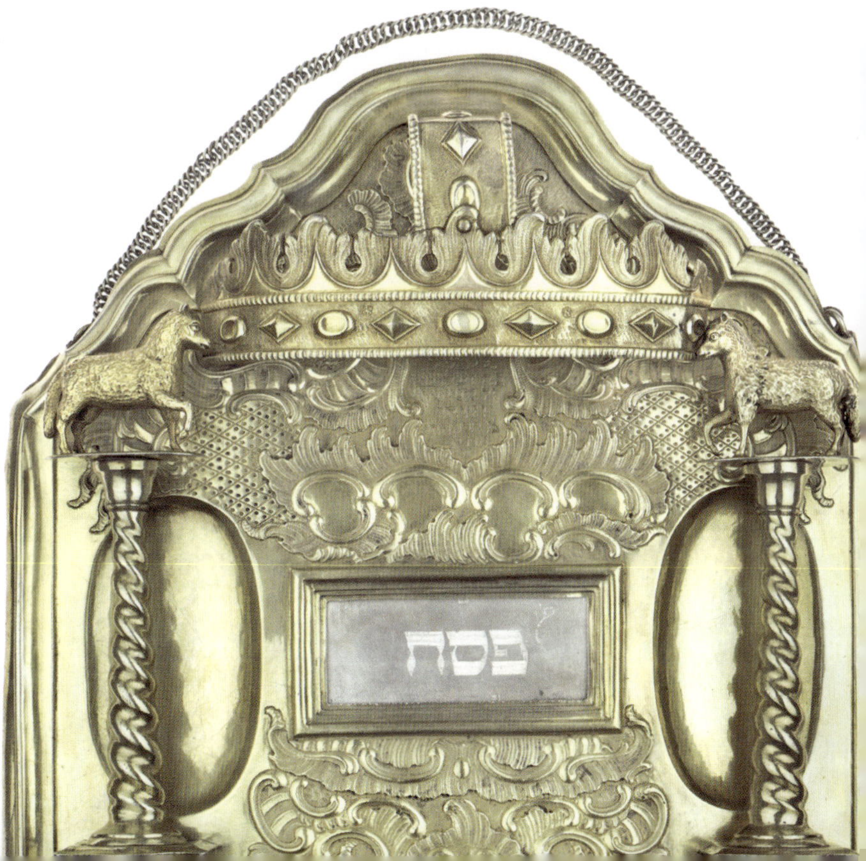

[9] Torah finials, inv. no. JMP 004.423/01, 02, cat. no. 161, manufactured by Vincenz Czokally Co.; cf. Neuwirth (2002), p. 235 and Neuwirth (1977/I), p. 138. Torah pointer, inv. no. JMP 012.648, cat. no. 258, manufactured by Hermann Südfeld Co.; cf. Neuwirth (1977/II), p. 240.

[10] Spice box, inv. no. 177.237, cat. no. 427, maker's mark GB. The spice box was purchased by the JMP in 1998; unfortunately we have not been able to determine when and by whom it was brought to the territory of today's Czech Republic.

[11] Burial Society beaker, inv. no. JMP 002.925, cat. no. 335; cf. Seling (1980/III), p. 67.

[12] See the chapter on the compulsory purchase of silver.

[13] Torah shield, inv. no. JMP 001.739, cat. no. 1. The shield is without hallmark and inscription (a tax mark of 1806–1807 is on each of the three small shields obviously added later). One possible way of dating it is to compare the forms of the ornamental elements applied, and this approach yields 1670–1680 as the approximate period for its production. Yet the same method does not help us identify the place of production. For the ornamentation and composition of similar shields, that is, unmarked, see Grafman (1996), pp. 124–125.

[14] Torah pointer, inv. no. JMP 001.968, cat. no. 171. On the artisan cf. Tebbe (2007/I), 1, pp. 438–439.

[15] Torah shield, inv. no. JMP 044.438, cat. no. 16 and Torah finials, inv. no. JMP 044.435/01, 02, cat. no. 103. On the maker see Tebbe, 2007/I, 1, pp. 42–45. Beckensteiner created a rather large number of Judaica pieces.

CAT. NO. 16 >

with the Western European type without an extended base of the shaft. They are capped by a multisided, tiered head in the shape of a tower with small bells hanging off it, and its entire surface is gilded. The shield is also completely gilded, but what is exceptional is its iconography: unlike the vast majority of contemporaneous shields, it does not bear on the tops of the flanking columns in relief lions or griffins but two lambs facing one another.[16] A smaller Torah shield from the same producer is also found in the collection.[17]

There are other German produced Torah shields in the collection from the latter half of the 18th century, largely the work of Nuremberg masters who were generally known for their Judaica: Johann Jonas Meyer, whose shield was made in the period from 1777 and 1781, and Wolfgang Schubert, from whose workshop most likely come two Torah shields found in the collection that date to the very end of the 18th century.[18] A Torah shield with a Moses and Aaron motif that is probably also the work of a German master from the latter 18th century could also be grouped with them, though we have not been able to identify the maker with certainty.[19] In the early 19th century, import of German-made silver Judaica steadily subsided for a time and only picked up again toward the end of the century, yet now these were factory-produced objects of rather low artistic and technical quality.[20]

In addition to the regions mentioned above, a smaller number of objects in the collection come from Poland, even though contact with this region was not especially extensive. A rather exceptional example of Polish work is a Torah shield ornamented with a cast central relief of a stag and set with semiprecious stones.[21] The great majority of the remaining objects of Polish provenance in the collection comprise spice boxes, which usually date to the 19th century, though several pieces come from the first decades of the 20th century.[22] Judging by the records of the collection points from which the objects came to the Jewish Museum, it was primarily the Moravian areas that maintained contact with the lands of Eastern Europe. In addition to a small set of Torah shields from Galicia, the collection also contains a number of the tower-shaped spice boxes executed in filigree, which

[16] This rare iconographic detail is explained in the donation inscription, which gives Lämel of Touškov and his wife Rebecca as the donors (lamb in German: "das Lamm"). It is unknown if the lamb motif is original or if it was added when the shield was refurbished. Related to it is a donation inscription from 1826 authored by the donor's son, Simon, the freeman Herr von Lämel (1766–1845), elevated to peerage in 1812 for his service in supplying the emperor's armies during the Napoleonic Wars. The inscription does not elaborate how the shield was refurbished. We might assume that Simon von Lämel had both the shield and finials brought from their original locality to Vienna, where he resided, and exact copies were produced and the originals then returned. The copies are today in the collection of the Jewish Museum in Vienna.

[17] Torah shield, inv. no. JMP 013.501, cat. no, 6. Though not dated, the shield also comes from the period around 1760. For other shields from the same silversmith see Shachar (1981), no. 348, or Grafman (1996), pp. 90–91 and for finials pp. 190–191.

[18] Torah shield, inv. no. JMP 079.821, cat. no. 21; from Schubert, Torah shield, inv. no. JMP 002.183, cat. no. 20 (cf. Grafman (1996), pp. 92–93), and probably also Torah shield, inv. no. JMP 001.956, cat. no. 7 (it has an illegible hallmark, but its style corresponds to Schubert's work). Schubert is also the maker of the Torah finials, inv. no. JMP 023.107/01, 02,

cat. no. 114. See Tebbe (2007/I), 1, pp. 274–275 on Johann Jonas Meyer and pp. 387–388 on Schubert.
[19] Torah shield, inv. no. JMP 001.573, cat. no. 19. The shield bears the hallmark HHK in a trefoil and an indistinct official city mark of a gate with towers (possibly Hamburg).
[20] The German-made ritual objects from the end of the 18th century that did appear were probably a result of individual needs to replenish the store of ritual objects at the start of the following century. The number of objects coming from abroad, however, is rather low. When there was a need to quickly replenish objects, the Jewish communities of Bohemia and Moravia largely turned to domestic producers of silver Judaica.
[21] Torah shield, inv. no. JMP 001.992. cat. no. 69.
[22] Spice box, inv. no. JMP 010.205, cat. no. 430, from Krakow, as is the spice box, inv. no. JMP 012.736, cat. no. 426.
[23] Torah shield, inv. no. JMP 001.515, cat. no. 8; spice boxes, inv. no. JMP 174.629, cat. no. 402 and inv. no. JMP 002.934, cat. no. 403.
[24] Catalogued as a Hanukkah lamp, inv. no. JMP 003.790, cat. no. 385.
[25] Spice box, inv. no. JMP 012.747, cat. no. 405.
[26] E.g.: Torah pointer, inv. no. JMP 037.502, cat. no. 269; menorah, inv. no. JMP 173.824, cat. no. 399; Kiddush cup, inv. no. JMP 178.885, cat. no. 381.

was common to Galicia.[23] From the same region come two Hanukkah lamps of the traditional type, what sometimes called a "Baal Shem Tov" menorah.[24]

The collection contains only the occasional individual piece from other regions. Of Russian origin are a few small boxes and filigree spice boxes from the 19th century; from Slovakia come two cups used for ancillary purposes and two very unusually shaped spice boxes produced in Banská Bystrica around 1800;[25] and Judaica from the former Hungarian lands is surprisingly not represented the collection at all. The last group of ritual objects originating abroad come from the workshops of the Bezalel School in Jerusalem and were brought to the Czech lands individually by travelers to Palestine probably soon after the school was established.[26]

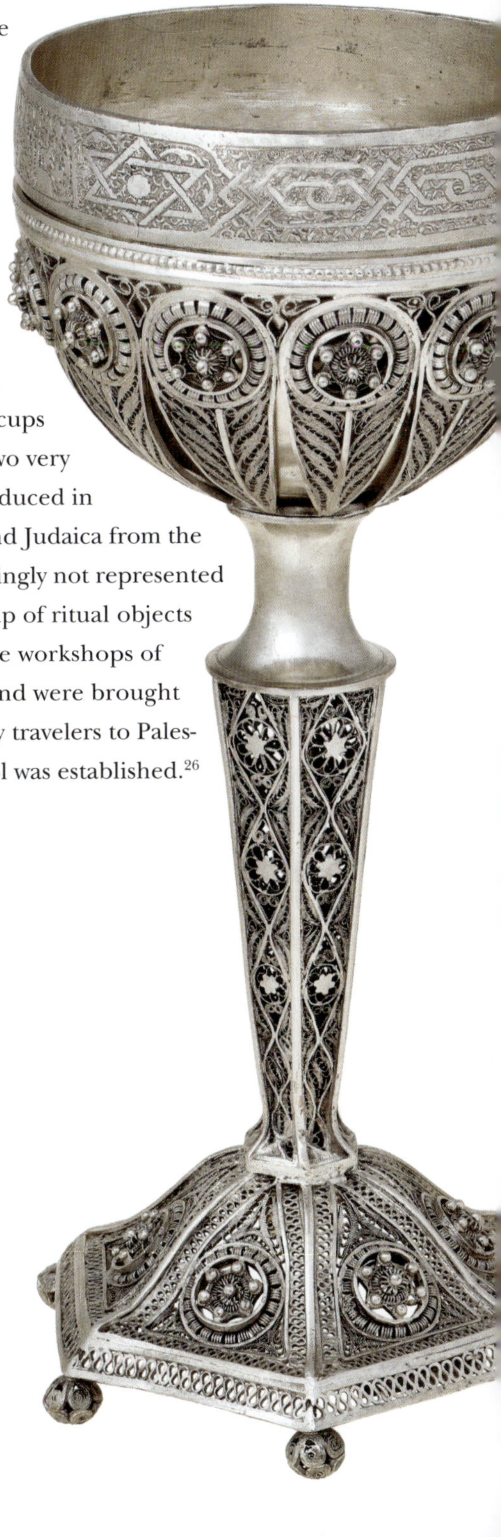

Cat. No. 381

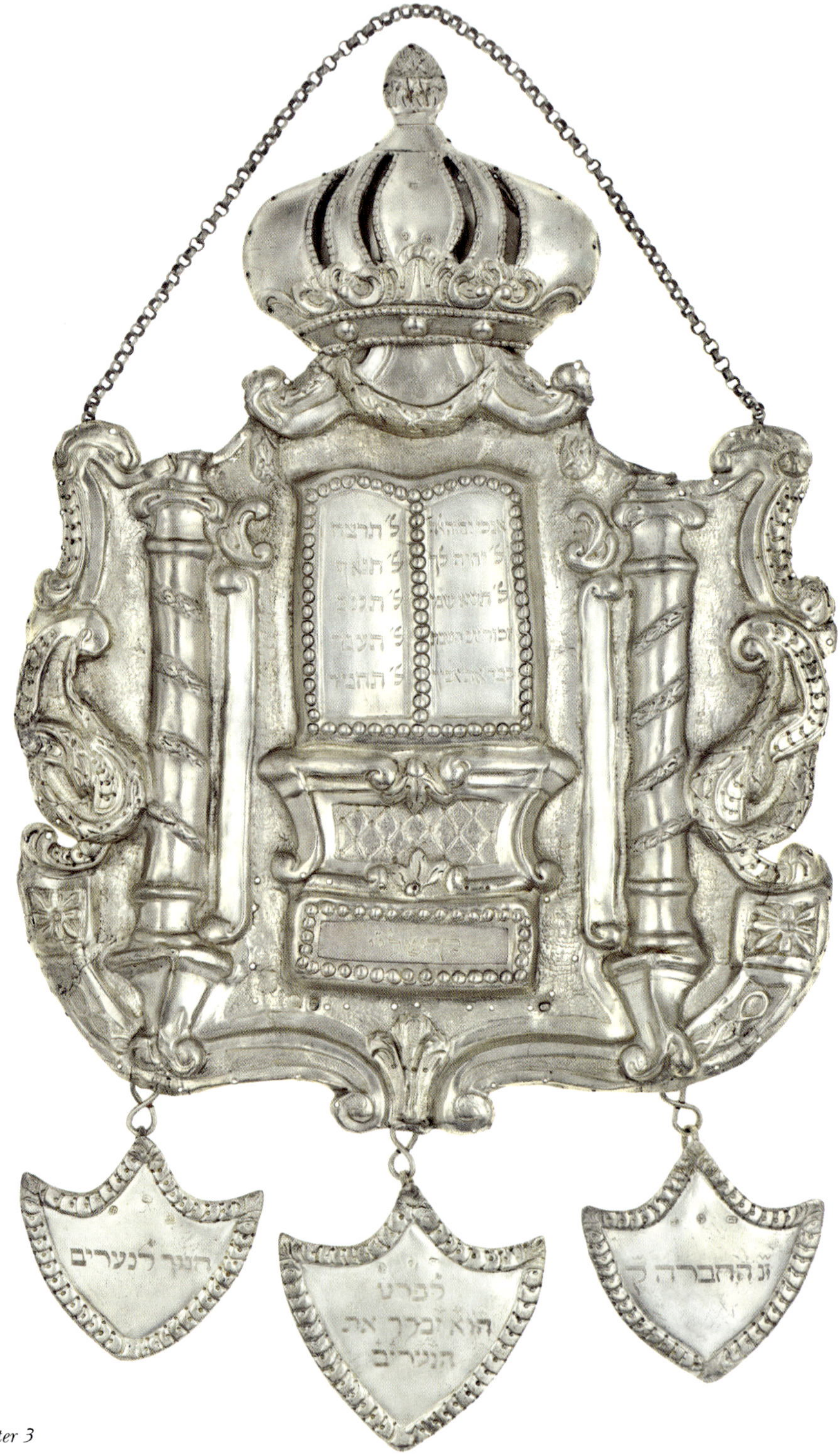

Cat. No. 61

CHAPTER 3

Characteristics and Typical Features of Domestic Production of Silver Judaica

The specific form of the silver objects used by the local Jewish communities and individuals was determined by several factors whose relationship to one another is today difficult to determine. While a relatively large number of extant objects of domestic production (at least in the period under discussion here) does allow us to formulate a general idea about the character of the ritual objects originating in Bohemia, Moravia, and Silesia, one should always bear in mind the circumstances, for which the objects give no evidence, and what information that does exist is hardly sufficient for us to draw any far-reaching conclusions. Silver Judaica in the Czech lands was made by both Christian and Jewish masters.

Jewish silversmiths, of course, were intimately aware of what issues were involved with ritual objects, but we do not know what level of knowledge Christian makers had.[1] I assume the client would instruct the silversmith on what the final shape should be for the object he had commissioned. Unfortunately, we do not know in what manner or in what detail a sketch, or specific written instructions, or sample were submitted for reference.[2] Moreover, it is still an open question to what extent non-Jewish silversmiths contributed to an object's design and iconographic representation. Given the lack of archival and source materials (particularly from the earliest periods) we can do nothing more than speculate.[3] Ritual objects repurposed from objects that were in common use by the majority, such as a Levite set, or cups, or an eternal light, do not provide us with any useful information. Their shape was not dependent on tradition or specific use, and the vast

[1] In my opinion, reliable information on the specific requirements for the form and function of Jewish ritual objects and on restrictions pertaining to their production was probably the reason why there existed only a small group of local Christian silversmiths producing the majority of items for Jewish clients.

[2] I am fairly certain that the silversmith Fleischmann was working from either a drawing or a graphic print as a model when making the Torah shield for the Pinkas Synagogue (see Torah shield, inv. no. JMP 046.075, cat. no. 24). For those who made copies later, they likely borrowed the original, even though this is questionable with regards to the last copy (Torah shield, inv. no. JMP 002.000, cat. no. 61).

[3] The appearance of a new element (iconographic or decorative) does not preclude its prior use on defunct objects which the client or the producer had had the opportunity to see for themselves; thus one should always exercise caution when considering such matters. An example is a pair of the oldest Torah shields made in the same year by the same person (Jan Kogler in 1708), but each

majority were made according to the era's style and general tastes.[4] So when surveying the characteristic features of domestically produced silver Judaica we have only those ritual objects that have no counterpart in the Christian milieu.

The object that offered an artisan the most rewarding opportunity to express himself was the Torah shield. In looking at the extant Torah shields from Bohemia we see a clear conservative orientation among local artisans, and the exceptions do not make this any less obvious. The majority of Torah shields from individual makers (up to the mid-19th century) could be classified as a single basic type. Its shape is square, or slightly oblong, and is capped at the top with a semicircular arch. The surface of the shield is worked with forms in mid-relief, flanked by columns or paired columns with paired lions on their capitals holding up a Baroque-style crown in relief. A box is situated in the middle of the shield on a removable plate and three shields with donation inscriptions hang from the bottom edge.[5] The form of the shield was usually enclosed (with a few exceptions), without additional plastic elements, such as crowns set at the top or the cast figures common to the German work of the day.[6] In some cases the iconography might be missing or replaced by other iconography. Instead of lions atop the columns there might be vases or birds, or the columns under the lions might be replaced by consoles, but in terms of type this is still the same shield.[7]

Objects conceived in such way can be identified in the work of all Christian master silversmiths who to a large extent worked for a Jewish clientele, although in some individual cases they showed that they were capable of producing work of a completely different type.[8] One such prominent exception is the Prague silversmith Tomáš Höpfel, albeit his work does include several Torah shields of the type described above. Even so, from the outset of his career Höpfel focused on producing a very unique type of shield that has no parallel among either domestic or foreign silversmiths. Höpfel used a classic technique to make his shields but their contours trace the form of the iconography used, such as winged dragons with entwined necks and tails wound around the vase-shaped columns.[9] We do not know what motivated him to produce

fashioned in an entirely different manner (Torah shields, inv. no. JMP 004.418, cat. no. 4 and inv. no. JMP 044.437, cat. no. 3). If only one of these two had been lost we would have a completely different idea about the particularities of production at that time.

[4] They are usually only distinguished from objects produced for common use by their inscription either mentioning an object's purpose or referencing the donor or owner. Not even in those cases when the date of production in the hallmark corresponds with the date of the donation in the inscription (the object was most likely produced on order from a Jewish client) are there any exterior elements that would directly identify the object as for Jewish ritual use.

[5] For example, Torah shield, inv. no. JMP 037.594, cat. no. 15, by the Prague master Kryštof Wild from 1762. He was naturally capable of taking different approaches, as evidenced by Torah shield, inv. no. JMP 001.871, cat. no. 22, from 1781, which was conceived with the basic compositional elements in its ornamentation but worked in an entirely different way.

[6] Cf. Torah shield, inv. no. JMP 002.183, cat. no. 20, by the Nuremberg master Wolfgang Schubert from the end of the 18th century.

[7] For birds see Torah shield, inv. no. JMP 037.615, cat. no. 44, and for consoles replacing columns see Torah shield, inv. no. JMP 010.540, cat. no. 46 – both are by Karel Skřemenec from 1810.

[8] It's interesting to compare the two oldest Torah shields, see note 3.

[9] Torah shield, inv. no. JMP 037.922, cat. no. 63. Master Höpfel also created two other similarly shaped types with motifs of horns

these shapes and ornamentation for his shields, that is, whether such unusual conceptions were what his clients had ordered or something he came up with on his own. As he made a number of these shields over the course of his career, it is fairly obvious that his clientele was accepting of such curiosities. Nevertheless, he was alone in creating this type of work, and his death marks the endpoint of such shields extant in the Museum's collection.[10] Torah shields made in Bohemia over the latter half of the 19th century are consistent in form with what was being produced in Vienna, and any sort of individual expression is absent.

Torah shields made in Moravia display much more diversity, and one sees traces of German as well as Viennese influences.[11] One possible reason why the objects display a greater variety is that a plethora of silver workshops were found all across the region of Moravia, while in Bohemia, Prague was the undisputed center for such work, and the masters had various religious affiliations. Unlike Torah shields coming from Bohemia, trying to identify a typical type of Moravian shield is an exercise in futility. A certain similarity does exist between those produced by Brno workshops during the early 19th century, but rather than

of plenty and ample seated lions. In both cases the shape of the shield is contoured according to the decorative elements in the composition. For the lions see Torah shield, inv. no. JMP 037.603, cat. no. 54.

[10] Höpfel died in 1847, and his wife ran the workshop until 1858. The only other evidence we have of a similar type (decorative lions and horns of plenty) from another master silversmith is a Torah shield from Antonín Maroušek, made during 1840–1849, inv. no. JMP 003.745, not included in the catalogue.

[11] The influence of older Viennese work can only be guessed at. The compulsory purchase program in the first decade of the 19th century had the same impact in Austria (a more detailed discussion in the chapter on the mandatory purchase of silver). Only from the 1810s does there begin to be enough material available for us to make comparisons with ritual objects of Viennese provenance.

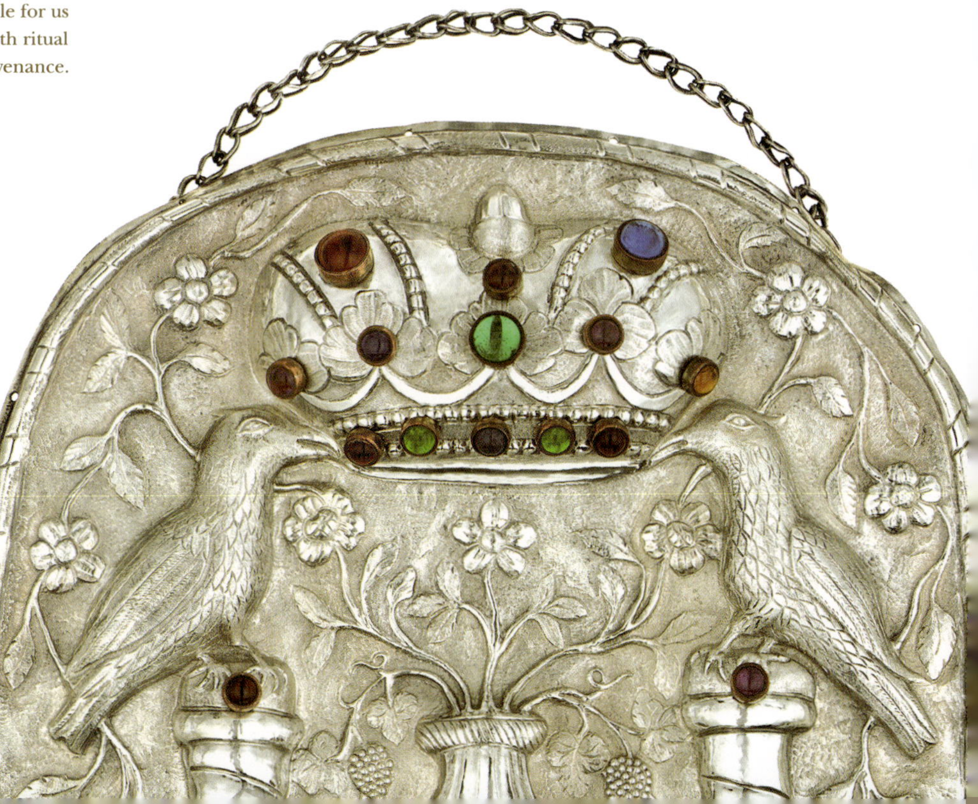

Cat. No. 44

this constituting a general type it has more to do with the fact that the work of the Brno master silversmith Franz Kaltenmarker was commonly copied. The typical shield of this group is oblong in shape and capped by a steep extended arch and closed contours. On the shield's surface, rampant lions on low columns hold aloft a Baroque-style crown. In the middle are the tablets of the Decalogue, under which is a rectangular box on a removable plate. The ornamentation is executed in bas-relief whose artistic quality differs from workshop to workshop.[12] One interesting detail on some of the shields from this group is the figures of Moses and Aaron on low columns rather than lions.[13] We see the use of these figural elements on shields of Silesian origin (Breslau) from the 18th century, and it can also be found on shields made in Vienna during the same period – the influence of both regions is noticeable in the work of Moravian silversmiths.[14] The techniques used in fashioning the shields are relatively diverse. Apart from the prevailing method of execution in a blanket bas-relief, we also see columns extended out and cast lions fastened to the surface. This design also appears in older Moravian work.[15] Over the following century (in particular the first decades), Moravian makers were increasingly inspired by the work coming from Vienna, which ultimately came to predominate in the region.[16] From Silesian silversmiths there is only a single Torah shield in the collection, the work of Breslau resident Georg Kahlert, Jr., from 1758–1760, with an entirely unique central motif of the tree of life.[17]

For the group of Torah crowns from Bohemia two basic types are prevalent: one with curved bands topped by a smaller crown and the other in the form of a closed crown of Baroque shape usually topped by a smaller crown in addition.[18] The oldest preserved crown of Bohemian origin dates to 1723 and has a relatively simple shape with a higher repoussé rim and six curved bands connected at the top and capped by a small crown.[19] The basic form of the Torah crown as described above was later modified by adapting the curved bands to follow the Rococo style and by increasing their number, and this form essentially remained the norm until the late 19th century.[20] The closed Baroque-shaped crown produced in Bohemia starts to appear uncommonly late, at the turn of the 20th century. In the set under discussion, however, the

[12] Typical for this group is Torah shield, inv. no. JMP 012.391, cat. no. 51.

[13] Torah shield, acq. no. JMP 1973/0195, cat. no. 56.

[14] Cf. Grafman (1996), pp. 125-126, 128, presented here in another basic type.

[15] For example, Torah shield, inv. no. JMP 005.346. cat. no. 12. A design with the crown extending out from the surface is clearly inspired by German Torah shields. For a similar technical conception also see Torah shield, inv. no. JMP 010.405, cat. no. 26.

[16] An example is the unmarked shield that probably comes from a Jewish silversmith, dated in the inscription to 1838, whose upper section with baldachin and crown at the apex undeniably shows a Viennese inspiration. Cf. Torah shield, inv. no. JMP 002.267, cat. no. 65.

[17] Torah shield, inv. no. JMP 005.344, cat. no. 11.

[18] In evaluating Torah crowns of an earlier period we are limited to a very small number of extant objects.

[19] Torah crown, inv. no. JMP 037.746, cat. no. 85, from the workshop of Filip Oberholzer.

[20] See Torah crown, inv. no. JMP 038.000, cat. no. 88, or Torah crown, inv. no. JMP 002.164, cat. no. 90.

youngest Torah crown, which was clearly produced by a Prague workshop in 1929–1931, somewhat curiously repeats the older type with arched bands.[21]

In Moravia, the situation was a bit different. The oldest extant dated crown comes from 1769, and its basic form (capped by only a single band) is representative of the German type, quite unique to both Bohemia and Moravia.[22] The only item produced in Silesia in this group is a Torah crown with cut-out and overlaid arched bands that comes from the workshop of Georg Kahlert, Jr., of Breslau from 1761–1772.[23] Other crowns of Moravian origin are extant from the beginning of the 19th century – all belonging to the simple type with curved bands. The majority come from Brno workshops, particularly that of Franz Kaltenmarker, but also extant are crowns that were produced in other localities.[24] Torah crowns were no longer produced in Moravia after the 1820s, and orders from the region for this type of ritual item was largely met by importing from Vienna.

For Torah finials it is easier to determine what shapes were prevalent in both Bohemia and Moravia. The oldest extant finials made in Bohemia come from the workshop of Jakub Kristián Ebner and are dated to 1743.[25] They are representative of a type in use for nearly the whole of the following century: an extended round base in the shape of a compressed bell with tubular shafts segmented by one or two knobs and capped by a small closed Baroque-shaped crown.[26] Over time, this type experienced slight modifications though the basic proportions of its shape remained the same. An example of such modification are Torah finials from 1767 produced by Michal Enzinger, who gave the base and shaft a Rococo ornamentation.[27]

Among the successive groups of Torah finials produced by Prague silversmiths there is very little deviation from the standard type.[28] An exception are the Torah finials made in 1783 by Richard Fleischmann for the Pinkas Synagogue, but in this case it was produced according to the wishes of the client.[29] Another exception are the finials made in neoclassical style by an unknown Prague master silversmith with the initials AK in 1786, but even here the artisan only replaced the crown at the top with a rosette.[30] More significant changes in the shape of finials came

[21] Torah crown, inv. no. JMP 017.561, cat. no. 98, and Torah crown, inv. no. JMP 044.295, cat. no. 99.

[22] Torah crown, inv. no. JMP 005.331, cat. no. 87. The crown is the work of Jan Michal Kaltenmarker of Brno. Of his work for Jewish clients only a single set of Torah adornments has been preserved, making it impossible to determine to what extent he worked in this style. Also see note 39.

[23] Torah crown, inv. no. JMP 005.332, cat. no. 86. For a nearly identical crown from the same maker see Grafman (1996), pp. 265-266.

[24] Torah crown, inv. no. JMP 007.157, cat. no. 91, from the workshop of a yet unidentified Jihlava master IB from 1821.

[25] Torah finials, inv. no. JMP 037.563/ 01, 02, cat. no. 101.

[26] This type could be seen as a modification of the Galician type, which usually does not have any sort of element segmenting the shaft and has a round ball at the top instead of a crown.

[27] Torah finials, inv. no. JMP 037.572/01, 02, cat. no. 104. The artisan made another, completely identical set of finials in 1769 (inv. no. JMP 037.571/01, 02, not in catalogue).

[28] Very similar in shape are Torah finials, inv. no. JMP 044.405/01, 02, cat. no. 106, by Jan Jiří Brullus in 1769, or Torah finials, inv. no. JMP 005.037/01, 02, cat. no. 109, by Michal Enzinger from 1780, and the work of other master silversmiths from the early 19th century.

[29] Torah finials, inv. no. JMP 046.002/01, 02, cat. no. 110; for more see the chapter on Christian makers of Judaica.

[30] Torah finials, inv. no. JMP 032.404/01, 02, cat. no. 111.

with the decline in demand for ritual objects over the first half of the 19th century as producers during this time tried to keep up with what was being ordered from Vienna.[31] The Prague silversmith Jan Novotný came up with a relatively original design for Torah finials, which were outfitted with boat-shaped leaves extending out and off which dangle small bells.[32] Over the last third of the 19th century and the beginning of the next the remaining silversmiths in Bohemia were entirely taken over by the Viennese types with either the bulbous or spherical top adorned by a cut-out or chased flower motif.[33] Only a single pair of finials – made in the early 20th century in Art-Nouveau style by unknown master JM – diverges from this relatively uniform group.[34]

What the majority of Torah finials produced in Moravia looked like is shown by the oldest extant pair, which comes from neighboring Silesia circa 1732–1737, made by the master silversmith Georg Kahlert, Jr., of Breslau.[35] This type has an extended base, tubular shaft with a central knob, and is capped by a small crown formed by curved bands.[36] This is an isolated case; there is no evidence (given the absence of extant material) that such a type was in wider circulation at that time. As these finials lack a donation inscription, we do not know when they were brought to Moravia. Comparing them with the majority of extant Torah finials produced in Moravia, however, it is clear that the Kahlert type of finial was adopted.[37] Its dissemination was thanks largely to Christian master silversmiths in Brno over the first decades of the 19th century. Slightly simplifying the form, their workshops produced numerous sets of virtually identical finials.[38] Of the older finials (18th century) whose shape differs, we could add a pair of the Galician type, dated in the donation inscription to 1749 (though their Moravian provenance is unclear), and a pair coming from the Brno workshop of Jan Michal Kaltenmarker in 1769.[39] An interesting example of the influence of work from Galicia on Moravian objects is two pairs of Torah finials produced in the area around Jihlava in 1800 by a Jewish master silversmith known only by the initials MG.[40] A small, but important group in terms of its divergence from the common type come from North Moravian silversmiths, whose finials are identified by their very wide base and thin shaft with spiraling, chased ornamentation and

[31] This is seen particularly by contrasting finials with a smooth shaft and those segmented by rings adorned with a chased tiny flower motif. Cf., for example, Torah finials, inv. no. JMP 037.749/01, 02, cat. no. 140 from Vienna in 1844 with Torah finials, inv. no. JMP 009.788/01, 02, cat. no. 146 from the workshop of Jan Novotný circa 1850–1860.

[32] Torah finials, inv. no. JMP 009.788/01, 02, cat. no. 146.

[33] Cf. one of the more recent extant Torah finials, inv. no. JMP 004.343/01, 02, cat. no. 170, produced by the Jindřich Grünfeld Co. after 1928.

[34] Torah finials, inv. no. JMP 001.675/01, 02, cat. no. 168.

[35] Torah finials, inv. no. JMP 010.386/01, 02, cat. no. 100.

[36] Unlike finials from Bohemia, which were only of the Baroque type with a closed crown.

[37] See Torah finials, inv. no. JMP 010.466/01, 02, cat. no. 115, produced in Mikulov in 1799.

[38] A typical example is Torah finials, inv. no. JMP 004.383/01, 02, cat. no. 129. An uncommon example is Torah finials, inv. no. JMP 004.486/01, 02, cat. no. 116, produced in 1799 in Brno, with the dividing ring positioned lower toward the base and capped by small crowns (these, however, might have been a later replacement for damaged elements).

[39] Torah finials, inv. no. JMP 012.207/01, 02, cat. no. 102, and Torah finials, inv. no. JMP 005.340/01, 02, cat. no. 107.

[40] Torah finials, inv. no. JMP 009.549/01, 02, not in the catalogue, and Torah finials, inv. no. JMP 009.550/01, 02, cat. no. 117.

[41] Torah finials, inv. no. JMP 002.944/01, 02, cat. no. 112.

capped by a spherical top formed by narrow bands.[41] In addition to the aforementioned Georg Kahlert, Jr., the extant work of Silesian silversmiths is represented by finials of an unidentified Breslau master, probably circa 1761–1776, and finials made in Opava in 1810 by master silversmith Oehler. The small number of such work in the collection does not permit a thorough evaluation of their output.[42]

The last group of objects preserved in numbers that allow identification by locale type is the ritual spice boxes. Bohemia is represented by a set of highly unique tiny filigree boxes with the space for the spices either spherical or oval-shaped, sitting on three legs of thick granulated wire attached to a circular base.[43] This type appears shortly after the beginning of the 19th century and seems to have no local precursor or model.[44] These spice boxes are the work of several Prague Jewish silversmiths with the surname Goldschmid[45] and were made over a relatively short period of time (the most recent come from the beginning of the 1820s, and none appear after this period).

A particular type of filigree spice box has likewise been identified with Moravia, and in this case it was clearly a modification and simplification of older models.[46] The spice boxes from Moravia are stamped with a Brno hallmark and were made by two master silversmiths one after the other, thus we can attribute the emergence of this type to the older of them, which are stamped with the initials JR.[47] Spice boxes of this type were made in two sizes. The larger had a cube shaped space for the spices with a small hatch and pennants on the corners; the bottom was edged with full strips. On the upper surface is a smaller filigree cube, and it is capped by a steep cone with a pennant (the cone is sometimes filigree and sometimes full). The legs of the spice box are made of four thick granulated wires or filigree bands in concave form and braced underneath by an oblong or lunette patterned strip of filigree that terminates in a semicircle.[48] The smaller version was without the smaller filigree cube above the spice container, on which the cone was placed directly.[49] The older extant spice boxes can be

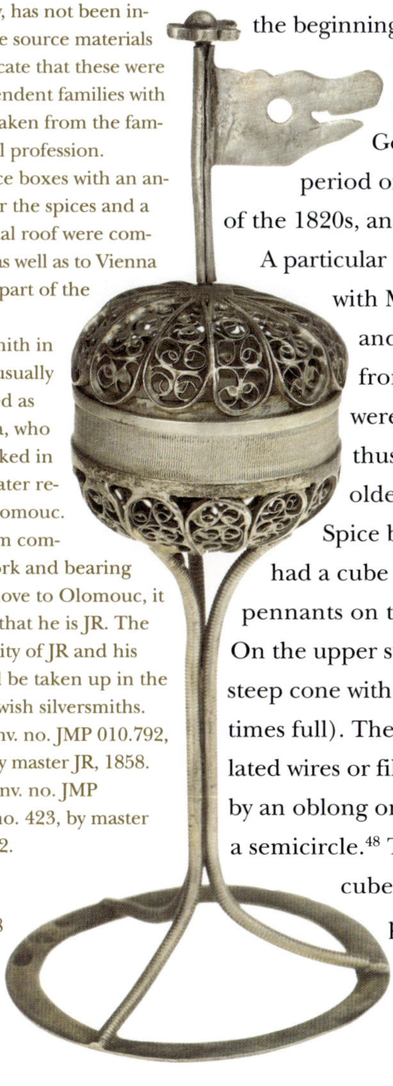

Cat. No. 408

[42] Torah finials, inv. no. JMP 005.339/01, 02, cat. no. 105, bearing a poorly stamped hallmark C.P., and Torah finials, inv. no. JMP 12.188/01, 02, not in the catalogue.
[43] Spice box, inv. no. JMP 037.735, cat. no. 408, from the workshop of Rafael Jonas Goldschmid, 1820.
[44] A distant precursor might be the spice boxes in the shape of fruit on small stems that were common to Eastern Europe.
[45] What their relation was to one another, if any, has not been investigated. The source materials there are indicate that these were several independent families with the surname taken from the family's traditional profession.
[46] Filigree spice boxes with an angular space for the spices and a small pyramidal roof were common to Brno as well as to Vienna from the first part of the 19th century.
[47] The silversmith in question has usually been identified as Johann Radda, who originally worked in Brno before later relocating to Olomouc. Given the form common to his work and bearing in mind his move to Olomouc, it is not certain that he is JR. The possible identity of JR and his successors will be taken up in the chapter on Jewish silversmiths.
[48] Spice box, inv. no. JMP 010.792, cat. no. 417, by master JR, 1858.
[49] Spice box, inv. no. JMP 037.932, cat. no. 423, by master EE, 1869–1872.

dated to 1844–1860, and the more recent from 1864 to 1872, at which point it is no longer possible to ascertain a precise date. In particular, there is the work of a later master silversmith who made many spice boxes of the type described, and one often encounters his work in most of the collections focused on Judaica.

Paradoxically, gleaning how the members of the Jewish communities in a given era typically perceived the form and function of other types of ritual objects in the Museum's collection with provenance in Bohemia, Moravia, and Silesia is nearly impossible given the paucity of such material (leaving aside those types of ritual objects that were easily adapted from more luxurious objects of daily use by the majority population or objects serving similar uses in the Christian milieu and reflecting only the general tastes of the day).[50] This might seem surprising given the breadth of the Jewish Museum in Prague's collection of silver, but if local demand is taken together with the requirements of specific Jewish use, then in many cases we discover that really only a minimum of a given type of object in the collection meets both conditions.[51]

In conclusion, it should be kept in mind that this brief typological sketch of the groups of ritual objects is based solely on extant material, in some fortunate cases surviving several centuries. Given that over the course of time ritual objects were replaced after being worn by use, destroyed, or falling out of fashion, any picture formed of the past will necessarily remain incomplete. Moreover, in Bohemia and Moravia the authorities instituted at the beginning of the 19th century a general reduction in ritual objects, and we can therefore only speculate what factors were considered when Jewish communities had to decide which objects to save and which to surrender.[52] The drastic reduction in ritual objects for the synagogue and home, and the hasty replenishment of their store that followed, has skewed the composition for a large part of the time frame under consideration, and this should always be remembered when interpreting the collection.

[50] E.g., Kiddush cups, Levite sets, the majority of plates and etrog containers, Shabbat candlesticks, as well as alms boxes, eternal lights, etc.

[51] E.g., the Hanukkah lamps. If the selection is limited to just local demand, then only two pieces are relevant, and each stands at one end of the time frame under consideration here.

[52] See the chapter on the compulsory purchase of silver.

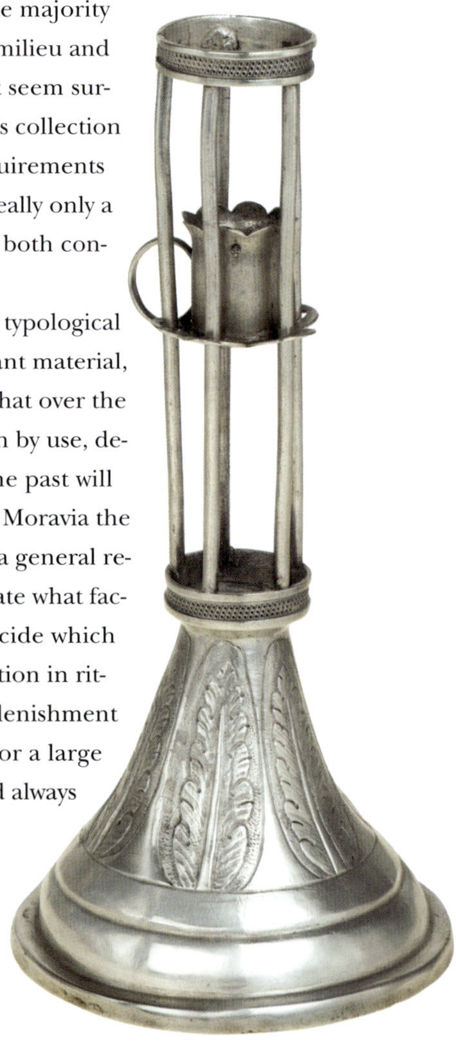

Cat. No. 389

CHAPTER 4

Jewish Makers in Bohemia, Moravia, and Silesia

Only a small part of the Jewish Museum in Prague's silver collection was made by Jewish goldsmiths and silversmiths. Surveying only the extant objects would likely give a distorted view of the extent and substance of their activity. When data in the archive is also considered, then the work of Jewish producers is seen in a different light than what is yielded by studying solely the objects in the collection. I should point out that for part of the period under review here (the 18th century), there is very little information to work with on Jewish goldsmiths and silversmiths. With regard to individual producers, all that is usually given in the register of residents is the name without any further details that might facilitate determining whether the person in question was indeed a practicing craftsman.[1] A more fruitful source is the correspondence between the individual levels of state administration, in particular the reports of the local administrators to the central offices.[2] From the end of the 18th century the primary source material becomes more copious, especially in connection with the change in the official attitude toward the practice of a trade by Jewish residents, and in the case of goldsmiths and silversmiths, the new law on hallmarking that came into effect in 1806 was also a factor.[3]

Attributing individual extant objects to specific 18th-century producers is, therefore, extremely difficult. It is influenced in some part by the relatively specific characteristics of the Museum's collection, which is almost exclusively focused on ritual objects. These, however, were usually not made for the common consumer market,

[1] Commonly the surname Goldschmid appears, or its Hebrew equivalent Tzoref. But most of the records do not make it known whether this surname comes from the person's profession or his family. And this lack of clarity is further exacerbated by the practice of the son apprenticing in his father's workshop, in which case the surname might refer to profession and family both. That a profession was handed down from father to son is testified to by the records of the Brno regional governor from 1732 in which the name of the Mikulov Jewish goldsmith Isaac Beer appears alongside the information that he was apprenticed to his father (cf. Schirek (1902), p. 45), or the records of the Bučovice governor from the same year on the local Jewish goldsmith Joachim Salomon (ibidem, p. 46).

[2] For this, the work of Schirek (1902) provides some interesting information from the reports of the local clerks on the number of goldsmiths and silversmiths in the individual Moravian localities, including Jewish makers.

[3] The law was proclaimed by a decree of Emperor Franz II on August 20, 1806, with effect from September 1, 1806. See *Vývoj českého*

and thus producers did not stamp their maker's mark, nor did they have an official hallmark.[4] That some Jewish goldsmiths and silversmiths owned die stamps with a maker's mark and commonly used it is documented in the archival sources, as are the rare impressions of maker's marks directly on ritual objects.[5] A maker's mark was reserved for items intended for general sale on the commercial market. Even when an artisan was working full-time on them, in the context of the total number of items produced the making of ritual objects was nothing more than a marginal activity, albeit a rather prestigious commission. Evidence on the form of items designated for the general market is found in the records on the specializations of the individual masters as contained in the official correspondence, the later records on the type of master-craftsman work made by new members of the Prague Jewish Guild, and the small number of these objects found in the collections of other museums.[6] This is largely filigree jewelry and other small objects. As these objects were mainly for the consumer market, only a small portion of the total number produced is extant today. Their value at the time of their making was probably not too high, and for the majority of Jewish artisans it was more a way to earn their livelihood, but failure to mention this activity would make the picture of Jewish goldsmiths and silversmiths less complete.

In the absence of a maker's mark, the only way to determine the authorship of specific objects, or match them with the archival records, is by a donation inscription that uncommonly includes the name of the maker along with the donors' names. These types of inscriptions are indeed unique, and for the great majority of extant silver objects without a mark but considered to be the work of a Jewish artisan, the name remains unknown.[7]

When appraising the number of extant objects and the structure of the collection it should be kept in mind that the intervention of the state at the beginning of the 19th century into the ownership of precious-metal objects (discussed in a subsequent chapter) resulted in radical changes, especially with the preservation of older silver objects.[8] Given that Jewish goldsmiths and silversmiths lacked proper professional training, their work is generally considered to be technically

puncovnictví [The Development of Hallmarking in Bohemia], p. 34.

[4] The mandatory hallmarking that was introduced later at the beginning of the 19th century, and with few exceptions it appeared on all silver objects, helps to some extent determine an object's date and movement, but it gives no clues to the maker's identity.

[5] The statement of the Holešov Jewish goldsmith Joachim Salomon from 1769 on stamps with the first initials of his name and surname (cf. Schirek (1902), p. 65), or the impression of a stamp with the letters MG on Torah finials, inv. no. JMP 009.550/01, 02, cat. no. 117, from 1800.

[6] On the above-mentioned Joachim Salomon of Bučovice (see note 1) the records note that he worked mostly with filigree and wire; cf. Schirek (1902), p. 46. The works of masters who were members of the Prague Association of Jewish Guilds, later the Prague Jewish Guild, are largely in filigree; cf. Hráský (1981), pp. 37-39. A set of tiny jewelry from the workshops of Prague Jewish master craftsmen is part of the collections of the Museum of Decorative Arts in Prague.

[7] This particularly concerns objects whose execution and style of ornamentation suggests the work of a Jewish master craftsman and that bear an unknown mark. The letters in the mark do not necessarily always correspond with the name given in the archival records or the name of a known maker. Therefore, identifying a craftsman could sometimes be misleading.

[8] If one assumes that the overwhelming majority of ritual silver objects made during 1810–1820 was to replace those surrendered by synagogues, then an assessment

inferior to that done by Christian master craftsmen, and thus it is probable that the majority of work by Jewish artisans was (taking this view into account) what got chosen to be handed over to the authorities.[9,10] Therefore, the actual proportional relationship between ritual objects coming from Jewish and Christian workshops and in use in an earlier period is impossible to ascertain. This fact needs to be taken into account in any study of the collection.

Jewish Goldsmiths and Silversmiths in Bohemia

Records of Jewish master goldsmiths in Bohemia appear as early as the latter half of the 16th century, yet no physical proof of their work from this period has been preserved.[11] The existence of Jewish goldsmiths and silversmiths in the following two centuries is substantiated by the register of ghetto inhabitants and by the numerous official restrictions and regulations directed at Jewish artisans to limit or completely prevent their professional activity.[12] Only a small number of ritual objects from this period have been preserved. Taking into account their function, a large number were likely surrendered at the beginning of the 19th century. One exception is a comb used by the Burial Society, which indicates how the work of Jewish masters might have looked during this period.[13] The comb has no maker's mark, and the donation inscription gives 1748 as the date and Hayyim Tzoref of

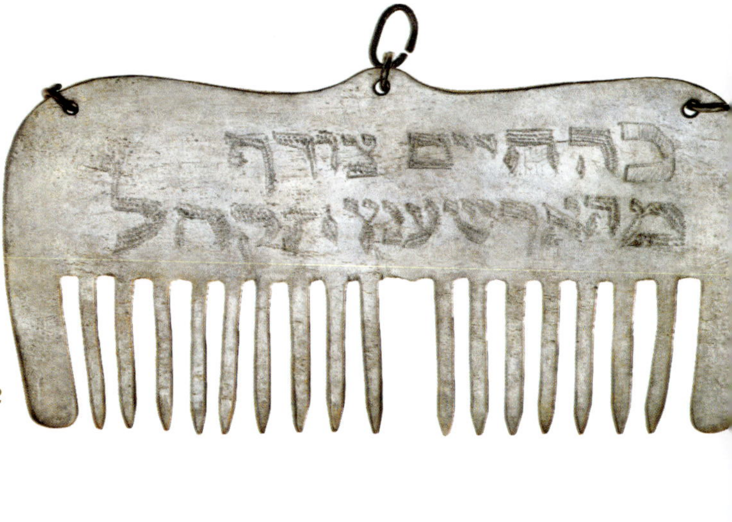

Cat. No. 322

of the extent of furnishings in Jewish communities prior to 1800 based solely on the objects found in the present collection would inevitably yield skewed conclusions.

9 See the chapter on the compulsory purchase of synagogue silver.

10 Inferior technical execution, particularly cracks and porous spots in the material indicating an unprofessional preparation of the alloy, is one of the distinctive features for determining what is presumed to be Jewish work from an earlier period.

11 This is Isaac Goldscheider, entered into the register in Prague in 1560, who later received from the Vice-regent of Bohemia, Archduke Ferdinand, privileges to operate as a goldsmith and to cast metals. After his death, his privileges were transferred upon the decision of Emperor Rudolf II to his son Jacob. Another master craftsman from this period with privileges granted by the emperor was Joseph de Tzervi (deHerz), who received his privileges in 1577. See Brilling (1968), pp. 21-26.

12 The register of Prague ghetto inhabitants from 1729 lists among the other trades 20 goldsmiths (Prokeš, pp. 297-332). For the regulations against the professional practice of goldsmithing or silversmithing by Jews see Hráský (1966), p. 19.

13 Burial Society comb, inv. no. JMP 049.443, cat. no. 322. The donor's name suggests that the comb could have been his own work, but this is not entirely clear given how the inscription is formulated. The material for the comb is of indistinct quality and it's not even clear if it can be considered silver (laboratory testing has not been done). Even so, given how

Hořenec as the donor.[14] Another Burial Society comb is also likely the work of a Jewish silversmith,[15] also lacking a maker's mark. In this case, the donation inscription does not give the maker, though it gives 1759 as the date and has an additional date corresponding to 1795.[16] A charity dish can also be dated to the 18th century (but not more precisely than that). It is unmarked and without donation inscription, but judging by the way it was made, it also is the work of a Jewish craftsman.[17]

Jewish silversmiths operated under more favorable conditions with the ascension of Joseph II to the throne of Holy Roman Emperor and his Edict of Tolerance issued in 1782 that granted religious freedom to the Jewish population. As a result, the Association of Jewish Guilds was formed, which served as an umbrella organization for the artisans of various trades.[18] Its membership also comprised goldsmiths and silversmiths. Other extant objects from the workshops of Jewish master craftsmen from Bohemia are dated to this period. The most informative value are provided by two silver Torah shields. The older was, according to the donation inscription, made in 1789 and belongs to those ritual objects whose inscription contains information about the maker.[19] The artisan is Elia Tzoref, a Jewish goldsmith from Kolín who stamped his finished work with the maker's mark MK.[20] The second shield, according to the donation inscription, comes from 1794 and has no maker's mark. Judging by the way it was executed (with the inscription chased) and the type of ornamentation applied, it is also the work of Elia Tzoref.[21] Why both shields were preserved (despite the purchase program) is unknown as there is very little material from other Jewish artisans with which to compare these pieces. If we compare the Tzoref Torah shields to similar shields from Christian masters, which were exempted from the compulsory transfer to the state treasury, the work of the Jewish master is clearly of a somewhat lesser artistic quality. The question remains whether and how donors considered this fact. An explanation for why these two shields were preserved might be the relatively short time that had elapsed from the time they were made and the deadline to surrender silver objects (twenty-one years in the case of the

exceptional it is, the comb has been included in the catalogue.

[14] Hořenec presently forms a municipality with Nezabylice, by Chomutov. A Jewish settlement from the end of the 17th century has been documented here.

[15] Burial Society comb, inv. no. JMP 037.731, cat. no. 323.

[16] The later dating is clearly for when the comb was repaired or altered.

[17] Charity dish, inv. no. JMP 037.771, cat. no. 320. It is not clear, however, if the dish actually originated in Bohemia. It was catalogued as such with respect to the locality from where it came to the Jewish Museum.

[18] Jewish guilds followed the model of Christian guilds and are listed in the records as early as the mid-17th century (the extant symbol of the guild of Jewish butchers is dated to 1620); their activity was by and large limited to their own community and did not extend beyond the confines of the ghetto. Cf. Wischnitzer, p. 152 and note. With regards to several organizational matters, the Association of Jewish Guilds was under the supervision of the members of Christian guilds, but in its relationship with state administrators it was considered an officially separate entity.

[19] Torah shield, inv. no. JMP 004.048, cat. no. 25.

[20] Elia Tzoref (Kolman), Goldarbeiter; cf. Register of Jewish Families, 1793, II, p. 63. The surname Kolman explains the presence of the letter "K" in the mark, though the first initial does not correspond to the maker's name. See note 7.

[21] Torah shield, inv. no. JMP 000.865, cat. no. 27.

older shield).[22] The buy-back of these objects, therefore, might have been arranged by the original donors. Three Torah pointers dating roughly to the same period should also be included with these shields (given the locality from where they came and their similarity of form) as possibly coming from Tzoref's workshop.[23]

In the collection is another set of Torah pointers without maker's marks, which according to a subsequent tax mark dates to the turn of the 19th century. Their specific form differs from the standard pointers made by Christian craftsmen, so they might very well have come from Jewish workshops.[24] Among objects without a mark that were made in the same period, roughly around the turn of the 19th century, there are those that are highly likely to have come from the workshops of Jewish goldsmiths and silversmiths. One such object is the silver personal seal with the haft in the shape of a rampant lion.[25] A Torah shield with clumsily chased ornamentation in the style of folk embroidery also almost certainly came from a Jewish workshop.[26] Prague Jewish goldsmiths and silversmiths soon grew disenchanted with being part of an association of guilds and began to consider forming their own separate guild. Its establishment was permitted by a decree of February 28, 1805, and the first meeting of the new guild was held on April 7, 1805.[27] The guild began with eleven master craftsmen, most of whom came from the association of guilds, but a few had joined the new guild directly.[28] The guild was in operation until all guild organizations were abolished in 1859.

Because a separate Jewish guild was already in existence at the time the new law on hallmarking was passed, we know the maker's marks of its members almost in their entirety from the time of the guild's establishment until it became defunct. During the founding meeting of the guild in 1805, the craftsmen present formally affirmed that they will adhere to the established regulation on using a maker's mark, though inspection imprints of the marks, however, were not required.[29] But after the Assay Office was established, guild members were requested at a meeting on December 7, 1806 to provide a sample impression of their die stamp on copper plates and the name affiliated with it.[30]

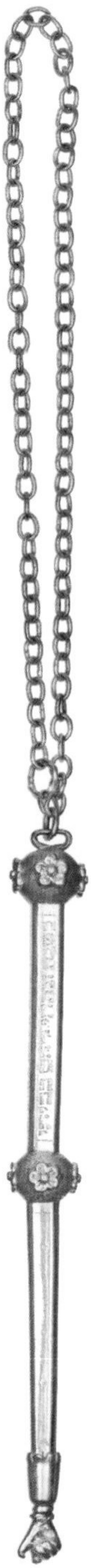

Cat. No. 177

[22] The injunction for handing over silver objects owned by synagogues was issued on January 17, 1810; see the chapter on the compulsory purchase of silver.

[23] The pointers have an identical material composition and are very similar in the shape of the hand. Also, the collection point is given as Kolín: Torah pointer, inv. no. JMP 004.104, dated in the donation inscription to 1791, cat. no. 183; Torah pointer, inv. no. JMP 004.028, with a later donation inscription, cat. no. 177; and Torah pointer, inv. no. JMP 004.042, without inscription and with illegible maker's mark, not included in the catalogue. Attribution to this artisan remains hypothetical.

[24] One should exercise caution here: the absence of a maker's mark does not guarantee they came from a Jewish artisan, and the subsequent tax mark from 1806–1807 does not indicate that the object was made in a given region. See, e.g., Torah pointer, inv. no. JMP 012.587, cat. no. 186.

[25] Personal seal, inv. no. JMP 012.792, cat. no. 437.

[26] Torah shield, inv. no. JMP 001.840, cat. no. 29.

[27] See Hráský (1966), pp. 29-30.

[28] See Hráský (1981), the commentary on the individual Jewish masters.

[29] See Hráský (1966), p. 103.

[30] Ibidem.

It is not known whether these impressions were actually submitted as physical proof of such has not been preserved. Until just recently there was at the Prague Assay Office a preserved oblong copper plate with the engraved inscription: *Verzeichnis der Prager israelitischen Goldarbeitermeistern 1807*, the name of the masters and their embossed mark.[31] This knowledge of the maker's marks of Prague Jewish masters from the 19th century allows us to match particular extant objects with specific names.

In evaluating the work of Prague Jewish guild masters found in the JMP's collection it is important to remember that this probably does not represent a cross-section of their characteristic work. The greatest number of objects in the collection comes from the years 1810–1820, which corresponds to the period when silver ritual objects were quickly replenished both in the synagogue and at home.[32] Objects from Prague Jewish craftsmen appear later only sporadically, the larger objects in particular, Torah shields and finials, being, with only a few exceptions, left to Christian masters to make. Likewise, extant records on test and master pieces of the individual artisans clearly indicate that they primarily concentrated on making jewelry, which had more mass appeal and was easier to sell.[33] So a more significant contribution by Jewish masters in producing ritual objects must be considered as having been within a limited period of time. For the majority of Prague Jewish guild members there are no extant ritual objects coming from their workshops, and it's likely that they were not even focused on producing any, giving priority instead to ordinary clients.[34]

The most typical object produced by Prague Jewish masters is the filigree spice box, known largely by an almost identical form that was characteristic of those made by the Goldschmid family (Gabriel Goldschmid, Michal Samuel Goldschmid, or Rafael Jonas Goldschmid).[35, 36] This type of spice box had a spherical or egg-shaped container for the spices capped by a pennant and resting on three legs of thick, granulated wire attached at the bottom to the surface of a circular base. This characteristically Prague object appears over a relatively short period, and by the mid-19th century is seen no more. Other types of representative ritual objects are above all Torah pointers, mostly from the

[31] Ibidem. The plate was, along with a similar plate of the same date with the names of Christian masters, stored at the Prague Assay Office. In the 1960s it was researched by PhDr. Josef Hráský, but today is missing. At the Prague Assay Office there is still deposited a more recent plate with the engraved inscription: *Tafel für israelitische Gold- und Silber Arbeiter der Stadt Prag*, including the impressions of the die stamps of Jewish craftsmen, containing, however, only ten names with their stamp impressions and clearly coming from the year 1853. All marks from these plates, both Jewish and Christian, are published; see Hráský (1981).

[32] See the chapter on the compulsory purchase of silver.

[33] See Hráský (1981). The quality of this information is naturally somewhat compromised by the fact that pieces made for tests at the journeyman and master level were intended for sale, and when the subject of the test was given the subsequent sale of the piece was taken into consideration.

[34] E.g., Samuel Elias (Goldschmid), from whom we have a gilded medallion with pendants, today in the Museum of Decorative Arts in Prague (on the artisan see Hráský (1981), p. 37 and Stehlíková (2003), p. 151), or Noe Simon Taussig (on the artisan see Hráský (1981), p. 99).

[35] Spice box, inv. no. JMP 037.735, cat. no. 408, Rafael Jonas Goldschmid.

[36] On Gabriel Goldschmid see Hráský (1981), p. 37 and Stehlíková (2003), p. 151. On Michal Samuel Goldschmid

workshop of Rafael Jonas Goldschmid, yet they do not go beyond what was the local standard.[37] From the same workshop come the majority of little bells for synagogue curtains.[38]

Given the character and period of his work, the Prague master Abraham David Kuh, who specialized on larger ritual objects, deserves special attention.[39] His extant work, however, comes largely from the last phases of his activity when the market was already becoming dominated by industrial factory production, which affected how objects were rendered. By mid-century the individual works of Jewish masters began, with a few exceptions, to disappear.[40] A special place among Jewish entrepreneurs in the manufacture of silver objects during this period of growing industrial production is occupied by Abraham Bernard Bächer. Though not a member

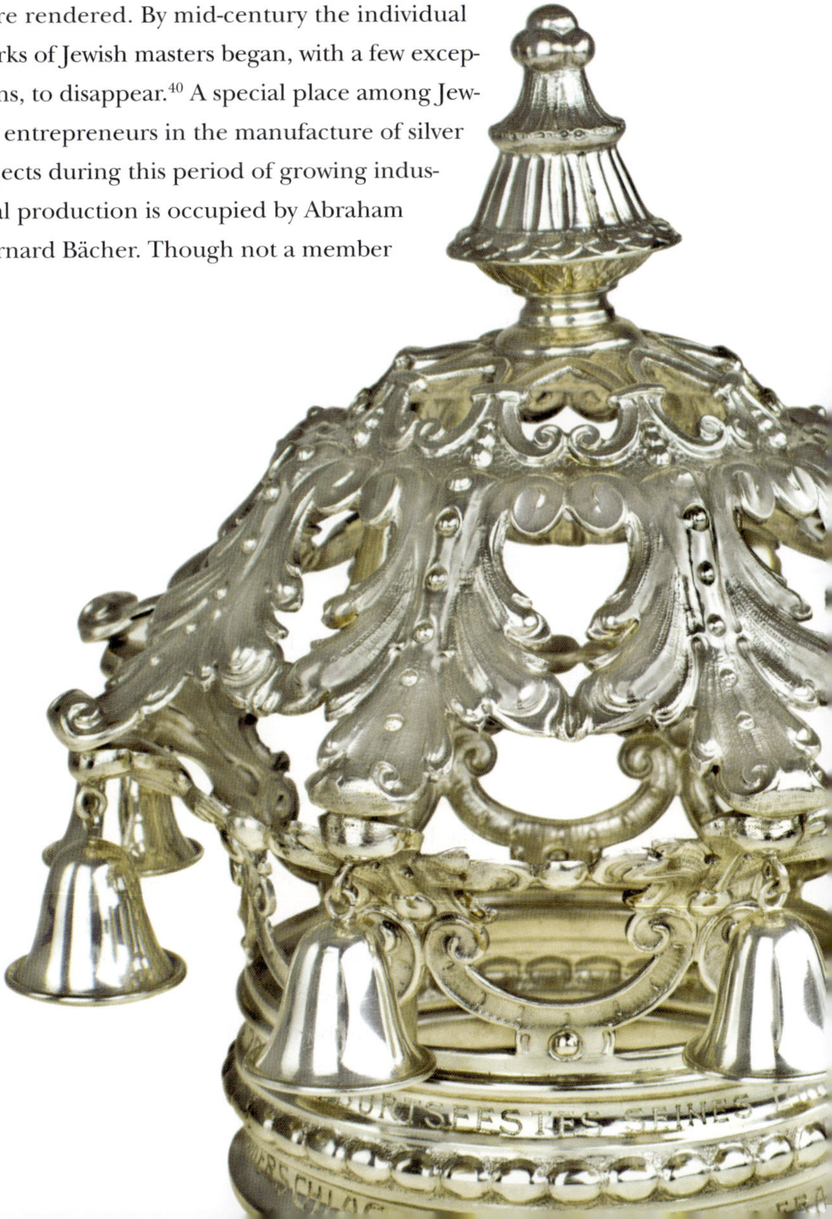

Cat. No. 97

see Hráský (1981), p. 38 and Stehlíková (2003), p. 151. For Rafael Jonas Goldschmid see Hráský (1981), p. 39 and Stehlíková (2003), p. 152.

[37] Torah pointer, inv. no. JMP 010.618, cat. no. 233, Rafael Jonas Goldschmid.

[38] Curtain bells, acq. no. JMP 1995/1164/01, 02, cat. no. 453.

[39] Torah crown, inv. no. JMP 037.443, cat. no. 97; on the maker see Hráský (1981), p. 57.

[40] The production of individual ritual objects probably declined under the pressure of imports of semi-industrial Judaica from Vienna, the rapid rise of which can be traced. For production for the consumer market, not represented in the Museum's collection, some of the objects allow us on the other hand to trace the rapid growth and emergence of large companies. This includes the aforementioned Michal Samuel Goldschmid, who in 1813 established a facility for the manufacture of garnet jewelry, which expanded to a factory by 1840 employing nearly 200 workers, and later as the Michal Goldschmidt Soehne Co. continued its operations until at least the end of the 19th century (see Stehlíková (2003), p. 151). Since we have a company receipt to the Jewish community in Březnice from the latter third of the 19th century for Torah finials weighing 586 grams and costing 70 gulden and 34 kreuzer, we know that the company offered a selection of ritual objects (The Central Archives for the History of the Jewish People, Jerusalem, Israel, Czechoslovakia fund, CS-273).

of the Jewish guild, he obtained a license to produce pressed silver and metal goods, and his company in Prague began operations in 1846 to make so-called "German" silver.[41] In 1853 he opened a branch in Vienna, where his sons relocated in 1872 (probably after his death) the company's head office, and ten years later the company went out of business.[42] The products of the Bächer Co. were supplied in large numbers and range to the general consumer market and certainly cannot be considered Judaica, even if the company's owner himself was Jewish. The cups he produced in particular were widely used as ritual objects, which is justification for their inclusion in the catalogue.[43]

Another who made ritual objects in Prague during the era of factory production was the son of Hermann Samuel Goldschmid, Alexander, owner of the H.S. Goldschmidt Sohn Co.[44] The company existed until the outbreak of the Second World War, and its assortment of Judaica was, in comparison to other producers of the time, relatively varied. The last of the local large-scale producers worthy of mention is Alfred Pollak, whose firm, one of the large jewelry manufacturers in the Austro-Hungarian Empire, was in operation until 1934.[45] Judaica, and Torah shields in particular, were only a small part of his company's production, and they were rather eclectic in form.[46] Given how long his company operated, a relatively large number of these objects from the end of the 19th and beginning of the 20th centuries have been preserved.

Jewish Goldsmiths and Silversmiths in Moravia and Silesia

The situation in Moravia and Silesia was different, and this is reflected in the structure of the collection of the objects coming from these regions. Unlike in Bohemia, Jewish inhabitants lived in a much larger number of smaller settlements across the whole region, with the highest concentration in southern Moravia. This is likely the reason why we have more extant ritual objects from these areas (as compared to Bohemia). Another basic difference is in how these ritual objects were cared for, particularly as evidenced in the number of redeemed objects over the

[41] Cf. Neuwirth (2002), p. 114. The term "German" silver should not be confused with a similar term for ersatz silver. In Bächer's case, he used a technology for pressing silver from thin sheets and then giving them a low repoussé ornamentation.

[42] Ibidem. Other sources give the company beginning in Vienna in 1830–32. Cf. Stehlíková (2003), p. 41.

[43] Kiddush cup, inv. no. JMP 001.988, cat. no. 371, or etrog container, inv. no. JMP 046.041, cat. no. 283, no doubt originally sold as a sugar container.

[44] Torah shield, inv. no. JMP 004.242, cat. no. 79, and alms box, inv. no. JMP 010.868, cat. no. 308. On the producers see Stehlíková (2003), p. 151. As a source, we have correspondence from 1884 between the producer and a representative of the Jewish community in Březnice, from where the Torah shield came; with regards to the order of Torah finials, cf. CAHJP, CS-273.

[45] See Stehlíková (2003), p. 384.

[46] Torah shield, inv. no. JMP 002.397, cat. no. 80; Torah finials, inv. no. JMP 004.397/01, 02, cat. no. 166; Torah pointer, inv. no. JMP 007.038, cat. no. 270.

[47] See the chapter on the compulsory purchase of synagogue silver.

[48] This fact also partially applies to what was produced by Christian workshops and used by the Jewish communities; this includes both objects made explicitly for Jewish clients or, more commonly, adapted for Jewish ritual use.

course of the state's invasive program to regulate the ownership of precious metal objects (1809–1810).[47] In the Museum's collection there are a greater number of objects made by Moravian Jewish goldsmiths and silversmiths from the earlier period, far more than the number of similarly dated extant objects from Bohemia.[48] The most simple explanation is that the Jewish communities in Moravia were better financed, and unlike some Jewish communities in Bohemia they did not have to face during the previous century the threat and then the actuality of being temporarily expelled from their traditional domiciles.[49] Given the historical losses that resulted from the compulsory purchase program, we must accept that this will skew any conclusions.

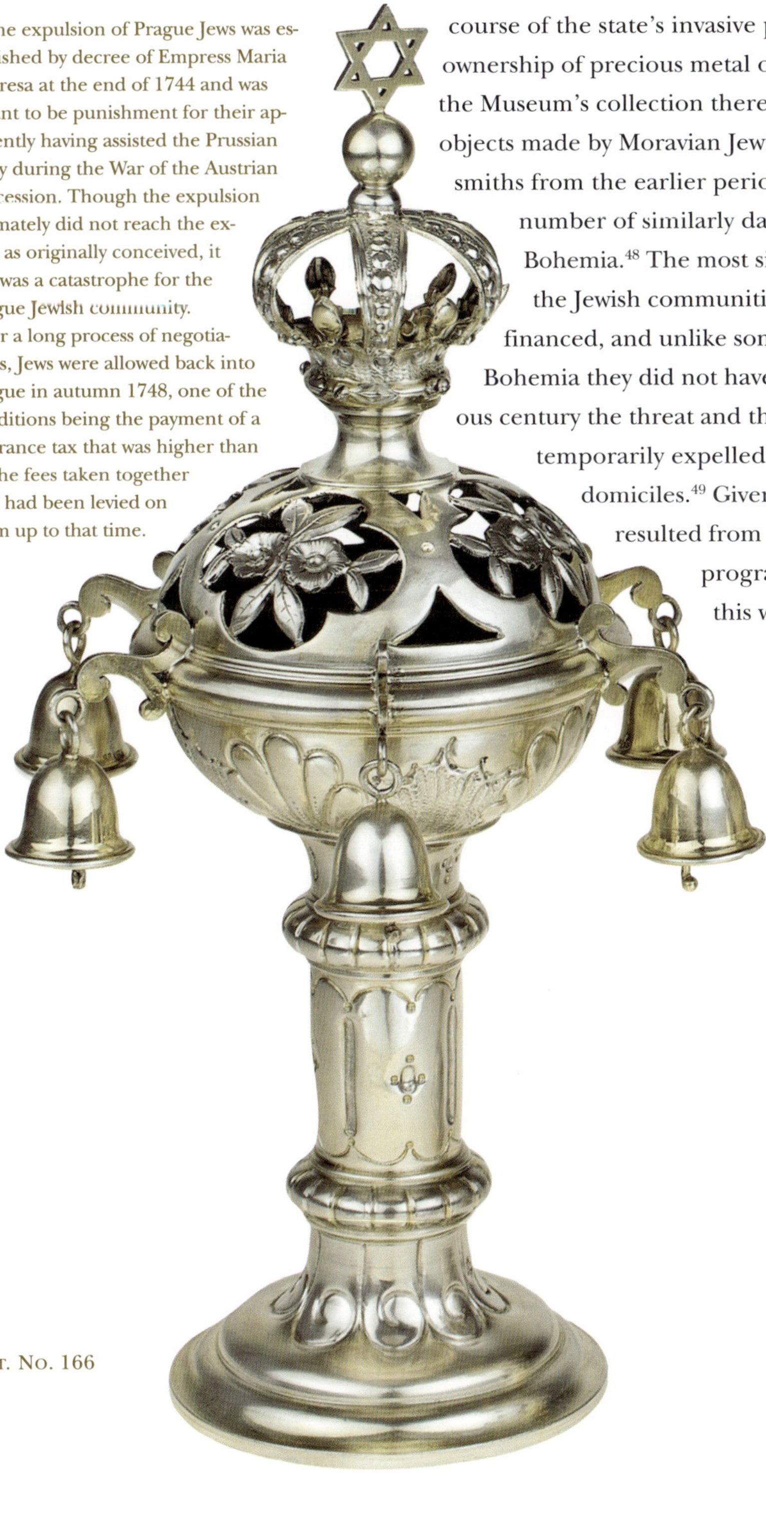

Cat. No. 166

[49] The expulsion of Prague Jews was established by decree of Empress Maria Theresa at the end of 1744 and was meant to be punishment for their apparently having assisted the Prussian army during the War of the Austrian Succession. Though the expulsion ultimately did not reach the extent as originally conceived, it still was a catastrophe for the Prague Jewish community. After a long process of negotiations, Jews were allowed back into Prague in autumn 1748, one of the conditions being the payment of a tolerance tax that was higher than all the fees taken together that had been levied on them up to that time.

The oldest archival evidence on a Jewish goldsmith from Moravia comes from a somewhat earlier period than similar sources on craftsmen in Bohemia. There is mention of an Isaac Goldarbeiter from Dolní Kounice between the years 1583 and 1594.[50] From this earlier period, however, no material proof in the form of an object has been preserved, and the same goes for the 17th century. Yet from this period there are individual records of Jewish goldsmiths living in Mikulov, Slavkov, Prostějov, Jevíčko, and Boskovice.[51] For the 18th century we can use the registry of Christian and Jewish goldsmiths and silversmiths that was compiled in the individual districts at the behest of the central office,[52] and we have out or disposal a few extant silver objects as well.

One of the oldest known works from the workshop of a Moravian Jewish master is a lid to a Burial Society pitcher.[53] Except for a tax mark applied later, the object bears neither maker's mark nor hallmark. The donation inscription that runs along the pitcher's circumference gives the date as 1725.[54] A cast figural group of men carrying a bier with corpse is affixed to the top of the lid.[55] In the absence of comparative material it is not possible to attribute the work to a specific master, but the donation inscription might at least allow one to determine *terminus ante quem.*[56] Another extant object from Moravia, likely the work of a Jewish craftsman, are Torah finials, which, like the previous object, have no maker's mark but are dated in the donation inscription to 1749.[57] The inscription identifies Isaac, son of Saul Levi, and gives the date the work was completed. From the specific form of ornamentation and how the inscription is formulated, we can assume it is the work of a Jewish master.[58] Another object from Moravia whose maker we are able to definitively identify is a Torah shield from 1753 that is published in much of the older literature. This piece belongs to a rare group of objects whose donation inscriptions give both the maker's name and the locality where it was made.[59] The master silversmith in the inscription is given as Joshua Tzoref, son of Maharam Litsch, in the holy community of Třebíč.[60] Another Torah shield from the same locality and dated to the same year is attributed in the older literature to the same master.[61] No maker is mentioned, however, in the donation

[50] Cf. Brilling (1969), p. 139. The term "Goldarbeiter" does not necessarily mean that the person in question worked with gold; it might very well be nothing more than his name.
[51] Ibidem.
[52] Cf. Schirek (1902), individual sections. For a survey of the references to Jewish producers using other sources see Brilling (1969), pp. 139-146.
[53] Lid for a Burial Society pitcher, inv. no. JMP 003.941, cat. no. 431.
[54] Over time the lid was part of several faience pitchers, the oldest of which was made between 1723 and 1724; even though it was not preserved, we get an idea of how it looked from an actual copy made in 1801 (Burial Society pitcher, inv. no. JMP 008.049), on which appears the exact wording of the original donation inscription with the original dating. After the pitcher was damaged, another copy was made in 1836, the second copy (Burial Society pitcher, inv. no. JMP 008.048). Cf. *The Precious Legacy*, catalogue (1983), p. 255.
[55] The technique of casting metal requires a high degree of technical knowledge and that the workshop be equipped to execute such work. Among Jewish silversmiths, the casting of figures of larger dimensions was rare, even though they theoretically might have had the experience with casting fragments of precious metals. Mikulov was the central Moravian Jewish settlement, and the lid is probably the work of a local master. The Jewish goldsmith Isaac Beer (see note 1) is mentioned by name in Mikulov in 1732, and in the records of the town's magistrate from the same

inscription on this shield, and the technique used to execute the ornamentation differs from the previous shield. Thus this is more likely the work of one of Joshua Tzoref's colleagues.[62]

A group of Moravian Burial Society alms boxes with a typical cylindrical form with convex lid can be dated to the mid-18th century. Yet even in this case the makers are unfortunately unknown.[63] Only one of the alms boxes is dated in the donation inscription (1764).[64] Of the objects from Moravia that do give the name of the maker, there is a Burial Society comb and cleaner pick, made by Moses, son of Itzak in, according to the donation inscription, 1770.[65] The collection of objects from Moravia contains two Torah pointers from the latter third of the 18th century, unmarked yet dated in the inscriptions to 1772 and 1786, and they also likely come from the workshops of Jewish masters.

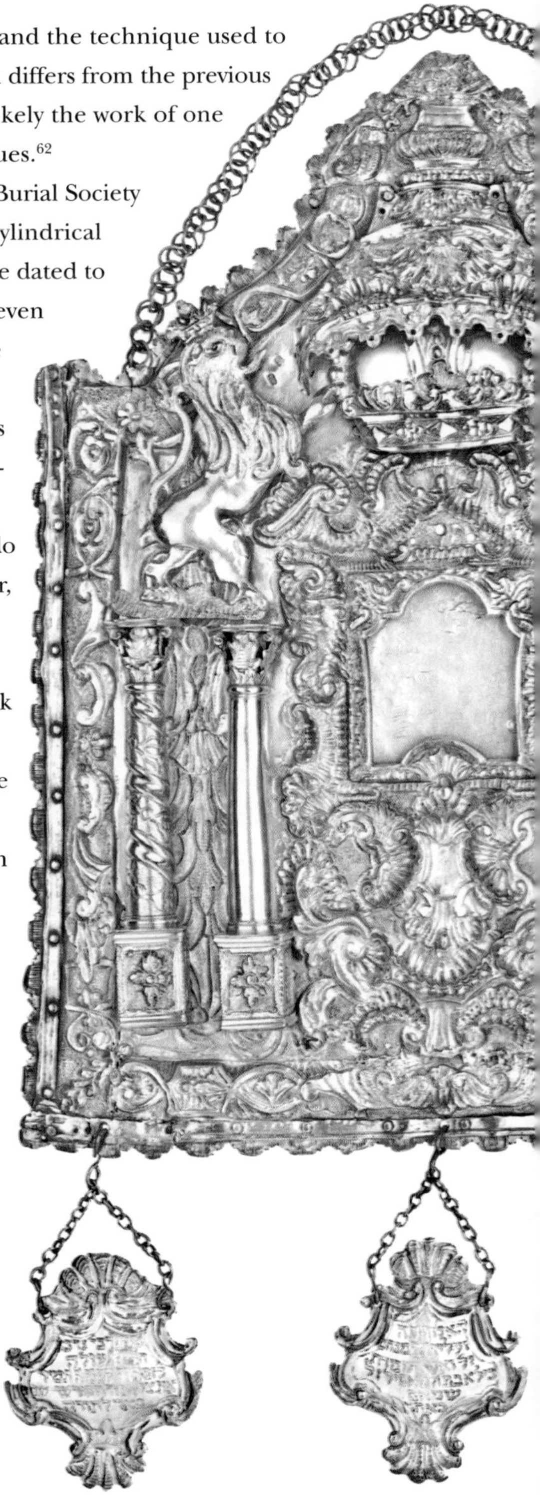

Cat. No. 9

year there appears mention of three unnamed Jewish goldsmiths (cf. Schirek (1902), p. 45).
[56] Though attributing the work to the aforementioned Isaac Beer might be tempting, active in Mikulov during the same period were at least two other Jewish craftsmen (see note 55).
[57] Torah finials, inv. no. JMP 012.207/01, 02, cat. no. 102.
[58] The finials were finished on 27 Elul 509 a.s.c. (= Sept. 10, 1749). It still has proven impossible to clarify the information on locality contained in the donation inscription. A comparison of the name of the donor with the official records of Jewish goldsmiths seems to give the master as "Jud Guttmann Isaac Löw" in Mikulov in 1769 (cf. Schirek (1902), p. 66).
[59] Torah shield, inv. no. JMP 012.222, cat. no. 9. Information on the maker is engraved on back of the small hatch of the box on the removable plate.
[60] The maker is mentioned in the official records from 1769 as Isaiah Mayram, as is his brother, Alexander Mayram, also a goldsmith, and another craftsman, Emanuel Polnauer (cf. Schirek (1902), p. 68). A note on their maker's marks is attached (ibidem, p. 164), but the shield unfortunately has none.
[61] Torah shield, inv. no. JMP 010.998, cat. no. 10; on the attribution cf. Flesch (1933), p. 33.
[62] See note 60.
[63] One of the alms boxes (inv. no. JMP 004.480, cat. no. 286) has a stamped maker's mark underneath, but it has suffered significant damage.
[64] Burial Society alms box, inv. no. JMP 010.355, cat. no. 287.
[65] Burial Society comb and cleaner pick, inv. no. JMP 004.520/01, 02, cat. no. 324. This set could be attributed hypothetically to the artisan recorded in Mikulov in 1769 as Moyses Isaac

For the whole of the period just outlined in Moravia, the independent activity of Jewish goldsmiths and silversmiths was in various ways either prohibited, limited, or at best tolerated. The change came, as it did in Bohemia, with Emperor Joseph II's Patent of Toleration, which was issued in Moravia on February 13, 1782.[66] Though it did not guarantee absolute equal rights to the Jewish population, it did improve its standing. In Moravia, however, the relaxing of religious restrictions surprisingly did not lead to the establishment of a separate Jewish guild for goldsmiths and silversmiths, as was the case in Bohemia. The reason might be that Moravia lacked a true economic center, and the fact that Jewish goldsmiths and silversmiths were uniformly spread out across the entire region might also have played a role.[67] Instead, Jewish goldsmiths and silversmiths began to join Christian guilds.[68] The absence of an independent Jewish guild in Moravia and any archival documents associated with it makes it very difficult to determine which extant work was made by whom.

The collection contains a relatively large group of unmarked Moravian Judaica, mostly Torah pointers, from the end of the 18th and the turn of the 19th centuries.[69] In the donation inscription, when one even exists, there is usually no date given, so the only aid is the tax mark that was applied later between 1806 and 1807, which provides only the latest possible time frame for when the object was made.[70] A smaller group of Moravian objects come from the same period, and they have full markings that allow for an exact dating and determination of the approximate locality where they were made.[71] The oldest of these is a Torah shield with a Mikulov hallmark with the year 1799 and a maker's mark with the initials SG.[72] The full name of the master is unknown, so we cannot say if he was Jewish, though the manner in which the object was executed would suggest it and supports the assumption that it was made in Mikulov.[73]

Another set of ritual objects have a Jihlava hallmark and are probably the work of a single Jewish master.[74] The oldest are two identical pairs of Torah finials with a Jihlava hallmark with the date 1800 and with a maker's mark MG located within the profile of the Decalogue tablets.[75] Another such object is a Torah shield with a Jihlava hallmark

Löw, Silber Arbeither (Schirek (1902), p. 66).

[66] See Brilling (1969), p. 139.

[67] The absence of a true economic center was also the reason for the existence of two separate goldsmith guilds, one in Brno and one in Olomouc. As their activity has yet to be thoroughly researched and published, the matching of objects with well-known Moravia craftsmen must be considered no more than conditional for the time being.

[68] In 1807, for example, the goldsmith Judah Safír from Velké Meziříčí requested permission to join the goldsmith guild in Olomouc (cf. Flesch (1933), p. 33).

[69] E.g., Torah pointer, inv. no. JMP 005.337, cat. no. 187, or Torah pointer, inv. no. JMP 012.219, cat. no. 193.

[70] Not even the donation inscription gives a reliable dating for when an object was made. For objects with full markings and a dating given in the inscription, a comparison of the two shows that the dates rarely correspond, and for some of the objects the dates are rather far apart.

[71] A craftsman was officially required to give the object a maker's mark as well as a hallmark. This mark was applied for a fee by an authorized clerk in a locality that might not necessarily have been the same as the artisan's place of residence.

[72] Torah shield, inv. no. JMP 007.424, cat. no. 31.

[73] On provenance see note 71.

[74] On provenance see note 71. This is undoubtedly the work of a Jewish craftsman judging by the manner of the object's execution and choice of motif for the ornamentation. Yet Jews

were prohibited from settling in Jihlava until 1848. The craftsman came, then, not from Jihlava proper but from the surrounding area. The provenance of the object as Jihlava is given here as a simplification.
[75] Torah finials, inv. no. JMP 009.549/01, 02 (not in the catalogue) and Torah finials, inv. no. JMP 009.550/01, 02, cat. no. 117
[76] Torah shield, inv. no. JMP 009.548, cat. no. 36.
[77] Torah shield, inv. no. JMP 001.543, cat. no. 43.
[78] Torah shield, inv. no. JMP 003.931, cat. no. 38.
[79] See note 76.
[80] Torah shield, inv. no. JMP 002.267, cat. no. 65. It is not clear from how the donation inscription is formulated whether the date relates to when the object was made or to the occasion for its donation mentioned in the inscription.

with the barely legible date of 1800–1806 and a maker's mark of MG within a rectangular frame.[76] The last object of the set, and the most interesting in terms of iconography, is a Torah shield with a Jihlava hallmark with the date 1810 and maker's mark of MG within a rectangular frame.[77] Its central section is ornamented with a chased relief depicting the Ark in the temple in Jerusalem. The full name of the craftsman is not known, but he might very well have lived in one of the Jewish communities nearby or in the wider region.

For the purposes of orientation, another Torah shield can be classified as belonging to the early 19th century. It has a crudely done fake maker's mark and hallmark simulating the Vienna hallmark from 1807–1809, and the engraved date is 1834.[78] What is interesting about the shield is that it is a rather exact, though ineptly made, copy of one of the shields mentioned above from the Jihlava master MG.[79] One more remarkable Torah shield, likely made as well by a Jewish craftsman, clearly comes from the first half of the 19th century, but it is unfortunately unmarked (the donation inscription gives 1838 as the date).[80]

Cat. No. 31

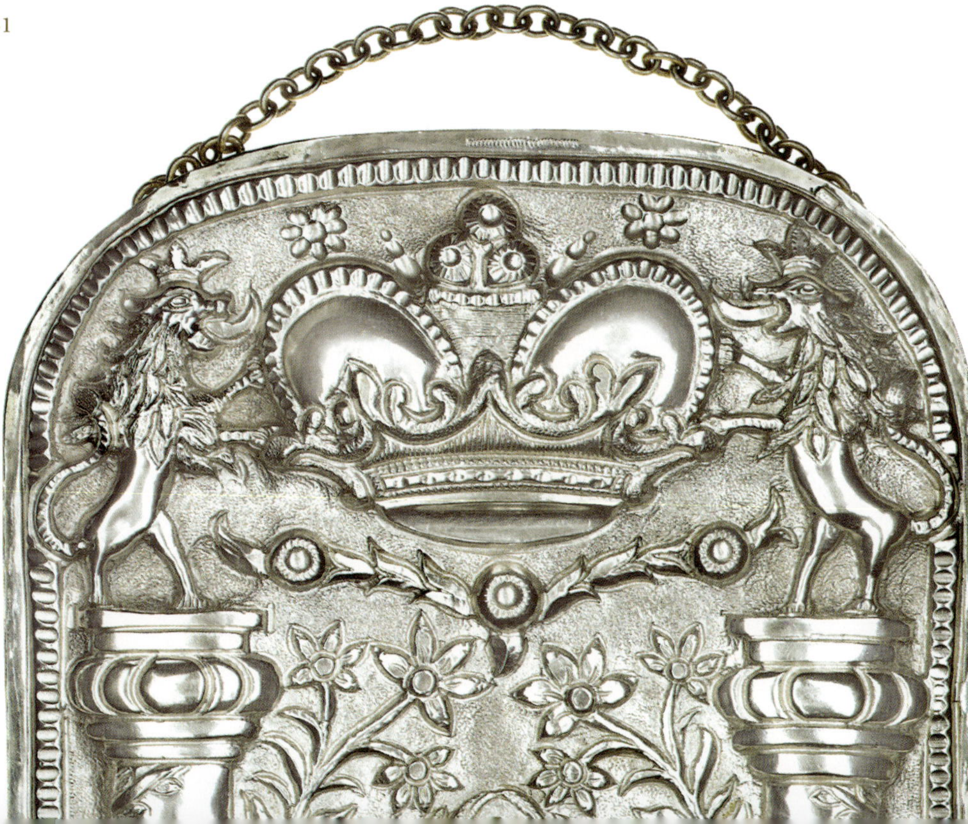

From roughly the 1810s the work of Moravian Jewish goldsmiths and silversmiths, easily identified by the technique employed and the ornamentation applied, stops appearing. One of the causes might have been the increase in production of the Brno workshops of Christian masters, who during this period were producing to replace the objects lost to the compulsory purchase program. Another cause might have been the import of ritual objects from nearby Vienna in the subsequent period. If we look at the situation in Bohemia for an analogy, where the activity of Jewish craftsmen is more easily followed, then the more likely explanation is that the relaxed access to technical education very quickly raised the quality level of work by Moravian Jewish masters, and to such an extent that it was no longer possible to surmise an object's origins by its distinguishing features. The fact that there is no collected research of the source materials has kept open the question on how to identify the activity of 19th century Jewish goldsmiths and silversmiths in Moravia. An example of a common problem encountered when trying to identify a maker is the case of two craftsmen whose work is preserved in relatively large number while their names and religious affiliation still remain unknown. These two theoretically could bring to a close the succession of Jewish goldsmiths and silversmiths operating in Moravia and Silesia. The first of the two used a maker's mark with the initials JR, and the hallmark stamped on the objects comes from his workshop in Brno. This is usually identified as Johann Radda, a goldsmith in the records from 1825 in Brno and from 1841 in Olomouc.[81] His maker's mark approximates the marks documented on objects in the Museum's collection, and his biographical data in the main agrees with the dating on the objects.[82] Yet an examination of the typological composition of the objects leads me to question whether the attribution of this work to this master is indeed correct. If this were the case, he would then be the maker of two Torah shields, an alms box, a Burial Society comb and cleaner picks, but chiefly several filigree spice boxes.[83] Work with filigree, however, is normally attributed only to Jewish craftsmen. When looking for an alternative master with similar data, the name Josef Rohmann suggests itself, and in 1823 he was registered as a member of the goldsmiths guild in Olomouc, listed there as a provincial master in Boskovice.[84] This hypothesis is supported as well by the fact

[81] Cf. Stehlíková (2003), p. 401.

[82] The extant objects can be dated to between 1830 and 1860.

[83] A selection of the work included in the catalogue comprises: Burial Society comb and cleaner picks, inv. no. JMP 010.344/01-05, cat. no. 330; Torah shield, inv. no. JMP 023.172, cat. no. 70; spice box, inv. no. JMP 003.665, cat. no. 415; and ritual spice box, inv. no. JMP 010.792, cat. no 417.

[84] Cf. Stehlíková (2003), p. 417.

[85] E.g., spice box, inv. no. JMP 003.694 from 1867–1868, cat. no. 420. The Jewish Museum's collection has no other work from this workshop than spice boxes. This master, however, was capable of working with other techniques. In 1990, Christie's offered at auction a circumcision set from 1864, which most probably came from this very same workshop. See the Christie's catalogue, no. 25 (1990), p. 17.

that Boskovice is recorded in the Jewish Museum's documentation as the provenance of the above-mentioned comb and cleaner picks. Yet for Josef Rohmann we do not possess any other biographical details, and we also do not know the form and content of his maker's mark, which means that the actual identity of the master who made this set of objects remains unclear.

The second master, known only by the initials EE, is somewhat connected to the first in his work. He is the maker of a group of extant pieces from 1864–1872 (afterwards, given the new hallmarks, it's not possible to precisely date the objects). He is also the maker of a remarkable number of filigree spice boxes.[85] The entire manner in which he constructs and structures the filigree wires is virtually identical to the work of master JR. Given the overlap in the time periods for their work, it is possible that master EE was trained in the workshop of his predecessor, because we have no records for any other Moravian artisan working with filigree during this period. No one has been able to ascertain any other information about this master, not even his name, or even enough information to make a guess. We can only hope that other scholars will have more success in the future.

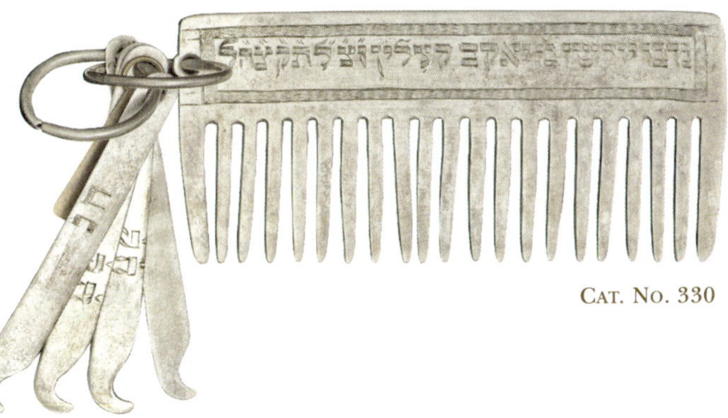

Cat. No. 330

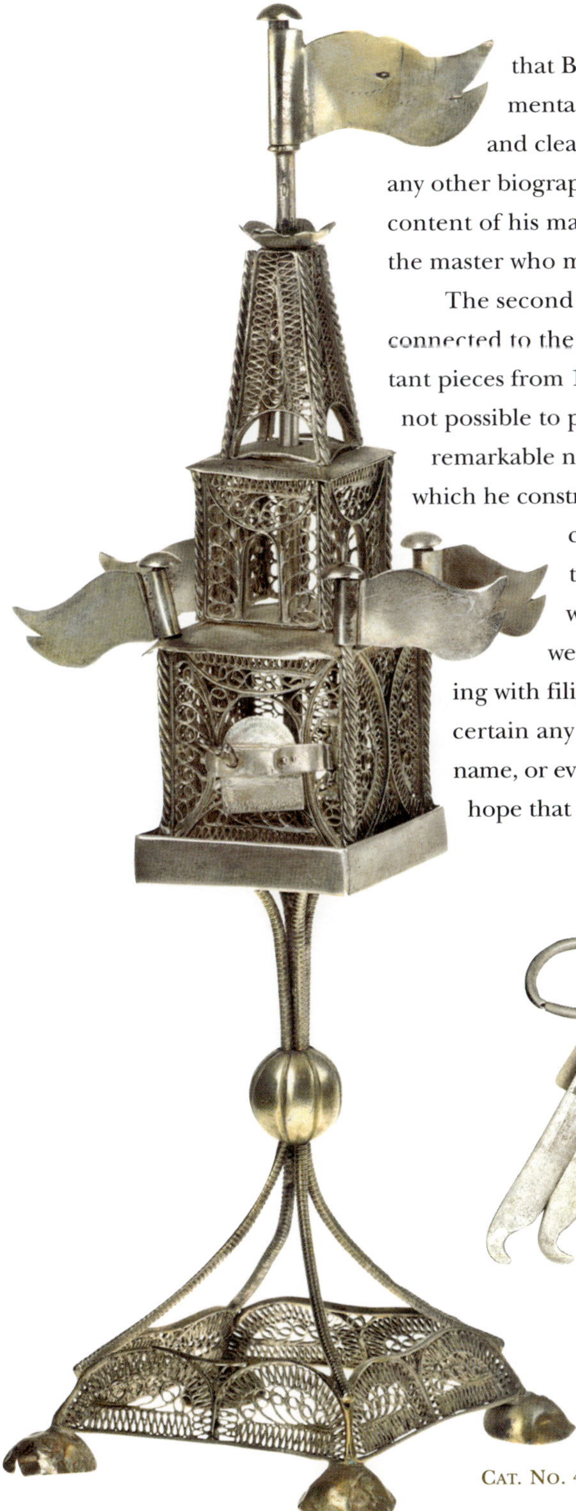

Cat. No. 420

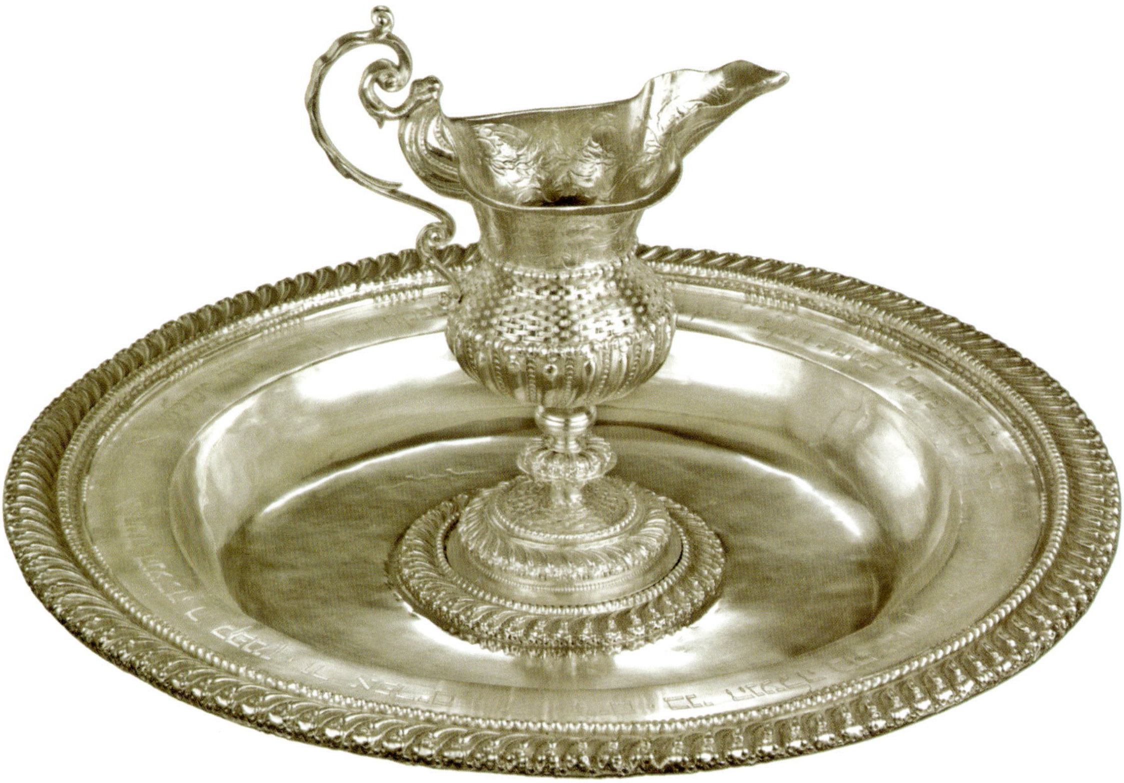

Cat. No. 272

CHAPTER 5

Christian Makers of Judaica in Bohemia

[1] The property of the communities located in the Nazi administered Protectorate of Bohemia and Moravia was part of a comprehensive confiscation and transfer to the Central Jewish Museum in Prague.

The extant silver ritual objects made by Christian craftsmen in Bohemia (the great majority of whom were in Prague) afford us the opportunity to partially reconstruct how local synagogues and Jewish households of the day were furnished, and to some extent we are able to map out the relationships between members of the Jewish communities and their Christian surroundings. At present, the work of Prague master silversmiths predominate in the Jewish Museum's collection of ritual objects. Yet it should be pointed out that for those objects that come from an older period (up to the end of the 18th century), which are sparsely represented, the collection does not provide, in terms of the provenance of objects for ritual use, a precise picture of the actual localities where they were made and who the specific makers were. Any conclusions that are drawn about this period must therefore be understood as hypothetical, and are impossible to verify due to the drastic reduction of the original silver furnishings of Jewish homes and synagogues. From the beginning of the 19th century, the sets of ritual objects from communities in Bohemia and Moravia have been nearly completely preserved and thereby give us a unique glimpse both into Jewish life of the day and to the craftsmanship and artistic level of the local master silversmiths.[1] The sets of silver ritual objects that were used by the communities in Bohemia can be divided by origin into several groups, the most numerous being the work of Prague silversmiths. Next is the work of Viennese makers, the majority of which dates to the second half of the 19th century; a smaller group is older work of German origin, largely from both of the goldsmith centers in Southern

Germany, Augsburg and Nuremberg. An even smaller group is represented by work from neighboring Moravia.[2]

The goldsmith and silversmith center in Bohemia was Prague. The Fellowship of Old Town Goldsmiths, an association of masters from the entire city, was founded in 1324. It later changed into a guild, which over the following centuries split into three separate guilds based on city districts.[3] These three guilds merged back into a single one in 1776 in which the majority of Czech Christian goldsmiths and silversmiths were affiliated until 1859 when the artisan guilds was definitively abolished.[4] In addition to the Prague guilds, there also existed a goldsmith guild in Kutná Hora that was founded in 1462 during a period of prosperity for the local silver mines.[5] As the town went into decline it also became less important for the guild, and in the first third of the 19th century it merged with the Prague guild.[6] Besides the craftsmen who operated their workshops in the places the guilds were located, there were also a handful of masters working in other towns. They had to be registered with one of the existing guilds, whose jurisdiction they were under, and they were designated as provincial masters.[7]

We are able to identify a great majority of the craftsmen by their maker's mark, the use of which was required and governed by established rules.[8] With the establishment of the Prague Assay Office in 1806 (to be exact, the following year), a copper plate was made that bore the imprint of the master's stamp with name affixed for all the current members of the guild.[9] Maker's marks and names were then added until the time the guilds were abolished.[10] The fact that these plates have been preserved to the present day has facilitated our ability to identify Prague craftsmen, and especially for the period in which the majority of the extant silver objects in the Jewish Museum's collection originated.

[2] The informative value of where an object was made should not, however, be overstated. In the case of some of the older objects coming from Germany, it is likely that they were used first in the Christian milieu for a longer period before being adapted for Jewish ritual use around the beginning of the 19th century as a replacement for objects that had been relinquished.

[3] Splitting off from the original guild, whose sphere remained limited to Prague's Old Town, were a New Town guild in 1478 and a Lesser Town guild in 1510–1547. Each had their own individual hallmark (cf. Stehlíková (2003), p. 378).

[4] The guilds were abolished in conjunction with the issuing of new trade regulations founded on principles quite different than those of the original guild system.

[5] Cf. Stehlíková (2003), p. 264.

[6] The Kutná Hora guild was abolished in 1820 by order of the regional governor of Bohemia (cf. Hráský (1981), p. 7). From the work of Kutná Hora silversmiths, the Jewish Museum has only one object in the collection (see note 20).

[7] It was customary for an artisan to become a member of the guild that trained him. His work was then stamped with the corresponding hallmark.

[8] The master's mark comprised the master's initials: given name followed by surname. As this order was strictly adhered to, it allows us to more easily identify the maker. Only one Prague master, František Müller, officially active from about 1800, used a mark with the order of the initials reversed.

[9] A set of two plates with the engraved samples of master's marks from 1807–1859 is deposited at the

Masters Silversmiths in Prague

For the oldest silver ritual objects extant in the Jewish Museum's collection that come from the workshops of Czech craftsmen it can be assumed with some certainty that they were not originally created for ritual purpose. As with the oldest extant objects from Moravia and abroad (mostly those of German provenance), these objects were adapted for ritual use only later. Leaving aside an etrog container, which was probably the work of Prague Old Town silversmith Matouš Fischer, who was active in the early 17th century and whose attribution and dating is unclear given the absence of other objects for comparison and poor legibility,[11] the oldest silver objects of Bohemian origin are two etrog containers both made in 1673 by Prague Lesser Town master Markus Hrbek.[12] One has the ornamental motif of tulips and thistles, the other with a group of various kinds of fruit surrounded by sprigs. Comparing these to similar dishes of German origin from the same period, which were made for the general market, it becomes clear that the ornamentation is conventional, and for that reason it cannot be assumed that they were made explicitly for a Jewish customer.[13] The oldest extant objects that can be said to definitely have been intended for a Jewish client is a Levite set, consisting of a pitcher and basin, made in 1702 in the workshop of renowned Lesser Town master Jan Jiří Lux.[14]

Prague Assay Office. The more recent of the plates contains the master's marks of craftsmen not resident in Prague and was clearly made around 1853.

[10] Josef Hráský published the plates and supplemented the archival data, including similar plates belonging to the Jewish goldsmith guild. For a brief description see Hráský (1981), p. 7.

[11] This is only hypothetical as the date in the Old Town hallmark is illegible, and we have no other object from this master with which we could compare. Stehlíková (2003), p. 128, with some reservations attributes the master's mark and the container's maker to Marek Fischer, who was indeed a master, but in another part of Prague, in Lesser Town.

[12] Etrog container, inv. no. JMP 012.729, cat. no. 277, and etrog container, inv. no. JMP 044.034, not included in the catalogue. For the maker cf. Hráský (1987), p. 136-137, and Stehlíková (2003), p. 185-186; for the master's mark cf. Rosenberg, Band IV, p. 589, no. 9335, given here without identifying the name.

[13] In the Christian milieu these dishes were used for small sweets, fruit, or to taste wine or brandy (in German "Fruchtschale" and "Branntweinschale"). Their shape and size later proved to be suitable for keeping the precious fruit, the etrog.

[14] Levite set, inv. no. JMP 046.036/01, 02, cat. no. 272. For the maker cf. Hráský (1987), p. 143, and Stehlíková (2003), p. 289; for the master's mark cf. Rosenberg, Band IV, p. 589, no. 9337, given here without identifying the name. The Levite set is remarkable not only for its exceptional quality, comparable to that of the Southern German masters, but for the Hebrew inscription that appears along the perimeter of the basin as well, which explains how it survived the conditions of the early 19th century.

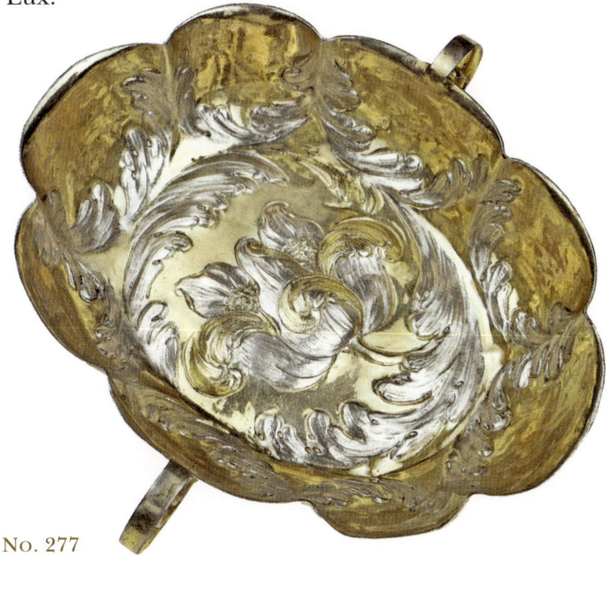

Cat. No. 277

The work of Bohemian silversmiths appears in the collection more often at the outset of the 18th century. Two Torah shields from 1708 were made by another well-known Lesser Town master, Jan Kogler.[15] These are the oldest Torah shields with precise dates that come from the workshops of artisans operating in Bohemia. Of particular note, the shield with the depiction of a Hanukkah lamp in the central field and the figures of Judith and the high priest Aaron on the sides is a rather remarkable object in terms of its iconography.[16] Another extant Torah shield in the collection, made in 1723, comes from the workshop of Old Town master Michal Josef Cocsell.[17] From the same year comes an alms box of the Burial Society in Libochovice, made by Old Town silversmith Martin Ketzner.[18] Another silver ritual object made in Bohemia is the oldest Torah crown in the collection, and precisely dated at that, also to 1723, and comes from the workshop of Old Town master Filip Oberholzer.[19] One could also place a closely dated etrog dish in this

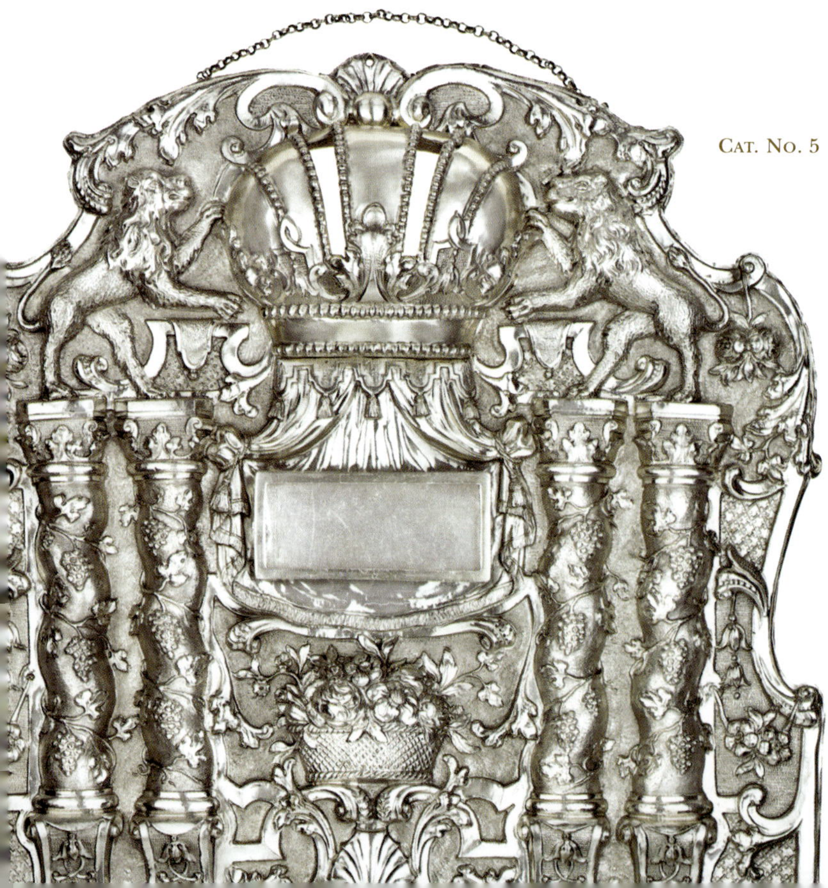

Cat. No. 5

[15] Torah shield, inv. no. JMP 044.437, cat. no. 3, and Torah shield, inv. no. JMP 004.418, cat. no. 4. For the maker cf. Hráský (1987), p. 138, and Stehlíková (2003), p. 235, here identified as Jan Jiří Kogler the elder. The question of to whom to attribute the master's marks has not been definitively answered; both shields are stamped with a double letter mark in an oval.

[16] The shield's form and iconography are very different from Kogler's other shield, as they are from all the other extant 18th-century Torah shields from Czech silversmiths. The person who commissioned the shield had a rather exact idea of how it should look, and to what extent its final form depended on the artisan is difficult to guess. The shield does not have a donation inscription, and who commissioned it is not known.

[17] Torah shield, inv. no. JMP 017.562, cat. no. 5. For the maker cf. Hráský (1987), p. 27, and Stehlíková (2003), p. 84.

[18] Alms box, inv. no. JMP 010.712, cat. no. 285. For the maker cf. Hráský (1987), pp. 32-33, and Stehlíková (2003), p. 226.

[19] Torah crown, inv. no. JMP 037.746, cat. no. 85. For the maker cf. Hráský (1987), p. 54, and Stehlíková (2003), p. 341.

[20] Torah finials, inv. no. JMP 037.563/01, 02, cat. no. 101. For the maker cf. Hráský (1987), p. 124, and Stehlíková (2003), p. 113. Ebner worked later as well for Jewish clients, and there is preserved a fragment of a Torah pointer from him dated to 1761, which was augmented in the 19th century to make it functional.

[21] Etrog container, inv. no. JMP 002.205, cat. no. 279. For the maker cf. Stehlíková (2003), p. 292. The dish bears an engraved date of purchase as 1855.

group. It comes from the first third of the 18th century and is attributed to a New Town master named Rinaldo Ranzani, even though the maker's mark is difficult to read. And just like older etrog containers in the collection, it is an object that had obviously been repurposed later for ritual use.

Only a few ritual objects made by Czech Christian masters for Jewish clients around the mid-18th century have been preserved. The only extant objects commissioned specifically for Jewish use during this period are a pair of Torah finials from the workshop of Lesser Town silversmith Jakub Kristián Ebner from 1743.[20] In addition, there is also preserved an object from a member of the Kutná Hora goldsmith guild: an undated etrog container by master Mikuláš Maden clearly from around 1750, which the inscription gives as belonging to the property of the Jewish community almost a century later.[21] The small number of objects that can be dated to this period could be explained by the uncertain situation of the local Jewish communities in regards to Empress Maria Theresa's policy to expel Jews from the land.[22] This would correspond with the higher number of ritual objects newly made by Prague masters after 1760.[23] Four Torah shields are dated to 1762: one is the work of Old Town master Jan Jiří Brullus the younger[24] and the other three come from the workshop of Kryštof Wild, which was also located in Prague's Old Town.[25] The number of preserved objects then slowly increases, though they come from a small circle of craftsmen.[26] For the first time the name Michal Enzinger appears; he was the maker of magnificent Rococo Torah finials from 1767 and their exact copy in 1769.[27] The Museum's collection also includes his Torah finials from 1780 and an etrog container from 1782.[28] Likewise from 1767 is a bench-type Hanukkah lamp, the work of unidentified master KV,

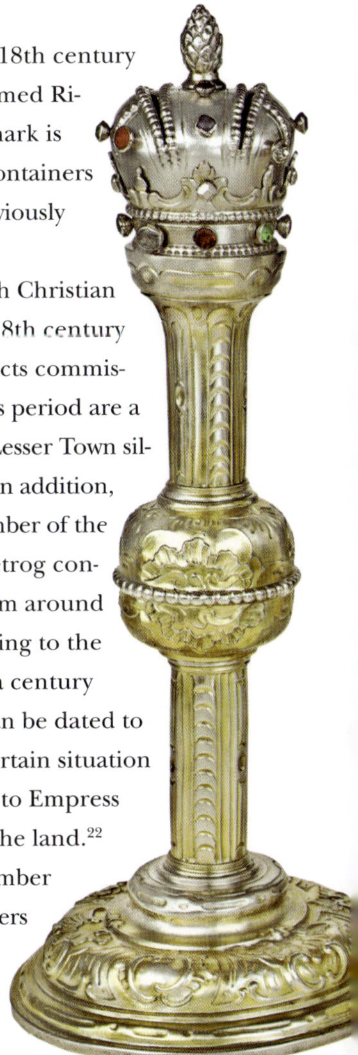

Cat. No. 101

[22] Even though the full extent of these measures never came into force, at the end of 1744 Prague Jews were banished to outside the city limits. They were not allowed to return until autumn 1748.

[23] It should be kept in mind, of course, the low informative value of the extant objects in the collection as a result of the losses of silver ritual objects at the beginning of the 19th century.

[24] Torah shield, inv. no. JMP 004.001, cat. no. 13. For the maker cf. Hráský (1987), p. 25 (with an erroneous version of the mark), and Stehlíková (2003), pp. 71-72.

[25] Torah shield, inv. no. JMP 001.555, cat. no. 14, Torah shield, inv. no. JMP 010.611, not included in the catalogue, and Torah shield, inv. no. JMP 037.594, cat. no. 15. For the maker cf. Hráský (1987), pp. 72-73, and Stehlíková (2003), p. 545.

[26] Given that we do not know how the synagogues were originally outfitted we are not able to know if those who commissioned ritual objects concentrated on a smaller number of quality pieces from the workshops of trusted masters or if they ordered less expensive pieces of lesser quality, which is what got surrendered during the seizure of synagogue silver in 1810. We need to also consider that only a short period of time had elapsed from the procurement of objects over the last third of the 18th century to when they were threatened with being either redeemed or surrendered, and their being preserved for posterity could have been in the interest of the original donor or the family members of the donor. The mere quality of a piece might have far less significance than we might assume.

[27] Torah finials, inv. no. JMP 037.572/01, 02, cat. no. 104

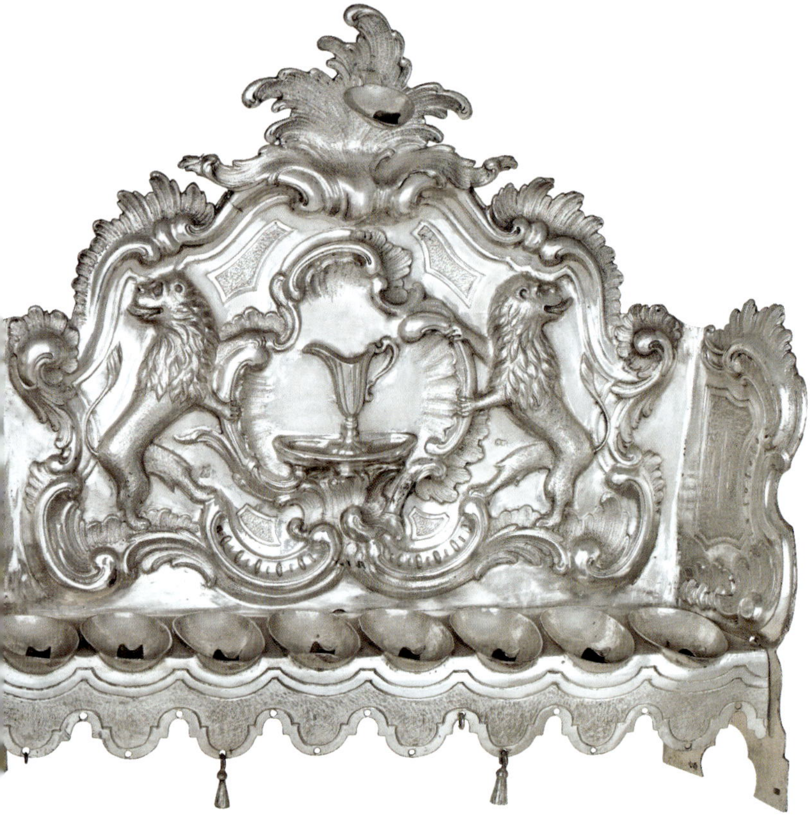

Cat. No. 384

and by its age a singular piece among the set of extant Hanukkah lamps.[29] From 1769 come Torah finials and a metal-fitted book cover from the workshop of the aforementioned Jan Jiří Brullus the younger.[30] The workshop of Kryštof Wild also produced pieces for Jewish clients and moreover continued to produce Torah shields, of which five have been preserved from the period 1774 to 1787. The most recent piece from this craftsman in the Museum's collection is a saltcellar from 1802.[31] Several objects from the period 1776 to 1795 come from the workshop of Josef Jakub Raspel.[32] Another master silversmith who during this period produced work for Jewish clients was Richard Fleischmann from Prague's Lesser Town. His oldest extant work is a Torah shield that can be dated to 1769–1776,[33] and several other objects in the collection come from his workshop as well, the most impressive of which is a set of Torah finials and shield from 1783–1784, made for

and Torah finials, inv. no. JMP 037.571/01, 02, not included in the catalogue. Both pairs of finials are identical in size and shape. For the maker cf. Hráský (1987), p. 28, and Stehlíková (2003), p. 119.

28 Torah finials, inv. no. JMP 005.037/01, 02, cat. no. 109, and etrog container, inv. no. JMP 010.860, cat. no. 280.

29 Hanukkah lamp, inv. no. JMP 066.185, cat. no. 384.

30 Torah finials, inv. no. JMP 044.405/01, 02, cat. not. 106, and metal-fitted book cover, inv. no. JMP 023.889, not included in the catalogue (the cover originally held a Hebrew text printed in Amsterdam in 1764).

31 Included in the catalogue are two Torah shields, inv. no. JMP 001.871, cat. no. 22, and inv. no. JMP 061.616, cat. no. 28, and a saltcellar, inv. no. JMP 173.618, cat. no. 439.

32 Torah pointer, inv. no. JMP 032.417, cat. no. 180 from 1776; Levite set, inv. no. JMP 032.420/01, 02, cat. no. 273 from 1780; circumcision shield, inv. no. JMP 012.784/04, cat. no. 434 from 1781; Burial Society comb, inv. no. JMP 049.444, not in catalogue, from 1795; and one Torah finial, inv. no. JMP 001.916, not in catalogue. For the maker cf. Hráský (1987), p. 58, and Stehlíková (2003), p. 402.

33 Torah shield, inv. no. JMP 004.391, cat. no. 17. For the maker cf. Hráský (1987), pp. 128-129, and Stehlíková (2003), p. 129.

34 Torah finials, inv. no. JMP 046.002/01, 02, cat. no. 110 and Torah shield, inv. no. JMP 046.075, cat. no. 24.

35 The way the Torah shield was made must have been even at that

time truly exceptional and impressed other donors as well as inspired other craftsmen as we have three extant copies of it that come from Bohemia over the following decades, and they more or less imitate the original. The first of them is from 1801, and it was made by an as yet unidentified Prague silversmith WK; the second copy is from 1819 from the workshop of Prague silversmith Antonín Kába; and the last is more of a free interpretation by Prague silversmith Karel Skřemenec from 1820. Another copy made by Prague silversmith Kašpar Duncker in 1816 is reportedly in an unspecified foreign collection (this information was kindly provided by Joschko Buxbaum of Vienna).

[36] Torah pointer, inv. no. JMP 046.074, not included in catalogue.

[37] They were: Jan Wolfgang Rossi, Ignatz Rudolf, Jan Matthias Seitz, Matthias Stuckel, and Josef Tomášek; cf. Hráský (1987), pp. 58, 60, 100-101, 104, 105. Also Hynek Prokop Gindle; cf. Hráský (1987), p. 36. According to his own account, Matthias Stuckel worked fifteen years for Zappert and Tomášek worked for him eighteen years. The engraving house of Jan Němec also worked for Zappert; cf. Hráský (1987), pp. 51-53.

[38] Curtain bells, inv. no. JMP 046.067/01-06, cat. no. 435.

[39] Cf. Hráský (1987), p. 68, and Stehlíková (2003), p. 98 (here as Antonín Dejl).

[40] Torah shield, inv. no. JMP 038.000, cat. no. 88; Torah finials, inv. no. JMP 007.062/01, 02, not in the catalogue; circumcision knife, inv. no. JMP 012.784/01, cat. no. 436.

the Aron Kodesh of Prague's Pinkas Synagogue.[34] Made in a neoclassical style, they are a very early example of this style in the Czech lands. Fleischmann's work on this Torah set is even more impressive by the technical skill and precision on display, and the pieces are executed in a way that uses the contrast of silver and gold details. The shield has emeralds and rubies set into its crown, which for Bohemia was entirely unique.[35] In both cases the craftsman was clearly working from either a drawn or printed diagram provided by the client himself, while one of his other works, a Torah pointer from 1785, also intended for the Pinkas Synagogue, does not bear traces of this new style.[36] The person who commissioned the set for the Pinkas Synagogue deserves closer attention. According to the donation inscription, he was Wolf Zappert, one of the elders of the synagogue and a wholesale merchant in precious metals. Zappert exported goods to other regions of the monarchy and to Germany (he attended the annual trade fair in Leipzig), and he also supplied the spa towns with gold and silver items. Several goldsmiths and silversmiths in Prague, members of the Christian guild, performed work for him over a long period of time.[37] Zappert's choice of craftsman for his expensive donation to the synagogue confirms that he must have had a rather good overview of who could do what and the technical abilities of each, even the ones who were directly employed by him. The last extant object made by Richard Fleischmann is a set of Ark curtain bells from 1793 and was most probably also commissioned by Zappert for the Pinkas Synagogue.[38]

From the 1780s and 1790s the Museum's collection has the work of other Prague Christian craftsmen. One is a master with the initials AD, identified (with some reservation) as the Old Town silversmith Ondřej Dejl.[39] From his workshop come a Torah shield and finials and a circumcision knife.[40] Another important craftsman was Jakub Vojtěch Fortner, from whom

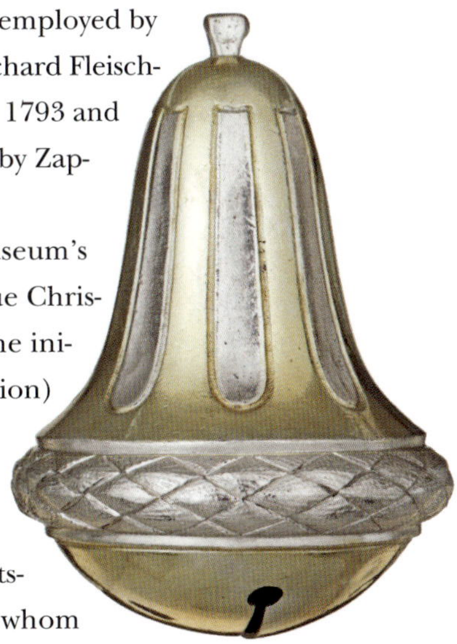

Cat. No. 435

the Museum's collection has two Torah shields dating to 1783.[41] Torah finials from 1786 were made by a thus far unidentified master AK.[42] Finally, Master IP, likely Josef Pscher, is the maker of a Burial Society alms box from 1793.[43]

The extant work of Karel Skřemenec appears at the very end of the 18th century.[44] The fact that such an extraordinary number and wide range of his work is in the Museum's collection makes him deserving of more attention. The archival records on Karel Skřemenec are relatively meager. He was from Prague, but the dates of his birth and death are not precisely known. He became a master silversmith at the end of 1768, and he received a town license in April of the following year. Probably due to the poor market conditions in Prague, he is listed in the records for 1772 as being in Český Krumlov, where he owned a house until 1785. He clearly came back to Prague some time later, but why is not known. One explanation could be that around that time he was able to establish contacts with Jewish clients, yet any material evidence for such a conclusion does not exist. The archival mention of Karel Skřemenec is from 1804, when he was voted a hallmark master, but the output

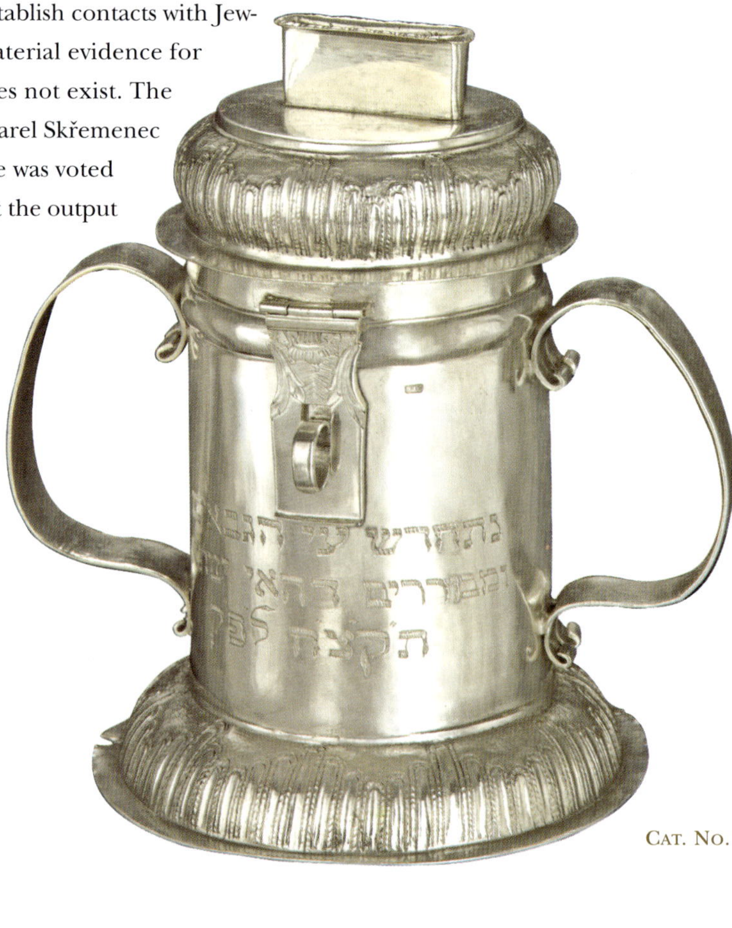

Cat. No. 288

[41] Torah shields, inv. no. JMP 023.094, cat. no. 23 and inv. no. JMP 017.464, not in catalogue; cf. Hráský (1987), pp. 29-30, and Stehlíková (2003), pp. 131-132.
[42] Torah finials, inv. no. JMP 032.404/01, 02, cat. no. 111.
[43] Burial Society alms box, inv. no. JMP 002.173, cat. no. 288; cf. Hráský (1981), p. 77, and Stehlíková (2003), p. 396.
[44] His oldest Torah shield can be dated to 1797, inv. no. JMP 001.957, cat. no. 30. Given their large number I am not presenting any other of his extant objects here; cf. Hráský (1981), p. 93, and Stehlíková (2003), p. 462.
[45] On Václav Rummel the elder cf. Hráský (1981), pp. 84-85; Jan Adam Řehořovský, ibidem, p. 85;

Jan Ferdinand Jakub Fleischmann, ibidem, p. 30; Jan Prokop Wild, ibidem, p. 104; Josef František Václav Fortner, ibidem, p. 31; Antonín Neubert; ibidem, p. 69. A. Neubert differs from the others in the number of extant ritual objects. Master IN has yet to be identified by name.

[46] Five objects from 1807–1816 made by one of Richard Fleischmann's sons, Jan Ferdinand Jakub, are extant, and some of them are included in the catalogue for comparison with the work of his father: Torah shield, inv. no. JMP 002.173, cat. no. 288; Torah pointer, inv. no. JMP 037.742, cat. no. 212; a pair of Sabbath candlesticks, inv. no. JMP 173.698/01, 02, cat. no. 390. The work of Jan Prokop Wild, the son of Kryštof Wild, is represented by nine Torah pointers from the years 1802–1807 (some have been attributed to him, however, on the basis of an analysis of the technology used in the detailing); we do not know of any other types of objects from his workshop.

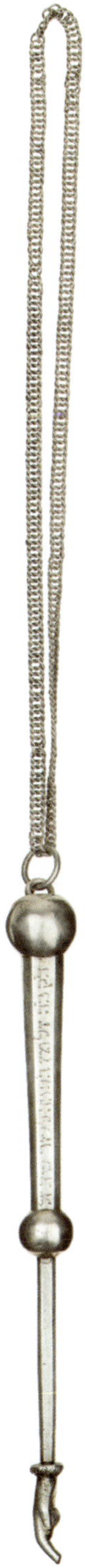

Cat. No. 212

of his workshop can be followed up to 1820. Up to 1810, his silver Judaica appears regularly in a quantity comparable to that being produced by the workshops of his peers, and it is of mid-level quality both in its technical skill and artistic execution. The sharp rise in the number of Jewish ritual objects his workshop subsequently produced is no doubt a result of the local communities trying to quickly replace the losses of synagogue property as a result of the measures instituted to appropriate silver objects. Why the bulk of this task fell to Karel Skřemenec is anyone's guess, but the subsequent drop in the quality of his work was likely tied to how quickly he could deliver a commission and the lower prices he offered, which his competitors simply could not match. Judging by the objects that have been preserved, the quality of the work from his workshop gradually declined, and in his last years his work could not compare with that of his peers either in artistry or technical skill. We have no information on how the Skřemenec workshop was managed, so we cannot know whether he met the volume of orders alone or whether he had the help of journeymen. The workshop suddenly ceased operation in 1820, no doubt because of his death.

At the turn of the century and into the early 19th century other Prague master craftsmen performed work for Jewish clients: Václav Rummel the elder, Jan Adam Řehořovský, master IN, Jan Ferdinand Jakub Fleischmann, Jan Prokop Wild, Josef František Václav Fortner, Antonín Neubert, and others.[45] In some cases the surnames are known from the latter third of the 18th century, and they are the sons of well-known Prague master silversmiths, who after setting up their own enterprises took some of their fathers' original clientele, which represented only a small part of overall production. Judging by the extant objects, their commissions were not that substantial.[46]

Other Prague silversmiths also contributed to the quick replenishing of silver Judaica in synagogues in Bohemia after

1810, but most of them only produced a small number. The majority of new objects came from the workshops of a small group of master silversmiths. Besides Karel Skřemenec, there were his younger contemporaries Tomáš Höpfel, Antonín Maroušek, and Antonín Kába. In the number of objects produced, Höpfel, who became a master in 1815, ranks second behind Skřemenec, and the oldest piece of his making in the collection is a Torah shield from 1816.[47] He worked for Jewish clients fairly regularly during his whole career, focusing on larger pieces (Torah shields and finials), but he also made smaller objects as well (a Torah pointer, a Burial Society comb). The extant ritual objects from Höpfel number in the dozens, and after his death in 1847 his widow continued the workshop's production, which ceased operations in 1858. Antonín Karel Maroušek, who became a master in 1814, was also instrumental in helping to replenish synagogue inventory.[48] Judaica from the beginning of his long professional career appears only rarely;[49] his greatest productivity comes relatively late, in the 1830s, and the latest object that can be attributed to him is a Torah pointer from 1859.[50] His work in the Museum's collection number in the dozens, and it comprises a variety of types of ritual objects. Antonín Kába, who also became a master in 1814,[51] is the last of this group. Given the short time he was active the number of ritual objects coming from his workshop is much lower than the others discussed here, yet for all that, what he did make is deserving of admiration. All extant objects from Kába come from a compressed seven-year period, 1817 to 1824.[52]

Starting around the mid-19th century, production from the traditional type of artisan was on the wane, and this of course includes those trades working with precious metals. Thanks to new technologies that allowed for quicker and cheaper production, ritual objects gradually came to be mass-produced. It simply was not possible for small producers to survive these changes. Even so, there were a few Prague master silversmiths who continued to make work. One was Jan Novotný, active between 1853 and 1876.[53] Despite all the difficulties associated with this period of vanishing individual artisans, he was surprisingly productive, and a great number of Judaica objects made by his workshop have been preserved. Most are Torah pointers, but there are also

[47] Torah shield, inv. no. JMP 037.603, cat. no. 54. Already this earliest piece bears the traits of Höpfel's unique method of working. In view of the number of his objects extant others are not listed here. Cf. Hráský (1981), p. 45, and Stehlíková (2003), p. 181 (erroneously given here as a Jewish craftsman).

[48] Cf. Hráský (1981), pp. 62-63, and Stehlíková (2003), p. 297.

[49] Alms box, inv. no. JMP 037.710, cat. no. 293. Other extant work by Maroušek is not given here due to their large number.

[50] Torah pointer, inv. no. JMP 004.366, not included in the catalogue.

[51] Cf. Hráský (1981), p. 50, and Stehlíková (2003), p. 210.

[52] Levite set, inv. no. JMP 037.546/01, 02, cat. no. 274. The catalogue also includes a Torah shield, inv. no. JMP 001.869, cat. no. 58, which is a copy of a shield made by Richard Fleischmann; see note 34. Other work by Kába is not given here due to their large number.

[53] Cf. Hráský (1981), p. 71, and Stehlíková (2003), p. 338. The fact that he relocated to Vienna in 1876 testifies to how difficult conditions had become in the trade.

[54] In the catalogue are: Torah finials, inv. no. JMP 009.788/01, 02, cat. no. 146; circumcision knife, inv. no. JMP 173.854/01, cat. no. 463; Torah pointer, inv. no. JMP 010.902, cat. no. 246; eternal light, inv. no. JMP 010.480, cat. no. 391. Given the large number of his work, other objects are not listed here.

Torah shields and finials, parts of Levite sets, charity dishes, Burial Society combs, and other objects that taken together number several dozen.[54] Another Prague artisan of this period was Václav Kabeš, active from 1846 to (probably) 1866.[55] The pieces produced by his workshop were also varied in type, and several have been preserved: a cup, two alms boxes, a Burial Society comb, and others. And from the latter third of the 19th century the collection has several Torah pointers from Gustav Karel Ferdinand Dittmann.[57]

From the last few decades of the 19th century there are no longer (save an exception here and there) any objects of an individual type made on the commission of a client. One now had to choose from a product range serially produced by large companies with sufficient capital to operate a manufacturing facility. As such, the distinction between Jewish and Christian makers also lost all relevance as production overall and the creation of particular models were no longer governed by individual religious affiliation. An example is the Prague gold and silver company Alfred Pollak,[58] for whom the manufacture of Jewish ritual objects was only a marginal part of their total output.[59] Another such firm was Sandrik,[60] whose production catalogue also included Hanukkah lamps.[61]

The time frame for the collection of silver ritual objects closes with the expressive shapes and simple ornamentation of the work coming from the Czech lands at the beginning of the 1930s. Without more detailed knowledge of what other objects these companies produced, however, we cannot determine whether it was the producer or the client who influenced how they were created and to what extent it was merely mechanical work based on a model.[62]

[55] Cf. Hráský (1981), p. 50, and Stehlíková (2003), pp. 210-211.
[56] The catalogue includes: cup, inv. no. JMP 037.548, cat. no. 365, a set of curtain bells, acq. no. JMP 1995/1166/01–07, cat. no. 461.
[57] Cf. Hráský (1981), p. 25, and Stehlíková (2003), p. 103.
[58] This was one of the largest producers of precious metal goods in the Austro-Hungarian Empire. The Prague factory was in operation until 1934. Cf. Stehlíková (2003), p. 384.
[59] Torah shield, inv. no. JMP 010.474, cat. no. 83.
[60] For more on the company see Stehlíková (2003), p. 438.
[61] Hanukkah lamp, inv. no. JMP 170.329/01, 02, cat. no. 400.
[62] E.g., Torah crown, inv. no. JMP 044.295, cat. no. 99.

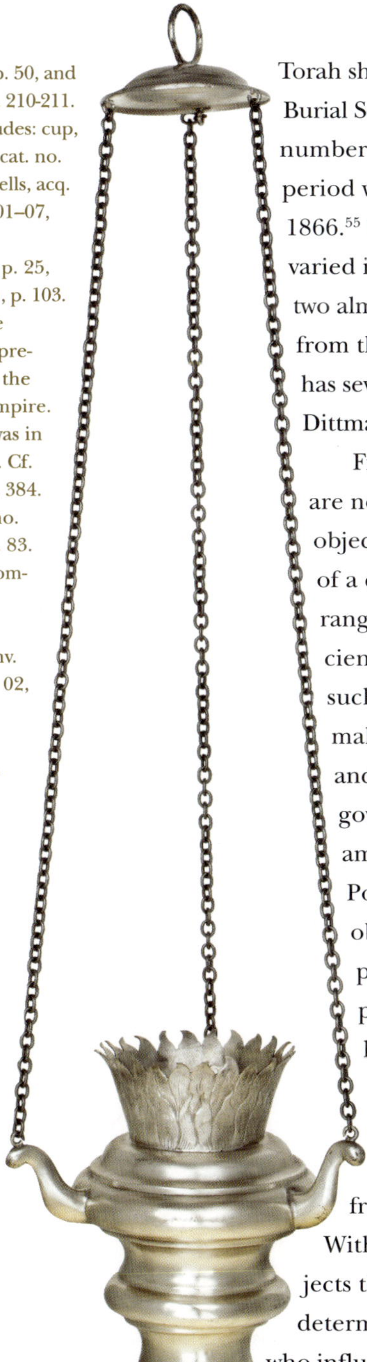

Cat. No. 391

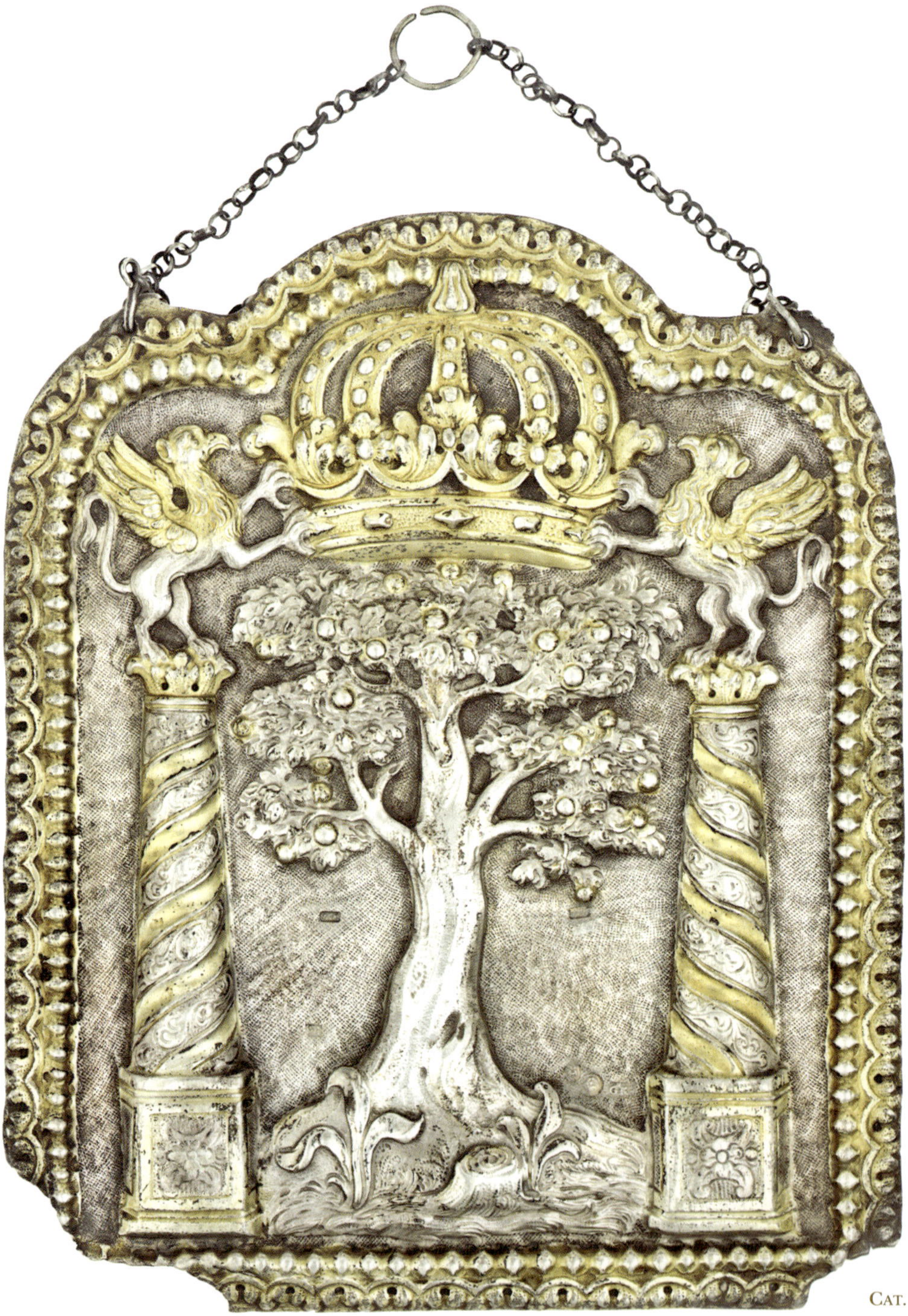

Cat. No. 11

CHAPTER 6

Christian Makers of Judaica in Moravia and Silesia

The set of extant silver Jewish ritual objects coming from the workshops of Moravian and Silesian goldsmiths and silversmiths gives us in comparison to neighboring Bohemia a somewhat different and, in some respects, richer picture of the collection's composition of ritual Judaica. What should be remembered, however, is that though this picture has been formed by extensive study of these objects, significant gaps still appear, particularly with the older objects, and our current research has thus far been unable to fill them. A more comprehensive identifying of Christian makers of Judaica is further hindered by the absence of a comprehensive overview of the information in the archival sources pertaining to local Moravian craftsmen for whom a closer association of the name with the extant work is missing.[1] Attributing concrete pieces to individual masters on the basis of a correspondence of initials and approximate biographical details is possible only in a few exceptional cases, and I should emphasize that even here this is a rather unreliable method.

The silver synagogue objects used by Moravian Jewish communities for liturgical purposes are rather varied (in terms of their provenance or where they were made). The work of Moravian craftsmen[2] is the most well represented, but we also find the work of Viennese silversmiths and a relatively large number of objects made by Galician craftsmen. On the other hand, work of Silesian origin is rare in the collection, no matter if it is from the Czech areas of Silesia (Opava) or the Polish (Wroclaw/Breslau). Yet the work of German silversmiths,

[1] Schirek (1902) is an exception. He is focused more on the period from which very few objects are extant. Save some passing references to hallmarks, he entirely passes over the 19th century, from which the great majority of three-dimensional comparative material comes.
[2] With work that is unmarked but whose style corresponds to objects made in Galicia it cannot be definitively stated that this is not the work of a Moravian Jewish master.

as well as that of Prague silversmiths, appears fairly regularly among the older Moravian synagogue objects.[3]

In regards to the dispersion of goldsmith and silversmith workshops in Moravia, it is possible to come up with a more tangible mapping out of the composition (as opposed to the situation in Bohemia) of their localities. The absence of a dominant economic center, like Prague for the region of Bohemia, is certainly one factor that stimulated the emergence and existence of two independent goldsmith guilds, one in Brno and one in Olomouc.[4] These two guilds brought together Moravian craftsmen from the larger towns who were registered as "provincial masters."[5] Brno is at the top of the list of localities where the individual masters had their workshops; it was where more craftsmen always worked at any given time and from where the most extant ritual objects come.[6]

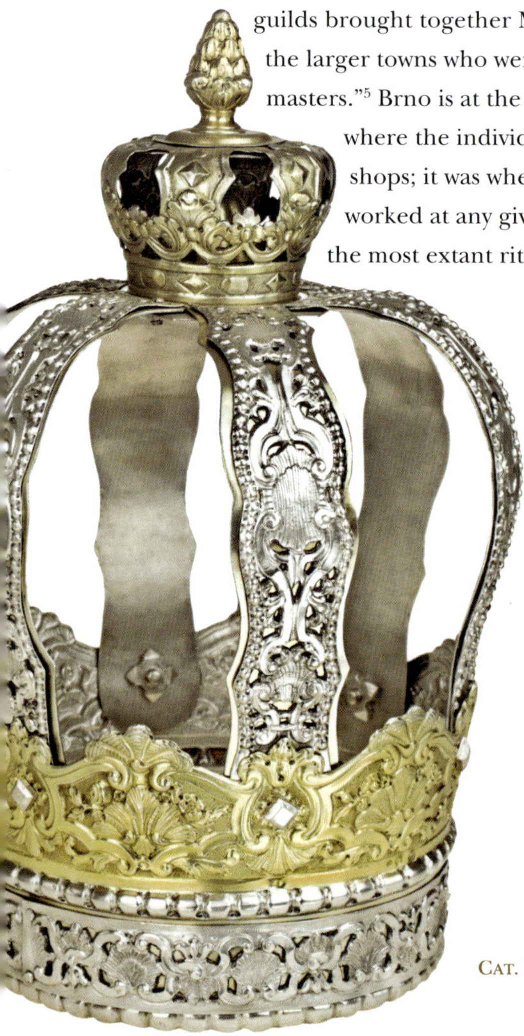

Cat. No. 86

[3] This inventory of the work coming from separate regions nearby surely could lead one to consider the commercial and personal relationships and connections that Moravian Jews had established with other Jewish communities. It goes without saying that one must exercise caution when connecting local trade and personal relationships with distant regions. Silver objects (including those intended for ritual use) were of course a generally desired article and over a period of time could therefore have traveled quite a distance from the maker to the user. We also need to consider the numerous waves of migration, both forced and voluntary, that Central European Jewry experienced. Some of the objects with a great distance between their place of production and their collection points, from where they came to the wartime Central Jewish Museum in Prague, also do not have conclusive donation inscriptions that would give evidence of the object being used in a specific time and in a specific place. To rely only on the place of production or even only on the location of the collection point without any other research would surely yield misleading results.

[4] The term "goldsmith guild" is chosen here for simplification. Members of a guild thus defined were not only goldsmiths, they were also silversmiths and makers of ornamentation from precious metals.

[5] The system then for assaying work and then giving it a maker's mark does not allow us (as there is very little data in the archives) to more precisely ascertain the location of a specific workshop; the hallmark of a town might cover a wider region. This is the case with Kroměříž, for example, whose hallmark as of 1769 encompassed the whole Přerov

region; cf. Schirek (1902), p. 137. Not even the adoption of a new marking practice in 1807 (with letters in the mark and a numerical index of Assay Office substitutions) really improve on the system that had been in place.
[6] It should be noted that Jews were prohibited from settling in the town from 1454. This prohibition was gotten around in various ways from the mid-18th century on and was later relaxed with Emperor Joseph II's Patent of Toleration in 1782, but it was not until 1848 that the prohibition was completely lifted (see Brunner (1929), p. 137 and note). A large number of silver Judaica produced in Brno at the beginning of the 19th century was, therefore, primarily intended for the Jewish communities in the provinces (outside Brno).
[7] Beaker, inv. no. JMP 010.349, cat. no. 334. The absence of a donation inscription means that attributing the beaker to use by the Burial Society cannot be verified with any certainty. On the markings see Rosenberg, p. 578, no. 9246 (master's mark) and no. 9234 (hallmark), listed here as by an unknown master. Cf. also Stehlíková (2003), p. 166 (instead of a beaker erroneously listed here as a type of Torah shield).
[8] From this maker we know of two other silver objects: a beaker that was once found in the Figdor Collection in Vienna (see Rosenberg, p. 578); and a spoon that was once in the collection of the former Františkovo Museum in Brno (see Schirek (1902), pp. 121-122). None of these objects is directly related to the Jewish cultural milieu. The Boskovice beaker was evidently used for ritual purposes by a Jewish association given its undoubted artistic and technical quality.

Master Silversmiths in Brno

The oldest silver object of Brno provenance extant in the Jewish Museum in Prague's collection is a beaker made by the silversmith Bernard Hartenach prior to 1618 that was once used by the Burial Society in Boskovice.[7] Clearly it was not originally intended for ritual purposes. It came to the Jewish Community of Boskovice only later (judging from the engraved initials in Latin).[8] When exactly is a matter of conjecture. Looking for an analogy among similar objects from roughly the same period with donation inscriptions, we can say that evidently it was not before the beginning of the

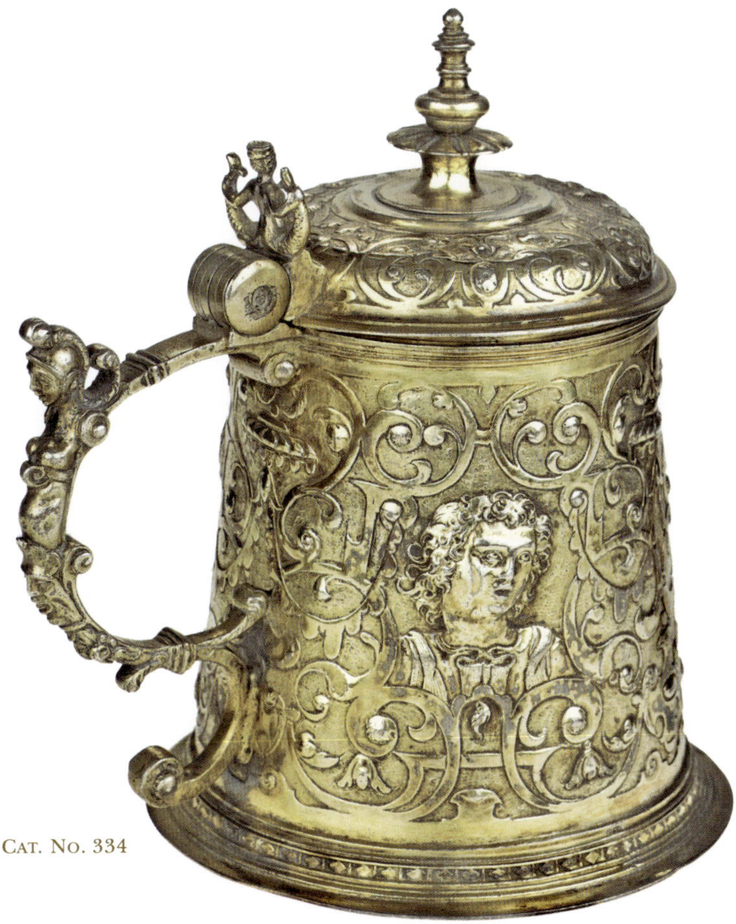

Cat. No. 334

19th century.[9] As with Bohemia, for the oldest period represented in the Museum's collection of silver (16th–17th centuries) there are no extant objects from Moravia and Silesia that are of local make that we would be able to reliably identify as having been produced primarily for Jewish clients. They surely did exist, but how many there were and what they looked like remain unknown.

The oldest extant Jewish ritual object of Brno origin, therefore, is a Torah shield made by Jan Michal Kaltenmarker in 1761.[10] Other pieces from this master are dated a bit later: Torah finials and a Torah crown are from 1769.[11] These three, or four if you will, objects, are to date the only known pieces of Judaica that are from the workshop of this Brno master, and so it is not possible to say unambiguously that those were his sole commissions from Jewish clients or if he did more work in this vein. All aforementioned objects came from the Holešov collection point and were most likely intended for the local Jewish community.[12]

Another object that comes from Moravia from the latter half of the 18th century is a Torah pointer made circa 1769–1776 by Johann Christian Fischer, a prominent member of the silversmiths guild in Brno.[13] After this period, the collection of ritual objects from Brno workshops has about a thirty-year gap. Right after the turn of the 19th century there appears the work of another generation of Christian masters. The first is Franz Kaltenmarker, son of the aforementioned Jan Michal Kaltenmarker.[14] His oldest extant work is a Torah crown from 1803.[15] Starting in this year, Kaltenmarker's workshop supplied Jewish clients fairly regularly: in addition to this crown, extant are several Torah finials and shields from 1807–1809. His workshop's production for Jewish clients over this initial period is estimated to have been several pieces yearly.

In 1810, the production of non-Jewish Moravian craftsmen took a sharp turn upward as a result of the need to replace Jewish ritual objects lost to the state's compulsory

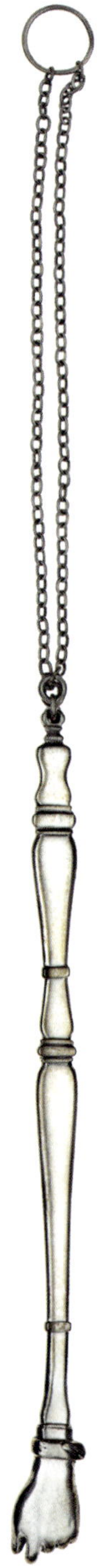

Cat. No. 174

[9] For example, a beaker, inv. no. JMP 002.268, not included in catalogue, from Augsburg circa 1635–1640 with a donation inscription from 1813, or an etrog container, inv. no. JMP 004.259, not included in catalogue, also from Augsburg circa 1670–1680 with a donation inscription from 1857.

[10] Torah shield, inv. no. JMP 005.346, cat. no. 12. Given the poor legibility of the hallmark, the object's dating is derived from the donation inscription. Stehlíková (2003), p. 216, indicates that this craftsman was given a town license only in 1763. On the maker also see Schirek (1902), pp. 66, 86, 92, 114.

[11] Torah finials, inv. no. JMP 005.340/01, 02, cat. no. 107; Torah crown, inv. no. JMP 005.331, cat. no. 87.

[12] A donation inscription appears only on the shield and does not give the names of donors or locality.

[13] Torah pointer, inv. no. JMP 012.176, cat. no. 174. On the maker see Schirek (1902), pp. 40, 44, 66, 86, 114, 118, 125, and Stehlíková (2003), p. 128.

[14] On the maker see Stehlíková (2003), p. 216. The assay master of the same name mentioned by Schirek (as Franz Kalchmarker) in 1774 most likely is not the same person; cf. Schirek (1902), pp. 84, 85, 125.

[15] Torah crown, inv. no. JMP 177.816, not included in catalogue due to heavy damage.

[16] How many his workshop employed is not known, but given the rather careful technical execution of the objects we have extant, such a volume of

purchase program. Franz Kaltenmarker, who had already proven himself a reliable producer, became over the next decade the most productive maker of silver Judaica in Moravia and Silesia. In 1810 alone he churned out (based on what's extant in the Museum's collection) ten Torah shields, two pairs of Torah finials, one Torah pointer, and one Torah crown, as well as a Burial Society comb and cleaners, a Burial Society alms box, and a charity dish.[16] With slight fluctuations, he continued this output over the following years, and the last extant piece of Judaica from his workshop in the Museum's holdings is from 1821.[17]

The greater part of Franz Kaltenmarker's extant work for Jewish clients is ornamentation for the Torah scrolls. These were the most painful losses for the Jewish communities. The typological composition of his work is, however, more varied and includes, in addition to the objects made for Burial Society use (alms boxes, charity dishes), Hanukkah lamps and eternal lights. Quite unique in the work of Christian craftsmen is the ritual spice box bearing Kaltenmarker's mark.[18] His distinctive means of expression, most noticeable with the Torah shields, were borrowed almost without any alteration by other Brno silversmiths. The objects produced in their workshops are virtually interchangeable, and I would infer from this that Kaltenmarker's early work served as a direct model for other local craftsmen.

Other Brno Christian masters from this period who contributed to making silver ritual objects for the Jewish communities were Carl Lackstampfer and his son Carl Michael Lackstampfer.[19] The oldest extant work of Carl Lackstampfer in the Museum's collection is dated to 1800.[20] From 1810, the workshops of both Lackstampfers produced to meet the demand for new ritual objects, though their output in this regard was somewhat lower than Kaltenmarker's workshop. Their extant work in the collection is represented primarily by adornments for the Torah scrolls and alms boxes; other types of objects seldom appear. By comparing their biographical data with the datings of the individual objects, we see that the elder Lackstampfer contributed a far greater share.[21] The work of both Lackstampfers can be distinguished from Kaltenmarker's work by the more crudely executed details and the almost folk treatment of zoomorphic motifs.[22]

commissions could not have been completed by the master alone.

[17] It is not possible to identify any work coming from him (at least not Judaica) after this date. It is unknown whether he gave up the trade or if his workshop ceased operations upon his death.

[18] Spice box, inv. no. JMP 010.291, cat. no. 406. Other known work by him is found in the holdings of the Spertus Institute in Chicago (Hanukkah lamp, inv. no. 68.1.42, personal conversation with Ilana Segal, Spertus' curator of collections) and probably in the holdings of the Jewish Museum of Vienna (Hanukkah lamp, Max Berger Collection, inv. no. 436).

[19] On both makers see Grossová (2006), pp. 119-142.

[20] Cup, inv. no. JMP 012.271, cat. no. 349. How the relationship between the maker and the Jewish communities developed after this year is not clear. The cup has no inscription. Similarly simple objects might have been made for a storehouse, coming into Jewish ownership only later. Unquestionable proof of work for a Jewish client can be dated to 1804: see Torah finials, inv. no. JMP 007.553/01, 02, not included in catalogue.

[21] Both used a similar, rather difficult to read mark with interlocked initials, and this was during a period when the operations of both workshops overlapped. This makes it extremely difficult to differentiate the individual work of each, especially since we have to consider that the son apprenticed in his father's workshop.

[22] This difference is most noticeable on the Torah shields. Cf. Torah shield, inv. no. JMP 012.391, cat. no. 51, by Franz

Another Brno Christian silversmith whose work we are able to identify among the extant Judaica ritual objects is Jakob Uhl, from whom the collection holds several cups, a pair of Torah finials, and one alms box from the period 1810–1816.[23] Uhl evidently relocated to Znojmo in 1816, after which time we know of no further pieces of Judaica of his make.[24]

After 1820 the production of silver Judaica in Moravia steeply drops off, and usually only single pieces are all that have been preserved from later craftsmen. The losses had been replaced, and the relative proximity of Vienna also played a role, as it was more technologically advanced, and from the 1830s on objects that followed the day's fashion gradually began to displace domestic production even in the specialty market of ritual products for Jewish use.

One Brno craftsman whose share of the production of silver Judaica was only marginal was Eduard Uhl,[25] who in 1819 is mentioned as an assistant in Carl Lackstampfer's workshop and is known to have become an independent master after 1830.[26] Its possible to identify other masters working in Brno only by the initials in their marks, yet associating concrete names found in the archives with these marks must remain hypothetical due to the absence of sufficient comparative material. With master FR, from whom we have two Torah shields and an alms box from 1826–1833, not even this proved fruitful. The only master to whom it is possible to identify a specific name is the author of an alms dish from 1837, Ludvík Plitschka, listed as an assistant in Lackstampfer's workshop from 1820.[27] Master WB, who made a Torah shield circa 1840–1842, could be Wilhelm Bartoňek, who in 1828 became a citizen of Brno.[28] Torah finials made by master BS, whose name we have not been able to identify, come from the same period.

To conclude the overview of Brno masters, two other makers should be mentioned, even though they have not been identified with certainty. The first is master JR, who according to his extant work was active circa 1830–1860. Based on his maker's mark he is usually identified as Johann Radda, who since 1833 had been a provincial member of the Olomouc guild and from 1841 a master in Olomouc.

Kaltenmarker in 1815 with Torah shield, inv. no. JMP 012.221, cat. no. 41, by Carl Lackstampfer in 1810.

[23] Cf. cup, inv. no. JMP 010.332, cat. no. 355, from 1815.

[24] All extant objects have a Brno hallmark. On the maker see Stehlíková (2003), p. 517.

[25] Whether he was a relative of Jakob Uhl has yet to be determined.

[26] On the maker see Stehlíková (2003), p. 517. Of his work, the Museum's collection holds an alms box, inv. no. JMP 010.346 from 1836, not included in the catalogue.

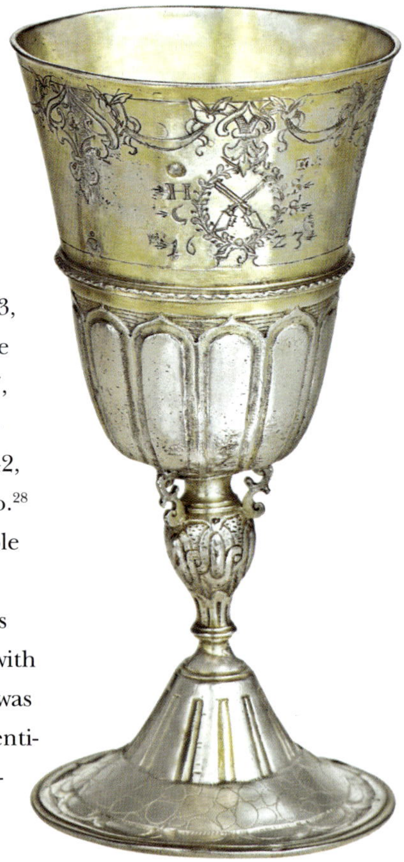

Cat. No. 338

All of his extant work that comes even after this date have a Brno hallmark.[29] Doubt over Radda's identity is cast by the typological composition of his extant objects, which are mostly spice boxes in filigree, and this is generally attributed to Jewish craftsmen. Given the initials, the name Josef Rohmann suggests itself here. He was a Jewish craftsman[30] who was registered in the Olomouc guild as of 1823 as a provincial master in Boskovice.[31]

Similarly, the extant work in the Museum's collection by the last master under discussion, known only by the initials EE and active circa 1860–1880, also comprises only filigree spice boxes.[32] Given the very similar structure of the filigree and the overlapping time frame to the above-mentioned master, he is usually taken to be an apprentice in JR's workshop. The work of master EE, however, is also stamped solely with a Brno hallmark, but the exact location of his workshop cannot be pinpointed.[33] The fact is, a lack of data makes it impossible to definitively place both masters in the group of Jewish craftsmen, even though their exclusive use of a filigree technique indicates that they probably should be.

Makers from Other Moravian and Silesian Locales

Extant work made for Jewish clients by Christian masters outside of Brno is not that numerous. The absence of such work from the earlier period is clearly a result of local demand being satisfied directly by Jewish masters. After the beginning of the 19th century, Christian workshops in Brno were extremely active in filling orders, and they were capable of meeting the volume of demand from the wider region. The most numerous group of extant silver Judaica from craftsmen outside of Brno bears a Jihlava hallmark.[34] The oldest work from this locality preserved in the Jewish Museum's collection is a kiddush cup made by master DK, with engraved ornamentation and the date 1623. But just as with the other older silver objects in our collection, this cup was not made originally for ritual use, ending up in Jewish hands only later.[35] After this singular artifact there follows a sizable gap in time,

[27] On the maker see Stehlíková (2003), p. 378.

[28] Torah shield, inv. no. JMP 002.294, cat. no. 66. The shield follows the model from the beginning of the century. During this period similar work no longer had an opportunity to attract clients on account of the competition from Vienna.

[29] Cf. Stehlíková (2003), p. 401.

[30] In addition to the great many spice boxes from his workshop, also extant are two Torah shields, an alms box, and a Burial Society comb.

[31] Cf. Stehlíková (2003), p. 417.

[32] A circumcision set by him was once offered at auction by Christie's. See Christie's Catalogue, 1990, p. 17, cat. no. 25.

[33] It could have been located in Brno proper or his pieces might have been transported for assaying from one of the towns nearby.

[34] In Jihlava there also was in effect until 1848 the prohibition on Jews settling in the town. Objects, therefore, were either intended for one of the surrounding communities or they could be brought into Jihlava for assaying by one of the provincial masters. Thus determining a Jewish craftsman outside of Jihlava is difficult without archival evidence.

[35] Cup, inv. no. JMP 002.195, cat. no. 338. Judging its ornamentation, its original use can be identified relatively easily: it was a prize for the winner of an annual shooting competition held by the Brotherhood of St. Sebastian in Jihlava.

and makers, whom we might assume are from the ranks of Jihlava Christian silversmiths, do not appear again until the 1820s. The first is master AF, again identified only by his initials, whose earliest extant work, an alms box in the form of a tomb, is dated to 1821.[36] Other examples of his work preserved in the Museum's collection are a Torah pointer, spice box, and an alms box from 1829. Another Jihlava craftsman is master IB. His work extant in the collection is represented by a Torah crown (also from 1821) and a charity dish from 1825.[37] Other objects of Jihlava provenance no longer appear over the subsequent years. Local craftsmen evidently took advantage of a temporary spike in demand after Brno workshops had scaled back their production.

Other Moravian localities contribute only individual pieces. A Znojmo hallmark and JS maker's mark are on Torah finials from 1790 and on two Torah shields from the same year. The master might very well be Josef Sartori, who was based in Moravský Krumlov and stamped his work with a Znojmo hallmark.[38]

A Torah shield from 1810 bears an Olomouc hallmark and JT as the master's mark, which most likely refers to Johann Tychi from Prostějov, a provincial member of the Olomouc silversmiths guild since 1804.[39] Also coming from Olomouc are two pairs of Torah finials, both dated to 1814, and bearing the maker's mark AS. This is likely the work of Antonín Schmidt, affirmed as an Olomouc master in 1804.[40] The latest extant piece bearing an Olomouc hallmark is a Burial Society comb dating to 1828 from a master EW, whom we have been unable to identify further.[41] Other finials, almost identical in form to those from Olomouc, have a master's mark AD and no hallmark. They might have been made by Andreas Domeni, who worked in Místek.[42] An alms box from 1781 made by master IS bears a Kroměříž hallmark.[43]

Ritual objects produced in Silesia number only a few in the Museum's collection. The earliest is a pair of Torah finials made by Breslau (Wroclaw) master Georg Kahlert the younger.[44] An Opava hallmark is found on two objects from the early 19th century: Torah finials from 1810, marked with the complete surname "Oehler"; a Torah pointer from the same year bearing a poorly legible master's mark (apparently the initials AG).[45]

[36] Alms box, inv. no. JMP 007.049, cat. no. 296.
[37] Torah crown, inv. no. JMP 007.157, cat. no. 91.
[38] Torah shield, inv. no. JMP 010.405, cat. no. 26. On the assumed maker see Schirek (1902), p. 67.
[39] Torah shield, inv. no. JMP 010.324, not included in catalogue. On the assumed maker see Schirek (1902), p. 163.
[40] Torah finials, inv. no. JMP 002.939/01, 02, not included in catalogue, and Torah finials, inv. no. JMP 010.995/01, 02, not included in catalogue. On the assumed maker see Stehlíková (2003), p. 451.
[41] Burial Society comb, inv. no. JMP 007.559, cat. no. 329.
[42] Torah finials, inv. no. JMP 002.944/01, 02, cat. no. 112. On the assumed maker see Stehlíková (2003), p. 104.
[43] Alms box, inv. no. JMP 007.042, not included in catalogue. The Kroměříž hallmark is from 1769 and applied to the whole Přerov region; cf. Schirek (1902), p. 137. The maker, that is, might not have come from Kroměříž proper.
[44] Torah finials, inv. no. JMP 010.386/02, 02, cat. no. 100, from 1732–1737. On the maker see Rosenberg, p. 294, no. 1449.
[45] Torah finials, inv. no. JMP 012.188/01, 02, not included in catalogue; Torah pointer, inv. no. JMP 010.705, cat. no. 211.

In conclusion, I should point out that when it comes to makers from Moravia and Silesia, particularly from the beginning of the 19th century, it is impossible without additional biographical details to distinguish between Christian and Jewish goldsmiths and silversmiths, especially if all we have to go on is their extant work. After the discriminatory measures were relaxed, Moravian Jews could become members of the already existing Christian guilds, which meant that the techniques and means of expression that had differentiated their work during the long years of isolation soon became homogenized. For the purposes of this study, the working method I have chosen for categorizing individual craftsmen as either Christian or Jewish is if an object bears a complete master's mark and hallmark, which is evidence of the object's readiness to be introduced into the standard commercial chain, and if there exist specific ornamental details.[46] This method, however, is not the most reliable, and as such there is the possibility that several masters whom we now classify as Christian might have to be reclassified in the future, as far as their religious affiliation is concerned, as Jewish.

[46] For ornamental details and motifs that identify Jewish masters with a high degree of probability, see, for example, Torah shield, inv. no. JMP 001.543, cat. no. 43, made in 1810 by master MG and stamped with a Jihlava hallmark, with the central motif of the Ark of the Covenant and offered bread, in slightly altered form from that known in drapery. The shield is marked in full, and if we were to rely solely on the complete markings as a key to categorizing this maker as Christian then our findings would clearly be misleading.

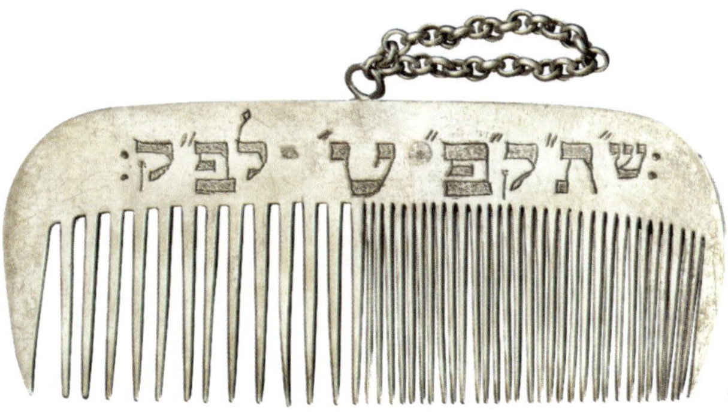

< Cat. No. 329

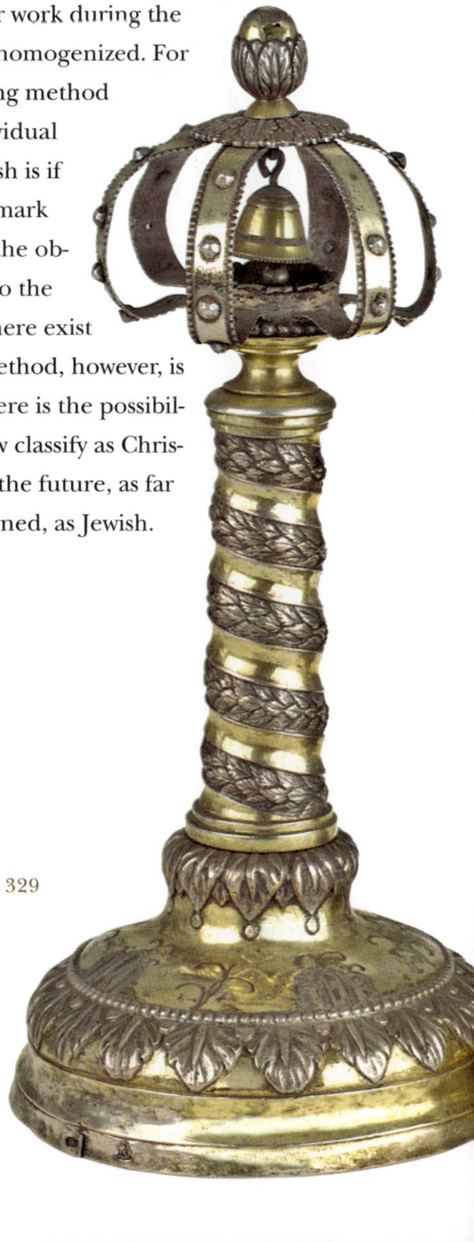

Cat. No. 112 >

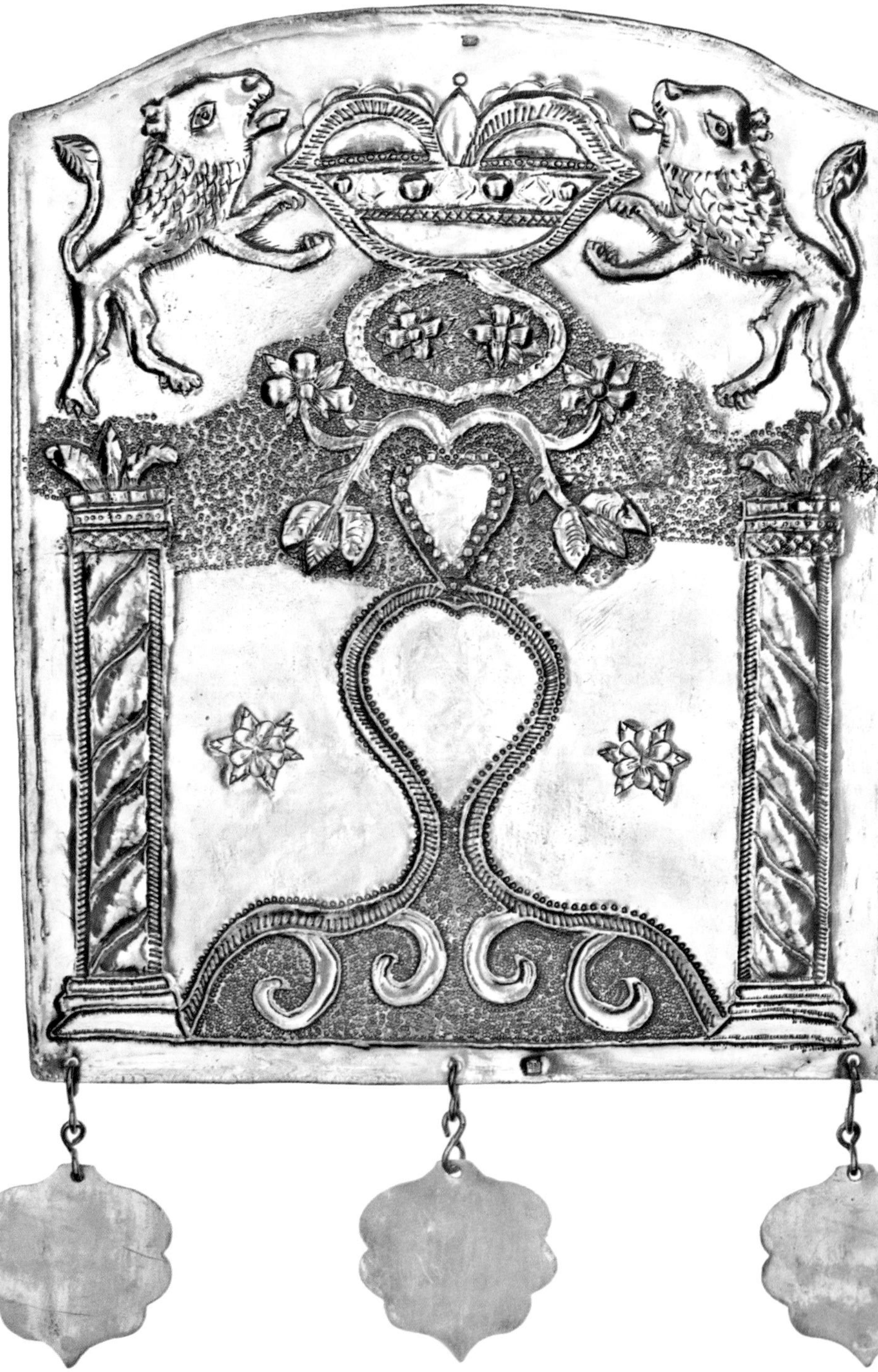

Cat. No. 29

CHAPTER 7

The Compulsory Purchase of Synagogue Silver 1809–10

Its impact on the Jewish communities, their reactions to the program, and how it has shaped the Museum's present holdings.

The structure of the Jewish Museum in Prague's holdings has to a large extent been shaped by historical events, some of which took place many years before the Museum was even established. One such event was an extraordinary levy placed on precious metals and a subsequent program for the compulsory purchase of gold and silver objects, which was instituted at the beginning of the 19th century and applied to private individuals as well as to professional and religious institutions.

The One-Time Tax and Compulsory Purchase

After 1800, the Austrian state found itself in financial straits largely as a result of the wars it was engaged in.[1] In searching for other sources of finances, the government decided to impose, among other measures, a supplemental tax on the ownership of gold and silver objects.[2] This measure was promulgated by an imperial patent of Emperor Francis I. on August 20, 1806, after which on August 24 the Regional Governor of Bohemia issued a circular.[3]

The measures were to come into effect on September 1, 1806, and end on May 1, 1807, but they were extended by three months

[1] Austria's joining the anti-Napoleon coalition brought rather than military success a string of defeats. The most germane to the discussion at hand was its defeat at the Battle of Wagram in 1809, after which it signed a punitive peace treaty with Napoleon that required it to pay large reparations, and this further contributed to the breakdown of an already exhausted economy.

[2] The tax was imposed in the German Hereditary Lands, that is, Upper and Lower Austria, Styria, Carinthia, Carniola, Gorizia, Tyrol, Bohemia, Moravia, and Silesia.

[3] Patent ref. no. 28876/1806 and the Order of the Governor no. 5970/1806; cf. Hráský (1987), p. 173, notes 1 and 2.

and in reality ended on July 31, 1807. After this deadline, objects made of precious metals were not to be marked post facto, and any unmarked objects were subject to confiscation. The obligation to tax precious metals applied to all citizens, including religious institutions, thus synagogues and the liturgical items in their possession. For this purpose, the Assay Office was reestablished in Vienna, with new branches opening up in the major metropolises of the individual lands in the Monarchy.[4] In the provincial towns, this was performed by an assay commission that fell under the jurisdiction of the branch Assay Office.[5]

All owners of gold and silver objects were required to submit in the given time frame these objects to one of the offices to be listed, weighed, and generally appraised. Smaller objects for personal use, garment elements, and other specifically designated types of objects were exempt from the mandatory hallmarking requirement. The proportion of precious metal in the alloy was not examined, and the fee was based solely on weight. The object was then stamped with the appropriate hallmark,[6] and according to its weight or its appraisal it was assessed an extraordinary assay fee, which in the case of gold was 20 kreuzer of conventionsmünze for the weight of one ducat (3.49 g) and in the case of silver 12 kreuzer of conventionsmünze for the weight of one lot (17.55 g).[7] Compared to the former standard assay fees levied by the authorized representative of the goldsmiths guild, this new fee represented a rather significant increase.[8]

Despite the undoubted boon to the state's coffers that resulted from these measures, it proved insufficient. The amount of income it contributed to the budget was still too small compared to the awful economic situation the Empire found itself in. For this reason, the state administration began to take further measures. The first was a patent announced on April 1, 1809, on the voluntary "loan" of precious metals, which should have gone a long way toward addressing the economic difficulties. This loan program, however, was not popularly received, so on December 19 of the same year another patent was issued that decreed the surrender to the state of all silver objects in private ownership. The objects were to be melted down, and then the precious metal that was extracted was to be used for the minting of coins.

[4] The Assay Office in Vienna had been provisionally established in 1783 with a fixed mandate until July of the following year. Its role was to supervise the adherence to fineness standards for precious metals that were processed by the craftsmen; in practice this entailed the extraction of sample material from the object submitted and then stamping it with a hallmark for which a fee was charged. The office was abolished during the reorganization of the state administration in 1790, and it was subsumed under the Central Mint Office, which performed assay services until the Assay Office was established (see Täubl et al (2001), p. 32). The main task of the reestablished Assay Office and its branches was to stamp all available silver objects with the appropriate hallmarks and collect the assay fee.

[5] Each individual assay office was given a separate composition of letters of the alphabet in a mark that had a unified form (see Knies (1896), Taf. I, Fig. 1-66).

[6] For Church silver, to ensure the objects would not be desecrated a priest was entrusted with the stamping, and the same approach likely applied to synagogue objects (cf. Hráský (1987), p. 167), which could explain the high incidences of illegible marks.

[7] With ducats and lots, the Vienna unit of weight is used. To address the dearth of coinage, banknotes were later allowed as payment for bills and fees, of course at a rate two times higher (see Täubl et al (2001), p. 36).

[8] The previous marking fee on silver was 4 kreuzer of conventionsmünze for a talent (16 lots), that is, the fee was raised by a factor of forty-eight (ibidem, p. 35).

The owners of the objects surrendered were given a provisional voucher for payment based on a fixed rate.[9] For the time being, the requirement to surrender silver only applied to individuals, and the surrender of gold was left to the voluntary decision of owners. Exempt from this requirement were objects of personal use, medical instruments, medals, works of art and antiques, mounts for jewels, and stored objects designated for sale. The measures gave owners several ways to absolve themselves of the obligation to surrender their objects, but none were exactly favorable to owners. The first option was to pay in coinage the price of the object at the rate established; the second was to pay in banknotes at a rate three times higher; and the third option was to surrender other silver objects of the same volume, in which case the object first had to go through a process of being released from surrender. Objects released from the compulsory purchase obligation through one of the above options were stamped at the appropriate location with a prescribed mark, what is known as the release mark.[10]

The quantity of precious-metal objects obtained from individuals did not, however, meet the expectations of the state organs, so on January 17, 1810, the Court Chamber issued an order that instituted the compulsory purchase of objects in the possession of Church and religious institutions, which of course included synagogue furnishings. This order also included gold objects, and the said institutions were required over the course of two months to surrender all non-essential liturgical objects made of precious metals. Compensation again took the form of a payment voucher or debenture. Yet the surrender of precious-metal liturgical objects became a long, drawn-out affair. This might have been a result of the huge volume of administrative work it entailed and delays in establishing the amount of remuneration for the released liturgical objects, either provisionally or permanently, that had been deemed absolutely essential, and the lack of clarity about the precise approach put forth in other circulars. Also greatly contributing to the delays was the understandable reluctance of custodians of religious objects to comply.

Even though by the beginning of 1814 not all documented precious-metal objects had yet to be handed over, an order was issued in June that all work in this program was to end in August of that year. Afterward there

[9] This amounted to 23 gulden and 36 kreuzer of a conventionsmünze for a talent of pure silver (cf. Hráský (1987), p. 168.

[10] The mark was composed of the letters FR ("frei" = free), and in some cases had the letters N and S on the sides (see Knies (1896), Taf. IV, Fig. 1-4). The compulsory purchase program was to have ended on May 1, 1810, yet the assay fee thus established remained in effect. To prevent any confusion and mistakes, objects made after 1810 were stamped with an additional mark indicating that the object had been released from surrender and a tax on it had been paid (ibidem, Taf. IV, Fig. 10-13).

was to be no more compensation paid for the metals handed in, yet the owners were still required to surrender objects. An imperial decree of August 1, 1817, discontinued the program and also set how the compensation plus interest accrued was to be paid. The measures were definitively ended when the new hallmark law went into effect on April 1, 1824, which superseded the validity of all preceding measures. None of the measures instituted between 1806 and 1810, however, did much to alleviate the critical financial situation. On March 15, 1811, Austria was forced to declare national bankruptcy,[11] and the currency was devalued to twenty percent its previous value. The bankruptcy affected nearly every citizen.

How the Measures Impacted the Jewish Communities' Property

Given the present composition of the Jewish Museum in Prague's holdings, it is evident that the measures described above had a drastic impact on the property of Jewish communities and associations. Compared to the period that followed, where we see in the collection a continuous chronology for silver objects of all types, the older objects are represented only by singular pieces. The individual Jewish communities and individual owners of silver in Bohemia and Moravia did not really have much choice when presented with the purchase restrictions, and they were expected to act as loyal subjects and citizens. As the marks on the preserved objects left to them indicate, the vast majority did just that. Almost all of the older objects in the collection, or those produced until the end of 1807, as the case may be, bear marks confirming the payment of the extraordinary assay fee. Given the projected quantity of silver objects, particularly those in the possession of synagogues and private shuls, this requirement represented an undoubted financial blow, and was a generally unpleasant experience. Nonetheless, after getting the objects newly stamped owners could freely use and do what they pleased with them without further restriction. For those objects lacking a mark confirming payment of the extraordinary assay fee, one could conclude from their provenance that rather than an attempt to keep them secret, at the time the measures were in force they were not in the regions where the new markings were required. Yet even in the early phase of the program there were attempts to reduce the amount of fees incurred. The extant evidence would suggest that there was a widely adopted practice to exploit the fact that the fee was based on an object's weight. It worked like this: an object of low weight would be submitted to the commission and stamped with a new mark, then the original mark would be carefully excised and soldered onto an area prepared on another object.[12] This was a relatively simple operation to execute, and if done carefully it could not be detected by the eye alone.[13] The practice was probably so widespread that after a while it did not escape the notice of state officials.[14]

[11] Decree of February 20, 1811.

[12] The majority of objects in the collection prepared in this way are Torah pointers.

[13] After two centuries now, such transferred marks are distinguished by the more rapid corrosion of the silver solder used, in which the line displays a slight depression and discoloration. Given the set shape and differences in sizes, we might consider that there are several instances where a forged stamp was used. This was not only the case for new hallmarks but also for the release marks.

[14] Cf. Neuwirth (2002), p. 11.

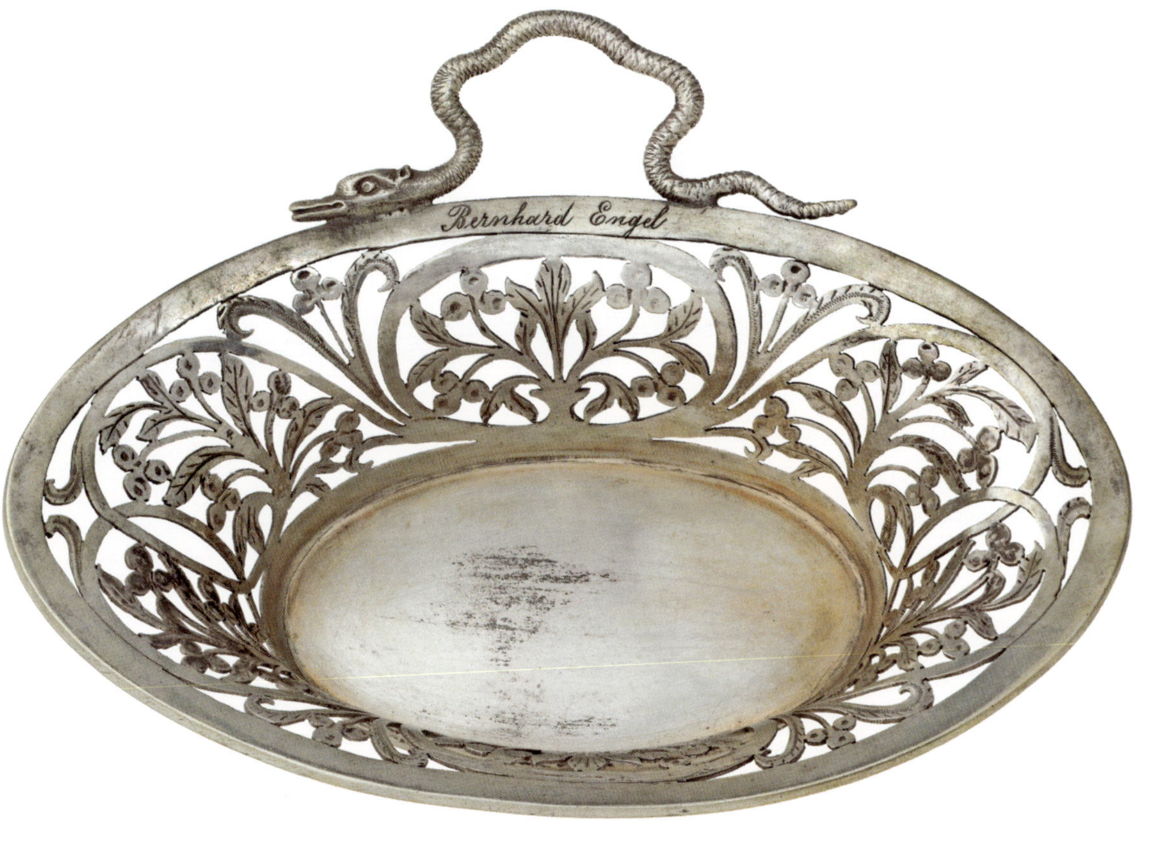

Cat. No. 281

From 1809 the situation becomes more complicated. It was no longer possible to redeem most of the objects, and owners had to decide for themselves which to sacrifice and which to keep. Given that we do not have in the collection today those objects surrendered, we cannot precisely say what factors guided these decisions, but analyzing the objects that were preserved through being redeemed does allow us to reach some general conclusions. A large number of these redeemed objects are above average in terms of their technical execution and artistic quality, though this by itself was not the sole criterion for saving them. The fact that a particular object might be connected to a specific locality or prominent individual was also an important consideration, and what's decisive here is the connection between an object and its donor and his descendants. To donate an item to the synagogue, particularly one made of costly silver, was a matter of great prestige, and this prestige was something subsequent generations of the donor would have an interest in seeing upheld. But this prestige might be attached not only to the donor but also to the person who saved the object by paying the fee to redeem it. An example is the engraved inscription on a Levite set coming from the Pinkas Synagogue in Prague, the work of Prague silversmith Jan Jiří Lux from 1702,[15] informing us that the pitcher and basin were according to an imperial decree of 1810 newly hallmarked by the brothers Kopman, Ephraim, and Hayyim,[16] sons of the elder of the Pinkas Synagogue, Isaac Epstein.[17] Another important factor in deciding which objects to save was the need to have at least the minimum number of liturgical items necessary for the proper functioning of a synagogue. All these considerations were in play, and we cannot determine today which was paramount with this or that object.

To what extent the compulsory purchase of ritual objects affected Jewish life is evidenced by the fact that the issue was addressed by Rabbi Bezalel Ranschburg in one of his responsa in which he discusses the legitimacy of the purchase requirement from the perspective of religious law.[18]

Certain regional distinctions are also noticeable in the composition of extant precious-metal objects that were redeemed. In Bohemia,

[15] Levite pitcher and basin, inv. no. JMP 046.036/01, 02, cat. no. 272.

[16] "Repuncirt" is the literal transcription of the German expression in Hebrew, and in this case it concerned an object redeemed from the requirement to hand over precious metals and then stamped with the appropriate hallmark. If we take into account the mass of both objects and the price established for the buyback of pure metals, then the brothers paid for the objects' release the rather large sum of 122 gulden of conventionsmünze.

[17] He is not directly mentioned in the inscription as the donor, though it is very likely that he was.

[18] The responsum is addressed to Rabbi Eleazar Flekeles, but in the wider sense it's possible to consider the Prague Jewish Community as the one who requested the explication. Cf. Ranschburg (1980), pp. 78-91.

these are overwhelmingly single pieces of high quality, largely from the workshops of local Christian silversmiths, and they are among the oldest extant silver Judaica of domestic make. A smaller number of redeemed metal objects in Bohemia come from the two German goldsmith centers, Nuremberg and Augsburg, and then there are as well individual pieces from other German regions.

Objects coming from Jewish workshops are, however, sporadic. Given the minimal amount of preserved evidence we cannot determine with certainty what sort of quantity and quality were generally achieved by Jewish goldsmiths and silversmiths, and whether it is possible to compare it with the work of Christian masters. Yet if we account for the limited opportunities for pursuing this trade, it would be commonly assumed that the work of Jewish masters did not reach the high level of craftsmanship of their Christian counterparts, and this is somewhat supported by the preponderance in the collection of objects made by Christian workshops. If the most important criterion when deciding an object's fate was the quality of its craftsmanship, this could explain the small number of preserved work from Jewish workshops.[19] Compared to Moravia, the number of older objects that have been preserved is quite small, and it is largely work from the beginning of the 19th century shortly before the compulsory purchase measures were instituted.

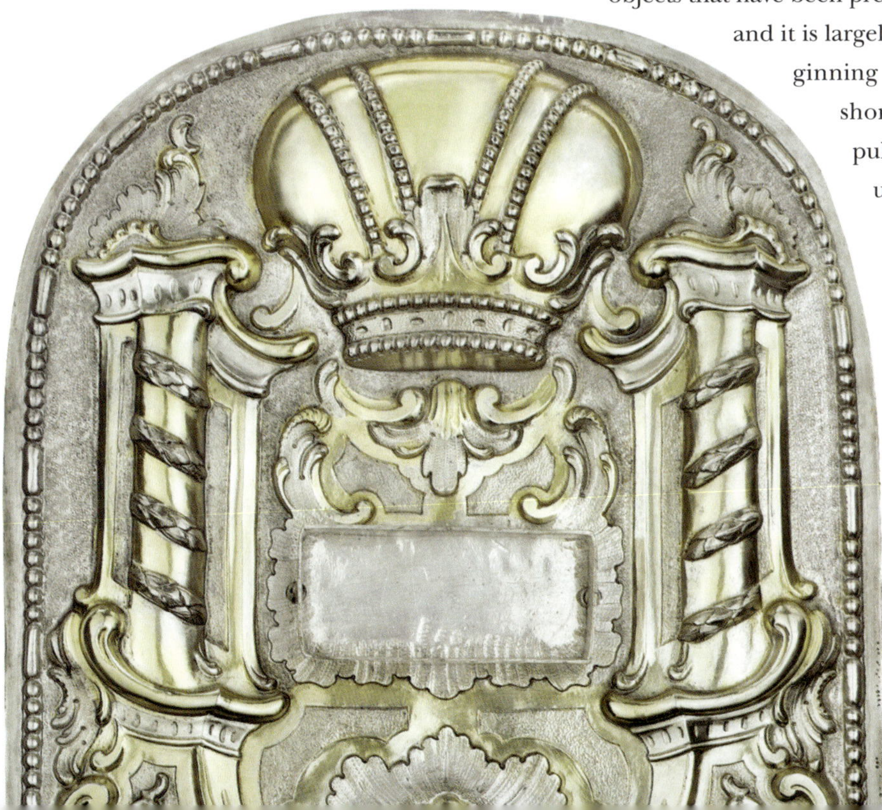

Cat. No. 30

[19] For the extant work of Jewish masters from Moravia, the quality of craftsmanship compared to Christian masters is indeed quite low.

The composition of extant objects from Moravia and Silesia is more varied, in particular in regards to provenance. A large part comprises silver objects from the very beginning of the 19th century, mainly from the workshops of Brno masters Franz Kaltenmarker and Carl Lackstampfer, but there is also somewhat older work from the smaller Moravian towns of Znojmo, Jihlava, and Mikulov. Other objects show the interaction with surrounding regions, and we see pieces with a Vienna or Silesia provenance. An interesting and relatively large group consists of old objects made in Augsburg that were adapted for ritual use. Yet we cannot say if these objects came into the possession of Jewish communities only later. To a great extent, redeemed objects were also assumed to have come from Moravian Jewish workshops (alms boxes being the most numerous). By comparing the composition and number of extant older objects in Bohemia and in Moravia, we see the communities in these two regions took different approaches in deciding on what objects to preserve. The communities in Moravia made a greater effort and devoted more finances to preserving their original ritual objects. Without more detailed knowledge of the situation at the time, however, we can only speculate as to why.

Efforts to Replenish

The Jewish communities very quickly reacted to the situation. The number of surrendered objects might partially be inferred from the accumulation of newly produced liturgical objects over the subsequent years. While such an analysis is not exact – not all newly made objects were necessarily intended as replacements for those surrendered – the sharp spike in production of silver objects is stunning and gives us an idea of the losses incurred by synagogues and homes as a result of the measures.[20] The lost objects had to be quickly replaced, and with as little financial outlay as practical. The task was given to Christian silversmiths who had performed work for Jewish clients in the past, and therefore had an idea of what was required. Jewish craftsmen only marginally contributed to replenishing the losses.

[20] For example, Karel Skřemenec produced in 1810 a total of 13 Torah pointers and over the following years (until he ceased operations in 1820) only 18 exactly dated pieces altogether.

[21] On Karel Skřemenec cf. Hráský (1981), p. 93, no. 422; on Tomáš Höpfel, cf. ibidem, p. 45, no. 160; on Antonín Kába, cf. ibidem, p. 50, no. 186; and on Antonín Maroušek, cf. ibidem, p. 62, no. 265.

[22] Compare the technical quality of an older Torah shield, inv. no. JMP 001.957, cat. no. 30, from 1797 with a later Torah shield, inv. no. JMP 037.427, cat. no. 53, from 1816.

[23] From Skřemenec the JMP's collection has 72 Torah shields, 48 Torah pointers, and dozens of various other objects. The paucity of information on him does not allow us to ascertain whether he worked alone or employed journeymen in his workshop.

In Bohemia, the primary supplier of new silver objects was the Prague silversmith Karel Skřemenec, who had already worked for Jewish clients at the end of the 18th century, followed by his fellow Prague craftsmen Tomáš Höpfel, Antonín Kába, and Antonín Maroušek.[21] From what we can judge from the preserved objects intended for a general clientele, Skřemenec produced standard, affordable pieces geared toward the middle class. The oldest extant ritual objects from his workshop – Torah shields and pointers from the end of the 18th century still executed in Rococo style – display a relatively high level of skill. As output grew quality quickly began to decline, but clients evidently were willing to accept a lower quality in exchange for promptness and affordable prices.[22] Nevertheless, the quantity of work produced by Skřemenec's workshop is remarkable. It seems that in the last phase of his career he worked exclusively for Jewish clients.[23]

Cat. No. 53

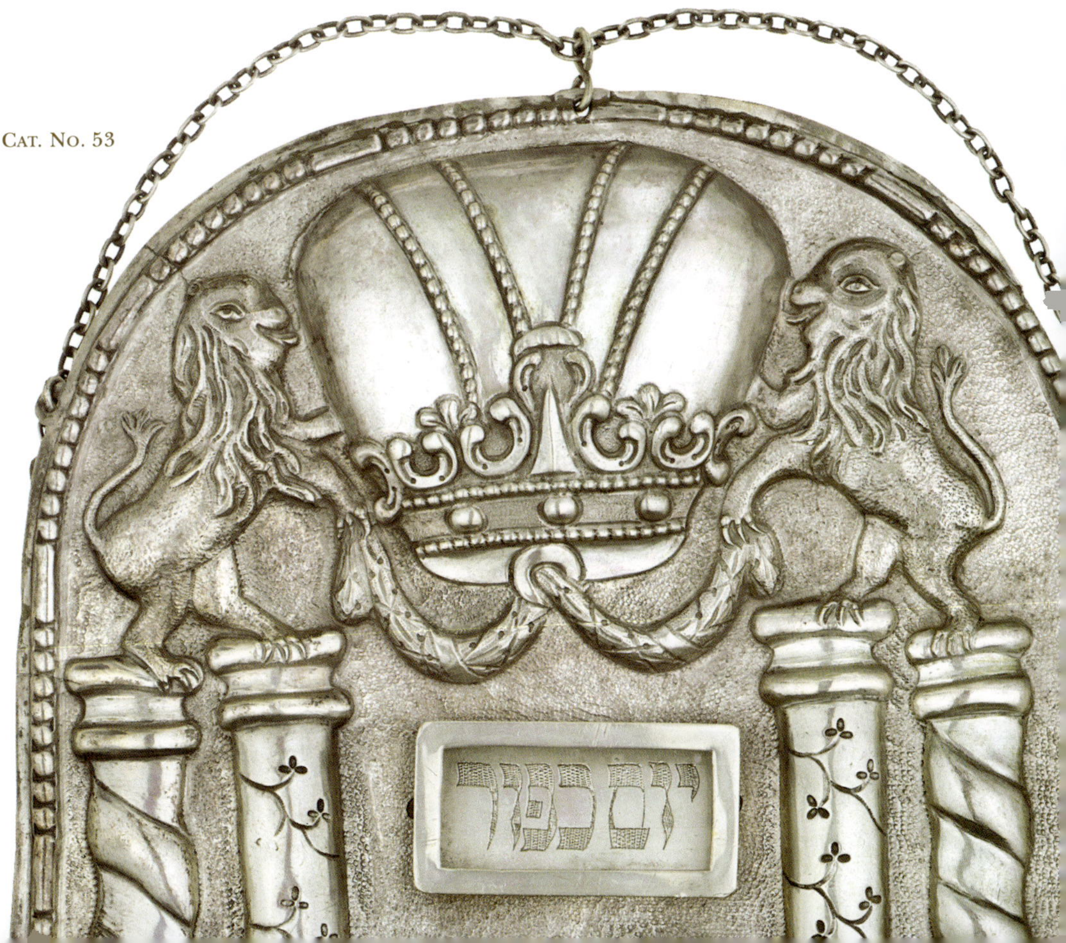

Tomáš Höpfel was another supplier. He did not become a master until 1815 so missed the beginning of the boom in demand to replace "expropriated" property. Still, his work for Jewish clients starts appearing as soon as 1816, and in the case of Torah shields, his work was distinguished by a rather original artistic interpretation.[24] The majority of his work falls between the years 1820 and 1840. It is likely that when Skřemenec closed his workshop in 1820 Höpfel was the one who took over his clients. The Höpfel workshop continued to produce ritual objects even after his death, until his widow closed the business in 1858.[25]

Antonín Kába became a master in 1814, and together with Höpfel and Maroušek can be classified among those craftsmen who produced both Judaica and general consumer goods. His earliest reliably dated work for Jewish clients is from 1817, and he stopped working in his trade in 1831. Antonín Maroušek likewise became a master in 1814, and his first extant work for Jewish clients is straightaway dated to the following year.[26] He worked for Jewish clients over the whole of his long career, and his later work comes from the latter half of the 19th century. Other artisans also contributed to replenishing the original inventory of liturgical and other precious-metal objects, including Antonín Neubert, Jan Adam Řehořovský, and as yet unidentified master IN. Their share of the work compared to those craftsmen mentioned above, however, constitutes only the odd individual piece. Of the Jewish masters, worthy of mention are Michal Samuel Goldschmid and Rafael Jonas Goldschmid, known in this period for their filigreed spice boxes, small Ark curtain bells, and Torah pointers.

The situation in replenishing the inventory of the numerous religious objects in Moravia and Silesia was similar to that in Bohemia. Even in these regions there were several Christian silversmiths who focused on this type of work or were chosen by members of the Jewish communities[27] to make objects. The Brno silversmith Franz Kaltenmarker became virtually the exclusive supplier of new ritual objects to Moravian Jewish communities. He had already performed work for Jewish clients in the past, and his position was clearly strengthened by the fact that he could point to older Judaica made by the workshop of his father, Jan Michael Kaltenmarker.[28] Compared to his counterpart

[24] Torah shield, inv. no. JMP 037.603, cat. no. 54.
[25] Torah pointer, inv. no. JMP 037.986, from 1853, not included in catalogue.
[26] Havdalah candle holders, inv. no. JMP 012.732, from 1815, not included in catalogue; cf. M. Veselská (2006), cat. Fig. 31.
[27] Cf. Stehlíková (2003), p. 216 (here listed as Franz Kaltenmarker II. the younger).
[28] E.g., Torah finials, inv. no. JMP 005.340/01, 02, cat. no. 107.
[29] About half of what we know Skřemenec accepted; the last known work of Judaica from his workshop (Torah finials) dates to 1821.
[30] Cf. Grossová (2006), pp. 119–142.
[31] The work of father and son are stylistically identical. Both used a similar, poorly legible maker's mark CL in an oval. The legibility is in many cases made even worse by the mark being clumsily stamped and the many years of use of the objects. Their contributions to the production numbers can be roughly estimated by the dating of the objects.
[32] Cf. Stehlíková (2003), p. 517.

in Bohemia, Karel Skřemenec, Kaltenmarker managed to maintain a relatively high level of craftsmanship for his whole career, which might be a result of having a somewhat smaller volume of orders to fill.[29] Other Brno masters contributing to replenishing the wide range of forms and functions of the lost objects included Carl Lackstampfer and his son, Carl Michael Lackstampfer, who worked in the same style as Kaltenmarker.[30 31]

In addition to these three silversmiths mention should also be made of Jakob Uhl, originally a master from Znojmo who in this period was obviously working in Brno or its environs,[32] even though his output, of course, does not compare quantitatively with the others. And there were other craftsmen from the towns of Moravia and Silesia who produced the sporadic object to replace what had been lost. This period of heightened silversmith production to replenish the losses incurred from the compulsory purchase program came to an end in the first half of the 1820s. While the number of objects made continued to grow, it happened at a much more moderate tempo, and in most cases they were produced by the next generation of artisans.

The objects testifying to the historical events outlined above, that is, the hallmarks used in the period from 1806 to 1824, offer rich material for the researcher. Several of the extant silver objects have neither maker's mark nor hallmark, and given the conservative style in which they were executed, not even an analysis along those lines would yield much in the way of a reliable dating for their making. Re-hallmarking stamps, release marks, and tax marks represent, therefore, along with the donation inscription where one exists, one of the few opportunities we have to derive a precise dating and (according to how the branches of the Assay Officer were distinguished by letters in their stamps), in some cases, even more specifically determine their provenance, or at least ascertain where the object was located during a given period. When a combination of the various aforementioned marks is present, then it is possible in these specific instances to come up with quite precise data on the object in question.

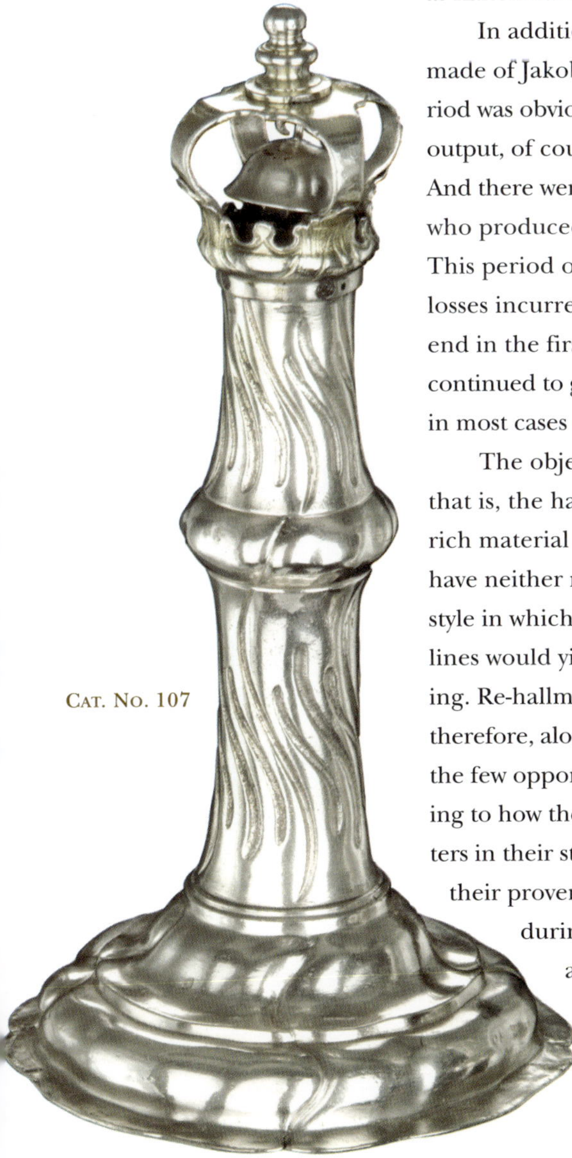

Cat. No. 107

CATALOGUE

Silver Judaica from the Collection of the Jewish Museum in Prague

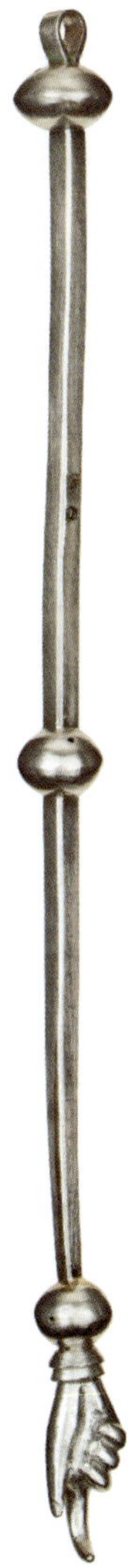

Cat. No. 225

A Note on the Catalogue

The objects included in the catalogue are for ease of reference divided into twelve groups by type. The number of objects from the more numerous groups was chosen so that 10% of a given type would be represented. Those object types whose usage was similar (for example, eternal lights and menorahs; etrog containers and dishes; cups and beakers) are included here as part of a larger group though by function they belong to separate smaller sets. The catalogue concludes with a group that comprises diverse types of objects from the Museum's collection that are either a single piece or were not used independently (for example, the small bells removed from Torah curtains). The objects within a group are arranged in chronological order and are numbered in that order. For the sake of brevity and simplicity, the entry headings are given without any extra information on when an object was published or exhibited, though most of these objects in fact are being published here for the first time. The data on maker's marks and hallmarks are given without reference to sources; these are cited in the footnotes to the individual chapters.

Each entry includes the following data:

Inventory or acquisition number:
This gives the basic identification of an object in the collection. When there is a slash followed by other numbers, this indicates an object set with more than one piece.

Techniques and materials:
All objects in the catalogue were made of silver alloy, in some cases in combination with other metals or non-metals. The precise fineness of an individual object's material has not been subjected to general laboratory testing. For those objects that include a hallmark, the fineness of the alloy roughly corresponds to the conditions set out by state regulations for the composition of precious metal in an alloy. For those objects without hallmark or any other sort of mark, a low alloy fineness should be assumed, though no general conclusions should be drawn based solely on the presence or absence of a mark. The techniques used in an object's production, and combination thereof, are briefly listed, and the same applies to an object's ornamentation – for example, if it is gilded or engraved. A more detailed discussion of production and ornamentation techniques would exceed the scope of this publication.

Maker, locality, date:
This data was derived almost exclusively from assessing the maker's (master's) marks and hallmarks found directly on the object. When there is some doubt or there is a lack of information required to precisely identify a maker, the name is give with a question mark beside it. In some cases a mark does not appear in the existing registers for a given region, the maker is identified only by his initials. If the mark is partially illegible, the initials are accompanied by a question mark. If an unmarked object in regards to maker and locality is identical in its level of artistry and technique to other work verified to be from a known master, then his name is given, with reservations, as the maker. It was not the usual practice for Jewish craftsmen to directly claim authorship for a work in the donation inscription, but when it does appear, this name is taken from the inscription. The production locality is given by the hallmark. When the location of a master has not been verified with other sources, this identification must not necessarily be exact as the location of the assay office or its branch did not have to be in the same place where a craftsman lived. The hallmark also serves as a basic piece of information for dating an object. If it is not possible to determine the exact date an object was made, a time frame is given within which it is assumed the object was made, and this is usually derived either from evaluating other marks on the object itself or on equivalent objects from the same maker, or in some cases from analyzing archival sources that mention the maker. For objects without marks and a dating in the donation inscription, an approximate date for its making is determined based on stylistic elements, perhaps also in comparison with analogous objects from the same period. When a dating appears in the donation inscription, it is used in several cases as a demarcation "ad quem."

Dimensions:
All dimensions are given in millimeters. The largest dimensions are always given, and for a better idea it is accompanied by other dimensions measured at a right angle to the first dimension. For objects that can be rotated, like Torah finials, the greatest diameter measurement is given.

Maker's mark:
Marks on the objects are written out in the following order: 1. maker's (master's) mark; 2. hallmark; 3. recharge mark; 4. tax mark(s). A brief wording was chosen to simplify the issues surrounding such marks, and for the same reason no dimensions of the marks are given.

Donation or ownership inscriptions:
For those objects with a donation or an ownership inscription the original language of the inscription is given, and in some cases where it appears, and then the translation. The standard Hebrew abbreviations in the tablets of the Decalogue, which appear as an ornamental motif on a great many objects, are not translated.

Collection point:
A collection point is always listed for those items recorded in the so-called German catalogue of the Central Jewish Museum. One should be aware that pinpointing a concrete place for a collection point only tells us where the object

was just before it was transferred to the Museum's warehouse in Prague, and it might not be the place where the object was originally used, a fact that also applies to the region at large. The information on a collection point, therefore, has to be verified from other sources. This problem is relatively complicated and requires further explication.

During the Second World War, as the German Occupation's political administration gradually spread and entrenched, the Jewish communities lost their independence and became part of a hierarchical structure whereby several local Jewish communities always fell under a "regional community," and these regional communities were centrally administered from Prague, the Jewish Religious Community there. As a result of this form of administration imposed on the communities' property, the continuing mass deportations, and an effort to save objects from the depopulated Jewish communities outside of Prague, a plan was adopted to concentrate the objects in one place (for example, objects from the whole Brno *Oberlandrat* were first concentrated in Brno and shortly thereafter transferred to Prague). So the objects moved between particular locations, and listed in the catalogue of the Central Jewish Museum in Prague, which was compiled in August 1942, are objects that were sent from the nearest city or larger town, not from the Jewish communities where they originated. This wartime collection, which brought in the majority of objects found in the catalogue today, has yet to be properly investigated because it is an issue of incredible complexity requiring a thoroughgoing cross-disciplinary approach.

Objects from Prague synagogues were collected at the beginning of 1942 and deposited in the Pinkas Synagogue, which was serving at that time as a depot. After the Central Jewish Museum was set up in August 1942, they were gradually included in the collections. In a number of cases, however, the original information on the synagogue where an object was actually in use before the war and from where it was transferred to a warehouse has not been preserved; the only information remaining was that it was stored in the Pinkas Synagogue before being included in the Jewish Museum's collection. When an object does not have a donation inscription with information on who donated it and to what synagogue it belonged, it is virtually impossible to ascertain the original place of its usage. Moreover, we should be mindful that a donation inscription might not always capture the full circumstances of an object's use: the urban renewal of Prague's Jewish ghetto at the turn of the 20th century saw several synagogues and private shuls abolished, and their objects were distributed among the separate Prague synagogue associations and synagogues proper before the First World War.

The same also applies to the moveable property (synagogue furnishings) of Jewish communities in the Protectorate of Bohemia and Moravia. Before the Second World War, objects were relocated as Jewish communities were merged due to historical circumstances, such as the declining populations of some communities as Jews moved from the countryside to the city or a shortage of rabbis, etc.

The Central Jewish Museum in Prague also housed the collections of prewar Jewish museums from across the Protectorate: the Jewish

Museum in Prague was founded in 1906, and we assume no further acquisitions were made for its collection after 1939; the Central Jewish Museum for Moravia and Silesia in Mikulov, Moravia, was open to the public from 1936 to 1938; the collection of the Jewish Religious Community in Mladá Boleslav was considered a local museum as of 1898/1899.

The property of individuals deported from Prague and its environs was stored in a warehouse known as the *Treuhandstelle* (Trustee's Office for the Property of Third Persons), and for those items that were not works of art identification information on the original owners (their transport number in particular) has unfortunately not been preserved save in a few exceptional cases. For these objects, the provenance is given as Prague, *Treuhandstelle* (if it has not been determined by a maker's/master's mark or hallmark).

The State Jewish Museum in Prague was established in 1950. For many years the staff largely focused on preparing exhibitions and publishing their research. Cataloguing the collections was not undertaken systematically until the 1970s. Since that time, objects in the Museum's depositories that over the years lost their original inventory or acquisition numbers have been re-catalogued. In these cases, the object is listed here as having been entered into the Jewish Museum's catalogue secondarily (in the acquisition records). Given the absence of any other data, we are not able to ascertain anything more about its origins.

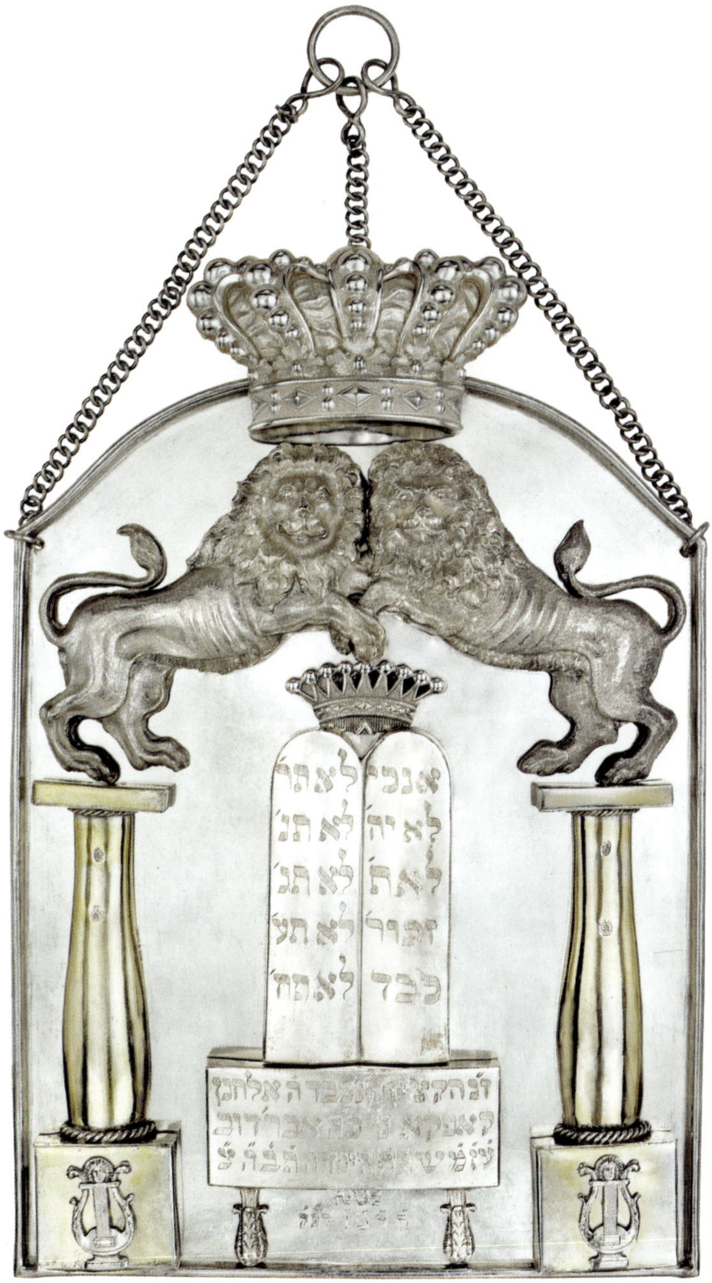

Cat. No. 70

I. Torah Shields

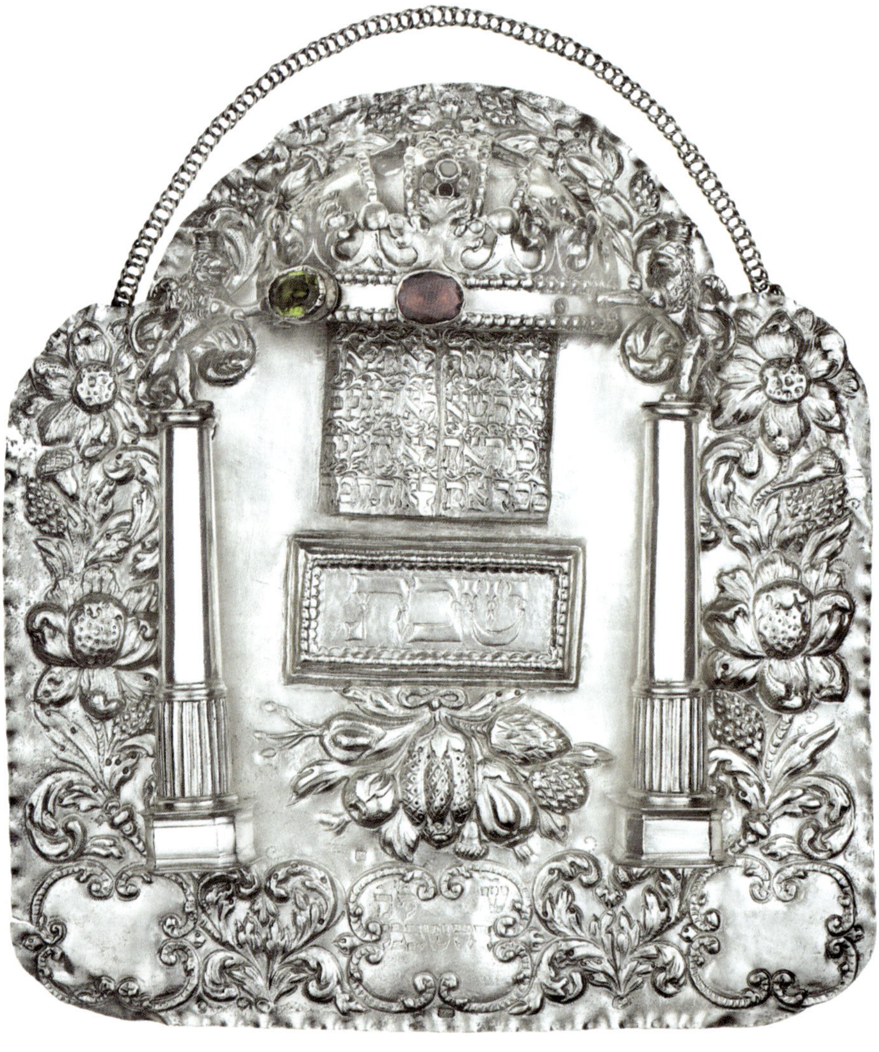

Cat. No. 2

Cat. No. 1
Torah Shield
Inv. No. JMP 001.739
Silver, repoussé
Maker unknown, Germany [?], ca 1670–80
Height: 185 mm, width: 166 mm
Hallmarks: 1. recharge mark Prague 1806–7
Without inscriptions.
Collection point: Sušice

Cat. No. 2
Torah Shield
Inv. No. JMP 005.347
Silver, repoussé, cast, glass stones
Maker unknown, Moravia [?], early 18th century [?], later additions
Height: 247 mm, width: 225 mm
Hallmarks: 1. unidentified mark, 2. recharge mark Brno 1806–7, 3. release mark 1809–10
Donation inscription in Hebrew; the first words of the Decalogue and name of the festival in Hebrew.
Translation:
In the year "early risers" [?] *a. s. c.*
[dating in the chronogram 565 = 1805].
Collection point: Holešov

Cat. No. 3
Torah Shield
Inv. No. JMP 044.437
Silver, repoussé, cast, parcel-gilt
Jan Kogler, Prague, 1708
Height: 325 mm, width: 290 mm
Hallmarks: 1. IK in oval, 2. city mark Prague–Malá Strana 1708, 3. recharge mark Prague 1806–7, 4. release mark 1809–10
Without inscriptions.
Collection point: Prague, Maisel Synagogue

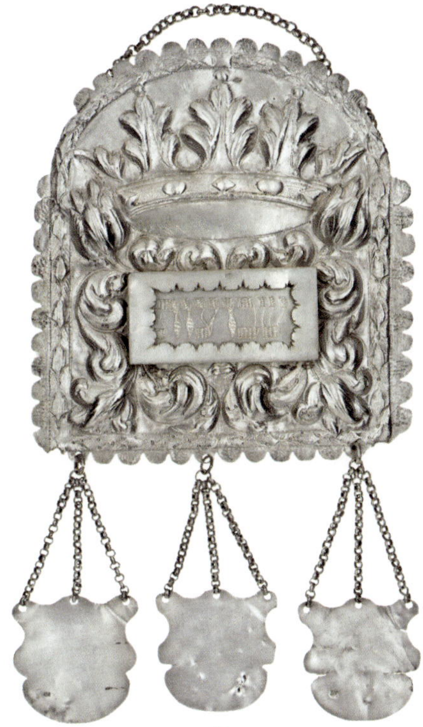

Cat. No. 1

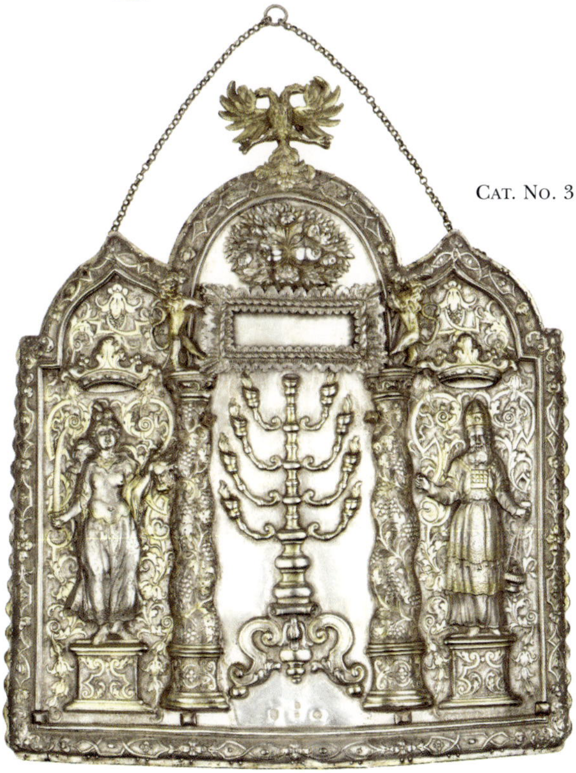

Cat. No. 3

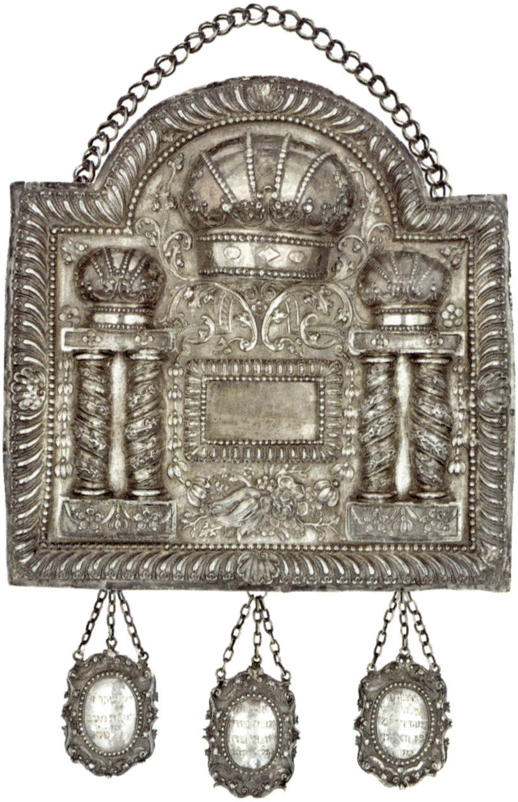

Cat. No. 4
Torah Shield
Inv. No. JMP 004.418
Silver, repoussé
Jan Kogler, Prague, 1708
Height: 280 mm, width: 278 mm
Hallmarks: 1. IK in oval, 2. city mark Prague–Malá Strana 1708, 3. recharge mark Prague 1806–7, 4. release mark 1809–10
Donation inscription in Hebrew.
Translation:
A gift of the prince, the elder MVHRR Zalman, son of the prince, MVHR Abraham Munk of Vienna, and his wife, the lady Hanel, daughter of HR Issachar of blessed memory, in the year 472 a.s.c. [= 1712].
Collection point: Rychnov nad Kněžnou

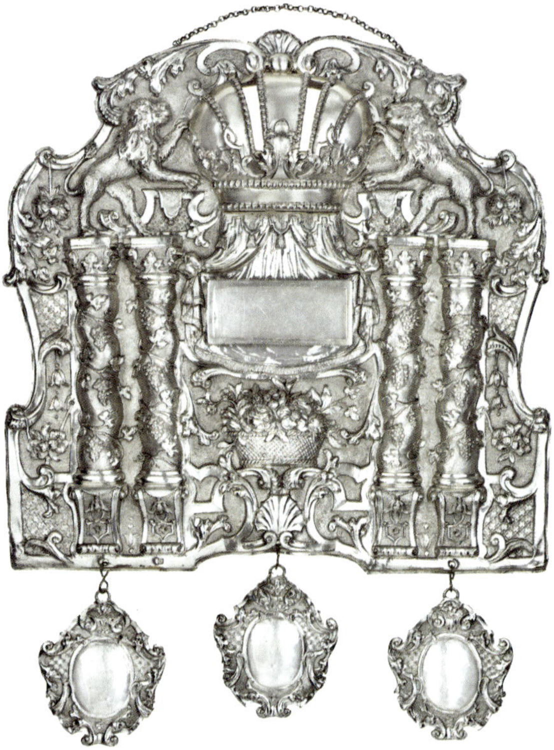

Cat. No. 5
Torah Shield
Inv. No. JMP 017.562
Silver, repoussé
Michal Josef Cocsell, Prague, 1723
Height: 340 mm, width: 336 mm
Hallmarks: 1. MIC in heart,
2. city mark Prague–Staré Město 1723,
3. recharge mark Prague 1806–7,
4. release mark 1809–10
Without inscriptions.
Collection point: Prague, Klausen Synagogue

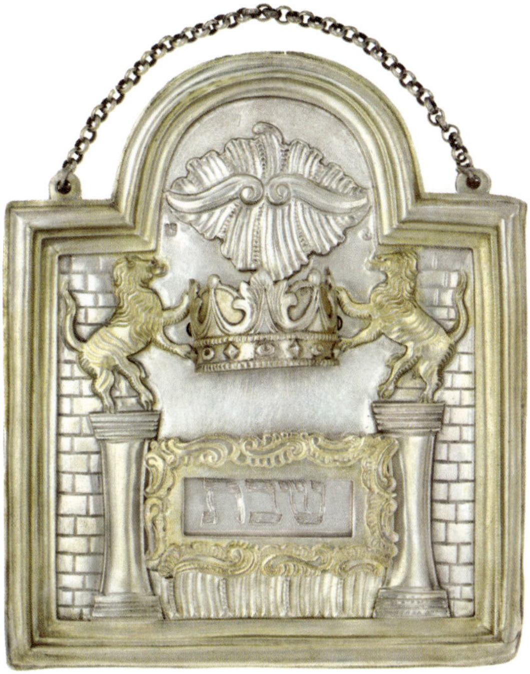

Cat. No. 6

Torah Shield

Inv. No. JMP 013.501

Silver, repoussé, parcel-gilt

Johann Samuel Beckensteiner,

Nuremberg, ca 1750

Height: 170 mm, width: 142 mm

Hallmarks: 1. stork in shield with letters IS,

2. city mark Nuremberg,

3. release mark 1809–10

Without inscriptions.

Collection point: České Budějovice

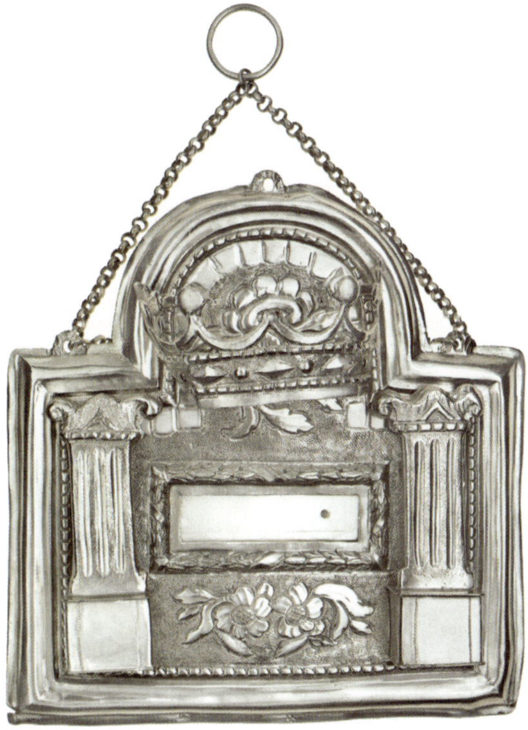

Cat. No. 7

Torah Shield

Inv. No. JMP 001.956

Silver, repoussé

Maker unknown, in the style of Wolfgang Schuberth,

Germany, 18th century

Height: 156 mm, width: 147 mm

Hallmarks: 1. unidentified mark,

2. release mark 1809–10 [?]

Without inscriptions.

Collection point: Nepomuk

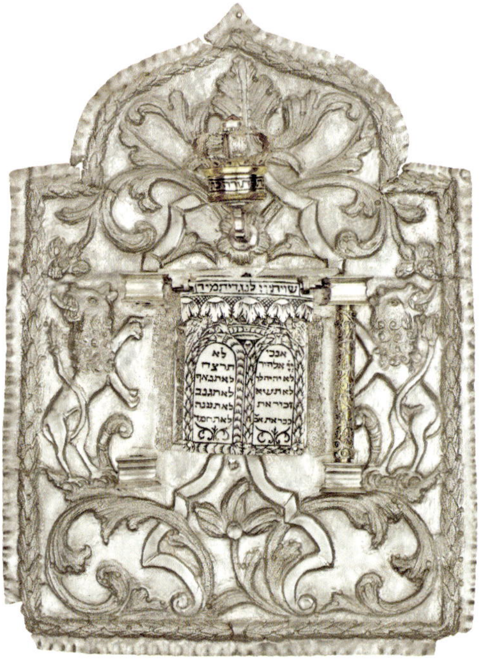

Cat. No. 8 ^
Torah Shield
Inv. No. JMP 001.515
Silver, repoussé, filigree, niello, parcel-gilt, almandin
Maker unknown, Eastern Europe, 18th century
Height: 213 mm, width: 155 mm
Hallmarks: unmarked
Inscription in Hebrew, the first words of the Decalogue in Hebrew.
Translation:
Crown of the Torah. The Crown [*of the priesthood, Crown of the kingdom*]. *"I have set the Lord always before me."* [Ps. 16:8].
Collection point: Pacov

Cat. No. 9
Torah Shield
Inv. No. JMP 012.222
Silver, repoussé
Joshua Tzoref, Třebíč, 1753 [inscription]
Height: 392 mm, width: 297 mm
Hallmarks: 1. recharge mark Brno 1806–7
Donation inscription in Hebrew.
Translation:
This is a donation exalted to the honor of the eternal Lord, a shield of the holy crown [Exod. 39:30], *an adornment for the Torah, is donated by prince KH Zelig, son K Menahem of blessed memory, and his wife, the lady Belah, daughter of H Kopel, the two as if one that You prolong their days and* [the days] *of their son K Abraham Judah and his sisters Leah and Edel, let them live and dwell in safety* [and] *peace. Made by HRR Joshua Tzoref, son of K Maharam Litsch of blessed memory, in the year 513 a.s.c.* [= 1753], *at this time, here in the holy community Třebíč.*
Collection point: Kounice

Cat. No. 10
Torah Shield
Inv. No. JMP 010.998
Silver, repoussé
Maker unknown, Moravia, 1753 [inscription]
Height: 172 mm, width: 140 mm
Hallmarks: 1. recharge mark 1806–7 [location letter unclear]
Donation inscription in Hebrew.
Translation:
This shield was made for the adornment of the tabernacle from a branch of a candelabrum recovered from the robbery of the New Synagogue. Executed through the agency of town supervisors in the year 513 a.s.c. [= 1753].
Collection point: Třebíč

Cat. No. 11
Torah Shield
Inv. No. JMP 005.344
Silver, repoussé, parcel-gilt
Georg Kahlert, Jr., Breslau, 1758–60
Height: 205 mm, width: 170 mm
Hallmarks: 1. GK in oval, 2. city mark Breslau, 3. date letter G, 4. recharge mark Prague 1806–7, 5. release mark 1809–10
Without inscriptions.
Collection point: Holešov

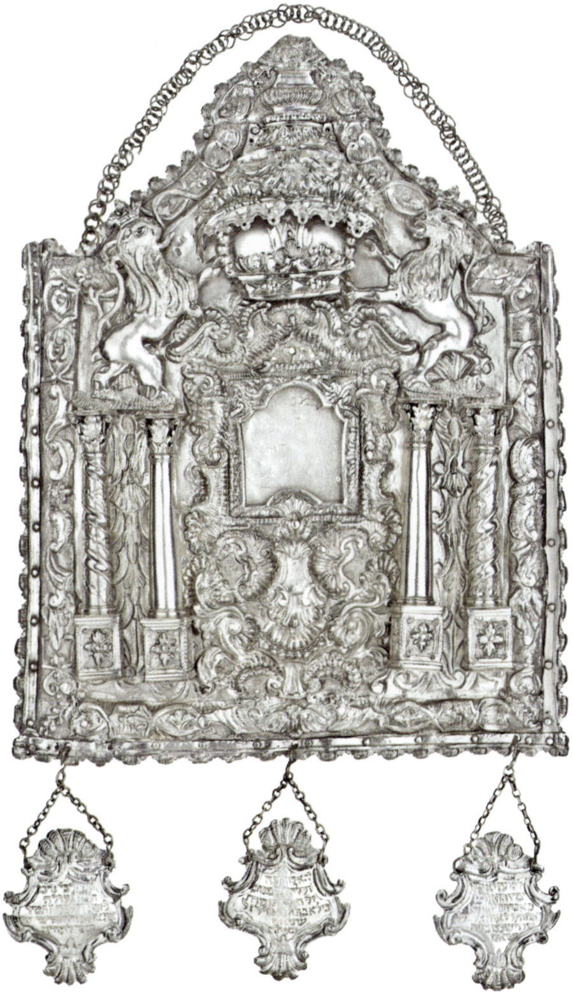

Cat. No. 9

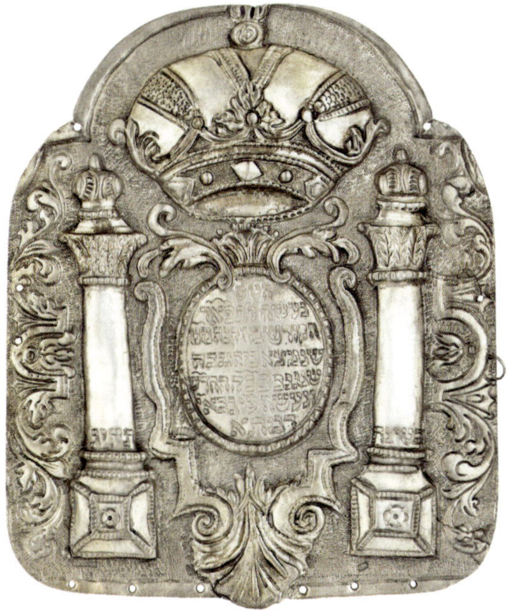

Cat. No. 10

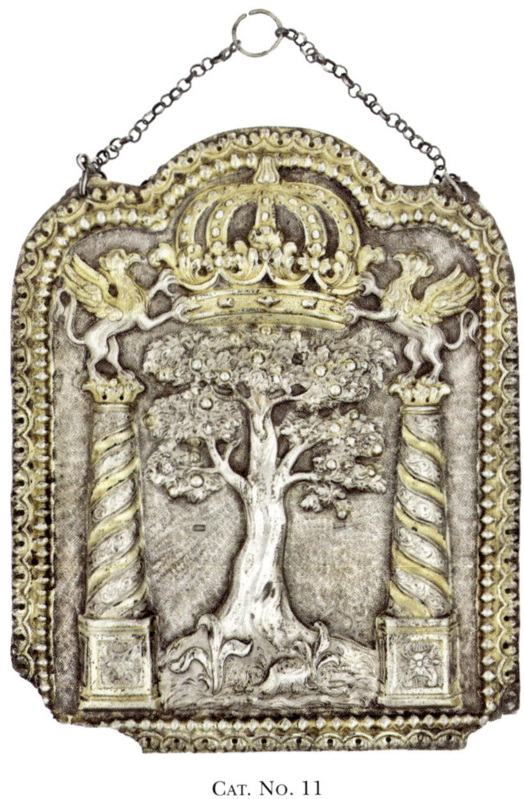

Cat. No. 11

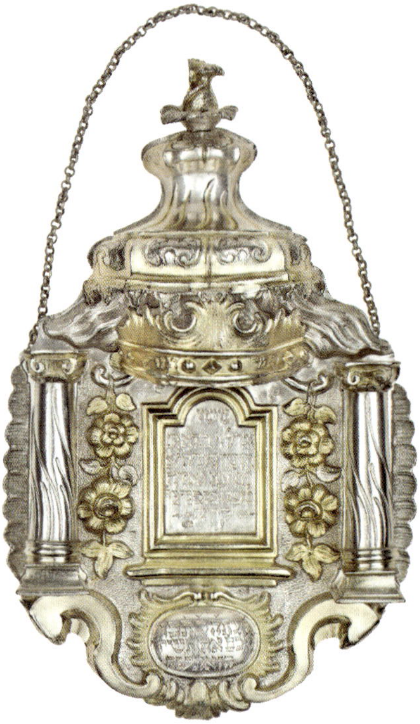

Cat. No. 12

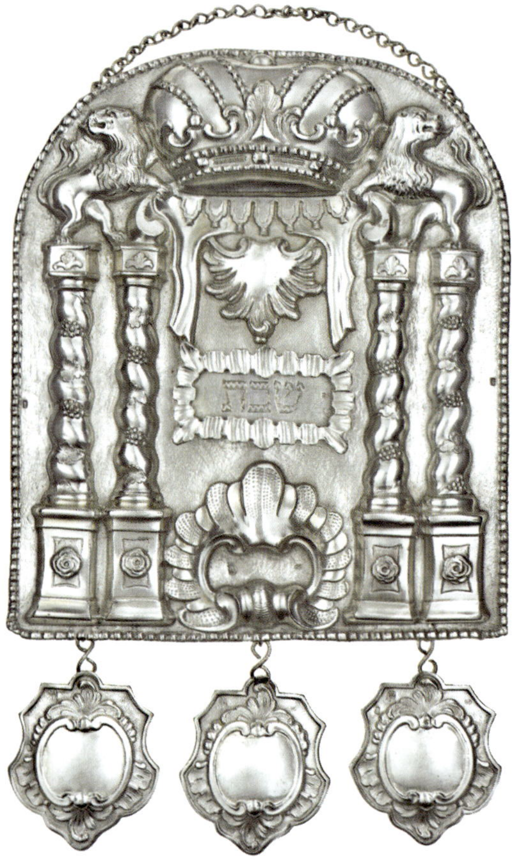

Cat. No. 14

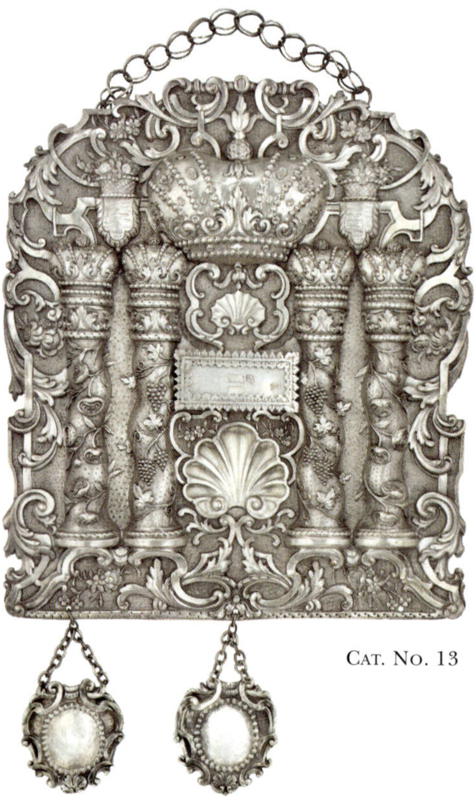

Cat. No. 13

Cat. No. 12
Torah Shield
Inv. No. JMP 005.346
Silver, repoussé, cast, parcel-gilt
Jan Michal Kaltenmarker, Brno, 1761
Height: 250 mm, width: 159 mm
Hallmarks: 1. IMK in trilob, 2. city mark Brno 1761, 3. recharge mark Brno 1806–7, 4. release mark 1809–10
Inscription in Hebrew.
Translation:
Crown of the Torah. Let us exult and rejoice with the Torah, as it is our strength and our light, dearer than gold and pearls [part of the Simchat Torah liturgy]. *"Now write down for yourselves this song." a. s .c.* [Deut. 31:19; dating in the chronogram 521 = 1761].
Collection point: Holešov

Cat. No. 13
Torah Shield
Inv. No. JMP 004.001
Silver, repoussé
Jan Jiří Brullus, Jr., Prague, 1762
Height: 347 mm, width: 298 mm
Hallmarks: 1. IGB in trilob,
2. city mark Prague–Staré Město 1762,
3. recharge mark Prague 1806–7,
4. release mark 1809–10
Without inscriptions.
Collection point: Rokycany

Cat. No. 14
Torah Shield
Inv. No. JMP 001.555
Silver, repoussé
Kryštof Wild, Prague, 1762
Height: 290 mm, width: 240 mm
Hallmarks: 1. CW in oval, 2. city mark Prague–Staré Město 1762, 3. recharge mark Prague 1806–7
Without inscriptions.
Collection point: Plzeň

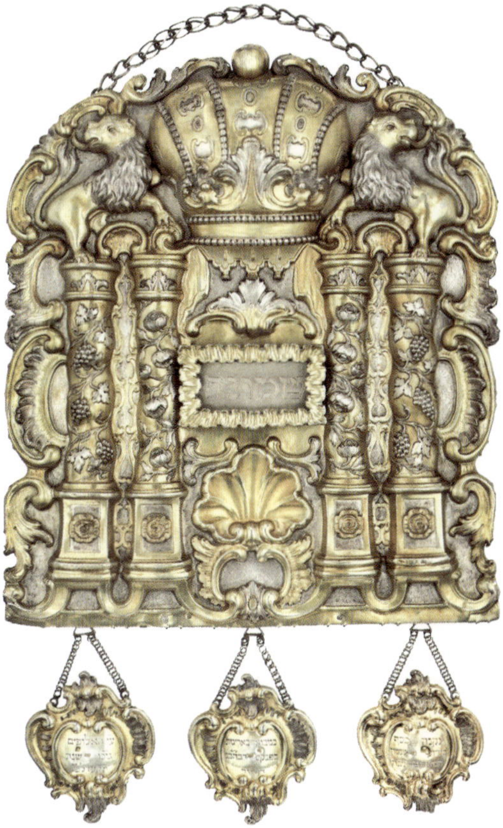

Cat. No. 15 ^
Torah Shield
Inv. No. JMP 037.594
Silver, repoussé, parcel-gilt
Kryštof Wild, Prague, 1762
Height: 365 mm, width: 310 mm
Hallmarks: 1. CW in oval, 2. city mark Prague–Staré Město 1762, 3. recharge mark Prague 1806–7, 4. release mark 1809–10
Donation inscription in Hebrew.
Translation:
[This] *that was discarded. Purchased with known money* [i.e., money whose origins are known] *and with money deposited in the coffers, as is given in detail in the Pinkas Synagogue on page 10, through the agency of the elders custodians, in the year 577 a. s. c.* [= 1817].
Collection point: Prague

Cat. No. 16
Torah Shield
Inv. No. JMP 044.438
Silver, repoussé, cast, gilt
Johann Samuel Beckensteiner, Nuremberg, 1763
[inscription]
Height: 348 mm, width: 296 mm
Hallmarks: 1. stork in shield with letters IS,
2. city mark Nuremberg, 3. tax mark Prague 1810–24
Donation inscription in Hebrew and name
of the festival in Hebrew.
Translation:
Made in the year 523 a. s .c. [= 1763]. *Lämel, son of H Zeligman from Touškov of blessed memory and his wife, the lady Rebecca, may she live, from Prague. This is a holy implement donated by my parents of blessed memory* [and] *was refurbished by their son, formerly known as Zelke Tuschkau and who through the compassion of our master Emperor Franz I was given the name of Edler von Lämel. 586 a. s. c.* [= 1826]. *And our master, the Emperor, let his majesty be exalted, has also shown compassion and kindness to me and my offspring, that he has granted his permission to engrave a seal as to one of the princes and nobles of the land who stand before you. In the year "and all his acts of power and might"* [Esther 10:2] *a. s. c.* [dating in the chronogram 586 = 1826].
Collection point: Prague, Maisel Synagogue

Cat. No. 17
Torah Shield
Inv. No. 004.391
Silver, repoussé
Richard Fleischmann, Prague, ca 1770
Height: 324 mm, width: 252 mm
Hallmarks: 1. RF in rectangle, 2. hallmark
Prague–Malá Strana, version before 1776,
3. recharge mark Prague 1806–7,
4. release mark 1809–10
Donation inscription in Hebrew.
Translation:
Donated by KH Meir Hirsch Poper with his wife, the lady Rezl, may she live, for their son, the boy Moses, may he live, in the year 598 a. s. c. [= 1838].
Collection point: Žamberk

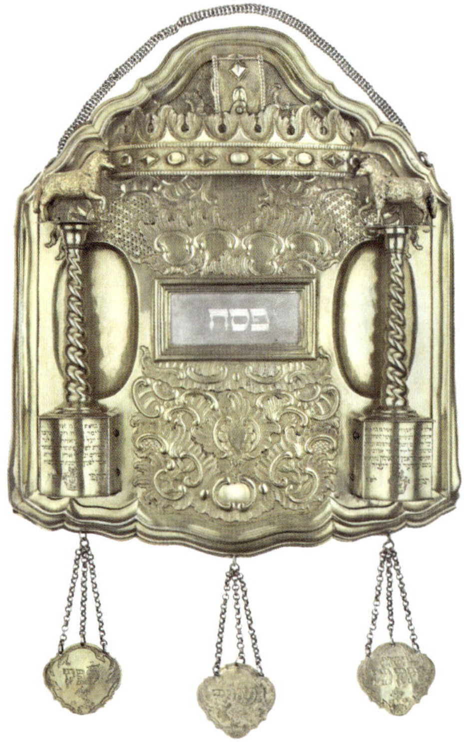

Cat. No. 16 ^ Cat. No. 17 v

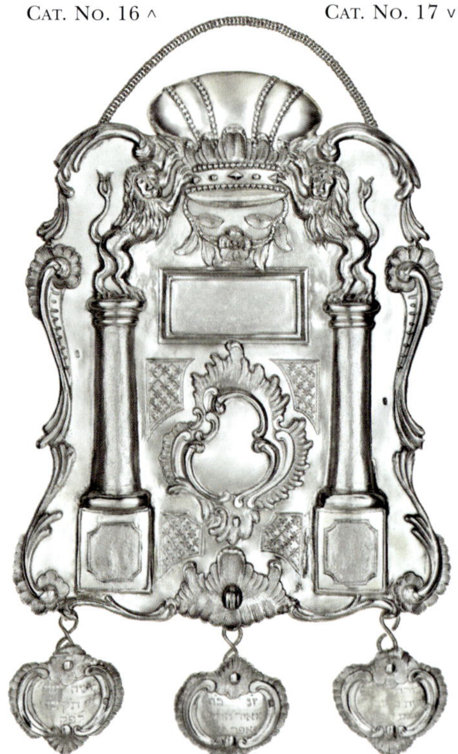

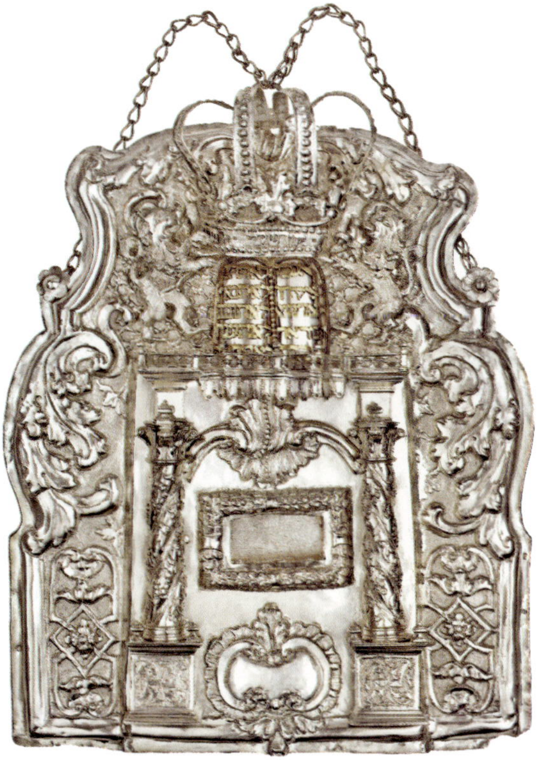

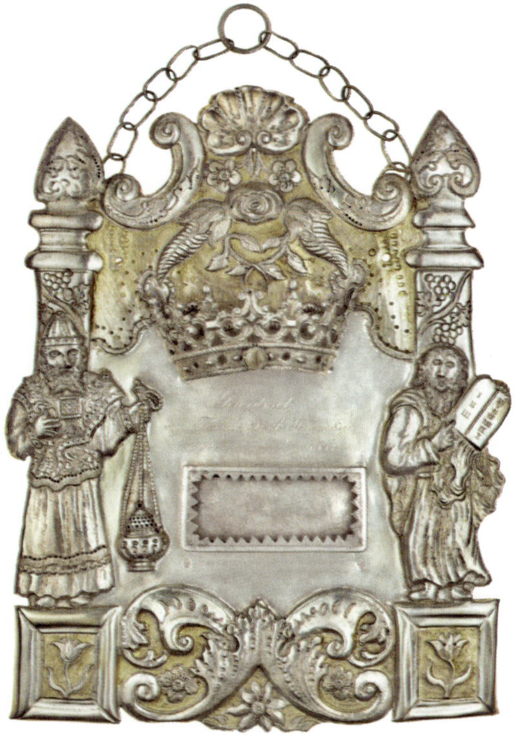

Cat. No. 18
Torah Shield
Inv. No. JMP 012.293
Silver, repoussé, cast, parcel-gilt
Maker unknown, Germany [?],
2nd half of 18th century
Height: 351 mm, width: 276 mm
Hallmarks: 1. recharge mark Vienna 1806–7,
2. unidentified mark
Without inscriptions.
Collection point: Brno, Ivančice

Cat. No. 19
Torah Shield
Inv. No. JMP 001.573
Silver, repoussé, parcel-gilt, glass stones
Maker HHK, Germany [Hamburg?],
2nd half of 18th century
Height: 332 mm, width: 260 mm
Hallmarks: 1. HHK in trilob,
2. unidentified city mark, maybe Hamburg
Donation inscription in German in Latin script.
Translation:
Donated by the family of Dr. A Stransky, 1894, 5664.
Collection point: Poděbrady

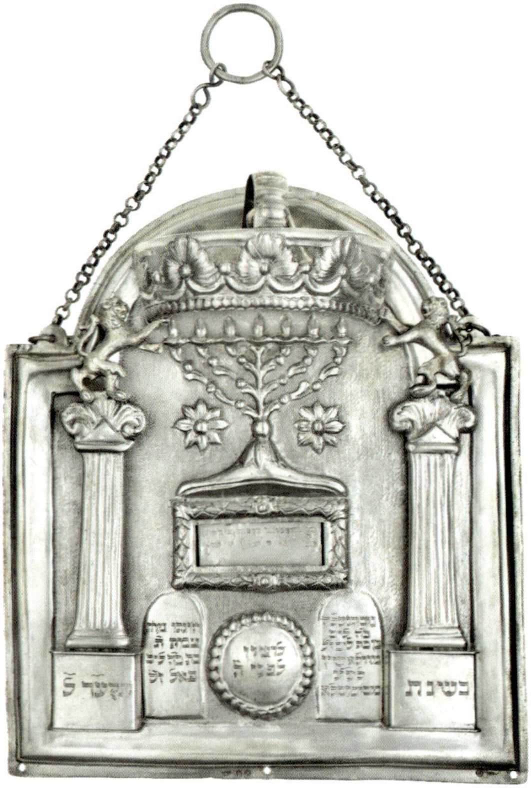

Cat. No. 20

Torah Shield

Inv. No. JMP 002.183

Silver, repoussé, cast, originally parcel-gilt

Wolfgang Schuberth, Nuremberg,

2nd half of 18th century

Height: 236 mm, width: 205 mm

Hallmarks: 1. WS in irregular rectangle,

2. city mark Nuremberg

3. unidentified mark, 4. tax mark Prague 1810–24

Donation inscription in Hebrew.

Translation:

Donated by the distinguished KH Leib, son of KH Leib of blessed memory, from Vlašim, presently from [Mladá] *Boleslav, and his wife, the lady Tzemach, may she live, daughter of KH Leib Pohl of blessed memory. In the year 574 a. s. c.* [= 1814]. *For the Lord's favor. Parshat Shekalim.*

Collection point: Mladá Boleslav

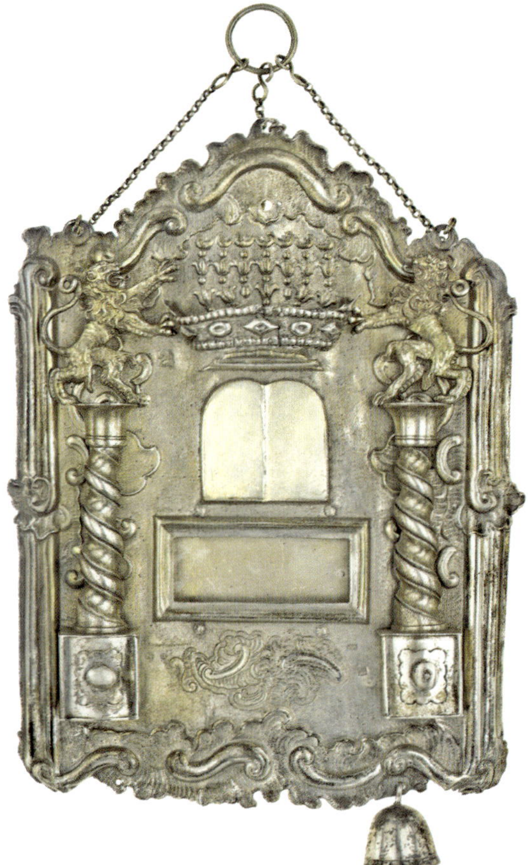

Cat. No. 21

Torah Shield

Inv. No. JMP 079.821

Silver, repoussé, parcel-gilt

Maker IM [Johann Jonas Meyer], Nuremberg,

1777–1781

Height: 267 mm, width: 199 mm

Hallmarks: 1. IM in rectangle,

2. city mark Nuremberg, 3. control letter D,

4. recharge mark Prague 1806–7,

5. release mark 1809–10

Without inscriptions.

Collection point: Prague

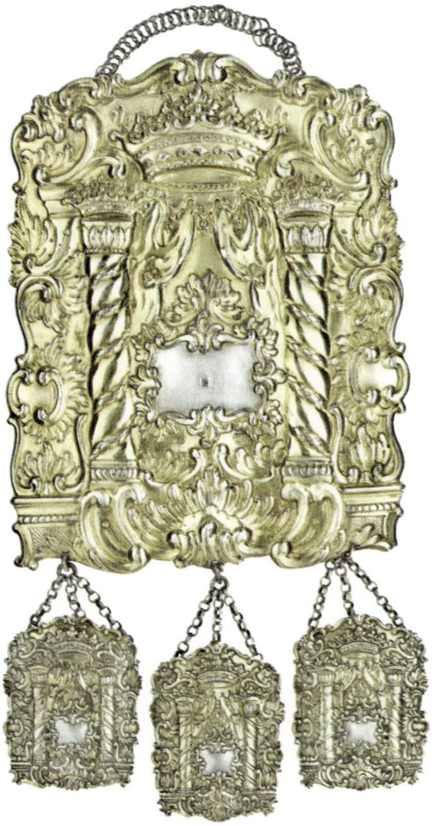

Cat. No. 22
Torah Shield
Inv. No. JMP 001.871
Silver, repoussé, parcel-gilt
Kryštof Wild, Prague, 1781
Height: 160 mm, width: 140 mm
Hallmarks: 1. CW in oval, 2. city mark Prague–Staré Město 1781, 3. recharge mark Prague 1806–7, 4. release mark 1809–10
Without inscriptions.
Collection point: Písek

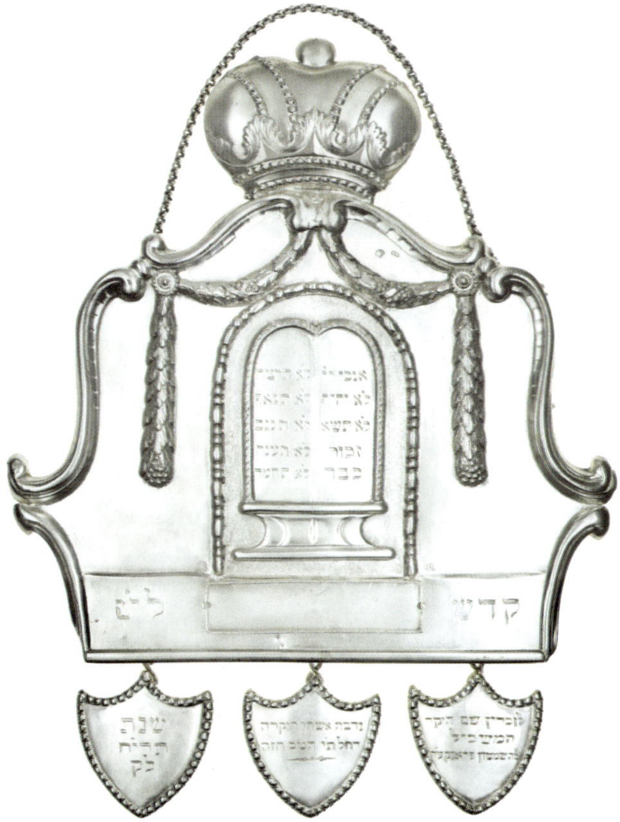

Cat. No. 23
Torah Shield
Inv. No. JMP 023.094
Silver, repoussé
Jakub Vojtěch Fortner, Prague, 1783
Height: 291 mm, width: 283 mm
Hallmarks: 1. IF in rectangle, 2. city mark Prague-Staré Město 1783, 3. recharge mark Prague 1806–7, 4. release mark 1809–10
Donation inscription and the first words of the Decalogue in Hebrew.
Translation:
Consecrated to the Lord. To the memory of the name of the esteemed, sage KH Samson Frank, peace to him, his dear wife Rachel, may she live, donated this shield in the year 618 a. s. c. [= 1858].
Collection point: Benešov

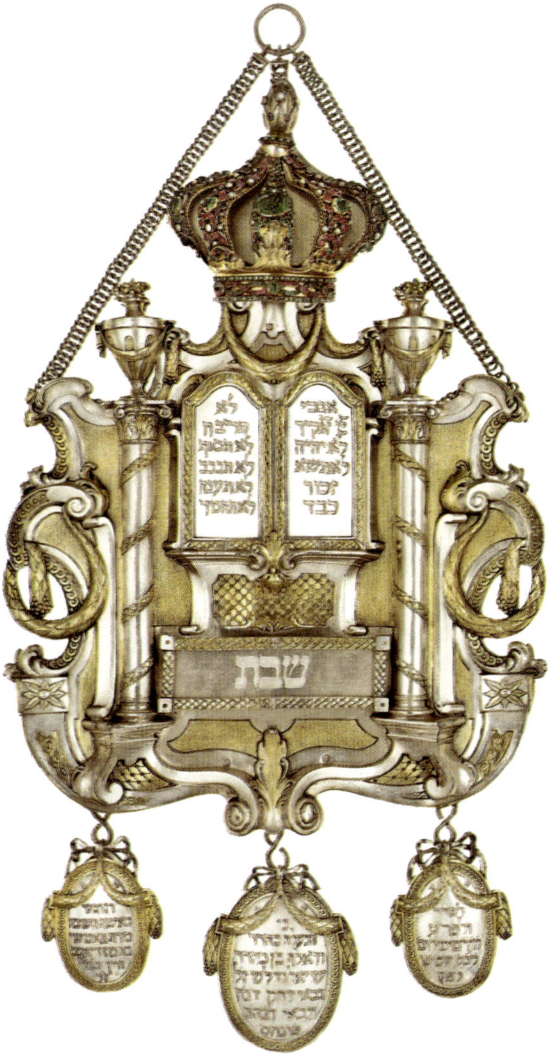

Cat. No. 24

< Cat. No. 24

Torah Shield

Inv. No. JMP 046.075

Silver, repoussé, cast, parcel-gilt, precious stones, pearls

Richard Fleischmann, Prague, 1784

Height: 419 mm, width: 302 mm

Hallmarks: 1. RF in rectangle, 2. city mark Prague–Malá Strana 1784, 3. recharge mark Prague 1806–7, 4. release mark 1809–10

Donation inscription in Hebrew; the first words of the Decalogue and name of the festival in Hebrew.

Translation:

A gift of the distinguished KHRR Wolf, son of KHRR Ezriel Gadeles of blessed memory, custodian of the Holy Benevolent Society [the Burial Society] *and custodian of the Pinkas Synagogue, and his wife, the esteemed lady Patscheh, daughter of KHRR Yokev Wien SGL of blessed memory, the order and count "may You grant them life and tranquility" a.s.c.* [dating in the chronogram 545 = 1785].

Collection point: Prague, Pinkas Synagogue

Cat. No. 25

Torah Shield

Inv. No. JMP 004.048

Silver, repoussé

Maker MK, Bohemia, 1789 [inscription]

Height: 264 mm, width: 223 mm

Hallmarks: 1. MK in rectangle, 2. purity mark 13, 3. recharge mark Prague 1806–7, 4. release mark 1809–10

Donation inscription in Hebrew and name of the festival in Hebrew.

Translation:

This esteemed gift was donated on behalf of the Society of the Seven Called [to the Torah and] made in the year "they gathered [it] *one after the other* [?] *" a.s.c.* [dating in the chronogram 549 = 1789]. *And the names of these men are engraved below. This is the work of Elijah Tzoref from the association LPK* [?] *MK* [from Kolín?; the initials' meaning is unclear]. *HRR Joseph, son of K R.; the sage Mordecai Leib, son of K R.; H Leib Hamrshlak; K Gershon of Konárovice* [Konarowitz]; *HRR Leib, son of H C.; KMR Mordecai, son of M.; KMR Berl, son of A.; KMR Ezriel Hayyat; the boy Moses, son of J.H.; K David, son of R G.; K Zanwil Bek; HH Hayyim, son of R C.; HRR Gershon, son of R J.H.; KMR Samuel, son of A.S.; KMR Shalom, son of L.R.; HRR Meir, son of H P.S.; KMR Joseph, son of M.H.; KMR Leib, son of R G.*

Collection point: Kolín

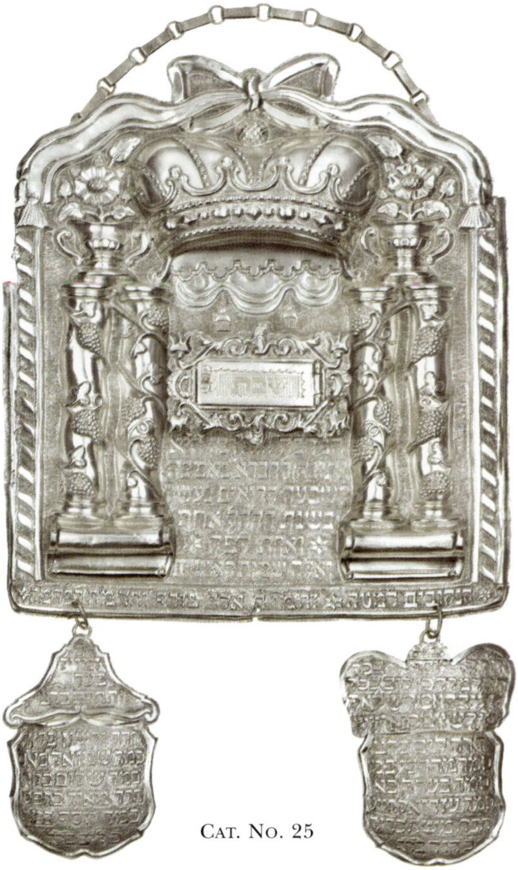

Cat. No. 25

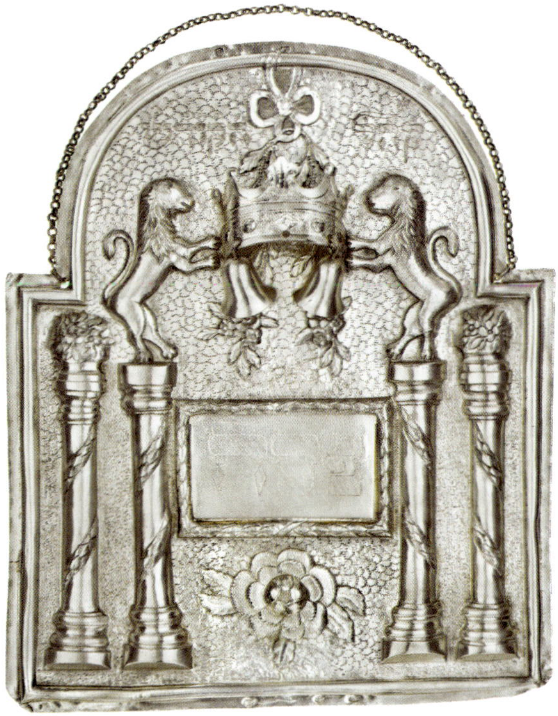

Cat. No. 26

Torah Shield

Inv. No. JMP 010.405

Silver, repoussé

Maker JS, Znojmo, 1790

Height: 270 mm, width: 220 mm

Hallmarks: 1. JS in oval, 2. hallmark Znojmo 1790, 3. recharge mark Brno 1806–7, 4. release mark 1809–10

Donation inscription in Hebrew.

Translation:

The holy community a. s .c. [dating in the chronogram 550 = 1790].

Collection point: Miroslav

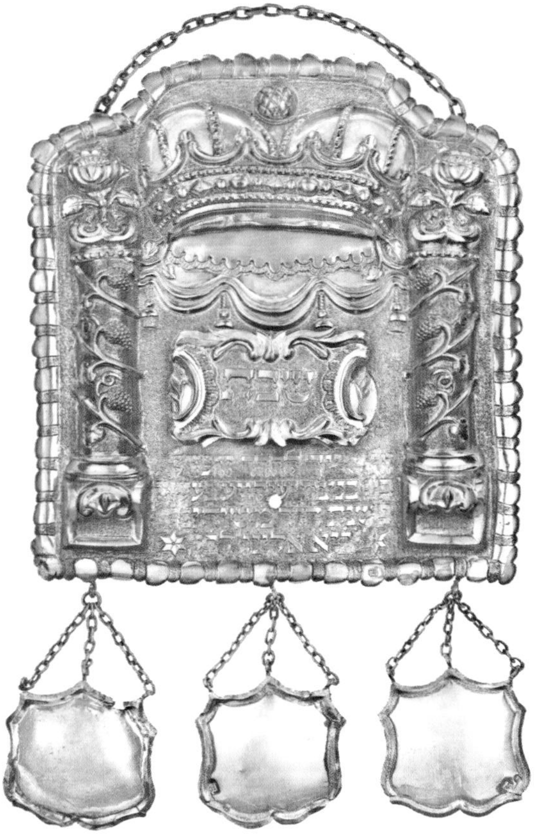

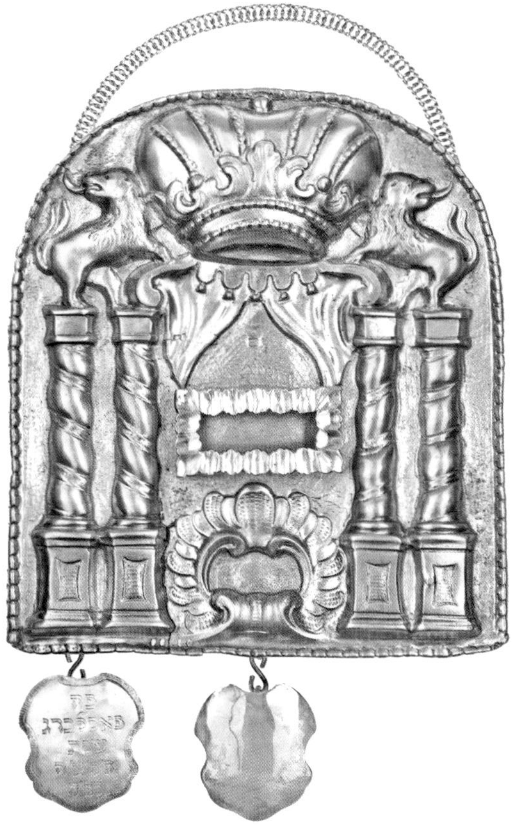

Cat. No. 27
Torah Shield
Inv. No. JMP 000.865
Silver, repoussé
Maker MK [?], Bohemia, 1794 [inscription]
Height: 216 mm, width: 195 mm
Hallmarks: 1. recharge mark 1806–7,
2. release mark 1809–10
Donation inscription in Hebrew and name of the festival in Hebrew.
Translation:
This belongs to HRR Zundel,
son of H Benjamin Yenkev. Made in the year
"May David, our Messiah, come to us" a.s.c.
[dating in the chronogram 554 = 1794].
Collection point: Plzeň

Cat. No. 28
Torah Shield
Inv. No. JMP 061.616
Silver, repoussé
Kryštof Wild, Prague, end of 18th century
Height: 208 mm, width: 180 mm
Hallmarks: 1. CW in oval, 2. recharge mark Prague 1806–7, 3. release mark 1809–10
Donation inscription in Hebrew.
Translation:
Here in Postoloprty in the year 575 a. s. c. [= 1815].
Collection point: Olomouc

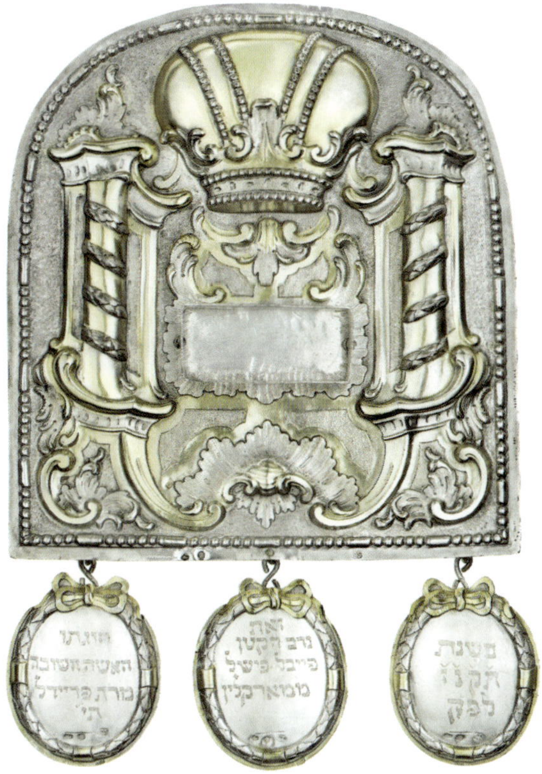

Cat. No. 29
Torah Shield
Inv. No. JMP 001.840
Silver, repoussé
Maker unknown, Bohemia [?], end of 18th century
Height: 213 mm, width: 178 mm
Hallmarks: 1. recharge mark Prague 1806–7,
2. release mark 1809–10
Without inscriptions.
Collection point: Klatovy

Cat. No. 30
Torah Shield
Inv. No. JMP 001.957
Silver, repoussé, parcel-gilt
Karel Skřemenec, Prague, 1797
Height: 250 mm, width: 224 mm
Hallmarks: 1. CS in oval, 2. hallmark Prague 1797,
3. purity mark 13, 4. recharge mark Prague 1806–7,
5. release mark 1809–10
Donation inscription in Hebrew.
Translation:
This was donated by the insignificant Faivel Fischl of Merklín and his wife, the esteemed lady Fraidlah, may she live, in the year 577 a. s. c. [= 1797].
Collection point: Nepomuk

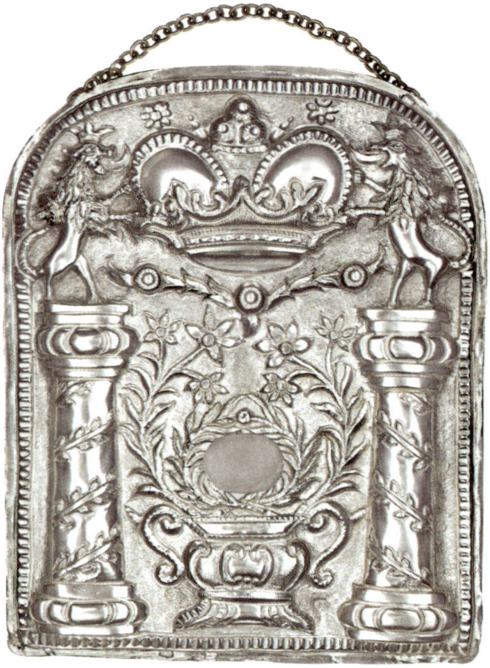

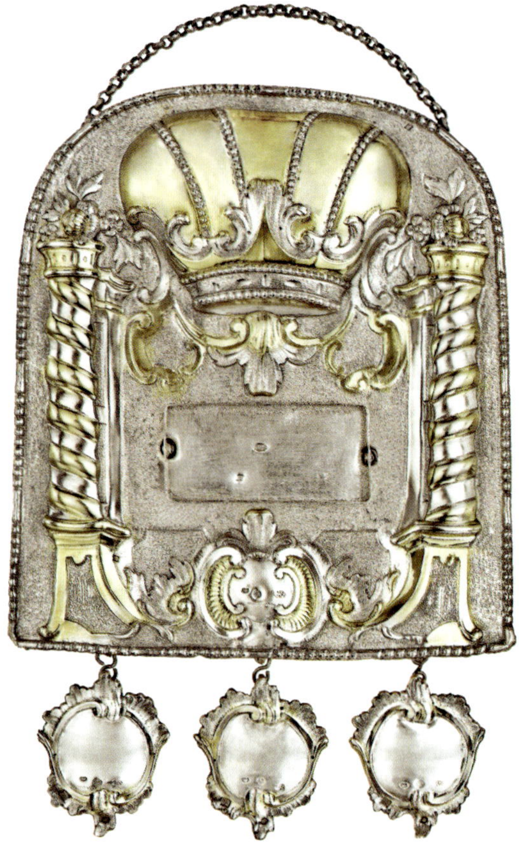

Cat. No. 31
Torah Shield
Inv. No. JMP 007.424
Silver, repoussé
Maker SG, Mikulov, 1799
Height: 179 mm, width: 141 mm
Hallmarks: 1. SG in oval, 2. hallmark Mikulov 1799, 3. recharge mark Brno 1806–7, 4. release mark 1809–10
Without inscriptions.
Collection point: Dambořice

Cat. No. 32
Torah Shield
Inv. No. JMP 001.841
Silver, repoussé, parcel-gilt
Karel Skřemenec, Prague, 1799
Height: 227 mm, width: 187 mm
Hallmarks: 1. CS in oval, 2. hallmark Prague 1799, 3. purity mark 13, 4. recharge mark Prague 1806–7, 5. release mark 1809–10
Without inscriptions.
Collection point: Klatovy

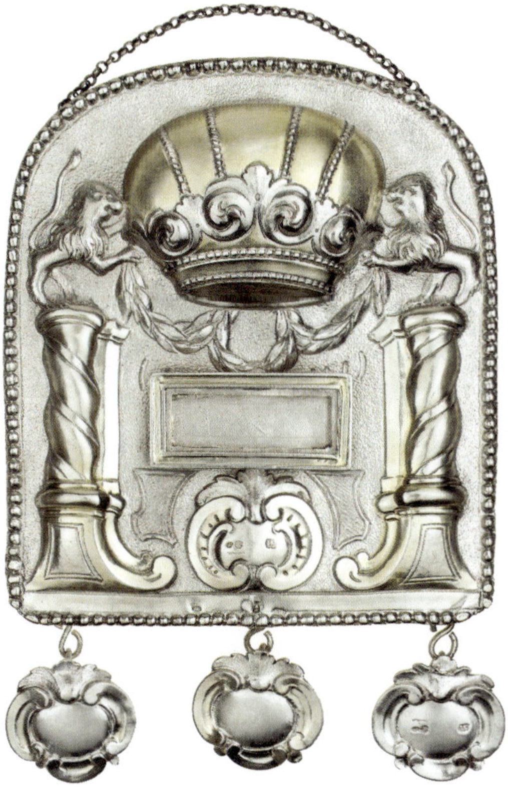

Cat. No. 33
Torah Shield
Inv. No. JMP 005.010
Silver, repoussé, parcel-gilt
Maker IN, Prague, 1800
Height: 210 mm, width: 180 mm
Hallmarks: 1. IN in rectangle, 2. hallmark Prague 1800, 3. purity mark 13, 4. recharge mark Prague 1806–7, 5. release mark 1809–10
Without inscriptions.
Collection point: Dobruška

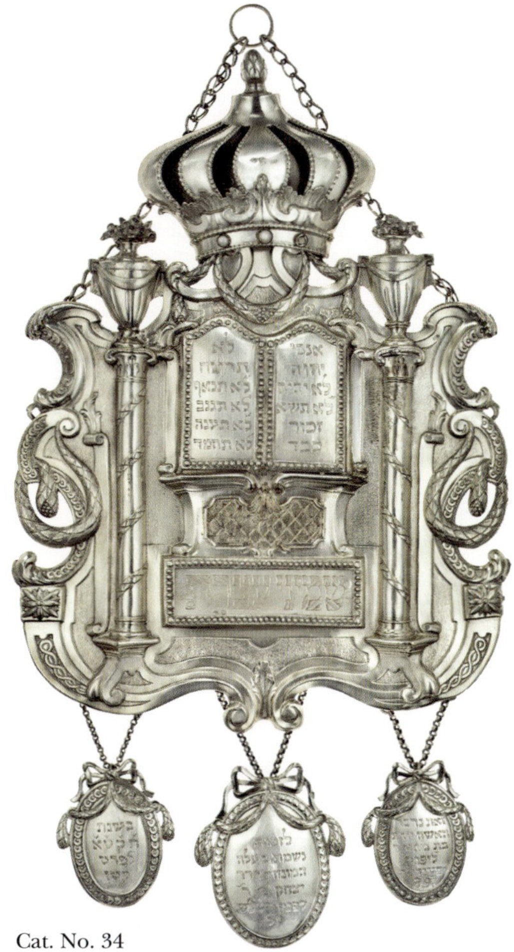

Cat. No. 34
Torah Shield
Inv. No. JMP 046.017
Silver, repoussé, cast, originally parcel-gilt, pearls
Maker WK, Prague, 1801
Height: 409 mm, width: 300 mm
Hallmarks: 1. WK in oval, 2. hallmark Prague 1801, 3. purity mark 13, 4. recharge mark Prague 1807–9
Donation inscription in Hebrew, the first words of the Decalogue in Hebrew.
Translation:
This was donated by Judith, daughter of MHVRR Lipman Bendiner, may the memory of the just be blessed, to the memory of the soul of her late husband, JHRR Isaac, son of R Kafman Jeiteles of blessed memory. In the year 561 a. s. c. [= 1801].
Collection point: Prague, Pinkas Synagogue

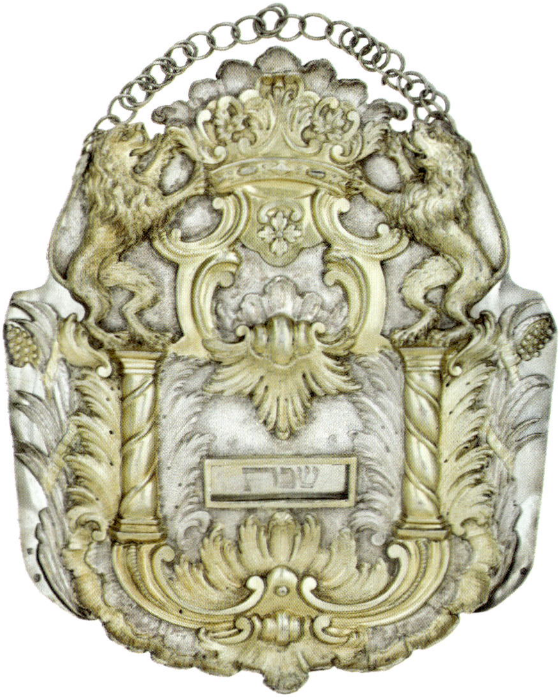

Cat. No. 35

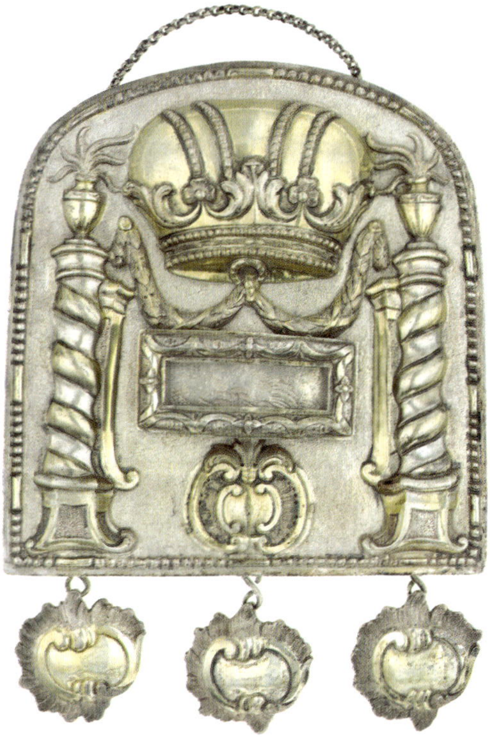

Cat. No. 37

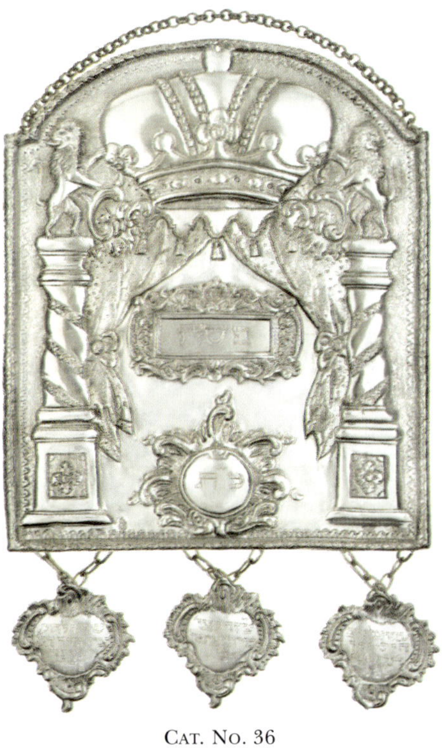

Cat. No. 36

Cat. No. 35
Torah Shield
Inv. No. JMP 007.134
Silver, repoussé, parcel-gilt
Josef Ignaz Fautz, Vienna, 1802
Height: 313 mm, width: 269 mm
Hallmarks: 1. JJF in oval, 2. hallmark Vienna 1802, 3. release mark 1809–10
Inscription in Hebrew.
Translation:
Belonging to the elder of the Burial Society, may his Rock protect him.
Collection point: Brno

Cat. No. 36
Torah Shield
Inv. No. JMP 009.548
Silver, repoussé
Maker MG, Jihlava, 1800–6
Height: 220 mm, width: 183 mm
Hallmarks: 1. MG in rectangle, 2. hallmark Jihlava 1800–6, 3. recharge mark Brno 1806–7, 4. release mark 1809–10
Donation inscription in Hebrew.
Translation:
KT. Belonging to the elder HRR Zalkind, let the Merciful protect and redeem him, and his wife the elder, lady Tziperl, may she live. Včelnice [Wtschelnitz], *18th of Sivan 569 a. s. c.* [=June 2, 1809].
Collection point: Kamenice nad Lipou

Cat. No. 37
Torah Shield
Inv. No. JMP 017.895
Silver, repoussé, parcel-gilt
Karel Skřemenec, Prague, 1805
Height: 200 mm, width: 186 mm
Hallmarks: 1. CS in oval, 2. hallmark Prague 1805, 3. purity mark 13, 4. recharge mark Prague 1806–7
Without inscriptions.
Collection point: Třeboň

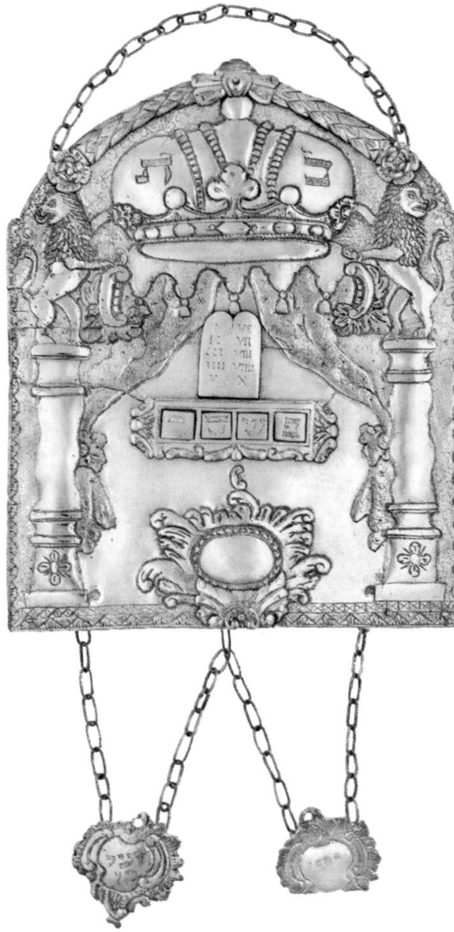

Cat. No. 38 ^
Torah Shield
Inv. No. JMP 003.931
Silver, repoussé
Maker unknown, Moravia [?], early 19th century
Height: 245 mm, width: 197 mm
Hallmarks: 1. fake maker's mark AG, 2. fake hallmark Vienna, version 1807–9
Donation inscription in Hebrew, the date 1834 in Latin script.
Translation:
KT. [...] [?]. *Lkáň* [Welkan].
Collection point: Central Jewish Museum for Moravia and Silesia, 1936–1938 in Nikolsburg

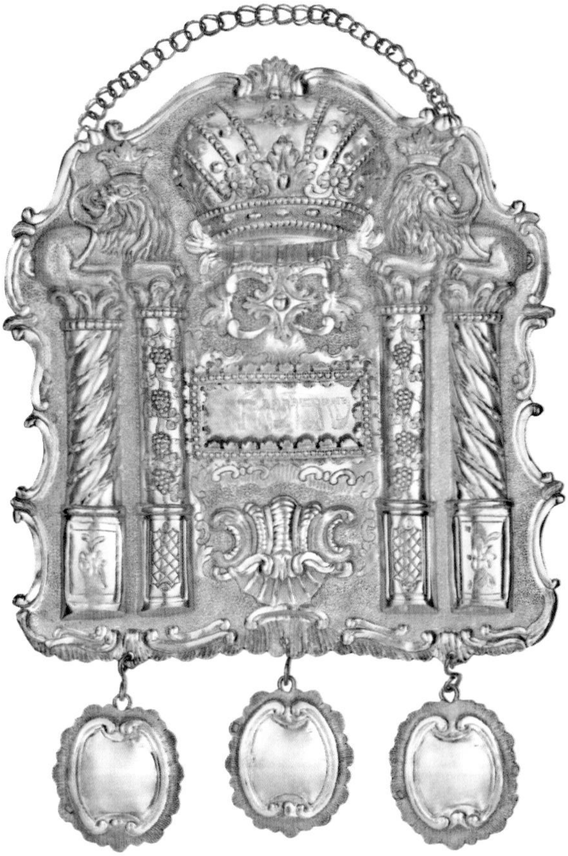

Cat. No. 39
Torah Shield
Inv. No. JMP 000.866
Silver, repoussé
Maker AD, Prague, 1807
Height: 297 mm, width: 207 mm
Hallmarks: 1. AD in rectangle, 2. hallmark Prague 1807–9, 3. recharge mark Prague 1806–7, 4. release mark 1809–10
Without inscriptions.
Collection point: Plzeň

Cat. No. 40
Torah Shield
Inv. No. JMP 023.104
Silver, repoussé, parcel-gilt
Karel Skřemenec, Prague, 1807
Height: 249 mm, width: 216 mm
Hallmarks: 1. CS in oval, 2. hallmark Prague 1807–9, 3. recharge mark Prague 1806–7, 4. release mark 1809–10
Without inscriptions.
Collection point: Světlá nad Sázavou

Cat. No. 41
Torah Shield
Inv. No. JMP 012.221
Silver, repoussé
Carl Lackstampfer, Sr., Brno, 1810
Height: 199 mm, width: 147 mm
Hallmarks: 1. CL in oval, 2. hallmark Brno 1810, 3. tax mark Brno 1810–24
Without inscriptions.
Collection point: Brno, Kounice

Cat. No. 42
Torah Shield
Inv. No. JMP 002.630
Silver, repoussé, cast
Carl Lackstampfer, Sr., Brno, 1810
Height: 269 mm, width: 235 mm
Hallmarks: 1. CL in oval, 2. hallmark Brno 1810, 3. tax mark Brno 1810–24
Without inscriptions.
Collection point: Holešov

Cat. No. 43
Torah Shield
Inv. No. JMP 001.543
Silver, repoussé
Maker MG, Jihlava, 1810
Height: 229 mm, width: 171 mm
Hallmarks: 1. MG in rectangle, 2. hallmark Jihlava 1810, 3. tax mark Jihlava 1810–24, 4. date mark Jihlava 1807 [variant for gold objects, likely stamped by mistake].
Without inscriptions.
Collection point: Bzenec

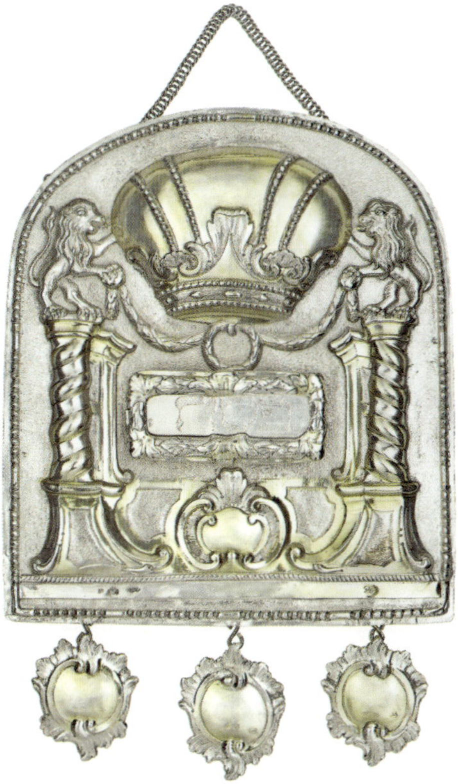

Cat. No. 40

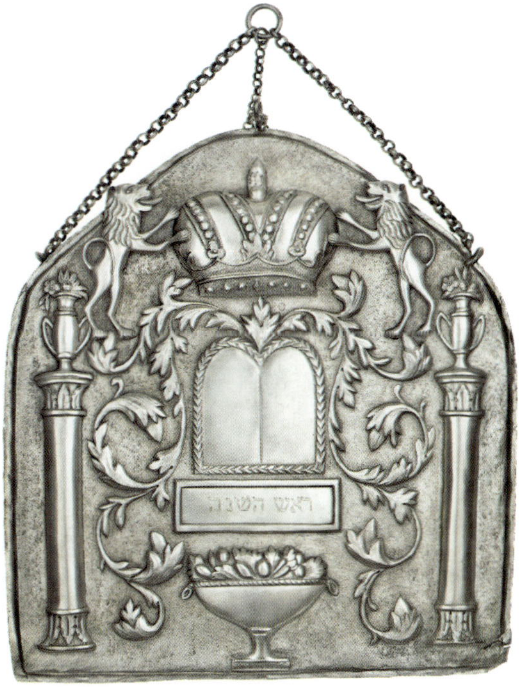

Cat. No. 42

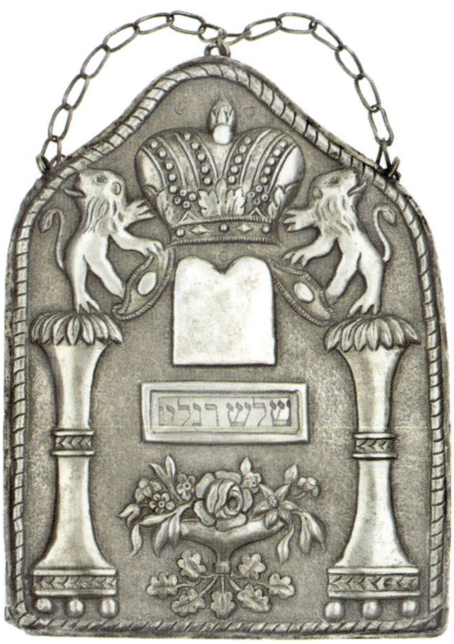

Cat. No. 41

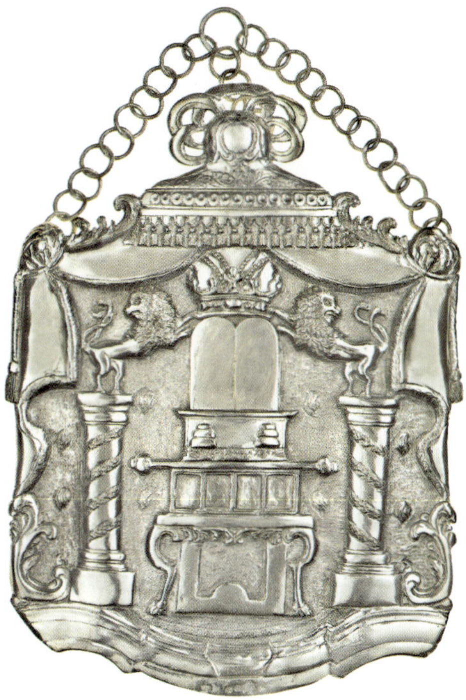

Cat. No. 43

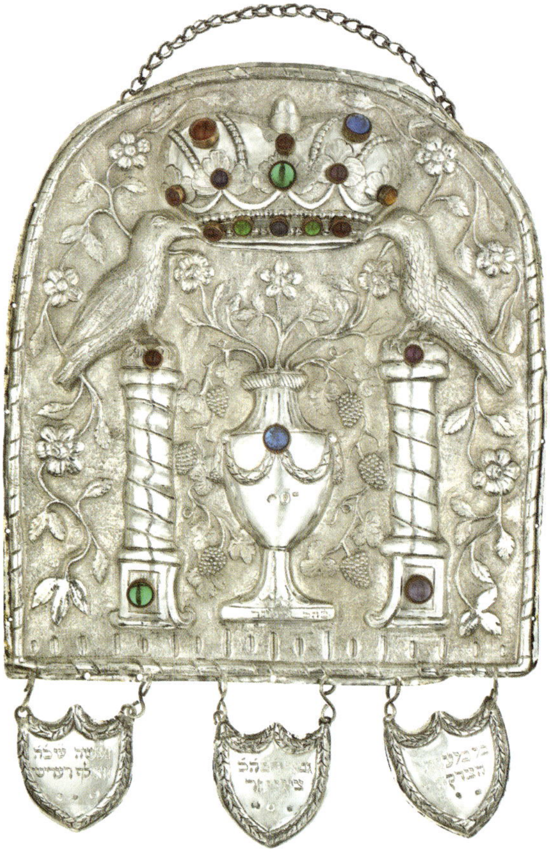

Cat. No. 44
Torah Shield
Inv. No. JMP 037.615
Silver, repoussé, glass stones
Karel Skřemenec, Prague, 1810
Height: 334 mm, width: 284 mm
Hallmarks: 1. CS in rectangle, 2. hallmark Prague 1810, 3. tax mark Prague 1810–24
Donation inscription in Hebrew.
Translation:
Zigeuner [Cikán] *Synagogue. From charitable funds. Made through the agency of KH Wolf Redisch, custodian of the Zigeuner Synagogue.*
Collection point: Prague

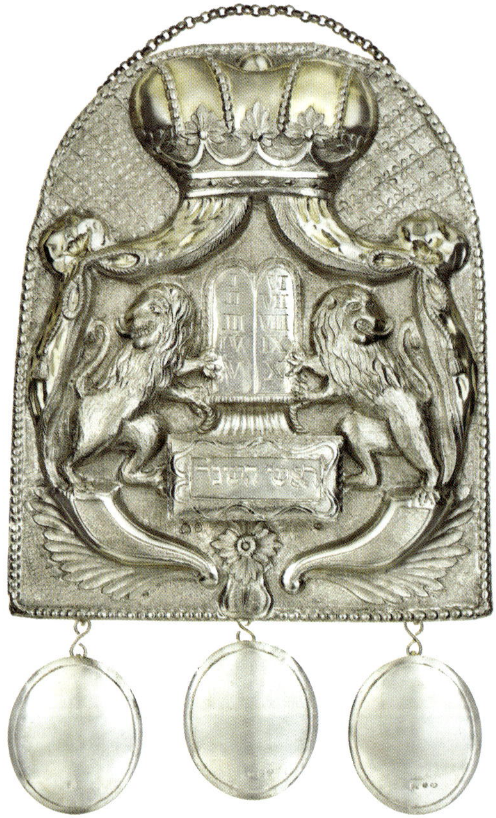

Cat. No. 45
Torah Shield
Inv. No. JMP 004.495
Silver, repoussé, parcel-gilt
Jan Fleischmann, Prague, 1810
Height: 244 mm, width: 201 mm
Hallmarks: 1. IF in heart, 2. hallmark Prague 1810, 3. tax mark Prague 1810–24
Without inscriptions.
Collection point: Tábor

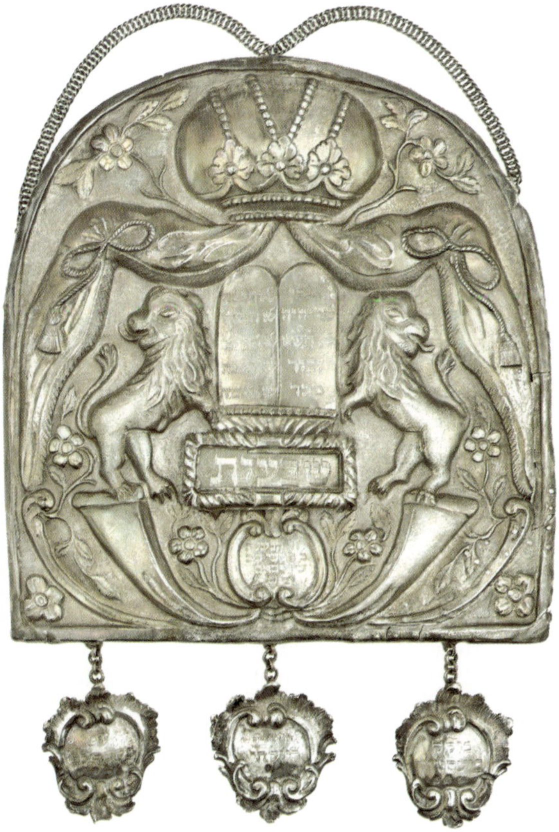

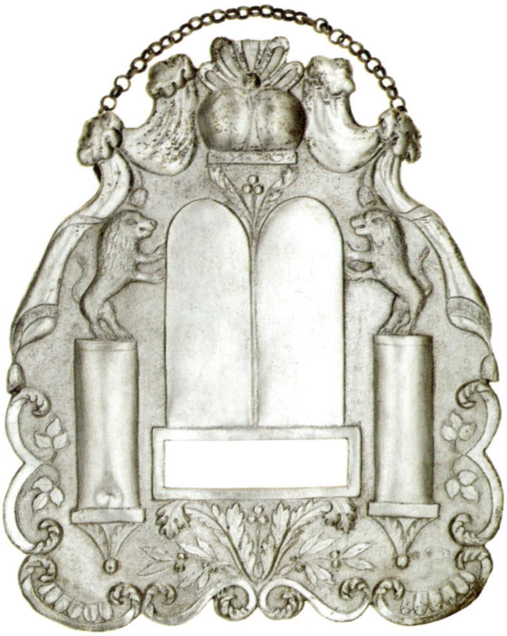

Cat. No. 46
Torah Shield
Inv. No. JMP 010.540
Silver, repoussé
Karel Skřemenec, Prague, 1810
Height: 280 mm, width: 260 mm
Hallmarks: 1. CS in rectangle, 2. hallmark Prague 1810, 3. tax mark Prague 1810–24
Donation inscription in Hebrew, the first words of the Decalogue and name of the festival in Hebrew.
Translation:
This was donated by the distinguished K. Hirsch, son of K Leib Bass from the holy community of Heřmanův Městec, with his wife, the lady Rezl, may she live, in the year 574 a.s.c. [= 1814].
Collection point: Heřmanův Městec

Cat. No. 47
Torah Shield
Inv. No. JMP 010.667
Silver, repoussé
Wenzel Nachtmann [?], Vienna, 1814
Height: 190 mm, width: 162 mm
Hallmarks: 1. WN in rectangle, 2. hallmark Vienna 1814, 3. tax mark Vienna 1810–24
Without inscriptions.
Collection point: Klatovy

Cat. No. 48
Torah Shield
Inv. No. JMP 002.187
Silver, repoussé
Karel Skřemenec, Prague, 1815
Height: 290 mm, width: 265 mm
Hallmarks: 1. CS in rectangle, 2. hallmark Prague 1815, 3. tax mark Prague 1810–24
Donation inscription in Hebrew.
Translation:
This was donated by the esteemed Mr. Judah Meisner with his wife, the lady Leah, may she live, for the Holy Society Visiting the Sick and the Holy Benevolent Society [the Burial Society] *in the holy community Mladá Boleslav, in the year 575 a. s. c.* [= 1815].
Collection point: Mladá Boleslav

Cat. No. 49
Torah Shield
Inv. No. JMP 010.318
Silver, repoussé
Franz Kaltenmarker, Brno, 1815
Height: 330 mm, width: 256 mm
Hallmarks: 1. FK in oval, 2. hallmark Brno 1815, 3. tax mark Brno 1810–24
Without inscriptions.
Collection point: Boskovice

Cat. No. 50
Torah Shield
Inv. No. JMP 009.839
Silver, repoussé
Maker AN, Prague, 1815
Height: 273 mm, width: 214 mm
Hallmarks: 1. AN in oval, 2. hallmark Prague 1815, 3. tax mark Prague 1810–24
Donation inscription in Hebrew and name of the festival in Hebrew.
Translation:
Consecrated to the Lord. This was purchased with money from the Holy Society for the Education of Boys in the holy community Mořina, in the year 580 a.s.c. [= 1820].
Collection point: Beroun

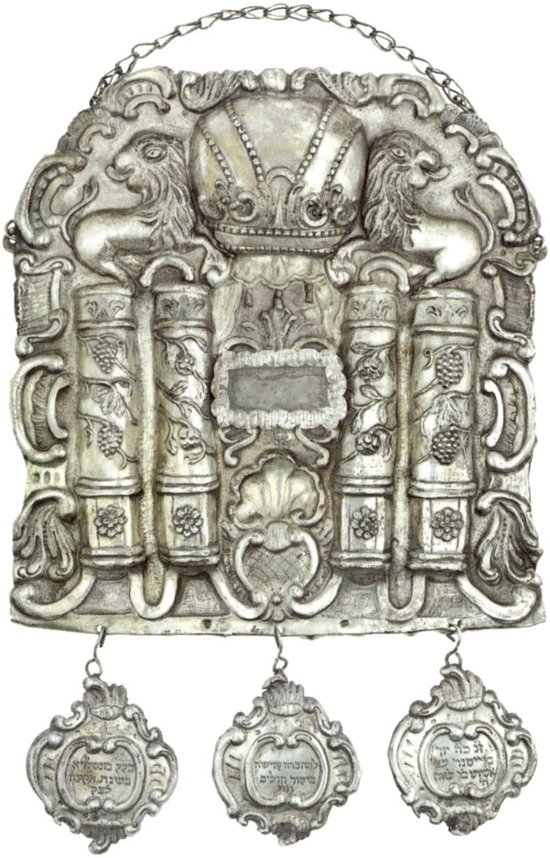

Cat. No. 48

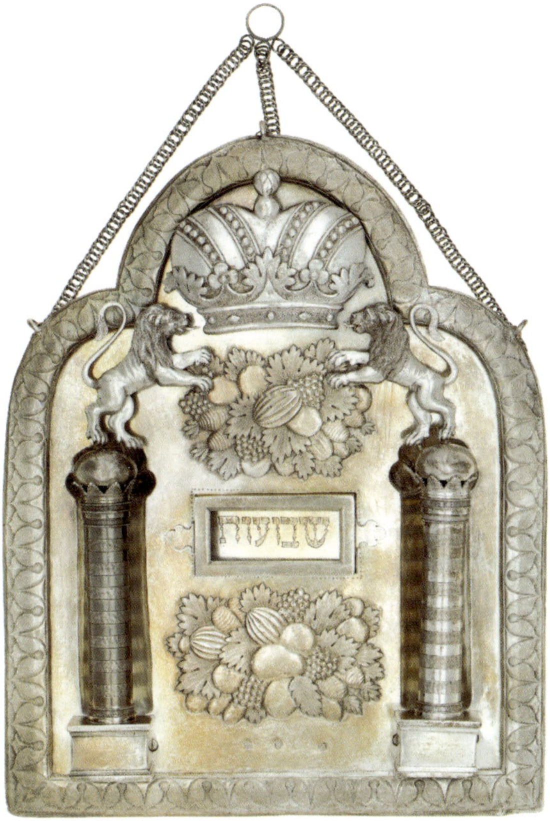

Cat. No. 49 ^

Cat. No. 50 v

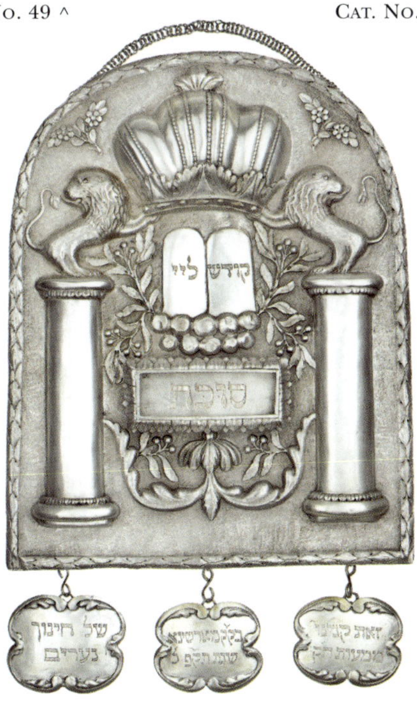

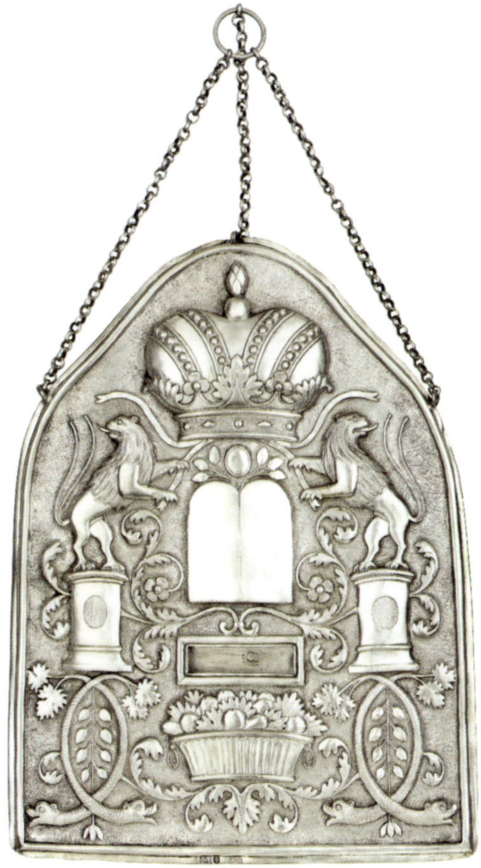

Cat. No. 51 ^

Torah Shield

Inv. No. JMP 012.391

Silver, repoussé

Franz Kaltenmarker, Brno, 1815

Height: 274 mm, width: 202 mm

Hallmarks: 1. FK in oval, 2. hallmark Brno 1815, 3. tax mark Brno 1810–24

Without inscriptions.

Collection point: Olomouc

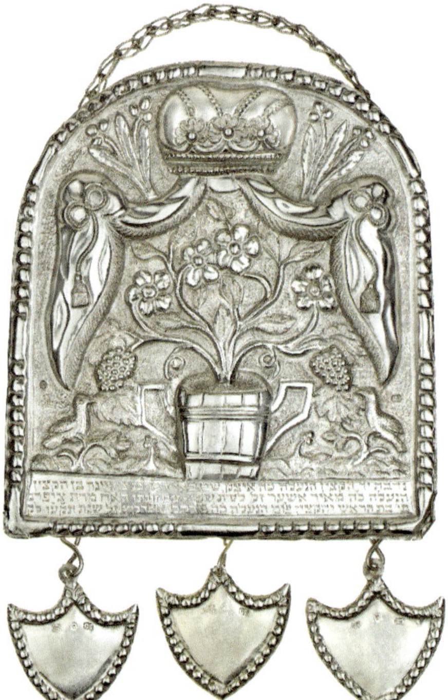

CAT. NO. 52 ^ CAT. NO. 53 v

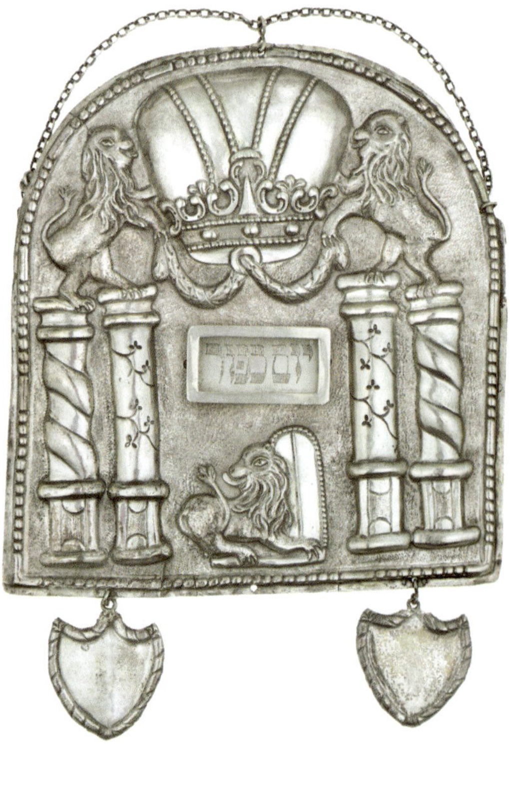

Cat. No. 52
Torah Shield
Inv. No. JMP 104.795
Silver, repoussé
Karel Skřemenec, Prague, 1816
Height: 175 mm, width: 155 mm
Hallmarks: 1. CS in rectangle, 2. hallmark Prague 1816, 3. tax mark Prague 1810–24
Donation inscription in Hebrew.
Translation:
A gift of the distinguished elder KH Itzak, may he live, custodian of the Zigeuner Synagogue, son of the distinguished elder, KH Meir Asher of blessed memory, for his Torah scroll. With his wife, the esteemed lady Tziperl, may she live, daughter of the head and elder, the distinguished Parnas and leader KH Mordecai Eidlitz of blessed memory, the year 576 a. s. c. [= 1816].
Purchased by the Jewish Museum in Prague.

Cat. No. 53
Torah Shield
Inv. No. JMP 037.427
Silver, repoussé
Karel Skřemenec, Prague, 1816
Height: 282 mm, width: 255 mm
Hallmarks: 1. CS in rectangle, 2. hallmark Prague 1816, 3. tax mark Prague 1810–24
Without inscriptions.
Collection point: Prague

Cat. No. 54
Torah Shield
Inv. No. JMP 037.603
Silver, repoussé
Tomáš Höpfel, Prague, 1816
Height: 220 mm, width: 204 mm
Hallmarks: 1. TH in rectangle, 2. hallmark Prague 1816, 3. tax mark Prague 1810–24
Without inscriptions.
Collection point: Prague

Cat. No. 55
Torah Shield
Inv. No. JMP 010.283
Silver, repoussé, parcel-gilt
Wenzel Nachtmann [?], Vienna, 1816
Height: 351 mm, width: 255 mm
Hallmarks: 1. WN in rectangle, 2. hallmark Vienna 1816, 3. tax mark Vienna 1810–24
Without inscriptions.
Collection point: Slavkov u Brna

Cat. No. 56
Torah Shield
Acq. No. JMP 1973/0195
Silver, repoussé
Franz Kaltenmarker, Brno, 1817
Height: 238 mm, width: 177 mm
Hallmarks: 1. FK in oval, 2. hallmark Brno 1817, 3. tax mark Brno 1810–24
Without inscriptions.
Catalogued secondarily into the inventory of the Jewish Museum in Prague.

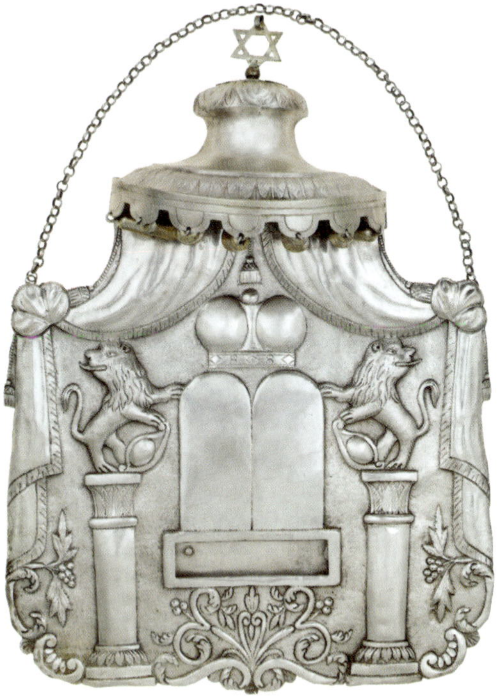

Cat. No. 55 ^

Cat. No. 54 v

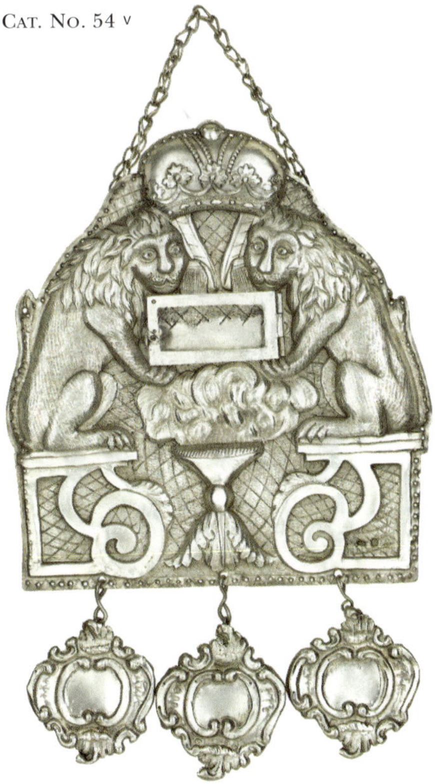

Cat. No. 56 v

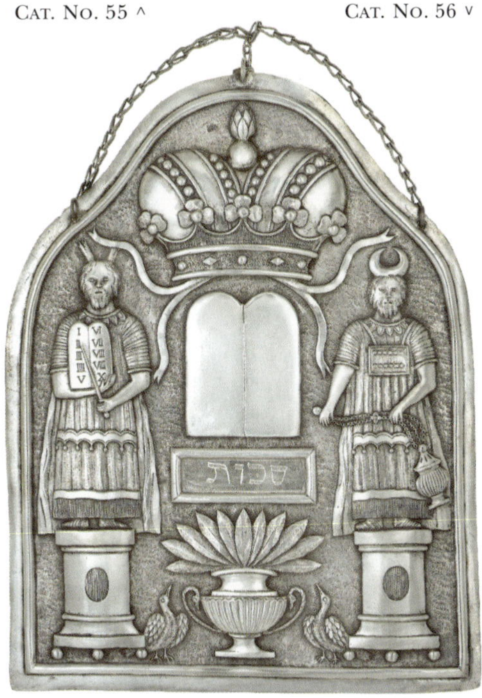

Cat. No. 57
Torah Shield
Inv. No. JMP 037.972
Silver, repoussé, parcel-gilt
Tomáš Höpfel, Prague, 1817
Height: 145 mm, width: 125 mm
Hallmarks: 1. TH in rectangle, 2. hallmark Prague 1817, 3. tax mark Prague 1810–24
Without inscriptions.
Collection point: Prague, Pinkas Synagogue

Cat. No. 58
Torah Shield
Inv. No. JMP 001.869
Silver, repoussé, parcel-gilt, stones
Antonín Kába, Prague, 1819
Height: 415 mm, width: 297 mm
Hallmarks: 1. AK in oval, 2. hallmark Prague 1819, 3. tax mark Prague 1810–24
Donation inscription in Hebrew, the first words of the Decalogue and name of the festival in Hebrew.
Translation:
In memory of the soul of our father, the distinguished KH Wolf Fürth of blessed memory.
Collection point: Písek

Cat. No. 59
Torah Shield
Inv. No. 004.390
Silver, repoussé
Franz Kaltenmarker (workshop), Brno, 1819
Height: 181 mm, width: 136 mm
Hallmarks: 1. hallmark Brno 1819, 2. tax mark Brno 1810–24
Without inscriptions.
Collection point: Žamberk

Cat. No. 60
Torah Shield
Inv. No. JMP 000.853
Silver, repoussé
Karel Skřemenec, Prague, 1820
Height: 230 mm, width: 215 mm
Hallmarks: 1. CS in rectangle, 2. hallmark Prague 1820, 3. tax mark Prague 1810–24
Without inscriptions.
Collection point: Plzeň

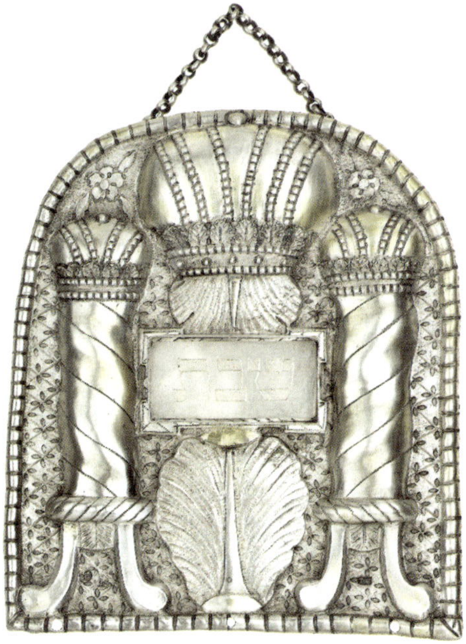

Cat. No. 57 ^

Cat. No. 58 v

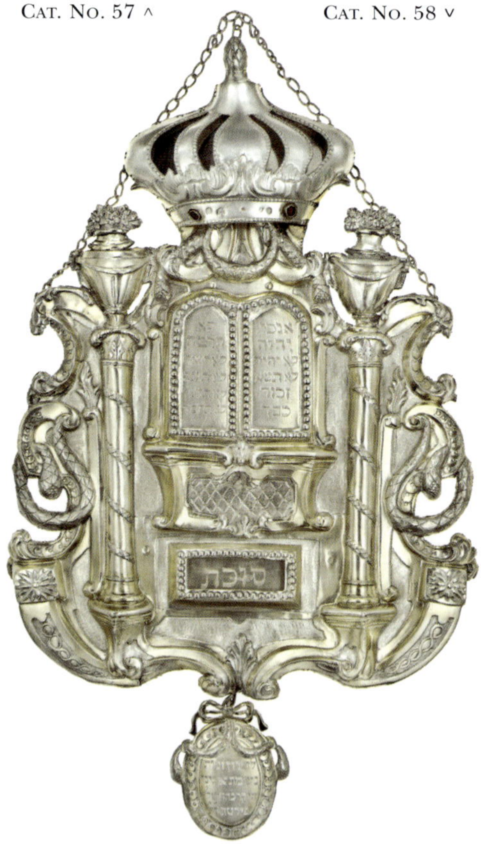

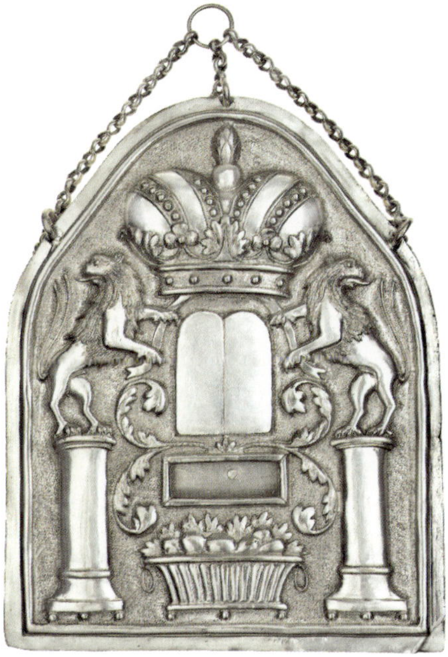

Cat. No. 59 ^   Cat. No. 60 v

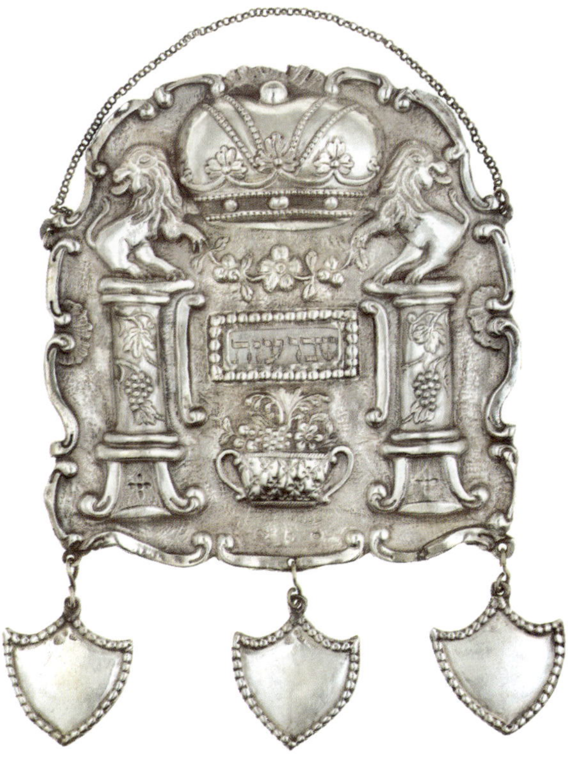

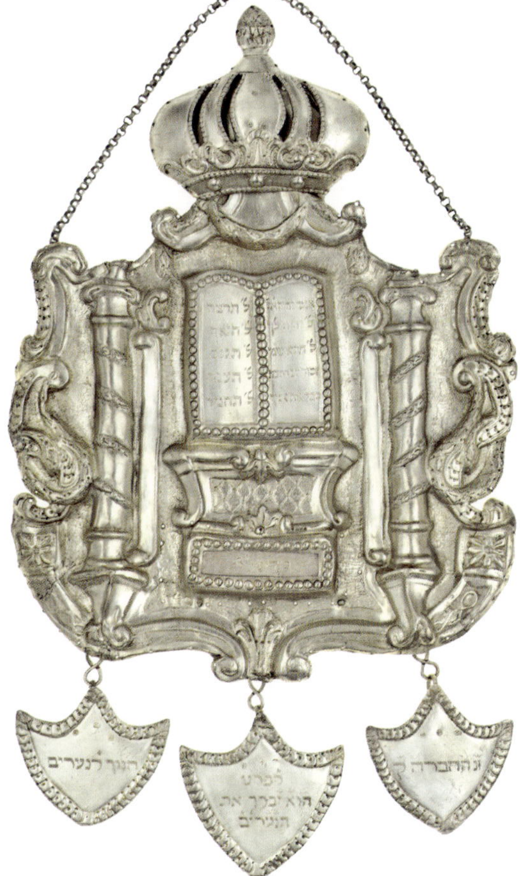

Cat. No. 61 ^
Torah Shield
Inv. No. JMP 002.000
Silver, repoussé
Karel Skřemenec, Prague, 1820
Height: 354 mm, width: 263 mm
Hallmarks: 1. CS in rectangle, 2. hallmark Prague 1820, 3. tax mark Prague 1810–24
Donation inscription in Hebrew, the first words of the Decalogue in Hebrew.
Translation:
Consecrated to the Lord. This was donated by the Society for the Education of Boys on the count "Bless the boys" [Gen. 48:16; dating in the chronogram 581 = 1821].
Collection point: Rokycany

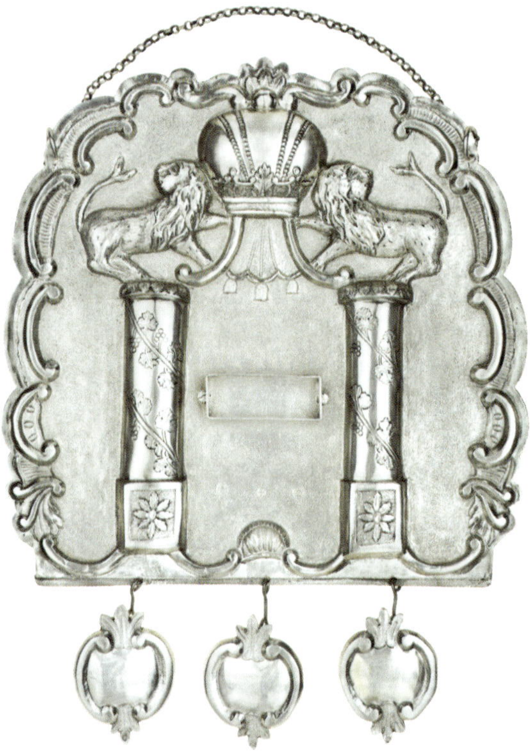

Cat. No. 62
Torah Shield
Inv. No. JMP 010.622
Silver, repoussé
Josef Rummel, Prague, 1822
Height: 205 mm, width: 204 mm
Hallmarks: 1. IR in oval, 2. hallmark Prague 1822,
3. tax mark Prague 1810–24
Without inscriptions.
Collection point: Mladá Vožice

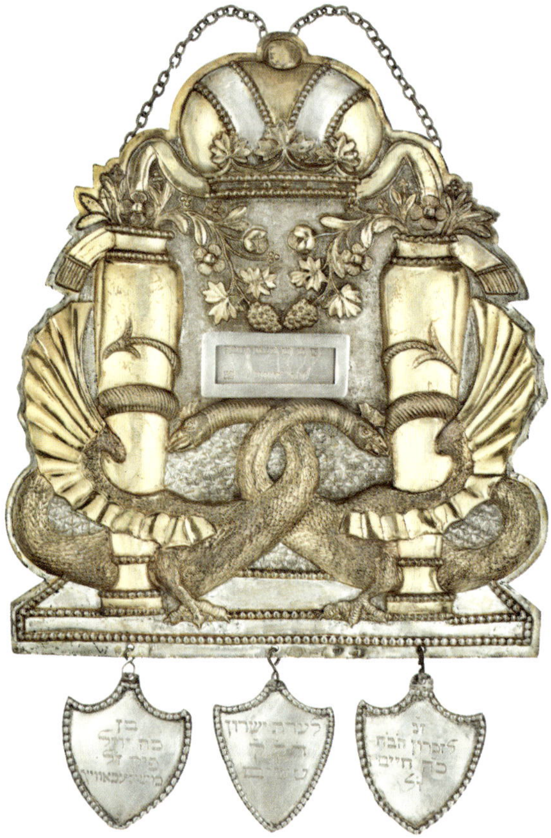

Cat. No. 63
Torah Shield
Inv. No. JMP 037.922
Silver, repoussé, parcel-gilt
Tomáš Höpfel, Prague, 1828
Height: 329 mm, width: 284 mm
Hallmarks: 1. TH in rectangle,
2. hallmark Prague 1828
Donation inscription in Hebrew and name
of the festival in Hebrew.
Translation:
This is a gift in remembrance of the boy KH Hayyim of blessed memory, the son of KH Jusel Pick of blessed memory, from Štěchovice for the holy community Čím [Tschim].
Collection point: Prague, Vinohrady Synagogue

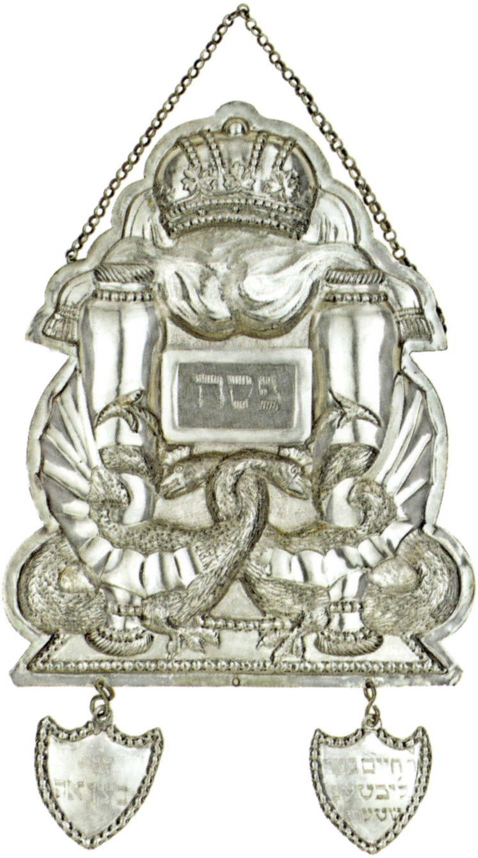

Cat. No. 64
Torah Shield
Inv. No. JMP 174.189
Silver, repoussé
Tomáš Höpfel, Prague, 1831
Height: 212 mm, width: 167 mm
Hallmarks: 1. TH in oval, 2. hallmark Prague 1831
Donation inscription in Hebrew and name of the festival in Hebrew.
Translation:
This was donated as a bequest from R Hayyim Beer Lichtenstern.
Acquired by the JMP via transfer.

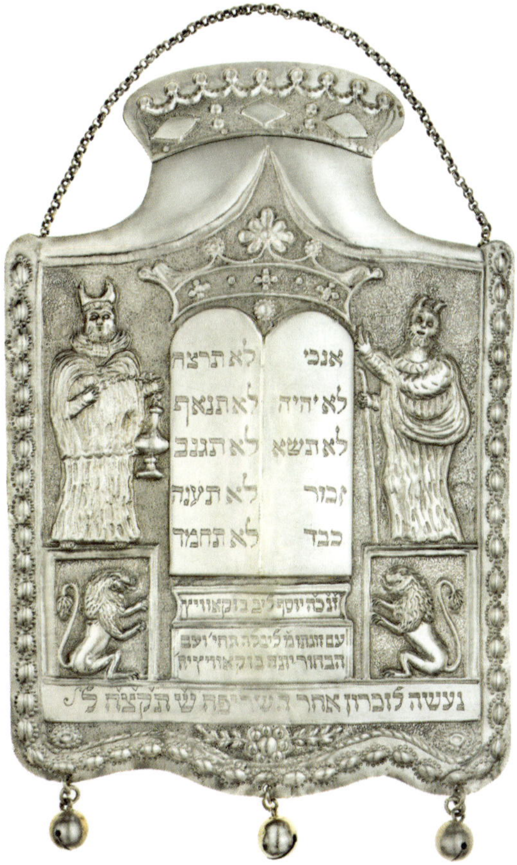

Cat. No. 65
Torah Shield
Inv. No. JMP 002.267
Silver, repoussé
Maker unknown, Moravia [?], 1838 [inscription]
Height: 292 mm, width: 203 mm
Hallmarks: unmarked
Donation inscription in Hebrew.
Translation:
This donated by KH Joseph Leib Bukowitz with his wife the lady Liblah, may she live, and with the boy Jonah Bukowitz, may he live. Made in memory of the fire of the year 598 a. s. c. [= 1838].
Collection point: Náchod

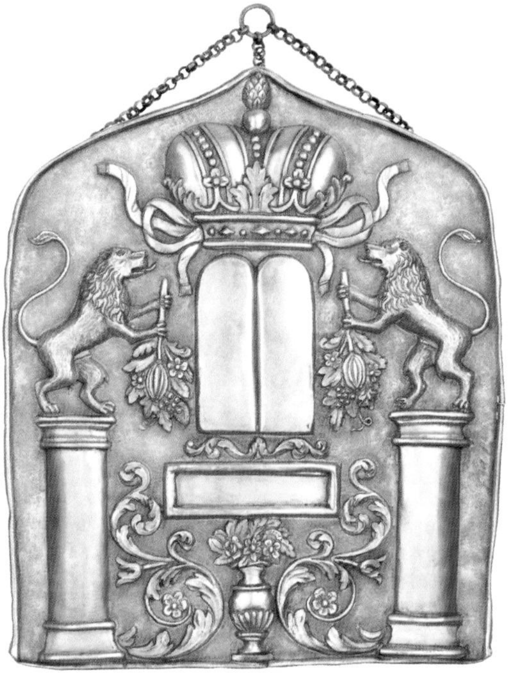

Cat. No. 66 ^
Torah Shield
Inv. No. JMP 002.294
Silver, repoussé
Maker WB, Brno, 1840
Height: 268 mm, width: 221 mm
Hallmarks: 1. WB in rectangle,
2. hallmark Brno 1840
Without inscriptions.
Collection point: Velké Meziříčí

Cat. No. 67
Torah Shield
Inv. No. JMP 037.711
Silver, repoussé, parcel-gilt
Benedict Raninger, Vienna, 1844
Height: 417 mm, width: 270 mm
Hallmarks: 1. BR in oval, 2. hallmark Vienna 1844
Donation inscription in Hebrew and the first words of the Decalogue in Hebrew.
Translation:
A solemn gift to the glory of the Lord and His Torah. To commemorate the love and memory of his mother, the esteemed woman Sarl, wife of the sage R Jehiel, who dwells on high, from her son Aaron Pollak, resident of Vienna. Brought to the temple on the last day of Passover in the year "And the glory of children is their parents" [Prov. 17:6; dating in chronogram 604 = April 11, 1844].
Collection point: Jewish Museum in Prague, 1906–1940

Cat. No. 68
Torah Shield
Inv. No. JMP 004.057
Silver, repoussé
Antonín Maroušek, Prague, 1845
Height: 206 mm, width: 184 mm
Hallmarks: 1. AM in oval, 2. hallmark Prague 1845
Donation inscription in Hebrew.
Translation:
Consecrated to the Lord. A solemn gift from the elder KH Abraham Stransky, may his Rock protect him, with his distinguished wife the lady Sarl, may she live, in the year 609 a. s. c. [= 1849].
Collection point: Kolín

Cat. No. 69
Torah Shield
Inv. No. JMP 001.992
Silver, repoussé, cast, parcel-gilt, natural and glass stones, red coral
Maker "M" [?], Poland, 19th century
Height: 290 mm, width: 273 mm
Hallmarks: 1. M in rhomboid, 2. unidentified mark, 3. purity mark 12 in circle, 4. walking deer in square
Donation inscription in Hebrew and name of the festival in Hebrew.
Translation:
This was donated by the esteemed R Yom Tov Polak with R Abraham Pereles in the holy community Prašný Újezd.
Collection point: Rokycany

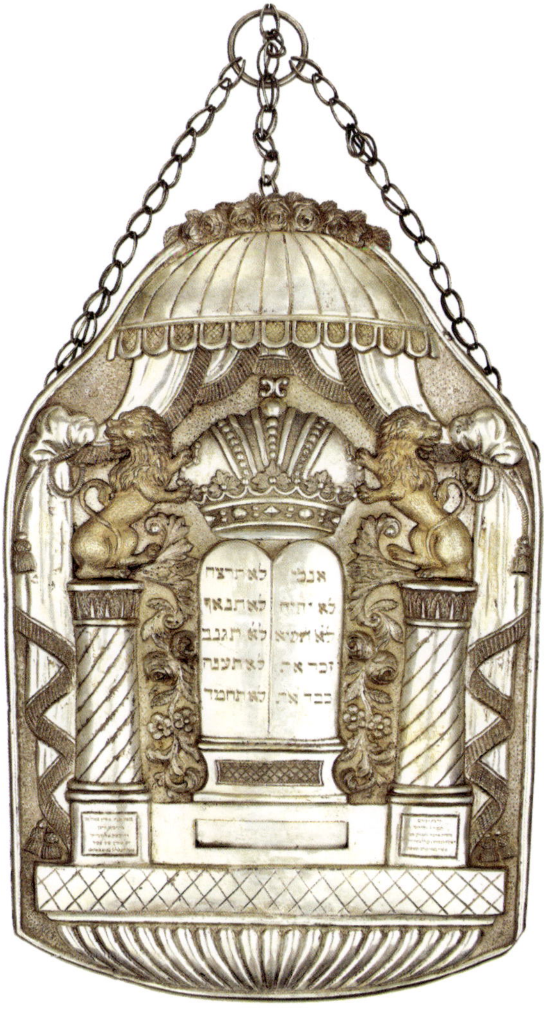

Cat. No. 67

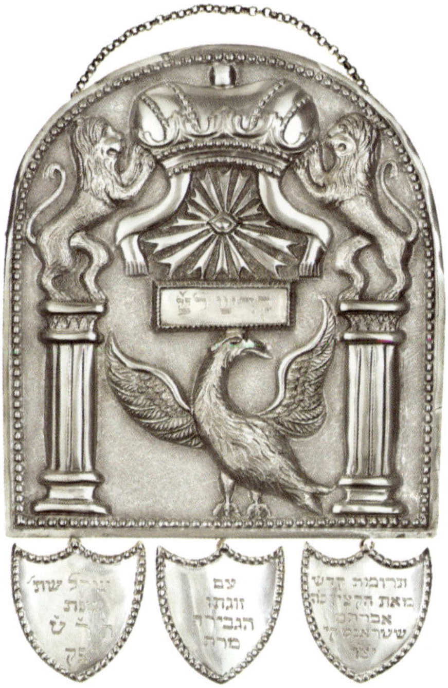

Cat. No. 68

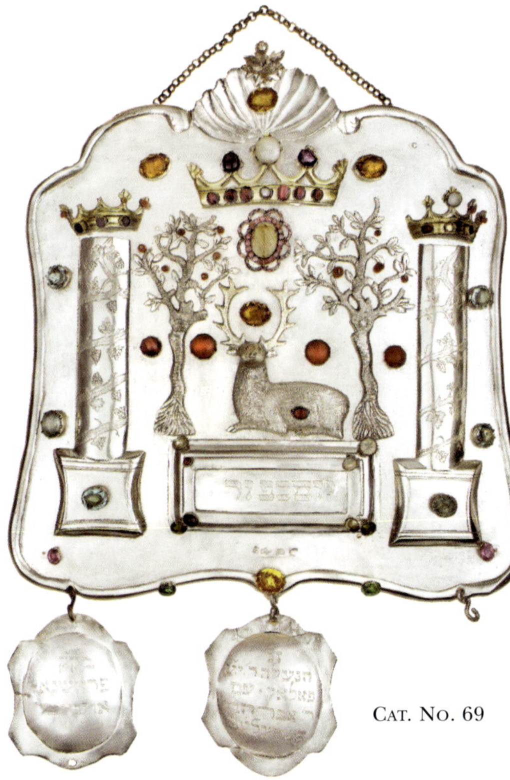

Cat. No. 69

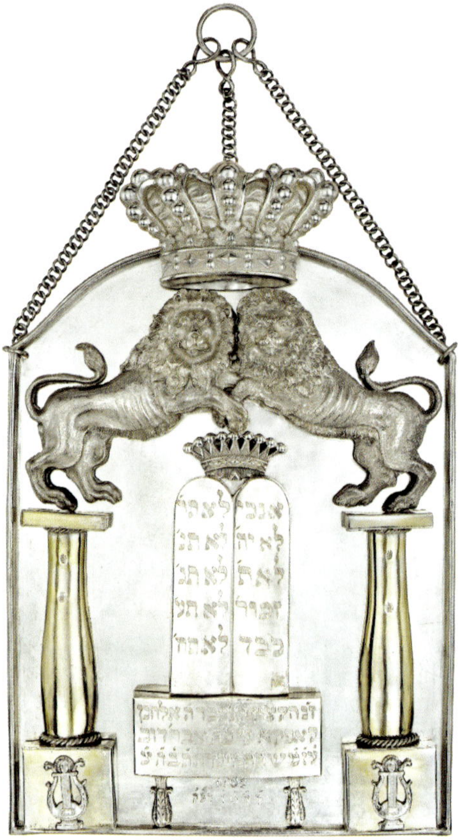

Cat. No. 70
Torah Shield
Inv. No. JMP 023.172
Silver, repoussé, cast, parcel-gilt
Johann Radda [?], Brno, 1854
Height: 275 mm, width: 182 mm
Hallmarks: 1. JR in oval, 2. hallmark Brno 1854
Donation inscription in Hebrew and the first words of the Decalogue in Hebrew.
Translation:
Donated by the esteemed elder H Elhanan Kafka, may his light shine, son of H Abraham Dov, with his wife the lady Sarah Hinda, may she live, daughter of H C. In the year 615 a.s.c. [= 1855].
Collection point: Vodňany

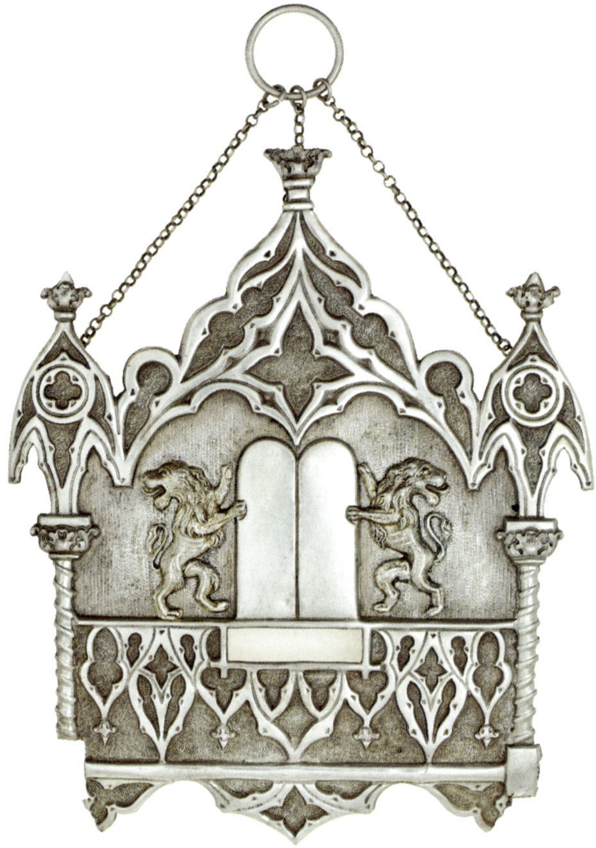

Cat. No. 71
Torah Shield
Inv. No. JMP 003.661
Silver, repoussé
Thomas Dub, Vienna, 1862
Height: 277 mm, width: 227 mm
Hallmarks: 1. TD in rectangle, 2. hallmark Vienna 1862
Without inscriptions.
Collection point: Brno

Cat. No. 72
Torah Shield
Inv. No. JMP 001.539
Silver, repoussé, parcel-gilt
Maker's mark illegible, Vienna, 1862
Height: 448 mm, width: 361 mm
Hallmarks: 1. illegible mark in rectangle,
2. hallmark Vienna 1862
Donation inscription in German
in Latin script.
Translation:
1863. Donated to the synagogue by Bernard and Karolina Eisler.
Collection point: Bzenec

Cat. No. 73
Torah Shield
Inv. No. JMP 010.401
Silver, repoussé, parcel-gilt
Eduard Gottlieb [?], Vienna, 1867–71
Height: 350 mm, width: 267 mm
Hallmarks: 1. EG in oval,
2. Austro-Hungary 1867–71
Without inscriptions.
Collection point: Brno, Miroslav

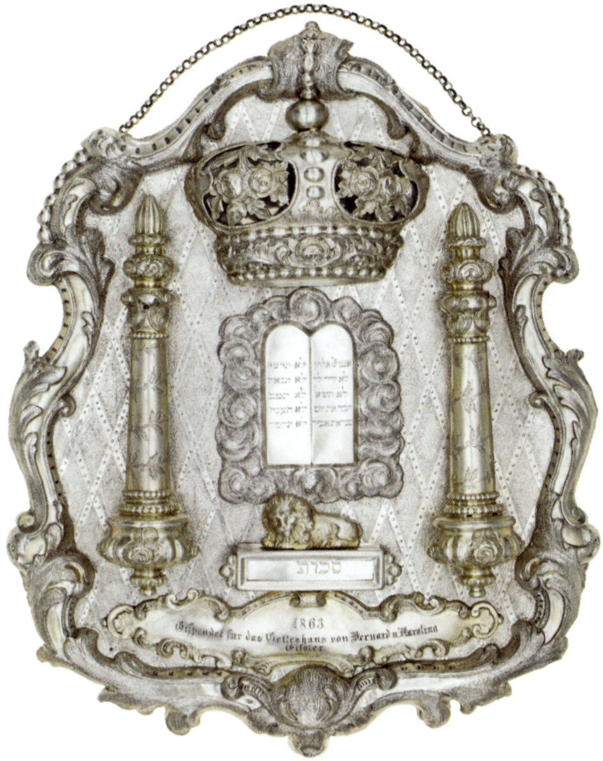

Cat. No. 72
Cat. No. 73

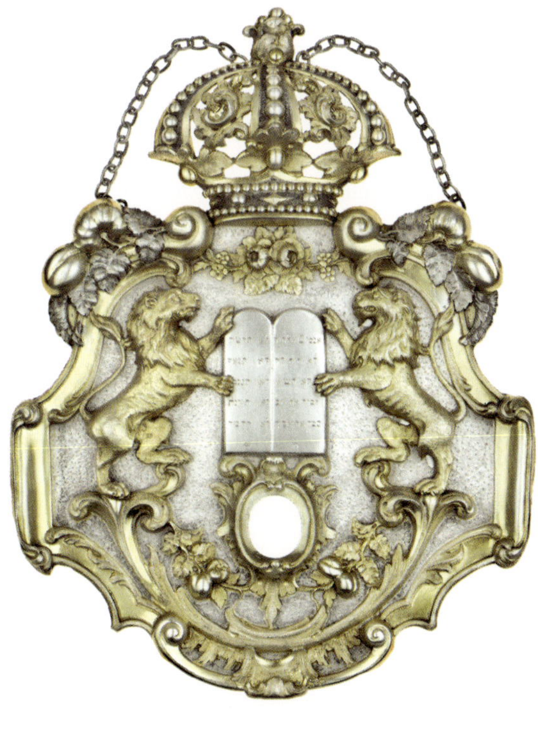

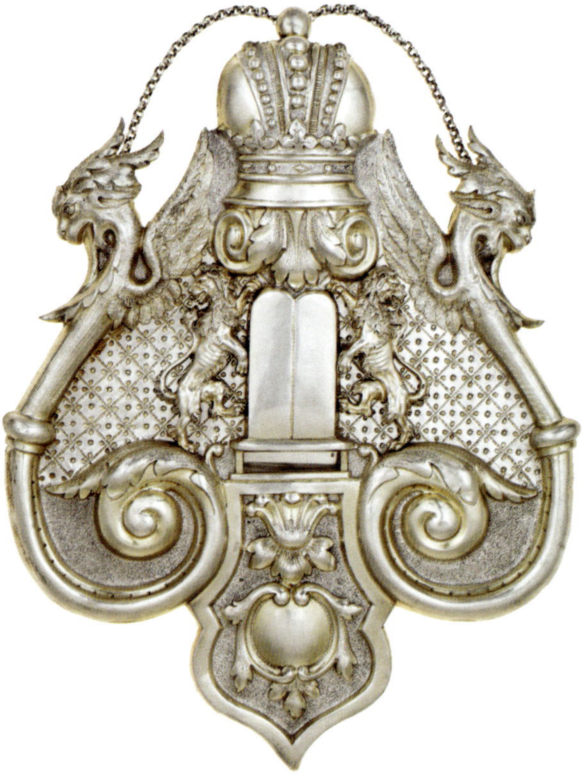

Cat. No. 74
Torah Shield
Inv. No. JMP 004.317
Silver, repoussé, cast, parcel-gilt
Vincenz Czokally (company), Vienna, after 1871
Height: 354 mm, width: 265 mm
Hallmarks: 1. VC in rectangle,
2. Austro-Hungary [Vienna] 1872–1921,
3. Vienna location letter “A”
Without inscriptions.
Collection point: Uherské Hradiště

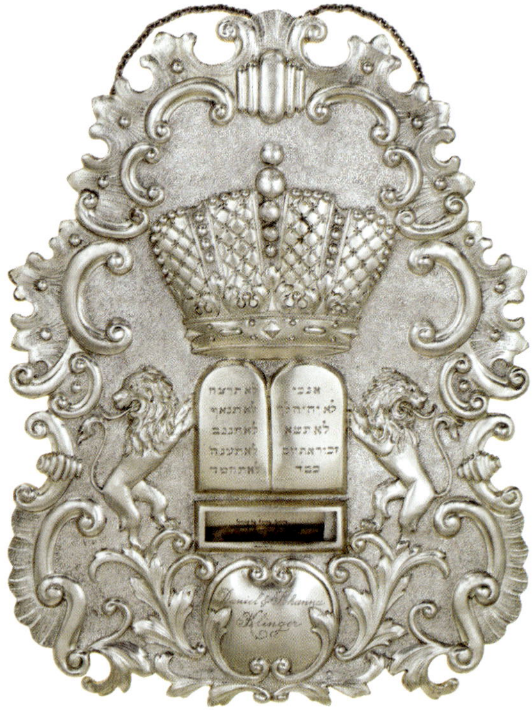

Cat. No. 75
Torah Shield
Inv. No. JMP 023.359
Silver, repoussé, originally parcel-gilt
Maker AK, Prague, after 1871
Height: 324 mm, width: 243 mm
Hallmarks: 1. AK in oval, 2. Austro-Hungary
[Prague] 1872–1921
Donation inscription in German in Latin script:
Daniel & Johanna Klinger.
Collection point: Velhartice

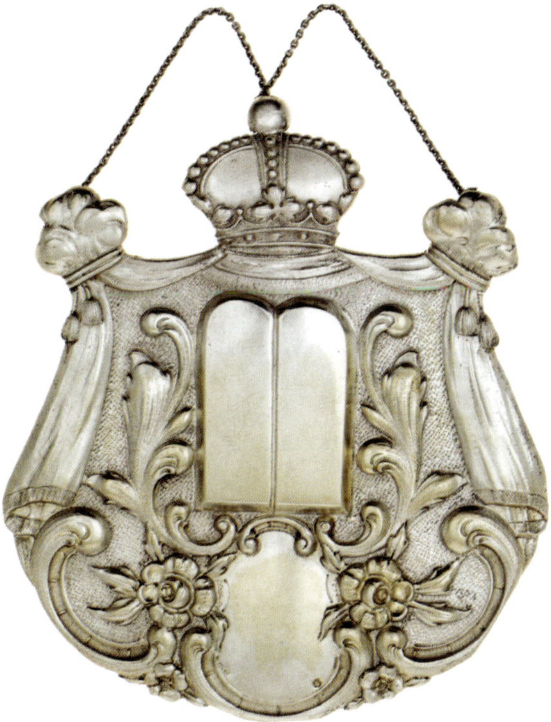

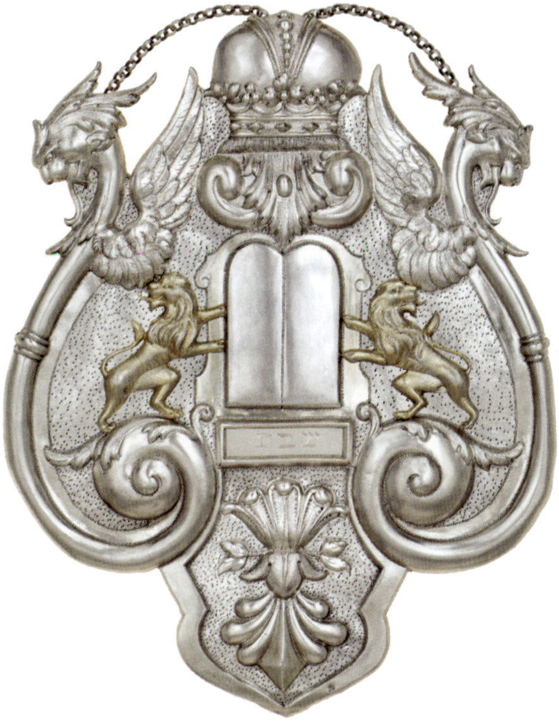

Cat. No. 76
Torah Shield
Inv. No. JMP 017.458
Silver, repoussé, originally parcel-gilt
Maker RK, Prague, after 1871
Height: 232 mm, width: 200 mm
Hallmarks: 1. RK in oval, 2. Austro-Hungary [Prague] 1872–1921
Without inscriptions.
Collection point: Prague, Klausen Synagogue

Cat. No. 77
Torah Shield
Inv. No. JMP 001.635
Silver, repoussé, parcel-gilt
Maker JZ [Josef Zauza Co.?],
Vienna, 1872–85
Height: 297 mm, width: 232 mm
Hallmarks: 1. JZ in rectangle,
2. Austro-Hungary [Vienna] 1872–1921
Donation inscription in German in Latin script.
Translation:
Presented to the religious society in Jablonec [nad Nisou] *by Emanuel Lederer from his income as registrar 1885, 645 a. s. c.* .
Collection point: Turnov

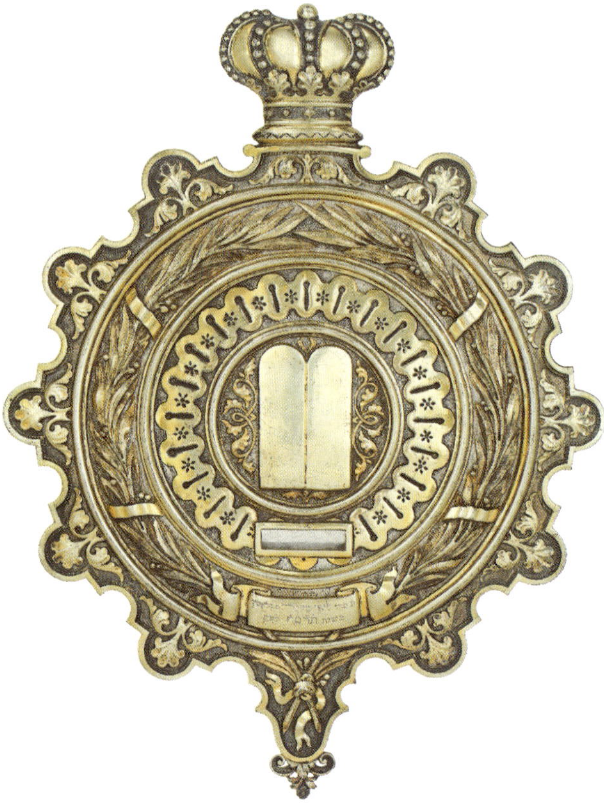

Cat. No. 78

Cat. No. 78
Torah Shield
Inv. No. JMP 004.070
Silver, repoussé, parcel-gilt
Vincenz Czokally (company), Vienna, 1872–85
Height: 428 mm, width: 324 mm
Hallmarks: 1. VC in rectangle, 2. Austro-Hungary [Vienna] after 1871, 3. Vienna location letter "A"
Donation inscription in Hebrew.
Translation:
This was a donation made by MHV Louis Menerl [Levi Mendl?] *of Galati* [Galatz] *in the year 645 a. s. c.* [= 1885].
Collection point: Tábor

Cat. No. 79
Torah Shield
Inv. No. JMP 004.242
Silver, repoussé
Goldschmidt H. S. (company), Prague, 1872–99
Height: 234 mm, width: 199 mm
Hallmarks: 1. HSG in rectangle, 2. HG in oval, 3. Austro-Hungary [Prague] after 1871
Donation inscription in Hebrew.
Translation:
This was a donation by KH Hayyim Luria with his wife the lady Gitl on behalf of their son Moses on Rosh Hashanah [?] *660 a. s. c.* [= Sept. 5, 1899].
Collection point: Březnice

Cat. No. 80
Torah Shield
Inv. No. JMP 002.397
Silver, repoussé
Alfred Pollak (company), Prague, 1878–99
Height: 340 mm, width: 246 mm
Hallmarks: 1. AP in rectangle, 2. Austro-Hungary [Prague] after 1871
Donation inscription in German in Latin script.
Translation:
Donated by Malvína, Olga, Wilhelm, and Ludwig Fischer in Rakovník on the festival of Pesach 5659 (D.W). 26/3 1899.
Collection point: Rakovník

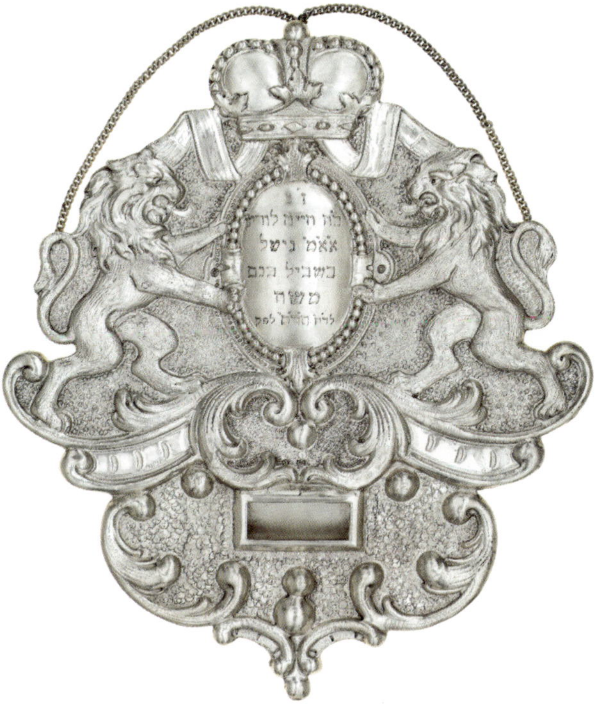

Cat. No. 79

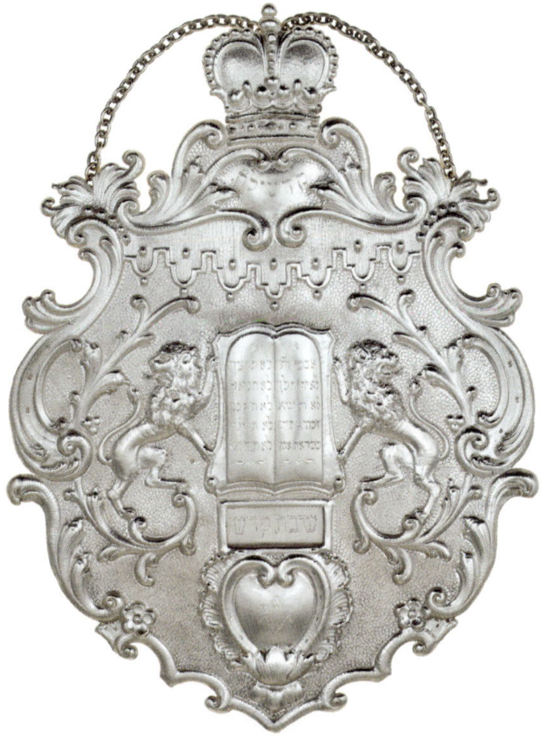

Cat. No. 80

Cat. No. 81 >
Torah Shield
Inv. No. JMP 001.678
Silver, repoussé, parcel-gilt
Maker AP, Prague, 1904 [inscription]
Height: 279 mm, width: 226 mm
Hallmarks: 1. AP in oval,
2. Austro-Hungary [Prague] after 1871
Donation inscription in Hebrew.
Translation:
From Kostelec nad Labem. This gift is made by R Simhah Bloch in the year 664 a. s. c. [= 1904].
Collection point: Brandýs nad Labem / Kostelec nad Labem

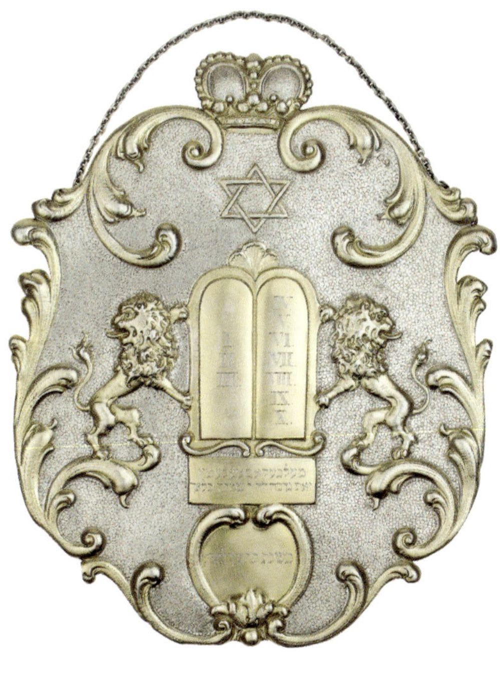

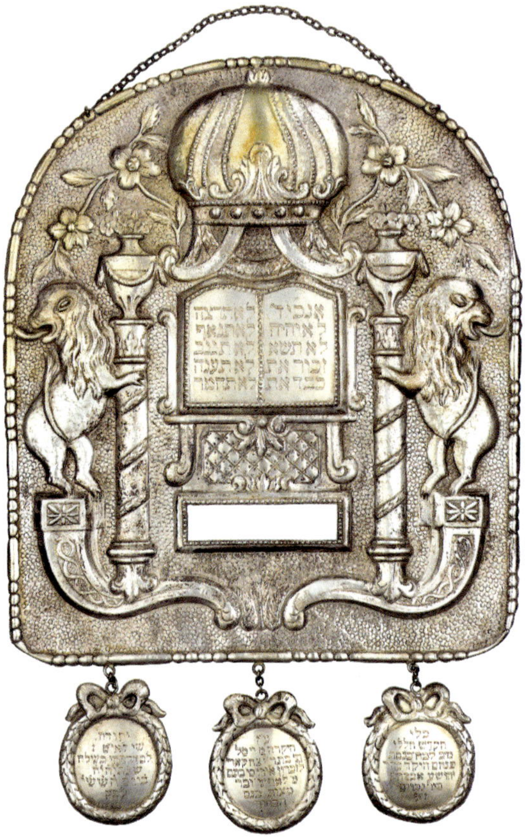

Cat. No. 82
Torah Shield
Inv. No. JMP 046.022
Silver, repoussé
Maker MV, Czechoslovakia, 1921–23
Height: 371 mm, width: 313 mm
Hallmarks: 1. MV in rectangle,
2. hallmark Czechoslovakia 1921–28
Donation inscription in Hebrew.
Translation:
This holy item is donated to the Pinkas Synagogue by the esteemed KHR Joshua Abraham Birnbaum of blessed memory, with his esteemed wife the lady Yitl, may she live, daughter of R Isaac Ari in remembrance of the wedding of their daughter the lady Leah, may she live, and bar mitzvah of their son, the boy Judah, may the days of his life be many and good. Sidra Va-yehi beshalach of the year "the sixth day" a. s. c.
[dating in the chronogram 5683 = Feb. 3, 1923].
Collection point: Prague, Pinkas Synagogue

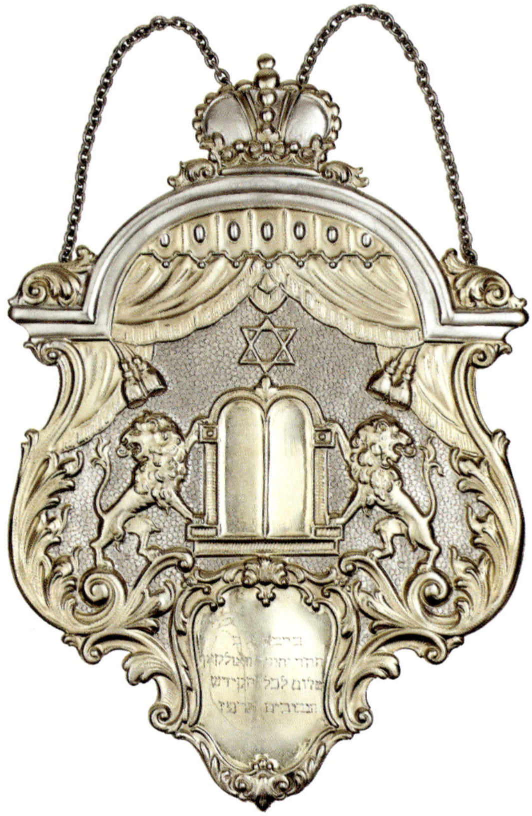

Cat. No. 83
Torah Shield
Inv. No. JMP 010.474
Silver, electroplated, parcel-gilt
Alfred Pollak (company), Prague, 1921–27
Height: 350 mm, width: 240 mm
Hallmarks: 1. AP in rectangle, 2. hallmark Czechoslovakia 1921–28
Donation inscription in Hebrew.
Translation:
A gift from the heart by H HR Judah Wulkan. Peace to stolen holy objects [?], *687 a. s. c.* [= 1927].
[In the inscription the letters "bet" and "nun" are indistinguishable, making it unclear.]
Collection point: Místek

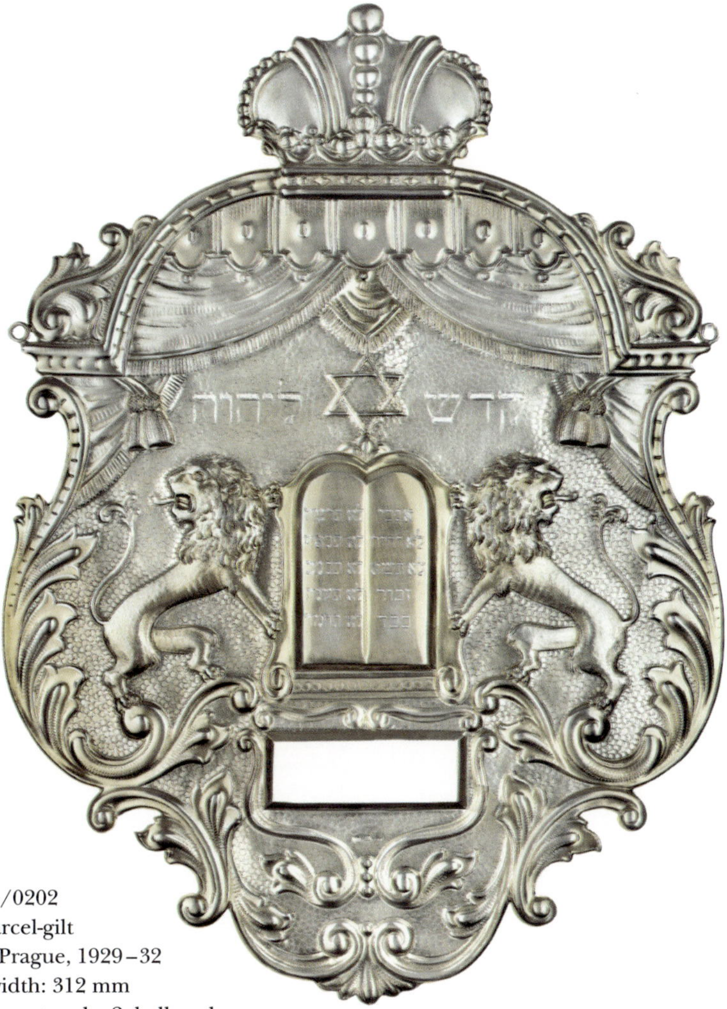

Cat. No. 84

Torah Shield

Acq. No. JMP 1973/0202
Silver, repoussé, parcel-gilt
Tomáš Procházka, Prague, 1929–32
Height: 436 mm, width: 312 mm
Hallmarks: 1. TP in rectangle, 2. hallmark Czechoslovakia 1929–40, 3. purity mark 800
Inscription in Hebrew and German and the first words of the Decalogue in Hebrew.
Translation:
Consecrated to the Lord [in Hebrew]. *Donated by the family of Ignaz Klein, Varnsdorf, Tamuz 5692* [= June 1932] [in German].
Catalogued secondarily into the inventory of the Jewish Museum in Prague.

II. Torah Crowns

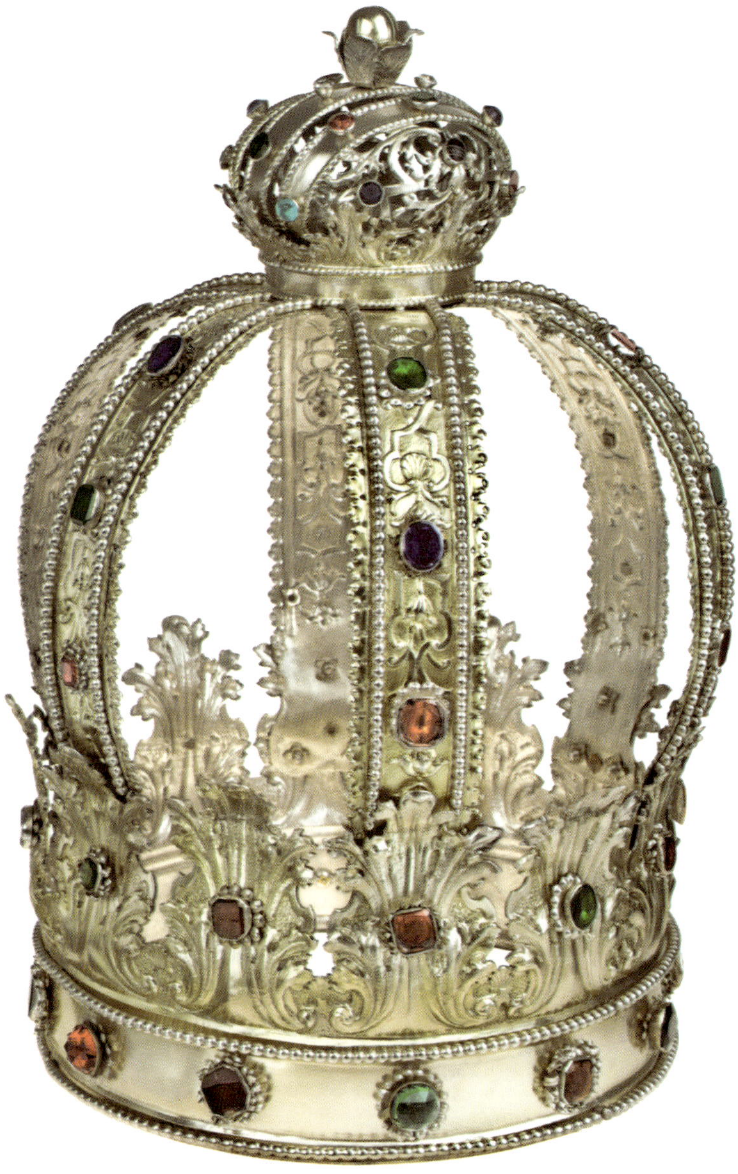

< Cat. No. 85
Torah Crown
Inv. No. JMP 037.746
Silver, repoussé, parcel-gilt
Filip Oberholzer, Prague, 1723
Height: 452 mm, diameter: 325 mm
Hallmarks: 1. PHO in heart,
2. city mark Prague – Staré Město 1723,
3. recharge mark Prague 1806–7
Without inscriptions.
Collection point: Jewish Museum
in Prague, 1906–1940

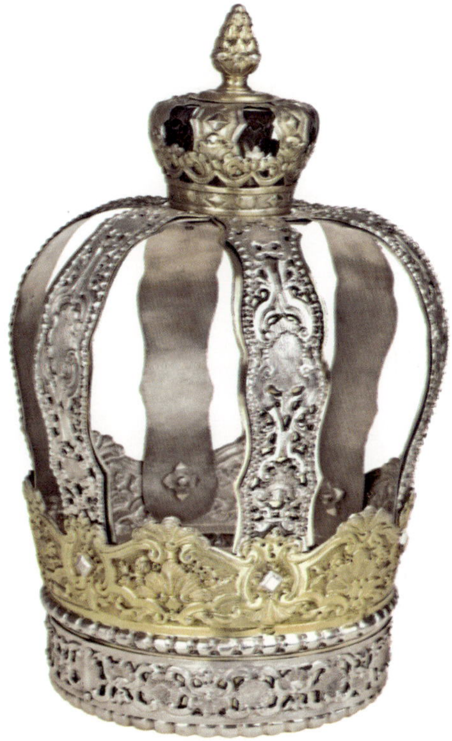

Cat. No. 86
Torah Crown
Inv. No. JMP 005.332
Silver, repoussé, parcel-gilt
Georg Kahlert, Jr., Breslau, 1761–1772
Height: 318 mm, diameter: 200 mm
Hallmarks: 1. GK in rectangle,
2. hallmark Breslau, 3. date letter G,
4. recharge mark Prague 1806–7,
5. release mark 1809–10
Without inscriptions.
Collection point: Holešov

Cat. No. 87
Torah Crown
Inv. No. JMP 005.331
Silver, repoussé, cast, parcel-gilt
Jan Michal Kaltenmarker, Brno, 1769
Height: 191 mm, width: 145 mm
Hallmarks: 1. IMK in trilob, 2. hallmark Brno 1769,
3. recharge mark Brno 1806–7
Without inscriptions.
Collection point: Holešov

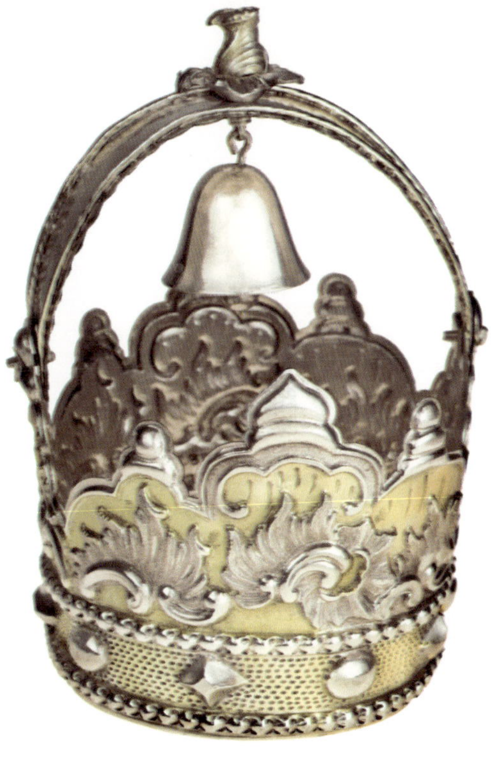

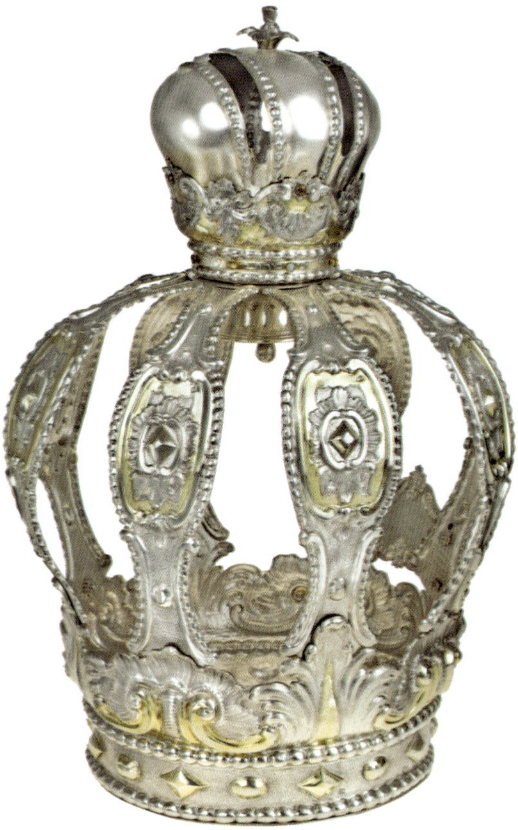

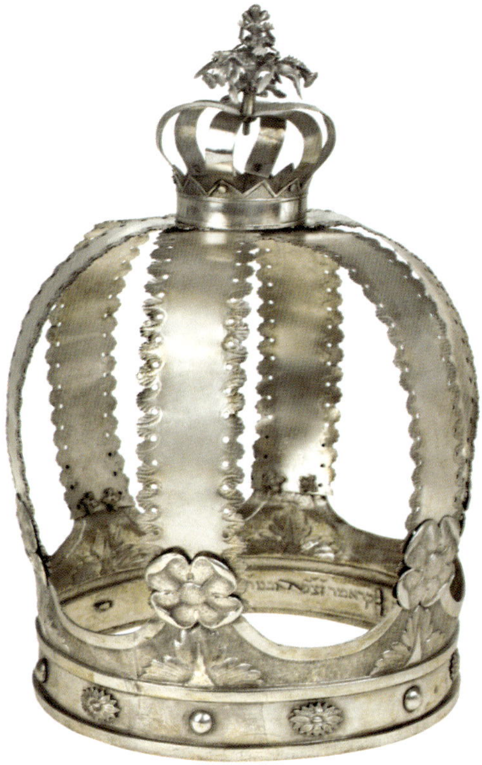

Cat. No. 88
Torah Crown
Inv. No. JMP 038.000
Silver, repoussé, parcel-gilt
Maker AD [Ondřej Dejl ?], Prague, 1782
Height: 473 mm, width: 310 mm
Hallmarks: 1. AD in irregular shape, 2. hallmark Prague 1782, 3. recharge mark Prague 1806–7
Donation inscription in Hebrew.
Translation:
KT. This was purchased from charitable funds together with contributions from eminent individuals, in the year 564 a. s. c. [= 1804]. *Refurbished by the sage R Jacob Kuranda, in the year 652 a. s. c.* [= 1892].
Collection point: Prague, Pinkas Synagogue

Cat. No. 89
Torah Crown
Inv. No. JMP 007.067
Silver, repoussé
Wilhelm Streithoff, Vienna, 1810
Height: 393 mm, diameter: 266 mm
Hallmarks: 1. WS in irregular shape, 2. hallmark Vienna 1810, 3. tax mark Vienna 1810–24
Donation inscription in Hebrew.
Translation:
R Wolf Kramer, may the memory of the just be blessed, and his son R Eizik.
Collection point: Třešť

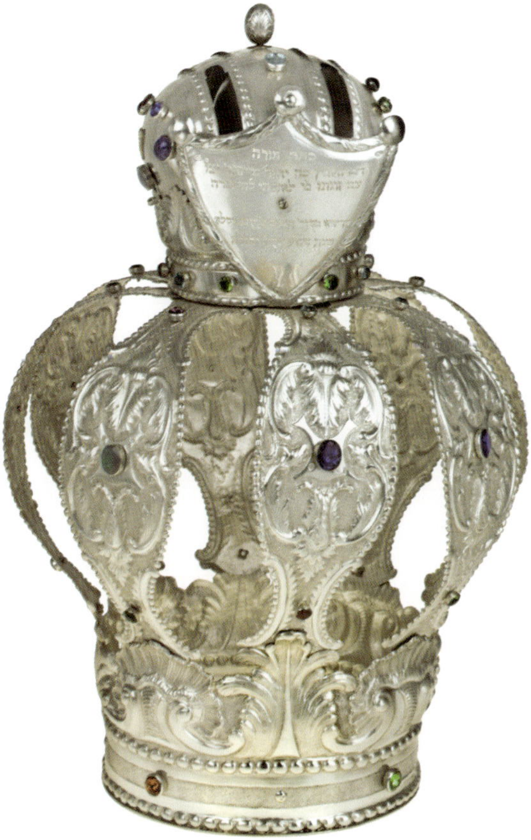

Cat. No. 90
Torah Crown
Inv. No. JMP 002.164
Silver, repoussé
Antonín Maroušek, Prague, 1817
Height: 520 mm, diameter: 335 mm
Hallmarks: 1. AM in oval, 2. hallmark Prague 1817, 3. tax mark Prague 1810–24
Donation inscription in Hebrew.
Translation:
Torah Crown. Donated by the eminent KH Judah Meissner, may his Rock and Redeemer protect him, and his wife, the lady Leah, may she live, for the Holy Society for Visiting the Sick in the holy community [Mladá] *Boleslav, in the year "Hear the voice of Judah"* [dating in the chronogram 578 = 1818].
Collection point: Mladá Boleslav

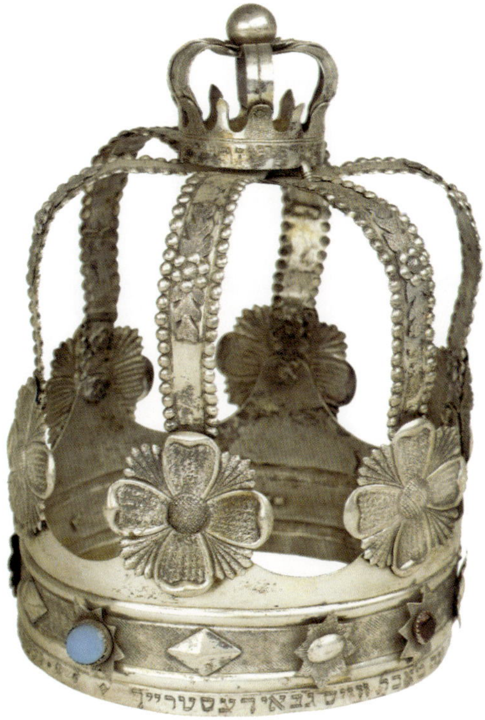

Cat. No. 91
Torah Crown
Inv. No. JMP 007.157
Silver, repoussé
Maker IB, Jihlava, 1821
Height: 239 mm, diameter: 175 mm
Hallmarks: 1. IB in rectangle, 2. hallmark Jihlava 1821, 3. tax mark Jihlava 1810–24
Donation inscription in Hebrew.
Translation:
Belonging to the Society of Boys in the holy community [Velké] *Meziříčí. Made through the agency of the elders, the custodians, the boys Abraham, son of R J.H. Ger, and KH Abraham, son of L. G Sch, and KH Hayyim, son of R. G Sch, and KH Mochel Weiss, custodian* [from] *Austria.*
Collection point: Brno

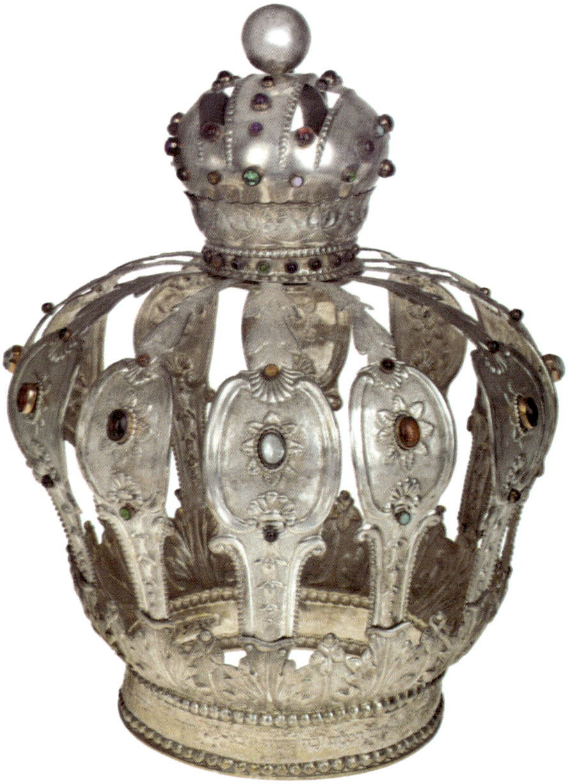

Cat. No. 92
Torah Crown
Inv. No. JMP 037.537
Silver, repoussé
Tomáš Höpfel, Prague, 1830
Height: 610 mm, diameter: 470 mm
Hallmarks: 1. TH in rectangle,
2. hallmark Prague 1830
Donation inscription in Hebrew.
Translation:
Made from charitable funds with a financial contribution from what was left from the sale of a silver crown that was donated by the late KH Moses Kicha with his wife Reizl of blessed memory, in memory of their souls bound to the bond of the living, in the year 590 a. s. c. [= 1830].
Collection point: Prague

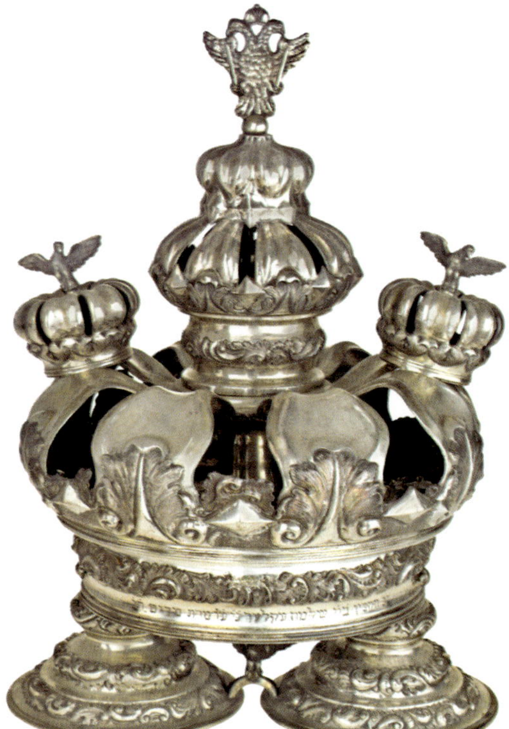

Cat. No. 93
Torah Crown
Inv. No. JMP 012.181
Silver, repoussé
Thomas Dub, Vienna, 1865
Height: 388 mm, diameter: 276 mm
Hallmarks: 1. TD in rectangle,
2. hallmark Vienna 1865
Donation inscription in Hebrew.
Translation:
This was donated by the elder KH Solomon Eckler, may his light shine, with his wife the lady Miriam, may she live.
Collection point: Rousínov

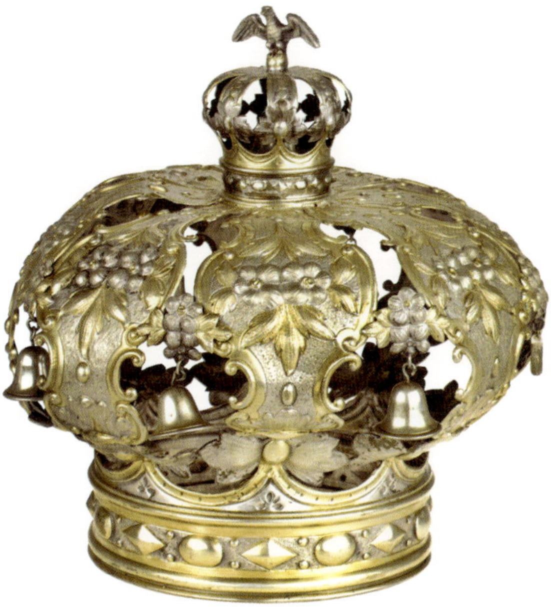

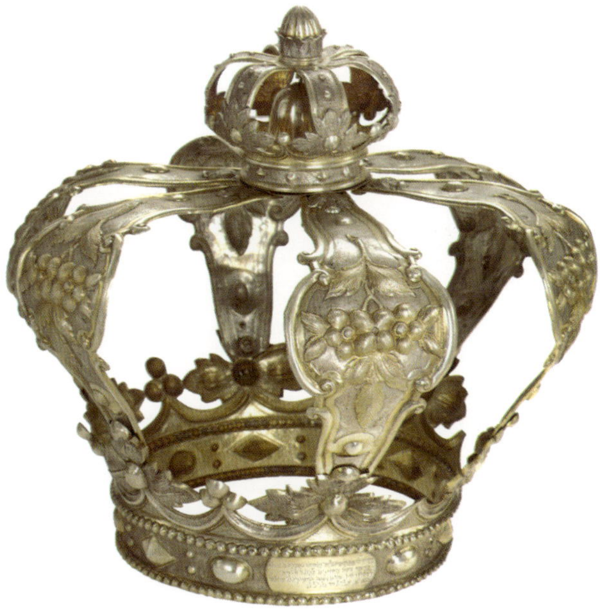

Cat. No. 94
Torah Crown
Inv. No. JMP 002.946
Silver, repoussé, parcel-gilt
Maker's mark illegible, Vienna, after 1871
Height: 292 mm, width: 290 mm
Hallmarks: 1. illegible maker's mark,
2. Austro-Hungary [Vienna] after 1871
Without inscriptions.
Collection point: Lipník nad Bečvou

Cat. No. 95
Torah Crown
Inv. No. JMP 010.057
Silver, repoussé, parcel-gilt
Maker TD [Thomas Dub Co.?],
Vienna, 1872–75
Height: 310 mm, diameter: 325 mm
Hallmarks: 1. TD in rectangle, 2. Austro-Hungary
[Vienna] after 1871
Donation inscription in Hebrew.
Translation:
The elder KH Aaron Käfler and his pious wife the lady Gitl have donated this Torah crown in memory of the wedding day of their young daughter the lady Figlah, 11 of Elul in the year 635 [= Sept. 11, 1875].
Collection point: Loštice

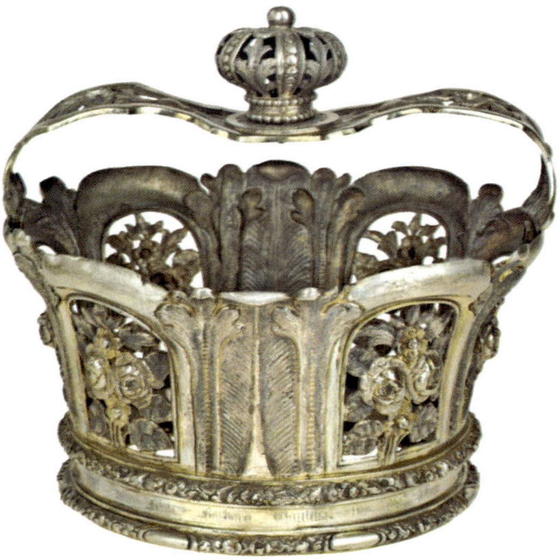

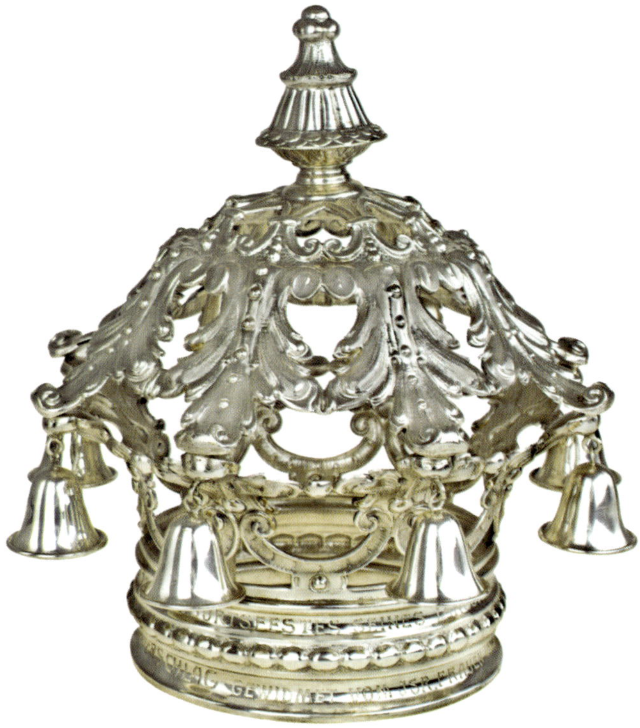

Cat. No. 96
Torah Crown
Inv. No. JMP 002.166
Silver, repoussé, parcel-gilt
Maker EG [Eduard Gottsleben?],
Vienna, 1872–79
Height: 216 mm, diameter: 237 mm
Hallmarks: 1. EG in rectangle,
2. Austro-Hungary [Vienna] after 1871
Donation inscription in German in Latin script.
Translation:
Donated by Mrs. Barbara Mautner in the year 1879.
Collection point: Mladá Boleslav

Cat. No. 97
Torah Crown
Inv. No. JMP 037.443
Silver, repoussé
Abraham David Kuh, Prague, 1872–82
Height: 390 mm, diameter: 330 mm
Hallmarks: 1. AK in oval,
2. Austro-Hungary [Prague] after 1871
Donation inscription in German in Latin script.
Translation:
Donated by the Society of Israelite Women in Ústí [nad Labem] *on the occasion of the 70th birthday of our long-time director, Mr. Löwi Hammerschlag, February 3, 1905.*
Collection point: Prague

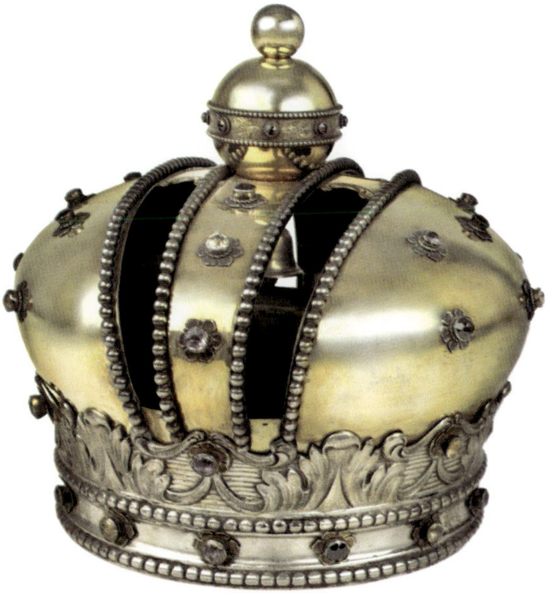

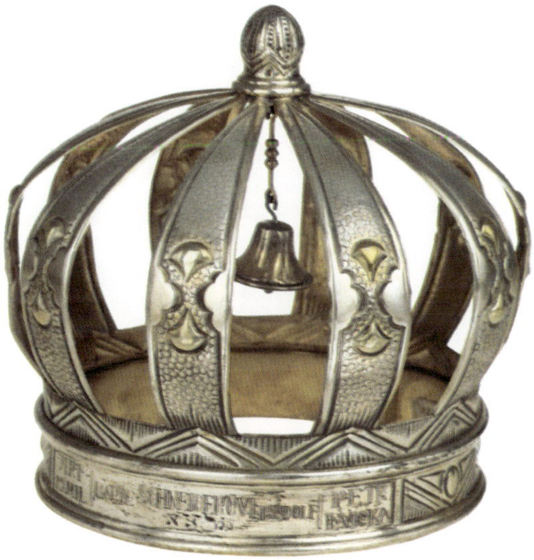

Cat. No. 98
Torah Crown
Inv. No. JMP 017.561
Silver, repoussé, parcel-gilt
František Hladík, Prague, 1913
Height: 280 mm, width: 290 mm
Hallmarks: 1. FH in rectangle,
2. Austro-Hungary [Prague] after 1871
Donation inscription in German in Latin script.
Translation:
On the 80th birthday of the elder of merit Mr. Moritz Austerlitz. Donated in remembrance by his devoted friend. Prague 2, February 1913. Fritz Winterbebg [Winterberg is likely the correct spelling], *designed and executed by Fr. Hladík.*
Collection point: Prague, Klausen Synagogue

Cat. No. 99
Torah Crown
Inv. No. JMP 044.295
Silver, repoussé
Maker MV, Czechoslovakia, 1929–31
Height: 172 mm, diameter: 192 mm
Hallmarks: 1. MV in rectangle,
2. hallmark Czechoslovakia after 1928
Donation inscription in Czech in Latin script, dating in Hebrew.
Translation:
The Schneiders Marie Rudolf Jiří Kamil Petr Evička, 691 a. s. c. [= 1931].
Collection point: Prague, Karlín Synagogue

III. Torah Finials

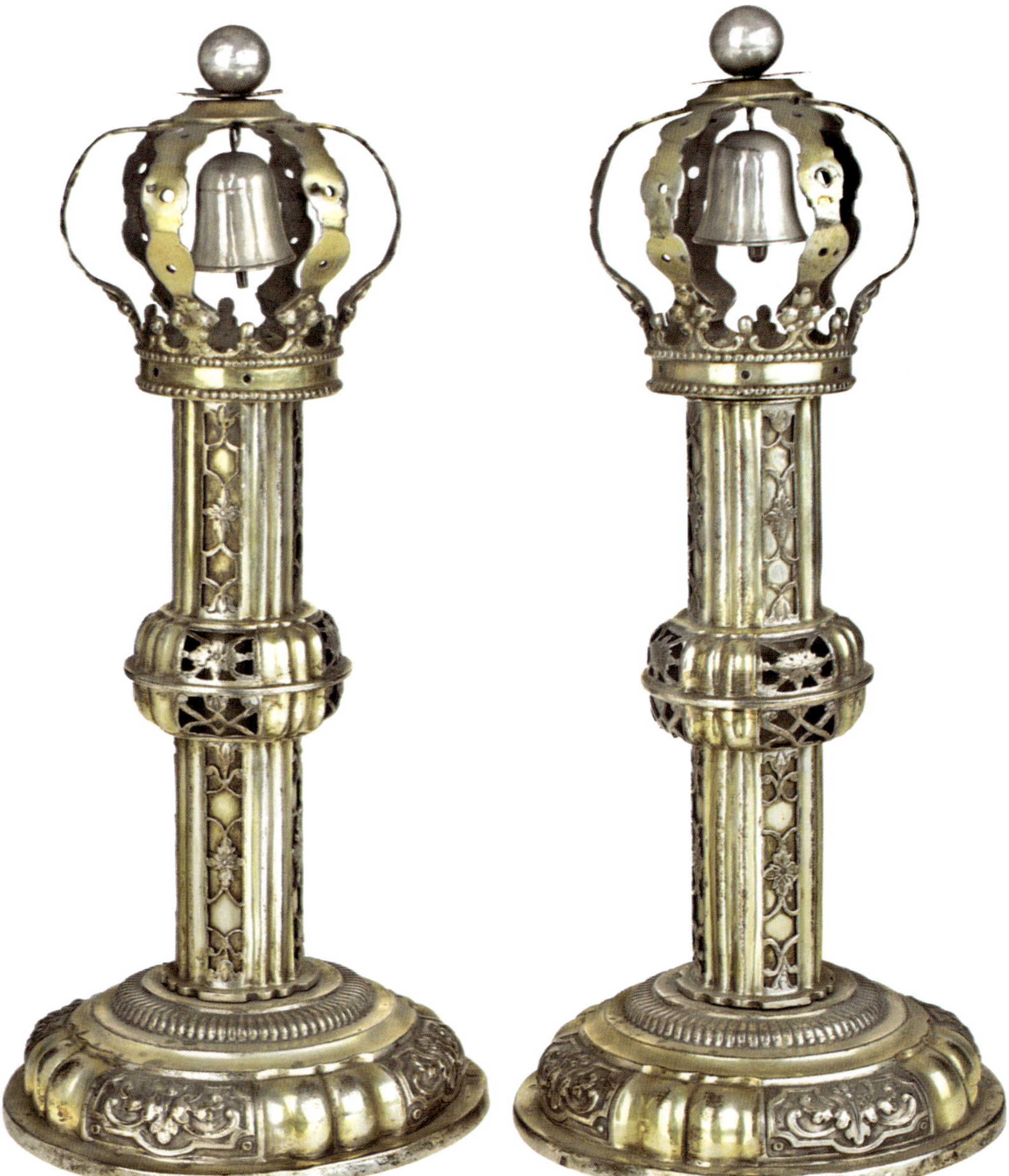

< Cat. No. 100
Torah Finials
Inv. No. JMP 010.386/01, 02
Silver, repoussé, parcel-gilt,
Georg Kahlert, Jr., Breslau, 1732–37
Height: 334 mm, diameter: 150 mm
Hallmarks: 1. GK in rectangle,
2. hallmark Breslau, 3. date letter C
Without inscriptions.
Collection point: Brno, Miroslav

Cat. No. 101
Torah Finials
Inv. No. JMP 037.563/01, 02
Silver, repoussé, engraving
Jakub Kristián Ebner, Prague, 1743
Height: 383 mm, diameter: 158 mm
Hallmarks: 1. IE in oval, 2. hallmark
Prague – Malá Strana 1743, 3. recharge mark
Prague 1806–7, 4. release mark 1809–10
Without inscriptions.
Collection point: Prague

Cat. No. 102
Torah Finials
Inv. No. JMP 012.207/01, 02
Silver, repoussé, engraving, gilt
Maker unknown, Moravia [?], 1749
[inscription]
Height: 208 mm, diameter: 109 mm
Hallmarks: 1. recharge mark Brno 1806–7,
2. release mark 1809–10
Donation inscription in Hebrew.
Translation:
The insignificant Isaac, son of the sage MVHRR Shaul ha-Levi, may the memory of the just be blessed, residing here in the holy community Šendšov [Schöndschow?] [the locality could not be determined]. *The holy object was completed the 7th of Elul 509 a. s. c.* [Aug. 21, 1749].
Collection point: Kounice

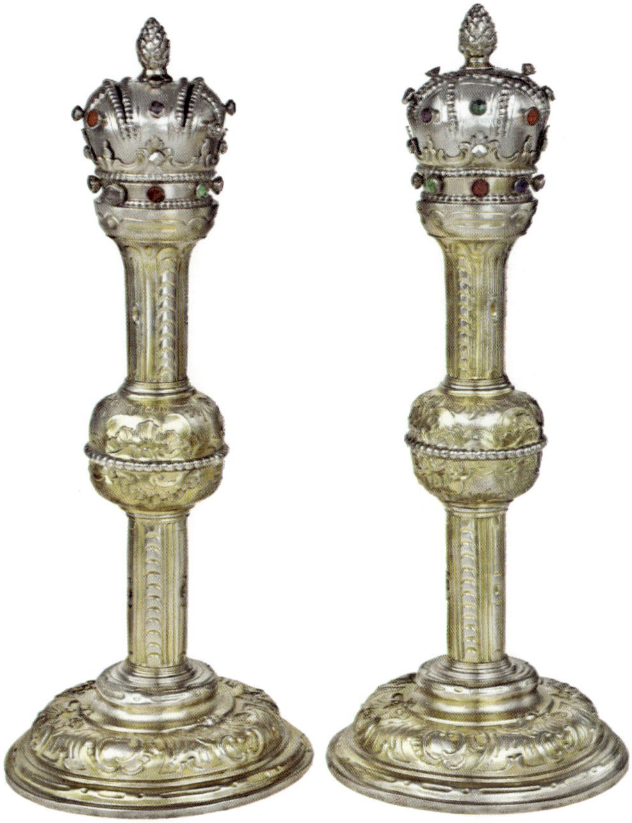

Cat. No. 101
Cat. No. 102

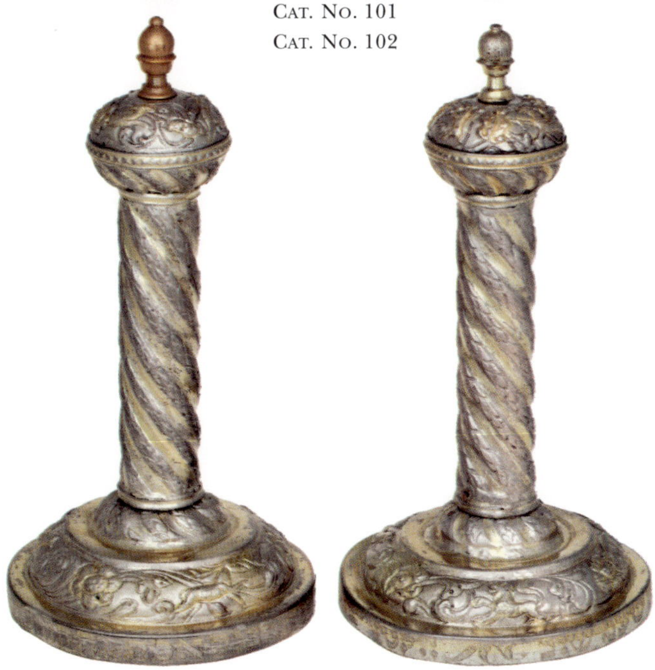

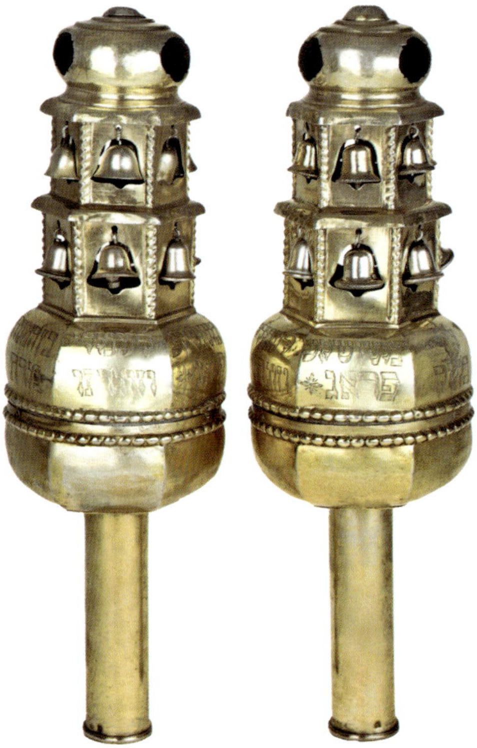

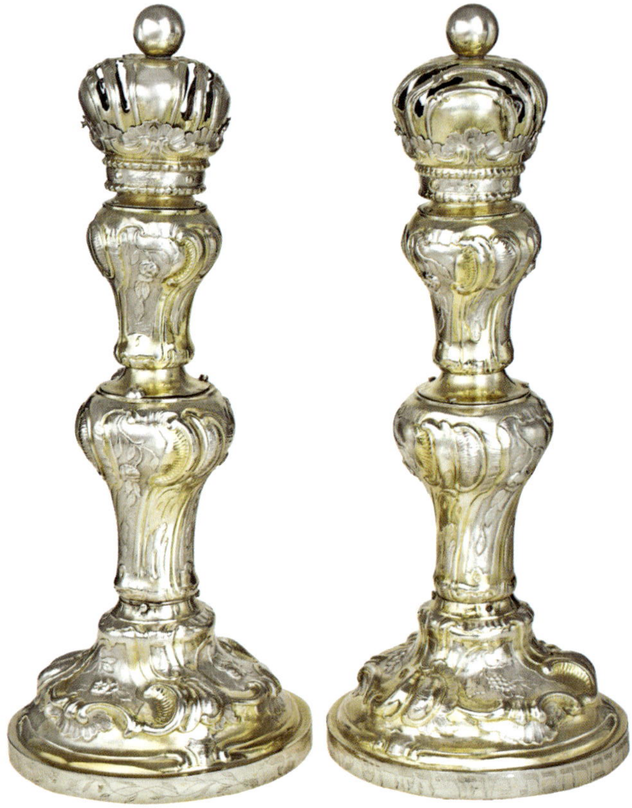

Cat. No. 103
Torah Finials
Inv. No. JMP 044.435/01, 02
Silver, repoussé
Johann Samuel Beckensteiner, Nuremberg, 1763
Height: 362 mm, diameter: 109 mm
Hallmarks: 1. stork in shield with letters IS,
2. hallmark Nuremberg
Donation inscription in Hebrew.
Translation:
Lämmel, son of the late KHTT Zeligman of blessed memory from Touškov and his wife the lady Rebecca, may she live, from the holy community Prague.
Collection point: Prague, Maisel Synagogue

Cat. No. 104
Torah Finials
Inv. No. JMP 037.572/01, 02
Silver, repoussé
Michal Enzinger, Prague, 1767
Height: 440 mm, diameter: 178 mm
Hallmarks: 1. ME in quadrilob, 2. hallmark Prague–Staré Město 1767, 3. recharge mark Prague 1806–7, 4. release mark 1809–10
Donation inscription in Hebrew.
Translation:
This was donated by the distinguished KHRR Abraham, son of KHRR Ephraim Ofner of blessed memory and his wife the lady Deborah, daughter of MHVRR, the holy [martyr] *Akiba, may the memory of the just be blessed, in the year 528 a. s. c.* [= 1768].
Collection point: Prague

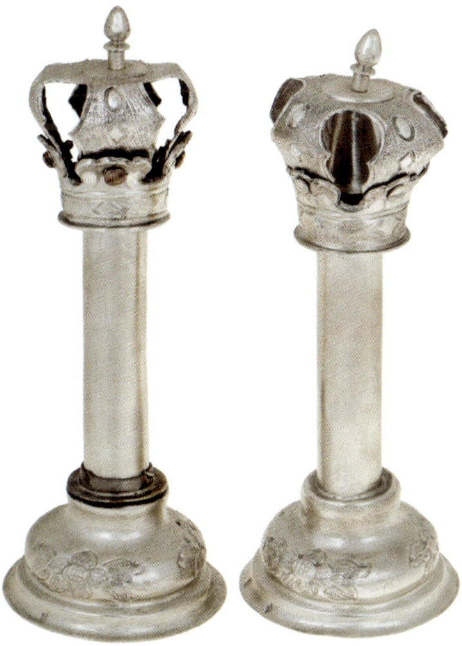

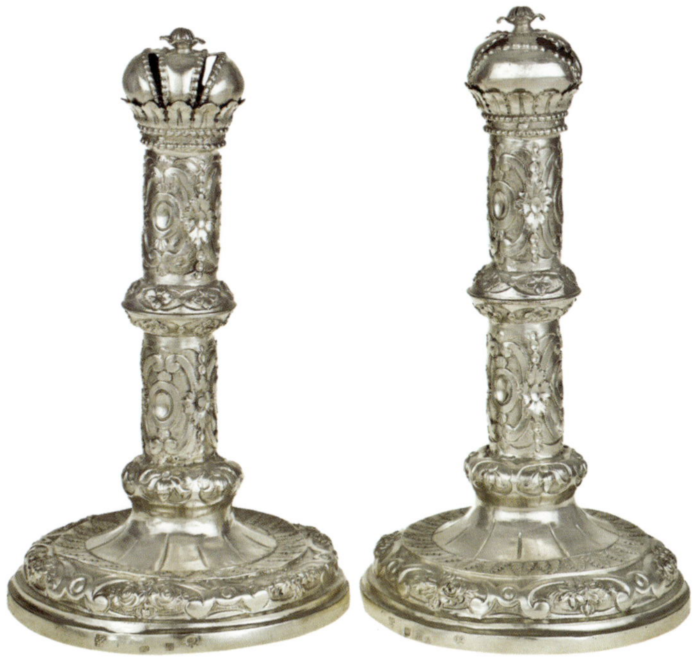

Cat. No. 105
Torah Finials
Inv. No. JMP 005.339/01, 02
Silver, repoussé, engraving
Maker C[?]P, Breslau, 1761–76
Height: 167 mm, diameter: 63 mm
Hallmarks: 1. C[?]P in irregular shape, 2. hallmark Breslau
Without inscriptions.
Collection point: Holešov

Cat. No. 106
Torah Finials
Inv. No. JMP 044.405/01, 02
Silver, repoussé, engraving
Jan Jiří Brullus, Jr., Prague, 1769
Height: 208 mm, diameter: 118 mm
Hallmarks: 1. IGB in trilob, 2. hallmark Prague–Staré Město 1769, 3. recharge mark Prague 1806–7, 4. release mark 1809–10
Without inscriptions.
Collection point: Prague, Maisel Synagogue

Cat. No. 107
Torah Finials
Inv. No. JMP 005.340/01, 02
Silver, repoussé
Jan Michal Kaltenmarker, Brno, 1769
Height: 190 mm, diameter: 103 mm
Hallmarks: 1. IMK in trilob,
2. hallmark Brno 1769,
3. recharge mark Brno 1806–7,
4. release mark 1809–10
Without inscriptions.
Collection point: Holešov

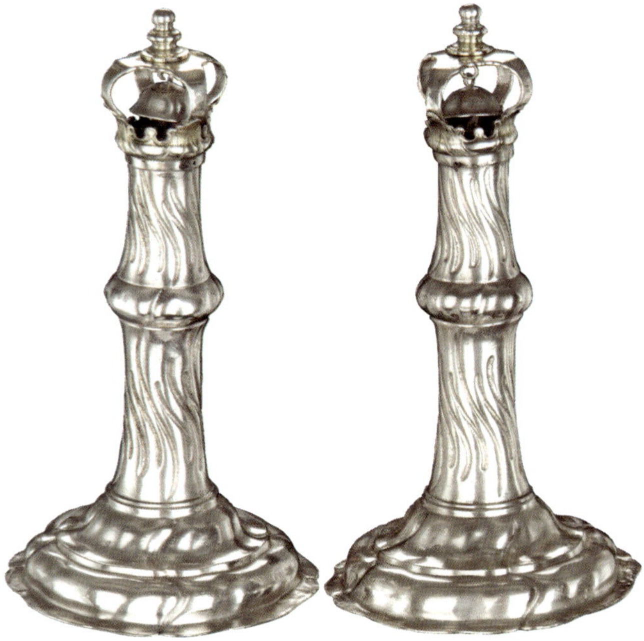

Cat. No. 107

Cat. No. 108
Torah Finials
Inv. No. JMP 001.949/01, 02
Silver, repoussé
Maker IR, Germany [?], 2nd half of 18th century
Height: 158 mm, diameter: 77 mm
Hallmarks: 1. IR in rectangle,
2. illegible city mark
Without inscriptions.
Collection point: Nepomuk

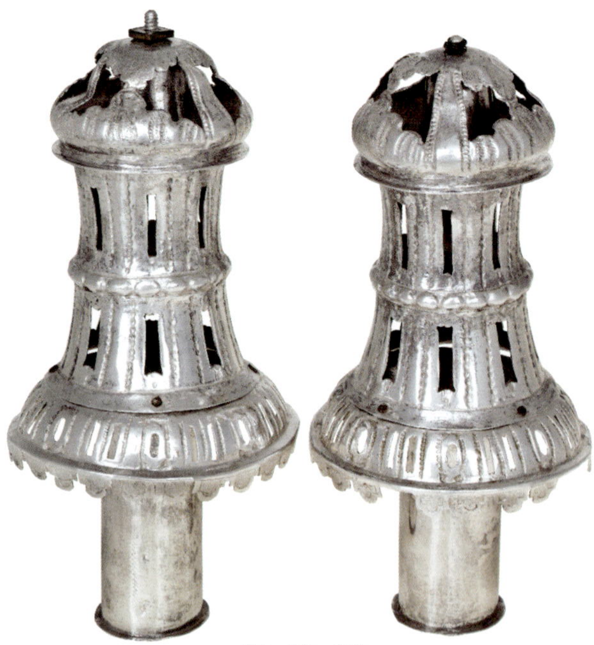

Cat. No. 108

Cat. No. 109
Torah Finials
Inv. No. JMP 005.037/01, 02
Silver, repoussé
Michal Enzinger, Prague, 1780
Height: 284 mm, diameter: 124 mm
Hallmarks: 1. ME in quadrilob, 2. hallmark
Prague 1780, 3. recharge mark Brno 1806–7,
4. release mark 1809–10
Donation inscription in German in Latin script.
Translation:
Donated by Markus Janowitzer in the year 1871.
Collection point: Strakonice

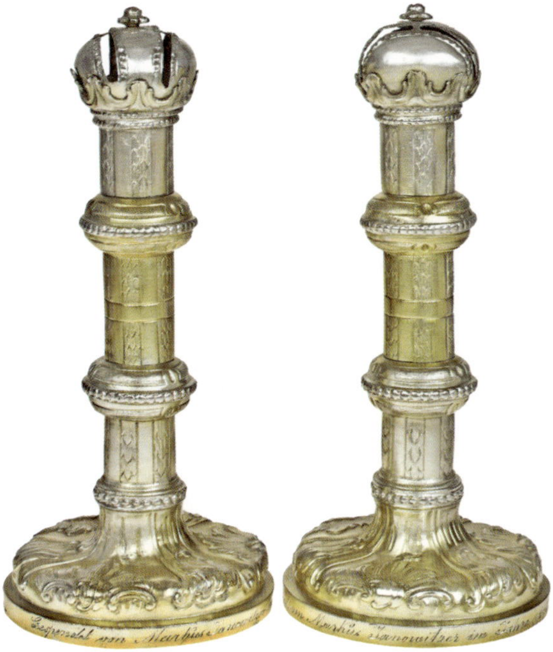

Cat. No. 109

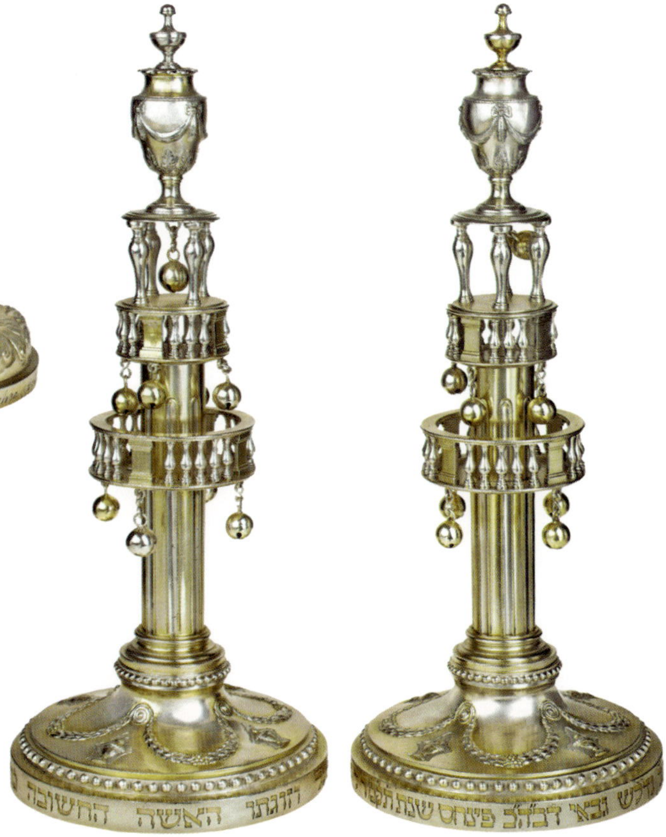

Cat. No. 110

Cat. No. 110
Torah Finials
Inv. No. JMP 046.002/01, 02
Silver, repoussé
Richard Fleischmann, Prague, 1783
Height: 419 mm, diameter: 177 mm
Hallmarks: 1. RF in irregular shape,
2. hallmark Prague 1783,
3. recharge mark Prague 1806–7,
4. release mark 1809–10
Donation inscription in Hebrew.
Translation:
This was donated by the distinguished KHRR Wolf, son of KHRR Ezriel Gadels, custodian of the Pinkas Synagogue, in the year 544 a. s. c. [= 1784], *and his wife, the esteemed lady Patscheh, daughter of KHRR Yokev Wien of blessed memory, SGL.*
Collection point: Prague, Pinkas Synagogue

Cat. No. 111
Torah Finials
Inv. No. JMP 032.404/01, 02
Silver, repoussé, engraving
Maker AK, Prague, 1786
Height: 215 mm, diameter: 153 mm
Hallmarks: 1. AK in oval, 2. hallmark Prague 1786, 3. recharge mark Prague 1806–7, 4. release mark 1809–10
Donation inscription in Hebrew.
Translation:
Donated by the distinguished KHRR Anshel, son of MHVRR Simon Wedeles, may the memory of the just be blessed [on one finial] *and his wife the lady Sheindl, daughter of MHVRR Abraham Bondi, may the memory of the just be blessed, in the year 546 a. s. c.* [= 1786] [on the other finial].
Collection point: Prague, Old-New Synagogue

Cat. No. 112
Torah Finials
Inv. No. JMP 002.944/01, 02
Silver, repoussé, parcel-gilt, engraving
Maker AD, Moravia [?], end of 18th century
Height: 258 mm, diameter: 118 mm
Hallmarks: 1. AD in irregular shape, 2. recharge mark Brno 1806–7, 3. release mark 1809–10
Without inscriptions.
Collection point: Lipník nad Bečvou

Cat. No. 113
Torah Finials
Inv. No. JMP 007.162/01, 02
Silver, repoussé
Maker unknown, Moravia [?], end of 18th century
Height: 184 mm, diameter: 82 mm
Hallmarks: 1. recharge mark Vienna 1806–7, 2. tax mark Vienna 1810–24
Donation inscription in Hebrew.
Translation:
This was donated by the late H Moses David Joseph Eisler of blessed memory and his wife, the esteemed lady [on one finial]. *Lady Sarah Milkah, may she live, in the year 621 a. s. c.* [= 1861] [on the other finial].
Collection point: Brno / Central Jewish Museum for Moravia and Silesia, 1936–1938 in Nikolsburg

Cat. No. 114
Torah Finials
Inv. No. JMP 023.107/01, 02
Silver, repoussé
Wolfgang Schuberth [?], Nuremberg, late 18th century
Height: 300 mm, diameter: 80 mm
Hallmarks: 1. WS in irregular shape, 2. hallmark Nuremberg, 3. standing animal in oval, 4. tax mark Prague 1810–24
Without inscriptions.
Collection point: Přerov

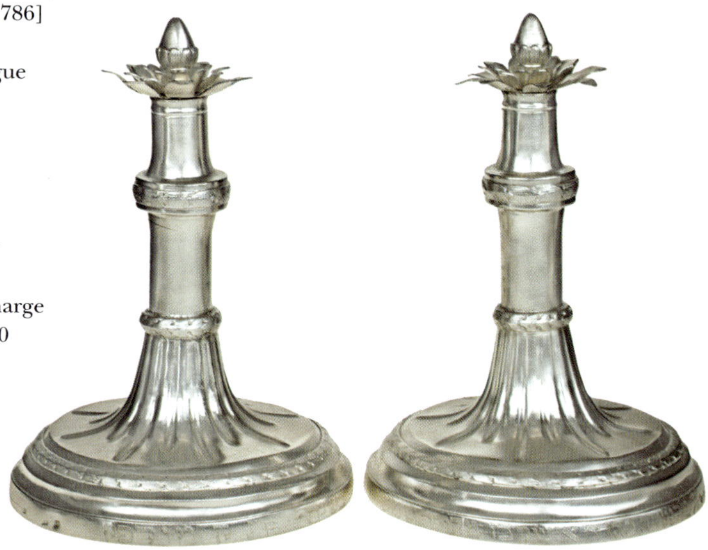

Cat. No. 111

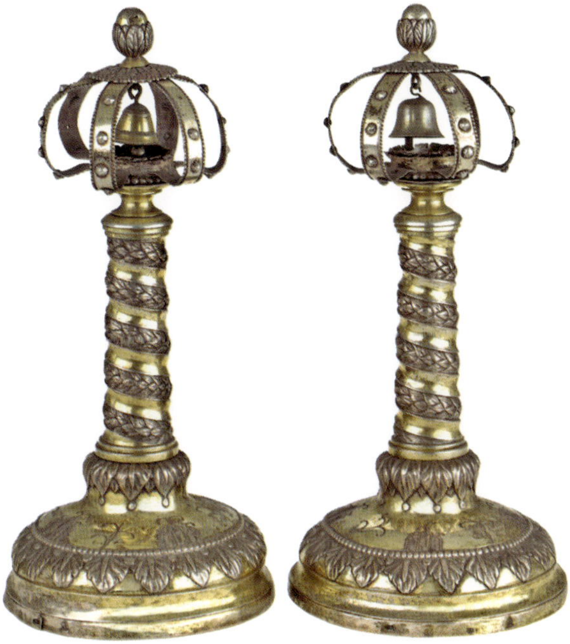

Cat. No. 112

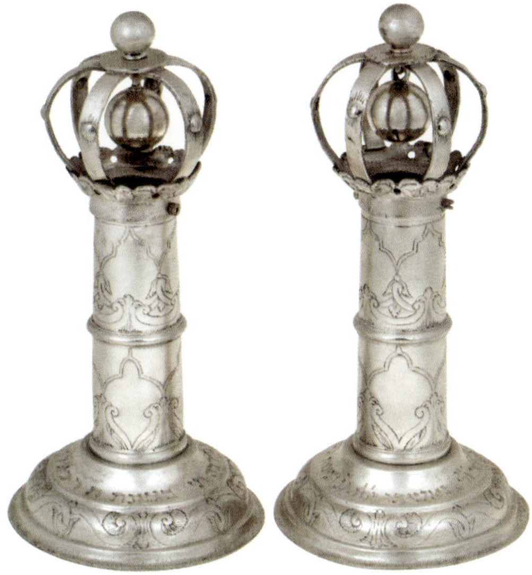

Cat. No. 113

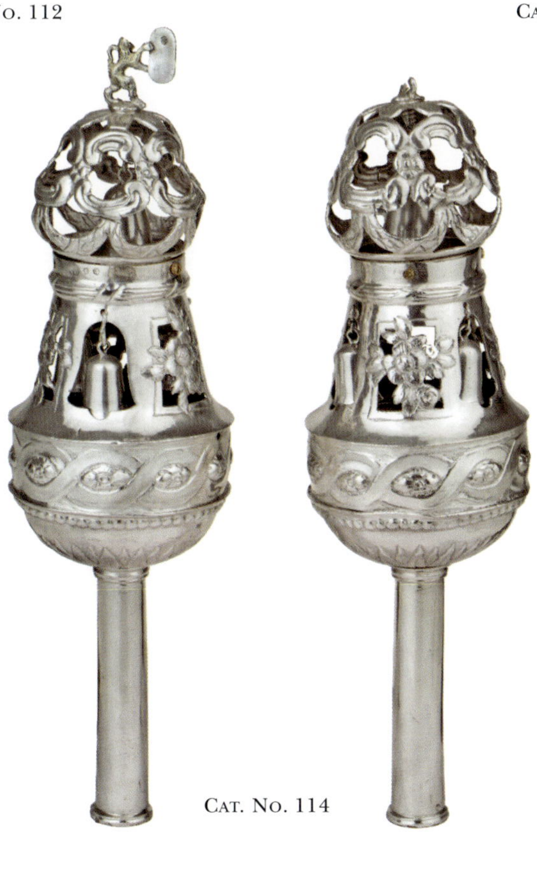

Cat. No. 114

Cat. No. 115
Torah Finials
Inv. No. JMP 010.466/01, 02
Silver, repoussé
Maker SG, Mikulov, 1799
Height: 234 mm, diameter: 98 mm
Hallmarks: 1. SG in oval, 2. hallmark Mikulov 1799,
3. recharge mark Brno 1806–7,
4. release mark 1809–10
Without inscriptions.
Collection point: Místek

Cat. No. 116
Torah Finials
Inv. No. JMP 004.486/01, 02
Silver, repoussé, engraving
Maker's mark illegible, Brno, 1799
Height: 290 mm, diameter: 147 mm
Hallmarks: 1. illegible maker's mark [maybe
Carl Lackstampfer, Sr.], 2. hallmark Brno 1799,
3. recharge mark Brno 1806–7,
4. release mark 1809–10
Donation inscription in Hebrew.
Translation:
This was donated for charity by the members of the Society of Early Risers in the New Synagogue, 612 a. s. c. [= 1852], *namely R A. Schidrowitz, R J. Stiassny, R A.H. Taussig, R.M. Löwenthal, R L. Schorer, R J.Ch. Sofer, R L. Subak, K D. Fürst, R H. Löwenthal.*
Collection point: Třebíč

Cat. No. 117
Torah Finials
Inv. No. JMP 009.550/01, 02
Silver, repoussé, engraving
Maker MG, Jihlava, 1800
Height: 187 mm, diameter: 124 mm
Hallmarks: 1. MG in rectangle, 2. hallmark Jihlava
1800, 3. recharge mark Brno 1806–7
Donation inscription in Hebrew.
Translation:
Belonging to the elder HRR Moses Sch C [cantor] *and his wife Hindl, may she live, in the year 561 a. s. c.* [= 1801]. *Also to their children Bezalel Hayyim, Nehamah, Mirl, and Leah, may they live.*
Collection point: Kamenice nad Lipou

Cat. No. 118
Torah Finials
Inv. No. JMP 007.063/01, 02
Silver, repoussé
Wilhelm Streithoff [?], Vienna, 1807
Height: 314 mm, diameter: 136 mm
Hallmarks: 1. WS in rectangle,
2. hallmark Vienna 1807–9,
3. recharge mark Vienna 1806–7
Without inscriptions.
Collection point: Třešť

Cat. No. 119
Torah Finials
Inv. No. JMP 007.064/01, 02
Silver, repoussé, parcel-gilt
Maker PH, Vienna, 1807
Height: 220 mm, diameter: 111 mm
Hallmarks: 1. PH in oval , 2. hallmark Vienna
1807–9, 3. recharge mark Vienna 1806–7
Without inscriptions.
Collection point: Třešť

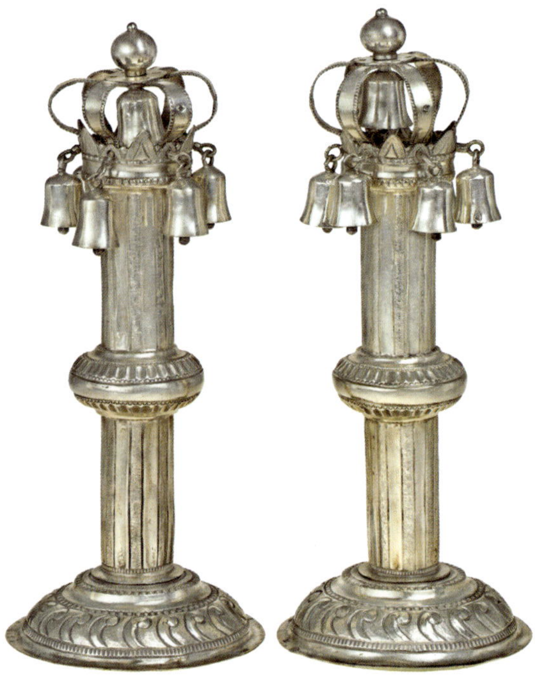

Cat. No. 115

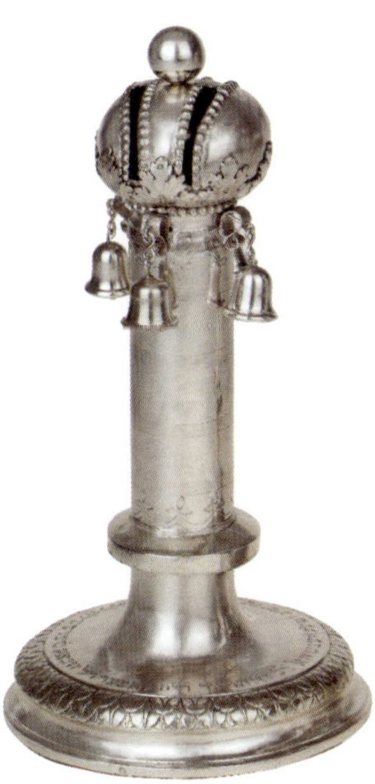

Cat. No. 116

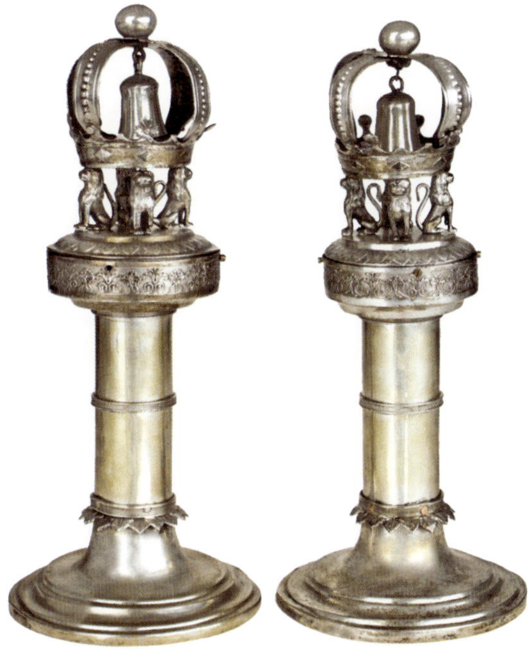

Cat. No. 118

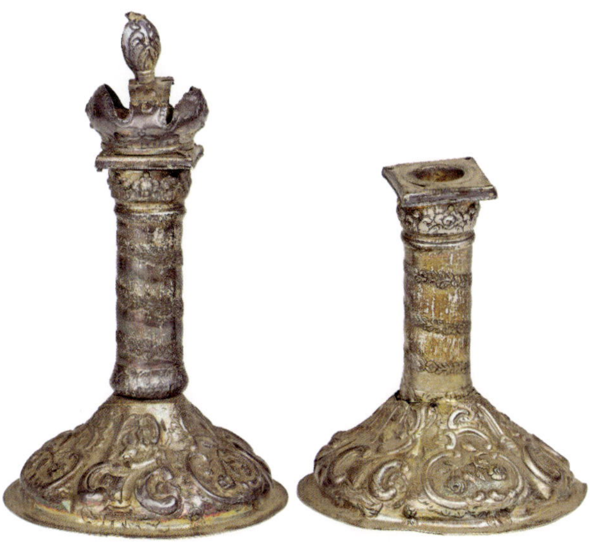

Cat. No. 117

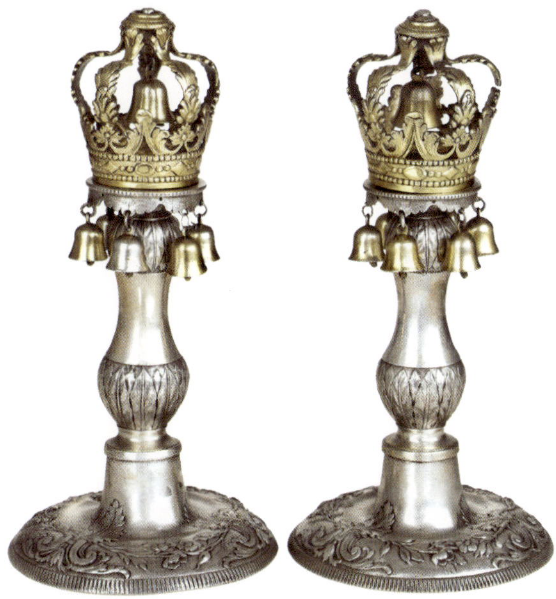

Cat. No. 119

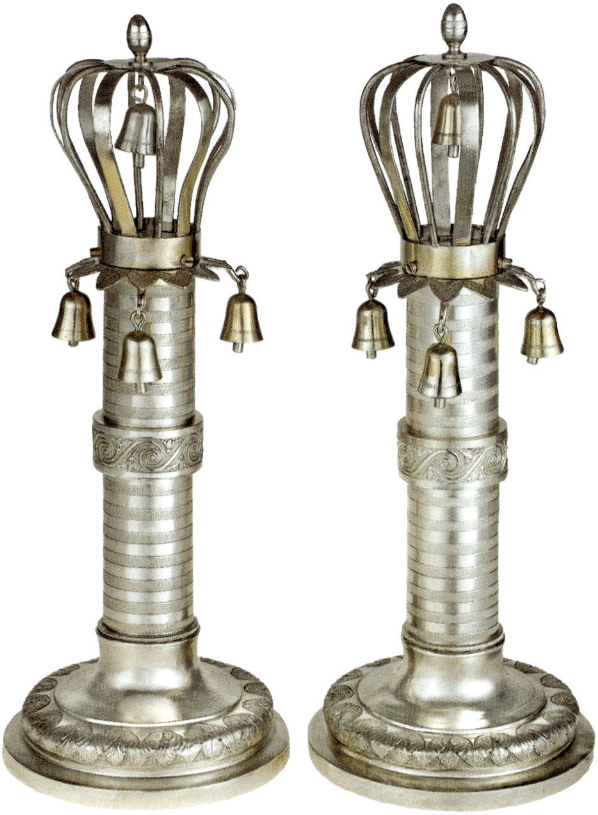

Cat. No. 120

Torah Finials

Inv. No. JMP 054.081/01, 02
Silver, repoussé
Carl Lackstampfer, Sr. [?], Brno, 1807
Height: 330 mm, diameter: 129 mm
Hallmarks: 1. CL in oval, 2. hallmark Brno 1807, 3. recharge mark Brno 1806–7, 4. release mark 1809–10
Without inscriptions.
Collection point: Jemnice

Cat. No. 121

Torah Finials

Inv. No. JMP 046.009/01, 02
Silver, repoussé
Jan Adam Řehořovský, Prague, 1807
Height: 225 mm, diameter: 177 mm
Hallmarks: 1. ARr in rectangle, 2. hallmark Prague 1807–9, 3. recharge mark Prague 1806–7, 4. release mark 1809–10
Donation inscription in Hebrew.
Translation:
A gift of the distinguished KHRR Wolf, son of KHRR Ezriel Gadels of blessed memory, custodian of the Pinkas Synagogue, and his wife, the esteemed lady Patscheh, daughter of KHRR Yokev Wien SGL of blessed memory. And [it] *was made in the year 570 a. s. c.* [= 1810].
Collection point: Prague, Pinkas Synagogue

Cat. No. 120 ^
Cat. No. 121 v

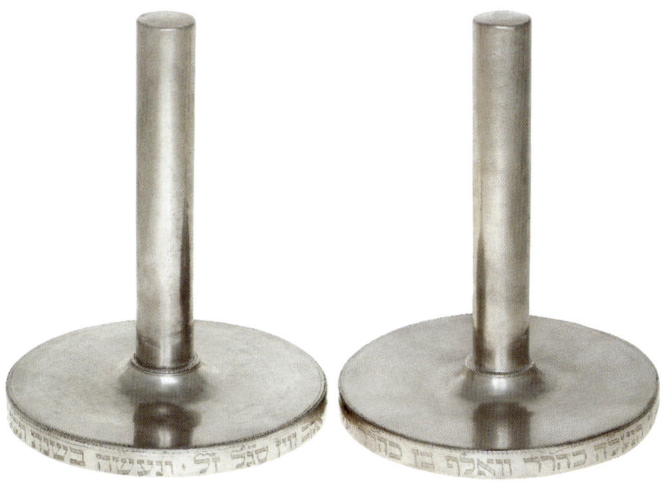

Cat. No. 122
Torah Finials
Inv. No. JMP 046.004/01, 02
Silver, repoussé, originally parcel-gilt
Jan Adam Řehořovský, Prague, 1810
Height: 315 mm, diameter: 170 mm
Hallmarks: 1. ARr in rectangle,
2. hallmark Prague 1810
Without inscriptions.
Collection point: Prague, Pinkas Synagogue

Cat. No. 123
Torah Finials
Inv. No. JMP 002.721/01, 02
Silver, repoussé
Carl Blasius, Vienna, 1810
Height: 335 mm, diameter: 90 mm
Hallmarks: 1. CB in oval,
2. hallmark Vienna 1810,
3. tax mark Vienna 1810–24,
4. stock mark 1807–24
Inscription in Hebrew.
Translation:
Belonging to the sage MVH Michael Leib, may his light shine, son of MVH Aaron Steinschneider, may the memory of the just be blessed [on the second]. *And his wife the honorable lady Haylah, may she live, daughter of MVH Faish Kelin, may his light shine, here* [in] *Prostějov,* [in the year] *573 a. s. c.* [= 1813] [on the first].
Collection point: Prostějov

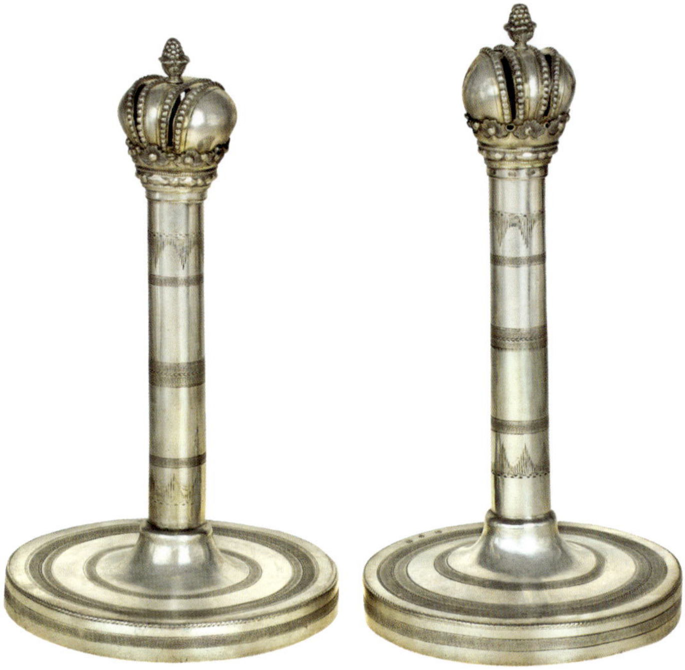

Cat. No. 122 ^
Cat. No. 123

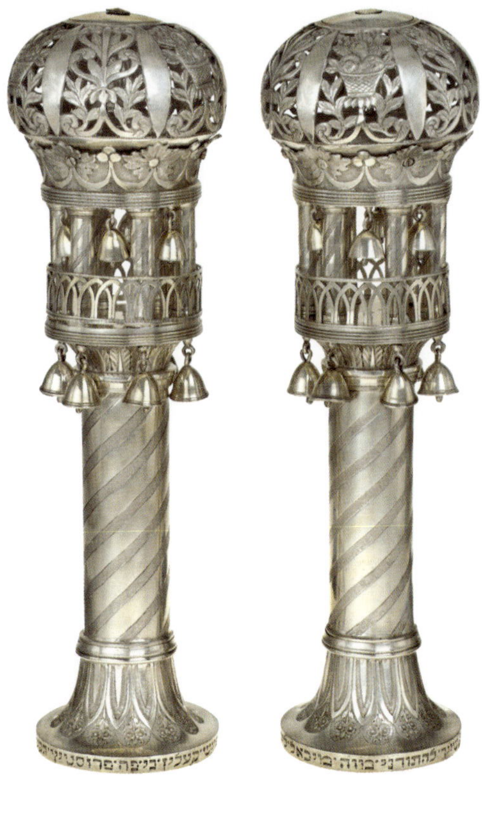

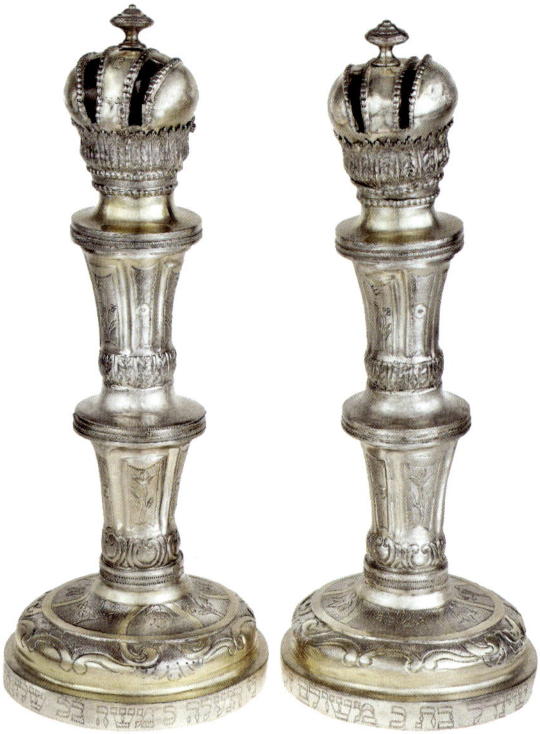

Cat. No. 124
Torah Finials
Inv. No. JMP 002.257/01, 02
Silver, repoussé, parcel-gilt
Karel Skřemenec, Prague, 1813
Height: 383 mm, diameter: 154 mm
Hallmarks: 1. CS in rectangle,
2. hallmark Prague 1813,
3. hallmark Prague 1815 [on the crowns],
4. tax mark Prague 1810–24
Inscription in Hebrew.
Translation:
A gift of the distinguished K Moses, son of K Solomon Feier of blessed memory, with his wife [on the second].
Lady Sheindl, daughter of K Meshulam of blessed memory, the year 575 a. s. c. [= 1815] [on the first].
Collection point: Náchod

Cat. No. 124 ^
Cat. No. 125 >

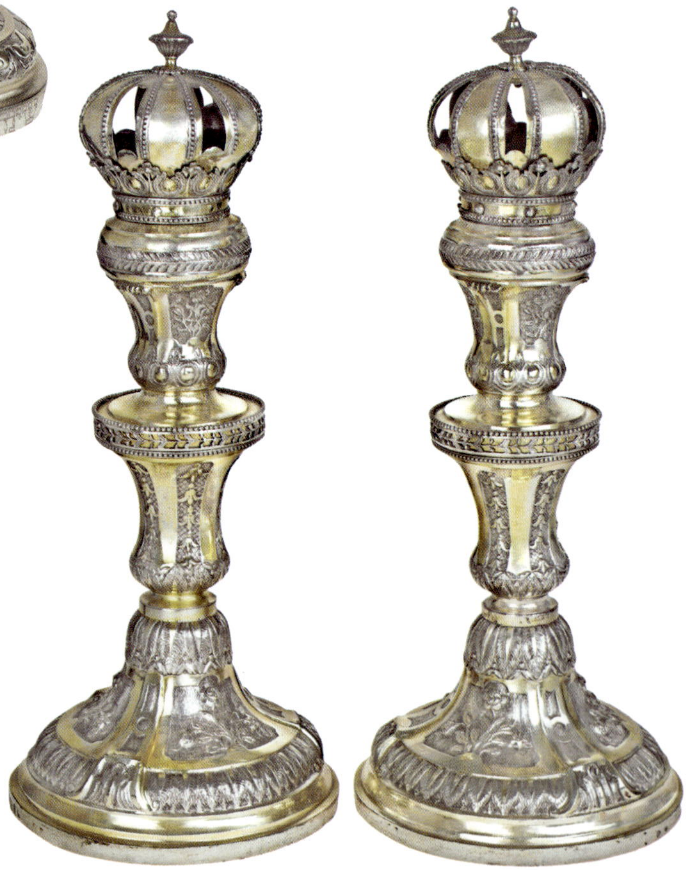

Cat. No. 125
Torah Finials
Inv. No. JMP 017.539/01, 02
Silver, repoussé
Maker AN, Prague, 1813
Height: 442 mm, diameter: 185 mm
Hallmarks: 1. AN in oval, 2. hallmark Prague 1813, 3. tax mark Prague 1810–24
Without inscriptions.
Collection point: Prague, Klausen Synagogue

Cat. No. 126
Torah Finials
Inv. No. JMP 001.524/01, 02
Silver, repoussé
Karel Skřemenec, Prague, 1814
Height: 350 mm, diameter: 109 mm
Hallmarks: 1. CS in oval, 2. hallmark Prague 1814, 3. tax mark Prague 1810–24
Without inscriptions.
Collection point: Plzeň

Cat. No. 127
Torah Finials
Inv. No. JMP 010.651/01, 02
Silver, repoussé, engraving
Maker WI [?], Vienna, 1814
Height: 159 mm, diameter: 95 mm
Hallmarks: 1. WI [?] in rectangle, 2. hallmark Vienna 1814, 3. tax mark Vienna 1810–24
Without inscriptions.
Collection point: Klatovy

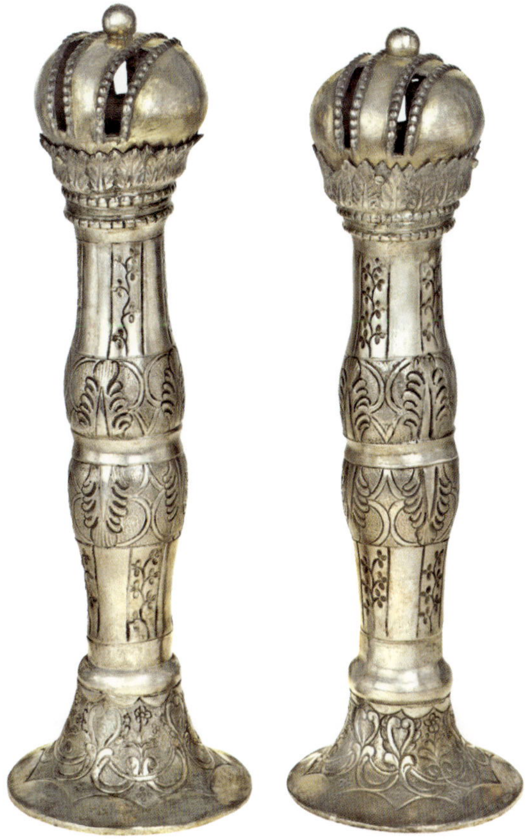

Cat. No. 126 ^
Cat. No. 127

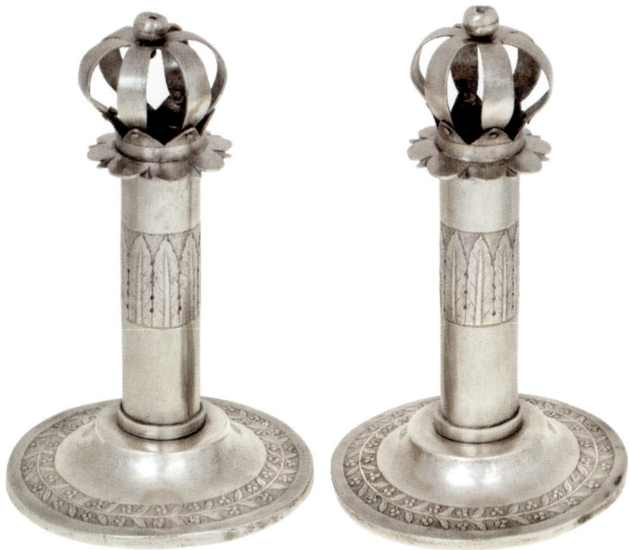

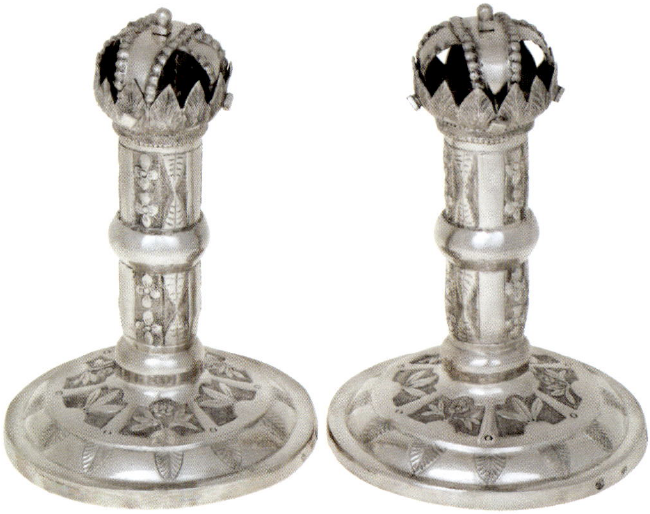

Cat. No. 128

Cat. No. 128
Torah Finials
Acq. No. JMP 1981/0078-01, 02
Silver, repoussé, engraving
Tomáš Höpfel, Prague, 1818
Height: 149 mm, diameter: 105 mm
Hallmarks: 1. TH in rectangle, 2. hallmark Prague 1818, 3. tax mark Prague 1810–24
Without inscriptions.
Catalogued secondarily into the inventory of the Jewish Museum in Prague.

Cat. No. 129
Torah Finials
Inv. No. JMP 004.383/01, 02
Silver, repoussé
Maker unknown, Brno [?], early 19th century
Height: 210 mm, diameter: 105 mm
Hallmarks: unmarked.
Inscription in Hebrew.
Translation:
This was donated by Mr. Nathan, son of Moses Mezritsch, [and it was] *made on the first day of slichot* [penitential prayers] [in the year] *579 a. s. c.* [= 1819] *here* [in] *Rokytnice.*
Collection point: Žamberk

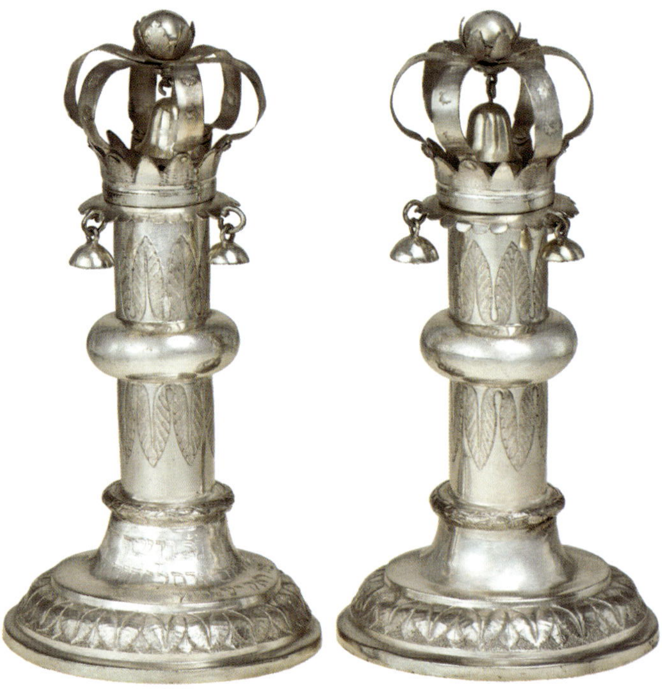

Cat. No. 129

Cat. No. 130
Torah Finials
Inv. No. JMP 007.108/01, 02
Silver, repoussé,engraving
Maker AN, Prague [?], 1820 [?]
Height: 340 mm, diameter: 108 mm
Hallmarks: 1. AN in oval, 2. illegible hallmark 1820 [?], 3. stock mark after 1807
Without inscriptions.
Collection point: Brno

Cat. No. 131
Torah Finials
Inv. No. JMP 007.552/01, 02
Silver, repoussé, engraving
Franz Kaltenmarker, Brno, 1821
Height: 236 mm, diameter: 104 mm
Hallmarks: 1. FK in oval, 2. hallmark Brno 1821, 3. tax mark Brno 1810–24
Without inscriptions.
Collection point: Kojetín

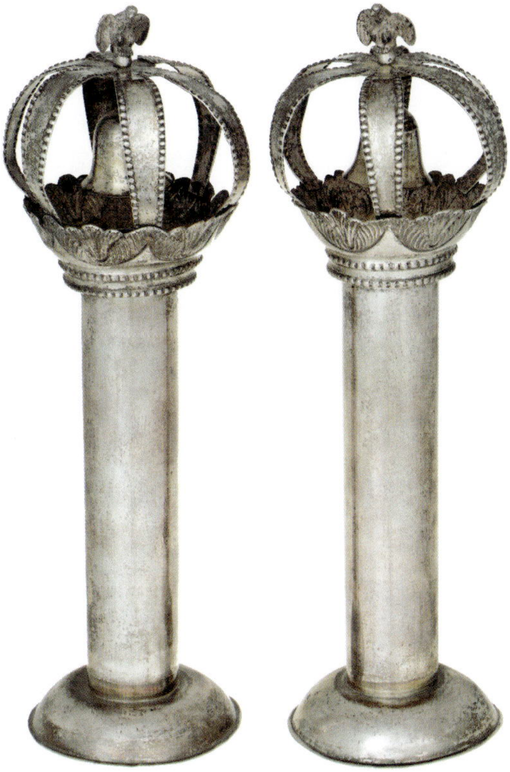

Cat. No. 130

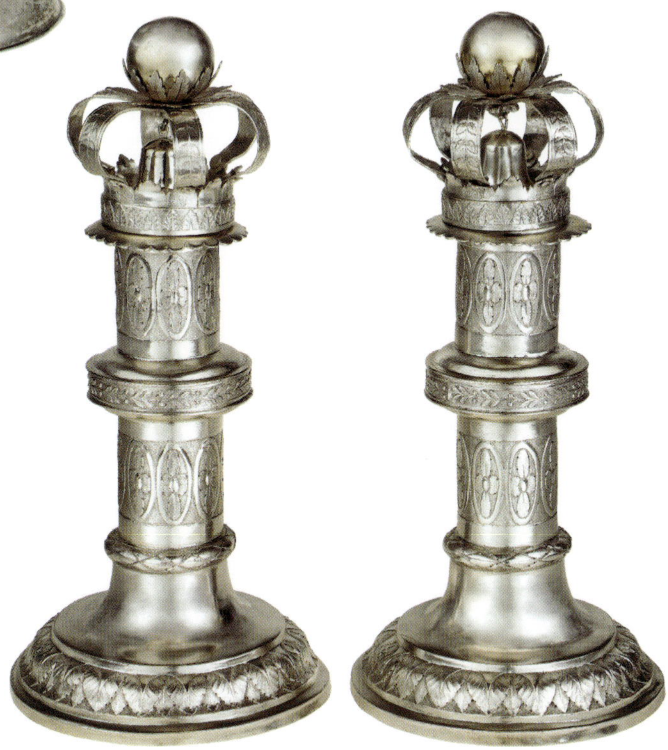

Cat. No. 131

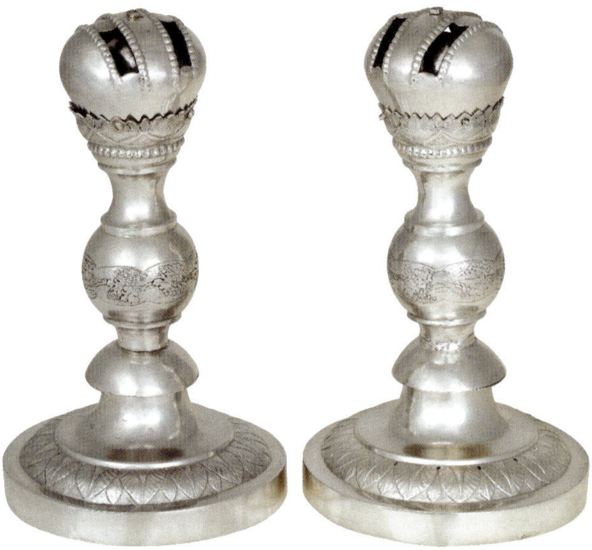

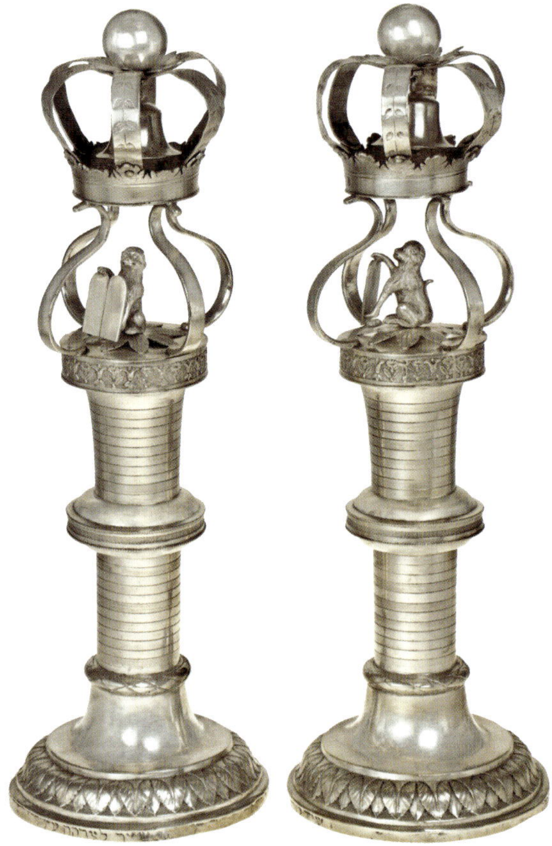

Cat. No. 132
Torah Finials
Inv. No. JMP 044.289/01, 02
Silver, repoussé
Antonín Kába, Prague, 1821
Height: 213 mm, diameter: 126 mm
Hallmarks: 1. AK in oval, 2. hallmark Prague 1821,
3. tax mark Prague 1810–24
Without inscriptions.
Collection point: Prague, Karlín Synagogue

Cat. No. 133
Torah Finials
Inv. No. JMP 004.820/01, 02
Silver, repoussé
Franz Kaltenmarker, Brno, 1821
Height: 375 mm, diameter: 120 mm
Hallmarks: 1. FK in oval, 2. hallmark Brno 1821,
3. tax mark Brno 1810–24
Donation inscription in Hebrew.
Translation:
Belonging to the charity coffers through the agency of the custodians Mr. Mendel Schulz and Mr. Leizer Fuchs [in] *the holy community Morchec* [in the year] *581 a. s. c.* [= 1821] [the identical inscription on both stems].
Collection point: Central Jewish Museum for Moravia and Silesia, 1936–1938 in Nikolsburg

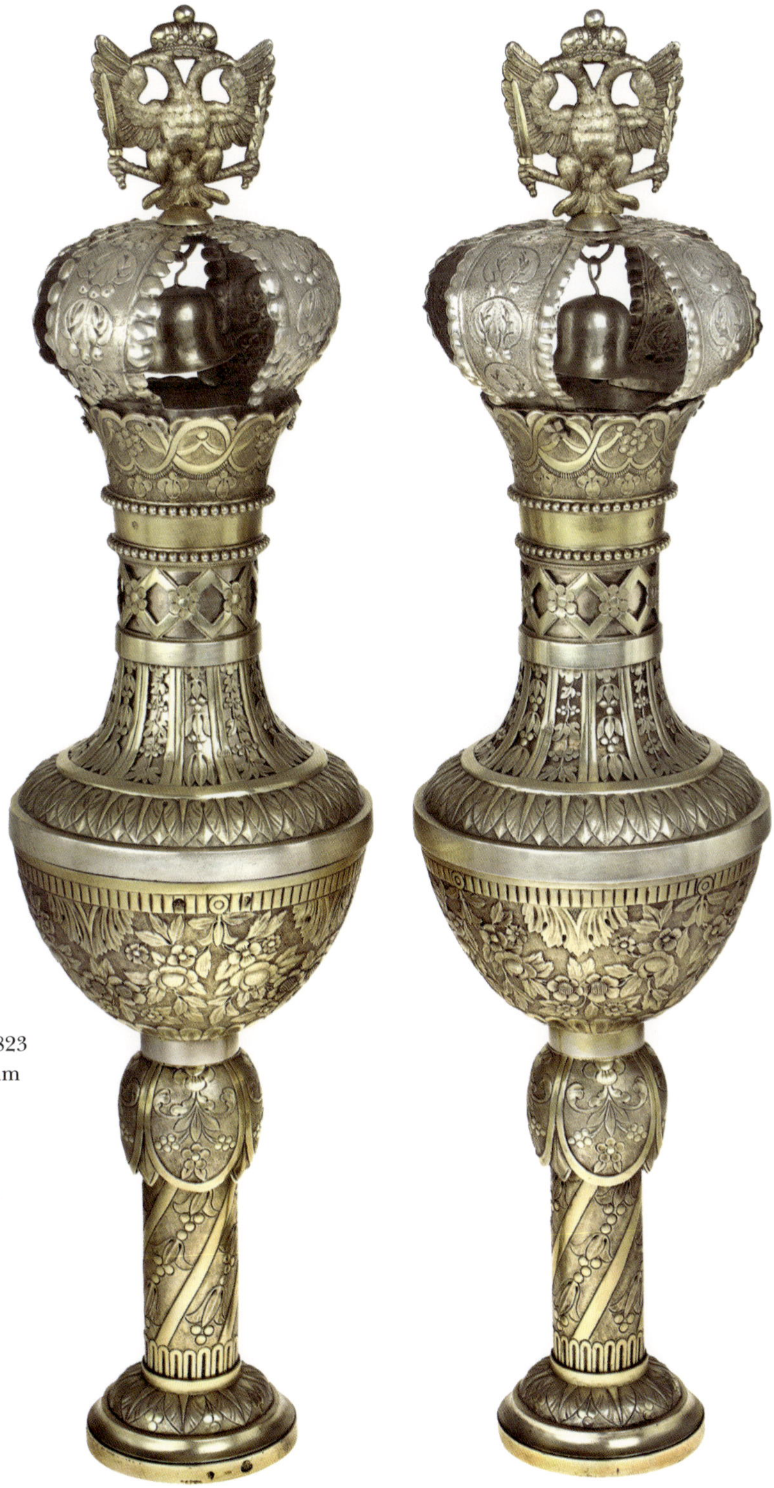

Cat. No. 134 >
Torah Finials
Inv. No. JMP 104.764/01, 02
Silver, repoussé, cast, gilt
Franz Lorenz Turinsky, Vienna, 1823
Height: 515 mm, diameter: 125 mm
Hallmarks: 1. FLT in shield,
2. hallmark Vienna 1823
Without inscriptions.
Purchased by the Jewish Museum
in Prague.

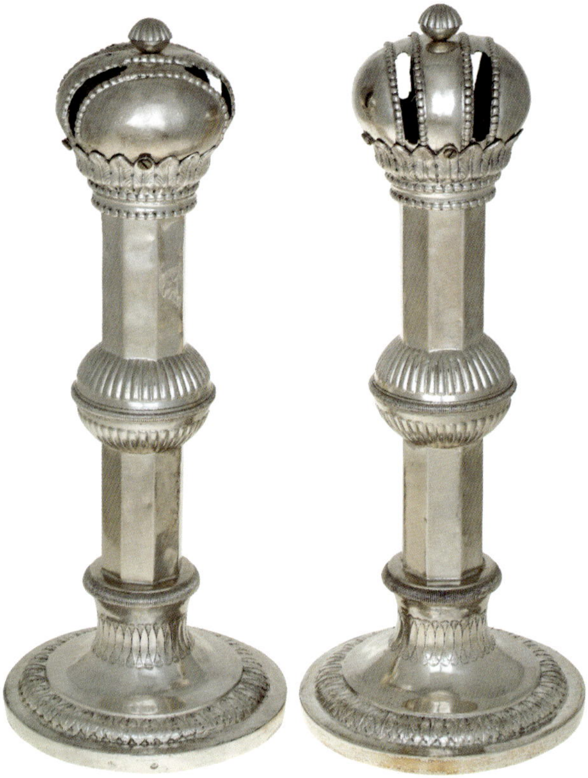

Cat. No. 135
Torah Finials
Inv. No. JMP 032.402/01, 02
Silver, repoussé
Antonín Maroušek, Prague, 1830
Height: 376 mm, diameter: 148 mm
Hallmarks: 1. AM in oval, 2. hallmark Prague 1830
Without inscriptions.
Collection point: Prague, Old-New Synagogue

Cat. No. 136
Torah Finials
Inv. No. JMP 017.026/01, 02
Silver, repoussé
Maker IW, Vienna, 1833
Height: 302 mm, diameter: 84 mm
Hallmarks: 1. IW in rectangle,
2. hallmark Vienna 1833
Without inscriptions.
Collection point: Týn nad Vltavou

Cat. No. 135 ^
Cat. No. 136

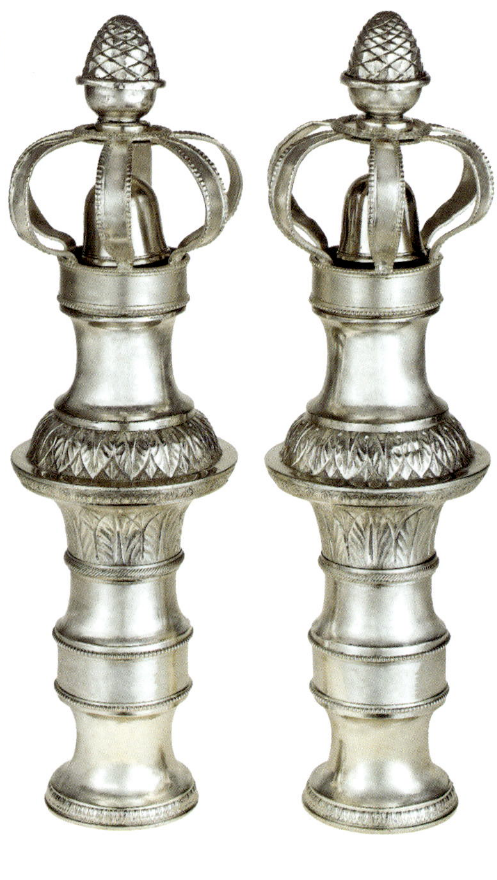

Cat. No. 137
Torah Finials
Inv. No. JMP 004.171/01, 02
Silver, repoussé
Maker AW [?], Vienna, 1838
Height: 383 mm, diameter: 137 mm
Hallmarks: 1. AW in rectangle,
2. hallmark Vienna 1838
Donation inscription in Hebrew.
Translation:
From the charity coffers of the Burial Society and [the Society] *for Visiting the Sick in the holy community Hořice through the agency of the custodians, the elder R Gumprecht Seegen and the elder R Meir Pokorny, in the year 598 a. s. c.* [= 1838].
Collection point: Hořice

Cat. No. 138
Torah Finials
Inv. No. JMP 009.500/01, 02
Silver, repoussé
Josef Wiederspeck, Vienna, 1840 [?]
Height: 210 mm, diameter: 110 mm
Hallmarks: 1. IW in shield,
2. hallmark Vienna 18[?]0
Donation inscription in Czech in Latin script.
Translation:
Donated by Eduard and Rosalie Witz in Polička in the year 1900.
Collection point: Polička

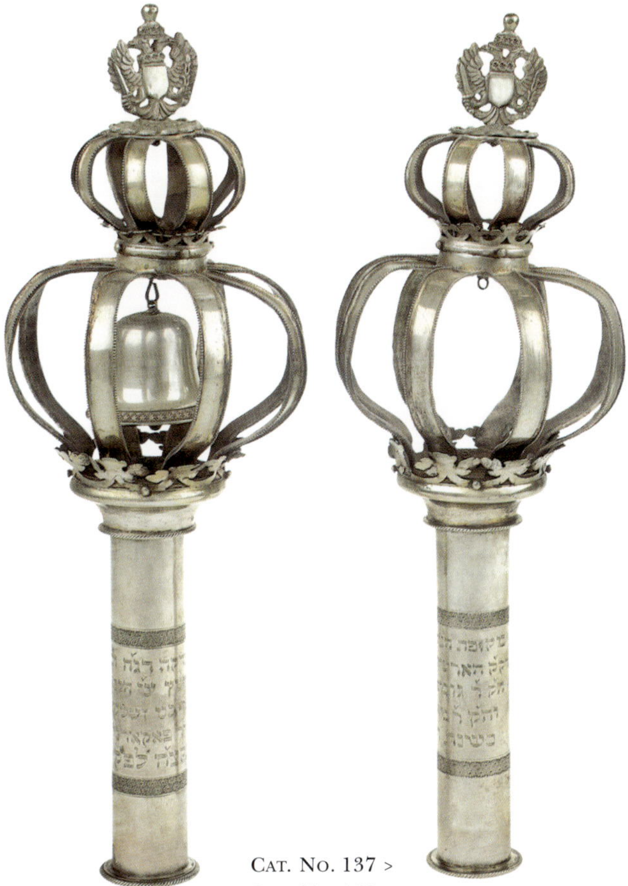

Cat. No. 137 >
Cat. No. 138

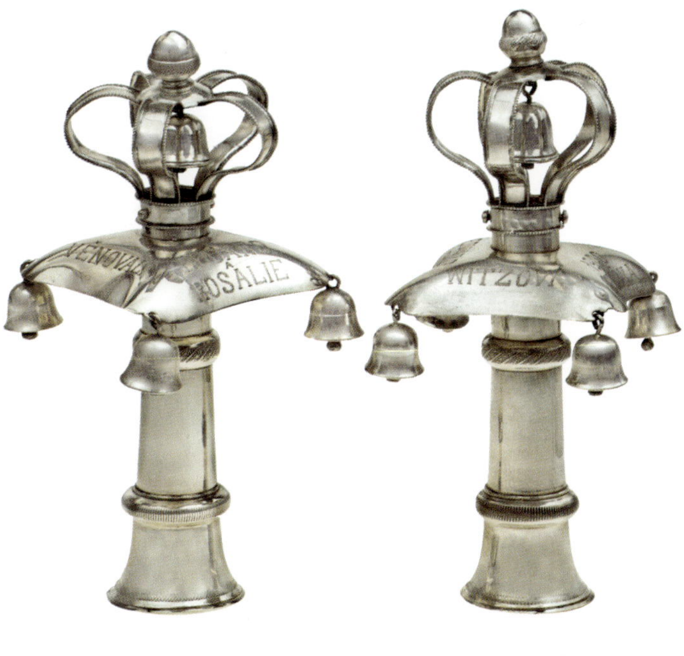

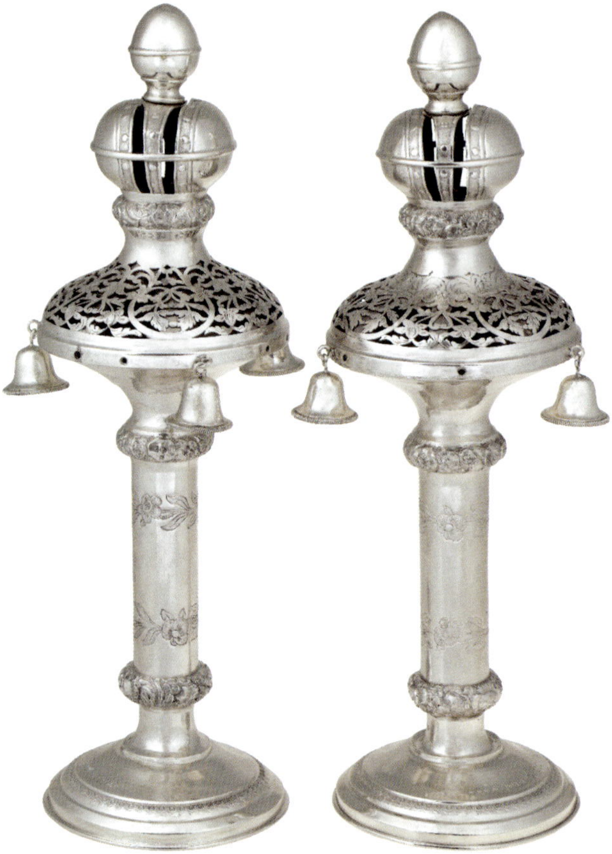

Cat. No. 139
Torah Finials
Inv. No. JMP 002.938/01, 02
Silver, repoussé
Maker AW, Vienna, 1842
Height: 385 mm, diameter: 119 mm
Hallmarks: 1. AW in rectangle,
2. hallmark Vienna 1842
Donation inscription in Hebrew.
Translation:
From the Society for Midrash Study [?],
Lipník [nad Bečvou], *638 a. s. c.* [= 1878].
Collection point: Lipník nad Bečvou

Cat. No. 140
Torah Finials
Inv. No. JMP 037.749/01, 02
Silver, repoussé, engraving
Maker SK [?], Vienna, 1844
Height: 308 mm, diameter: 140 mm
Hallmarks: 1. SK [?] in rectangle,
2. hallmark Vienna 1844
Donation inscription in Hebrew.
Translation: *Aaron Pollak.*
Collection point: Jewish Museum
in Prague, 1906–1940

Cat. No. 139
Cat. No. 140 >

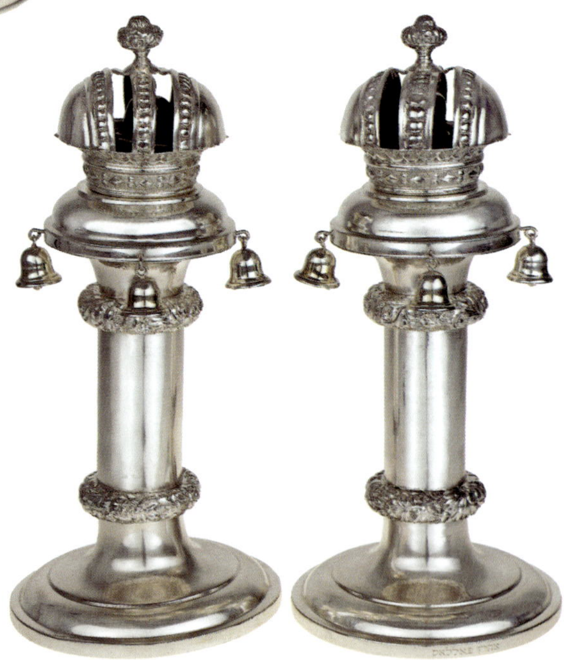

Cat. No. 141
Torah Finials
Inv. No. JMP 023.036/01, 02
Silver, repoussé
Antonín Maroušek, Prague, 1848
Height: 305 mm, diameter: 77 mm
Hallmarks: 1. AM in oval, 2. hallmark Prague 1848
Donation inscription in Hebrew.
Translation:
A gift from the boy of the sage R Leizer Gerson. As he instructed before his death, to do so in his memory.
[In the year] *"which loves* [loved] *righteousness" a. s. c.*
[dating in the chronogram 608 = 1848, cf. Ps. 11:7].
Collection point: Havlíčkův Brod

Cat. No. 142
Torah Finials
Inv. No. JMP 005.377/01, 02
Silver, repoussé, originally parcel-gilt, engraving
Maker JW, Vienna, 1853
Height: 236 mm, diameter: 104 mm
Hallmarks: 1. JW in rectangle,
2. hallmark Vienna 1853
Without inscriptions.
Collection point: Boskovice

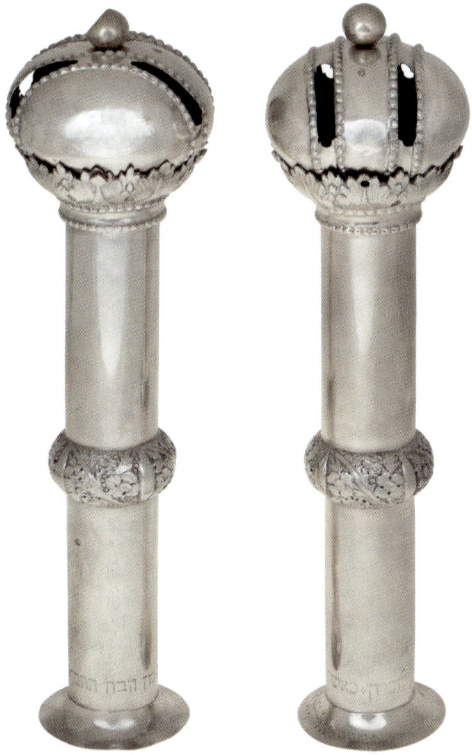

Cat. No. 141
Cat. No. 142

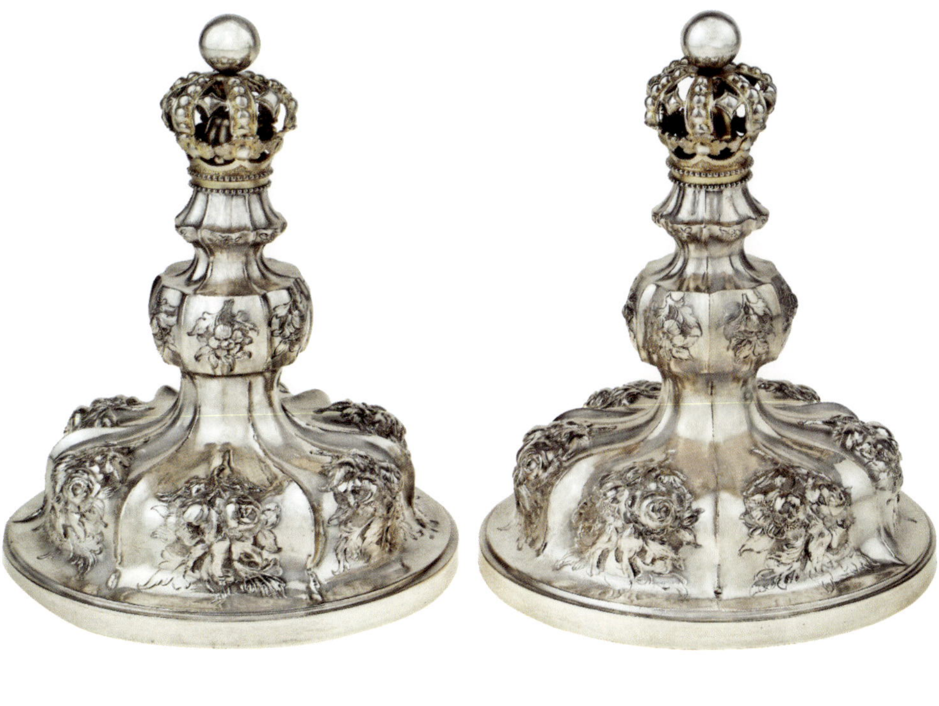

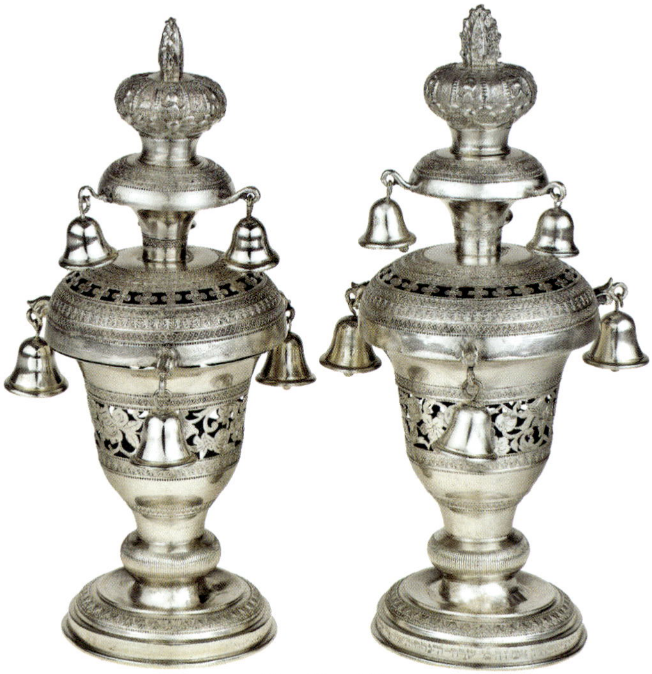

Cat. No. 143
Cat. No. 144

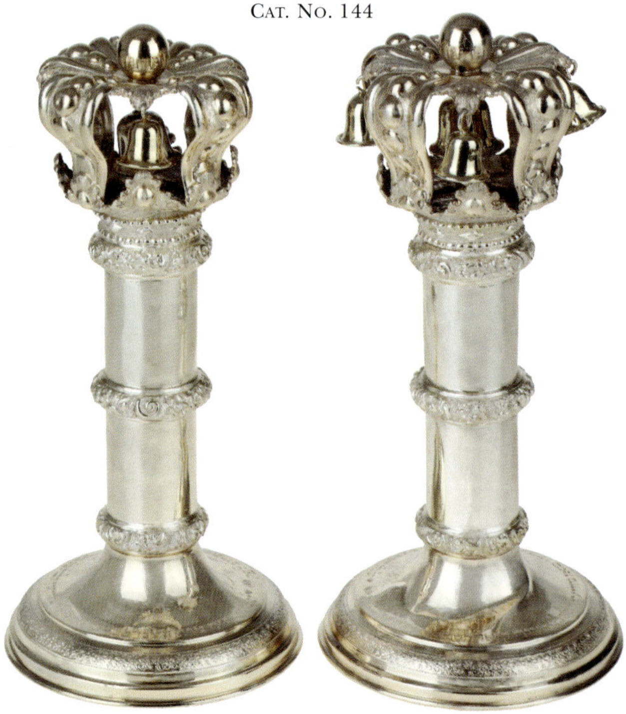

Cat. No. 143
Torah Finials
Inv. No. JMP 023.183/01, 02
Silver, repoussé
Maker CS, Vienna, 1854
Height: 237 mm, diameter: 82 mm
Hallmarks: 1. CS [unframed],
2. hallmark Vienna 1854
Inscription in Hebrew.
Translation:
This was donated by the elder HKH Elhanan Kafka, may his light shine, son of KH Abraham Dov Kafka, may the memory of the just be blessed, with his wife, the esteemed lady Sarah Hinda, may she live, daughter of KH Zevi Hirsch, may the memory of the just be blessed, in the year 615 a. s. c. [= 1855].
Collection point: Vodňany

Cat. No. 144
Torah Finials
Inv. No. JMP 046.006/01, 02
Silver, repoussé, engraving
Josef Wieninger, Vienna, 1854
Height: 255 mm, diameter: 126 mm
Hallmarks: 1. JW in rectangle,
2. hallmark Vienna 1854
Donation inscription in Hebrew.
Translation:
I.S.C. [the meaning of the initials is unclear]. *This was donated by KH Joseph and his wife, the lady Hendl Biedermann of Vienna, for the synagogue in the town of Karlovy Vary, in the year 612 a. s. c.* [= 1852] [sic].
Collection point: Prague,
Pinkas Synagogue

Cat. No. 145
Torah Finials
Inv. No. JMP 004.811/01, 02
Silver, repoussé, engraving
Maker TR, Vienna, 1854
Height: 303 mm, diameter: 95 mm
Hallmarks: 1. TR in rectangle,
2. hallmark Vienna 1854
Without inscriptions.
Collection point: Central Jewish Museum for Moravia and Silesia,
1936–1938 in Nikolsburg

Cat. No. 146
Torah Finials
Inv. No. JMP 009.788/01, 02
Silver, repoussé, parcel-gilt, engraving
Jan Novotný, Prague, ca. 1850–1860
Height: 224 mm, diameter: 62 mm
Hallmarks: 1. JN in rectangle,
2. hallmark Prague [date illegible]
Without inscriptions.
Collection point: Uhříněves

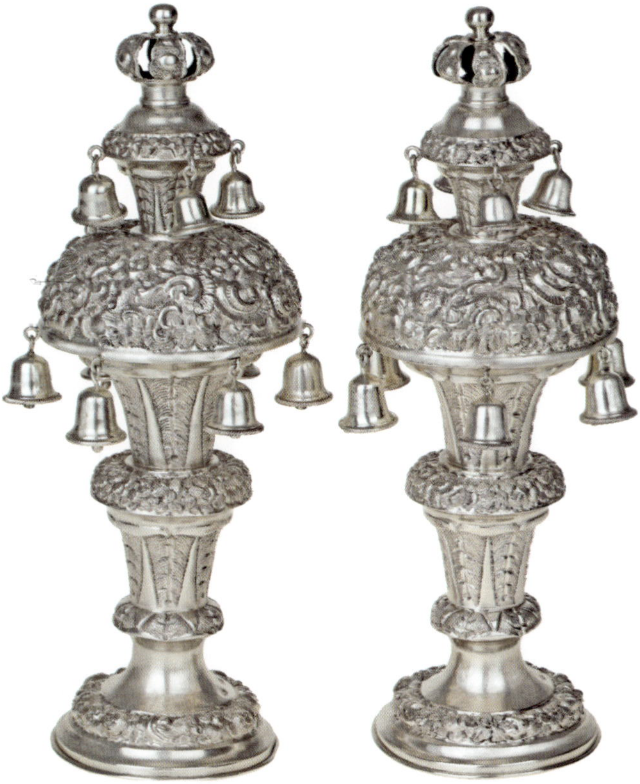

CAT. NO. 145
CAT. NO. 146

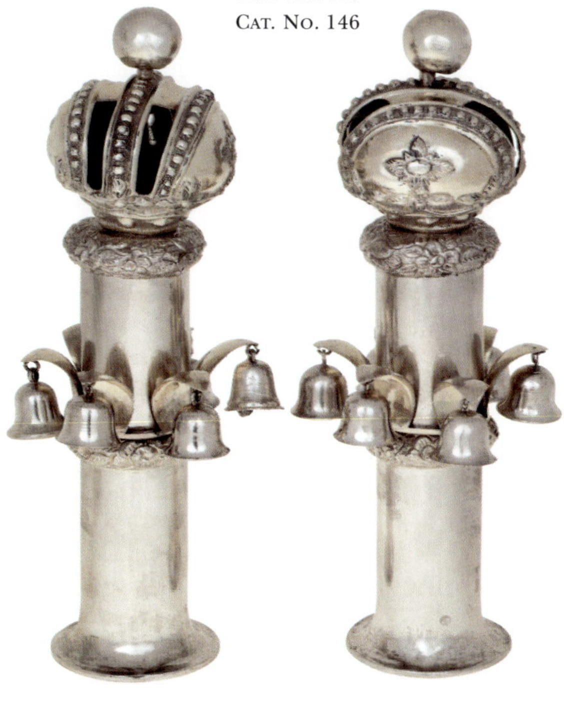

Cat. No. 147
Torah Finials
Inv. No. JMP 004.123/01, 02
Silver, repoussé, parcel-gilt
Isaac Joel Goldschmid, Prague, 1856
Height: 275 mm, diameter: 100 mm
Hallmarks: 1. IG in rectangle,
2. hallmark Prague 1856
Donation inscription in Hebrew.
Translation:
This was donated for the synagogue in Hříškov by the distinguished KH Elijah Glaser, alderman of Cítoliby, and his wife the lady Telah, in the year 616 a. s. c. [= 1856]. *This was donated for the synagogue in Hříškov by the distinguished KH Leib Glaser and his wife the lady Jares, in the year 616 a. s. c.* [= 1856].
Collection point: Louny

Cat No. 148
Torah Finials
Inv. No. JMP 007.161/01, 02
Silver, repoussé, gilt, engraving
Maker AW, Vienna, 1859
Height: 202 mm, diameter: 77 mm
Hallmarks: 1. AW in rectangle,
2. hallmark Vienna 1859
Without inscriptions.
Collection point: Brno

Cat. No. 149
Torah Finials
Inv. No. JMP 010.390/01, 02
Silver, repoussé, engraving
Maker TR [Thomas Regscheck?], Vienna, 1861
Height: 332 mm, diameter: 88 mm
Hallmarks: 1. TR in rectangle,
2. hallmark Vienna 1861
Without inscriptions.
Collection point: Miroslav

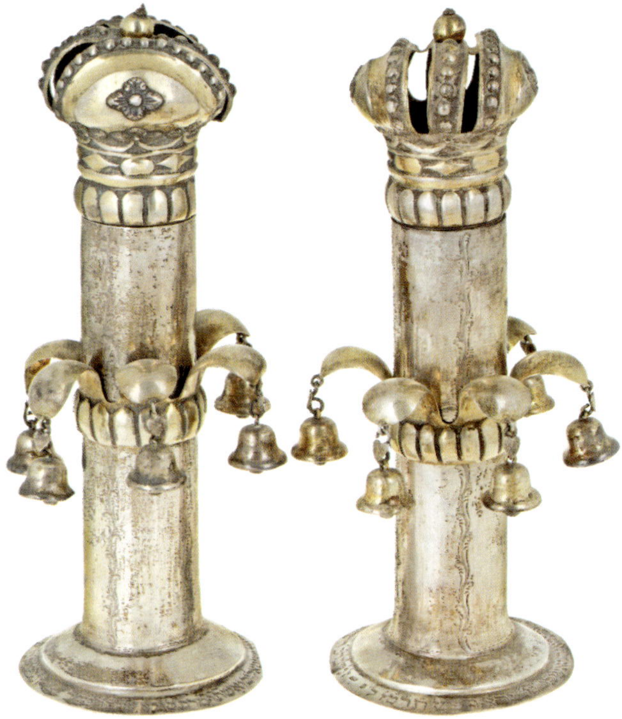

Cat. No. 147
Cat. No. 148

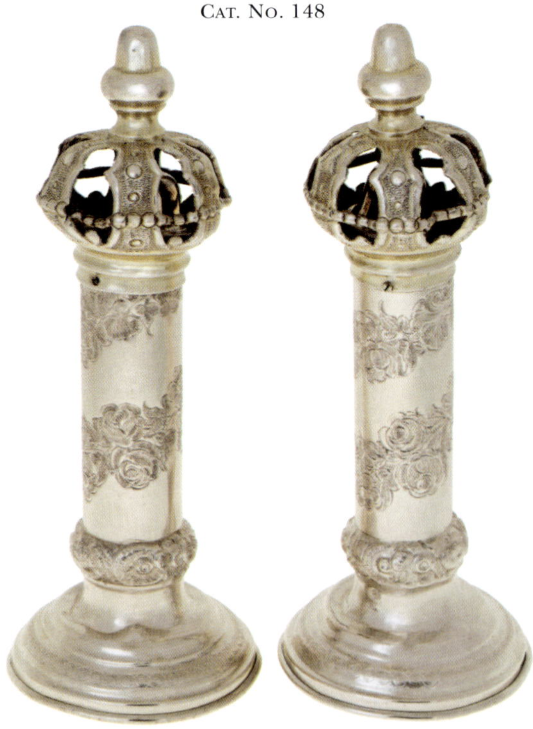

Cat. No. 150

Torah Finials

Inv. No. JMP 017.533/01, 02

Silver, repoussé, parcel-gilt, engraving

Maker JE, Vienna, 1864

Height: 368 mm, diameter: 160 mm

Hallmarks: 1. JE in rectangle,

2. hallmark Vienna 1864

Without inscriptions.

Collection point: Prague, Klausen Synagogue

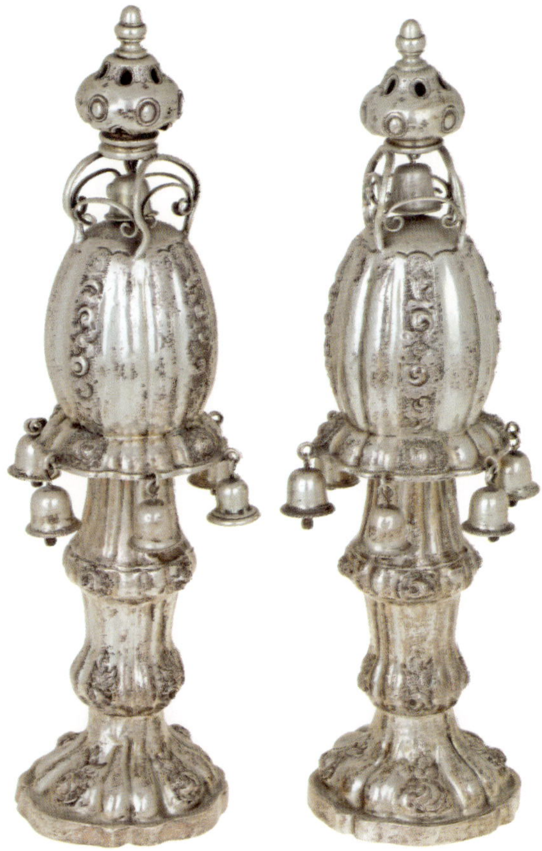

Cat. No. 149

< Cat. No. 150

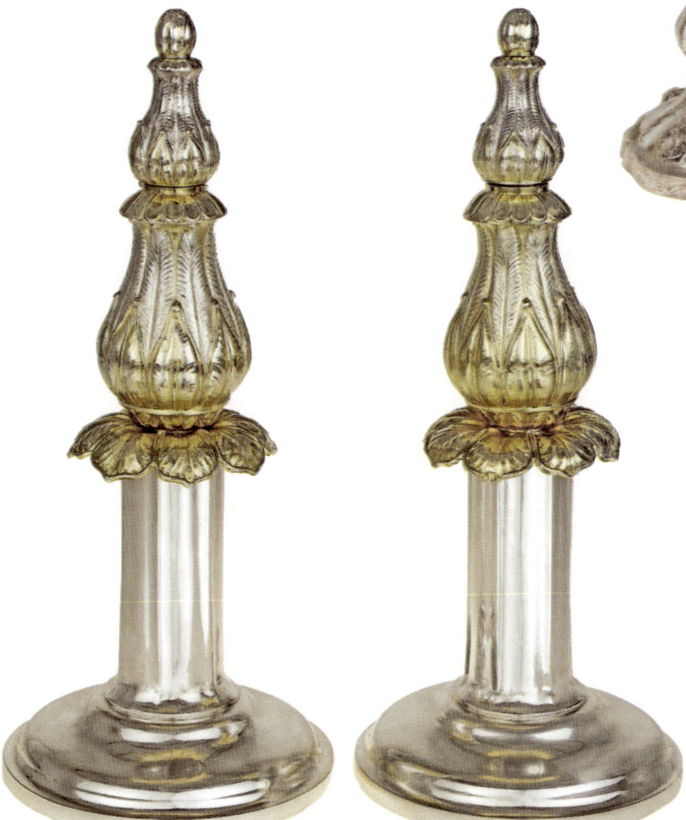

Cat. No. 151
Torah Finials
Inv. No. JMP 001.738/01, 02
Silver, repoussé, cut-out, engraving
Maker JE, Vienna, 1865
Height: 168 mm, diameter: 60 mm
Hallmarks: 1. JE in rectangle,
2. hallmark Vienna 1864
Without inscriptions.
Collection point: Sušice

Cat. No. 152
Torah Finials
Inv. No. JMP 037.903/01, 02
Silver, repoussé
Maker KC, Prague, 1867–71
Height: 283 mm, diameter: 115 mm
Hallmarks: 1. KC in rectangle,
2. Austro-Hungary 1867–71,
3. localization letter C [Prague]
Donation inscription in German
in Latin script.
Translation:
A gift on the occasion of the silver wedding anniversary of August and Helen Redisch, May 24, 1916.
Collection point:
Prague, Vinohrady

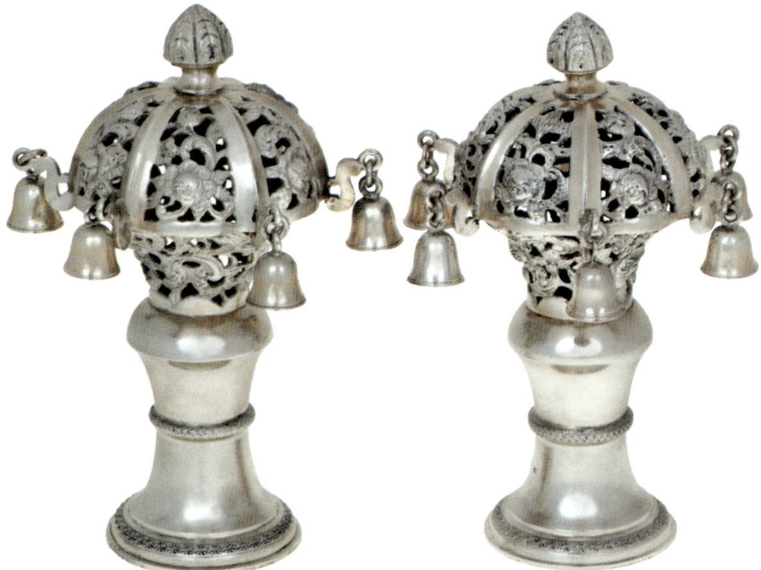

Cat. No. 151

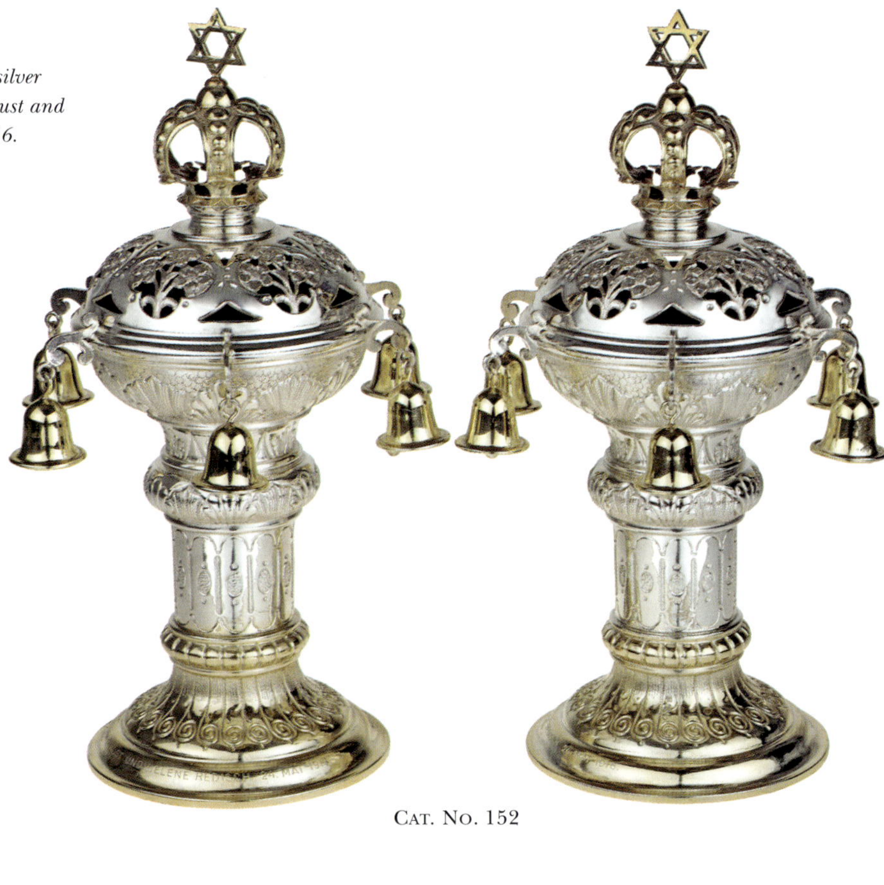

Cat. No. 152

Cat. No. 153
Torah Finials
Inv. No. JMP 010.865/01, 02
Silver, repoussé
Maker VC [Vincenz Czokally Co.],
Vienna, after 1871
Height: 255 mm, diameter: 86 mm
Hallmarks: 1. VC in rectangle,
2. Austro-Hungary [Vienna] after 1871
Without inscriptions.
Collection point: Soběslav

Cat. No. 154
Torah Finials
Inv. No. JMP 010.754/01, 02
Silver, repoussé, parcel-gilt, glass stones
Maker TD [Thomas Dub?], Vienna, after 1871
Height: 245 mm, diameter: 85 mm
Hallmarks: 1. TD in rectangle,
2. Austro-Hungary [Vienna] after 1871
Without inscriptions.
Collection point: Olomouc

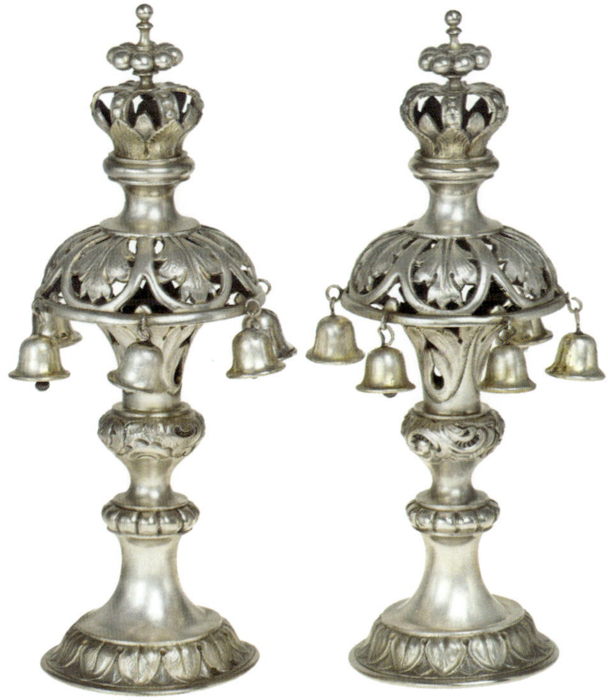

Cat. No. 153

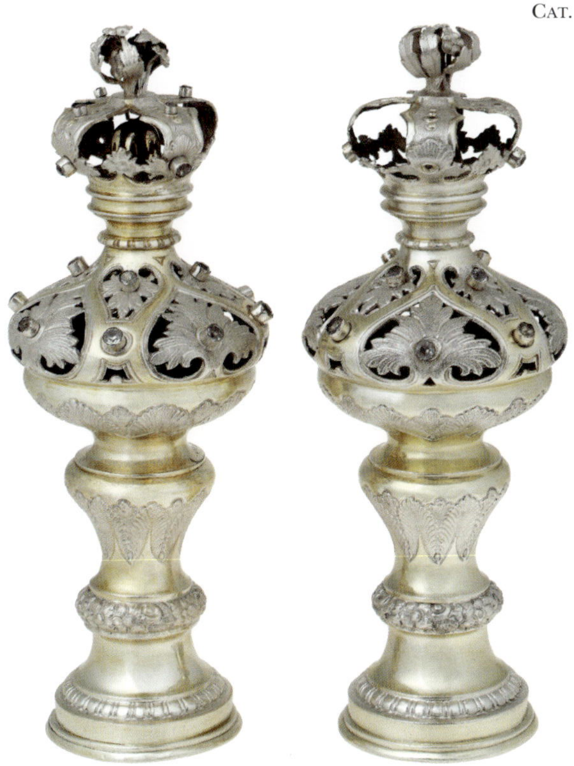

Cat. No. 154

Cat. No. 155
Torah Finials
Inv. No. JMP 102.430/01, 02
Silver, repoussé, originally parcel-gilt
Maker AP [Alfred Pollak Co.],
Prague, after 1871
Height: 280 mm, diameter: 115 mm
Hallmarks: 1. AP in rectangle,
2. Austro-Hungary [Prague] after 1871,
3. localization letter C [Prague]
Donation inscription in German
in Latin script and in Hebrew.
Translation:
Donated by Alfred and Camille Bruml, September 28, 1916. [in German]. *This was donated by Abraham, son of Joseph Bruml, and his wife the lady Rone, daughter of Sender Hirsch, in the year 674 a. s. c. [= 1914].* [in Hebrew].
Collection point: Prague

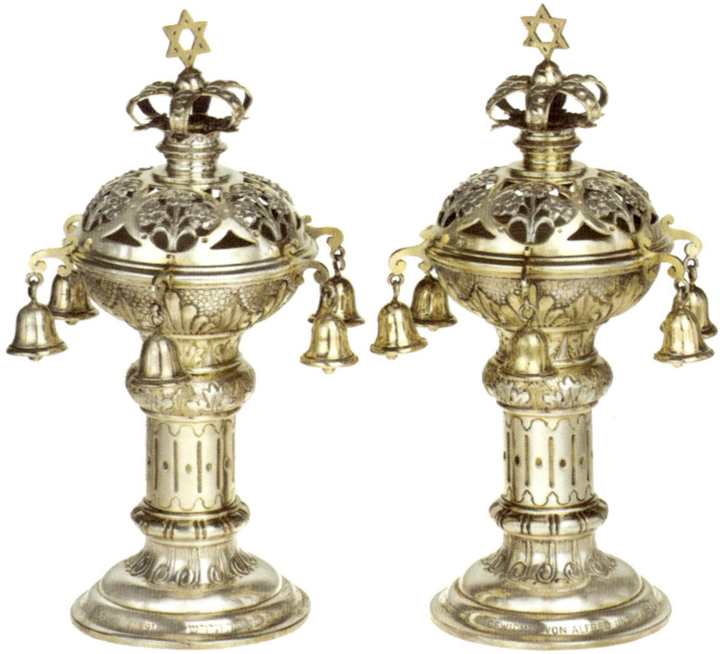

Cat. No. 155

Cat. No. 156
Torah Finials
Inv. No. JMP 004.222/01, 02
Silver, repoussé, parcel-gilt
Maker KW, Vienna, after 1871
Height: 300 mm, diameter: 96 mm
Hallmarks: 1. KW in oval,
2. Austro-Hungary [Vienna] after 1871
Without inscriptions.
Collection point: Uherský Brod

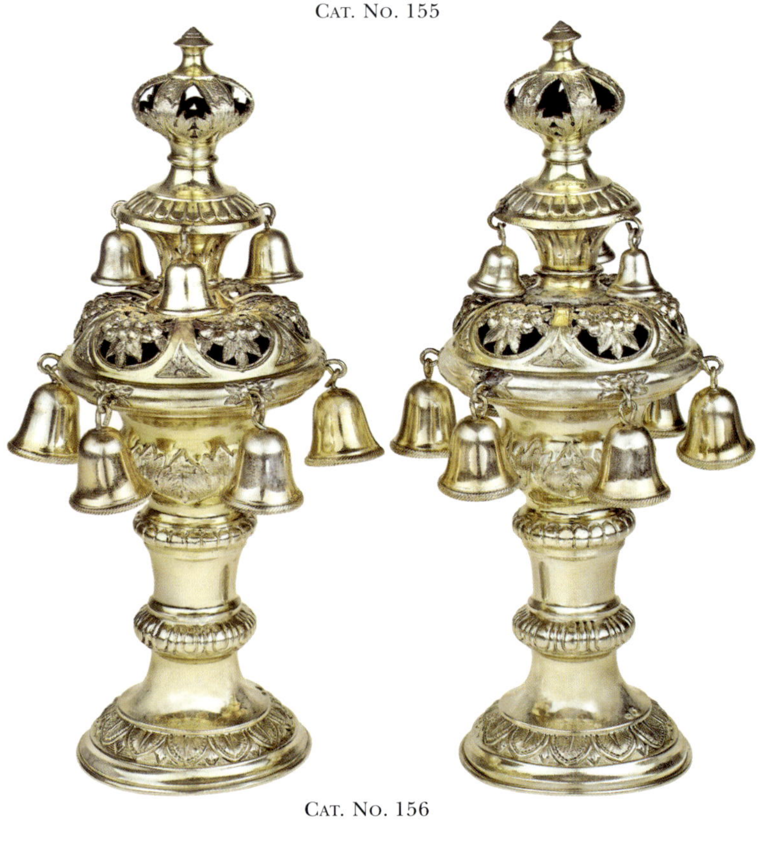

Cat. No. 156

Cat. No. 157
Torah Finials
Inv. No. JMP 002.655/01, 02
Silver, repoussé, engraving
Maker VC [Vincenz Czokally Co.],
Vienna, after 1871
Height: 215 mm, diameter: 93 mm
Hallmarks: 1. VC in rectangle,
2. Austro-Hungary [Vienna] after 1871
Without inscriptions.
Collection point: Holešov

Cat. No. 158
Torah Finials
Inv. No. JMP 007.187/01, 02
Silver, repoussé,gilt
Maker VC [Vincenz Czokally Co.],
Vienna, after 1871
Height: 272 mm, diameter: 90 mm
Hallmarks: 1. VC in rectangle,
2. Austro-Hungary [Vienna] after 1871
Without inscriptions.
Provenance: Brno-Pohořelice

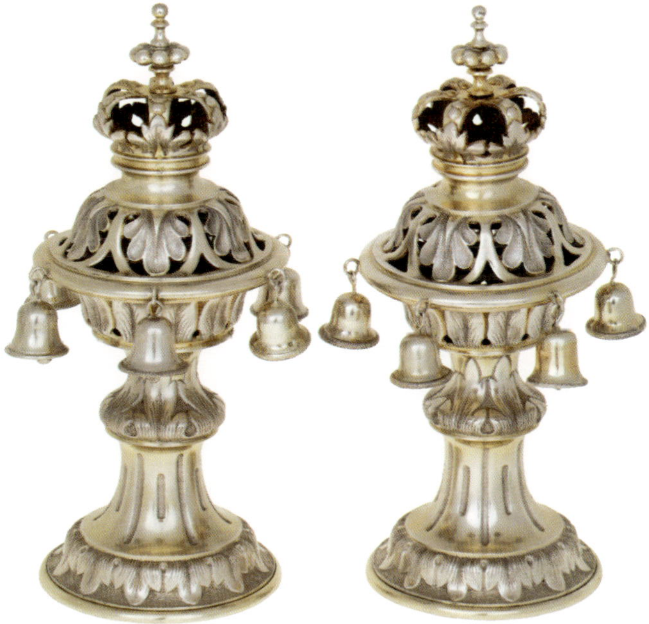

Cat. No. 157

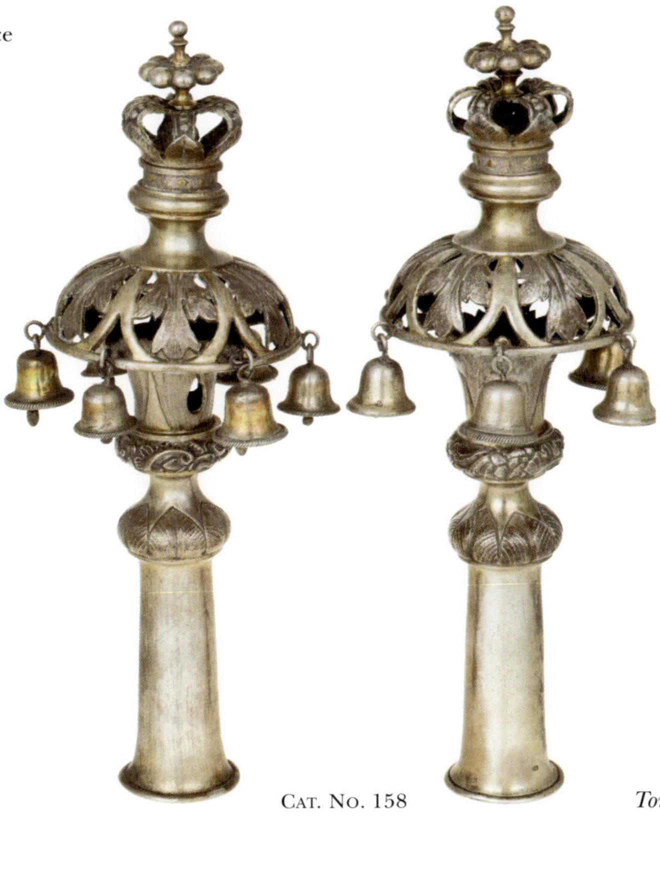

Cat. No. 158

Cat. No. 159
Torah Finials
Inv. No. JMP 004.277/01, 02
Silver, repoussé
Maker HS [Hermann Südfeld Co.],
Vienna, after 1871
Height: 364 mm, diameter: 125 mm
Hallmarks: 1. HS in rectangle,
2. Austro-Hungary [Vienna] after 1871
Without inscriptions.
Collection point: Kyjov

Cat. No. 160
Torah Finials
Inv. No. JMP 037.910/01, 02
Silver, repoussé
Maker VCD [Vincenz Carl Dub Co.],
Vienna, after 1871
Height: 305 mm, diameter: 124 mm
Hallmarks: 1. VCD in rectangle,
2. Austro-Hungary [Vienna] after 1871
Without inscriptions.
Collection point: Prague, Vinohrady

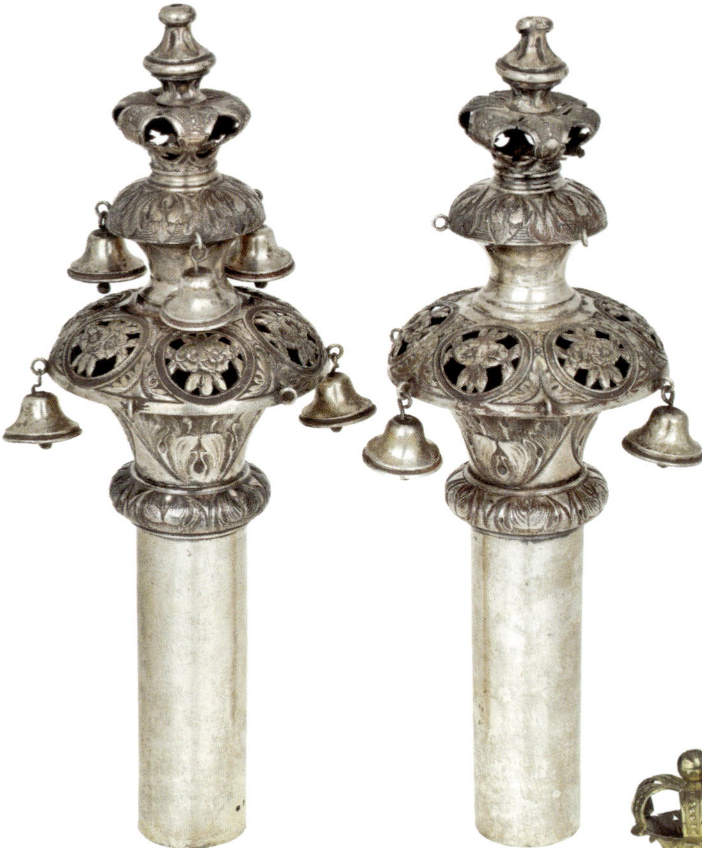

Cat. No. 159

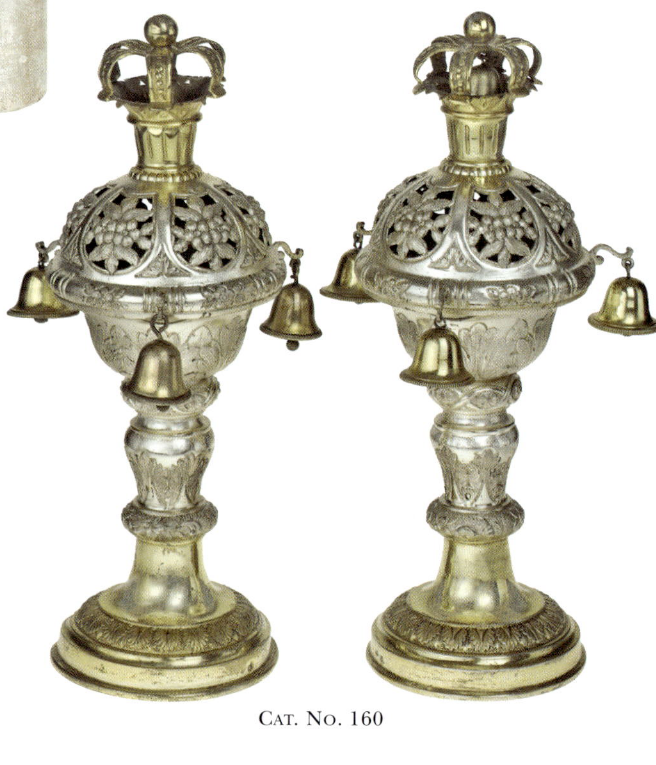

Cat. No. 160

Cat. No. 161
Torah Finials
Inv. No. JMP 004.423/01, 02
Silver, repoussé, gilt
Maker VC [Vincenz Czokally Co.],
Vienna, after 1871
Height: 286 mm, diameter: 87 mm
Hallmarks: 1. VC in rectangle,
2. Austro-Hungary [Vienna] after 1871
Without inscriptions.
Collection point: Rychnov nad Kněžnou

Cat. No. 162
Torah Finials
Inv. No. JMP 012.653/01, 02
Silver, repoussé, originally parcel-gilt
Maker JZ, Vienna, after 1871
Height: 221 mm, diameter: 101 mm
Hallmarks: 1. JZ in rectangle,
2. Austro-Hungary [Vienna] after 1871
Donation inscription in Hebrew.
Translation:
This was donated by the sons of KH Simon Klein [in the year] *655 a. s. c.* [= 1895].
Collection point: Nový Bydžov

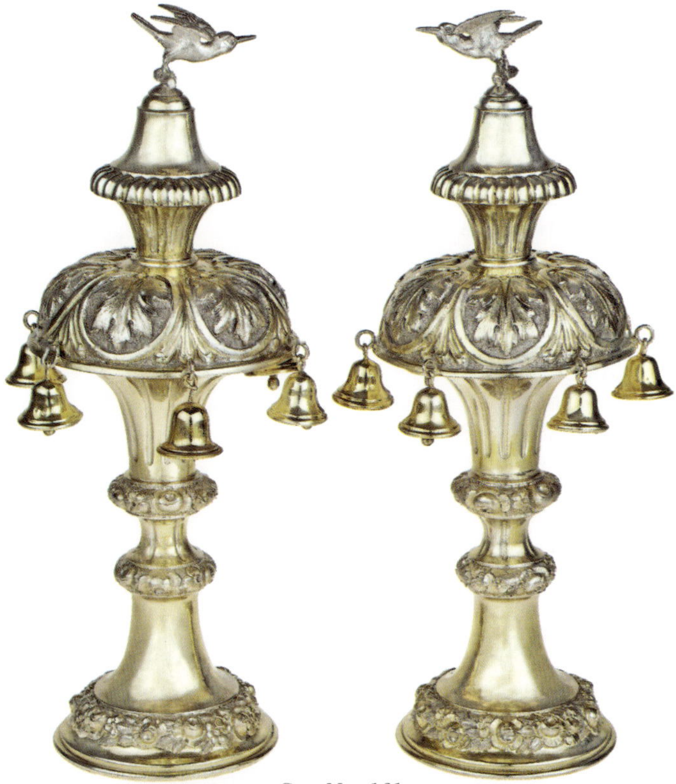

Cat. No. 161

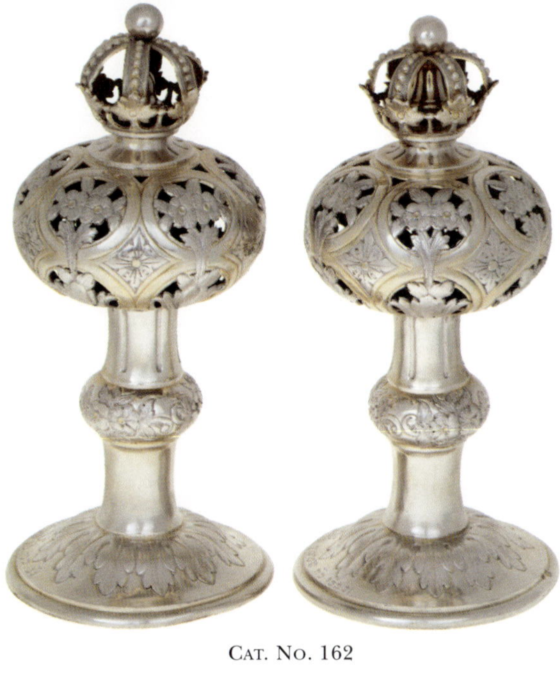

Cat. No. 162

Cat. No. 163
Torah Finials
Inv. No. JMP 002.167/01, 02
Silver, repoussé
Maker JZ, Vienna, after 1871
Height: 264 mm, diameter: 100 mm
Hallmarks: 1. JZ in rectangle,
2. Austro-Hungary [Vienna] after 1871
Without inscriptions.
Collection point: Mladá Boleslav

Cat. No. 164
Torah Finials
Inv. No. JMP 001.856/01, 02
Silver, repoussé
Maker JE, Vienna, after 1871
Height: 320 mm, diameter: 120 mm
Hallmarks: 1. JE in rectangle,
2. Austro-Hungary [Vienna] after 1871
Without inscriptions.
Collection point: Klatovy

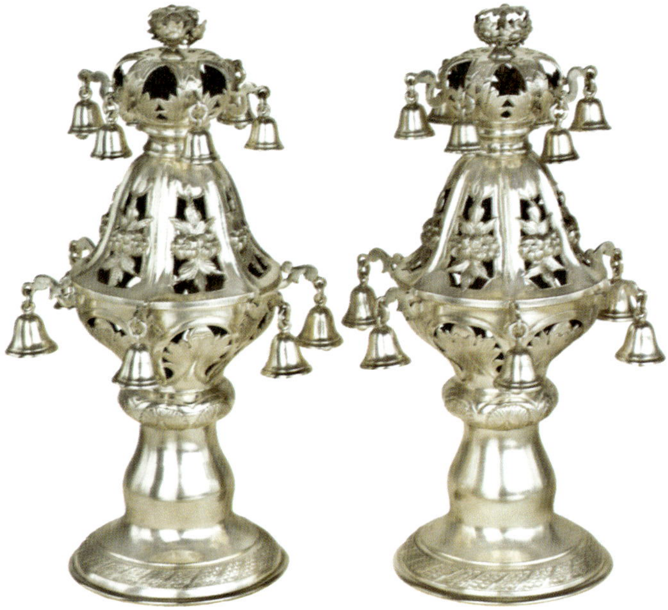

Cat. No. 163

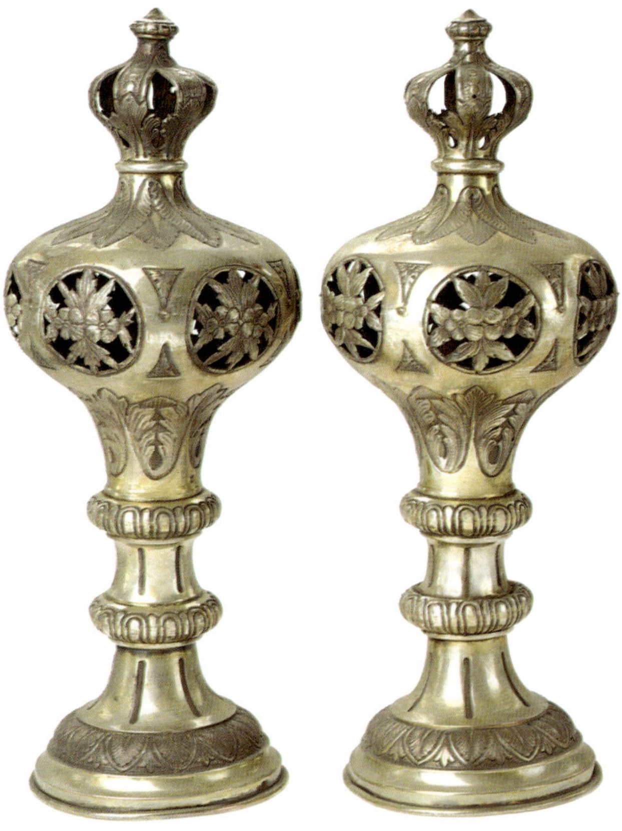

Cat. No. 164

Cat. No. 165
Torah Finials
Inv. No. JMP 017.531/01, 02
Silver, repoussé, parcel-gilt, engraving
Bruckmann & Söhne Co., Heilbronn [?],
Germany, end of 19th century
Height: 315 mm, diameter: 90 mm
Hallmarks: 1. eagle with outspread wings,
2. German hallmark for silver, 3. purity number 800,
4. POSEN in rectangle [the seller], 5. import mark
Austro-Hungary [Prague] after 1871
Without inscriptions.
Collection point: Prague, Klausen Synagogue

Cat. No. 166
Torah Finials
Inv. No. JMP 004.397/01, 02
Silver, repoussé, engraving
Maker AP [Alfred Pollak Co.], Prague, ca. 1900
Height: 278 mm, diameter: 135 mm
Hallmarks: 1. AP in rectangle, 2. Austro-Hungary
[Prague] after 1871, 3. imperial eagle,
4. localization letter C [Prague]
Without inscriptions.
Collection point: Kamenice nad Lipou

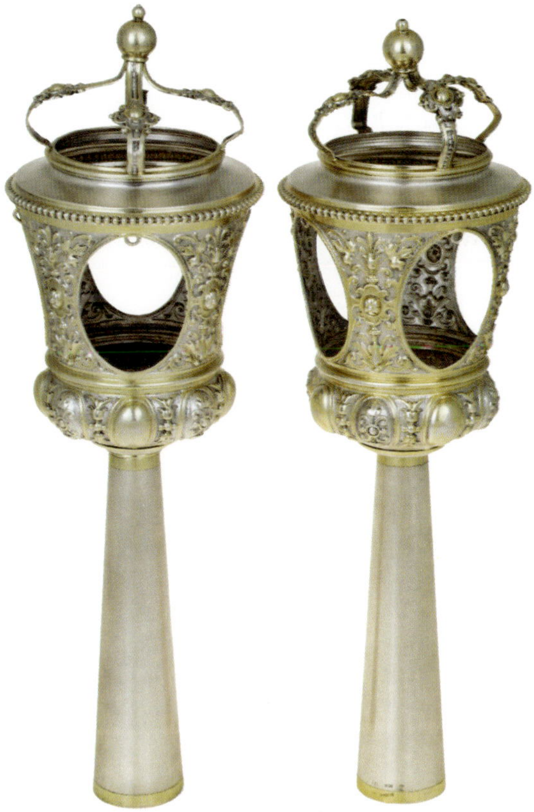

Cat. No. 165

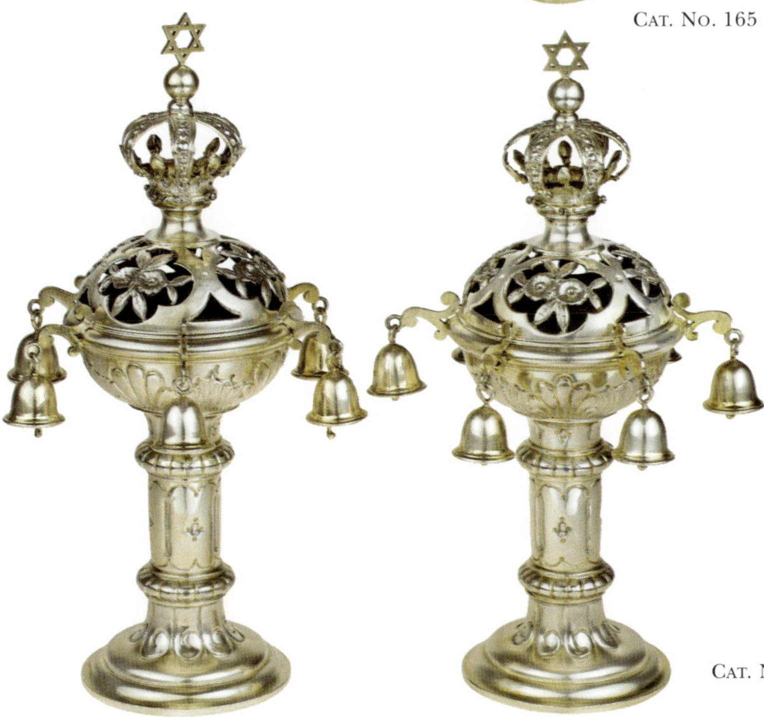

Cat. No. 166

Cat. No. 167
Torah Finials
Inv. No. JMP 012.409/01, 02
Silver, filigree
Bezalel workshops, Palestine, early 20th century
Height: 265 mm, diameter: 64 mm
Hallmarks: import mark Austro-Hungary [Vienna] after 1902
Donation inscription in Hebrew.
Translation:
"This is the law that Moses set before the people of Israel" [Deut. 4:44] [from the back is the text of the Decalogue].
Collection point: Olomouc

Cat. No. 168
Torah Finials
Inv. No. JMP 001.675/01, 02
Silver, repoussé, engraving
Maker JM, Prague, early 20th century
Height: 236 mm, diameter: 104 mm
Hallmarks: 1. JM in rectangle,
2. Austro-Hungary [Prague] after 1871
Without inscriptions.
Collection point:
Brandýs nad Labem / Kostelec nad Labem

Cat. No. 169
Torah Finials
Inv. No. JMP 012.556/01, 02
Silver, repoussé, engraving
Maker AP [Alfred Pollak Co.],
Prague, 1921–26
Height: 320 mm, diameter: 150 mm
Hallmarks: 1. AP in rectangle,
2. hallmark Czechoslovakia 1921–28
Donation inscription in Hebrew.
Translation:
A donation from Hayyim Joseph Schlachet and his wife Bellah in the year 686 [a. s. c.] [= 1926].
Collection point: Moravská Ostrava

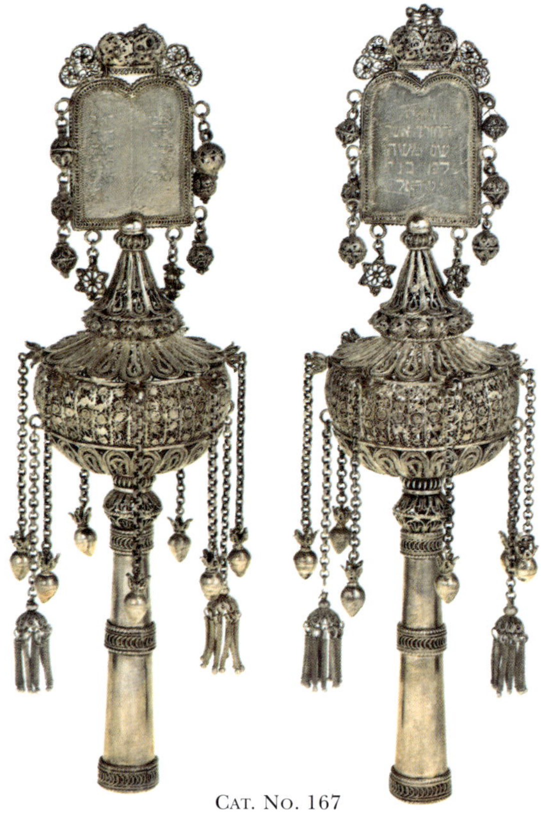

Cat. No. 167

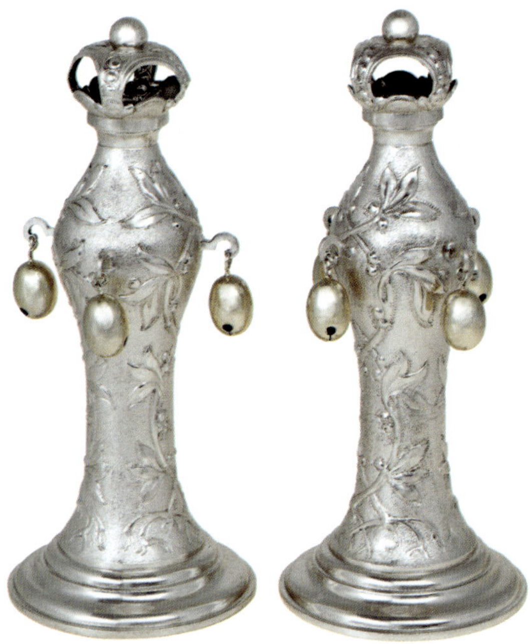

Cat. No. 168

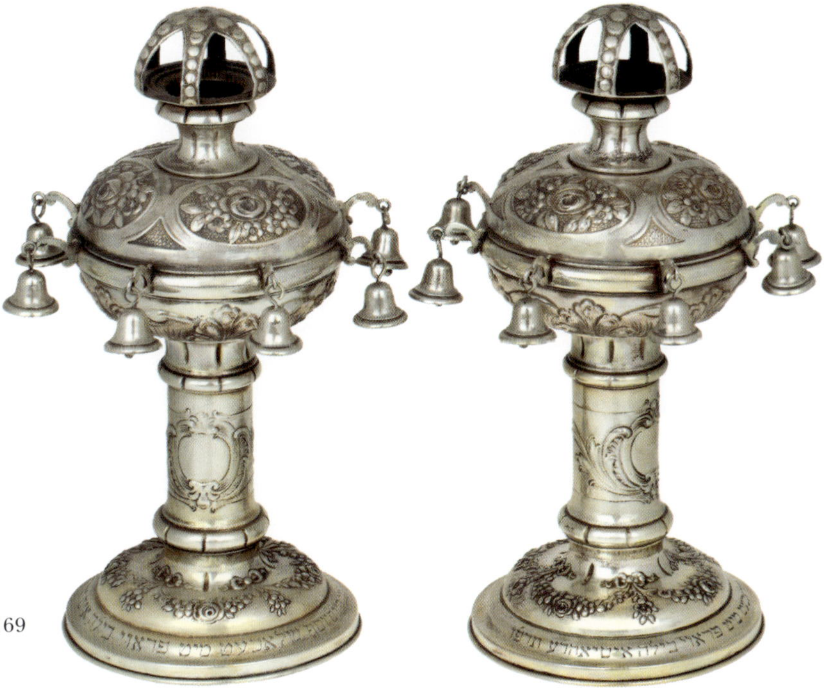

Cat. No. 169

Cat. No. 170 >

Torah Finials

Inv. No. JMP 004.343/01, 02

Silver, repoussé

Maker HG [Jindřich Grünfeld Co.],

Czechoslovakia, after 1928

Height: 325 mm, diameter: 120 mm

Hallmarks: 1. HG in oval,

2. hallmark Czechoslovakia 1929–1941

Donation inscription in Hebrew.

Translation:

This was donated by late HRR Dr. Jehiel ha-kohen Beer, may the memory of the just be blessed.

Collection point: Moravská Ostrava

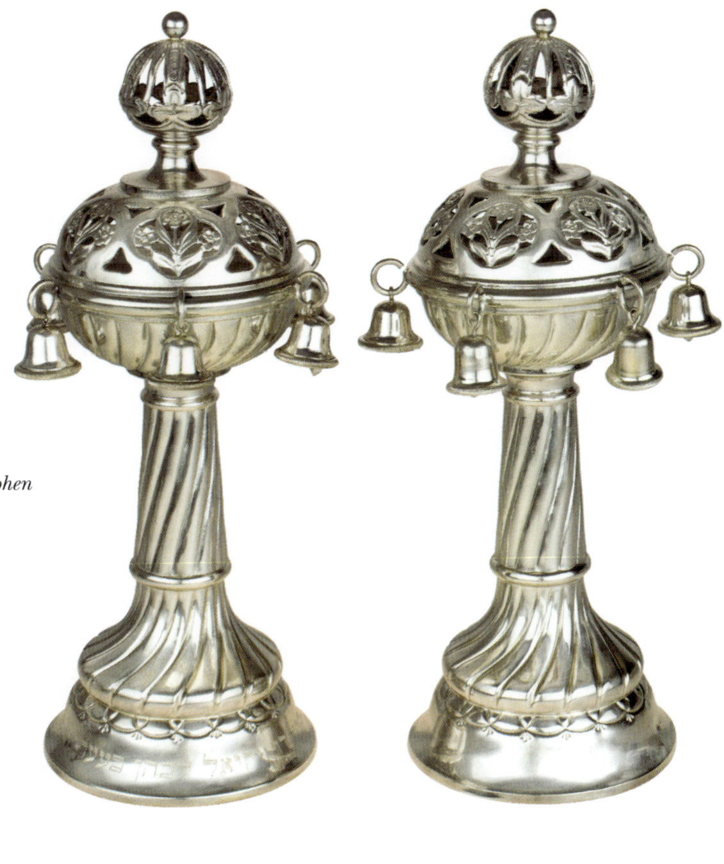

IV. Torah Pointers

Cat. No. 171
Torah Pointer
Inv. No. JMP 001.968
Silver, carved coral, repoussé, turned, parcel-gilt
Johann Conrad Weiss, Nuremberg,
1st third of 18th century
Length: 149 mm, diameter: 11 mm
Hallmarks: 1. ICW in trilob,
2. city mark Nuremberg
Without inscriptions.
Collection point: Nepomuk

Cat. No. 172
Torah Pointer
Inv. No. JMP 005.335
Silver, repoussé, cast
Maker unknown, Eastern Europe [?],
18th century
Length: 148 mm, diameter: 14 mm
Hallmarks: 1. recharge mark Brno 1806–7,
2. release mark 1809–10
Without inscriptions.
Collection point: Holešov

Cat. No. 173
Torah Pointer
Inv. No. JMP 177.818
Silver, repoussé, cast, turned, engraving
No maker's mark, Moravia [?], before 1772
Length: 278 mm, diameter: 24 mm
Hallmarks: unmarked
Donation inscription in Hebrew.
Translation:
Belonging to H David, son of R.W. and the name of his wife is Nehamah, 532 a. s. c. [= 1772].
Purchased by the Jewish Museum in Prague.

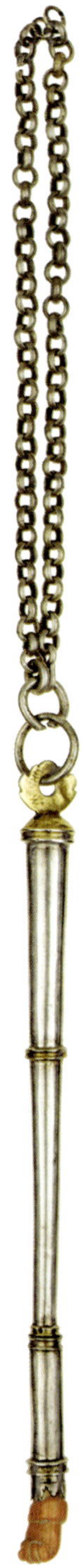
Cat. No. 171

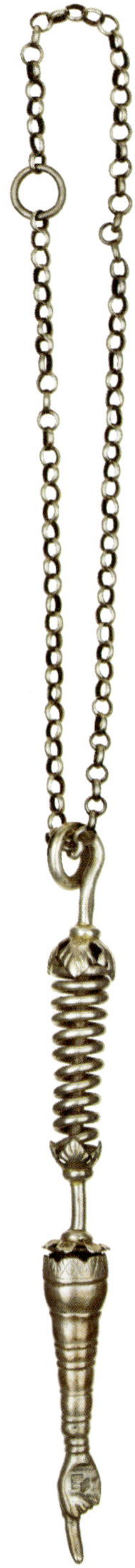
Cat. No. 172

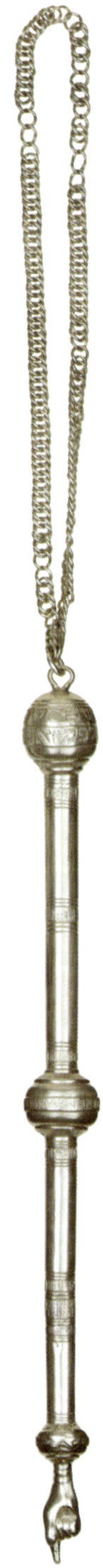
Cat. No. 173

Cat. No. 174
Torah Pointer
Inv. No. JMP 012.176
Silver, repoussé, cast
Johann Christian Fischer, Brno, 1769–76
Length: 264 mm, diameter: 21 mm
Hallmarks: 1. ICF in trilob, 2. hallmark
Brno 1769–76, 3. recharge mark Vienna 1806–7,
4. release mark 1809–10
Without inscriptions.
Collection point: Brno, Nový Rousínov

Cat. No. 175
Torah Pointer
Inv. No. JMP 003.962
Silver, repoussé, cast, engraving
No maker's mark, Moravia [?],
2nd half of 18th century
Length: 301 mm, diameter: 33 mm
Hallmarks: 1. recharge mark Vienna 1806–7,
2. release mark 1809–10
Donation inscription in Hebrew.
Translation:
Treasurer MR Itzak […]
[inscription is partially illegible].
Collection point: Central Jewish Museum for
Moravia and Silesia, 1936–1938 in Nikolsburg

Cat. No. 176
Torah Pointer
Inv. No. JMP 005.333
Silver, repoussé, cast, originally parcel-gilt
No maker's mark, Moravia [?],
2nd half of 18th century
Length: 376 mm, diameter: 36 mm
Hallmarks: 1. recharge mark Brno 1806–7
Without inscriptions.
Collection point: Holešov

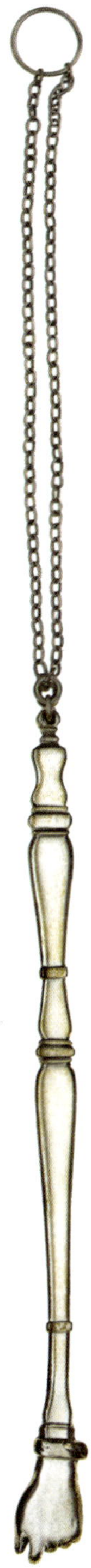

Cat. No. 174

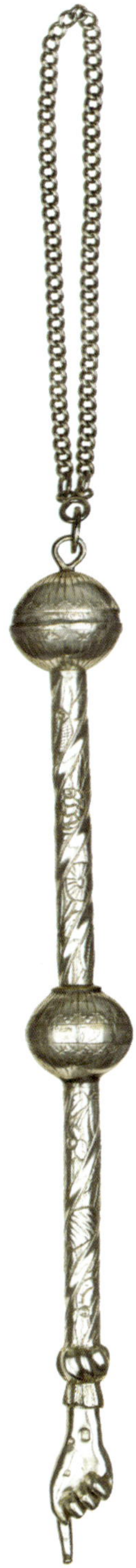

Cat. No. 175

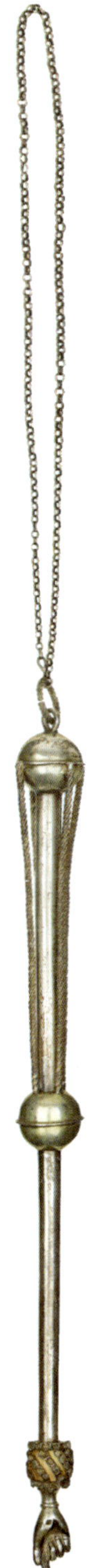

Cat. No. 176

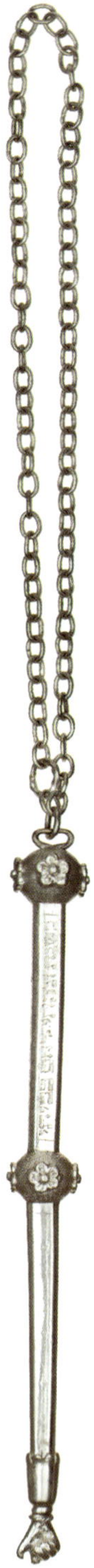

Cat. No. 177

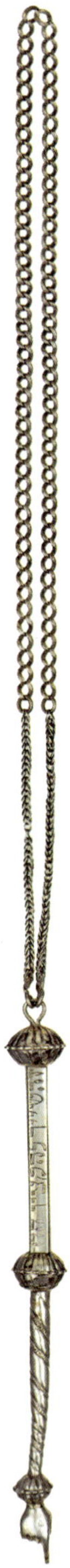

Cat. No. 178

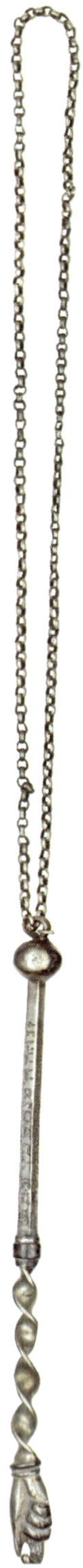

Cat. No. 179

Cat. No. 177
Torah Pointer
Inv. No. JMP 004.028
Silver, repoussé, cast
No maker's mark, Bohemia [?],
2nd half of 18th century
Length: 228 mm, diameter: 24 mm
Hallmarks: 1. release mark 1809–10
Donation inscriptions in Hebrew.
Translation:
A gift of the holy society known as "Shas Chevra" [The Society of the Six Orders of the Mishnah] *here in the holy community Kolín "I will give them, in my house and within my walls, a fine inheritance"* [cf. Is. 56:5; dating in the chronogram 549 = 1789, may also be read as 564 = 1804] *a. s. c.*
Collection point: Kolín

Cat. No. 178
Torah Pointer
Inv. No. JMP 007.053
Silver, repoussé, cast
No maker's mark, Moravia, 2nd half of 18th century
Length: 208 mm, diameter: 23 mm
Hallmarks: 1. recharge mark Brno 1806–7,
2. release mark 1809–10
Donation inscription in Hebrew.
Translation:
This belongs to the elder HRR Itzak Eibeschütz.
Collection point: Třešť

Cat. No. 179
Torah Pointer
Inv. No. JMP 001.767
Silver, repoussé, cast
No maker's mark, Moravia [?],
2nd half of 18th century
Length: 183 mm, diameter: 14 mm
Hallmarks: 1. recharge mark Vienna 1806–7,
2. release mark 1809–10
Donation inscription in Hebrew.
Translation:
This was donated by HH H Mendel Katz with his wife Miriam, may she live, in the year 566 a. s. c. [= 1806]
Collection point: Podivín

Cat. No. 180
Torah Pointer
Inv. No. JMP 032.417
Silver, cast, turned
Josef Jakub Raspel, Prague, 1776–79
Length: 182 mm, diameter: 10 mm
Hallmarks: 1. IR in rectangle, 2. hallmark
Prague 177x [?], 3. release mark 1809–10
Without inscriptions.
Collection point: Prague, Old-New Synagogue

Cat. No. 181
Torah Pointer
Inv. No. JMP 007.054
Silver, repoussé, cast
No maker's mark, Moravia [?], 1787 [inscription]
Length: 268 mm, diameter: 20 mm
Hallmarks: 1. recharge mark Brno 1806–7
Donation inscription in Hebrew.
Translation:
A gift of the elder H Zanwil, may his Rock protect him, son of H Zelig of blessed memory, and his wife the lady Hadas, daughter of H Jacob David of blessed memory, in the year 547 a. s. c. [= 1787].
Collection point: Třešť

Cat. No. 182
Torah Pointer
Inv. No. JMP 004.466
Silver, repoussé, cast, engraving
Maker IS [Ignaz Schubert?], Vienna, 1784–94
Length: 253 mm, diameter: 23 mm
Hallmarks: 1. IS in rectangle, 2. hallmark
Vienna 17x4 [?], 3. release mark 1809–10
Donation inscription in German in Latin script.
Translation:
Donated by Rosalie and Judah Kohnberger in the year 1848.
Collection point: Třebíč

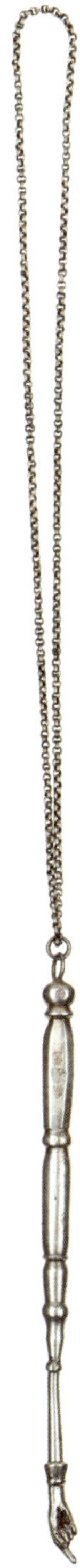

Cat. No. 180

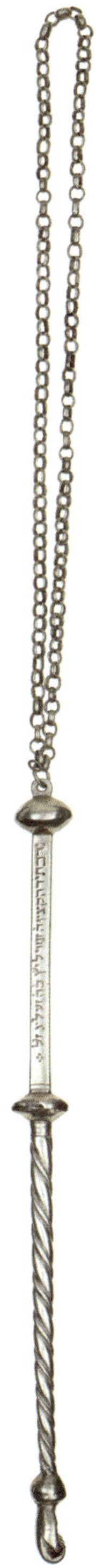

Cat. No. 181

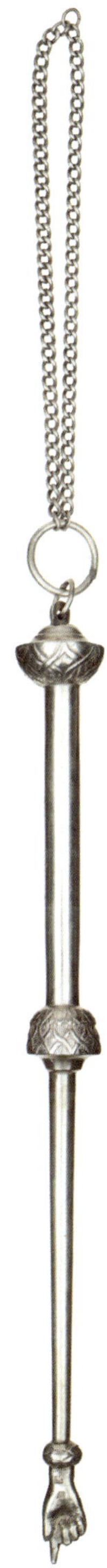

Cat. No. 182

Cat. No. 183
Torah Pointer
Inv. No. JMP 004.104
Silver, repoussé, cast, engraving
No maker's mark, Bohemia [?], 1791 [inscription]
Length: 292 mm, diameter: 28 mm
Hallmarks: 1. recharge mark Prague 1806–7,
2. release mark 1809–10
Donation inscription in Hebrew.
Translation:
A gift of the elder HRR Yokev Wolf, may his Rock and Redeemer protect him, and his wife, the elder lady Deborah, in the year 551 a. s. c. [= 1791].
Collection point: Chotěboř

Cat. No. 184
Torah Pointer
Inv. No. JMP 009.800
Silver, repoussé, cast, engraving
Maker unknown, Jihlava [?], early 19th century
Length: 210 mm, diameter: 19 mm
Hallmarks: 1. hallmark illegible,
2. tax mark Jihlava 1810–24
Without inscriptions.
Collection point: Bzenec

Cat. No. 185
Torah Pointer
Inv. No. JMP 010.874
Silver, repoussé, cast
No maker's mark, Bohemia [?], end of 18th century
Length: 249 mm, diameter: 20 mm
Hallmarks: 1. stock mark after 1776,
2. release mark 1809–10
Without inscriptions.
Collection point: Soběslav

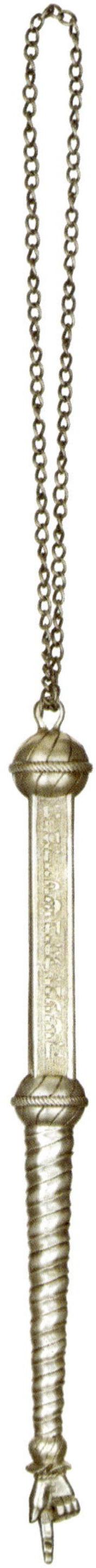

Cat. No. 183

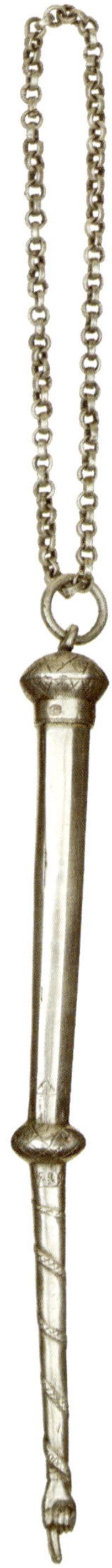

Cat. No. 184

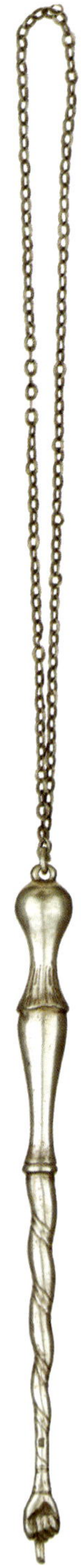

Cat. No. 185

Cat. No. 186
Torah Pointer
Inv. No. JMP 012.587
Silver, repoussé, cast, engraving
No maker's mark, Bohemia [?],
end of 18th century
Length: 300 mm, diameter: 27 mm
Hallmarks: 1. recharge mark Prague 1806–7,
2. release mark 1809–10 [not original]
Donation inscription in Hebrew.
Translation:
A gift from the boys here [in] *Strážovice.*
Collection point: Mirovice/Březnice

Cat. No. 187
Torah Pointer
Inv. No. JMP 005.337
Silver, repoussé, cast
No maker's mark, Moravia [?],
end of 18th century
Length: 235 mm, diameter: 28 mm
Hallmarks: 1. recharge mark Brno 1806–7,
2. release mark 1809–10
Without inscriptions.
Collection point: Holešov

Cat. No. 188
Torah Pointer
Inv. No. JMP 004.195
Silver, repoussé, cast, originally parcel-gilt, engraving
No maker's mark, Moravia [?],
end of 18th century
Length: 270 mm, diameter: 32 mm
Hallmarks: 1. recharge mark Brno 1806–7,
2. release mark 1809–10
Donation inscription in Hebrew.
Translation:
This was donated by the elder HRR Moses Hirsch, son of R B Kohen.
Collection point: Uherský Brod

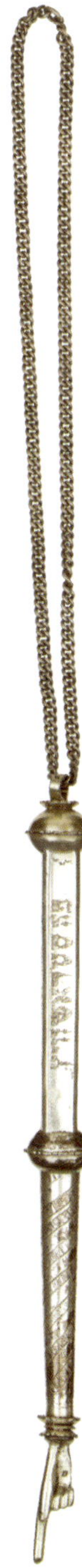

Cat. No. 186

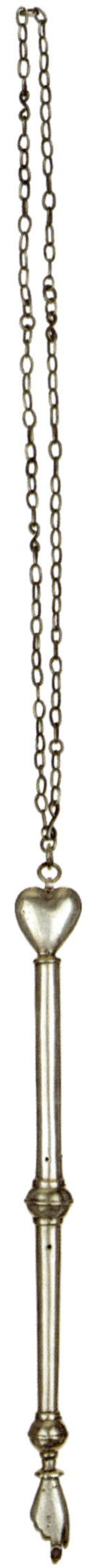

Cat. No. 187

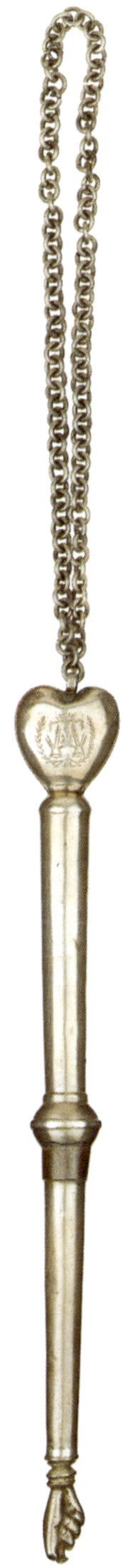

Cat. No. 188

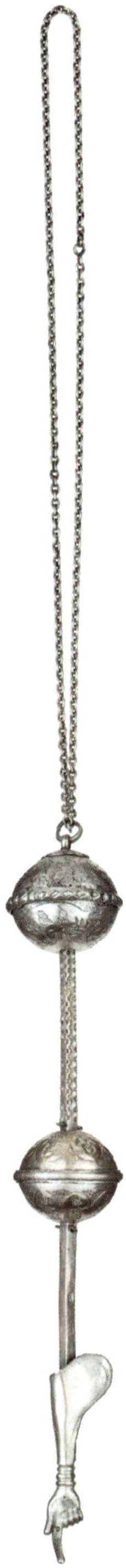

Cat. No. 189

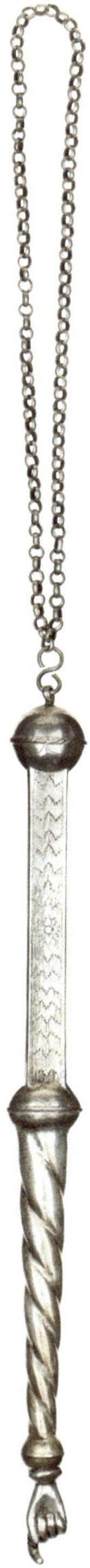

Cat. No. 190

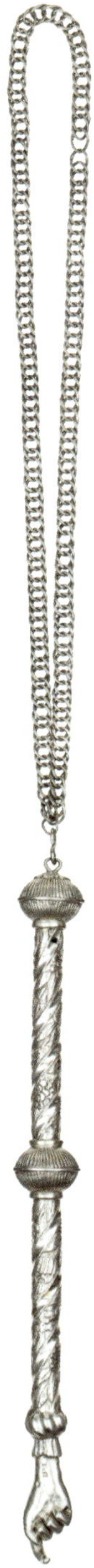

Cat. No. 191

Cat. No. 189
Torah Pointer
Inv. No. JMP 003.967
Silver, repoussé, cast
No maker's mark, Galicia, end of 18th century
Length: 268 mm, diameter: 41 mm
Hallmarks: 1. fake recharge mark
Lemberg 1806–7
Without inscriptions.
Collection point: Central Jewish Museum for Moravia and Silesia, 1936–1938 in Nikolsburg

Cat. No. 190
Torah Pointer
Inv. No. JMP 037.790
Silver, repoussé, cast, engraving
No maker's mark, Bohemia [?],
end of 18th century [?]
Length: 322 mm, diameter: 29 mm
Hallmarks: unmarked
Without inscriptions.
Collection point: Prague, Pinkas Synagogue

Cat. No. 191
Torah Pointer
Inv. No. JMP 037.402
Silver, repoussé, cast
No maker's mark, Moravia [?],
end of 18th century
Length: 273 mm, diameter: 26 mm
Hallmarks: 1. recharge mark Brno 1806–7,
2. release mark 1809–10
Without inscriptions.
Collection point: Batelov

Cat. No. 192
Torah Pointer
Inv. No. JMP 009.680
Silver, cast, turned
Kryštof Wild, Prague, 1797
Length: 201 mm, diameter: 16 mm
Hallmarks: 1. CW in oval, 2. hallmark Prague 1797, 3. purity mark 13, 4. recharge mark Prague 1806–7, 5. release mark 1809–10
Without inscriptions.
Collection point: Hluboká nad Vltavou

Cat. No. 193
Torah Pointer
Inv. No. JMP 012.219
Silver, cast, twisted
No maker's mark, Moravia,
turn of 18th/19th century
Length: 258 mm, diameter: 17 mm
Hallmarks: 1. recharge mark Brno 1806–7, 2. release mark 1809–10
Without inscriptions.
Collection point: Brno, Kounice

Cat. No. 194
Torah Pointer
Inv. No. JMP 012.771
Silver, repoussé, cast, engraving, cut-out
No maker's mark, Galicia [?],
turn of 18th/19th century
Length: 230 mm, diameter: 43 mm
Hallmarks: unmarked
Donation inscription in Hebrew.
Translation:
The elder Simhah Isaiah, son of MVHRR Isaac SGL [dating in the chronogram most likely 593 = 1833] *a. s. c.*
Collection point: Jewish Museum in Prague, 1906–1940

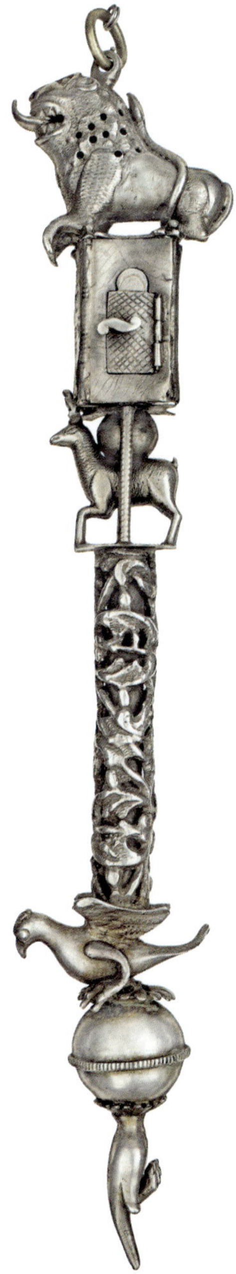

Cat. No. 194

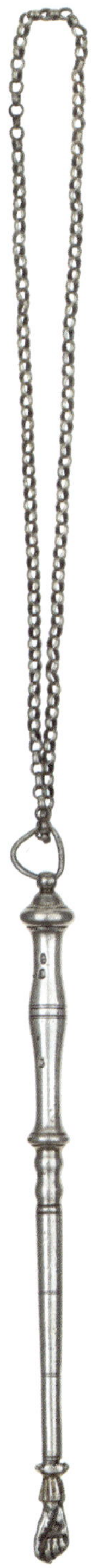

Cat. No. 192

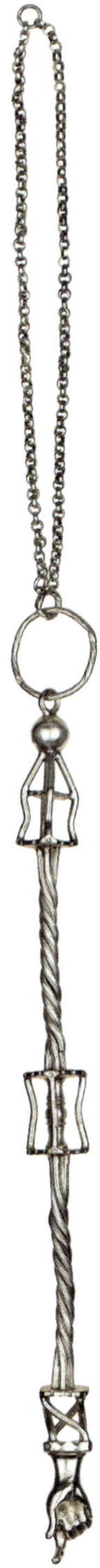

Cat. No. 193

Cat. No. 195
Torah Pointer
Inv. No. JMP 007.565
Silver, repoussé, cast
No maker's mark, Central Europe, ca. 1800
Length: 275 mm, diameter: 22 mm
Hallmarks: 1. recharge mark 1806–7,
2. release mark 1809–10
Inscription in Hebrew.
Translation:
This was donated by Mr. Gabriel, son of the esteemed M. of blessed memory, with his wife the lady Gitl, may she live, on behalf of their son Samuel, may his light shine, [in the year] *577 a. s. c.* [= 1817].
Collection point: Kojetín

Cat. No. 196
Torah Pointer
Inv. No. JMP 010.576
Silver, repoussé, cast
Karel Skřemenec, Prague, ca. 1800
Length: 243 mm, diameter: 18 mm
Hallmarks: 1. CS in oval, 2. hallmark Prague 1795–1806, 3. purity number 13 in oval,
4. recharge mark Prague 1806–7
Without inscriptions.
Collection point: Horažďovice

Cat. No. 197
Torah Pointer
Inv. No. JMP 002.523
Silver, cast, turned
No maker's mark, Bohemia [?],
turn of 18th/19th century
Length: 162 mm, diameter: 8 mm
Hallmarks: 1. recharge mark Prague 1806–7,
2. release mark 1809–10
Without inscriptions.
Collection point: Jindřichův Hradec

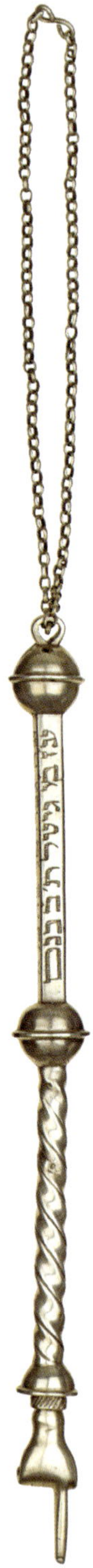
Cat. No. 195

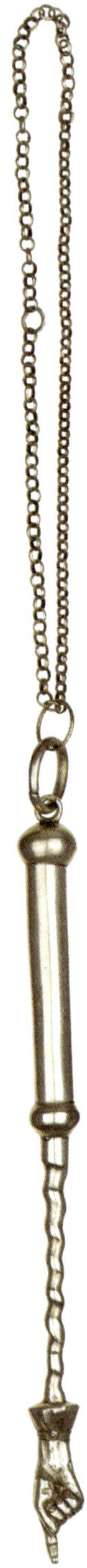
Cat. No. 196

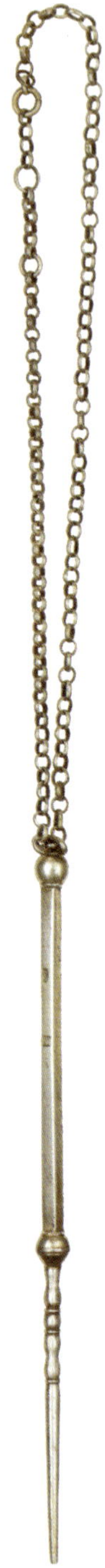
Cat. No. 197

Cat. No. 198
Torah Pointer
Inv. No. JMP 005.336
Silver, filigree, cast
No maker's mark, Eastern Europe,
turn of 18th/19th century
Length: 233 mm, diameter: 32 mm
Hallmarks: 1. recharge mark Brno 1806–7,
2. release mark 1809–10
Without inscriptions.
Collection point: Holešov

Cat. No. 199
Torah Pointer
Inv. No. JMP 010.453
Silver, repoussé, cast
No maker's mark, Eastern Europe,
turn of 18th/19th century
Length: 257 mm, diameter: 34 mm
Hallmarks: unmarked
Donation inscription in Hebrew.
Translation:
The Law of the Lord is perfect, rejoicing the heart. [Ps. 19:8] *The Lord protects all who love Him. Hear O Israel! The Lord is our God, the Lord is one.* [Deut. 6:4] *A gift to the Lord from the elder Judah Wolkan, 659 a. s. c.* [= 1899].
Collection point: Místek

Cat. No. 200
Torah Pointer
Inv. No. JMP 023.024
Silver, repoussé, cast
No maker's mark, Bohemia,
turn of 18th/19th century
Length: 253 mm, diameter: 22 mm
Hallmarks: 1. recharge mark Prague 1806–7,
2. release mark 1809–10
Without inscriptions.
Collection point: Český Brod

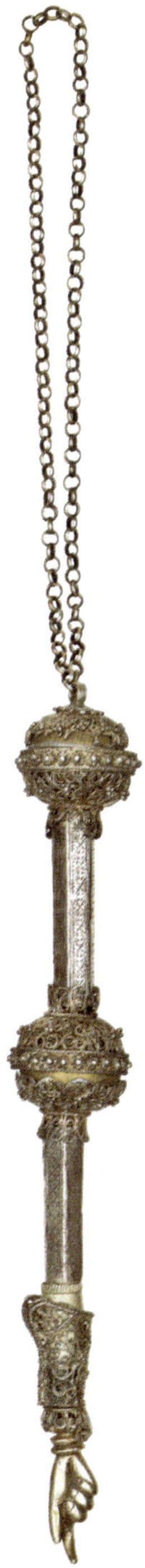

Cat. No. 198

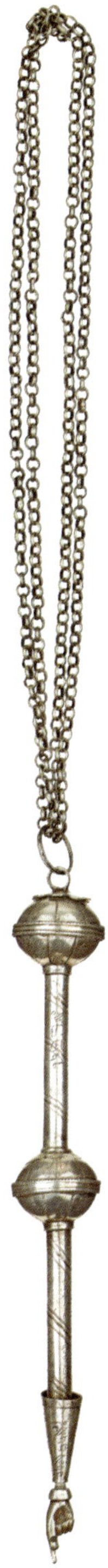

Cat. No. 199

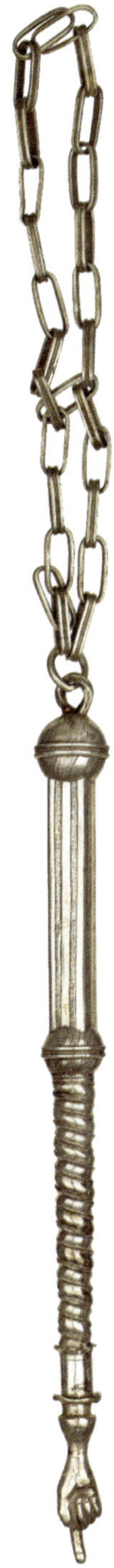

Cat. No. 200

Cat. No. 201
Torah Pointer
Inv. No. JMP 001.661
Silver, repoussé, cast
Maker WK, Prague, 1800–5
Length: 324 mm, diameter: 26 mm
Hallmarks: 1. WK in oval, 2. hallmark Prague 1800–6,
3. purity mark 13, 4. recharge mark Prague 1806–7,
5. release mark 1809–10
Donation inscription in Hebrew.
Translation:
To the honor of the Lord [locale] *and to the honor of the Torah on the festival of Shavuot. This was donated by HKHR HRR Josl son of Mr. Jonah Janowitz and his companion in study HKH HRR Abraham, son of Mr. Faivel Bischitzki, here in the holy community Brandýs to the glory of the Lord and to the glory of the Torah on the festival of Shavu'ot, in the year 565 a. s. c.* [= 1805].
Collection point: Brandýs nad Labem / Kostelec nad Labem

Cat. No. 202
Torah Pointer
Inv. No. JMP 010.373
Silver, repoussé, cast
Johann Kaba, Vienna, 1802
Length: 250 mm, diameter: 25 mm
Hallmarks: 1. JK in oval, 2. hallmark Vienna 1802,
3. recharge mark Vienna 1806–7
Without inscriptions.
Collection point: Brno, Miroslav

Cat. No. 203
Torah Pointer
Inv. No. JMP 175.885
Silver, repoussé, cast, parcel-gilt
Karel Skřemenec, Prague, 1803
Length: 265 mm, diameter: 26 mm
Hallmarks: 1. CS in oval, 2. hallmark Prague 1803,
3. purity mark 13, 4. recharge mark Prague 1806–7,
5. tax mark Prague 1810–24
Donation inscription in Hebrew.
Translation:
This was donated by the distinguished KH Jehiel, son of KH Aaron Beer of [Mladá] *Vožice and his wife, the esteemed lady Rezl, may she live, in the year 563 a. s. c.* [= 1803].
Purchased by the Jewish Museum in Prague.

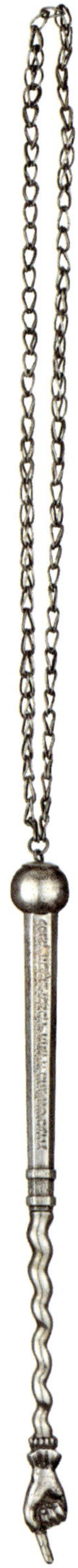
Cat. No. 201

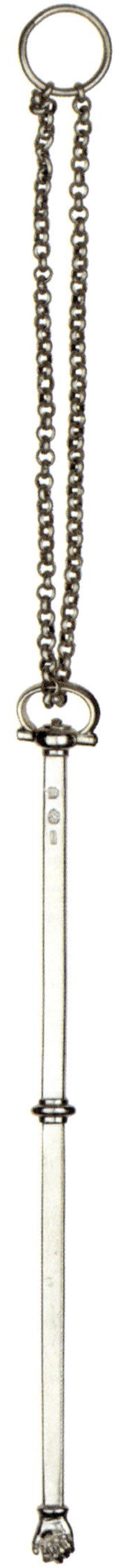
Cat. No. 202

Cat. No. 204
Torah Pointer
Inv. No. JMP 002.159
Silver, repoussé, cast
Karel Skřemenec, Prague, 1800–6
Length: 262 mm, diameter: 24 mm
Hallmarks: 1. CS in oval, 2. hallmark Prague 1800–6, 3. purity mark 13, 4. recharge mark Prague 1806–7, 5. release mark 1809–10
Donation inscriptions in Hebrew.
Translation:
A gift of the Holy Gaon Society, the chief judge of the Rabbinical Court, may the Merciful protect and redeem him, MHV Ezekiel Gloga SGL. Custodian R David Hirsch, son of R L. Brandes, R Wolf B Sch, son of our teacher, R Hayyim B Sch SGL, [judge] *and teacher of halacha* [justice on the Rabbinical Court], *in the year "Your stature"* [dating in the chronogram 566 = 1806] *a. s. c.*
Collection point: Mladá Boleslav

Cat. No. 205
Torah Pointer
Inv. No. JMP 007.393
Silver, repoussé, cast, originally parcel-gilt
No maker's mark, Moravia [?], early 19th century
Length: 310 mm, diameter: 29 mm
Hallmarks: unmarked
Without inscriptions.
Collection point: Uherský Ostroh

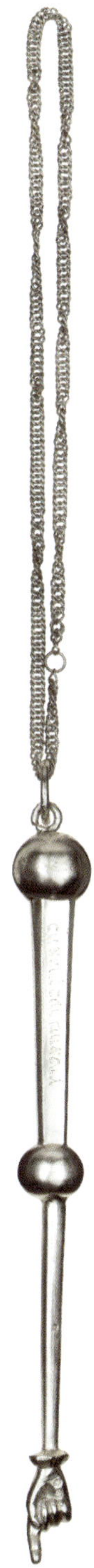
Cat. No. 203

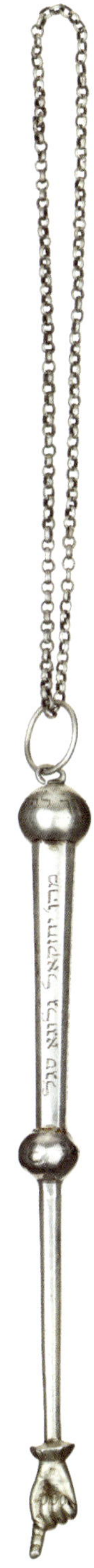
Cat. No. 204

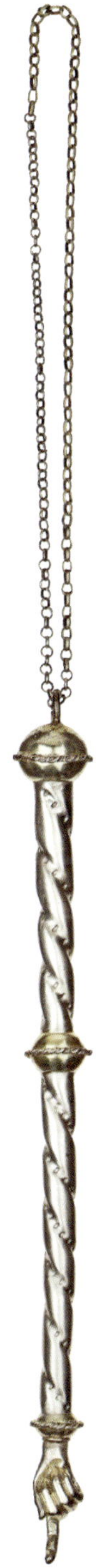
Cat. No. 205

Cat. No. 206
Torah Pointer
Inv. No. JMP 013.540
Silver, repoussé, cast
No maker's mark, Bohemia [?], early 19th century
Length: 250 mm, diameter: 22 mm
Hallmarks: unmarked
Without inscriptions.
Collection point: Dobříš

Cat. No. 207
Torah Pointer
Inv. No. JMP 007.395
Silver, repoussé, cast
Maker ML, Poland [?], early 19th century
Length: 274 mm, diameter: 32 mm
Hallmarks: 1. ML in rectangle, 2. purity mark 13 in shield
Without inscriptions.
Collection point: Uherský Ostroh

Cat. No. 208
Torah Pointer
Inv. No. JMP 012.398
Silver, repoussé, cast, engraving
Maker JB, Central Europe [Vienna?], early 19th century
Length: 245 mm, diameter: 27 mm
Hallmarks: 1. JB in circle, 2. JB in oval
Without inscriptions.
Collection point: Olomouc

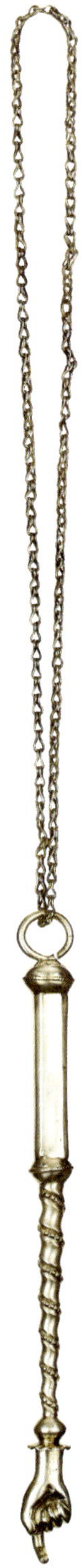

Cat. No. 206

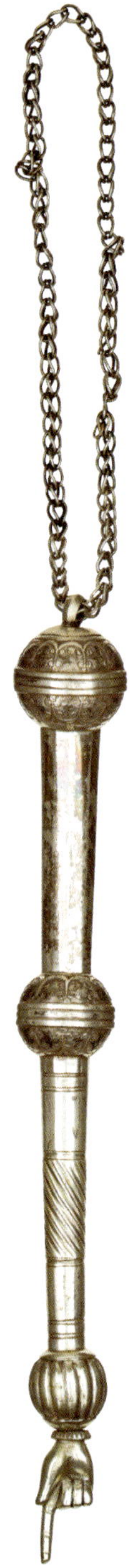

Cat. No. 207

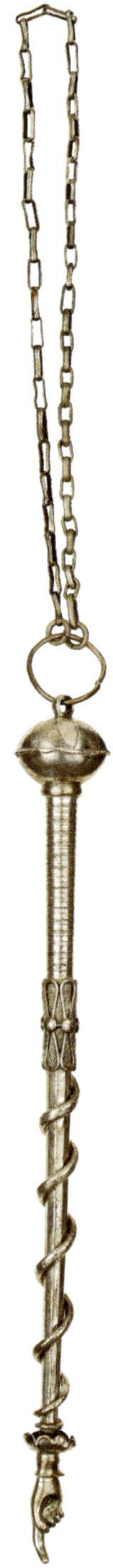

Cat. No. 208

Cat. No. 209
Torah Pointer
Inv. No. JMP 003.986
Silver, repoussé, cast
No maker's mark, Moravia [?], early 19th century
Length: 261 mm, diameter: 37 mm
Hallmarks: 1. recharge mark Vienna 1806–7
Donation inscription in Hebrew.
Translation:
This pointer belongs to the elder Nehemiah, son of H Benjamin Zeev of blessed memory, and his wife the lady Pesel, daughter of R Elazar.
Collection point: Central Jewish Museum for Moravia and Silesia, 1936–1938 in Nikolsburg

Cat. No. 210
Torah Pointer
Inv. No. JMP 017.843
Silver, repoussé, cast
Maker's mark illegible, Vienna, 1807
Length: 256 mm, diameter: 13 mm
Hallmarks: 1. illegible maker's mark, 2. hallmark Vienna 1807–9, 3. recharge mark Vienna 1806–7, 4. tax mark Prague 1810–24
Without inscriptions.
Collection point: Vlašim

Cat. No. 211
Torah Pointer
Inv. No. JMP 010.705
Silver, repoussé, cast, parcel-gilt,
Maker AG [?], Opava, 1810
Length: 251 mm, diameter: 22 mm
Hallmarks: 1. AG [?] in oval, 2. hallmark Opava 1810, 3. tax mark Opava 1810–24
Without inscriptions.
Collection point: Dvůr Králové nad Labem

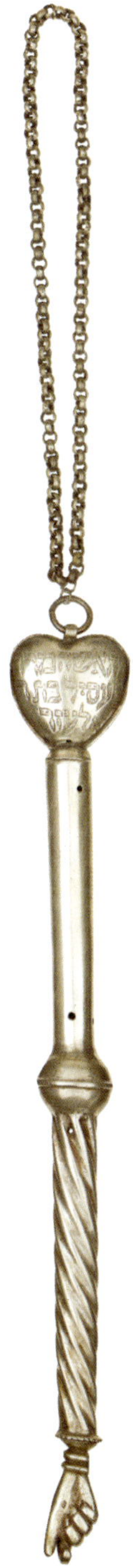

Cat. No. 209

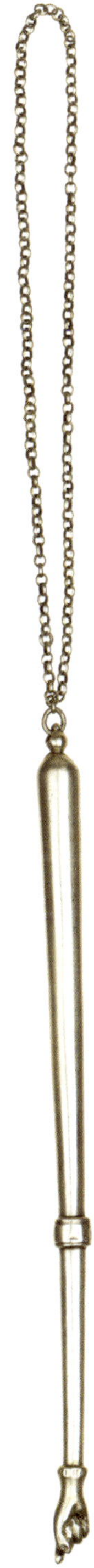

Cat. No. 210

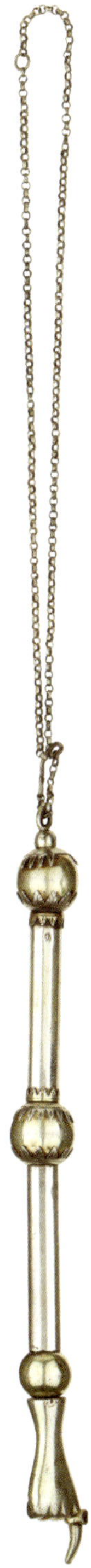

Cat. No. 211

Cat. No. 212
Torah Pointer
Inv. No. JMP 037.742
Silver, repoussé, cast
Jan Fleischmann, Prague, 1810
Length: 255 mm, diameter: 26 mm
Hallmarks: 1. IF in heart, 2. hallmark Prague 1810, 3. tax mark Prague 1810–24
Inscription in Hebrew.
Translation:
The elder KH Zalman, son of H KH Leizer Sch 'H [Schulhof] *of blessed memory.*
Collection point: Jewish Museum in Prague, 1906–1940

Cat. No. 213
Torah Pointer
Inv. No. JMP 037.406
Silver, repoussé, cast
No maker's mark, Vienna, 1810
Length: 294 mm, diameter: 21 mm
Hallmarks: 1. hallmark Vienna 1810, 2. tax mark Vienna 1810–24
Inscription in Hebrew.
Translation:
This was donated by HR Abraham Benjamin SGL with his wife Hayyah Sarah, may she live, in the year 574 a. s. c. [=1814].
Collection point: Batelov

Cat. No. 214
Torah Pointer
Inv. No. JMP 017.019
Silver, repoussé, cast,
Maker SHC [?], Linz, 1810–12
Length: 216 mm, diameter: 25 mm
Hallmarks: 1. SHC [?] in oval, 2. hallmark Linz 1810–12, 3. tax mark 1810–24
Inscription in Hebrew.
Translation:
Donated by Mr. [...], *son of P.* [in the year] *572* [a. s. c.] [= 1812] [text partially illegible].
Collection point: Týn nad Vltavou / Koloděje

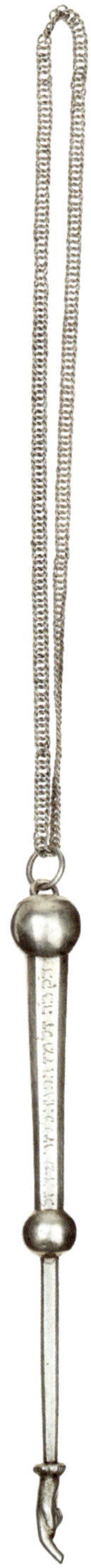
Cat. No. 212

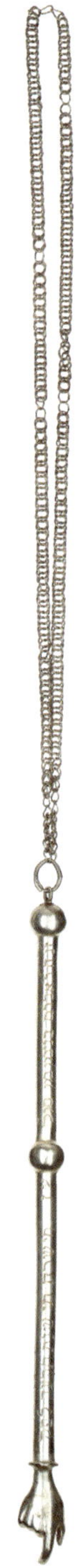
Cat. No. 213

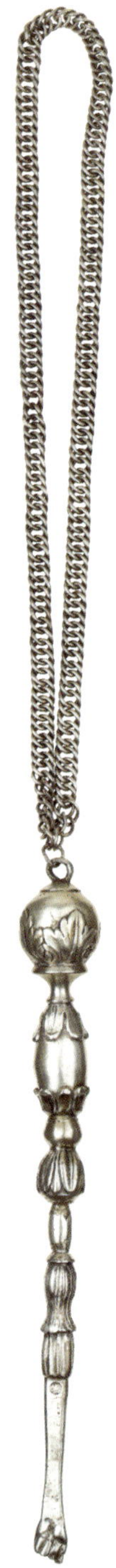
Cat. No. 214

Cat. No. 215
Torah Pointer
Inv. No. JMP 002.151
Silver, repoussé, cast
Antonín Neubert, Prague, 1813
Length: 265 mm, diameter: 23 mm
Hallmarks: 1. AN in oval, 2. hallmark Prague 1813, 3. tax mark Prague 1810–24
Donation inscription in Hebrew.
Translation:
This was donated by the Holy Society for Visiting the Sick, GR R Meir BR LB GSh Ziskind Horowitz, in the year 562 a. s. c. [= 1802] [sic].
Collection point: Mladá Boleslav

Cat. No. 216
Torah Pointer
Inv. No. JMP 023.019
Silver, repoussé, cast
Franz Kaltenmarker, Brno, 1813
Length: 204 mm, diameter: 21 mm
Hallmarks: 1. FK in oval, 2. hallmark Brno 1813, 3. tax mark Brno 1810–24
Without inscriptions.
Collection point: Havlíčkův Brod

Cat. No. 217
Torah Pointer
Inv. No. JMP 010.372
Silver, repoussé, cast, engraving, parcel-gilt
Franz Kaltenmarker, Brno, 1813
Length: 335 mm, diameter: 26 mm
Hallmarks: 1. FK in oval, 2. hallmark Brno 1813, 3. tax mark Brno 1810–24
Without inscriptions.
Collection point: Miroslav

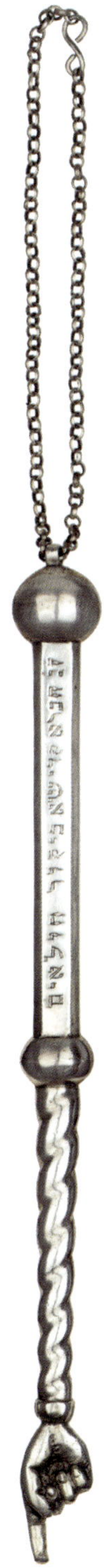

Cat. No. 215

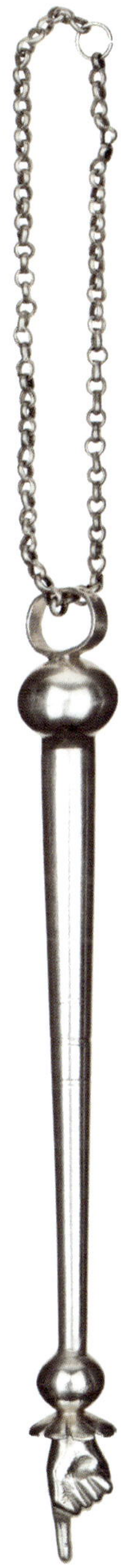

Cat. No. 216

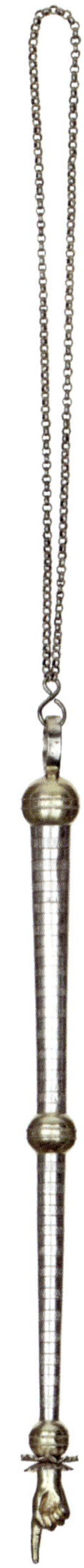

Cat. No. 217

Cat. No. 218
Torah Pointer
Inv. No. JMP 002.509
Silver, repoussé
No maker's mark, Brno, 1813
Length: 200 mm, diameter: 14 mm
Hallmarks: 1. hallmark Brno 1813,
2. tax mark Brno 1810–24
Without inscriptions.
Collection point: Kojetín

Cat. No. 219
Torah Pointer
Inv. No. JMP 017.017
Silver, repoussé, cast
Michal Samuel Goldschmid, Prague, 1814
Length: 203 mm, diameter: 19 mm
Hallmarks: 1. MG in rectangle, 2. hallmark
Prague 1814, 3. tax mark 1810–24
Donation inscription in Hebrew.
Translation:
This was donated by HRR Zanwil, son of K Simhah of blessed memory, with his wife the lady Gitl, may she live, for the Holy Benevolent Society [the Burial Society], *in the year 576 a. s. c.* [= 1816] *from the holy community Koloděje.*
Collection point: Týn nad Vltavou / Koloděje

Cat. No. 220
Torah Pointer
Inv. No. JMP 032.451
Silver, repoussé, cast
Antonín Novák [?], Prague, 1814–15
Length: 267 mm, diameter: 26 mm
Hallmarks: 1. AN in oval, 2. hallmark Prague
1814–15, 3. tax mark 1810–24
Donation inscription in Hebrew.
Translation:
This was donated by Edler von Lämel, may he live, for the synagogue in Postřižín in the year 575 a. s. c. [= 1815].
Collection point: Prague, Old-New Synagogue

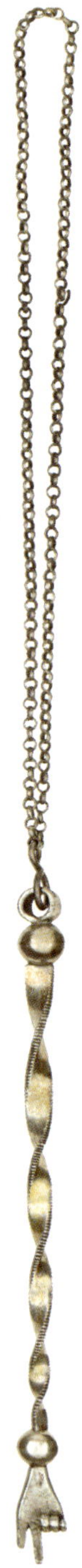
Cat. No. 218

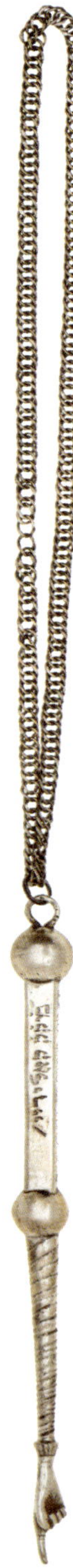
Cat. No. 219

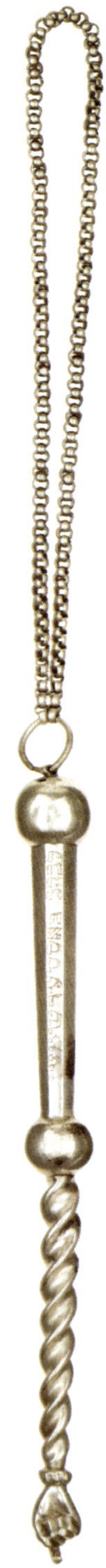
Cat. No. 220

Cat. No. 221
Torah Pointer
Inv. No. JMP 001.928
Silver, repoussé, cast
Maker's mark illegible [probably Franz Kaltenmarker], Brno, 1815
Length: 213 mm, diameter: 22 mm
Hallmarks: 1. illegible maker's mark, 2. hallmark Brno 1815, 3. tax mark Brno 1810–24
Without inscriptions.
Collection point: Polná

Cat. No. 222
Torah Pointer
Inv. No. JMP 004.468
Silver, repoussé, cast
Franz Kaltenmarker, Brno, 1815
Length: 257 mm, diameter: 15 mm
Hallmarks: 1. FK in oval, 2. hallmark Brno 1815, 3. tax mark Brno 1810–24
Without inscriptions.
Collection point: Třebíč

Cat. No. 223
Torah Pointer
Inv. No. JMP 017.545
Silver, repoussé, cast
Maker IN, Prague, 1816
Length: 251 mm, diameter: 24 mm
Hallmarks: 1. IN in oval, 2. hallmark Prague 1816, 3. tax mark Prague 1810–24
Donation inscription in Hebrew.
Translation:
This silver pointer belongs to K R David Natan, may he live, and his virtuous wife. To the good memory of lady Rachel Böhm, peace to her, from Svojšín.
Collection point: Prague, Klausen Synagogue

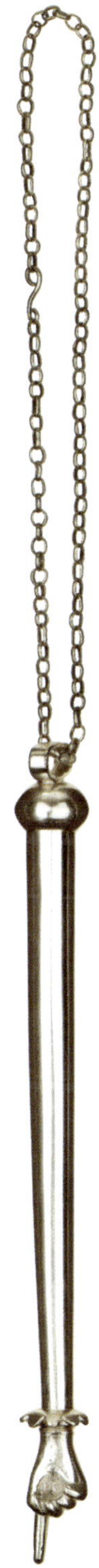

Cat. No. 221

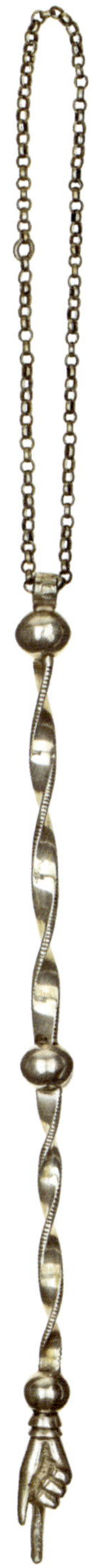

Cat. No. 222

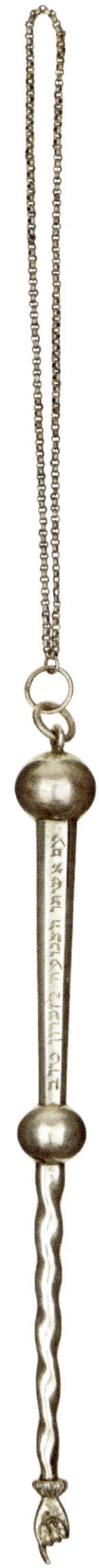

Cat. No. 223

Cat. No. 224
Torah Pointer
Inv. No. JMP 004.263
Silver, repoussé, cast
No maker's mark, Opava [?], 1810–24
Length: 305 mm, diameter: 36 mm
Hallmarks: 1. tax mark Opava 1810–24
Without inscriptions.
Collection point: Prostějov

Cat. No. 225
Torah Pointer
Inv. No. JMP 010.374
Silver, repoussé, cast
No maker's mark, Vienna, 1817
Length: 268 mm, diameter: 17 mm
Hallmarks: 1. hallmark Vienna 1817,
2. tax mark Vienna 1810–24
Without inscriptions.
Collection point: Boskovice

Cat. No. 226
Torah Pointer
Inv. No. JMP 037.580
Silver, repoussé, cast
Karel Skřemenec, Prague, 1817
Length: 161 mm, diameter: 18 mm
Hallmarks: 1. CS in rectangle, 2. hallmark
Prague 1817, 3. tax mark Prague 1810–24
Donation inscription in Hebrew.
Translation:
A gift from the distinguished R Moses Gerschelse and his wife the lady Estherl, daughter of R Elijah Mendel Bunzl for the bar mitzvah of his son, the boy Abraham, in the year 590 a. s. c. [= 1830].
Collection point: Prague

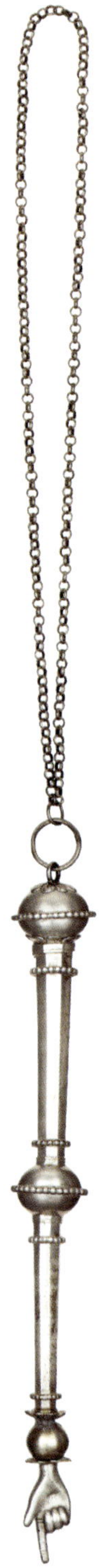
Cat. No. 224

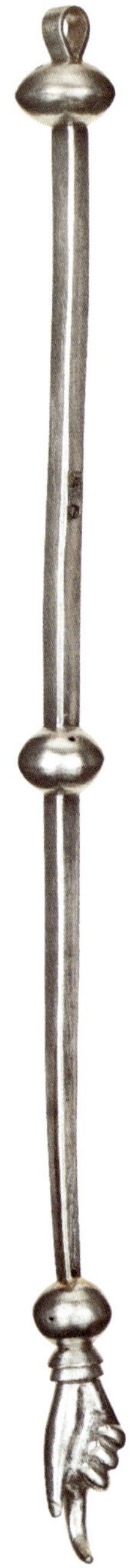
Cat. No. 225

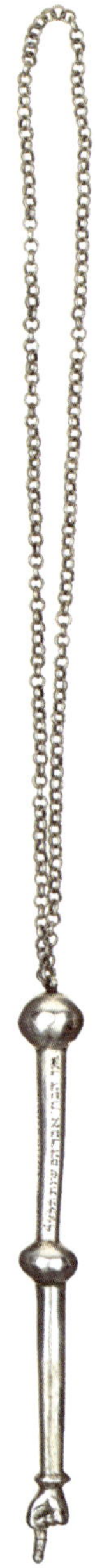
Cat. No. 226

Cat. No. 227
Torah Pointer
Inv. No. JMP 002.955
Silver, repoussé, cast, filigree
No maker's mark, Olomouc, 1817
Length: 244 mm, diameter: 25 mm
Hallmarks: 1. hallmark Olomouc 1817,
2. tax mark 1810–24
Without inscriptions.
Collection point: Lipník nad Bečvou

Cat. No. 228
Torah Pointer
Inv. No. JMP 037.501
Silver, repoussé, cast, engraving
No maker's mark, Bohemia, 1810–24
Length: 298 mm, diameter: 27 mm
Hallmarks: 1. tax mark Prague 1810–24
Without inscriptions.
Collection point: Prague

Cat. No. 229
Torah Pointer
Inv. No. JMP 007.404
Silver, hammered, cast
Johann Würth, Vienna, 1814–19
Length: 183 mm, diameter: 20 mm
Hallmarks: 1. JW in rectangle,
2. hallmark Vienna 1814–19,
3. tax mark Vienna 1810–24
Donation inscription in Hebrew.
Translation:
This was donated by HRR Isaac Lamberg with his wife the lady Esther, may she live.
Collection point: Uherský Ostroh

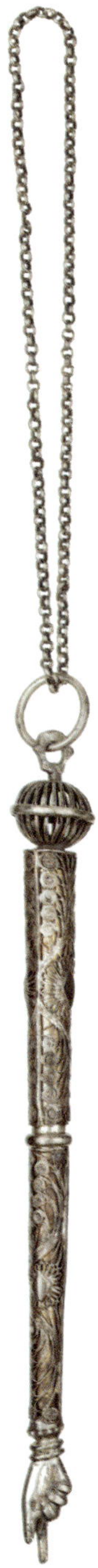

Cat. No. 227

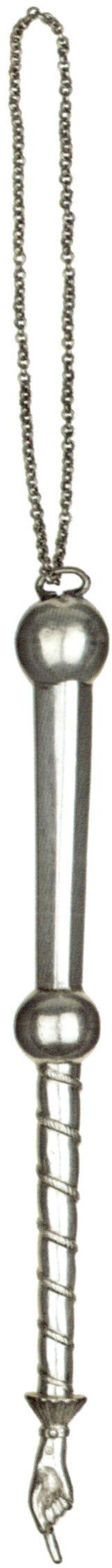

Cat. No. 228

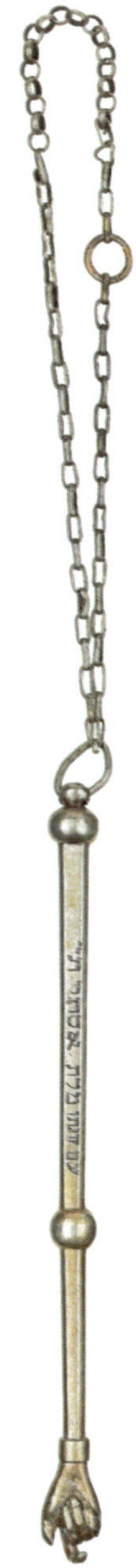

Cat. No. 229

Cat. No. 230
Torah Pointer
Inv. No. JMP 010.455
Silver, repoussé, cast
Maker AD [Andreas Domeni?], Olomouc [?], 1814–19
Length: 242 mm, diameter: 30 mm
Hallmarks: 1. AD in oval, 2. hallmark Olomouc [?] 1814–19, 3. tax mark 1810–24
Without inscriptions.
Collection point: Místek

Cat. No. 231
Torah Pointer
Inv. No. JMP 066.682
Silver, repoussé, cast
Antonín Kába, Prague, 1818
Length: 253 mm, diameter: 22 mm
Hallmarks: 1. AK in oval, 2. hallmark Prague 1818, 3. tax mark 1810–24
Without inscriptions.
Collection point: Prague, Treuhandstelle

Cat. No. 232
Torah Pointer
Inv. No. JMP 046.044
Silver, repoussé, cast
Antonín Kába, Prague, 1818
Length: 279 mm, diameter: 28 mm
Hallmarks: 1. AK in oval, 2. hallmark Prague 1818, 3. tax mark 1810–24
Donation inscription in Hebrew.
Translation:
"And [this] *shall serve you as a sign on your hand."* [Exod. 13:9] *It belongs to the Holy Society of the Seven Called in the Pinkas Synagogue, in the year 572 a. s. c.* [= 1812] [sic].
Collection point: Prague, Pinkas Synagogue

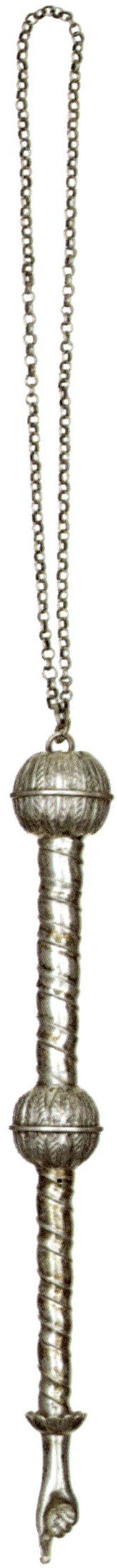

Cat. No. 230

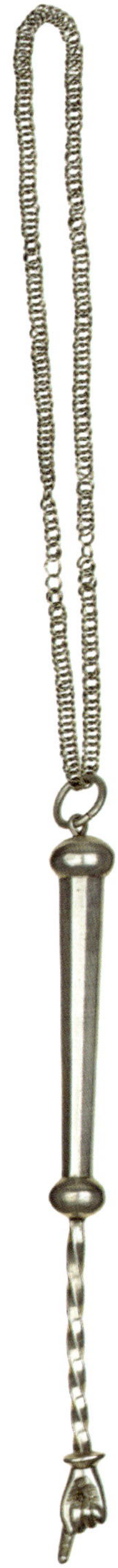

Cat. No. 231

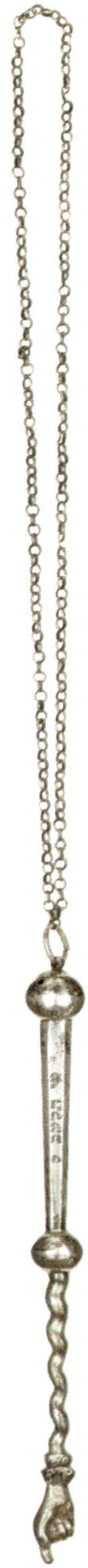

Cat. No. 232

Cat. No. 233
Torah Pointer
Inv. No. JMP 010.618
Silver, repoussé, cast, engraving
Rafael Jonas Goldschmid, Prague, 1814–24
Length: 223 mm, diameter: 17 mm
Hallmarks: 1. RG in rectangle, 2. hallmark Prague 1814–24, 3. tax mark 1810–24
Without inscriptions.
Collection point: Mladá Vožice

Cat. No. 234
Torah Pointer
Inv. No. JMP 007.566
Silver, repoussé, cast
No maker's mark, Vienna, 1830–39
Length: 234 mm, diameter: 14 mm
Hallmarks: 1. hallmark Vienna 1830–39
Without inscriptions.
Collection point: Kojetín

Cat. No. 235
Torah Pointer
Inv. No. JMP 004.177
Silver, repoussé, cast
Maker AW, Vienna, 1838
Length: 243 mm, diameter: 30 mm
Hallmarks: 1. AW in rectangle,
2. hallmark Vienna 1838
Without inscriptions.
Collection point: Hořice

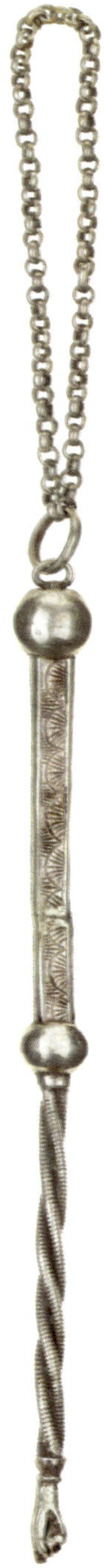

Cat. No. 233

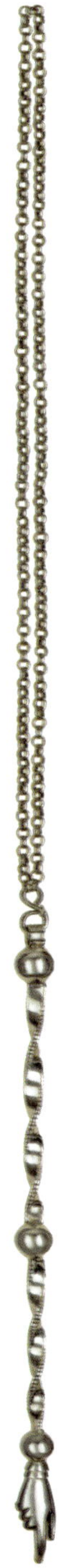

Cat. No. 234

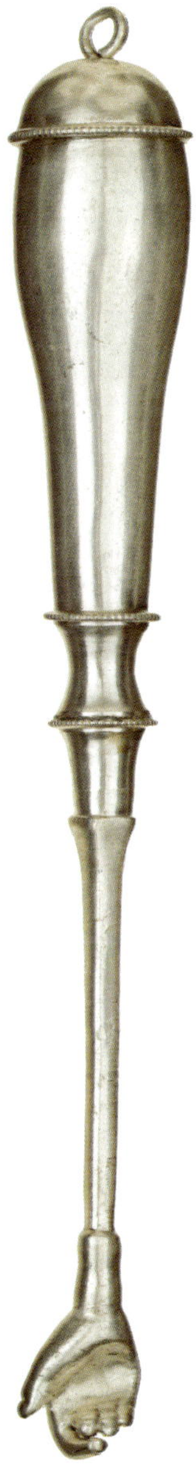

Cat. No. 235

Cat. No. 236
Torah Pointer
Inv. No. JMP 001.640
Silver, repoussé, cast, engraving
Tomáš Höpfel, Prague, 1840–41
Length: 290 mm, diameter: 25 mm
Hallmarks: 1. TH in oval,
2. hallmark Prague 1840
Inscription in Hebrew.
Translation:
From the Holy Society [of Singers] *of Psalms in the holy community Turnov, may God protect it, in the year 601 a. s. c.* [= 1841].
Collection point: Turnov

Cat. No. 237
Torah Pointer
Inv. No. JMP 001.980
Silver, repoussé, cast, engraving
Maker IS, Prague, 1844
Length: 315 mm, diameter: 27 mm
Hallmarks: 1. IS in oval,
2. hallmark Prague 1844
Without inscriptions.
Collection point: Rokycany

Cat. No. 238
Torah Pointer
Inv. No. JMP 066.605
Silver, repoussé, cast
Maker TR, Vienna, ca. 1840–50
Length: 220 mm, diameter: 22 mm
Hallmarks: 1. TR in rectangle,
2. hallmark Vienna 18[??]
Without inscriptions.
Collection point: Prague

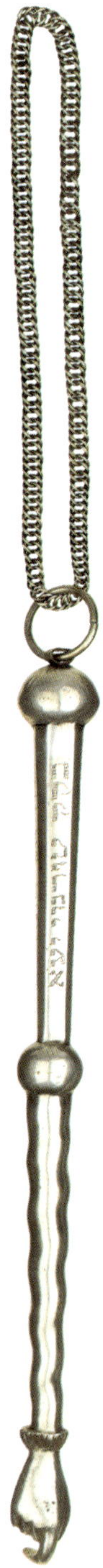
Cat. No. 236

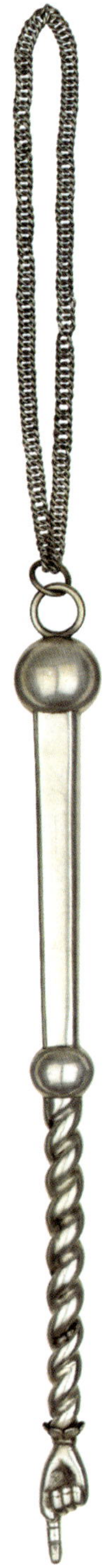
Cat. No. 237

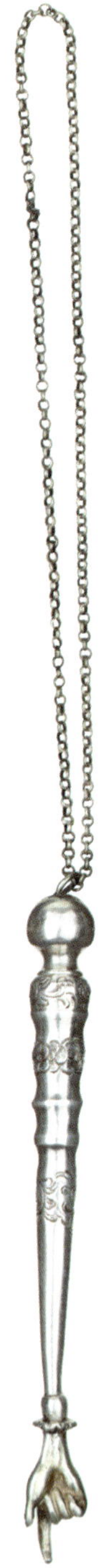
Cat. No. 238

Cat. No. 239
Torah Pointer
Inv. No. JMP 178.539
Silver, repoussé, cast
Tomáš Höpfel, Prague, 1840–49
Length: 278 mm, diameter: 24 mm
Hallmarks: 1. TH in oval,
2. hallmark Prague 184[?]
Without inscriptions.
Collection point: Prague

Cat. No. 240
Torah Pointer
Inv. No. JMP 003.965
Silver, repoussé, cast, filigree, originally parcel-gilt
No maker's mark, Eastern Europe, 19th century
Length: 278 mm, diameter: 24 mm
Hallmarks: unmarked
Inscription in Hebrew:
Sch. M. B. [?].
Collection point: Central Jewish Museum for Moravia and Silesia, 1936–1938 in Nikolsburg

Cat. No. 241
Torah Pointer
Inv. No. JMP 046.046
Silver, red coral, repoussé, cast, engraving
No maker's mark, Eastern Europe [?], 19th century
Length: 191 mm, diameter: 17 mm
Hallmarks: unmarked
Without inscriptions.
Collection point: Prague, Pinkas Synagogue

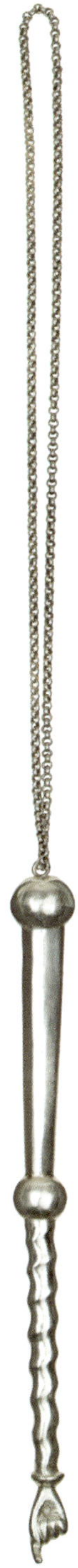

Cat. No. 239

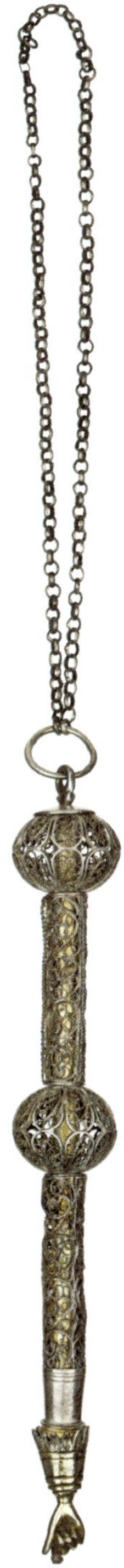

Cat. No. 240

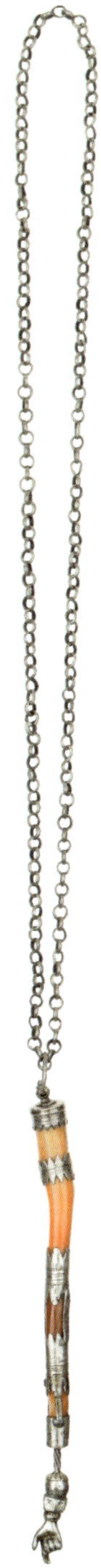

Cat. No. 241

Cat. No. 242
Torah Pointer
Inv. No. JMP 001.520
Silver, repoussé, cast, engraving
Maker CS, Vienna, 1842–62
Length: 301 mm, diameter: 29 mm
Hallmarks: 1. CS [unframed],
2. hallmark Vienna 18[?]2
Without inscriptions.
Collection point: Pacov

Cat. No. 243
Torah Pointer
Inv. No. JMP 032.327
Silver, repoussé, cast,
No maker's mark, Germany [?],
1853 [inscription]
Length: 218 mm, diameter: 14 mm
Hallmarks: unmarked
Donation inscription in Hebrew.
Translation:
This was donated by R Abraham with his wife the lady Leviah, may she live, in the holy community Geiering [Germany] *in the year 613 a. s. c.* [= 1853].
Collection point: Brno

Cat. No. 244
Torah Pointer
Inv. No. JMP 017.542
Silver, repoussé, cast
Josef Wieninger, Vienna, 1857
Length: 258 mm, diameter: 26 mm
Hallmarks: 1. JW in shield,
2. hallmark Vienna 1857
Donation inscription in Hebrew.
Translation:
This was donated by the elder Eizik Kohn, 619 a. s. c. [= 1859].
Collection point: Prague,
Klausen Synagogue

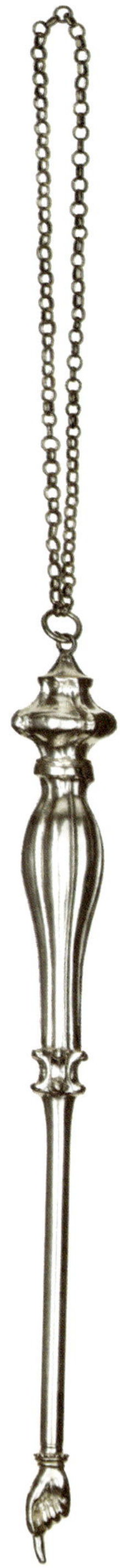
CAT. NO. 242

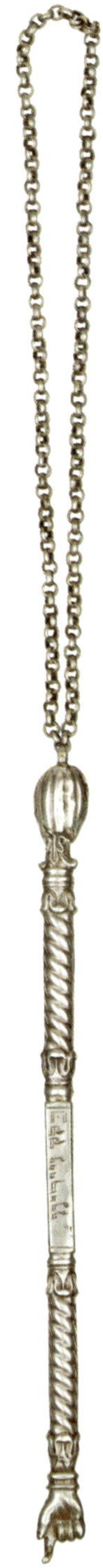
CAT. NO. 243

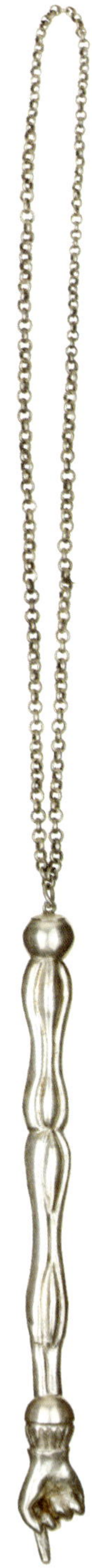
CAT. NO. 244

Cat. No. 245
Torah Pointer
Inv. No. JMP 001.929
Silver, repoussé, cast
Thomas Dub, Vienna, 1862
Length: 250 mm, diameter: 22 mm
Hallmarks: 1. TD in rectangle,
2. hallmark Vienna 1862
Donation inscription in Hebrew.
Translation:
A gift of the sage Jonathan Basch for the Holy Benevolent Society [the Burial Society] *on the day of the bar mitzvah of his son, the boy Menahem Isaac, parsha Shoftim, 620 a. s. c.* [= Aug. 25, 1860] [sic].
Collection point: Polná

Cat. No. 246
Torah Pointer
Inv. No. JMP 010.902
Silver, repoussé, cast, parcel-gilt
Jan Novotný, Prague, 1860–66
Length: 279 mm, diameter: 25 mm
Hallmarks: 1. JN in oval,
2. hallmark Prague 186[?]
Without inscriptions.
Collection point: Sedlčany

Cat. No. 247
Torah Pointer
Inv. No. JMP 003.604
Silver, repoussé, cast
Thomas Dub, Vienna, 1863
Length: 265 mm, diameter: 18 mm
Hallmarks: 1. TD in rectangle,
2. hallmark Vienna 1863
Without inscriptions.
Collection point: Brno

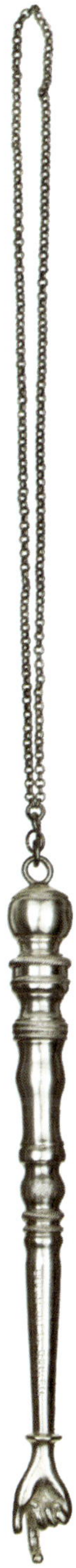

Cat. No. 245

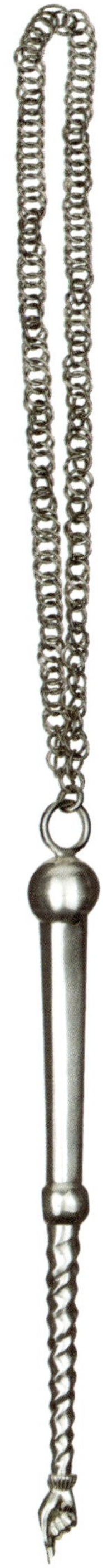

Cat. No. 246

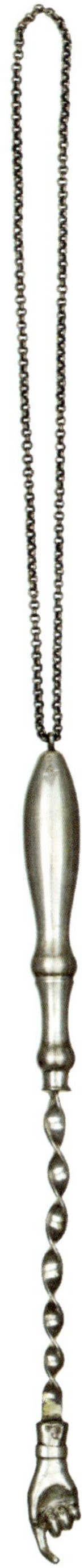

Cat. No. 247

Cat. No. 248
Torah Pointer
Inv. No. JMP 010.367
Silver, repoussé, cast
Maker AW, Vienna, 1867–71
Length: 231 mm, diameter: 26 mm
Hallmarks: 1. AW in rectangle,
2. Austro-Hungary 1867–71,
3. localization letter A (Vienna) 1867–71
Without inscriptions.
Collection point: Miroslav

Cat. No. 249
Torah Pointer
Inv. No. JMP 004.371
Silver, repoussé, cast
Maker KM, Prague, 1867–70
Length: 300 mm, diameter: 30 mm
Hallmarks: 1. KM in oval, 2. Austro-Hungary 1867–71, 3. localization letter C [Prague] 1867–71
Donation inscription in Hebrew.
Translation:
This was donated by the esteemed lady Tziperl, daughter of KH Wolf Stein of blessed memory, widow of KH Wolf Stein of blessed memory and of her first husband KH Wolf Fried of blessed memory, to the glory of the Lord and to the glory of the Torah, the holy community Koleč, in the year 630 a. s. c. [= 1870].
Collection point: Slaný

Cat. No. 250
Torah Pointer
Inv. No. JMP 037.512
Silver, repoussé, cast
Maker EK, Prague, 1867–71
Length: 220 mm, diameter: 24 mm
Hallmarks: 1. EK [unframed],
2. Austro-Hungary 1867–71,
3. localization letter C [Prague] 1867–71
Without inscriptions.
Collection point: Prague

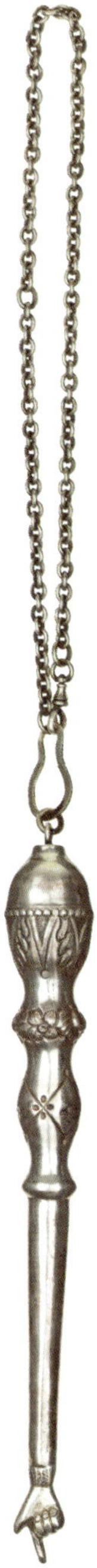
Cat. No. 248

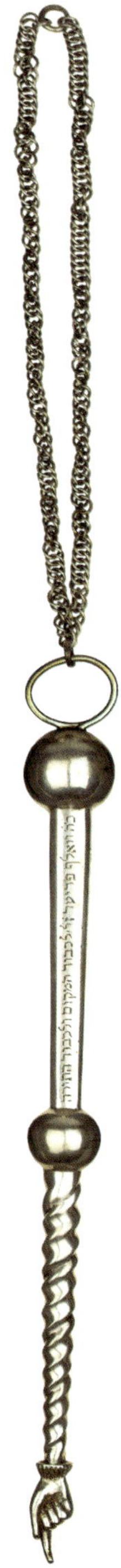
Cat. No. 249

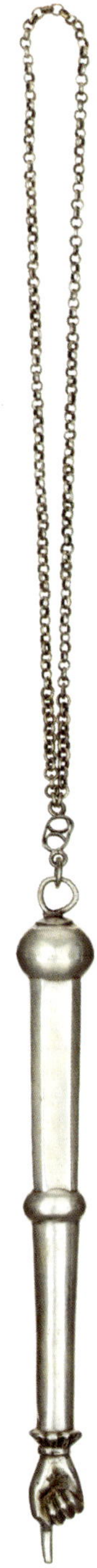
Cat. No. 250

Cat. No. 251
Torah Pointer
Inv. No. JMP 012.262
Silver, repoussé, cast, engraving
Maker JE, Vienna, 1867–71
Length: 300 mm, diameter: 38 mm
Hallmarks: 1. JE in rectangle,
2. Austro-Hungary 1867–71
Donation inscription in Hebrew.
Translation:
For the soul of the girl Leah, daughter of KH Nathan Fischer.
Collection point: Jevíčko

Cat. No. 252
Torah Pointer
Inv. No. JMP 037.963
Silver, repoussé, cast
Maker KM, Prague, 1867–71
Length: 179 mm, diameter: 21 mm
Hallmarks: 1. KM in oval,
2. Austro-Hungary 1867–71,
3. localization letter C [Prague] 1867–71
Donation inscription in Hebrew.
Translation:
Abraham Lichtenstern.
Collection point: Prague, Pinkas Synagogue

Cat. No. 253
Torah Pointer
Inv. No. JMP 001.642
Silver, repoussé, cast, parcel-gilt
Maker JZ, Vienna, after 1871
Length: 261 mm, diameter: 30 mm
Hallmarks: 1. JZ in rectangle,
2. Austro-Hungary [Vienna] after 1871
Without inscriptions.
Collection point: Turnov

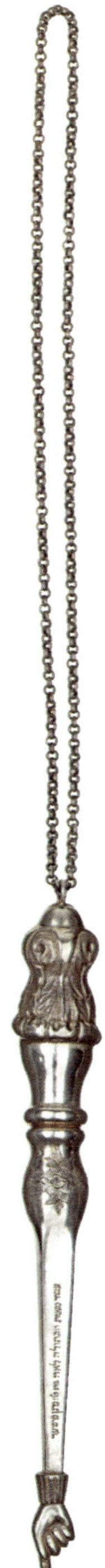

Cat. No. 251

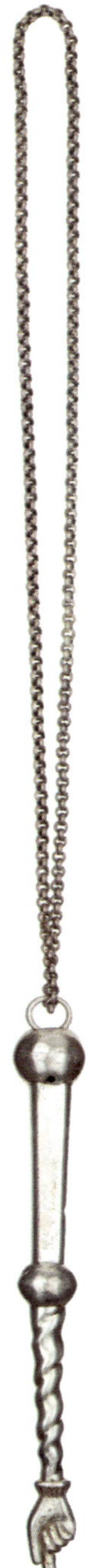

Cat. No. 252

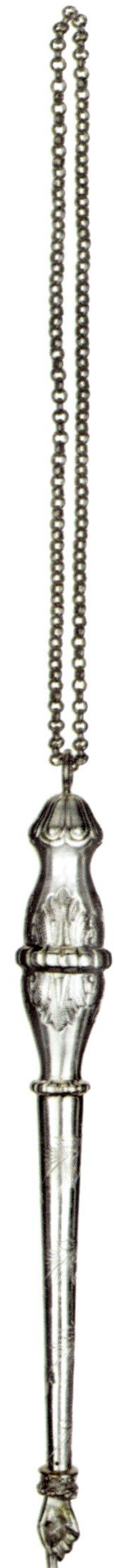

Cat. No. 253

Cat. No. 254
Torah Pointer
Inv. No. JMP 037.489
Silver, repoussé, cast
Maker VN, Prague, after 1871
Length: 245 mm, diameter: 23 mm
Hallmarks: 1. VN in oval,
2. Austro-Hungary [Prague] after 1871
Donation inscription in Hebrew.
Translation:
This was donated by KH Jacob, son of Joseph and his wife, peace to her, the lady Pesl Raubitzek. The Israelite Temple Society in Prague VII, 5663 [= 1903].
Collection point: Prague

Cat. No. 255
Torah Pointer
Inv. No. JMP 007.006
Silver, repoussé, cast, engraving
Maker HS, Vienna, after 1871
Length: 284 mm, diameter: 28 mm
Hallmarks: 1. HS in rectangle,
2. Austro-Hungary [Vienna] after 1871
Without inscriptions.
Collection point: Hodonín

Cat. No. 256
Torah Pointer
Inv. No. JMP 002.714
Silver, repoussé, cast, engraving
Maker TD [Thomas Dub Co.?],
Vienna, after 1871
Length: 296 mm, diameter: 26 mm
Hallmarks: 1. TD in rectangle,
2. Austro-Hungary [Vienna] after 1871
Without inscriptions.
Collection point: Prostějov

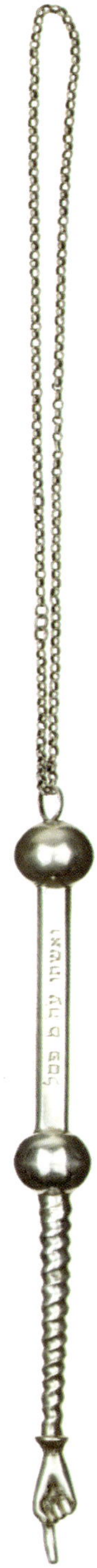
Cat. No. 254

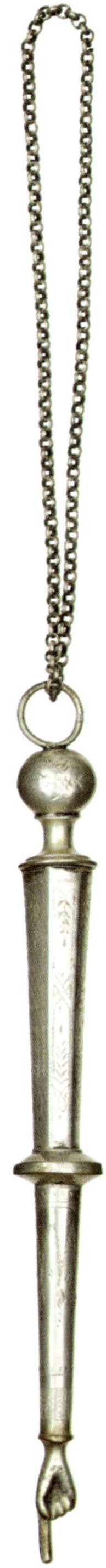
Cat. No. 255

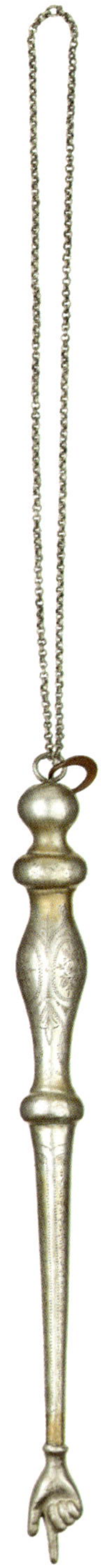
Cat. No. 256

Cat. No. 257
Torah Pointer
Inv. No. JMP 010.452
Silver, repoussé, cast, originally parcel-gilt
Maker AC, Austro-Hungary, after 1871
Length: 334 mm, diameter: 31 mm
Hallmarks: 1. AC in rectangle,
2. Austro-Hungary after 1871
Without inscriptions.
Collection point: Místek

Cat. No. 258
Torah Pointer
Inv. No. JMP 012.648
Silver, repoussé, cast, parcel-gilt
Hermann Südfeld (company), Vienna, after 1871
Length: 290 mm, diameter: 42 mm
Hallmarks: 1. HS in rectangle,
2. Austro-Hungary [Vienna] after 1871
The initials *J. P. B.* are in Latin script.
Collection point: Nový Bydžov

Cat. No. 259
Torah Pointer
Inv. No. JMP 004.429
Silver, repoussé, cast, parcel-gilt
Maker JE, Vienna, after 1871
Length: 270 mm, diameter: 29 mm
Hallmarks: 1. JE in rectangle,
2. Austro-Hungary [Vienna] after 1871,
3. localization letter A [Vienna]
Without inscriptions.
Collection point: Rychnov nad Kněžnou

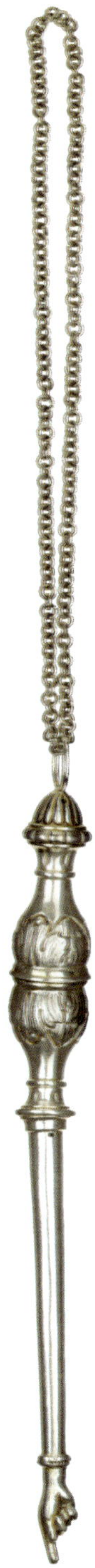

Cat. No. 257

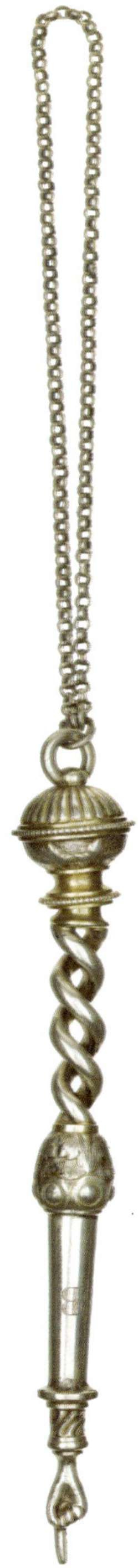

Cat. No. 258

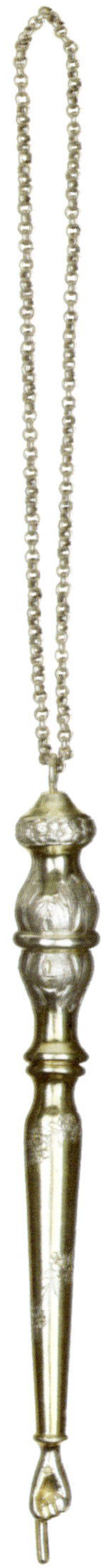

Cat. No. 259

Cat. No. 260
Torah Pointer
Inv. No. JMP 003.617
Silver, repoussé, cast
Vincenz Czokally (company), Vienna, after 1871
Length: 201 mm, diameter: 27 mm
Hallmarks: 1. VC in rectangle,
2. Austro-Hungary [Vienna] after 1871
Without inscriptions.
Collection point: Brno

Cat. No. 261
Torah Pointer
Inv. No. JMP 004.240
Silver, repoussé, cast
Maker RK, Prague, after 1871
Length: 190 mm, diameter: 25 mm
Hallmarks: 1. RK in rectangle,
2. Austro-Hungary [Prague] after 1871
Donation inscription in Hebrew.
Translation:
This was donated by Moses Lederer and his wife, Bresnitz.
Collection point: Březnice

Cat. No. 262
Torah Pointer
Inv. No. JMP 001.666
Silver, repoussé, cast
Maker JZ, Vienna, 1872–82
Length: 373 mm, diameter: 48 mm
Hallmarks: 1. JZ in rectangle,
2. Austro-Hungary [Vienna] after 1871,
3. localization letter A [Vienna]
Donation inscription in Hebrew.
Translation:
This was donated by KH Jacob, son of KH Isaac Freund, and his wife Hawwah, daughter of KH Leib Kohn, for the holy community Brandýs nad Labem in the year 642 a. s. c. [= 1882].
Collection point: Brandýs nad Labem / Kostelec nad Labem

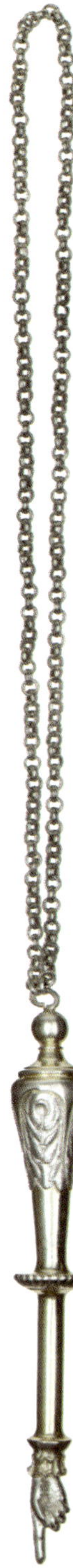
Cat. No. 260

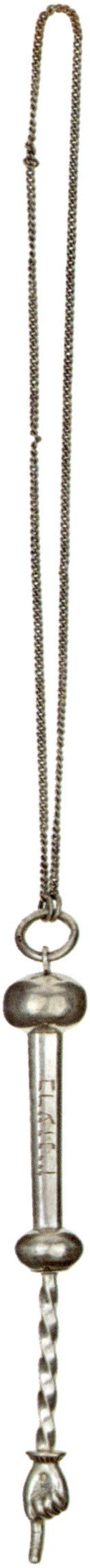
Cat. No. 261

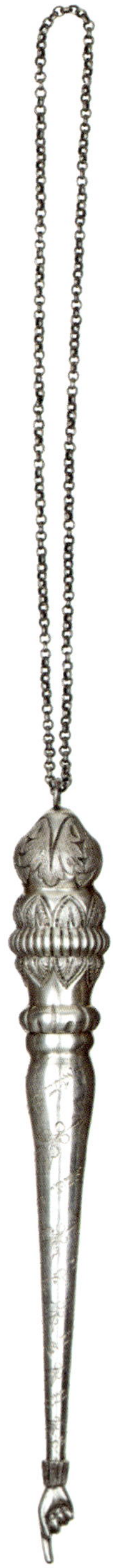
Cat. No. 262

Cat. No. 263
Torah Pointer
Inv. No. JMP 001.185
Silver, repoussé, cast
Maker VN, Prague, 1872–87
Length: 262 mm, diameter: 29 mm
Hallmarks: 1. VN in oval,
2. Austro-Hungary [Prague] after 1871
Donation inscription written in Latin script:
Joseph & Franziska Taussig 1887.
Collection point: Kladno

Cat. No. 264
Torah Pointer
Inv. No. JMP 010.604
Silver, repoussé, cast, originally parcel-gilt
Maker HS [?], Vienna, 1872–92
Length: 269 mm, diameter: 28 mm
Hallmarks: 1. HS [?] in rectangle,
2. Austro-Hungary [Vienna] after 1871,
3. Austro-Hungary [Vienna] after 1871
[small version]
Donation inscription in Hebrew.
Translation:
This was donated by the sage R Solomon, son of the sage R Hayyim Fleischner, with his wife the lady Figlah, daughter of the sage R Abraham David Falkenau, on the day of the bar mitzvah of their son the boy Hayyim. On the holy Shabbat, parsha Zachor, in the year 652 a. s. c. [= March 12, 1892].
Collection point: Jičín

Cat. No. 265
Torah Pointer
Inv. No. JMP 102.447
Silver, repoussé, cast
Maker KG, Prague, after 1871
Length: 286 mm, diameter: 32 mm
Hallmarks: 1. KG in rectangle,
2. Austro-Hungary [Prague] after 1871,
3. localization letter C [Prague]
Donation inscription in Hebrew.
Translation:
This is a gift from the eminent David Jellinek and his wife the lady Rachel, in the year 678 a. s. c. [= 1918].
Collection point: Praha

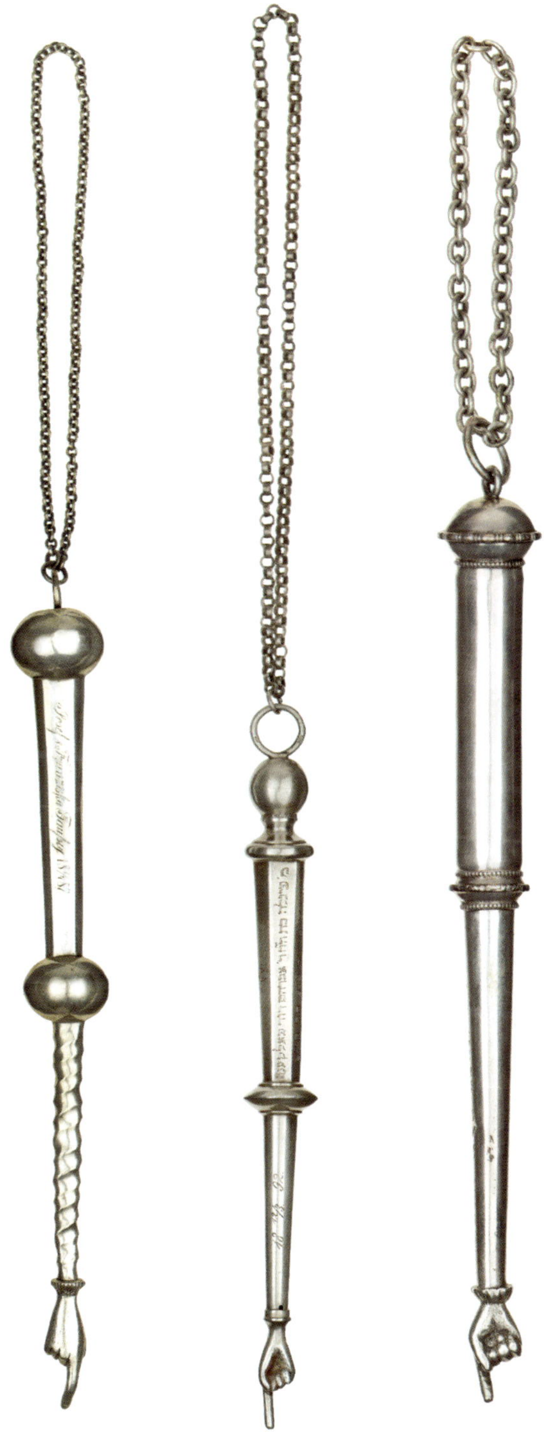

Cat. No. 263 Cat. No. 264 Cat. No. 265

Cat. No. 266
Torah Pointer
Inv. No. JMP 037.591
Silver, repoussé, cast
No maker's mark, Germany,
turn of 19th/20th century
Length: 241 mm, diameter: 22 mm
Hallmarks: 1. German hallmark for silver,
2. purity mark 800
Without inscriptions.
Collection point: Prague

Cat. No. 267
Torah Pointer
Inv. No. JMP 010.424
Silver, filigree, cast
Bezalel workshops [?], Palestine, early 20th century
Length: 205 mm, diameter: 23 mm
Hallmarks: 1. import mark Austro-Hungary
[Vienna] 1902–21
Without inscriptions.
Collection point: Kutná Hora

Cat. No. 268
Torah Pointer
Inv. No. JMP 002.715
Silver, repoussé, cast, filigree, glass stones
Bezalel workshops, Palestine, early 20th century
Length: 281 mm, diameter: 28 mm
Hallmarks: 1. import mark Austro-Hungary
[unclear city letter] 1902–21
Maker’s mark in Hebrew: *Bezalel, Jerusalem.*
Collection point: Prostějov

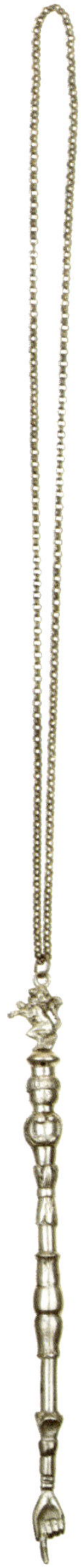
Cat. No. 266

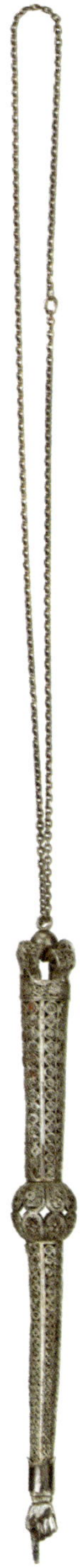
Cat. No. 267

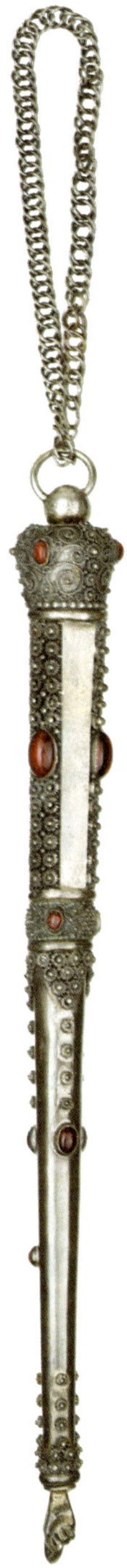
Cat. No. 268

Cat. No. 269
Torah Pointer
Inv. No. JMP 037.502
Silver, filigree, cast
Bezalel workshops, Palestine, 1912 [inscription]
Length: 313 mm, diameter: 32 mm
Hallmarks: 1. import mark Austro-Hungary
[Prague] 1902–20
Donation inscription in German in Latin script
and maker's mark in Hebrew: *Bezalel.*
Translation:
1872–1912. For Mr. Löwi Hammerschlag as appreciation and gratitude for his service in the function of chairman of the Burial Society [CHK] *from the Women's Association.*
Collection point: Prague

Cat. No. 270
Torah Pointer
Inv. No. JMP 007.038
Silver, repoussé, cast, engraving
Alfred Pollak (company), Prague, 1921–28
Length: 264 mm, diameter: 25 mm
Hallmarks: 1. AP in rectangle,
2. hallmark Czechoslovakia 1921–28
Inscription in Hebrew.
Translation:
The holy community Přerov 688 a. s. c. [= 1928].
Collection point: Přerov

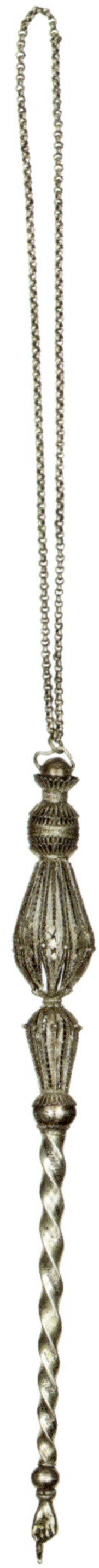

Cat. No. 269

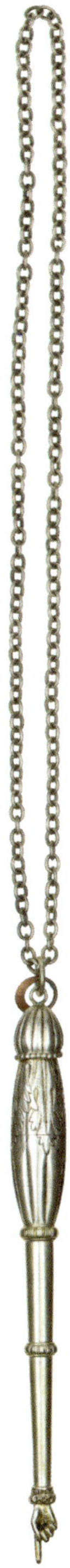

Cat. No. 270

V. Levite Pitchers and Basins

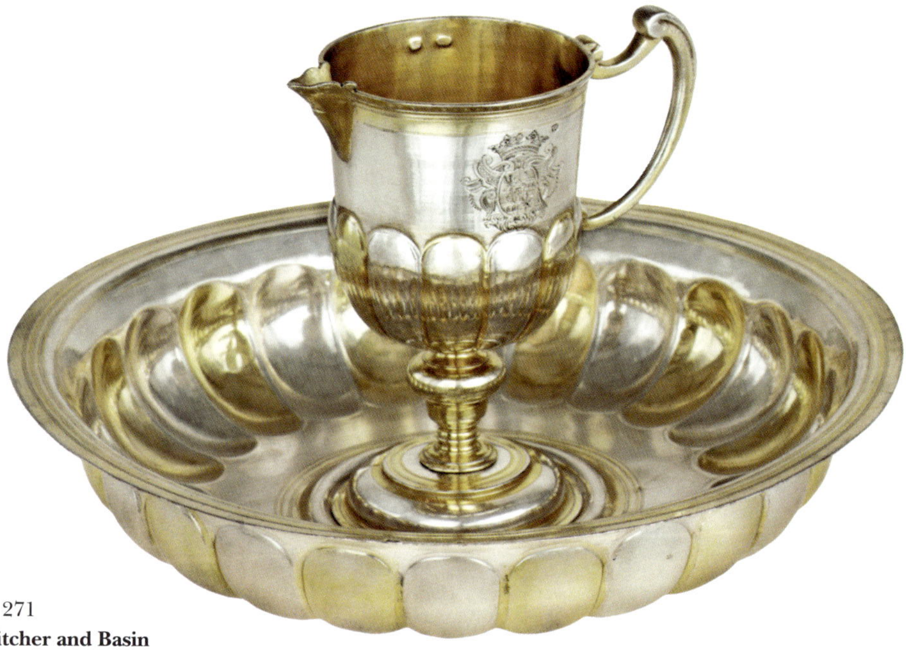

Cat. No. 271
Levite Pitcher and Basin
Inv. No. JMP 003.804/01, 02
Silver, repoussé, engraving, parcel-gilt
Johann Wagner, Augsburg, 1690–95
Levite pitcher [/01]: height: 155 mm, width: 140 mm
Basin [/02]: diameter: 280 mm
Hallmarks: 1. IW in oval, 2. hallmark Augsburg 1690–95, 3. recharge mark Brno 1806–7, 4. release mark 1809–10
Without inscriptions.
Collection point: Central Jewish Museum for Moravia and Silesia, 1936–1938 in Nikolsburg

Cat. No. 272

Levite Pitcher and Basin

Inv. No. JMP 046.036/01, 02

Silver, repoussé, cast, engraving

Jan Jiří Lux, Prague, 1702

Levite pitcher [/01]:

height: 248 mm, width: 195 mm

Basin [/02]: diameter: 460 mm

Hallmarks: 1. IGL in shield,

2. hallmark Prague – Malá Strana 1702,

3. recharge mark Prague 1806–7,

4. release mark 1809–10

Donation inscription in Hebrew.

Translation:

Hallmarked at the behest of the Emperor, may his majesty be exalted, by these three brothers: the distinguished R Kopman and R Ephraim and R Hayyim, son of the distinguished KH Isaac Epstein SGL of blessed memory, custodian of Pinkas Synagogue, the year 570 a. s. c. [= 1810].

Collection point: Prague, Pinkas Synagogue

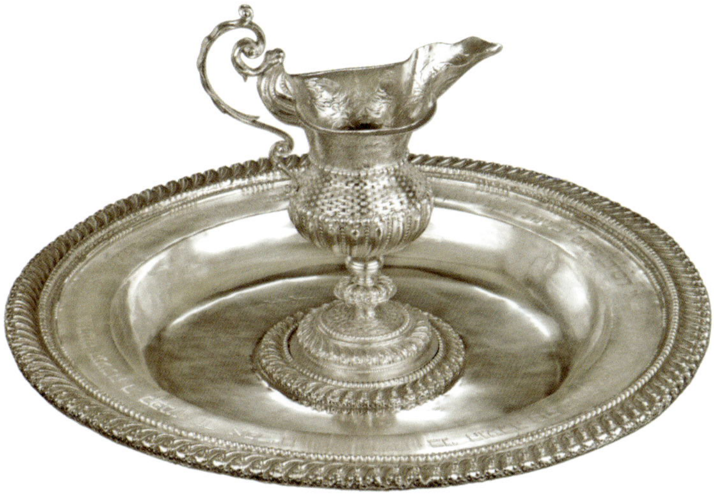

Cat. No. 272

Cat. No. 273

Levite Pitcher and Basin

Inv. No. JMP 032.420/01, 02

Silver, repoussé

Josef Jakub Raspel, Prague, 1780

Levite pitcher [/01]: height: 156 mm, width: 122 mm

Basin [/02]: length: 308 mm, width: 217 mm

Hallmarks: 1. IR in irregular shape,

2. hallmark Prague 1780,

3. recharge mark Prague 1806–7,

4. release mark 1809–10

Donation inscription in Hebrew.

Translation:

A gift of KH Simon, son of R Leib SGL Kuh [on the pitcher]. *A gift of KH Simon, R Leib SGL Kuh, in the Old-New Synagogue* [on the basin].

Collection point: Prague, Old-New Synagogue

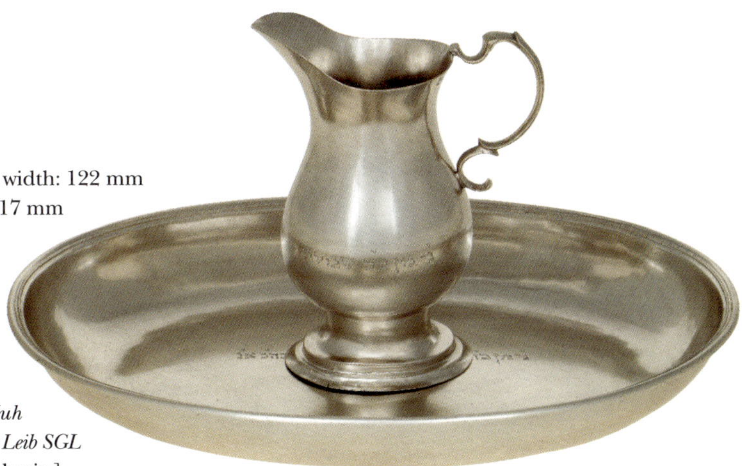

Cat. No. 273

Cat. No. 274
Levite Pitcher and Basin
Inv. No. JMP 037.546/01, 02
Silver, repoussé, engraving
Antonín Kába, Prague, 1818
Levite pitcher [/01]: height: 238 mm, width: 230 mm
Basin [/02]: length: 467 mm, width: 318 mm
Hallmarks: 1. AK in oval, 2. hallmark Prague 1818,
3. tax mark 1810–24
Donation inscription in Hebrew.
Translation:
Belonging to the Zigeuner [Cikán] *Synagogue and* [it] *was completed on Tuesday, Rosh Chodesh of Nisan the year 578 a. s. c.* [= April 7, 1818] [on the pitcher]. *And ordered by the head and elder, the distinguished KHRR Wolf Fleckeles, head of the community, may his Rock protect him,* [it] *was made from the treasury of the Ziegeuner Synagogue through the agency of the princes, the custodians, namely the distinguished elder KHRR Wolf Redisch, may his Rock and Redeemer protect him, the distinguished elder KHRR Meir Welhartitz, may his Rock and Redeemer protect him.* [It] *was completed on Tuesday, Rosh Chodesh of Nisan the year 578 a. s. c.* [= April 7, 1818] [on the basin].
Collection point: Prague

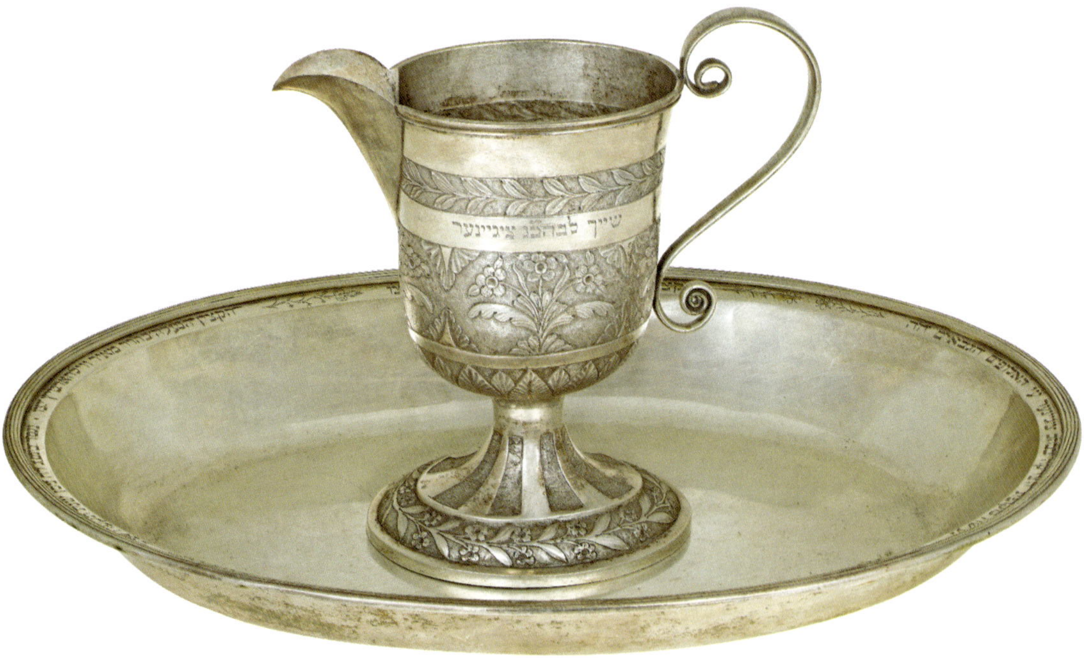

Cat. No. 274

Cat. No. 275
Levite Pitcher and Basin
Inv. No. JMP 002.703/01, 02
Silver, repoussé
Christian Sander, Sr., Vienna, 1833
Levite pitcher [/01]: height: 226 mm, width: 143 mm
Basin [/02]: length: 348 mm, width: 272 mm
Hallmarks: 1. CS in rectangle,
2. hallmark Vienna 1833
Donation inscription in Hebrew.
Translation:
This was donated by K Michael Leib Jahn on New Year 628 [a. s. c.] [= 1868] [on the pitcher] *to the glory of the New Synagogue and to the memory of the soul of his dear wife the lady Hendl, the daughter of Mr. Fishl of blessed memory, who left for eternity on Tuesday, 2nd of Adar 625 a. s. c.* [= 1865] [on the basin].
Collection point: Prostějov

Cat. No. 276
Levite Pitcher and Basin
Inv. No. JMP 002.252/01, 02
Silver, repoussé, engraving
Vincenz Czokally, Vienna, 1867–71
Levite pitcher [/02]: height: 262 mm, width: 135 mm
Basin [/01]: length: 331 mm, width: 259 mm
Hallmarks: 1. VC in rectangle, 2. Austro-Hungary 1867–71, 3. localization letter A [Vienna]
Donation inscription in Hebrew.
Translation:
A gift of KH Zevi Hirsch Doctor Kohen. This basin and his son for service in the temple. [on the basin] *On the day his heart rejoiced, at the age his dear son, the learned boy K Isaac, reached his 13th year, may he live many good days. "Let Aaron and his sons wash their hands and feet"* [Ex. 30:19] *a. s. c.* [dating in the chronogram 631 = 1871] [on the pitcher].
Collection point: Náchod

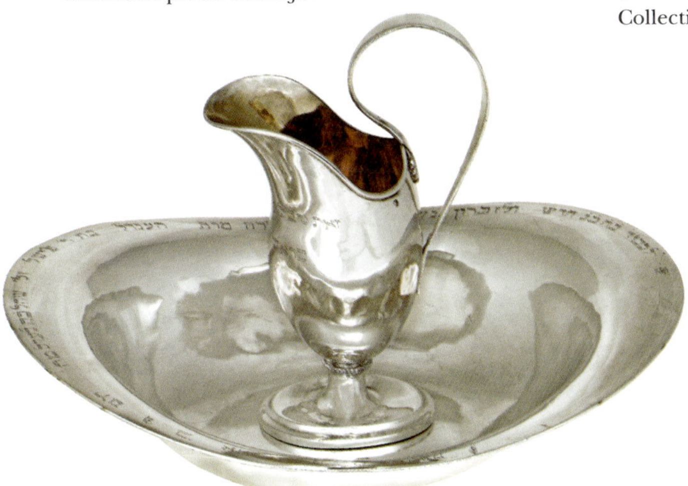

Cat. No. 275

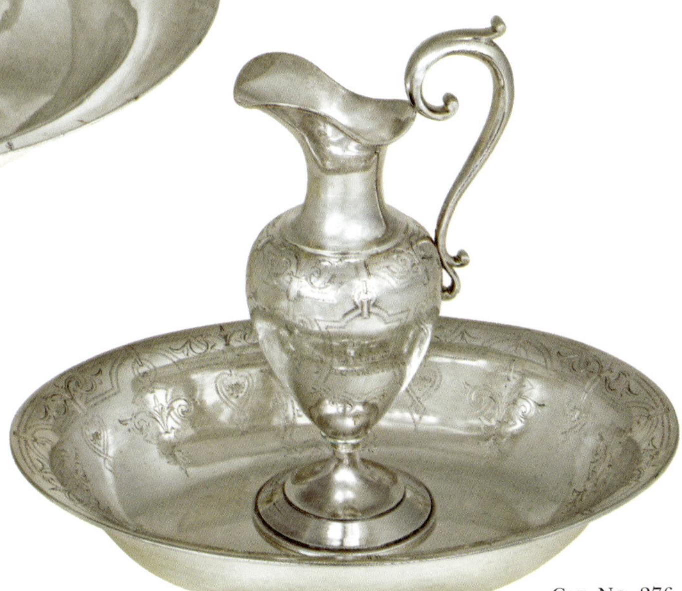

Cat. No. 276

VI. Etrog Containers

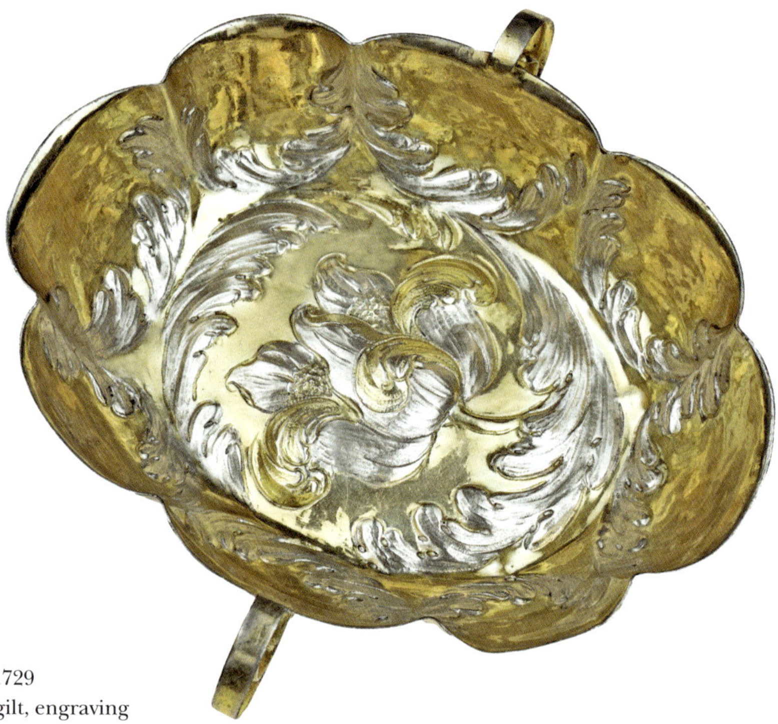

Cat. No. 277
Etrog Container
Inv. No. JMP 012.729
Silver, repoussé, gilt, engraving
Markus Hrbek, Prague, 1673
Height: 29 mm, length: 134 mm
Hallmarks: 1. MHR in quadrilob, 2. hallmark
Prague 1673, 3. tax mark Prague 1810–24
Without inscriptions.
Collection point: Jewish Museum in Prague, 1906–1940

Cat. No. 278
Etrog Container
Inv. No. JMP 037.566/01, 02
Silver, repoussé, engraving
Maker IS, Munich, 1768
Length: 145 mm, height: 108 mm
Hallmarks: 1. IS in double circle,
2. hallmark Munich 1768,
3. tax mark Prague 1810–24
Donation inscription in Hebrew.
Translation:
Purchased with charitable funds a.s.c. [dating in the chronogram 580 = 1820] *through the agency of the princes custodians and leaders of the Great Court Synagogue.*
Collection point: Prague

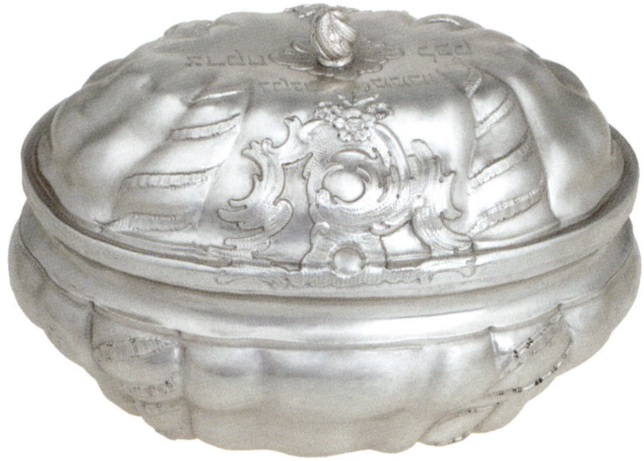

Cat. No. 278

Cat. No. 279
Etrog Container
Inv. No. JMP 002.205
Silver, repoussé, cut-out, engraving
Mikuláš Maden [?], Kutná Hora,
2nd half of 18th century
Height: 52 mm, length: 187 mm
Hallmarks: 1. NM in irregular shape,
2. hallmark Kutná Hora,
3. recharge mark Prague 1806–7
Donation inscription in Hebrew.
Translation:
This was purchased from treasury funds in the year 615 a. s. c. [= 1855].
Collection point: Mladá Boleslav

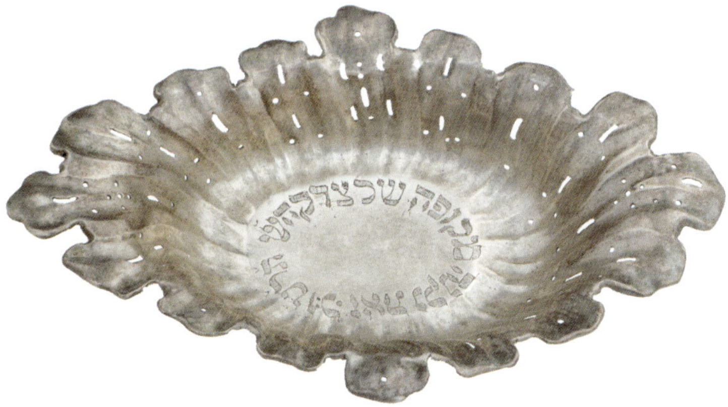

Cat. No. 279

Cat. No. 280
Etrog Container
Inv. No. JMP 010.860
Silver, repoussé, cast
Michal Enzinger, Prague, 1782
Height: 51 mm, length: 169 mm
Hallmarks: 1. ME in quadrilob,
2. hallmark Prague 1782,
3. recharge mark Prague 1806–7,
4. release mark 1809–10
Without inscriptions.
Collection point: Soběslav

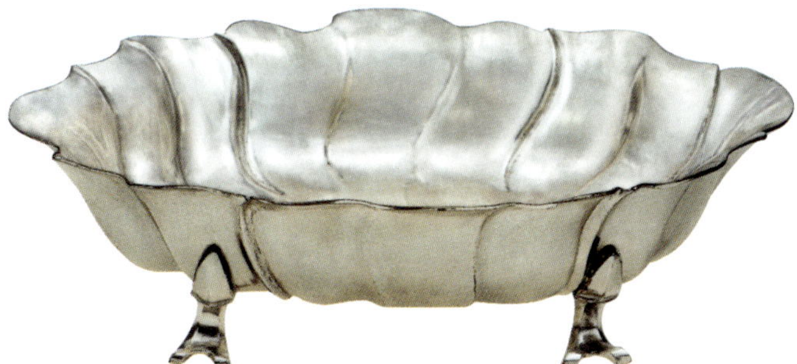

Cat. No. 280

Cat. No 281
Etrog Container
Inv. No. JMP 012.268
Silver, repoussé, engraving, cut-out
Michael Wiener, Sr., Vienna, 1807–9
Height: 38 mm, length: 127 mm
Hallmarks: 1. MW in shield, 2. hallmark Vienna 1807–9, 3. stock mark after 1807
Donation inscription in Latin script: *Bernhard Engel.*
Collection point: Brno, Jevíčko

Cat. No. 282
Etrog Container
Inv. No. JMP 104.769/01, 02
Silver, repoussé, engraving
Maker's mark illegible, Poland [?], mid-19th century
Height: 124 mm, length: 145 mm
Hallmarks: 1. illegible maker's mark, 2. purity number 13 in rectangle
Without inscriptions.
Purchased by the Jewish Museum in Prague.

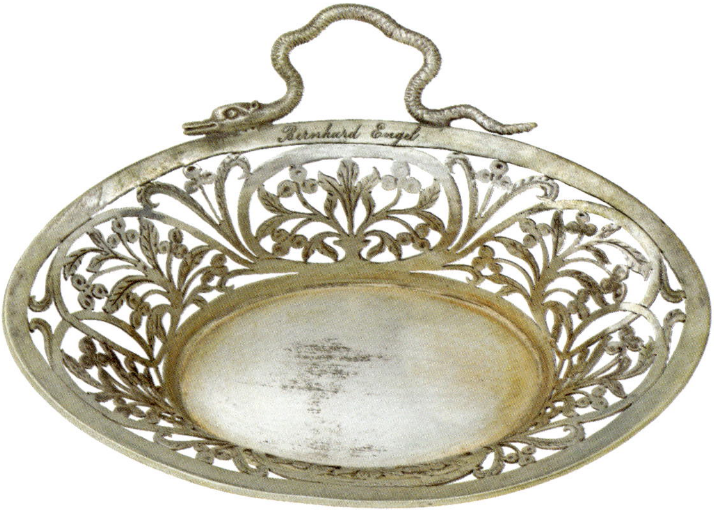

Cat. No. 281

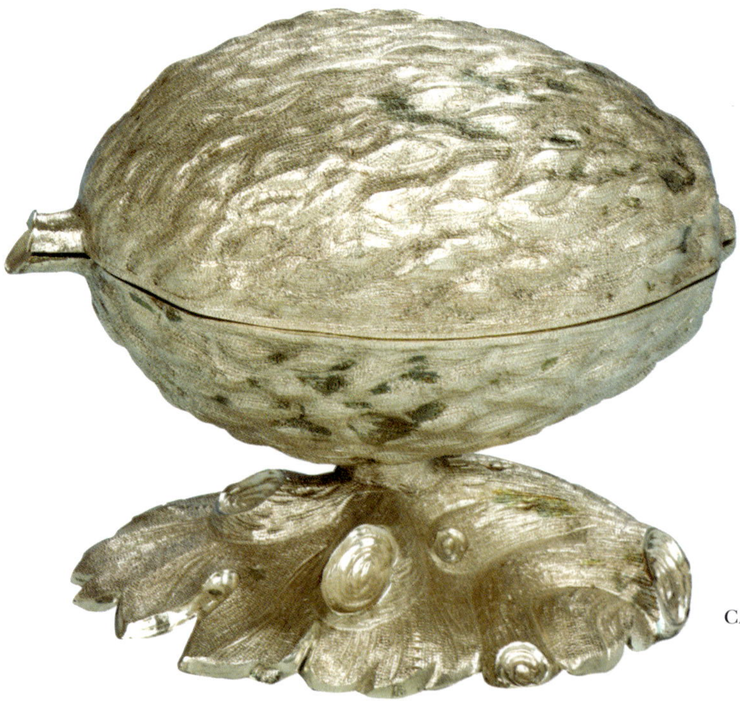

Cat. No. 282

Cat. No. 283
Etrog Container
Inv. No. JMP 046.041
silver, repoussé, engraving, parcel-gilt
Abraham Bernard Bächer (company), Prague, 1865
Height: 88 mm, length: 152 mm
Hallmarks: 1. AB in oval,
2. hallmark Prague 1865
Donation inscription in Hebrew.
Translation:
Raphael Kauders
Collection point: Prague, Pinkas Synagogue

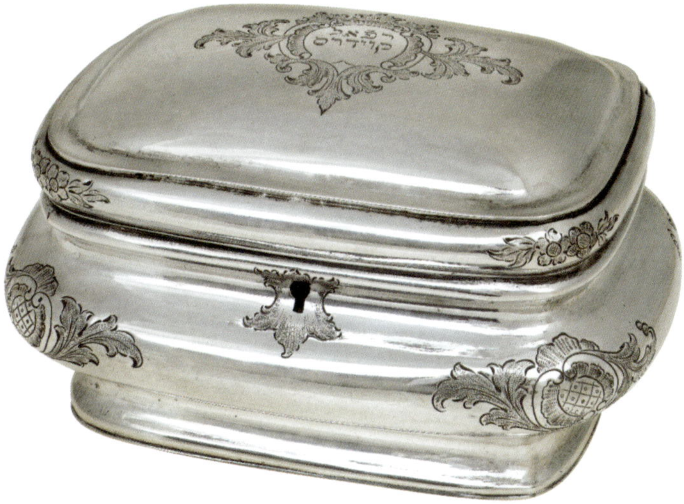

Cat. No. 283

Cat. No. 284
Etrog Container
Inv. No. JMP 010.643
Silver, repoussé, engraving, cast, parcel-gilt
Maker JZ, Vienna, 1872–82
Height: 119 mm, length: 128 mm
Hallmarks: 1. JZ in rectangle,
2. hallmark Vienna after 1871
The donation inscription is a combination of German in Latin script and Hebrew in Hebrew script:
A gift [in Hebrew] *of Mr. Markus Ehrlich, rabbi emeritus, Klatovy 1882* [in German].
Collection point: Klatovy

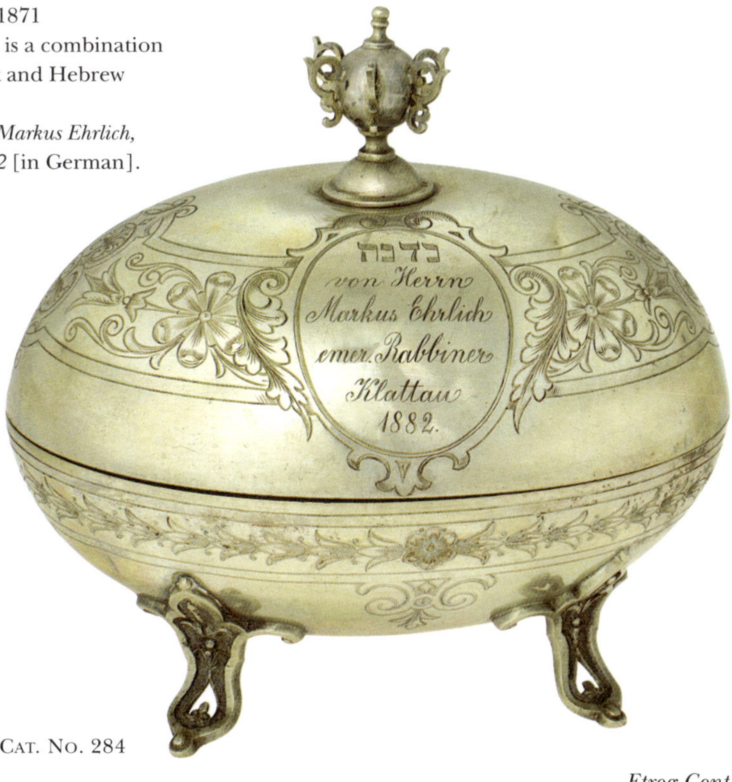

Cat. No. 284

VII. Alms Boxes

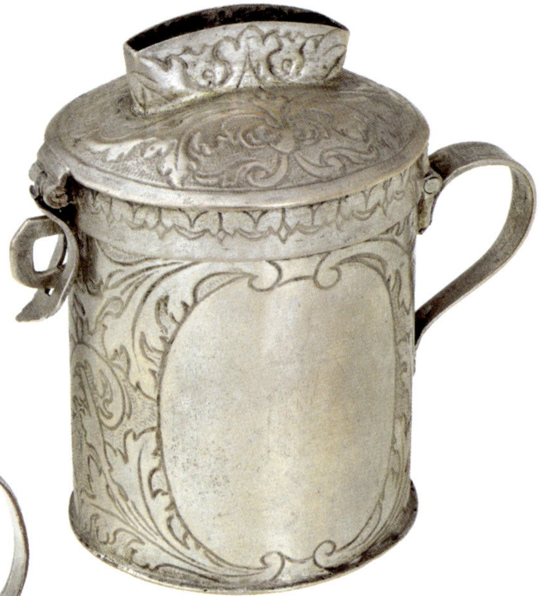

Cat. No. 286

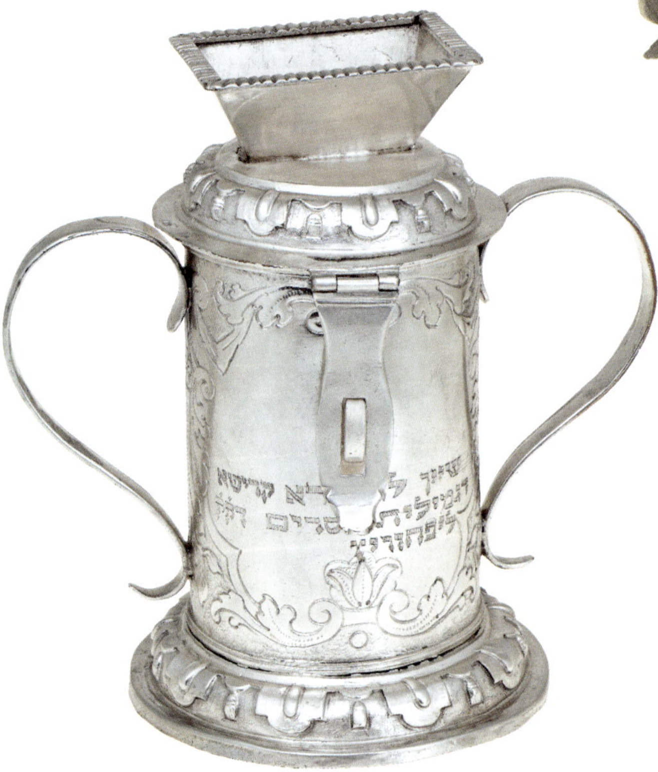

Cat. No. 285

Cat. No. 285
Alms Box
Inv. No. JMP 010.712
Silver, repoussé, engraving
Martin Ketzner, Prague, 1723
Height: 175 mm, width: 173 mm
Hallmarks: 1. MK in quadrilob, 2. hallmark Prague – Staré Město 1723, 3. recharge mark Prague 1806–7, 5. release mark 1809–10
Donation inscription in Hebrew.
Translation:
Belonging to the Holy Benevolent Society [Burial Society] *of the holy community Libochovice.*
Collection point: Libochovice

Cat. No. 286
Alms Box
Inv. No. JMP 004.480
Silver, repoussé, engraving
Maker IK [?], Moravia, 18th century
Height: 97 mm, length: 95 mm
Hallmarks: 1. IK [?] in oval,
2. recharge mark Brno 1806–7
Fragment of Hebrew inscription.
Translation:
Righteousness [saves] [incomplete inscription].
Collection point: Třebíč

Cat. No. 287
Alms Box
Inv. No. JMP 010.355
Silver, repoussé
No maker's mark, Moravia, 1764 [inscription]
Height: 155 mm, width: 110 mm
Hallmarks: 1. recharge mark Brno 1806–7
Donation inscription in Hebrew.
Translation:
Belonging to the custodians of the treasury of the holy community Miroslav. Made through the agency of H Wolf Eretz and H David Trebitsch and KMR Petahiah, son of G. "Those in her who repent, [shall be redeemed] *by righteousness"* [Is 1:27] *a. s. c.* [dating in the chronogram 524 = 1764].
Collection point: Brno, Miroslav

Cat. No. 288
Alms Box
Inv. No. JMP 002.173
Silver, repoussé, engraving
Maker IP [Josef Pscher?], Prague, 1793
Height: 178 mm, width: 168 mm
Hallmarks: 1. IP in rectangle, 2. hallmark Prague 1793, 3. purity mark 13,
4. recharge mark Prague 1806–7,
5. release mark 1809–10
Donation inscription in Hebrew.
Translation:
Refurbished through the agency of the custodians and elders of this year 598 a. s. c. [= 1838].
Collection point: Mladá Boleslav

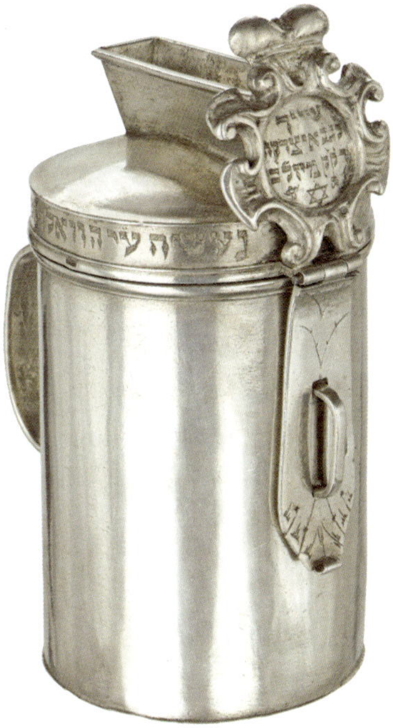

Cat. No. 287

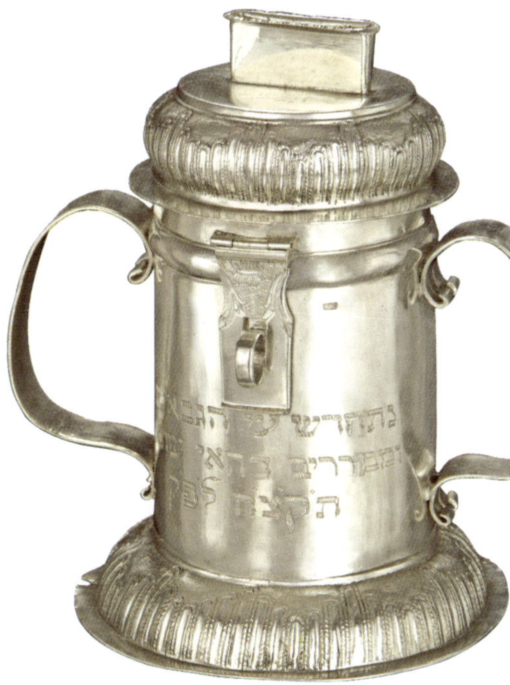

Cat. No. 288

Cat. No. 289
Alms Box
Inv. No. JMP 046.090
Silver, repoussé, engraving
Karel Skřemenec, Prague, 1807
Height: 184 mm, width: 195 mm
Hallmarks: 1. CS in oval, 2. hallmark Prague 1807–9, 3. recharge mark Prague 1806–7, 4. release mark 1809–10
Donation inscription in Hebrew.
Translation:
Made from the charitable funds of the Holy Benevolent Society [Burial Society] *in the holy community Smíchov and Popelka* [defunct settlement in the Prague Košíře district] *in the year 570 a. s. c.* [= 1810].
Collection point: Prague

Cat. No. 290
Alms Box
Inv. No. JMP 004.268
silver, repoussé, engraving
Franz Kaltenmarker, Brno, 1810
Height: 151 mm, width: 136 mm
Hallmarks: 1. FK in oval, 2. hallmark Brno 1810, 3. tax mark Brno 1810–24
Donation inscription in Hebrew.
Translation:
This was donated by the princes, the 18 men of the Holy Benevolent Society [Burial Society]*, the year 572 a. s. c.* [= 1812] [on the circumference].
Solomon Gans [underneath the bottom].
Collection point: Prostějov

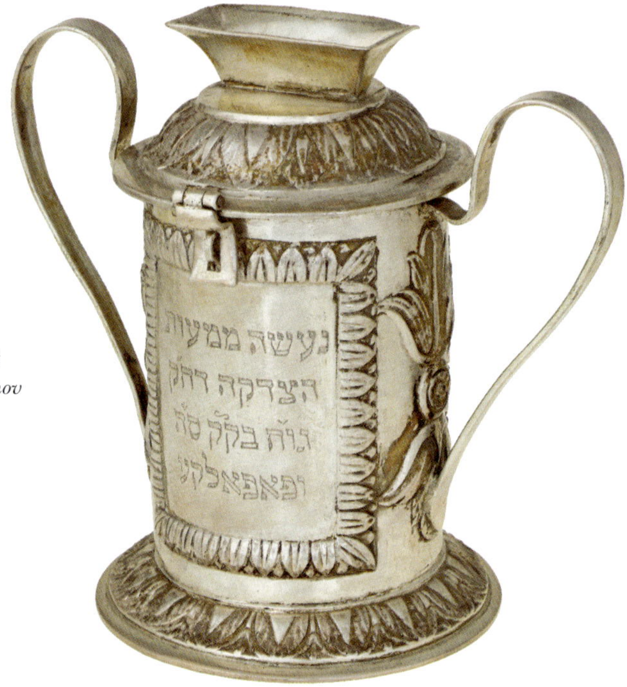

Cat. No. 289

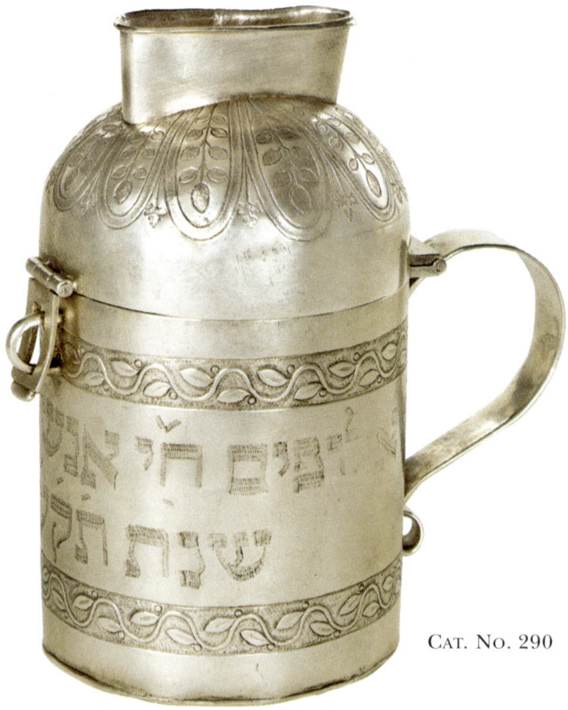

Cat. No. 290

Cat. No. 291
Alms Box
Inv. No. JMP 003.676
Silver, repoussé
Maker IM [Johann Mayerhofer?], Vienna, 1814
Height: 143 mm, width: 145 mm
Hallmarks: 1. IM in heart, 2. hallmark Vienna 1814,
3. tax mark Vienna 1810–24, 4. stock mark after 1807
Donation inscription in Hebrew.
Translation:
The Holy Benevolent Society [Burial Society]
of the holy community Šafov.
Collection point: Central Jewish Museum for
Moravia and Silesia, 1936–1938 in Nikolsburg

Cat. No. 292
Alms Box
Inv. No. JMP 010.273
Silver, repoussé, engraving
Carl Lackstampfer, Jr., Brno, 1814–17
Height: 187 mm, width: 150 mm
Hallmarks: 1. CL in oval,
2. hallmark Brno 1814–19,
3. tax mark Brno 1810–24
Donation inscription in Hebrew.
Translation:
"Righteousness saves from death" [Prov. 10:2],
[in the year] *577 a. s. c.* [= 1817]. *For the holy*
society of gravediggers [Burial Society]
in the holy community Slavkov.
Collection point: Slavkov u Brna

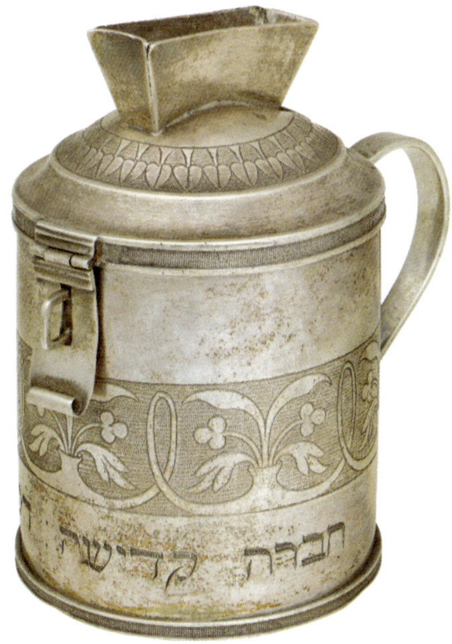
Cat. No. 291

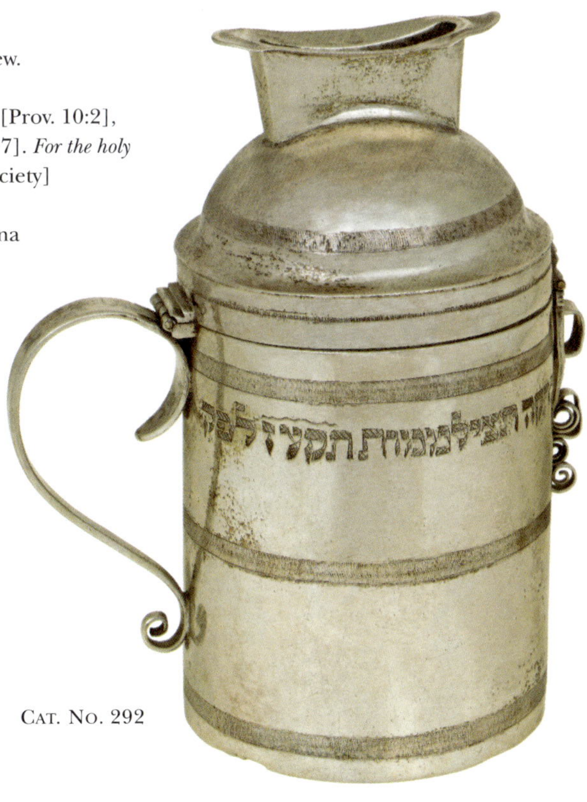
Cat. No. 292

Cat. No. 293
Alms Box
Inv. No. JMP 037.710
Silver, repoussé, engraving
Antonín Maroušek, Prague, 1818
Height: 152 mm, diameter: 122 mm
Hallmarks: 1. AM in oval, 2. hallmark Prague 1818, 3. tax mark Prague 1810–24
Inscription in Hebrew.
Translation:
The Holy Society of Mohels.
Collection point: Jewish Museum in Prague, 1906–1940

Cat. No. 294
Alms Box
Inv. No. JMP 003.797
Silver, repoussé, engraving
Wilhelm Berghaus, Vienna, 1819
Height: 170 mm, width: 130 mm
Hallmarks: 1. WB in shield, 2. hallmark Vienna 1819, 3. tax mark Vienna 1810–24
Donation inscription in Hebrew.
Translation:
"Righteousness saves from death" [Prov. 10:2]. *This alms box belongs to the Holy Benevolent Society* [Burial Society] *and was made through the agency of the custodians Mr. Joshua Beer, his son Mr. Aaron Böhm, Mr. Hayyim, son of Mr. Leib Teltsch Halfan, son of Solomon Tzoref, HRR Nahum, son of Mr. Eliakim Glaser, in the year 579 a. s. c.* [= 1819].
Collection point: Central Jewish Museum for Moravia and Silesia, 1936–1938 in Nikolsburg

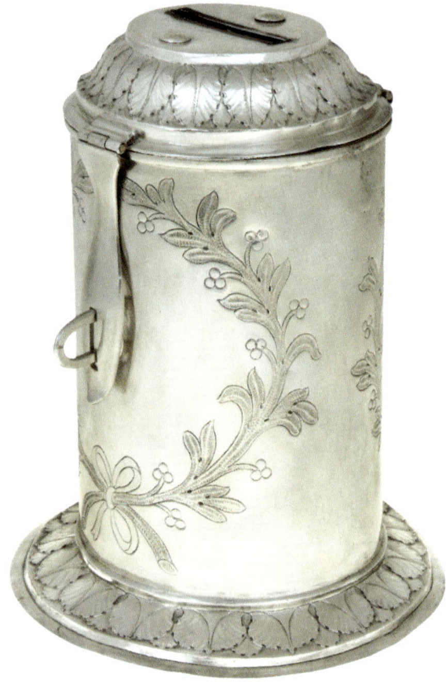

Cat. No. 293

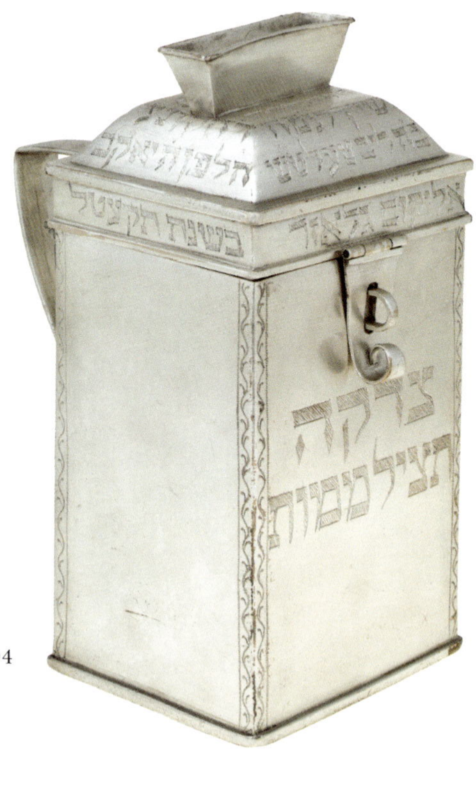

Cat. No. 294

Cat. No. 295
Alms Box
Inv. No. JMP 102.475
Silver, repoussé, engraving
Caspar Duncker, Prague, 1820
Height: 192 mm, width: 200 mm
Hallmarks: 1. CD in oval,
2. hallmark Prague 1820,
3. tax mark Prague 1810–24
Donation inscription in Hebrew.
Translation:
This was donated from the treasury of the eternal light for the Holy Benevolent Society [Burial Society] [in] *Libeň, in the year 581 a. s. c.* [= 1821].
Collection point: Prague

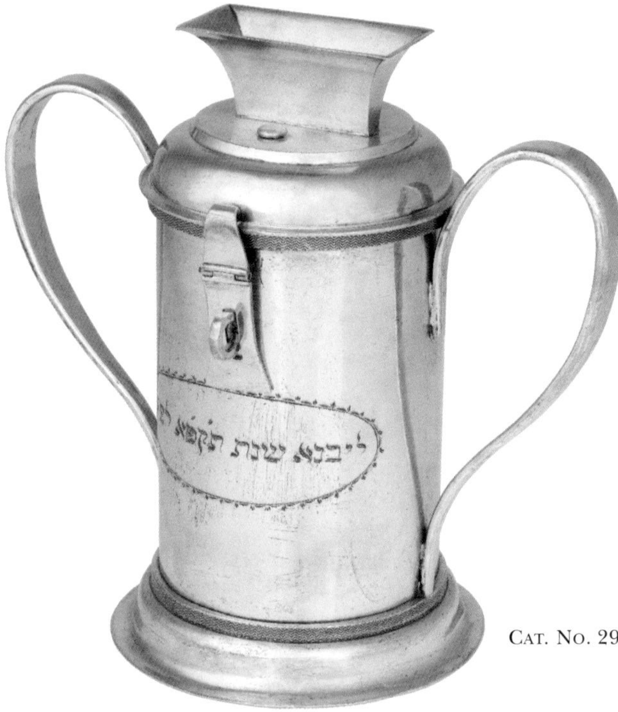

Cat. No. 295

Cat. No. 296
Alms Box
Inv. No. JMP 007.049
Silver, repoussé, engraving
Maker AF, Jihlava, 1821
Height: 127 mm, length: 180 mm
Hallmarks: 1. AF in shield,
2. hallmark Jihlava 1821,
3. tax mark Jihlava 1810–24
Donation inscription in Hebrew.
Translation:
The house for the assembly of all the living [cemetery]. *"Righteousness saves from death"* [Prov. 10:2]. *Executed and completed according to the will of the members of the Society, may their Rock and Redeemer protect them, on the behest of the princes custodians, may their light shine, and at their head the distinguished KH Itzik Eisenchütz, may his light shine, who also contributed from* [his] *money one part to creating this vessel, in the year 584 a. s. c.* [= 1824].
Collection point: Třešť

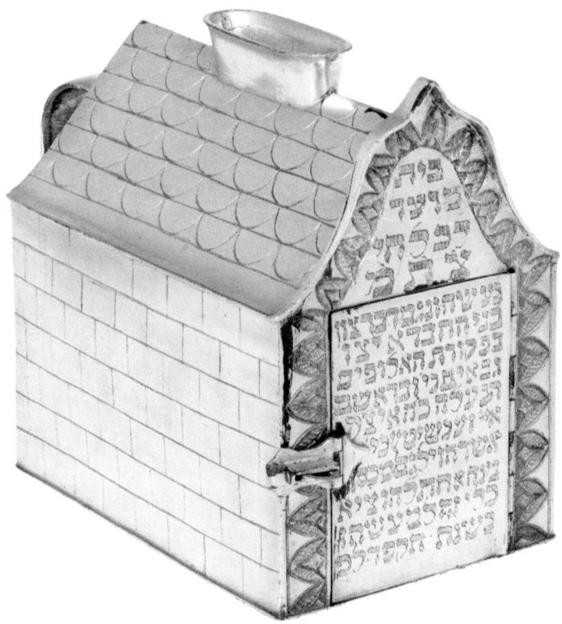

Cat. No. 296

Cat. No. 297
Alms Box
Inv. No. JMP 001.920
Silver, repoussé, engraving
Maker AF, Jihlava, 1829
Height: 165 mm, width: 145 mm
Hallmarks: 1. AF in shield,
2. hallmark Jihlava 1829
Donation inscription in Hebrew.
Translation:
In the year "The righteousness of the upright saves them" [Prov. 11:6] *a. s. c.* [dating in the chronogram 590 = 1830]. *Belonging to the Burial Society of the holy community Polná.*
Collection point: Polná

Cat. No. 298
Alms Box
Inv. No. JMP 027.805
Silver, repossé, engraving
Tomáš Höpfel, Prague, 1834
Height: 169 mm, width: 153 mm
Hallmarks: 1. TH in oval,
2. hallmark Prague 1834
Donation inscription in Hebrew.
Translation:
This silver alms box is a gift to the eternal memory of the elder KH Isaac Backofen, may his Rock and Redeemer protect him, custodian of the New Synagogue, so that in it money from the dish [?] *may be collected and a gift for wood to heat with, "And it will be righteousness for us"* [Deut. 6:25; dating in the chronogram 594 = 1834] *a. s. c.*
Collection point: Jewish Museum in Prague, 1906–1940

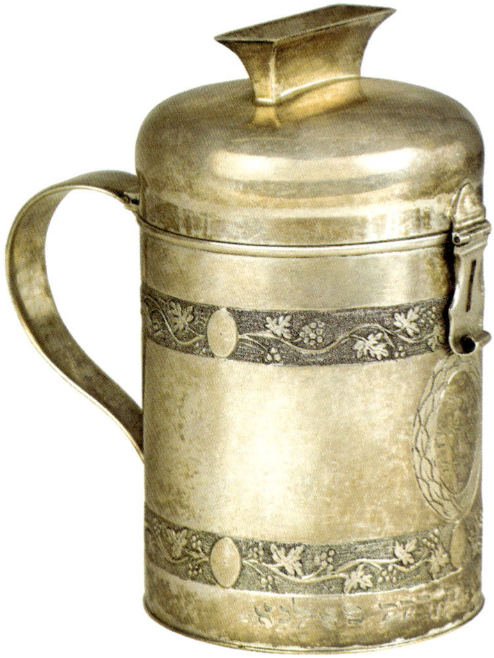

Cat. No. 297
Cat. No. 298

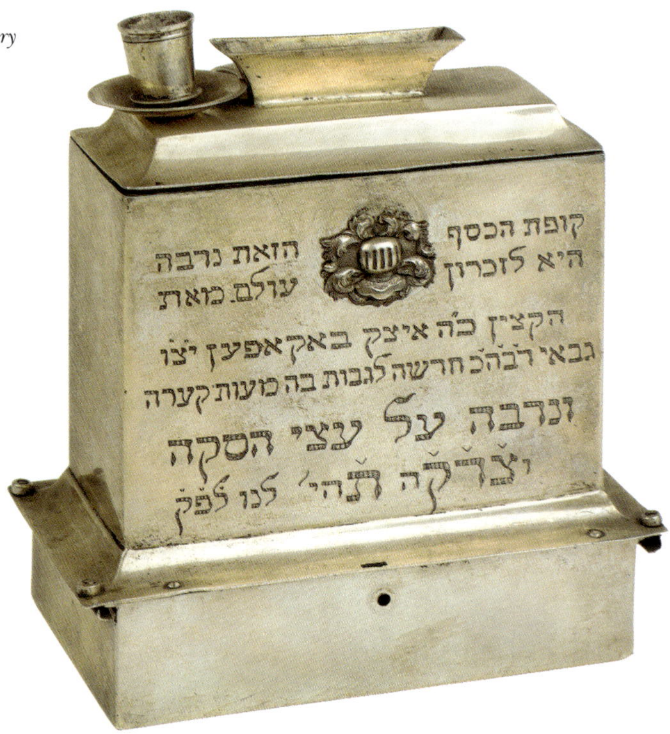

Cat. No. 299
Alms Box
Inv. No. JMP 002.288
Silver, repoussé, engraving
Not original marking [soldered in], Moravia [?], 1837 [inscription]
Height: 124 mm, width: 112 mm
Hallmarks: 1. IS in rectangle,
2. hallmark Vienna 1805
Inscription in Hebrew.
Translation:
Made through the agency of the matron, the esteemed lady Liblah, wife of the distinguished Abraham Pollak, may his Rock and Redeemer protect him, in the year 597 [a. s. c.] [= 1837] [in] *the holy community Meziříčí* [Velké Meziříčí].
Collection point: Velké Meziříčí

Cat. No. 300
Alms Box
Inv. No. JMP 046.169
Silver, repoussé, engraving
Joachim Anton Kaisberger, Prague, 1850–57
Height: 65 mm, width: 162 mm
Hallmarks: 1. JAK in rectangle, 2. hallmark Prague 1850–59
Donation inscription in Hebrew.
Translation:
Righteous women [in the year] *617* [a. s. c.] [= 1857]. *Made from the charitable funds of the Holy Benevolent Society* [Burial Society] *here* [in] *Prague through the agency of custodians and the committee of the chosen, may their Rock and Redeemer protect them, 369 a. s. c.* [= 1609].
Collection point: Prague

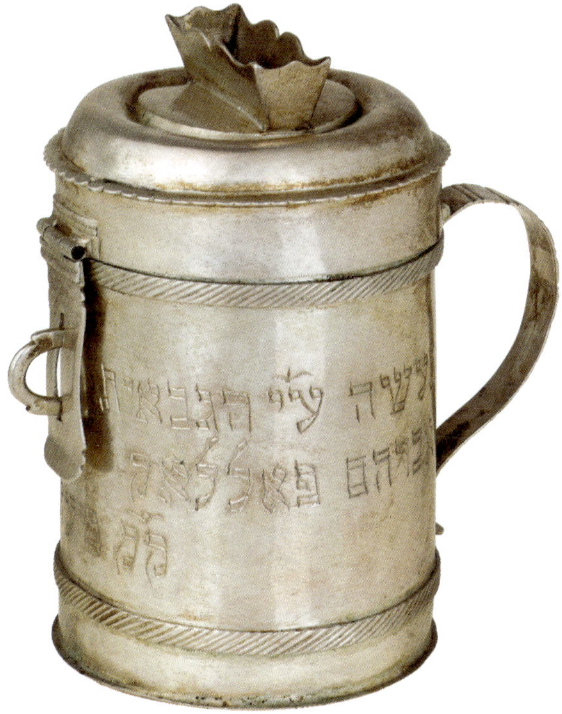

Cat. No. 299
Cat. No. 300

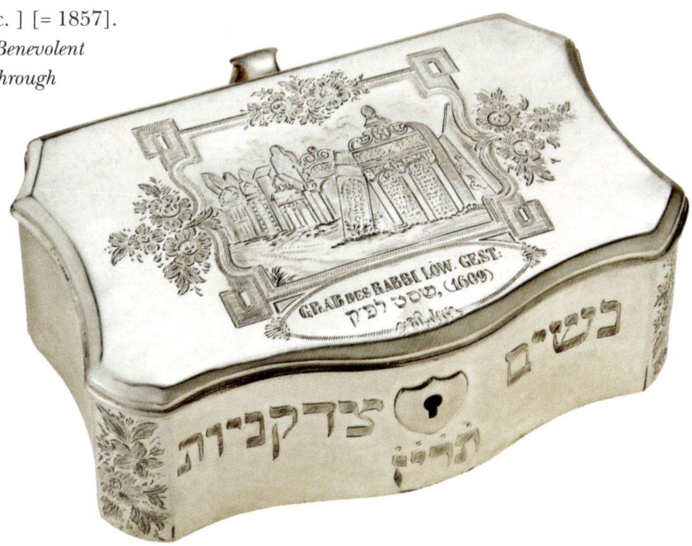

Cat. No. 301
Alms Box
Inv. No. JMP 007.445
Silver, repoussé
Maker ES, Vienna, 1867–69
Height: 132 mm, width: 123 mm
Hallmarks: 1. ES in oval, 2. Austro-Hungary 1867–71, 3. localization letter A [Vienna]
Donation inscription in Hebrew.
Translation:
R Joseph Polatschek, R Mordecai Stein, R Gerschon Mondschein, custodians performing good deeds [Burial Society] *of the town, the holy community Kyjov, 629 a. s. c.* [= 1869].
Collection point: Kyjov

Cat. No. 302
Alms Box
Inv. No. JMP 002.498
Silver, repoussé, engraving
Maker CS, Austro-Hungary, 1867–71
Height: 165 mm, width: 146 mm
Hallmarks: 1. CS in rectangle,
2. Austro-Hungary 1867–71
Without inscriptions.
Collection point: Kojetín

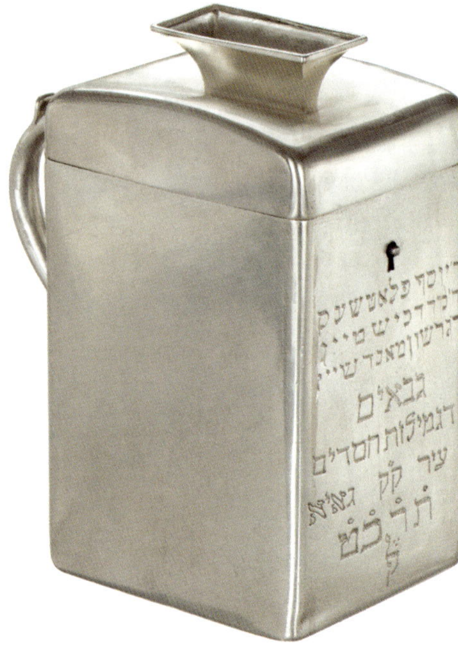

Cat. No. 301

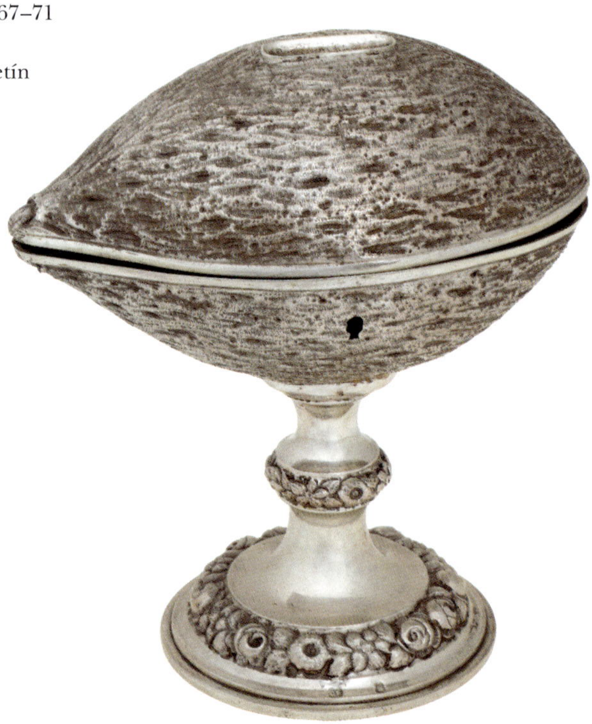

Cat. No. 302

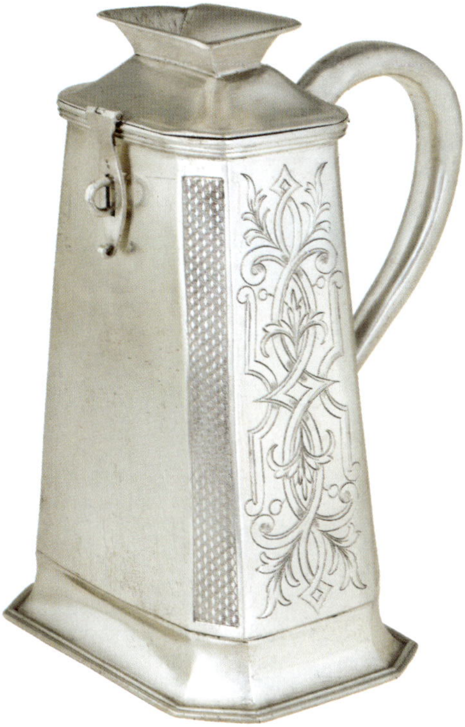

Cat. No. 303

Cat. No. 303
Alms Box
Inv. No. JMP 002.518
Silver, repoussé, engraving, guilloché
Maker TD, Vienna, after 1871
Height: 167 mm, width: 122 mm
Hallmarks: 1. TD in oval,
2. Austro-Hungary [Vienna] after 1871,
3. localization letter A [Vienna]
Without inscriptions.
Collection point: Jindřichův Hradec

Cat. No. 304
Alms Box
Inv. No. JMP 010.517
Silver, repoussé, engraving
Maker SK, Prague, after 1871
Height: 154 mm, width: 140 mm
Hallmarks: 1. SK in rectangle,
2. Austro-Hungary [Prague] after 1871,
3. localization letter C [Prague]
Donation inscription in German in Latin script.
Translation:
The Society of Israelite Women in Heřmanův Městec, founded in the year 1850.
Collection point: Heřmanův Městec

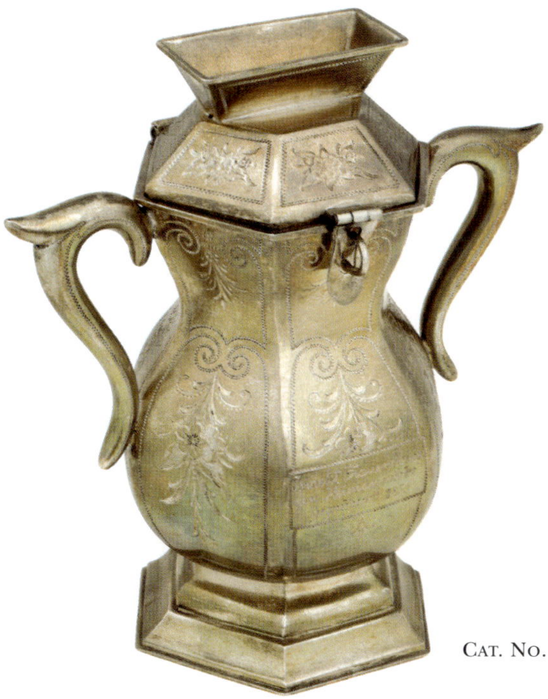

Cat. No. 304

Cat. No. 305
Alms Box
Inv. No. JMP 023.334
Silver, repoussé
Thomas Dub, Vienna, 1867–71
Height: 152 mm, width: 110 mm
Hallmarks: 1. TD in rectangle,
2. Austro-Hungary 1867–71
Donation inscription in German
in Hebrew script.
Translation:
Donated to the Women's Association from Yentl Neumann, Mirl Kohen, Rezl Neumann.
Collection point: Podivín

Cat. No. 306
Alms Box
Inv. No. JMP 010.693
silver, repoussé
Maker FR, Vienna, after 1871
Height: 170 mm, width: 137 mm
Hallmarks: 1. FR in rectangle,
2. Austro-Hungary [Vienna] after 1871
Inscription in Hebrew and German
in Latin script.
Translation:
Donated by Leopold Popper 1886
[in German] *The Holy Benevolent Society*
[Burial Society][in Hebrew].
Collection point:
Dvůr Králové nad Labem

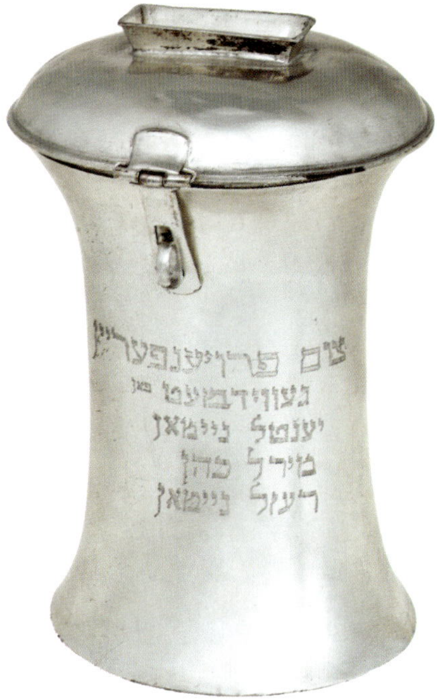

Cat. No. 305
Cat. No. 306

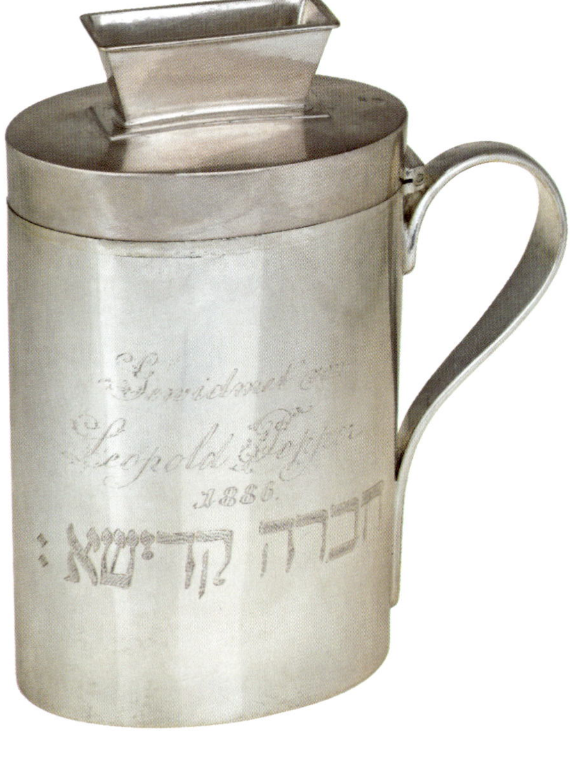

Cat. No. 307
Alms Box
Inv. No. JMP 017.014
Silver, repoussé, engraving
Maker EK, Prague, 1867–71
Height: 163 mm, width: 145 mm
Hallmarks: 1. EK in oval, 2. Austro-Hungary 1867–71, localization letter C [Prague]
Donation inscription in Hebrew.
Translation:
Belonging to the Holy Benevolent Society [Burial Society] *of the holy community Koloděje, made in the year 632 a. s. c.* [= 1872].
Collection point: Týn nad Vltavou / Koloděje

Cat. No. 308
Alms Box
Inv. No. JMP 010.868
Silver, repoussé
Goldschmidt H. S. (company), Prague, 1872–83
Height: 146 mm, width: 135 mm
Hallmarks: 1. HSG in rectangle, 2. Austro-Hungary [Prague] after 1871
Dating in Hebrew, donation inscription in German in Latin script.
Translation:
In the year 644 a. s. c. [= 1884]. *Donated by Emanuel and Therese Pollak to the Israelite Burial Society in Soběslav in the year 1883.*
Collection point: Soběslav

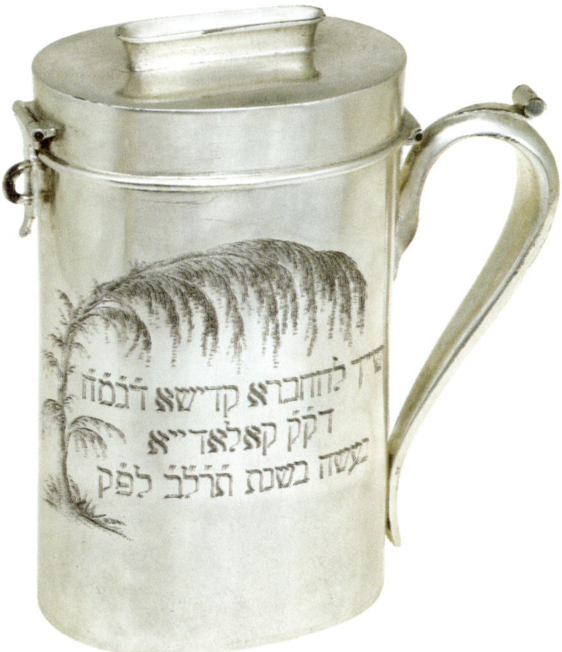

Cat. No. 307
Cat. No. 308

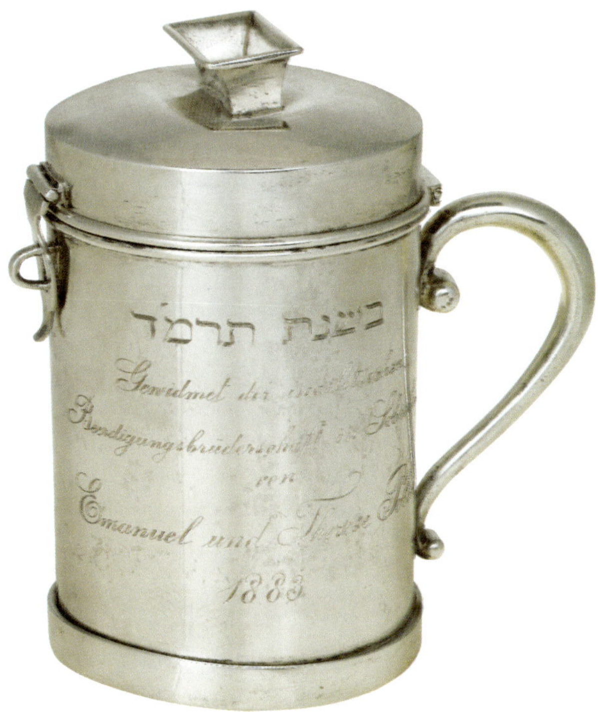

VIII. Charity Dishes

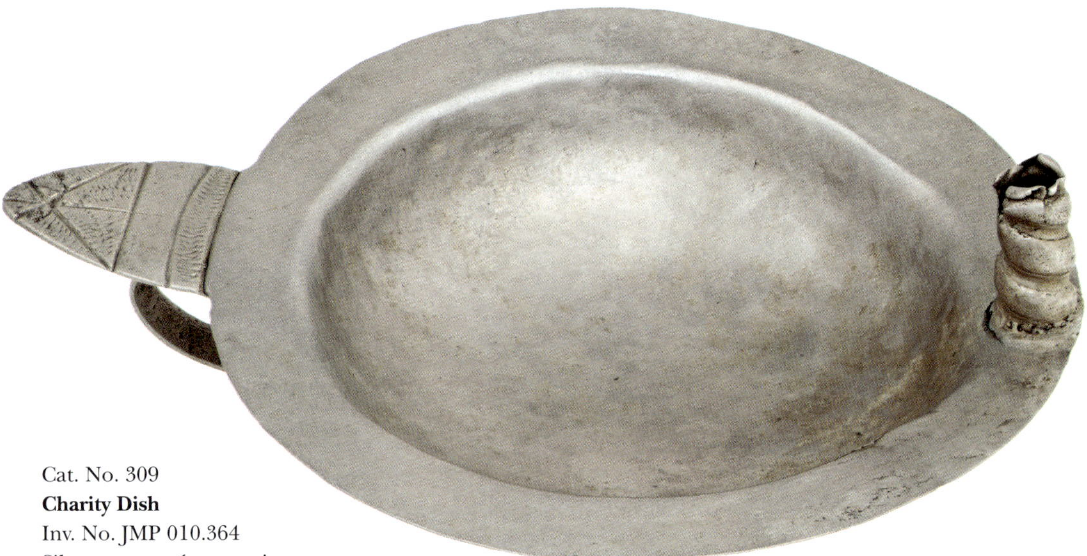

Cat. No. 309
Charity Dish
Inv. No. JMP 010.364
Silver, repoussé, engraving
No maker's mark, Moravia [?], 18th century
Length: 156 mm, diameter: 126 mm
Hallmarks: unmarked
Without inscriptions.
Collection point: Miroslav

Cat. No. 310
Charity Dish
Inv. No. JMP 037.771
Silver, repoussé, engraving
No maker's mark, Bohemia [?], 18th century
Length: 145 mm, diameter: 112 mm
Hallmarks: 1. recharge mark Prague 1806–7
Without inscriptions.
Collection point: Jewish Museum in Prague, 1906–1940

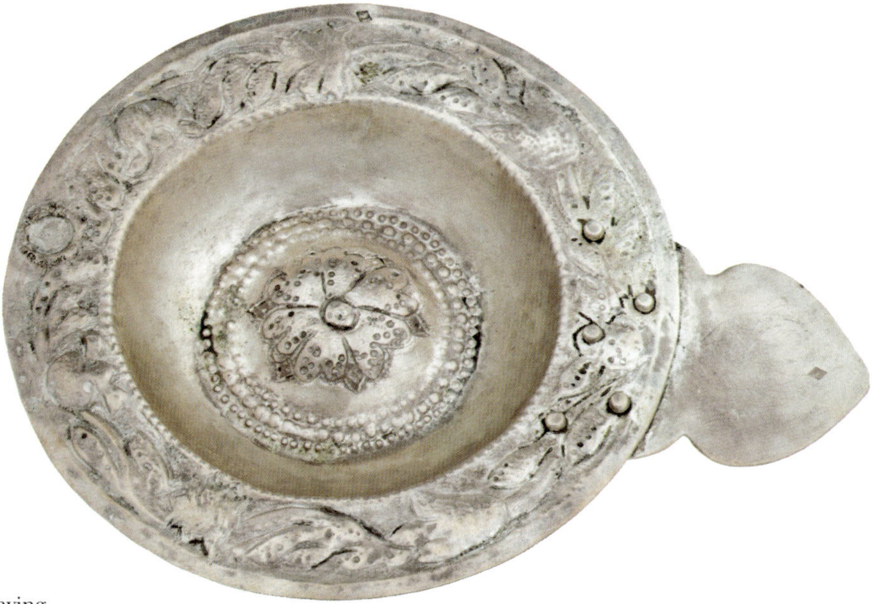

Cat. No. 310

Cat. No. 311
Charity Dish
Inv. No. JMP 002.211
Silver, repoussé
No maker's mark, Bohemia [?], 2nd half of 18th century
Length: 170 mm, diameter: 135 mm
Hallmarks: 1. recharge mark Prague 1806–7
Without inscriptions.
Collection point: Mladá Boleslav

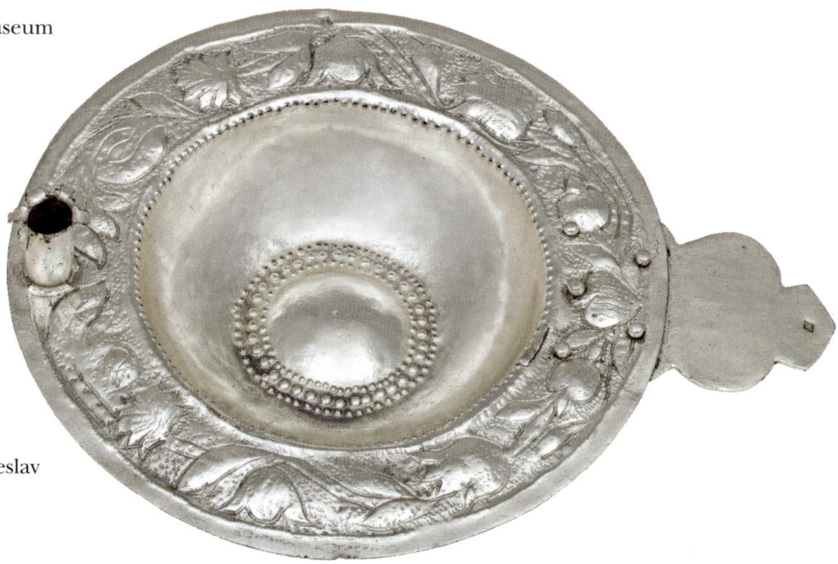

Cat. No. 311

Cat. No. 312
Charity Dish
Inv. No. JMP 003.751
Silver, repoussé
Jakob Uhl, Brno, 1807
Length: 177 mm, diameter: 125 mm
Hallmarks: 1. JU in oval, 2. hallmark Brno 1807–9, 3. recharge mark Brno 1806–7, 4. release mark 1809–10
Without inscriptions.
Collection point: Central Jewish Museum for Moravia and Silesia, 1936–1938 in Nikolsburg

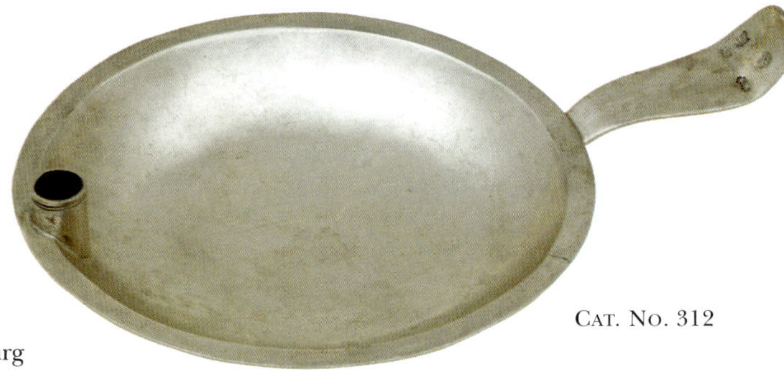

Cat. No. 312

Cat. No. 313
Charity Dish
Inv. No. JMP 027.804
Silver, repousssé, engraving
Antonín Neubert, Prague, 1813
Length: 290 mm, diameter: 225 mm
Hallmarks: 1. AN in oval, 2. hallmark Prague 1813, 3. tax mark Prague 1810–24
Donation inscription in Hebrew.
Translation:
Made from the charitable funds [of the society] *of those who pray morning and evening in the New Synagogue through the agency of the custodian KH Zechariah Gerschelis, Rosh Chodesh Iyar 573 a. s. c.* [= April 30, 1813].
Collection point: Jewish Museum in Prague, 1906–40

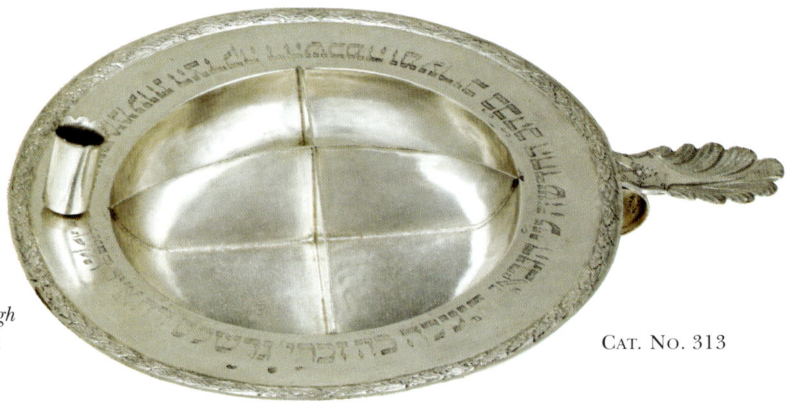

Cat. No. 313

Cat. No. 314
Charity Dish
Inv. No. JMP 044.170
Silver, repoussé
Karel Skřemenec, Prague, 1813
Length: 274 mm, diameter: 203 mm
Hallmarks: 1. CS in rectangle, 2. hallmark Prague 1813, 3. tax mark Prague 1810–24
Donation inscription in Hebrew.
Translation:
This was donated by the distinguished R Shalom, son of R Samuel Tzoref, may the memory of the just be blessed, in the year 574 a. s. c. [= 1814].
Collection point: Prague, High Synagogue

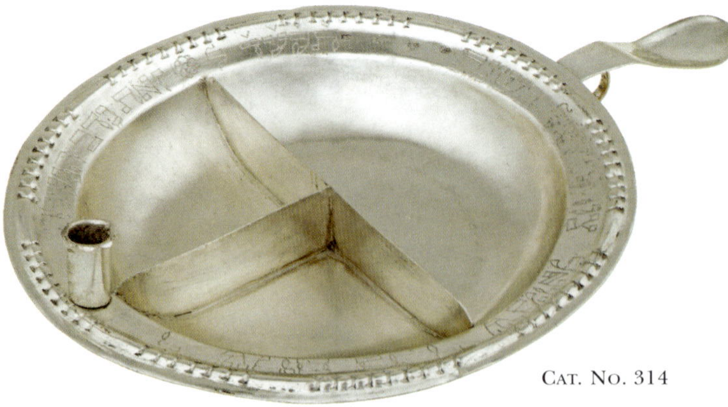

Cat. No. 314

Cat. No. 315
Charity Dish
Inv. No. JMP 012.179
Silver, repoussé
Carl Lackstampfer, Jr., Brno, 1816
Length: 240 mm, diameter: 189 mm
Hallmarks: 1. CL in oval,
2. hallmark Brno 1816,
3. tax mark Brno 1810–24
Donation inscription in Hebrew.
Translation:
Made throught the agency of the princes, custodians, the elder H Mendel Rosauer, the elder H Jacob Hickel, the sage H Israel Braunfeld, and the sage H Meir Bass. And [it] *was completed on the 28th day of the month of Sivan in the year 576 a. s. c.* [= June 24, 1816].
Collection point: Brno, Nový Rousínov

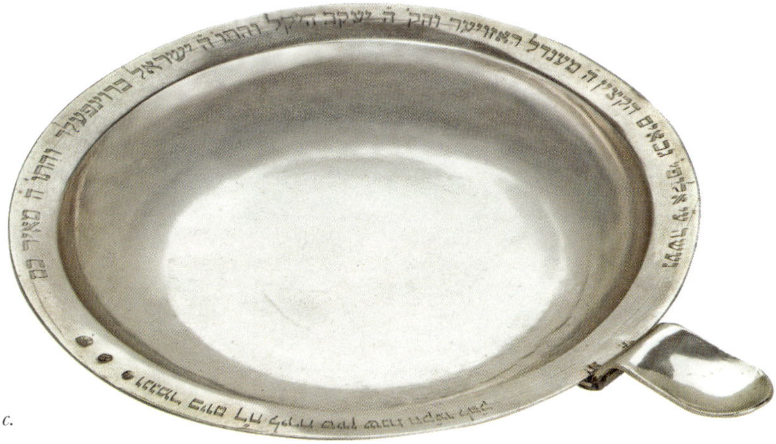

Cat. No. 315

Cat. No. 316
Charity Dish
Inv. No. JMP 001.774
Silver, repoussé
Maker JA [Josef Auer?], Vienna, 1821
Length: 149 mm, diameter: 134 mm
Hallmarks: 1. JA in oval, 2. hallmark Vienna 1821, 3. tax mark Vienna 1810–24
Donation inscription in Hebrew.
Translation:
Belonging to charity [. . .]
in [the year] *582 a. s. c.* [= 1822].
[Part of the inscription is illegible from being worn away by use.]
Collection point: Podivín

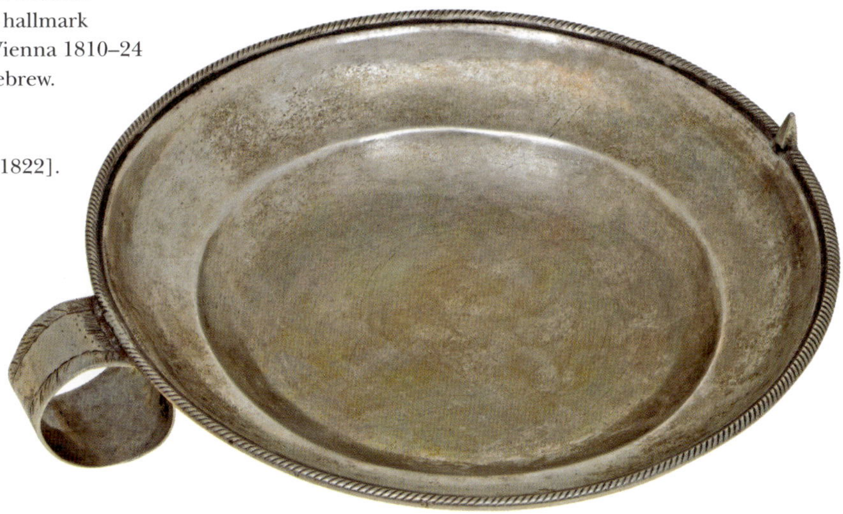

Cat. No. 316

Cat. No. 317
Charity Dish
Inv. No. JMP 010.135
silver, repoussé, stamping
Maker IW [Josef Wiederspeck?],
Vienna, after 1824
Length: 156 mm, diameter: 143 mm
Hallmarks: 1. IW in shield,
2. hallmark Vienna [illegible]
Without inscriptions.
Collection point: Loštice

Cat. No. 318
Charity Dish
Inv. No. JMP 004.476
Silver, repoussé, engraving
Maker IB, Jihlava, 1825
Length: 195 mm, diameter: 126 mm
Hallmarks: 1. IB in oval, 2. hallmark Jihlava 1825
Donation inscription in Hebrew.
Translation:
Made through the agency of the custodians [Burial Society?], *K Samuel Pollak, R Abraham Sch"W* [Schlackenwerth], *R Gabriel L"Sch* [Lasch / Lichtenstadt], *R Itzak R"B* [Rosenbaum / Rosenberg / Ranschburg]. *Rosh Chodesh Cheshvan 587 a. s. c.* [= Oct. 31, 1826].
Collection point: Třebíč

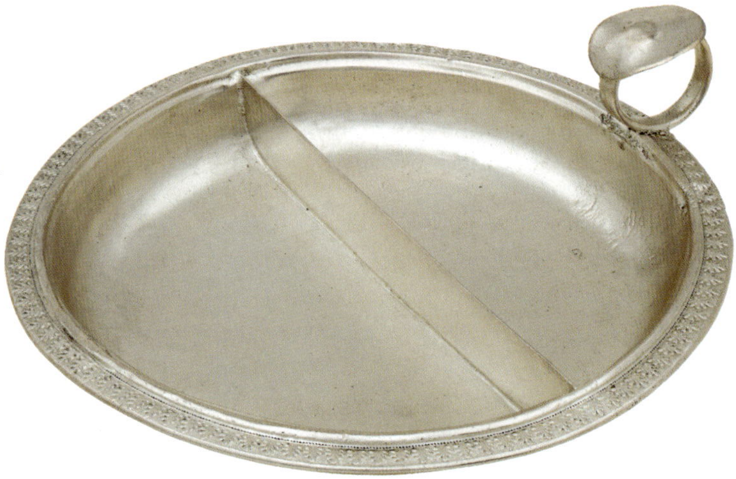

Cat. No. 317

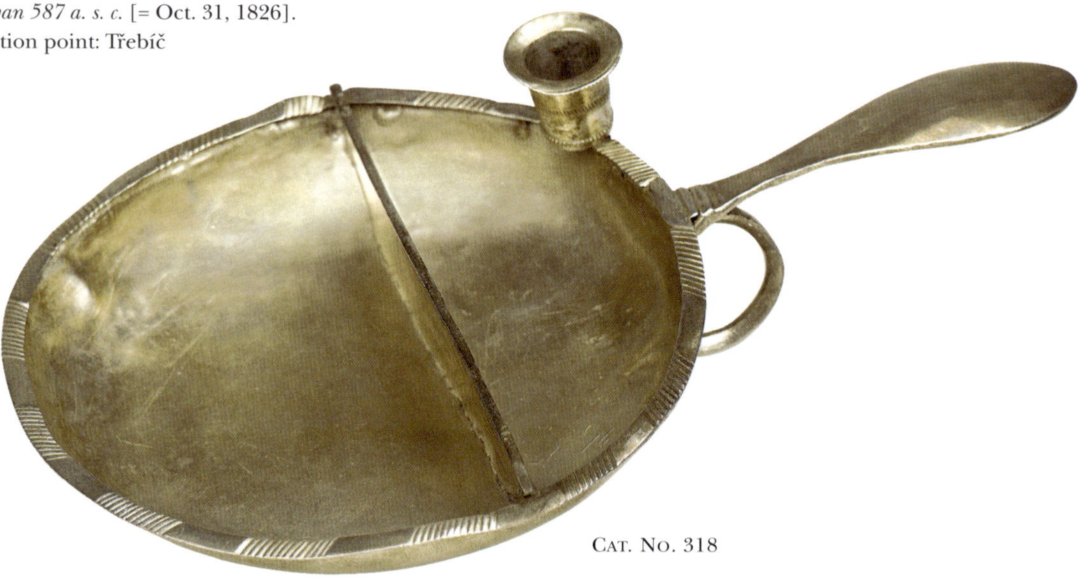

Cat. No. 318

Cat. No. 319
Charity Dish
Inv. No. JMP 002.928
Silver, repoussé
Maker IW, Vienna, 1834
Length: 148 mm, diameter: 119 mm
Hallmarks: 1. IW in oval 2. hallmark Vienna 1834
Donation inscription in Hebrew.
Translation:
Made through the agency of the treasurers HH H Solomon Hirsch Klein, H Pinhas Gold, H Wolf Gross, and H Gabriel Kulky, may they live, for the charity of the holy community Lipník [nad Bečvou] [in the year] *595* [=1835].
Collection point: Lipník nad Bečvou

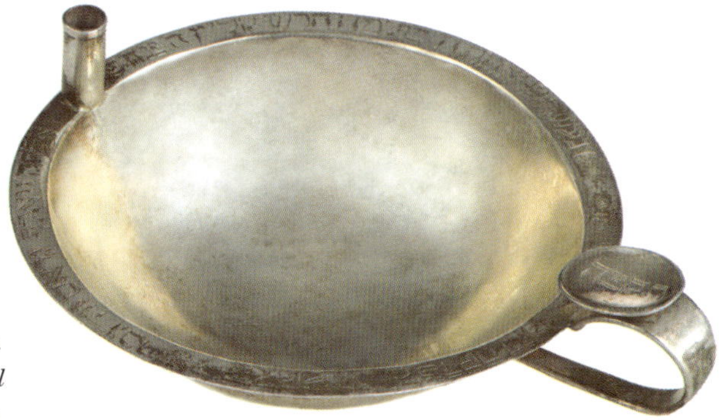

Cat. No. 319

Cat. No. 320
Charity Dish
Inv. No. JMP 032.438/02
Silver, repoussé
Joachim Anton Kaisberger,
Prague, 1860
Length: 258 mm, diameter: 179 mm
Hallmarks: 1. JAK in rectangle,
2. hallmark Prague 1860
Donation inscription in Hebrew.
Translation:
This was donated by the sage KH Isaiah, son of R Mordecai, son of the sage, departed, brilliant in Torah and outstanding in piety, MVH Gershon Wiener of blessed memory, in the year 620 a. s. c. [= 1860].
Collection point: Prague, Old-New Synagogue

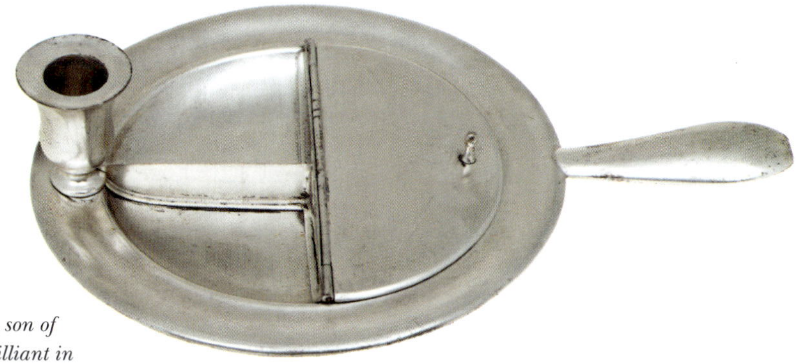

Cat. No. 320

Cat. No. 321
Charity Dish
Inv. No. JMP 010.956
Silver, repoussé, cast, engraving
Maker HS, Vienna, after 1871
Length: 275 mm, diameter: 197 mm
Hallmarks: 1. HS in rectangle,
2. Austro-Hungary [Vienna]
after 1871
Donation inscription in Hebrew.
Translation:
This charity dish was made through the agency of the custodians KH Ayzik Winter, KH David Weiner, KH Beer Rebenwurzel for the holy community Strážnice in the year 669 a. s. c. [= 1909].
Collection point: Strážnice

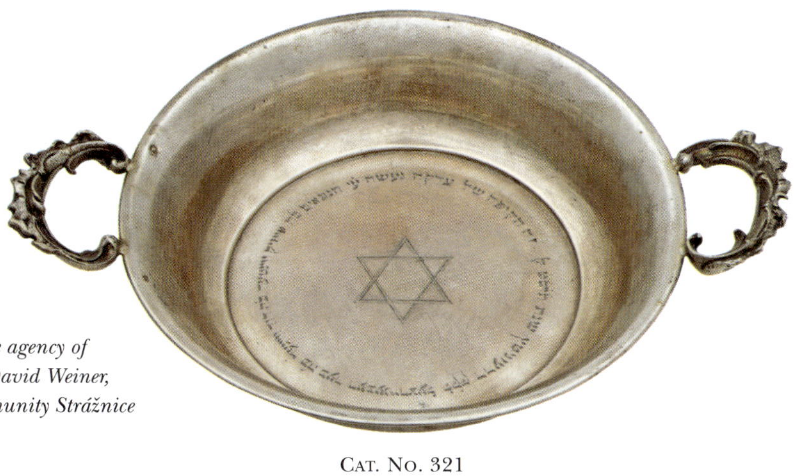

Cat. No. 321

IX. Combs

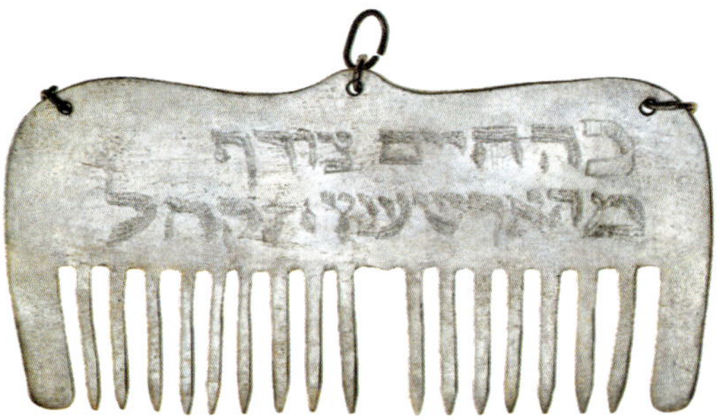

< Cat. No. 322
Burial Society Comb
Inv. No. JMP 049.443
Silver, cut-out
Hayyim Tzoref [?], Bohemia [?], 1748 [inscription]
Length: 113 mm, width: 55 mm
Hallmarks: unmarked
Donation inscription in Hebrew.
Translation:
This was donated to the holy society [Burial Society] *by KH Hayyim Tzoref of Hořenice* [in the year] *508 a. s. c.* [= 1748].
Collection point: Prague

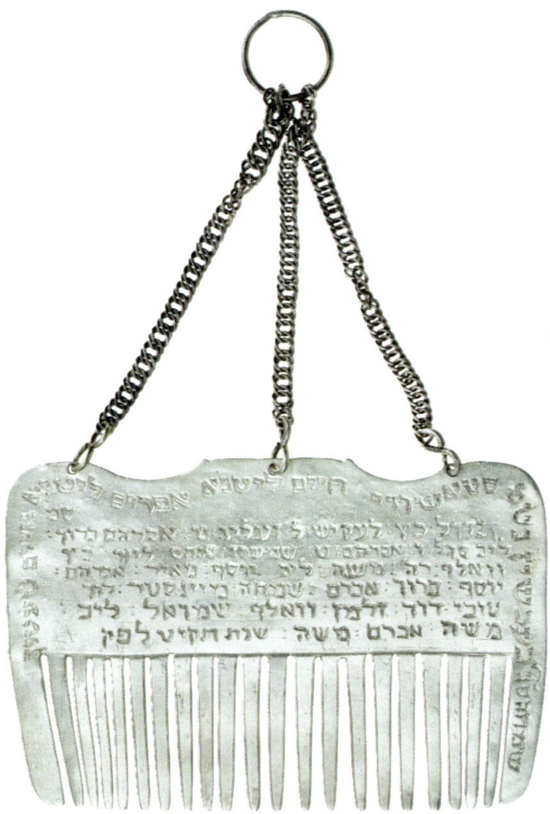

< Cat. No. 323
Burial Society Comb
Inv. No. JMP 037.731
Silver, cut-out
No maker's mark, Bohemia [?], 1759 [inscription]
Length: 149 mm, width: 97 mm
Hallmarks: 1. recharge mark Prague 1806–7
Donation inscription in Hebrew.
Translation:
Simhah SGL Bechschin; Netel Staschovy; Hayyim Littna; Ephraim Littna; Hayyim Tettin; Zanwil KC; Lekisch L.; Zelig M.; Abraham Baruch; Leib SGL R.; Abraham T.; Simon; Pinhas; Leizer KC; Wolf, head of the community; Moses; Leib; Joseph; Meir; Abraham; Joseph; Baruch; Abram; Simhah; Meinster; David; Tuvja [?]; *David; Zalman; Wolf; Samuel; Leib; Moses; Abram; in the year 519 a. s. c.* [= 1759]. *R Henich, custodian of the Burial Society; R Elijah, custodian of the Burial Society; R Joseph SGL; R Leib K P; R Meier KP, head of the community; R Leib Bondi; R Itzak SGL; R J. Merian; R W. Mishke, son of R Hirsch; R Hayyim Taschenk, son of R J.; R Itzak, son of Jusel; R Abraham L.; R Leib, son of R Aaron Engel; R Anschel Hecht, 555 a. s. c.* [= 1795].
Collection point: Jewish Museum in Prague, 1906–1940

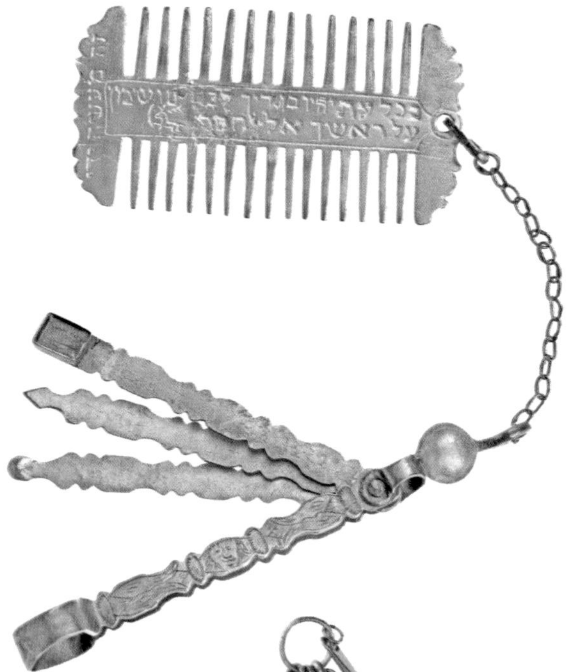

Cat. No. 324 >
Burial Society Comb and Cleaner Picks
Inv. No. JMP 004.520/01-02
Silver, cut-out
No maker's mark, Moravia [?], 1770 [inscription]
Comb: [/01]: length: 96 mm, width: 51 mm
Cleaner: [/02]: length: 102 mm
Hallmarks: unmarked
Donation inscription in Hebrew.
Translation:
Moses, son of Itzik [diagonal inscription]. *"A good name is better than fragrant oil, and the day of death than the day of birth"* [Eccles. 7:1], *in the year 530 a. s. c.* [= 1770] [lengthwise inscription]. *This is the work of my hand* [diagonal inscription]. *"Let your garments be always white, and your head never lack ointment"* [Eccles. 9:8] [lengthwise inscription].
Collection point: Central Jewish Museum for Moravia and Silesia, 1936–1938 in Nikolsburg

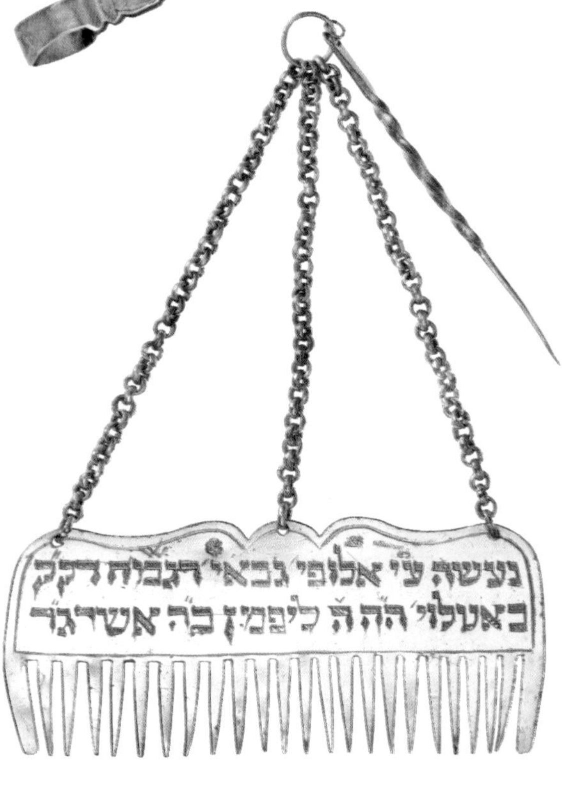

Cat. No. 325 >
Burial Society Comb and Cleaner Pick
Inv. No. JMP 037.398/01,02
Silver, cut-out
Maker KS, Jihlava, 1803
Comb: [/01]: length: 122 mm, width: 53 mm
Cleaner Pick: [/02]: length: 94 mm
Hallmarks: 1. KS in rectangle,
2. hallmark Jihlava 1803
Donation inscription in Hebrew.
Translation:
Made through the agency of the princes, custodians [of the holy society] *performing good deeds of the holy community Batelov, HH H Lipman, son of H Asher GR, and HH H Abraham Meir, son of H Joshua GSch, in the year 563 a. s. c.* [= 1803]. *VSch LK* [?].
Collection point: Batelov

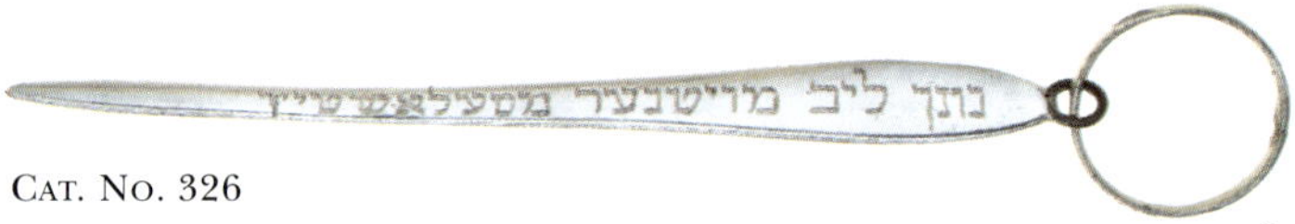

Cat. No. 326

Cat. No. 326

Burial Society Cleaner Pick

Inv. No. JMP 010.920

Silver, cut-out

Jan Fleischmann, Prague, 1807

Length: 139 mm, width: 13 mm

Hallmarks: 1. IF in heart, 2. hallmark Prague 1807, 3. recharge mark Prague 1806–7

Donation inscription in Hebrew.

Translation:

Donated by Leib Mautner of Selaštice.

Collection point: Prčice

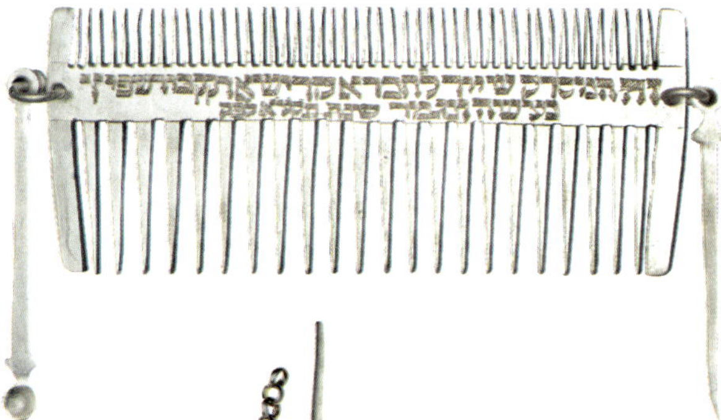

Cat. No. 327

Cat. No. 327

Burial Society Comb and Cleaner Picks

Inv. No. JMP 010.245/01–03

Silver, cut-out

Franz Kaltenmarker, Brno, 1810

Comb: [/01]: length: 134 mm, width: 57 mm

Cleaner Pick: [/02]: length: 73 mm

Cleaner Pick: [/03]: length: 74 mm

Hallmarks: 1. FK in oval, 2. hallmark Brno 1810, 3. tax mark Brno 1810–24

Donation inscription in Hebrew.

Translation:

This comb belongs to the Burial Society in the holy community Bučovice. Made and completed in the year 571 a. s. c. [= 1811].

Collection point: Bučovice

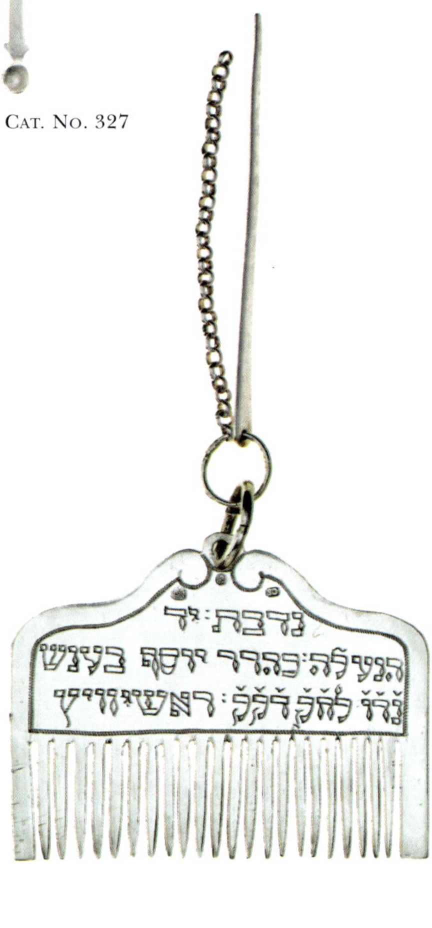

Cat. No. 328

Cat. No. 328

Burial Society Comb and Cleaner Pick

Inv. No. JMP 010.577/01,02

Silver, cut-out

Karel Skřemenec, Prague, 1814

Comb: length: 110 mm, width: 86 mm

Cleaner pick: length: 114 mm

Hallmarks: 1. CS in rectangle, 2. hallmark Prague 1814, 3. tax mark Prague 1810–24

Donation inscription in Hebrew.

Translation:

A gift of the distinguished KHRR Joseph Beneš, may the Merciful protect and redeem him, for the holy society [Burial Society] *in the holy community Rašivice / Rosivice / Rossitz.*

Collection point: Horažďovice

Cat. No. 329
Burial Society Comb
Inv. No. JMP 007.559
Silver, cut-out
Maker EW, Olomouc, 1828
Length: 155 mm, width: 75 mm
Hallmarks: 1. EW in rectangle,
2. hallmark Olomouc 1828
Donation inscription in Hebrew.
Translation:
This was donated by the esteemed lady Malkah, wife of Mr. Koppel of blessed memory for the prayers on behalf of their souls and to the glory of the Holy Benevolent Society [Burial Society] *in the year 589 a. s. c.* [= 1829].
Collection point: Kojetín

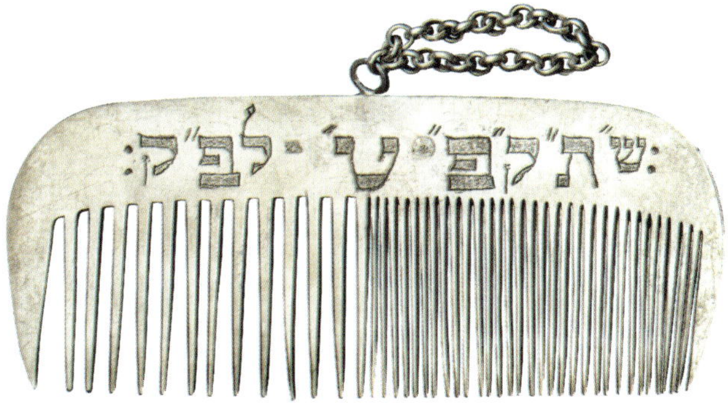

Cat. No. 329

Cat. No. 330
Burial Society Comb and Cleaner Picks
Inv. No. JMP 010.344/01-05
Silver, engraving, cut-out
Johann Radda [?], Brno, 183[5]
Comb: [/01]: length: 110 mm, width: 52 mm
Cleaner Pick: [/02 –/05]: length: 75 mm
Hallmarks: 1. JR in oval, 2. hallmark Brno 183[5]
Donation inscription in Hebrew.
Translation:
A gift and bequest of Yokev Klein, may the memory of the just be blessed. 595 a. s. c. [= 1835] [on the comb]. *Ch N, Ch K* [?] [on the cleaner pick].
Collection point: Boskovice

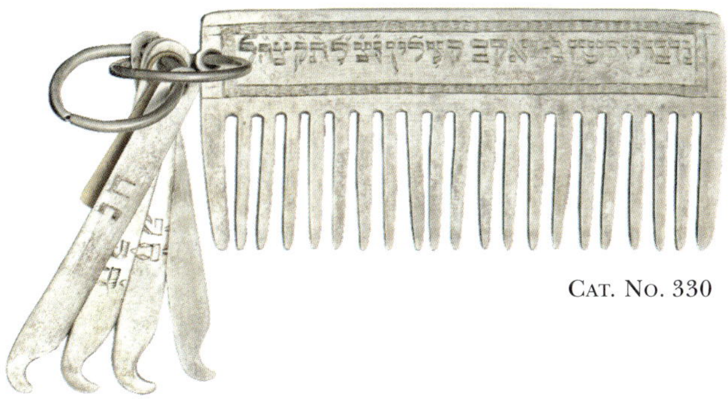

Cat. No. 330

Cat. No. 331
Burial Society Comb and Cleaner Pick
Inv. No. JMP 010.100/01-02
Silver, engraving, cut-out
Maker IB, Vienna, 1858
Comb: [/01]: length: 153 mm, width: 75 mm
Cleaner Pick: [/02]: length: 31 mm
Hallmarks: 1. IB in rectangle,
2. hallmark Vienna 1858
Without inscriptions.
Collection point: Loštice

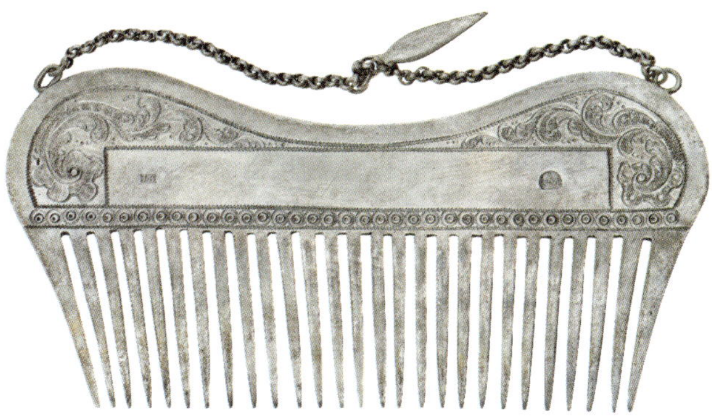

Cat. No. 331

Cat. No. 332
Burial Society Comb
Inv. No. JMP 023.338
Silver, cut-out
Maker EZ, Brno, 1864 [inscription]
Length: 176 mm, width: 36 mm
Hallmarks: 1. EZ in rectangle,
2. hallmark Brno 1865
[mark likely added later]
Donation inscription in Hebrew.
Translation:
This was donated by the elder R Joel Rosenberger for the Holy Benevolent Society [Burial Society] *of the holy community Podivín the 7th of Adar 624 a. s. c.* [= 1864] *with his wife the lady Pesl, may she live.*
Collection point: Podivín

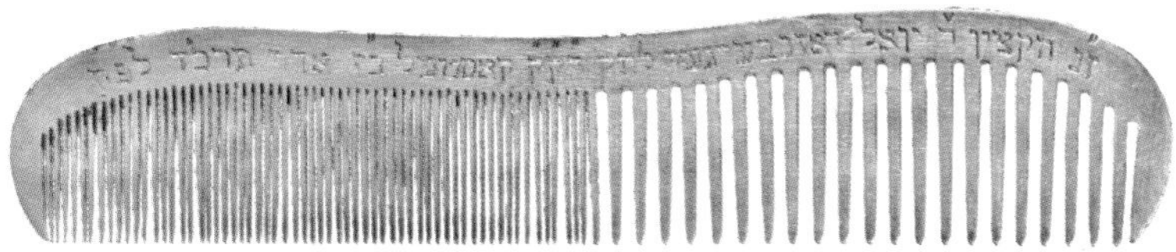

Cat. No. 332

Cat. No. 333
Burial Society Comb and Cleaner Pick
Inv. No. JMP 009.860/01, 02
Silver, cut-out
Maker AK, Prague, after 1871
Comb: [/01]: length: 130 mm, width: 92 mm
Cleaner Pick : [/02]: length: 148 mm
Hallmarks: 1. AK in rectangle,
2. Austro-Hungary [Prague] after 1871
Donation inscription in Hebrew.
Translation:
The Holy Benevolent Society
[Burial Society] [in] *Beroun.*
Collection point: Beroun

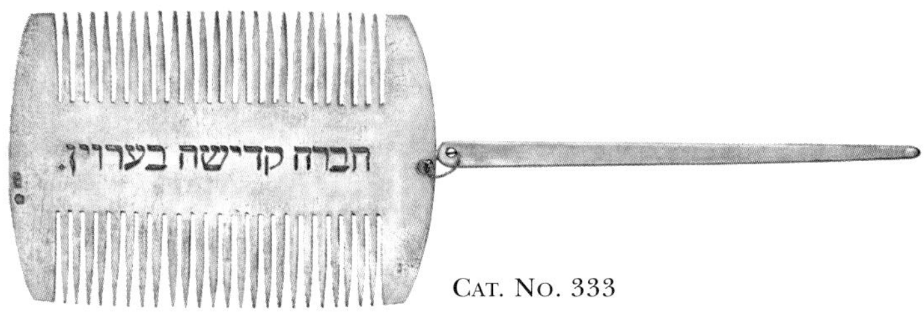

Cat. No. 333

X. Cups and Beakers

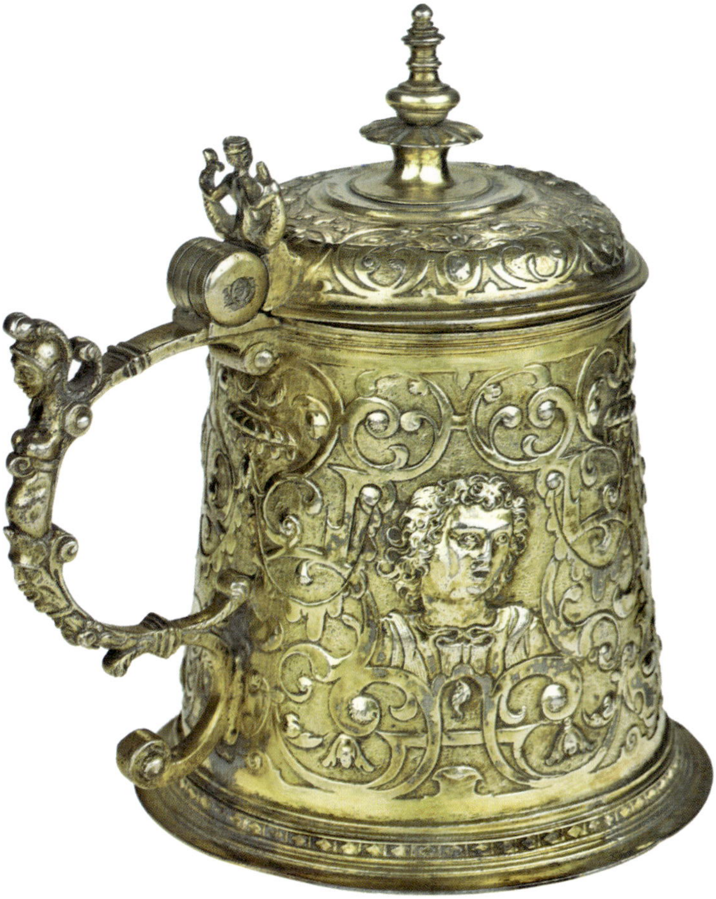

Cat. No. 334
Beaker
Inv. No. JMP 010.349
Silver, repoussé, gilt, engraving
Bernard Hartenach, Brno, ca. 1580 – before 1618
Height: 162 mm, width: 159 mm
Hallmarks: 1. BH in shield, 2. hallmark Brno,
3. recharge mark Brno 1806–7, 4. release mark 1809–10
Initials in Latin script:
S. C. E. E. G. B. W. [inside the lid].
I. O. I. I. [lower edge].
Collection point: Boskovice

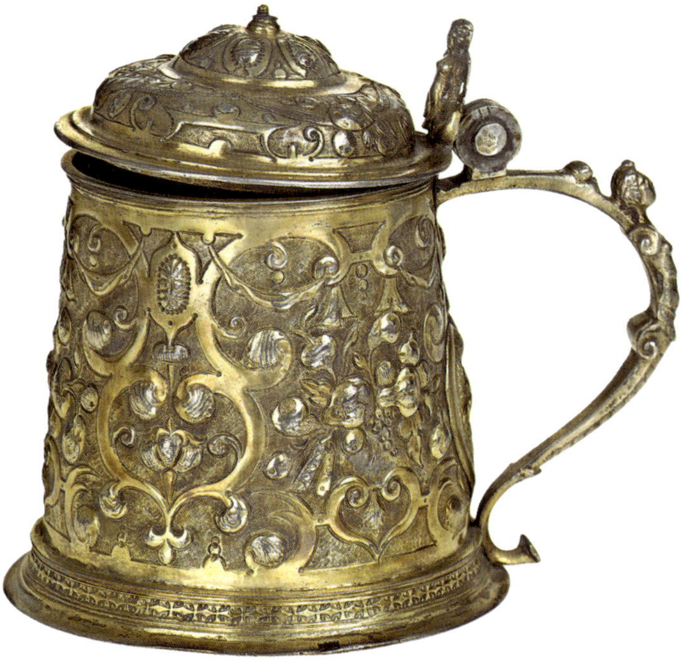

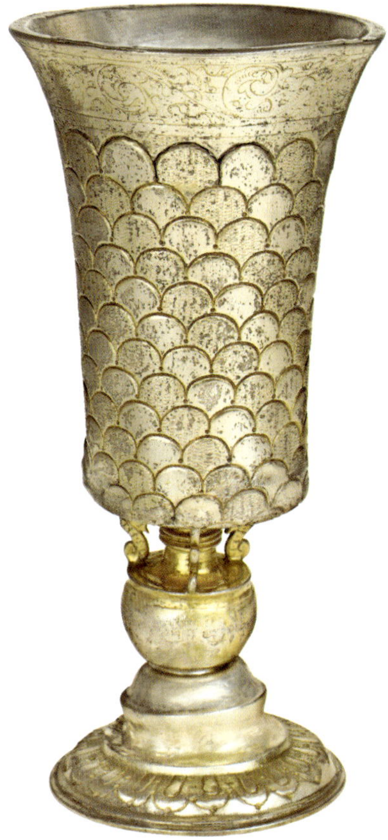

Cat. No. 335
Beaker
Inv. No. JMP 002.925
Silver, repoussé, engraving, gilt
Salomon II Spitzmacher, Augsburg, 1595–1600
Height: 123 mm, width: 135 mm
Hallmarks: 1. zigzag in shield, 2. hallmark Augsburg 1595–1600, 3. recharge mark Brno 1806–7
Initials in Latin script and date underneath the bottom: *V. W. 1638.*
Collection point: Lipník nad Bečvou

Cat. No. 336
Cup
Inv. No. JMP 003.939
Silver, repoussé, cast, gilt, engraving
No maker's mark, Central Europe, ca. 1600
Height: 176 mm, diameter: 81 mm
Hallmarks: unmarked
Donation inscription in Hebrew.
Translation:
Kiddush cup of the Maharal of Prague.
Collection point: Brno

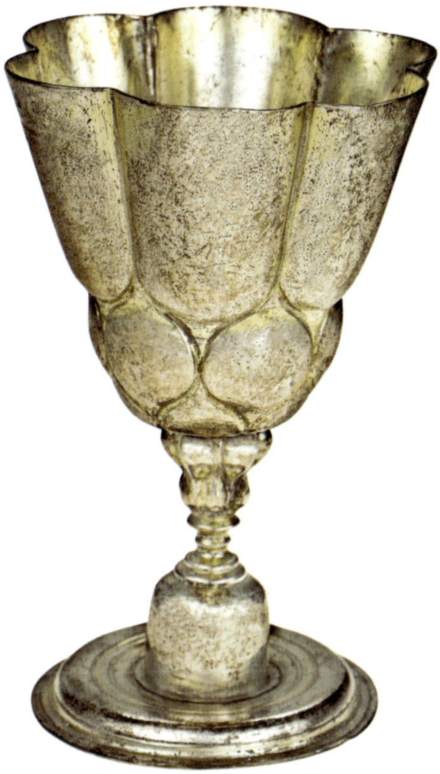

Cat. No. 337
Cup
Inv. No. JMP 012.223
Silver, repoussé, originally gilt
Emanuel Kessbair, Augsburg, 1620 [?]
Height: 142 mm, diameter: 89 mm
Hallmarks: 1. I in shield,
2. hallmark Augsburg 1620 [?],
3. recharge mark Brno 1806–7,
4. release mark 1809–10
Without inscriptions.
Collection point: Kounice

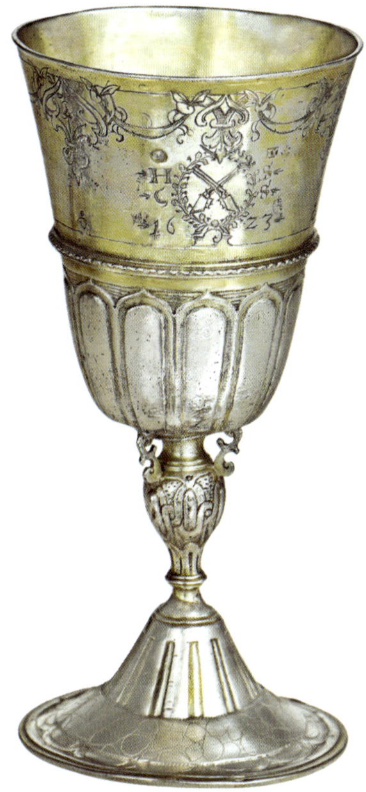

Cat. No. 338
Cup
Inv. No. JMP 002.195
Silver, repoussé, engraving, parcel-gilt
Maker DK [?], Jihlava, 1623 [inscription]
Height: 155 mm, diameter: 78 mm
Hallmarks: 1. DK [?] in rectangle, 2. hallmark Jihlava, 3. recharge mark Prague 1806–7,
3. release mark 1809–10
Initials in Latin script and date:
HS GS 1623.
Collection point: Mladá Boleslav

Cat. No. 339
Cup
Acq. No. JMP 2011/0091
Silver, repoussé, engraving
Jeronymus Gilg, Augsburg, 1630–35
Height: 135 mm, diameter: 76 mm
Hallmarks: 1. IG in oval,
2. hallmark Augsburg 1630–35
Without inscriptions.
Catalogued secondarily into the inventory of the Jewish Museum in Prague.

Cat. No. 340
Cup
Inv. No. JMP 010.269
Silver, repoussé, engraving
Philipp Plapert, Nuremberg, mid-17th century
Height: 85 mm, diameter: 72 mm
Hallmarks: 1. FP in shield, 2. hallmark Nuremberg,
3. recharge mark Brno 1806–7,
4. release mark 1809–10
Without inscriptions.
Collection point: Slavkov u Brna

Cat. No. 341
Cup
Inv. No. JMP 002.921
Silver, engraving
Ulrich Schnell, Augsburg, 1665–70
Height: 112 mm, diameter: 90 mm
Hallmarks: 1. VS in oval, 2. hallmark Augsburg 1665–70, 3. recharge mark Brno 1806–7,
3. release mark 1809–10
Donation inscription in Hebrew.
Translation:
This was donated by the lady Rosa for herself and her late husband H David D W [Dewidels ?] *of blessed memory.*
Collection point: Lipník nad Bečvou

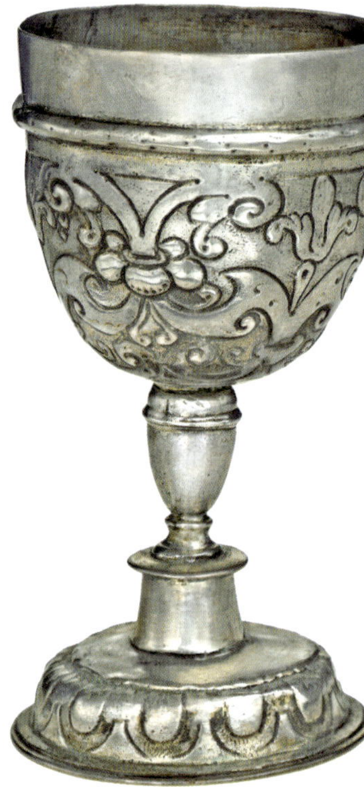

Cat. No. 339

Cat. No. 342
Cup
Inv. No. JMP 037.449
Silver, repoussé
Maker CL, Central Europe, 1668 [inscription]
Height: 80 mm, diameter: 68 mm
Hallmarks: 1. CL in shield
Initials in Latin script and date:
1. 6. M. D. RP. 6. 8. [RP not separated by a period]
Collection point: Prague

Cat. No. 343
Beaker
Inv. No. JMP 010.385
Silver, repoussé, gilt
Marx II Schaller [?], Augsburg, 1680 [?]
Height: 170 mm, width: 157 mm
Hallmarks: 1. standing bird in oval, 2. hallmark Augsburg 1680 [?], 3. recharge mark Brno 1806–7
Without inscriptions.
Collection point: Miroslav

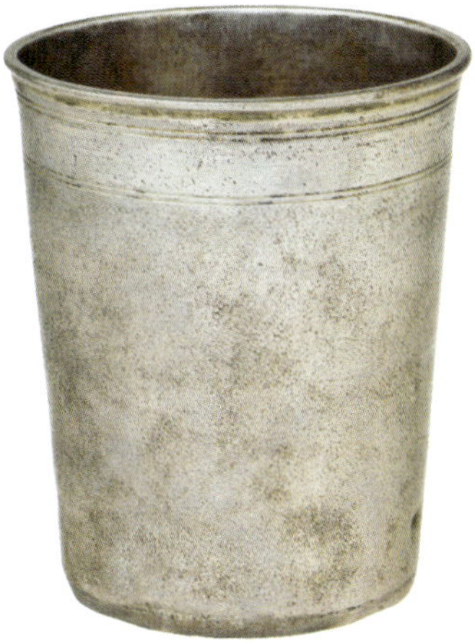

Cat. No. 340

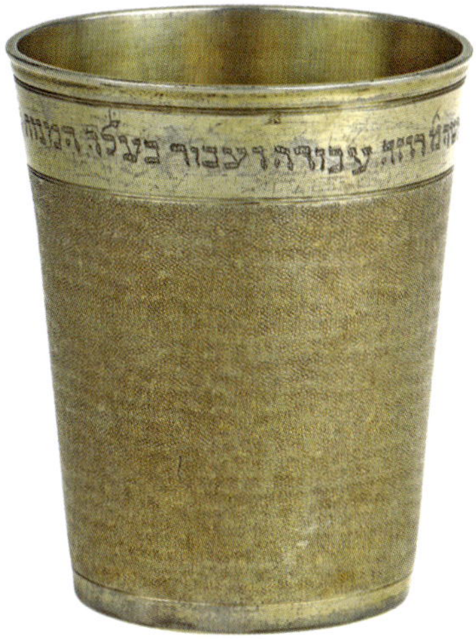

Cat. No. 341

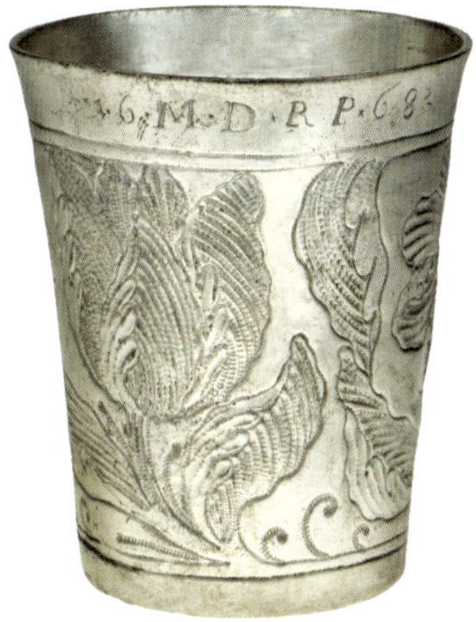

Cat. No. 342

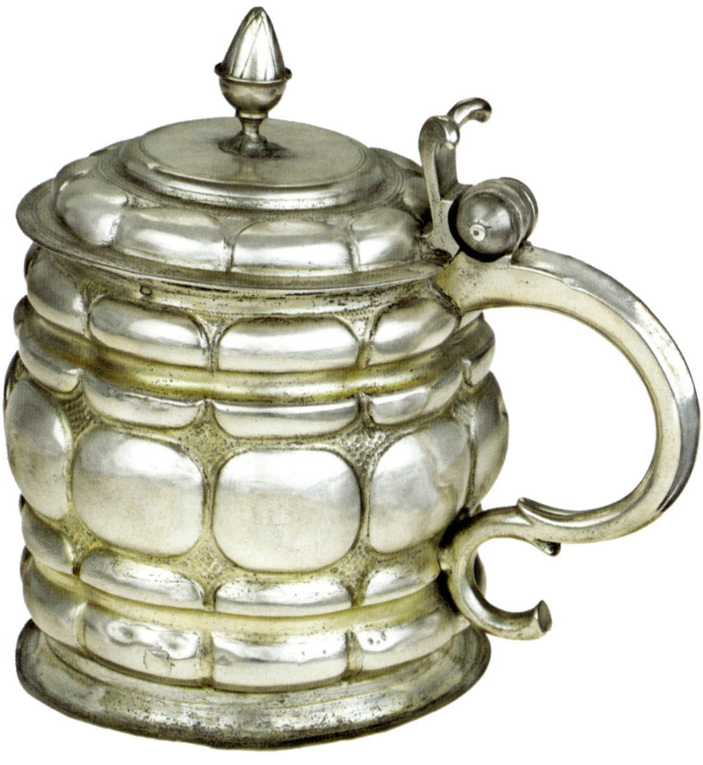

Cat. No. 343

Cat. No. 344
Cup
Inv. No. JMP 003.701
Silver, repoussé, engraving
Carl Schuh, Augsburg, 1695–1700 [?]
Height: 80 mm, diameter: 69 mm
Hallmarks: 1. CS in oval, 2. hallmark Augsburg 1695–1700 [?], 3. recharge mark Brno 1806–7
Donation inscription in Hebrew.
Translation:
This was donated by HH Simon Pulitz with his wife the lady Mindl on behalf of their son, the boy Eizak, to the charitable funds of the synagogue of the holy community A G [evidently Eisgrub = Lednice] *in the year 564 a. s. c.* [= 1804].
Collection point: Central Jewish Museum for Moravia and Silesia, 1936–1938 in Nikolsburg

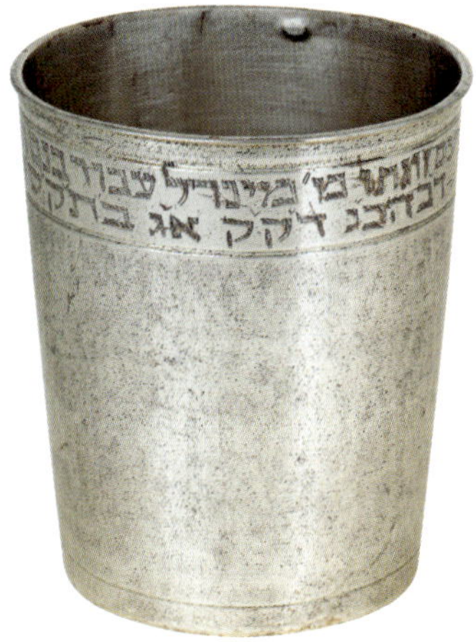

Cat. No. 344

Cat. No. 345
Cup
Inv. No. JMP 023.176
Silver, repoussé
Konrad Wolter, Oława, 1693–1710
Height: 83 mm, diameter: 74 mm
Hallmarks: 1. CW in circle, 2. hallmark Oława, 3. tax mark Prague 1810–24
Without inscriptions.
Collection point: Vodňany

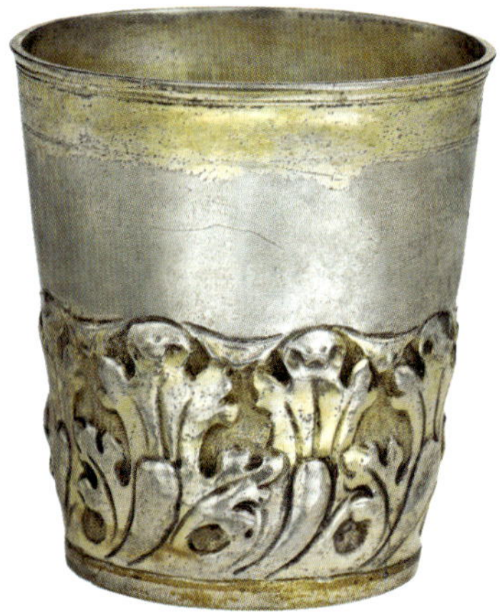

Cat. No. 345

Cat. No. 346
Cup
Inv. No. JMP 007.456
Silver, repoussé, parcel-gilt, engraving
Alexander Kraudy, Bánská Bystrica, mid-18th century
Height: 70 mm, diameter: 60 mm
Hallmarks: 1. AK in irregular shield, 2. hallmark Bánská Bystrica, 3. recharge mark Brno 1806–7
Without inscriptions.
Collection point: Kyjov

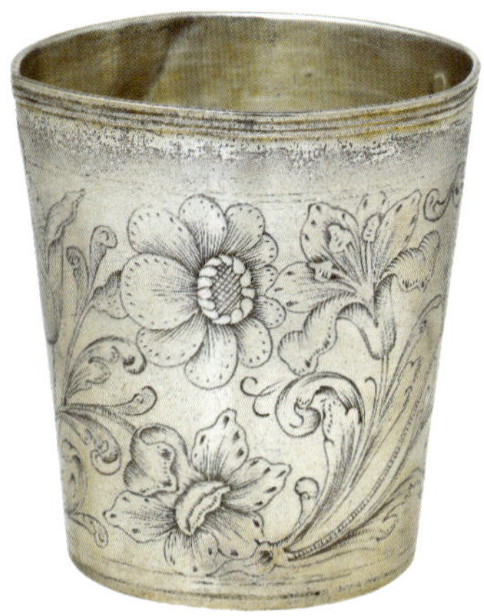

Cat. No. 346

Cat. No. 347
Cup
Inv. No. JMP 007.167
Silver, repoussé, parcel-gilt, engraving
No maker's mark, Central Europe, 18th century
Height: 57 mm, diameter: 55 mm
Hallmarks: unmarked
Donation incription in Hebrew.
Translation:
This was donated by the sage R Mordecai Blum with his wife the esteemed lady Elka [in the year] *630 a. s. c.* [= 1870].
Collection point: Brno

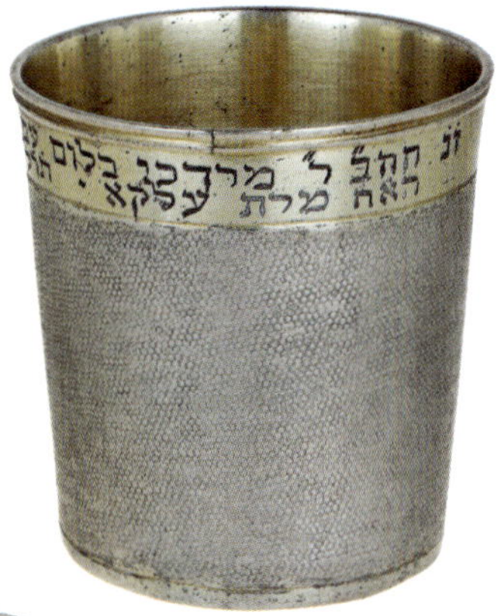

Cat. No. 347

Cat. No. 348
Cup
Inv. No. JMP 037.835
Silver, repousssé, engraving
Johann Friedrich Ehe, Nuremberg, 1793–97
Height: 101 mm, diameter: 59 mm
Hallmarks: 1. IFE in trilob, 2. hallmark Nuremberg, 3. mark of the elder H in circle [1793–97], 4. tax mark Prague 1810–24
Donation inscription in Hebrew.
Translation:
"I will lift up the cup of salvation" [Ps. 116:13] *a gift for the Kauder Synagogue. In the year 634 a. s. c.* [= 1874]. *Abraham, son of his master, father, and teacher MVH Hayyim Jaffe of blessed memory.*
Collection point: Prague, Pinkas Synagogue

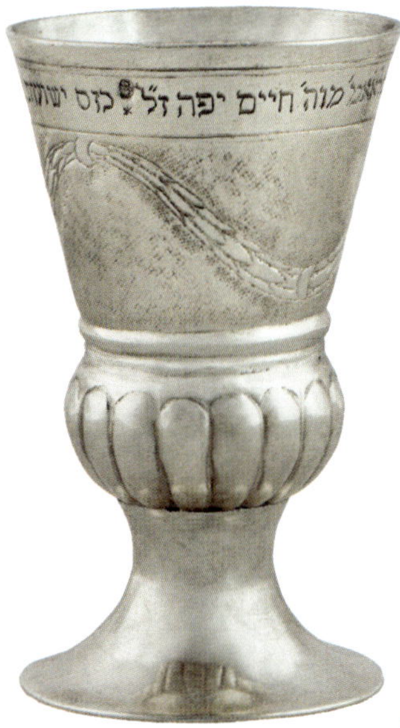

Cat. No. 348

Cat. No. 349
Cup
Inv. No. JMP 012.271
Silver, repoussé, originally parcel-gilt
Carl Lackstampfer, Sr., Brno, 1800
Height: 90 mm, diameter: 64 mm
Hallmarks: 1. CL in oval, 2. hallmark Brno 1800, 3. recharge mark Brno 1806–7, 4. release mark 1809–10
Without inscriptions.
Collection point: Brno, Jevíčko

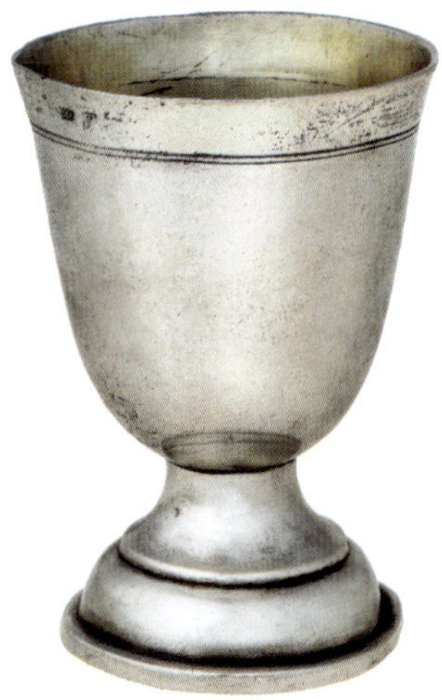

Cat. No. 349

Cat. No. 350
Cup
Inv. No. JMP 004.846
Silver, repoussé
Franz Lorenz Turinsky, Vienna, 1804
Height: 91 mm, diameter: 62 mm
Hallmarks: 1. FLT in shield,
2. hallmark Vienna 1804, 3. recharge mark
Brno 1806–7, 4. release mark 1809–10
Without inscriptions.
Collection point: Central Jewish Museum for
Moravia and Silesia, 1936–1938 in Nikolsburg

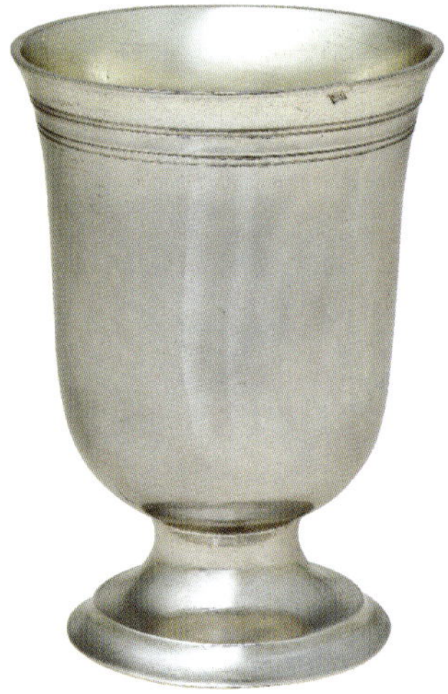

Cat. No. 350

Cat. No. 351
Cup
Inv. No. JMP 002.922
Silver, repoussé
Maker JV [?], Opava, 1807
Height: 112 mm, diameter: 84 mm
Hallmarks: 1. JV [?] in rectangle,
2. hallmark Opava 1807–9, 3. recharge mark
Brno 1806–7, 4. release mark 1809–10
Without inscriptions.
Collection point: Lipník nad Bečvou

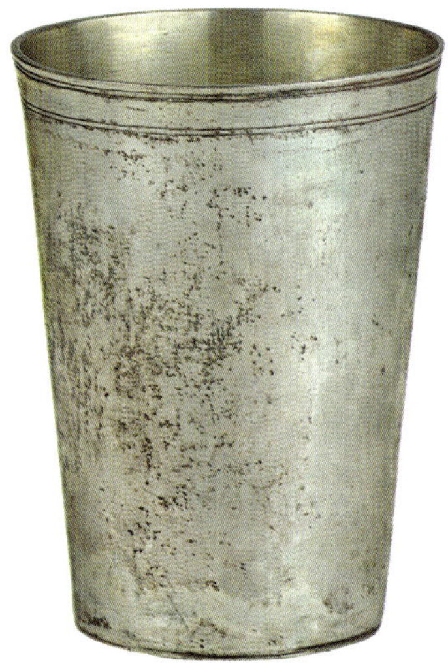

Cat. No. 351

Cat. No. 352
Cup
Inv. No. JMP 032.432
Silver, repoussé
Karel Skřemenec, Prague, 1807
Height: 47 mm, diameter: 67 mm
Hallmarks: 1. CS in oval, 2. hallmark Prague
1807–9, 3. recharge mark 1806–7,
4. release mark 1809–10
Without inscriptions.
Collection point: Prague, Old-New Synagogue

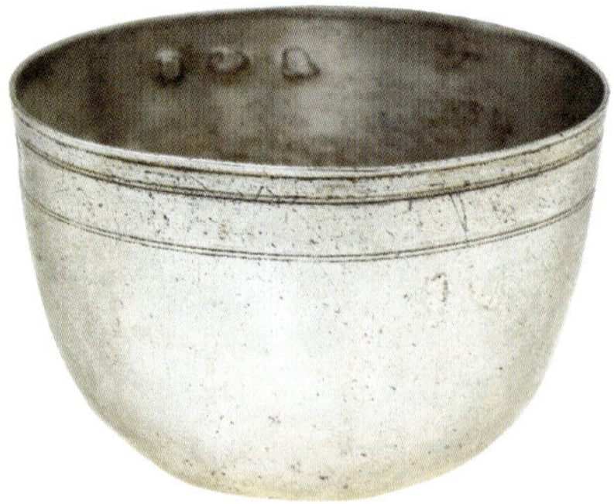

Cat. No. 352

Cat. No. 353
Cup
Inv. No. JMP 010.951
Silver, repoussé
Maker's mark illegible, Vienna, 1810–12
Height: 103 mm, diameter: 65 mm
Hallmarks: 1. illegible maker's mark,
2. hallmark Vienna 1810–12,
3. tax mark Vienna 1810–24
Without inscriptions.
Collection point: Strážnice

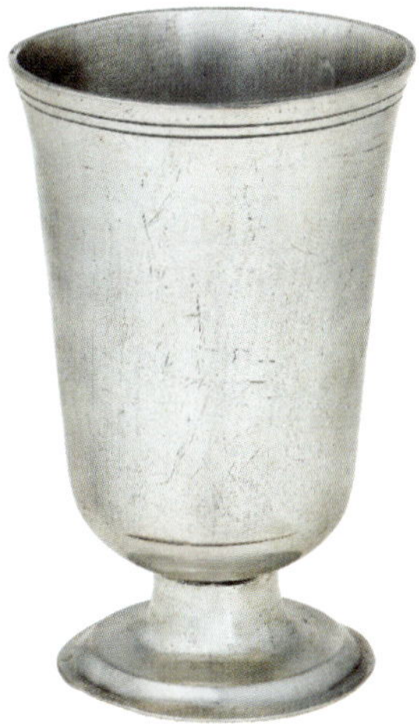

Cat. No. 353

Cat. No. 354
Cup
Inv. No. JMP 002.930
Silver, repoussé
Franz Lorenz Turinsky, Vienna, 1813
Height: 205 mm, diameter: 83 mm
Hallmarks: 1. FLT in shield, 2. hallmark
Vienna 1813, 3. tax mark Vienna 1810–24
Donation inscription in Hebrew.
Translation:
This was donated by HRR Abraham Heller,
571 [= 1811] [sic] *a. s. c.* .
Collection point: Lipník nad Bečvou

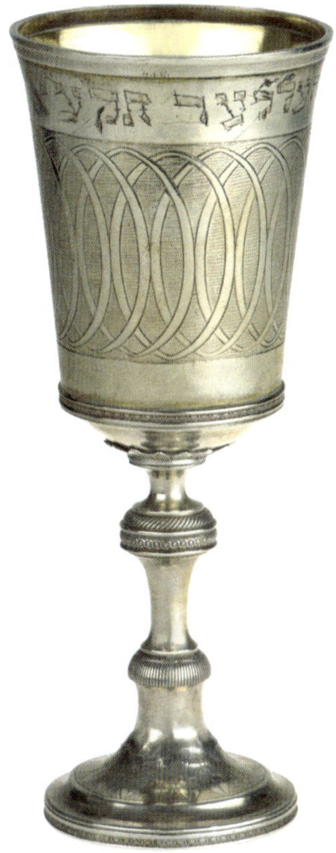

Cat. No. 354

Cat. No. 355
Cup
Inv. No. JMP 010.332
Silver, repoussé
Jakob Uhl, Brno, 1815
Height: 88 mm, diameter: 58 mm
Hallmarks: 1. JU in oval, 2. hallmark Brno 1815,
3. tax mark Brno 1810–24
Inscription in Hebrew.
Translation:
"I said to you in your blood, 'Live!' Yes, I said to you in your blood, 'Live!'" [Ezek. 16:6; part of the blessing following the circumcision, according to the Sichat Yitzhak siddur].
Collection point: Boskovice

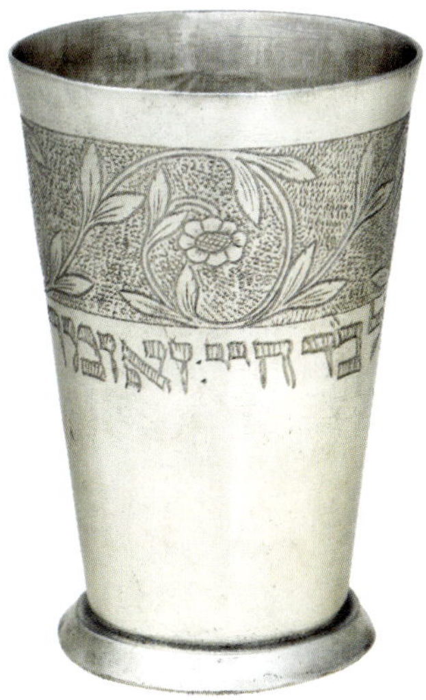

Cat. No. 355

Cat. No. 356
Inv. No. JMP 152.211/04
Circumcision Cup
silver, repoussé, engraving
Maker AN, Prague, 1815
Height: 75 mm, diameter: 58 mm
Hallmarks: 1. AN in oval, 2. hallmark Prague 1815,
3. tax mark Prague 1810–24
Without inscriptions.
Purchased by the Jewish Museum in Prague

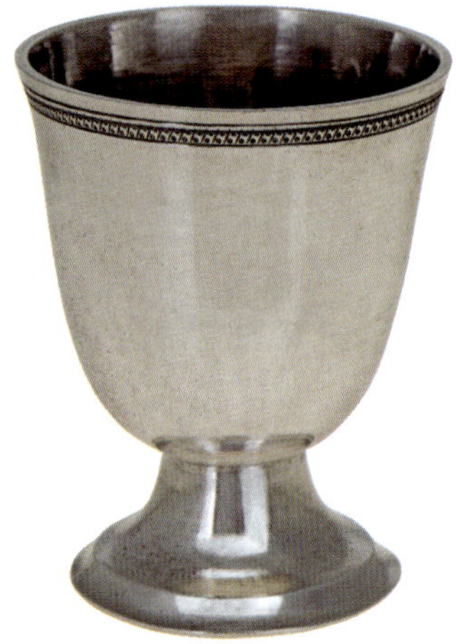

Cat. No. 356

Cat. No. 357
Cup
Inv. No. JMP 005.043
Silver, repoussé, originally parcel-gilt
Tomáš Höpfel, Prague, 1816
Height: 77 mm, diameter: 55 mm
Hallmarks: 1. TH in rectangle,
2. hallmark Prague 1816,
3. tax mark Prague 1810–24
Initials in Latin script:
MJ.
Collection point: Strakonice

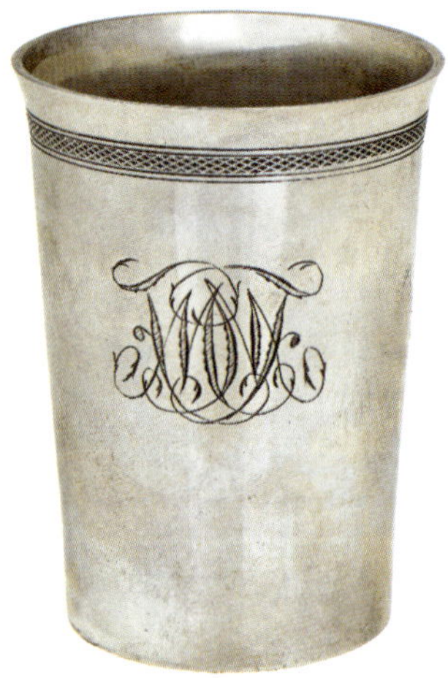

Cat. No. 357

Cat. No. 358
Cup
Inv. No. JMP 102.472
Silver, repoussé, engraving
Antonín Kába, Prague, 1818
Height: 78 mm, diameter: 65 mm
Hallmarks: 1. AK in oval, 2. hallmark
Prague 1818, 3. tax mark Prague 1810–24
Donation inscription in Hebrew.
Translation:
This was donated by three men leading prayers, KH Elijah Rosenwasser, KH David Hayyim Stern, KM Baruch Leib Weinschenk in the holy community Libeň. In the year 582 a.s.c. [= 1822].
Catalogued secondarily into the inventory of the Jewish Museum in Prague.

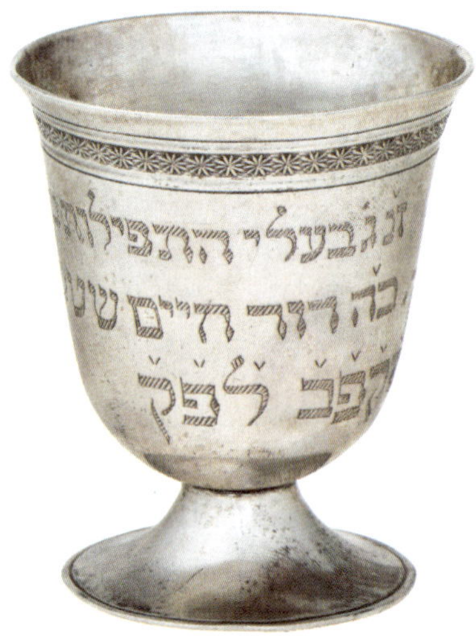

Cat. No. 358

Cat. No. 359
Cup
Inv. No. JMP 010.270
Silver, repoussé, engraving
No maker's mark, Germany [?],
1st half of 19th century
Height: 70 mm, diameter: 53 mm
Hallmarks: 1. purity number 13 in shield
Donation inscription in Hebrew.
Translation:
[In the year] *"He executed the justice of the Lord"*
[Deut. 33:21; dating in chronogram
594 = 1834] *a. s. c.* .
Collection point: Slavkov u Brna

Cat. No. 360
Cup
Inv. No. JMP 007.166
Silver, repoussé
Josef Wieninger, Vienna, 1825–29
Height: 80 mm, diameter: 65 mm
Hallmarks: 1. JW in rectangle,
2. hallmark Vienna 1820–29
Inscription in Hebrew.
Translation:
This belongs to the New Synagogue
and [it] *was donated in*
the year 694 a. s. c. [= 1834].
Collection point: Brno

Cat. No. 361
Cup
Inv. No. JMP 012.224
Silver, repoussé
Maker EU [Eduard Uhl?], Brno, 1830–39
Height: 139 mm, diameter: 89 mm
Hallmarks: 1. EU in oval,
2. hallmark Brno 1830–39
Without inscriptions.
Collection point: Kounice

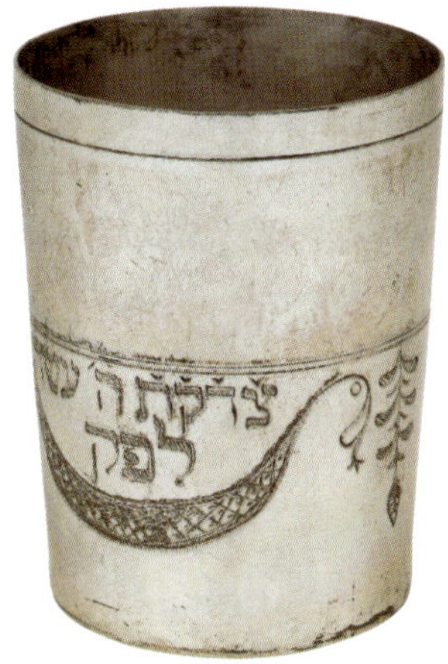

Cat. No. 359

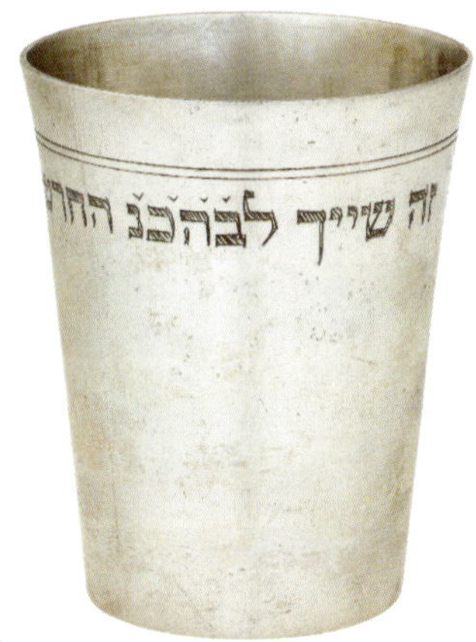

Cat. No. 360

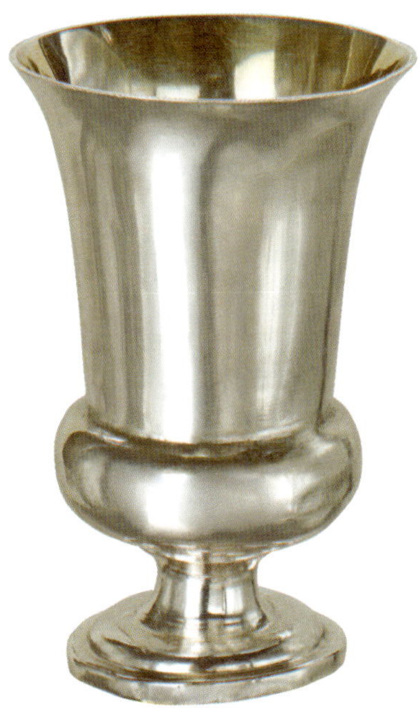

Cat. No. 361

Cat. No. 362
Cup
Inv. No. JMP 023.177
Silver, repoussé
Christian Sander, Sr., Vienna, 1846
Height: 99 mm, diameter: 67 mm
Hallmarks: 1. CS in rectangle,
2. hallmark Vienna 1846
Donation inscription in Hebrew.
Translation:
This was donated by the insignificant Aaron Neumann with his wife Frumet [in the year] *620* [a. s. c.] [= 1860].
Collection point: Vodňany

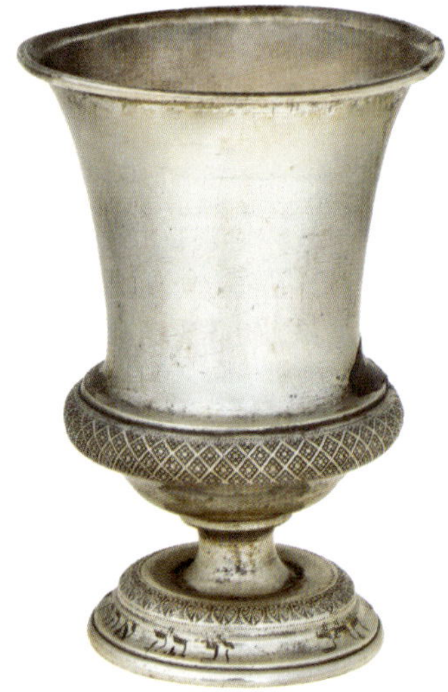

Cat. No. 362

Cat. No. 363
Beaker
Inv. No. JMP 004.265
Silver, repoussé, engraving
Thomas Regscheck, Vienna, 1849
Height: 170 mm, width: 150 mm
Hallmarks: 1. TR in rectangle,
2. hallmark Vienna 1849
Donation inscription in Hebrew.
Translation:
Through the agency of the matron the lady Zelda Husserl in the year 613 [a. s. c.] [= 1853].
Collection point: Prostějov

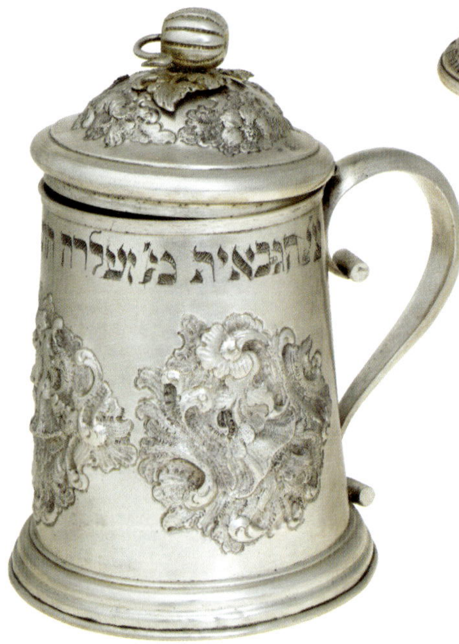

Cat. No. 363

Cat. No. 364
Cup
Inv. No. JMP 174.348
Silver, repoussé, engraving
No maker's mark, Poland [?],
mid-19th century
Height: 63 mm, diameter: 57 mm
Hallmarks: 1. purity number 12 in rectangle
Inscription in Hebrew.
Translation:
A cup of sanctity made from temple shekels.
Acquired by the JMP via transfer.

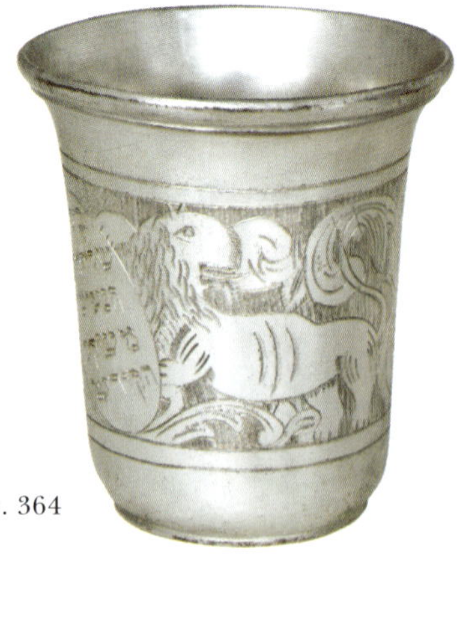

Cat. No. 364

Cat. No. 365
Cup
Inv. No. JMP 037.548
Silver, repoussé
Václav Kabeš, Prague, 1852
Height: 76 mm, diameter: 55 mm
Hallmarks: 1. WK in oval, 2. hallmark Prague 1852
Without inscriptions.
Collection point: Prague

Cat. No. 366
Cup
Inv. No. JMP 010.691
Silver, repoussé
Carl Lejolle, Vienna, 1856
Height: 87 mm, diameter: 80 mm
Hallmarks: 1. CL in rectangle,
2. hallmark Vienna 1856
Donation inscription in German in Latin script.
Translation:
Donated by Julius and Amalie Bauer,
February 26, 1862.
Collection point: Dvůr Králové nad Labem

Cat. No. 367
Cup
Inv. No. JMP 017.507
Silver, repoussé, engraving
Tomáš Hlaváč, Prague, 1857
Height: 81 mm, diameter: 64 mm
Hallmarks: 1. TH in irregular shape,
2. hallmark Prague 1857
Inscription in Hebrew and German in Latin script.
Translation:
Remember the Sabbath day and keep it holy
[in Hebrew]. *A gift to the Klausen Synagogue*
from Veit E. Bondi 1907–5667 [in German].
Collection point: Prague, Klausen Synagogue

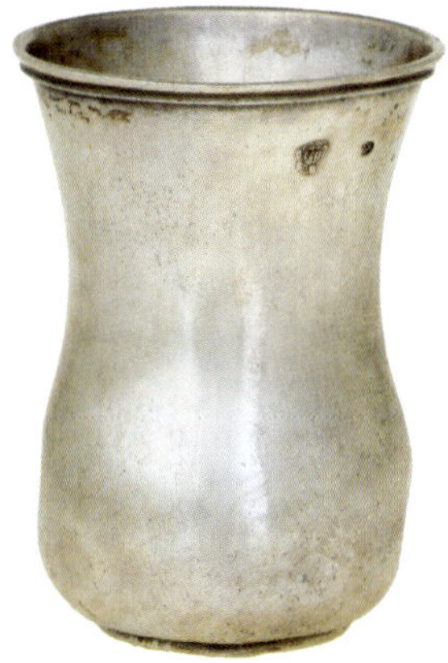

Cat. No. 365

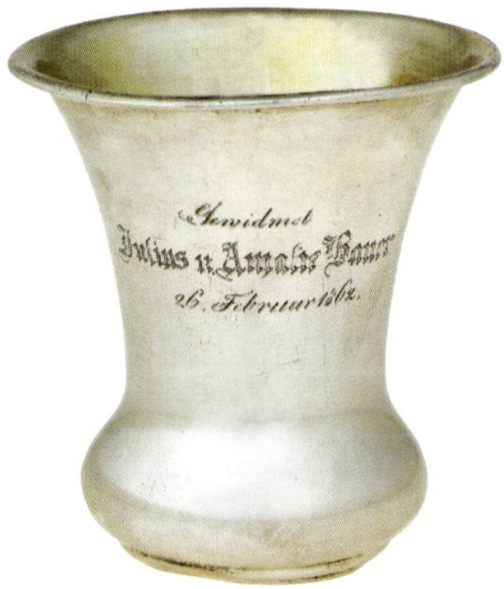

Cat. No. 366

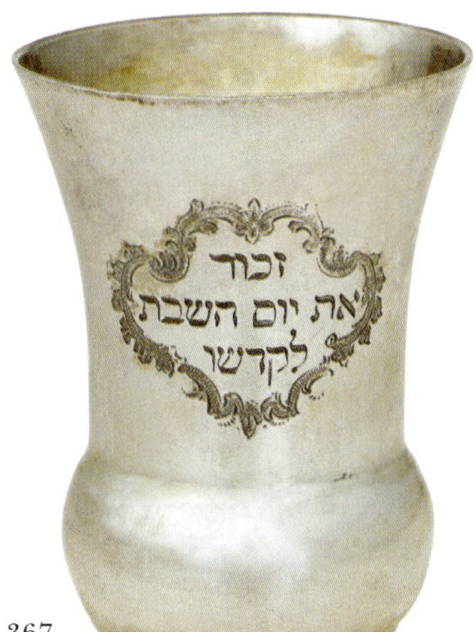

Cat. No. 367

Cat. No. 368
Cup
Inv. No. JMP 003.733
Silver, repoussé
Abraham Bernard Bächer (company), Prague, 1858
Height: 220 mm, diameter: 100 mm
Hallmarks: 1. AB in oval, 2. hallmark Prague 1858
Donation inscription in German in Latin script.
Translation:
Donated by J. Altmann and his spouse to commemorate the celebration of their silver wedding anniversary, February 18, 1859.
Collection point: Central Jewish Museum for Moravia and Silesia, 1936–1938 in Nikolsburg

Cat. No. 369
Cup
Inv. No. JMP 066.600
Silver, repoussé
Maker LW [Ludwig Wastl?], Vienna, 1858
Height: 104 mm, diameter: 73 mm
Hallmarks: 1. LW in rectangle,
2. hallmark Vienna 1858
Initials in Fraktur:
EP.
Collection point: Prague

Cat. No. 370
Cup
Inv. No. JMP 007.177
Silver, repoussé
Maker JS [?], Vienna, ca 1860
Height: 101 mm, diameter: 53 mm
Hallmarks: 1. JS [?] in oval,
2. hallmark Vienna [date illegible]
Donation inscription in Hebrew.
Translation:
A gift for the soul of Mindl, daughter of the lady Getzel.
Collection point: Brno

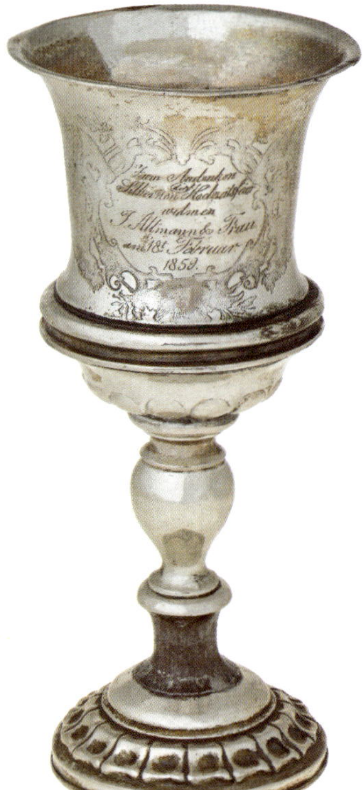

Cat. No. 368

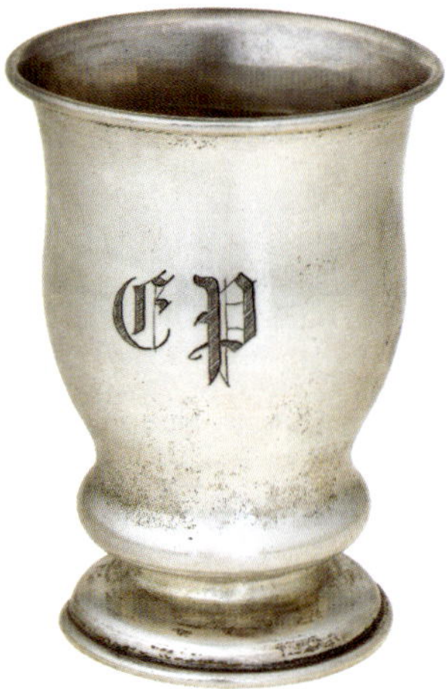

Cat. No. 369

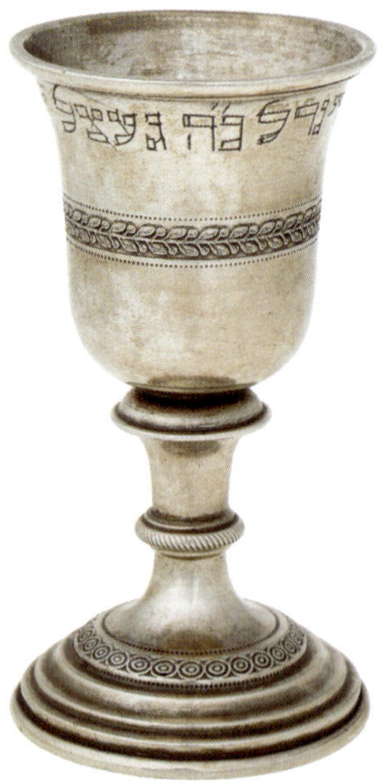

Cat. No. 370

Cat. No. 371
Cup
Inv. No. JMP 001.988
Silver, repoussé
Abraham Bernard Bächer (company), Prague, 1865
Height: 57 mm, diameter: 56 mm
Hallmarks: 1. AB in oval, 2. hallmark Prague 1865
Donation inscription in Hebrew.
Translation:
To the glory of the Lord. A gift of the esteemed Mr. Nathan Weim, may his light shine, and his wife the lady Pesl, may she live, "as a blessing" [dating in the chronogram 642 = 1882] *a. s. c.* [inscription on one side]. *Kiddush cup* [inscription on the other side].
Collection point: Rokycany

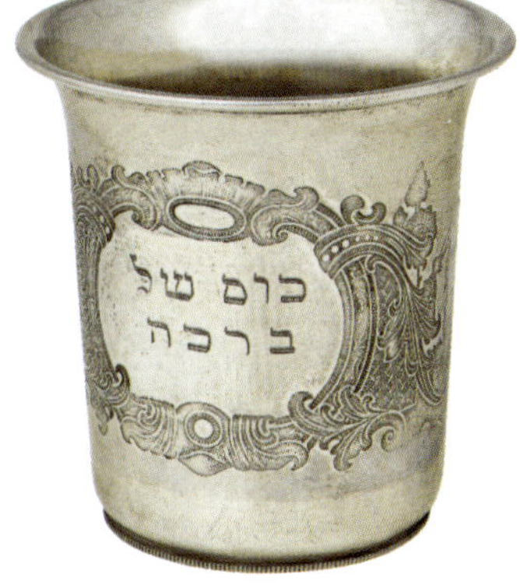

Cat. No. 371

Cat. No. 372
Cup
Inv. No. JMP 037.450
Silver, repoussé
No maker's mark, Germany [?], 1867 [inscription]
Height: 104 mm, diameter: 70 mm
Hallmarks: 1. import mark Austro-Hungary 1867–71, 2. localization letter C [Prague], 3. purity number 13 in rectangle,
Donation inscription in Hebrew.
Translation:
"I will lift up the cup of salvation" [Ps. 116:13]. *A gift from Miriam Kohn (née Eckstein) of Horní Cerekev, 627 a. s. c.* [= 1867].
Collection point: Prague

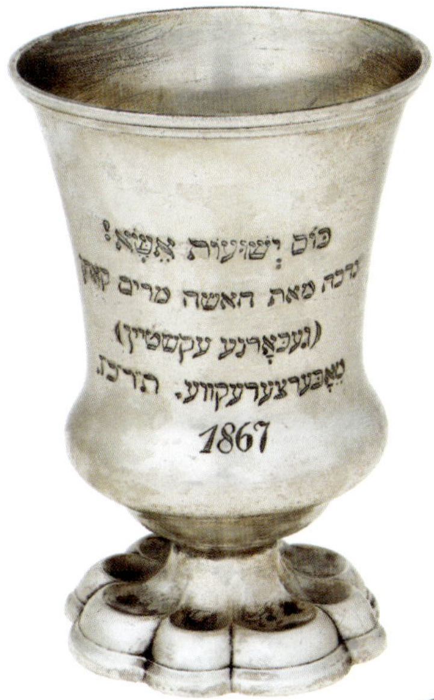

Cat. No. 372

Cat. No. 373
Cup
Inv. No. JMP 001.548
Silver, repoussé, engraving
Maker GK, Vienna [?], 1867–71
Height: 77 mm, diameter: 51 mm
Hallmarks: 1.GK in oval, 2. Austro-Hungary 1867–71, 3. illegible location letter
Without inscriptions.
Collection point: Plzeň

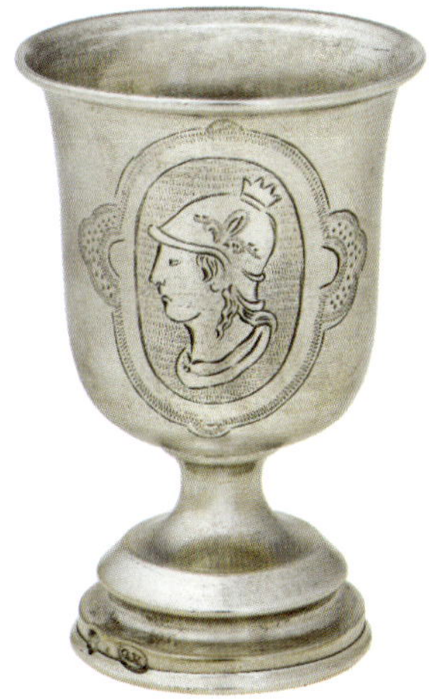

Cat. No. 373

Cat. No. 374

Cup

Inv. No. JMP 010.551
Silver, repoussé, engraving
Maker HS, Vienna, after 1871
Height: 73 mm, diameter: 53 mm
Hallmarks: 1. HS in rectangle,
2. Austro-Hungary [Vienna] after 1871
Donation inscription in Czech and Hebrew.
Translation:
Donated by Mr. B. Bondi, 664 a. s. c. [= 1904].
Collection point: Heřmanův Městec

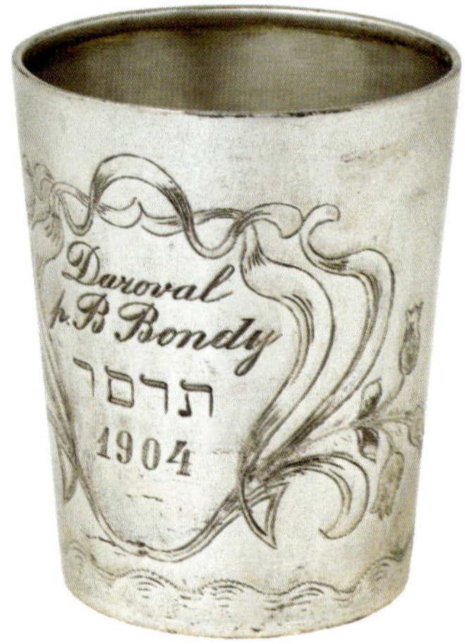

Cat. No. 374

Cat. No. 375

Cup

Inv. No. JMP 173.049
Silver, repoussé, engraving
Maker MJ, Krakow, after 1871
Height: 68 mm, diameter: 59 mm
Hallmarks: 1. MJ in rectangle,
2. Austro-Hungary [Krakow] after 1871
Inscription in Hebrew.
Translation:
A gift of the Holy Society for Love of the Torah.
Purchased by the Jewish Museum in Prague.

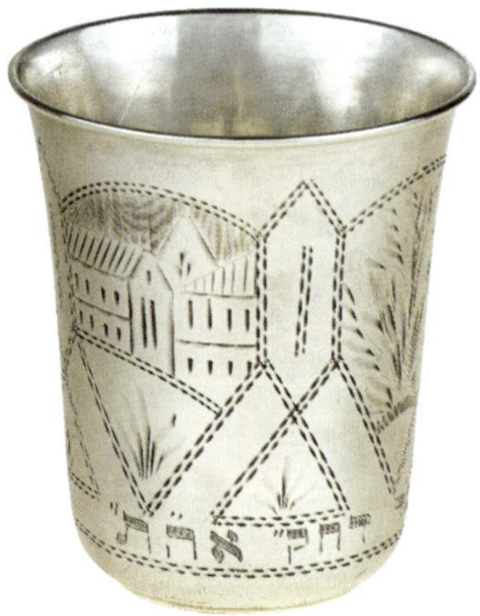

Cat. No. 375

Cat. No. 376

Cup

Inv. No. JMP 012.250
Silver, repoussé, engraving
Maker FT, Vienna, after 1871
Height: 79 mm, diameter: 68 mm
Hallmarks: 1. FT in oval,
2. Austro-Hungary [Vienna] after 1871
Without inscriptions.
Collection point: Brno, Vyškov

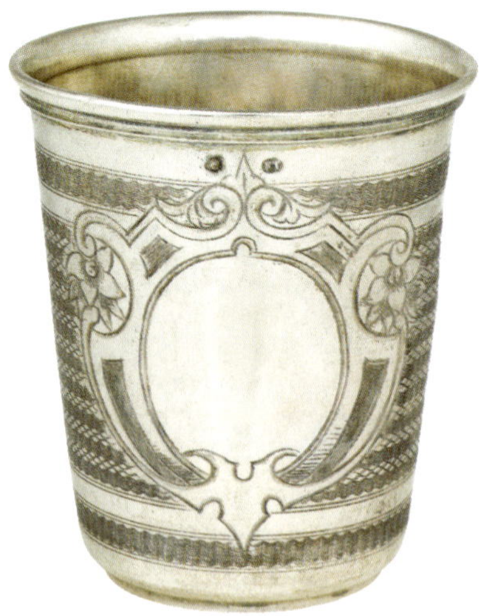

Cat. No. 376

Cat. No. 377

Cup

Inv. No. JMP 037.397
Silver, engraving, repoussé
No maker's mark, Germany [?], 1872–75
Height: 185 mm, diameter: 84 mm
Hallmarks: 1. import mark Austro-Hungary [Vienna] after 1871
Donation inscription in Hebrew and German.
Translation:
A gift for the synagogue from R Yom Tov Zevi and from his wife the lady Hindl Antscherl, may they live, on the day of the bar mitzvah of their son Joshua, may he live, on the holy Sabbath, parshat Miketz, 636 a. s. c. [= Dec. 25, 1875] [in Hebrew, on the front side]. *December 23, 1875 for the 13th birthday of our son Joseph* [in German in Latin script on the back side].
Collection point: Batelov

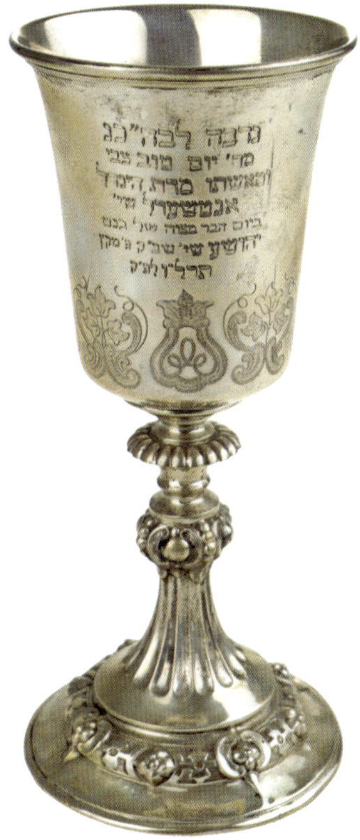

Cat. No. 377

Cat. No. 378

Cup

Inv. No. JMP 001.857
Silver, repoussé
Maker AS, Germany, end of 19th century
Height: 154 mm, diameter: 95 mm
Hallmarks: 1. AS in rectangle , 2. German hallmark for silver, 3. purity number 800, 4. import mark Austro-Hungary [Linz] after 1871
Donation inscription in Hebrew and Czech.
Translation:
A gift from me, Yom Tov ha-Kohen, 658 a. s. c. [= 1898] *5658* [on the front side]. *A kiddush cup to the joy and happiness of the wedding ceremony to commemorate the 50th anniversary of the rule* [in Hebrew]. *Of Franz Joseph I* [in Latin script on the back side].
Collection point: Klatovy

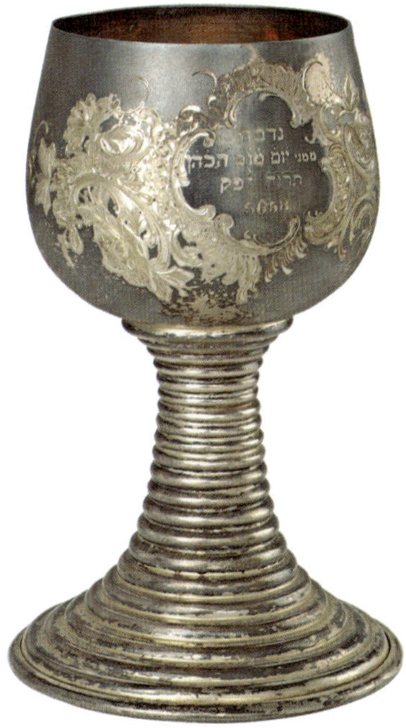

Cat. No. 378

Cat. No. 379
Cup
Inv. No. JMP 046.086
Silver, repoussé, engraving
No maker's mark, Germany [?],
end of 19th century
Height: 90 mm, diameter: 66 mm
Hallmarks: 1. import mark Austro-Hungary [Prague] 1872–1901
Donation inscription in Czech in Latin script.
Translation:
The religious community Slaný. 18 21/5 99.
Collection point: Prague

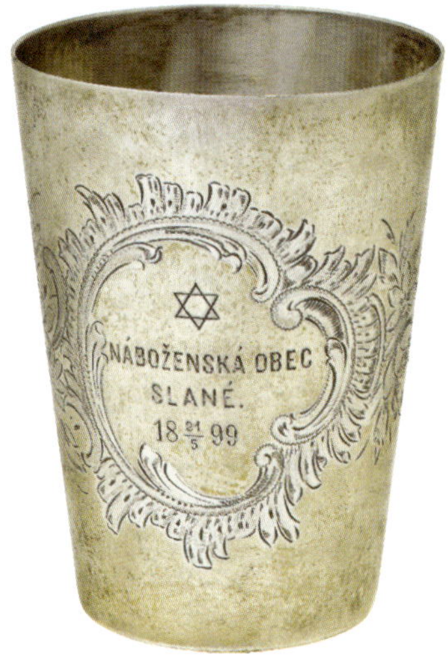

Cat. No. 379

Cat. No. 380
Cup
Inv. No. JMP 004.253
Silver, repoussé
No maker's mark, Germany,
early 20th century
Height: 308 mm, diameter: 98 mm
Hallmarks: 1. import mark
Austro-Hungary [Prague] after 1871
Donation inscription in Hebrew.
Translation:
To the memory of the soul of our teacher, Moses, son of Abraham Isaac Lederer, from the holy community Březnice and his wife the lady Yitl, the daughter of our teacher Abraham Solomon Zimelis, in the year 674 a. s. c. [= 1914].
Collection point: Březnice

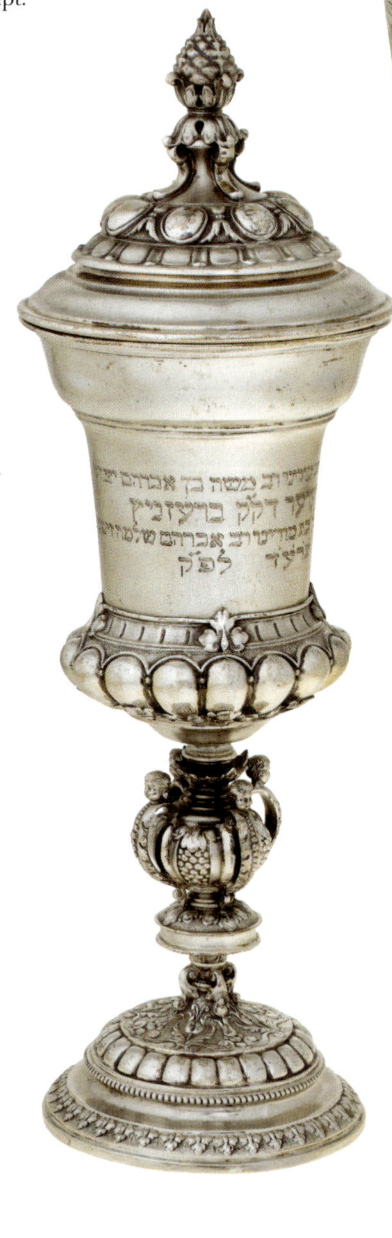

Cat. No. 380

Cat. No. 381
Cup
Inv. No. JMP 178.885
Silver, repoussé, filigree, etched
Bezalel workshops, Palestine, early 20th century
Height: 214 mm, diameter: 90 mm
Hallmarks: unmarked
Inscription in Hebrew and maker's mark
in Hebrew: *Bezalel.*
Translation:
"And wine to gladden the hearts of men" [Ps. 104:15].
Purchased by the Jewish Museum in Prague.

Cat. No. 382
Cup
Inv. No. JMP 001.611
Silver, repoussé
František Bibus (company), Czechoslovakia, 1929–35
Height: 121 mm, diameter: 78 mm
Hallmarks: 1. FB in rectangle, 2. hallmark
Czechoslovakia 1929–41, 3. purity number 800
Donation inscription in Czech in Latin script,
Hebrew abbreviation for Consecrated to the Lord.
Translation:
Donated by Otilie Taussigová on the occasion of the wedding of her son Jaroslav with Gerta Beranová. June 9, 1935.
Collection point: Hradec Králové

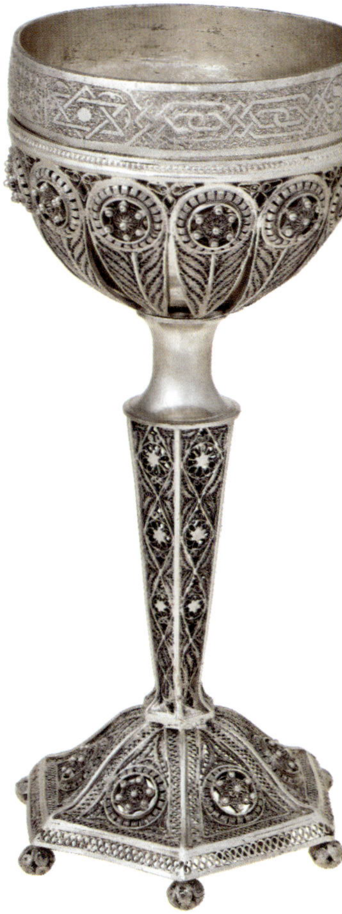

Cat. No. 381

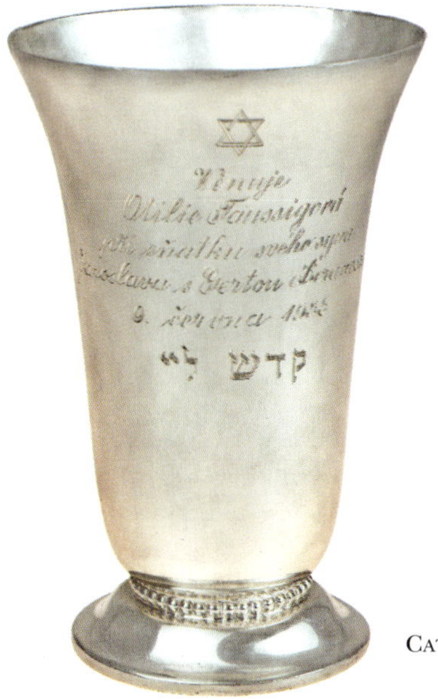

Cat. No. 382

XI. Lights

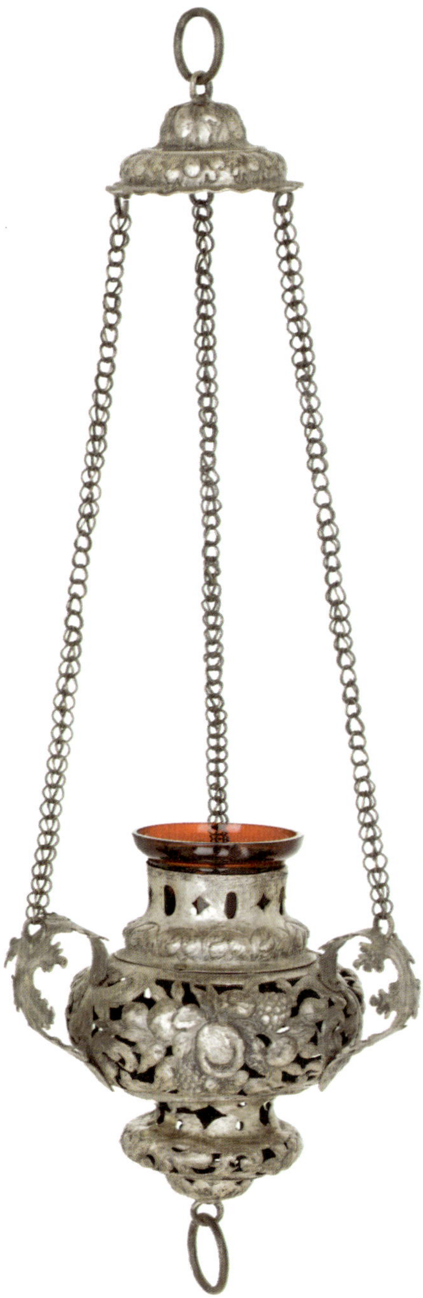

Cat. No. 383

Cat. No. 383
Eternal Light
Inv. No. JMP 003.787
Silver, repoussé, engraving
Johann Zeckel, Augsburg, early 18th century
Height: 139 mm, diameter: 137 mm
Hallmarks: 1. IZ in oval, 2. city mark Augsburg,
3. recharge mark Brno 1806–7,
4. release mark 1809–10
Without inscriptions.
Collection point: Central Jewish Museum
for Moravia and Silesia, 1936–1938 in Nikolsburg

Cat. No. 384
Hanukkah Lamp
Inv. No. JMP 066.185
Silver, repoussé
Maker KV, Prague, 1767
Height: 294 mm, width: 324 mm
Hallmarks: 1. KV in oval, 2. hallmark Prague 1767
Without inscriptions.
Collection point: Votice

Cat. No. 385
Hanukkah Lamp
Inv. No. JMP 003.790
Silver, filigree, repoussé, cast, engraving
No maker's mark, Galicia [?], early 19th century
Height: 277 mm, width: 295 mm
Hallmarks: unmarked
Without inscriptions.
Collection point: Central Jewish Museum
for Moravia and Silesia, 1936–1938 in Nikolsburg

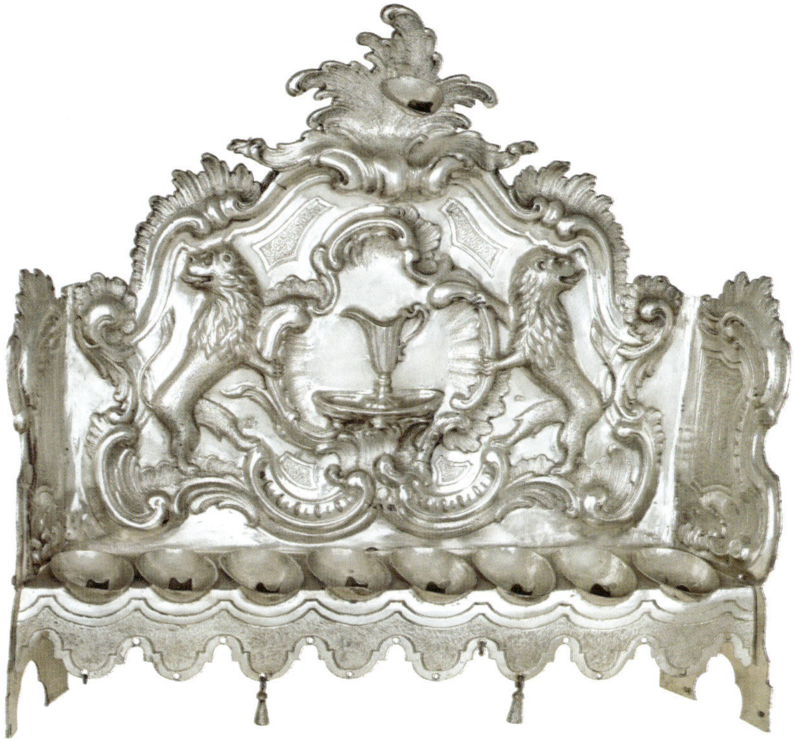

Cat. No. 384

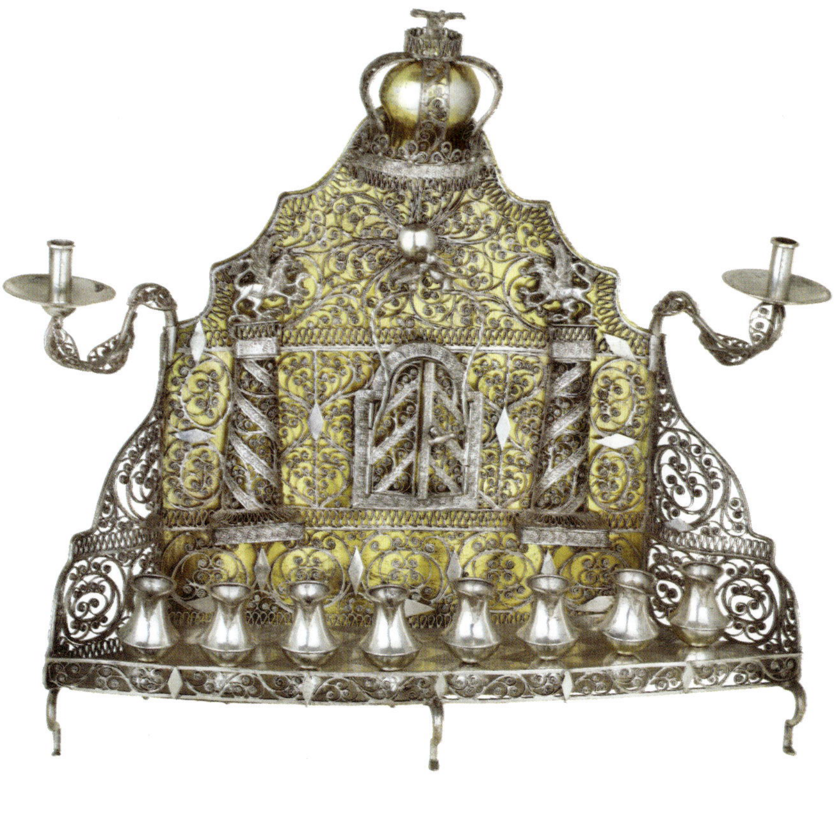

Cat. No. 385

Cat. No. 386
Sabbath Candlesticks
Inv. No. JMP 007.173/01, 02
Silver, repoussé
Eduard Uhl [?], Brno, 1843
Height: 273 mm, diameter: 132 mm
Hallmarks: 1. EU in oval, 2. hallmark Brno 1843
Without inscriptions.
Collection point: Brno

Cat. No. 387
Hanukkah Lamp
Inv. No. JMP 005.343
Silver, repoussé, engraving
Maker SK [?], Vienna, 1867–71
Height: 271 mm, width: 295 mm
Hallmarks: 1. SK [?] in rectangle,
2. Austro-Hungary 1867–71,
3. localization letter A [Vienna]
Without inscriptions.
Collection point: Holešov

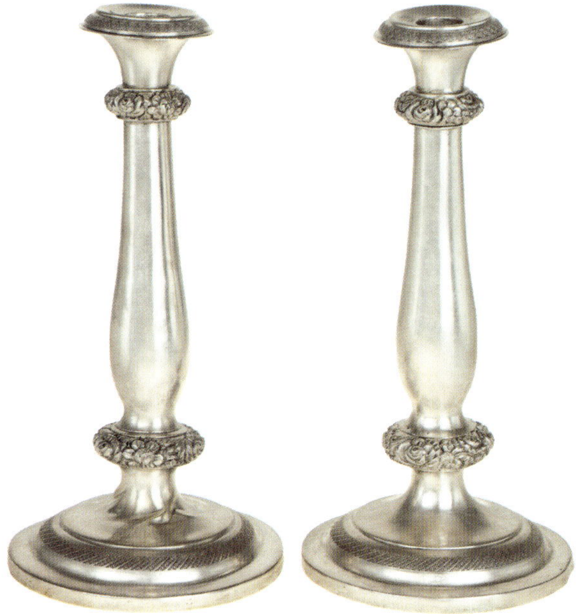

Cat. No. 386

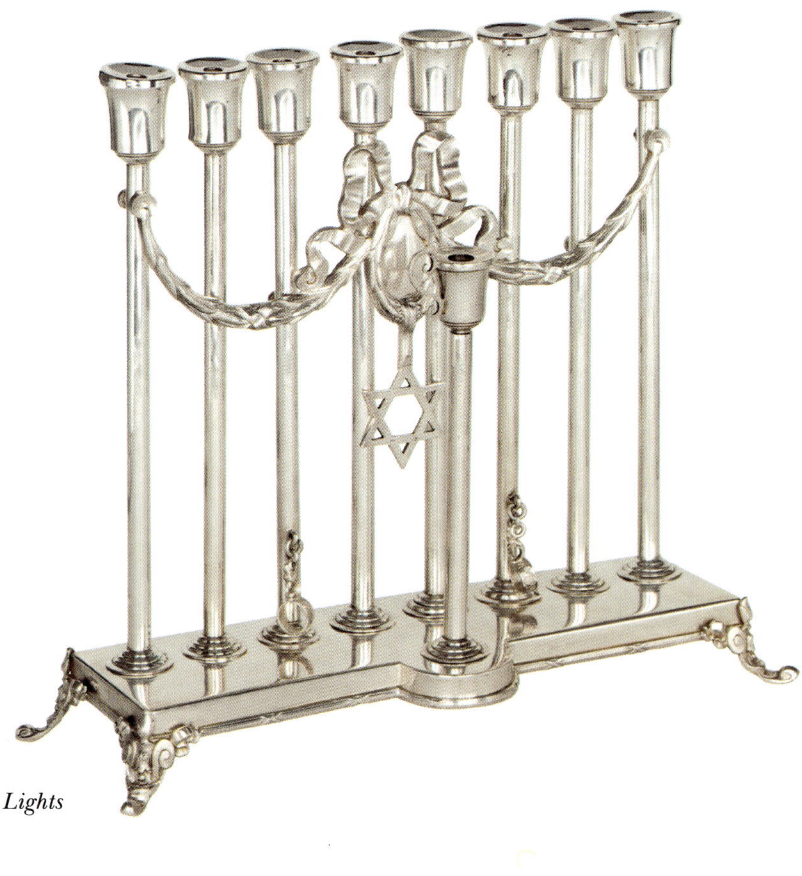

Cat. No. 387

Cat. No. 388
Eternal Light
Inv. No. JMP 002.947
Silver, repoussé, cut-out
Maker's mark illegible, Vienna, 1810
Height: 237 mm, diameter: 128 mm
Hallmarks: 1. illegible maker's mark in oval,
2. hallmark Vienna 1810, 3. stock mark after 1807
Without inscriptions.
Collection point: Lipník nad Bečvou

Cat. No. 389
Havdalah Candleholder
Inv. No. JMP 044.190
Silver, repoussé
Karel Skřemenec, Prague, 1814–19
Height: 225 mm, diameter: 108 mm
Hallmarks: 1. CS in rectangle 2. hallmark Prague 1814–19,
3. tax mark Prague 1810–24
Without inscriptions.
Collection point: Prague, High Synagogue

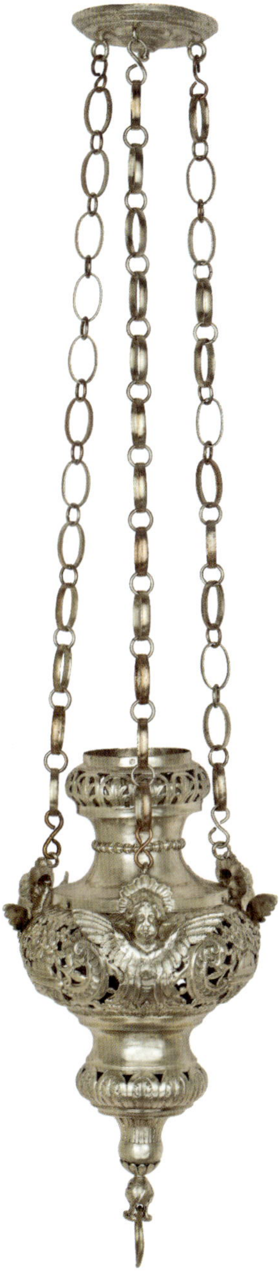

Cat. No. 388

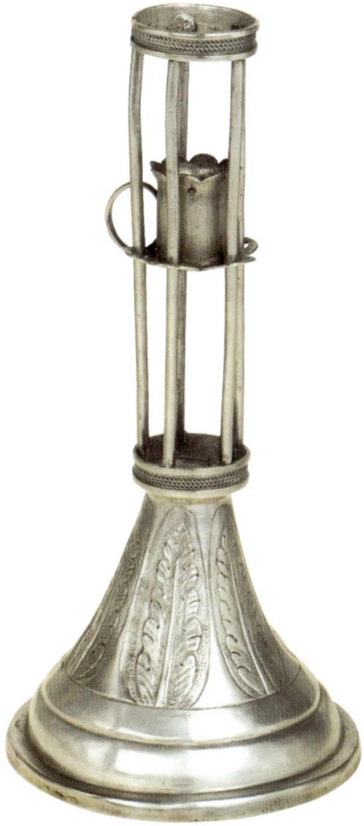

Cat. No. 389

Cat. No. 390

Sabbath Candlesticks

Inv. No. JMP 173.698/01, 02
Silver, repoussé, engraving
Jan Fleischmann, Prague, 1816
Height: 283 mm, diameter: 120 mm
Hallmarks: 1. JF in oval, 2. hallmark Prague 1816, 3. tax mark Prague 1810–24
Without inscriptions.
Catalogued secondarily into the inventory of the Jewish Museum in Prague.

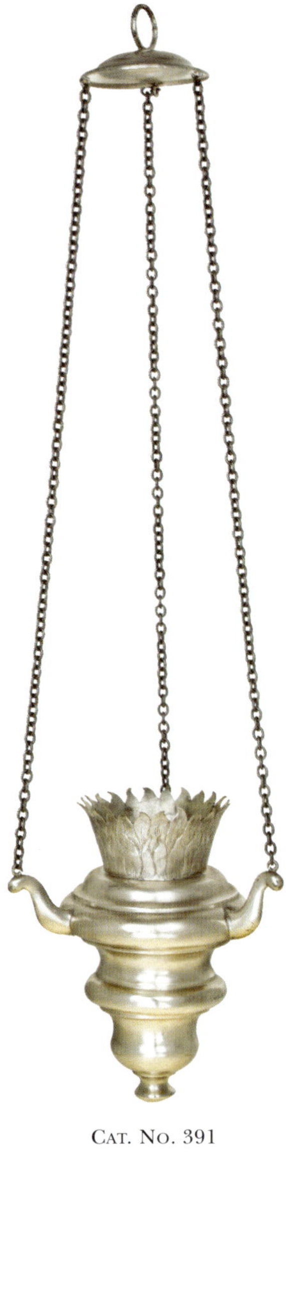

Cat. No. 391

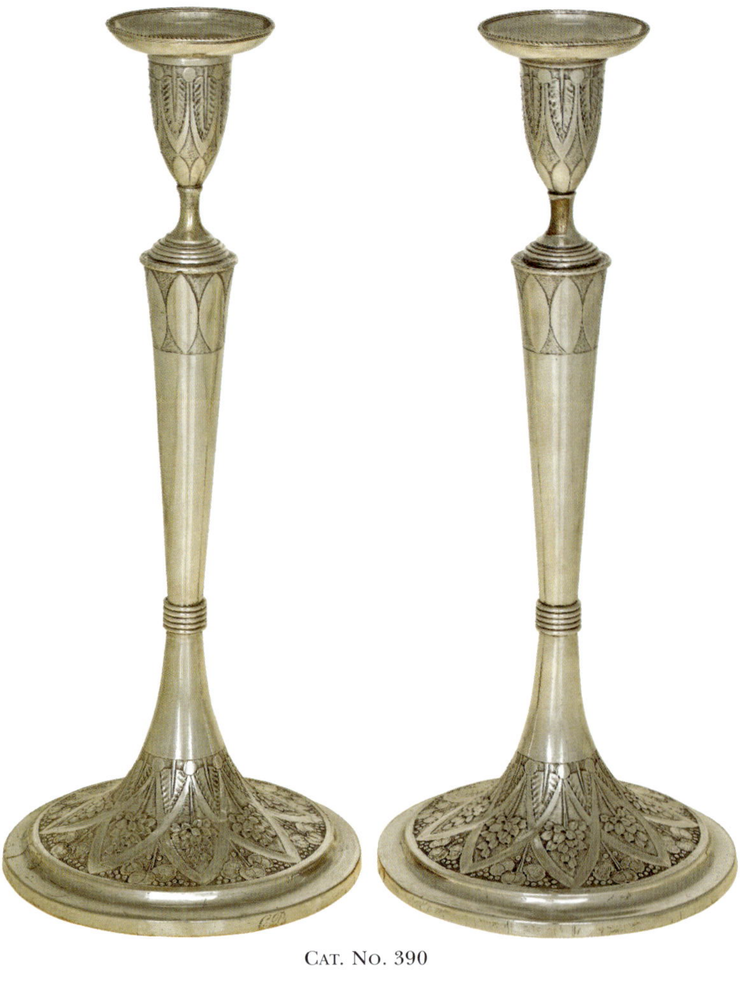

Cat. No. 390

Cat. No. 391
Eternal Light
Inv. No. JMP 010.480
Silver, repoussé, engraving
Jan Novotný, Prague, 1861
Height: 166 mm, diameter: 134 mm
Hallmarks: 1. JN in oval, 2. hallmark Prague 1861
Donation inscription in Hebrew and German
in Latin script:
Translation:
Donated by Emanuel Winternitz in the year 1861
[in German]. *"Your word is a lamp to my feet and*
a light to my path" [Ps. 119:105] [in Hebrew].
Collection point: Dobruška

Cat. No. 392
Hanukkah Lamp
Inv. No. JMP 009.802
Silver, repoussé, engraving
Maker FT, Vienna, 1860–66
Height: 227 mm, width: 340 mm
Hallmarks: 1. FT in rectangle,
2. hallmark Vienna 1860–66
Donation inscription in German in Latin script:
Donated by Jakob Eissler.
Collection point: Bzenec

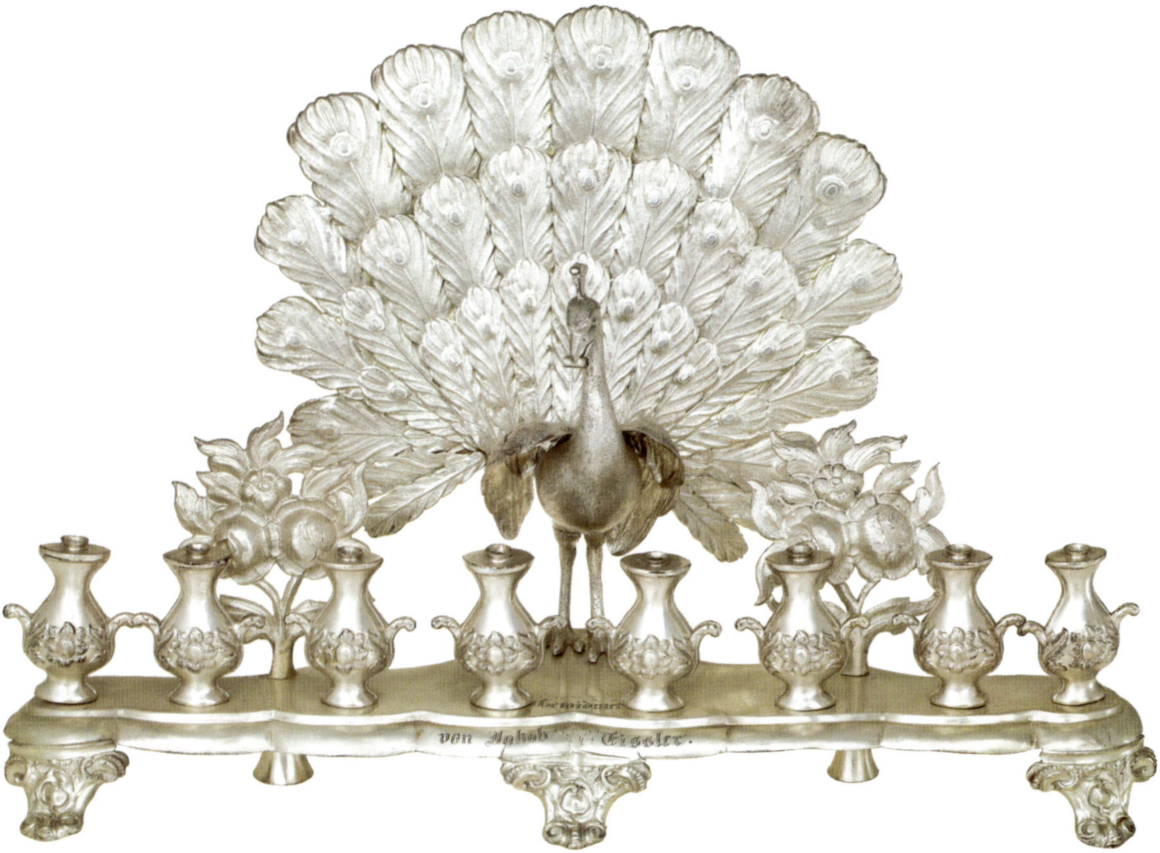

CAT. NO. 392

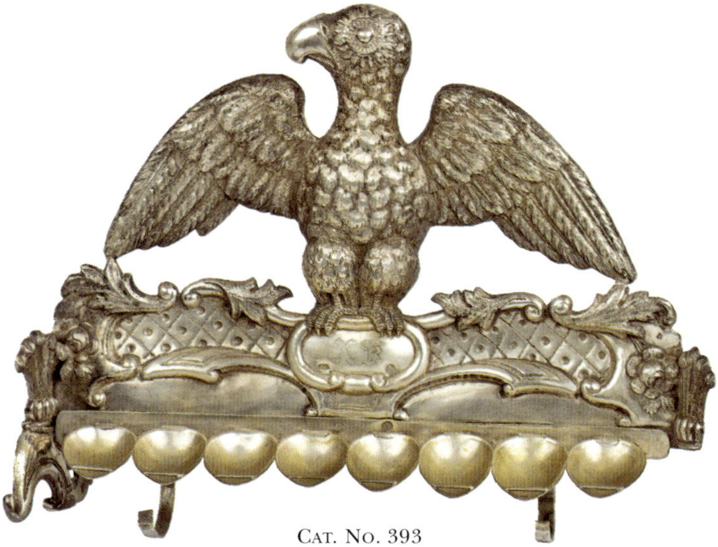

Cat. No. 393

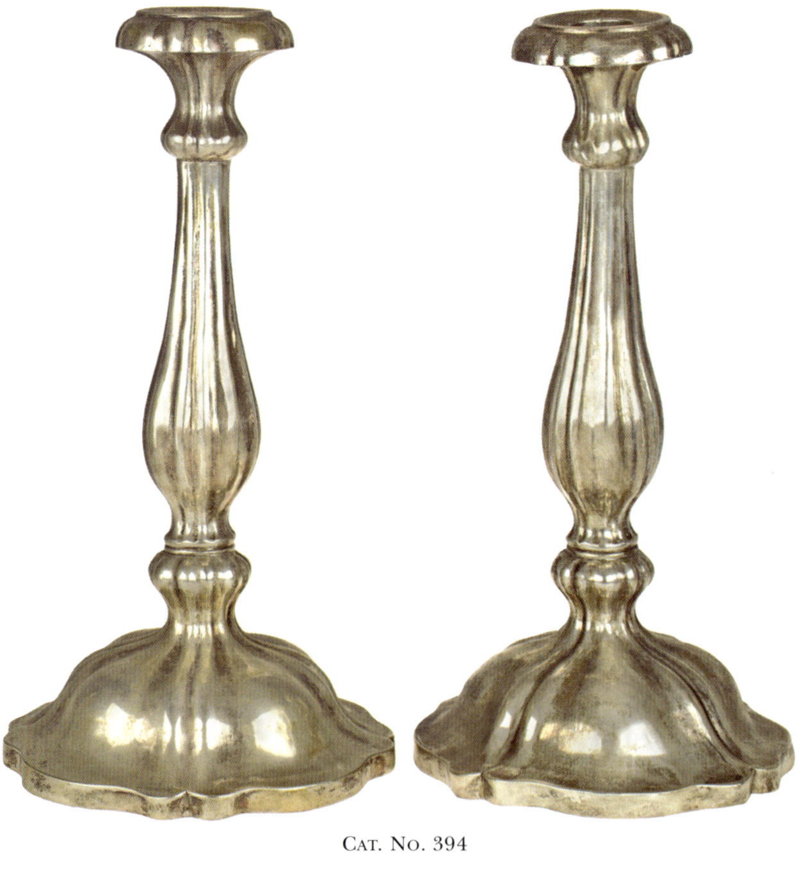

Cat. No. 394

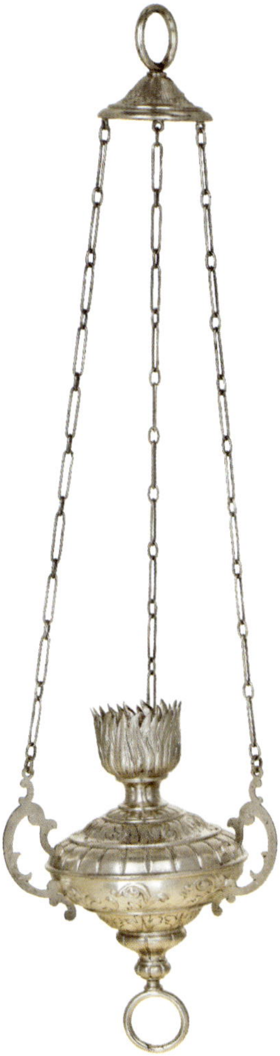

Cat. No. 395

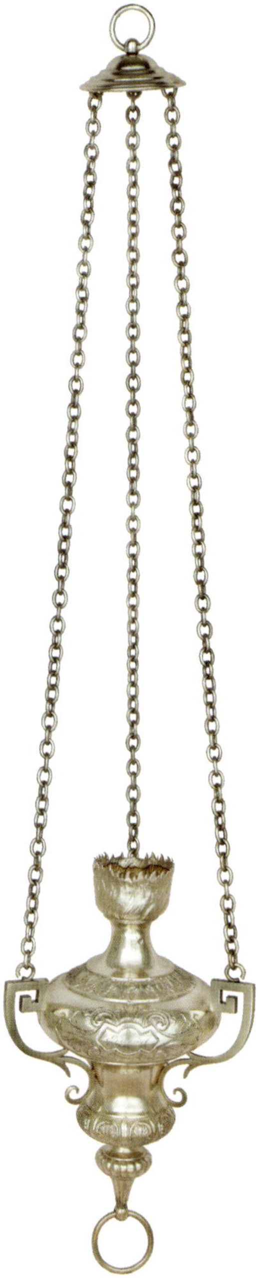

Cat. No. 396

Cat. No. 393
Hanukkah Lamp
Inv. No. JMP 032.151
Silver, repoussé, engraving
Maker AK, Vienna, 1863 [?]
Height: 208 mm, width: 277 mm
Hallmarks: 1. AK in hexagon,
2. hallmark Vienna 1863 [?]
Initials in Fraktur:
XK [?]
Collection point: Jewish Museum in Prague, 1906–1940

Cat. No. 394
Sabbath Candlesticks
Inv. No. JMP 002.936/01, 02
Silver, repoussé
Thomas Dub (company), Vienna, 1867–71
Height: 345 mm, diameter: 178 mm
Hallmarks: 1. TD in rectangle,
2. Austro-Hungary 1867–71
Without inscriptions.
Collection point: Lipník nad Bečvou

Cat. No. 395
Eternal Light
Inv. No. JMP 001.569
Silver, repoussé, engraving
Maker AP, Prague, after 1871
Height: 214 mm, diameter: 155 mm
Hallmarks: 1. AP in rectangle,
2. Austro-Hungary [Prague] after 1871
Without inscriptions.
Collection point: Plzeň

Cat. No. 396
Eternal Light
Inv. No. JMP 037.448
Silver, repoussé, engraving
Maker JZ, Vienna, 1872–82
Height: 260 mm, diameter: 154 mm
Hallmarks: 1. JZ in rectangle,
2. Austro-Hungary [Vienna] after 1871
Donation inscription in German in Latin script.
Translation:
Donated by Ignaz and Klara Dasch, 10. 9. 1882.
Collection point: Prague

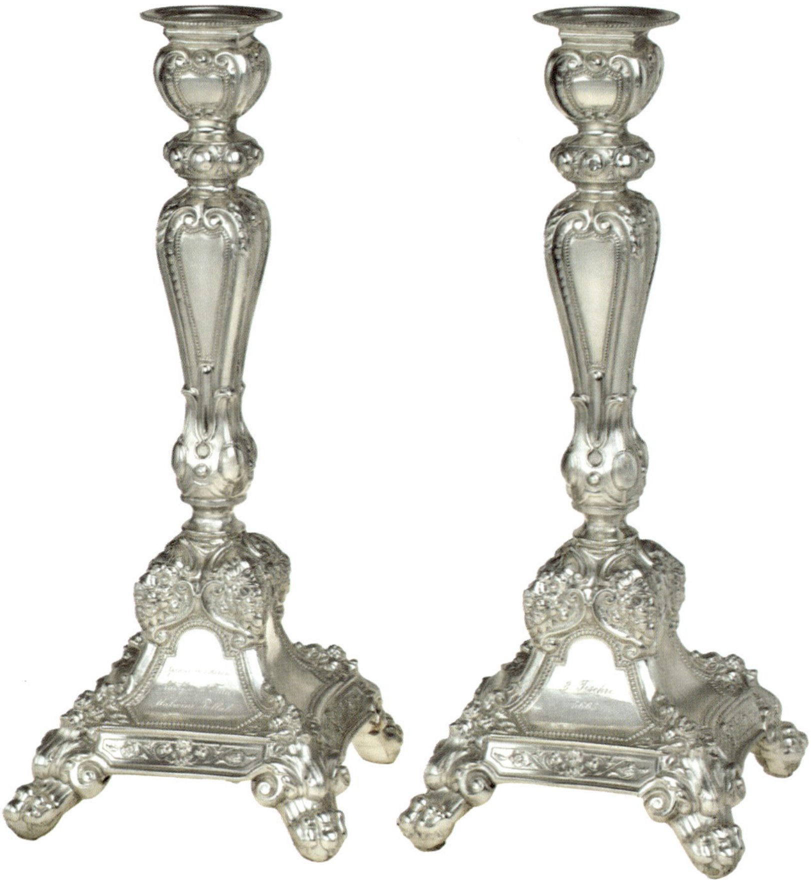

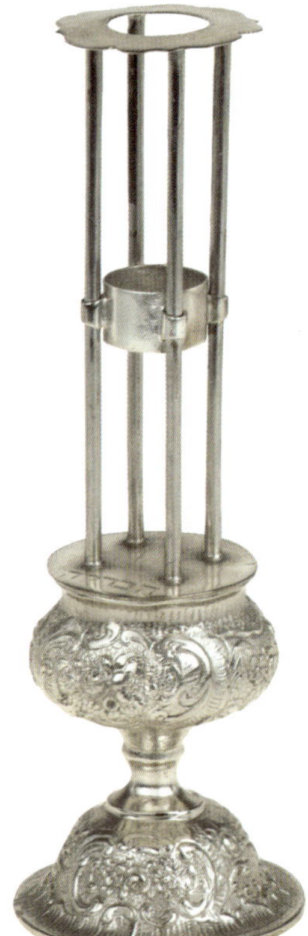

CAT. NO. 398

Cat. No. 397 ^
Sabbath Candlesticks
Inv. No. JMP 002.700/01, 02
Silver, repoussé
Maker HS, Vienna, end of 19th century
Height: 355 mm, width: 150 mm
Hallmarks: 1. HS in rectangle,
2. Austro-Hungary [Vienna] after 1871
Donation inscription in German in Latin script.
Translation:
A gift of Adolph and Malwin Pollak on the occasion of the bar mitzvah of their son Alois. The 8th of Tishrei 5665. 17 September 1904.
Collection point: Prostějov

Cat. No. 398
Havdalah Candleholder
Inv. No. JMP 012.748
Silver, repoussé, engraving
No maker's mark, Germany, end of 19th century
Height: 185 mm, diameter: 60 mm
Hallmarks: 1. German hallmark for silver,
2. purity number 800
Inscription in Hebrew.
Translation:
Havdalah.
Collection point: Jewish Museum in Prague, 1906–1940

Cat. No. 399
Menorah
Inv. No. JMP 173.824
Silver, repoussé, filigree
Bezalel workshops, Palestine,
early 20th century
Height: 296 mm, width: 228 mm
Hallmarks: 1. import mark Austro-Hungary
[Vienna] after 1902
Inscription in Hebrew.
Maker's mark in Hebrew: *Bezalel.*
Translation:
Remember the Sabbath day and keep it holy
[Exod. 20:8].
Purchased by the Jewish Museum in Prague.

Cat. No. 400
Hanukkah Lamp
Inv. No. JMP 170.329/01, 02
Silver, cast, repoussé
Sandrik Co., Czechoslovakia, after 1928
Height: 264 mm, width: 278 mm
Hallmarks: 1. Sandrik Co. mark,
2. hallmark Czechoslovakia 1929–41,
3. purity number 800
Without inscriptions.
Purchased by the Jewish Museum
in Prague.

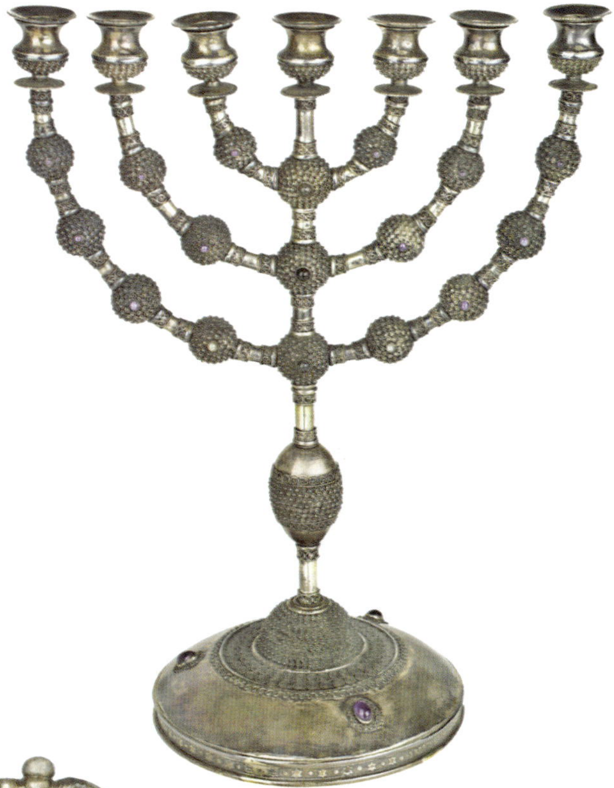

Cat. No. 399

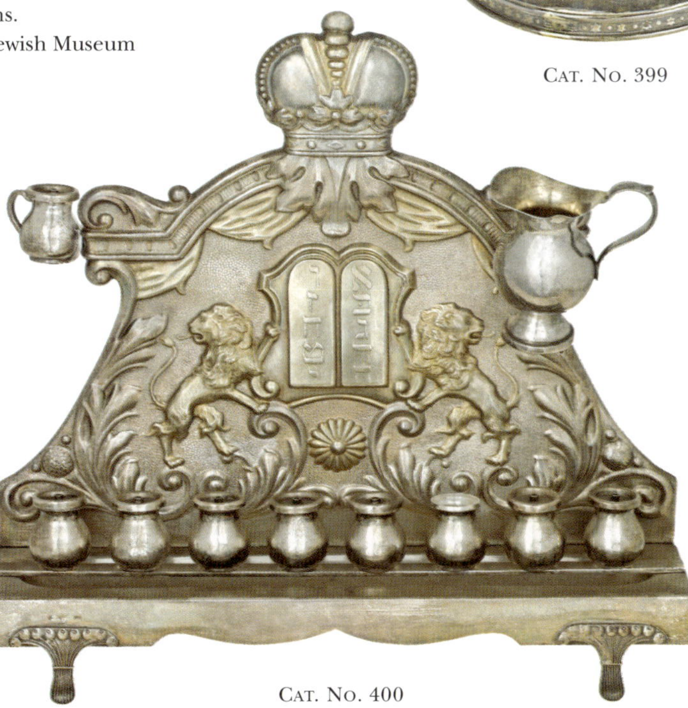

Cat. No. 400

XII. Spice Boxes

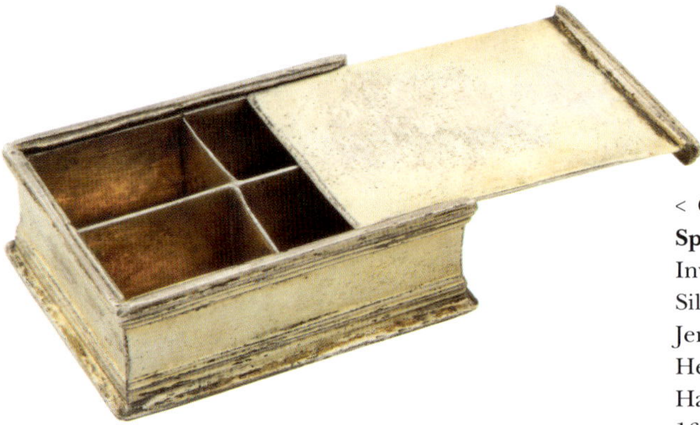

< Cat. No. 401
Spice Box
Inv. No. JMP 001.646
Silver, repoussé, gilt
Jerg Hainlin, Augsburg, 1613–15
Height: 22 mm, length: 63 mm
Hallmarks: 1. IH in oval, 2. hallmark Augsburg 1613–15, 3. recharge mark Prague 1806–7
Without inscriptions.
Collection point: Turnov

Cat. No. 402
Spice Box
Inv. No. JMP 174.629
Silver, filigree
No maker's mark, Galicia, 18th century
Height: 295 mm, diameter: 84 mm
Hallmarks: unmarked
Without inscriptions.
Catalogued secondarily into the inventory of the Jewish Museum in Prague.

Cat. No. 403
Spice Box
Inv. No. JMP 002.934
Silver, filigree
No maker's mark, Galicia, 18th century
Height: 279 mm, width: 64 mm
Hallmarks: unmarked
Without inscriptions.
Collection point: Lipník nad Bečvou

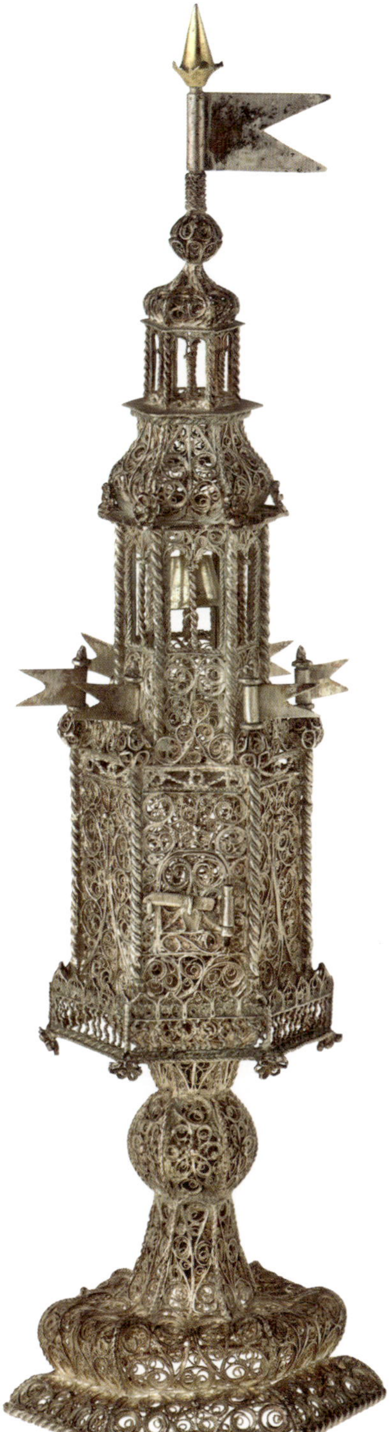

Cat. No. 402

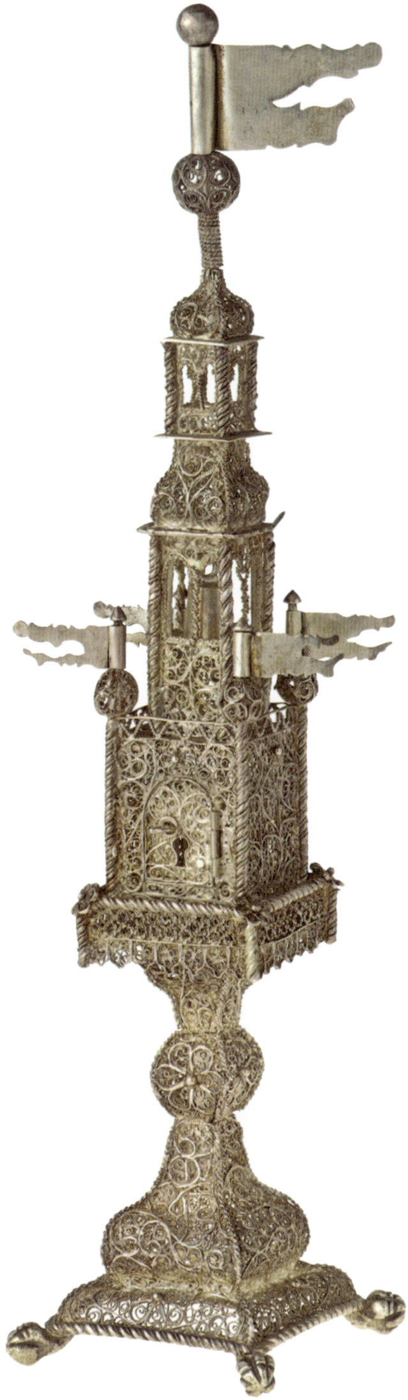

Cat. No. 403

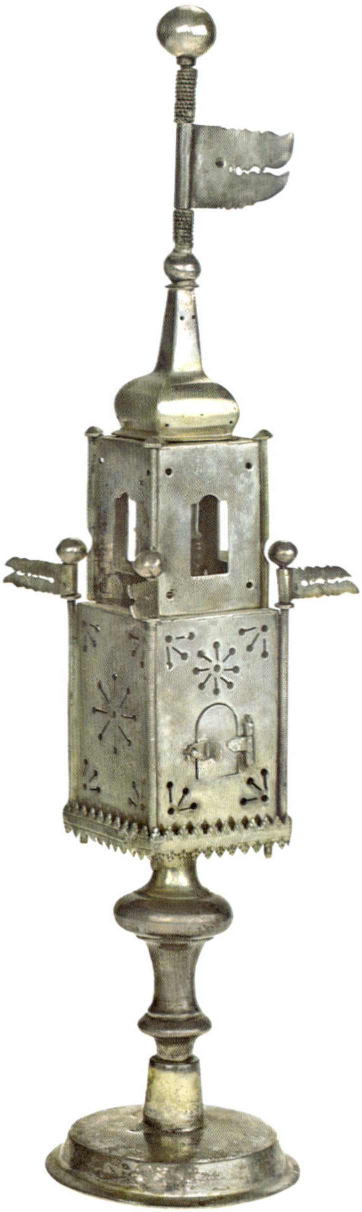

Cat. No. 404

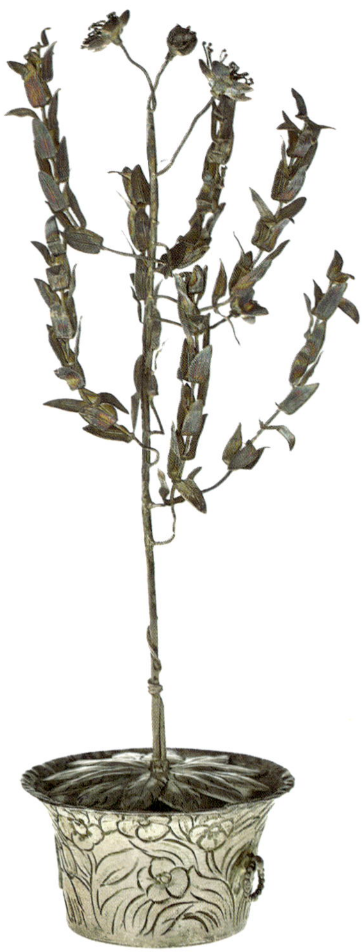

Cat. No. 405

Cat. No. 404
Spice Box
Inv. No. JMP 177.271
Silver, repoussé, originally gilt, cut-out
No maker's mark, Moravia [?],
end of 18th century
Height: 312 mm, diameter: 70 mm
Hallmarks: 1. recharge mark Brno
1806–7, 2. tax mark Brno 1810–24
Without inscriptions.
Purchased by the Jewish Museum
in Prague

Cat. No. 405
Spice Box
Inv. No. JMP 012.747
Silver, repoussé, engraving
No maker's mark, Banská Bystrica, ca. 1800
Height: 187 mm, diameter: 75mm
Hallmarks: 1. hallmark Banská
Bystrica, ca. 1800
Without inscriptions.
Collection point: Jewish Museum
in Prague, 1906–1940

Cat. No. 406
Spice Box
Inv. No. JMP 010.291
Silver, repoussé, cut-out, engraving
Franz Kaltenmarker, Brno, 1814
Height: 400 mm, diameter: 114 mm
Hallmarks: 1. FK in oval,
2. hallmark Brno 1814,
3. tax mark Brno 1810–24
Donation inscription in Hebrew.
Translation:
Made from charitable funds through the agency of the treasurers, the elder MVH Jacob, son of MSch, MVH Shalom, son of Mr. DR, the elder Solomon, son of Rabbi L, the elder Joseph, son of Rabbi MS, in the year 573 a. s. c. [= 1813] [sic].
Collection point: Boskovice

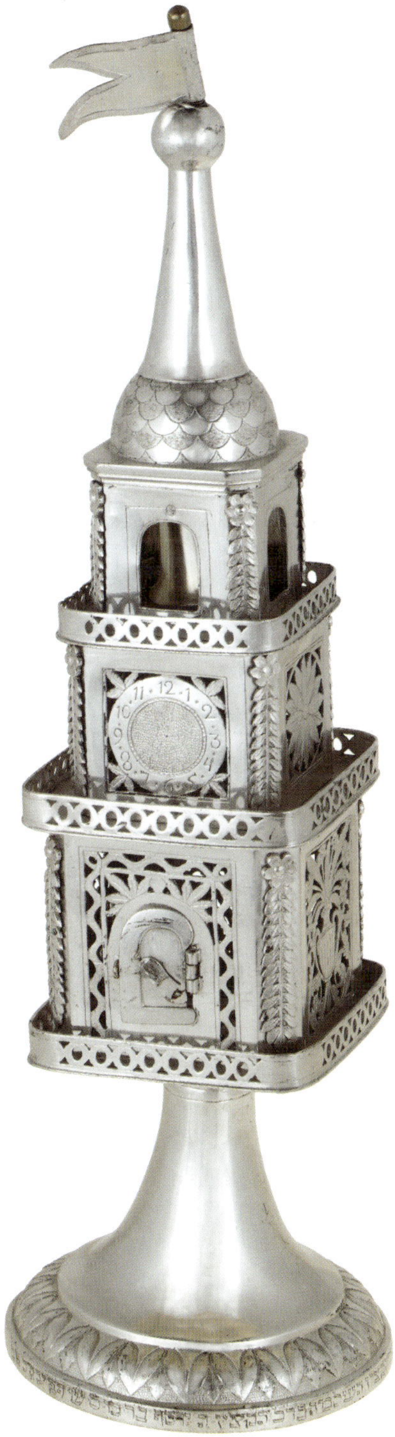

Cat. No. 406

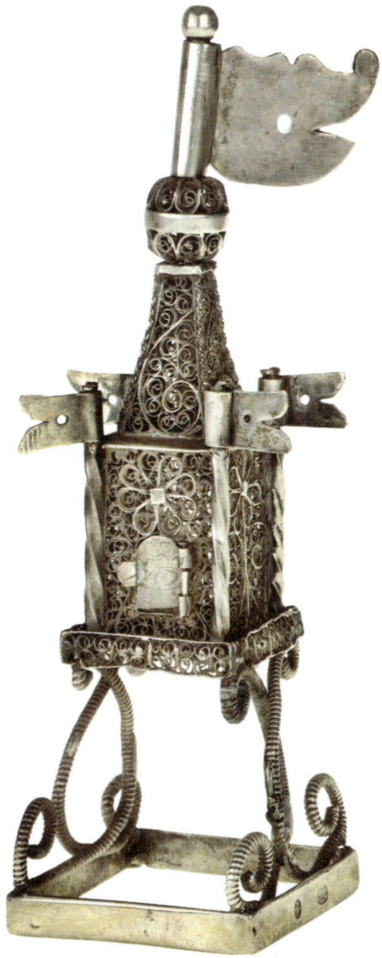

Cat. No. 407 ^
Spice Box
Inv. No. JMP 007.207
Silver, filigree
No maker's mark, Brno, 1816
Height: 164 mm, diameter: 51 mm
Hallmarks: 1. hallmark Brno 1816,
2. tax mark Brno 1810–24
Without inscriptions.
Collection point: Brno, Pohořelice

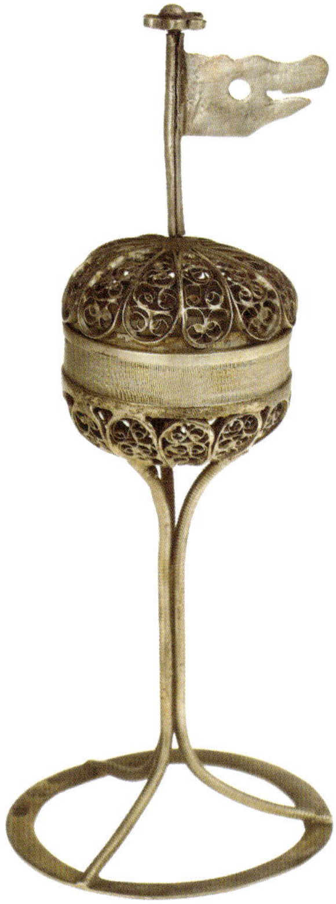

Cat. No. 408

Cat. No. 408
Spice Box
Inv. No. JMP 037.735
Silver, filigree
Rafael Jonas Goldschmid, Prague, 1820
Height: 131 mm, diameter: 52 mm
Hallmarks: 1. RG in rectangle, 2. hallmark Prague 1820, 3. tax mark Prague 1810–24
Without inscriptions.
Collection point: Jewish Museum in Prague, 1906–1940

Cat. No. 409
Spice Box
Inv. No. JMP 007.352
Silver, repoussé, cut-out, engraving
No maker's mark, Central Europe [Vienna?], early 19th century
Height: 197 mm, diameter: 66 mm
Hallmarks: 1. recharge mark Brno 1806–7, 2. release mark 1809–10
Without inscriptions.
Collection point: Kroměříž

Cat. No. 410
Spice Box
Inv. No. JMP 054.106
Silver, filigree
No maker's mark, Central Europe, early 19th century
Height: 222 mm, diameter: 63 mm
Hallmarks: 1. fake hallmark Vienna 1807–9, 2. [fake?] recharge mark 1806–7, 3. [fake?] release mark 1809–10
Without inscriptions.
Collection point: Jemnice

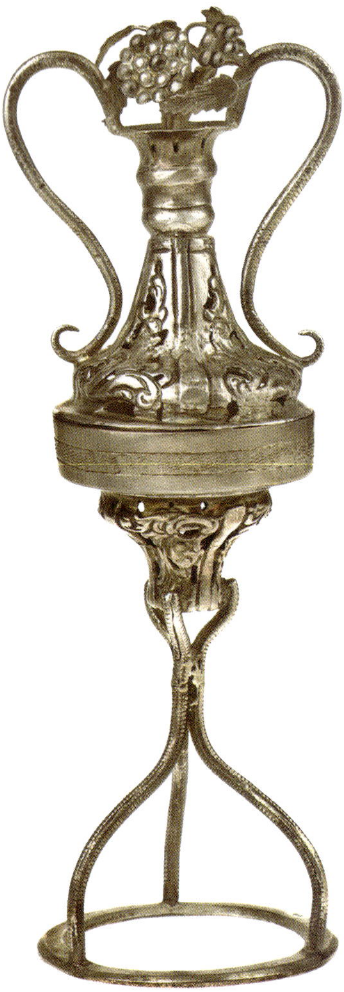

Cat. No. 409

Cat. No. 411
Spice Box
Inv. No. JMP 102.000
Silver, repoussé, cast, engraving
No maker's mark, Eastern Europe,
early 19th century
Height: 145 mm, diameter: 52 mm
Hallmarks: 1. purity number 12
in rectangle
Donation inscription in Hebrew.
Translation:
Jacob, son of R W.
Acquired by the JMP via transfer.

Cat. No. 412
Spice Box
Inv. No. JMP 004.369
Silver, repoussé, filigree
No maker's mark, Prague [?],
early 19th century
Height: 23 mm, diameter: 33 mm
Hallmarks: unmarked
Donation inscription and date
in Latin script:
Josef Fischer. 1880.
Collection point: Slaný

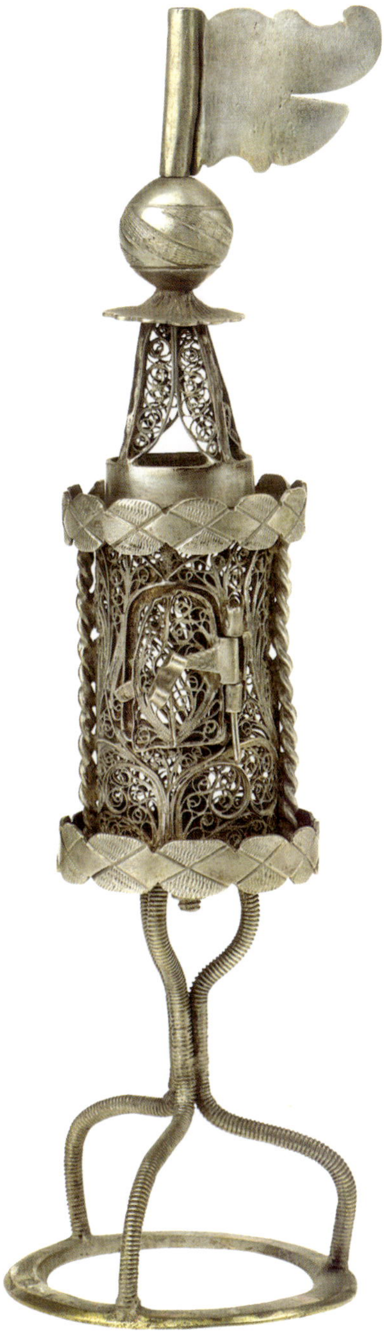

Cat. No. 410

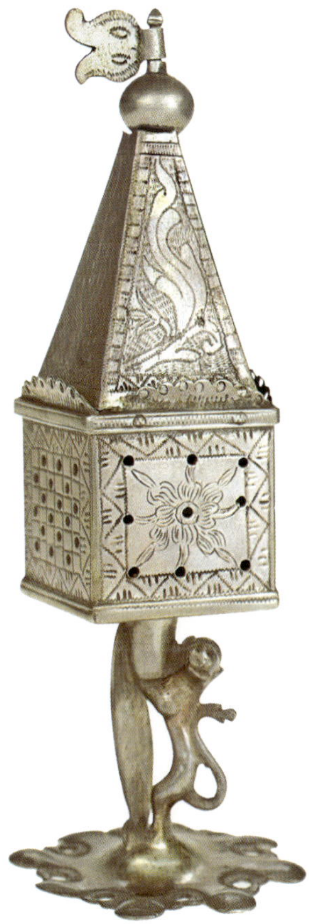

Cat. No. 411

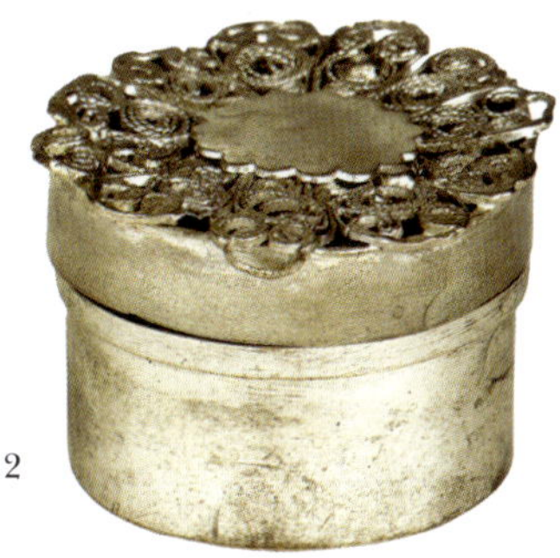

Cat. No. 412

Cat. No. 413
Spice Box
Inv. No. JMP 003.663
Silver, repoussé, engraving, cut-out
Maker's mark illegible, Poland [?], 19th century
Height: 161 mm, diameter: 63 mm
Hallmarks: 1. illegible maker's mark, 2. purity number 12 in rectangle
Donation inscription in Hebrew.
Translation:
This myrtle belongs to MHVRR Jacob.
Collection point: Central Jewish Museum for Moravia and Silesia, 1936–1938 in Nikolsburg

Cat. No. 414
Spice Box
Inv. No. JMP 102.001
Silver, repoussé, filigree, parcel-gilt
Maker PK, Eastern Europe [?], 19th century
Height: 185 mm, width: 125 mm
Hallmarks: 1. PK (unframed), 2. unidentified hallmark
Without inscriptions.
Acquired by the JMP via transfer.

Cat. No. 415
Spice Box
Inv. No. JMP 003.665
Silver, filigree
Johann Radda [?], Brno, 1856
Height: 123 mm, width: 51 mm
Hallmarks: 1. JR in oval, 2. hallmark Brno 1856
Without inscriptions.
Collection point: Central Jewish Museum for Moravia and Silesia, 1936–1938 in Nikolsburg

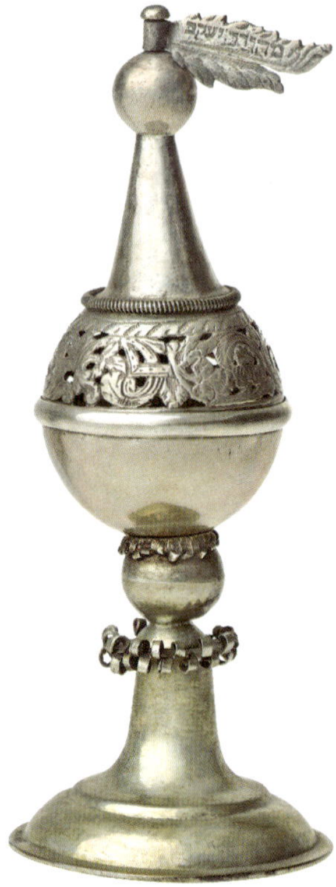

Cat. No. 413

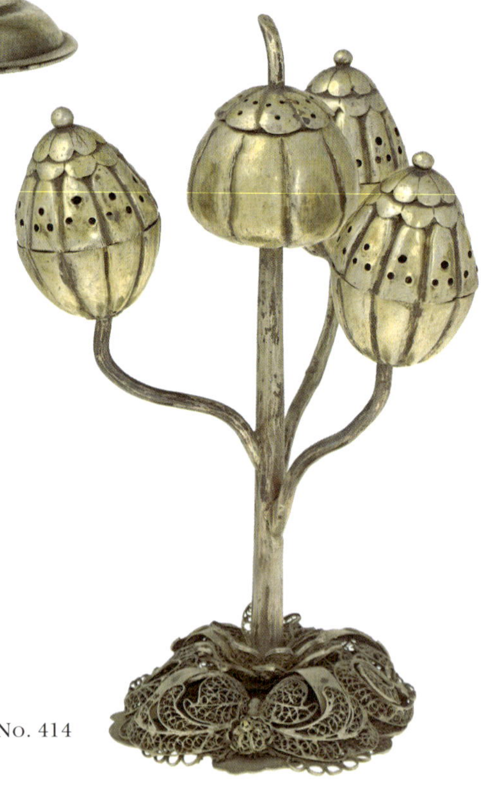

Cat. No. 414

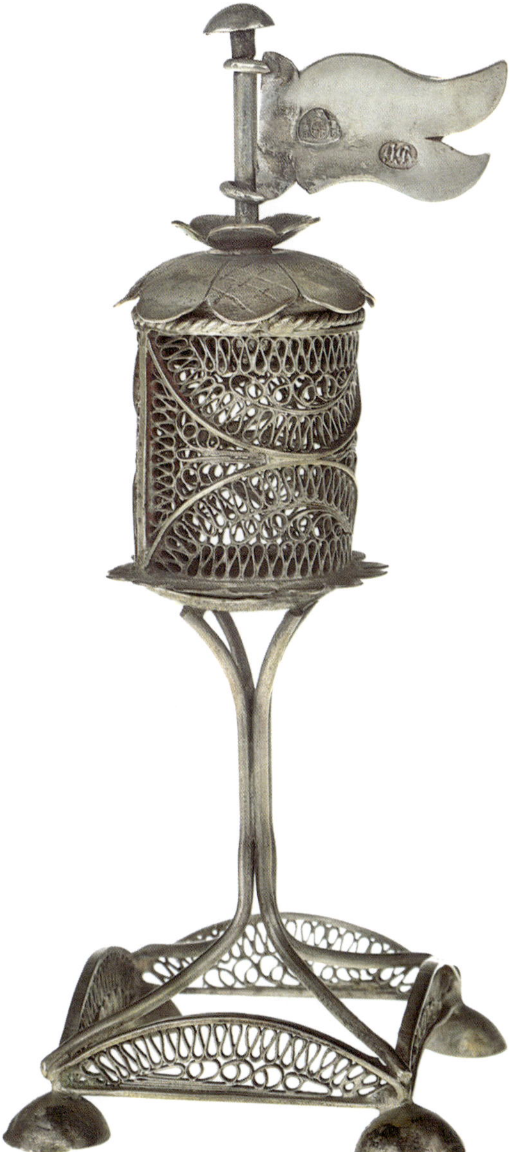

Cat. No. 415

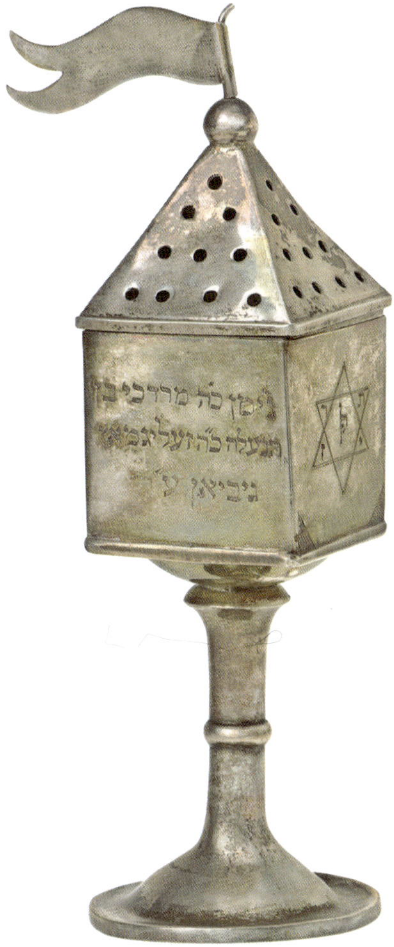

Cat. No. 416 ^

Spice Box

Inv. No. JMP 037.720

Silver, repoussé, engraving

Tomáš Hlaváč, Prague, 1857

Height: 166 mm, diameter: 55 mm

Hallmarks: 1. TH in irregular shape,
2. hallmark Prague 1857

Donation inscription in Hebrew.

Translation:

A gift from KH Mordecai, son of the distinguished KH Zeligman Gibian, peace to him, on behalf of his son, the boy Moses, may the Lord extend his days and years, 617 a. s. c. [= 1857].

Collection point: Jewish Museum in Prague, 1906–1940

Cat. No. 417
Spice Box
Inv. No. JMP 010.792
Silver, filigree
Johann Radda [?], Brno, 1858
Height: 248 mm, width: 80 mm
Hallmarks: 1. JR in oval, 2. hallmark Brno 1858
Inscription in Hebrew:
MLI.
Collection point: Písek

Cat. No. 418
Spice Box
Inv. No. JMP 037.725
Silver, repoussé, cut-out, engraving
Josef Reiner, Vienna, 1859
Height: 188 mm, diameter: 60 mm
Hallmarks: 1. REINER in rectangle,
2. hallmark Vienna 1859
Without inscriptions.
Collection point: Jewish Museum in Prague, 1906–1940

Cat. No. 419
Spice Box
Inv. No. JMP 177.233
Silver, filigree
Maker SB, Vienna, 1863
Height: 187 mm, width: 54 mm
Hallmarks: 1. SB in rectangle,
2. hallmark Vienna 1863
Without inscriptions.
Purchased by the Jewish Museum in Prague.

Cat. No. 420
Spice Box
Inv. No. JMP 003.694
Silver, filigree, originally parcel-gilt
Maker EE, Brno, 1867–68
Height: 236 mm, width: 70 mm
Hallmarks: 1. EE in oval,
2. Austro-Hungary 1867–71,
3. localization letter D [Brno] 1867–68
Without inscriptions.
Collection point: Central Jewish Museum for Moravia and Silesia, 1936–1938 in Nikolsburg

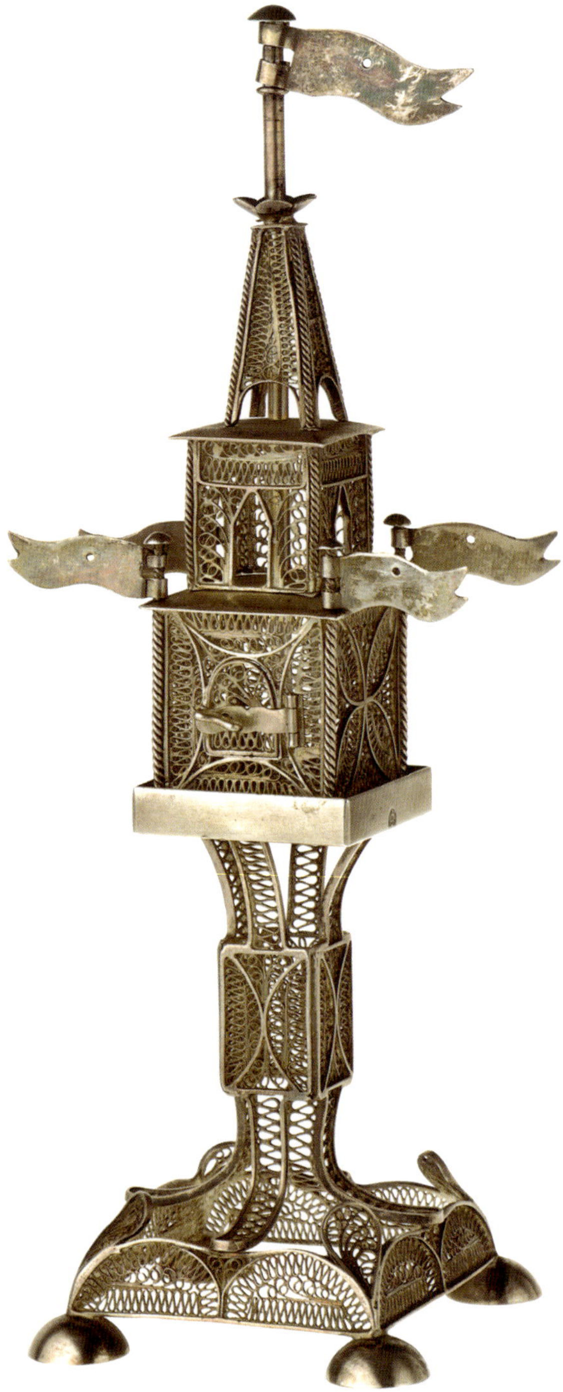

Cat. No. 417

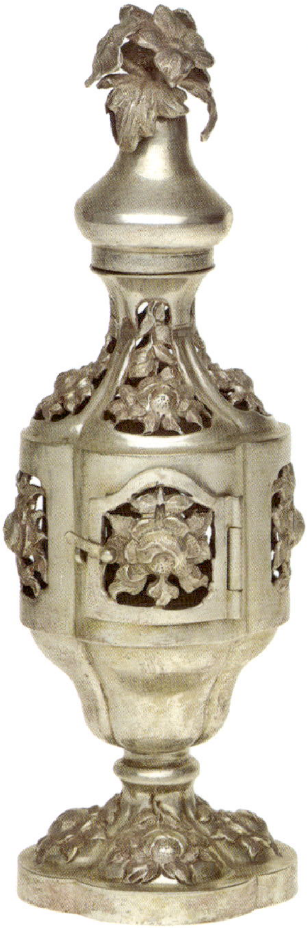

Cat. No. 418

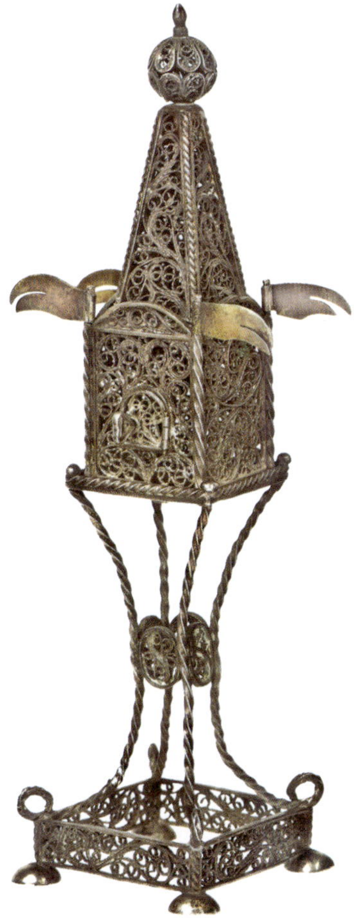

Cat. No. 419

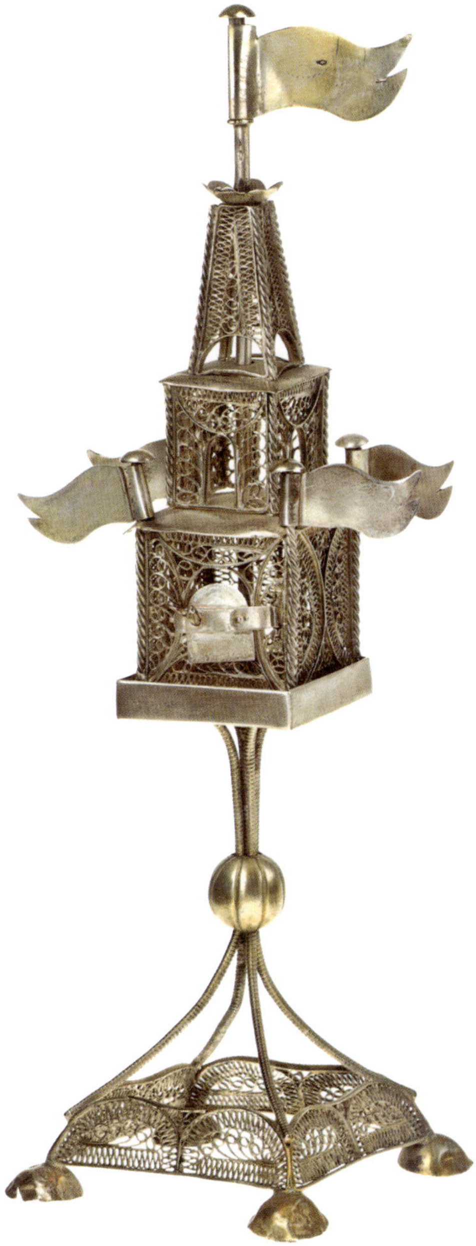

Cat. No. 420

Cat. No. 421
Spice Box
Inv. No. JMP 027.650
Silver, filigree
Maker EE, Brno, 1867–71
Height: 236 mm, width: 60 mm
Hallmarks: 1. EE in rectangle, 2. Austro-Hungary 1867–71
Without inscriptions.
Collection point: Prague, Treuhandstelle
depository Ca 345

Cat. No. 422
Spice Box
Inv. No. JMP 003.671
Silver, filigree
Maker EE, Brno, 1869–71
Height: 221 mm, width: 68 mm
Hallmarks: 1. EE in rectangle, 2. Austro-Hungary 1867–71,
3. localization letter A6 [Brno] after 1868
Without inscriptions.
Collection point: Central Jewish Museum for Moravia
and Silesia, 1936–1938 in Nikolsburg

Cat. No. 423
Spice Box
Inv. No. JMP 037.932
Silver, filigree
Maker EE, Brno, 1869–71
Height: 199 mm, width: 61 mm
Hallmarks: 1. EE in rectangle, 2. Austro-Hungary 1867–71,
3. localization letter A6 [Brno] after 1868
Without inscriptions.
Collection point: Prague, Pinkas Synagogue

Cat. No. 424
Spice Box
Inv. No. JMP 7.550
Silver, filigree
Maker EE, Brno, after 1871
Height: 238 mm, width: 77 mm
Hallmarks: 1. EE in rectangle,
2. Austro-Hungary [Brno] after 1871,
3. localization letter A6 [Brno] after 1868
Without inscriptions.
Collection point: Kojetín

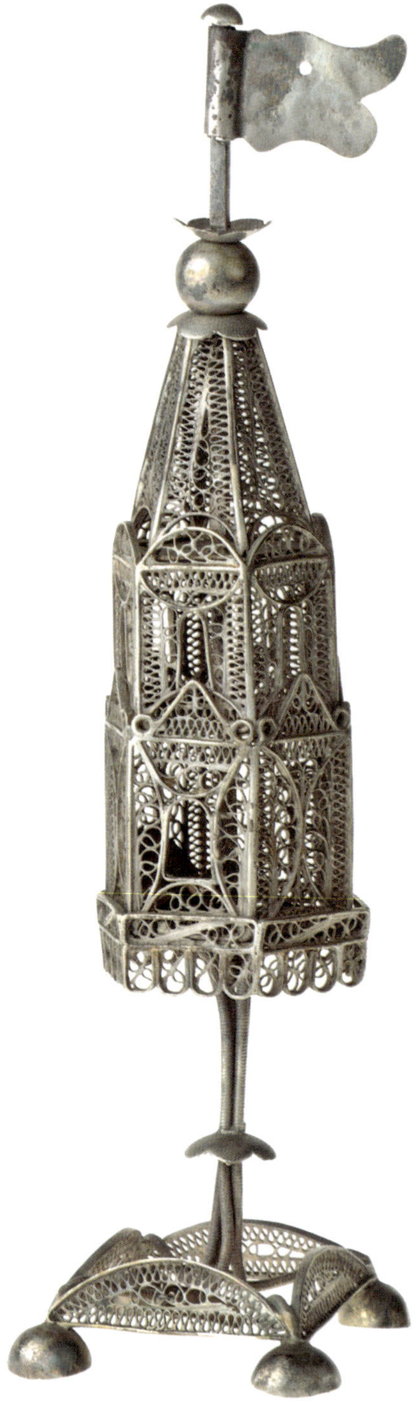

Cat. No. 421

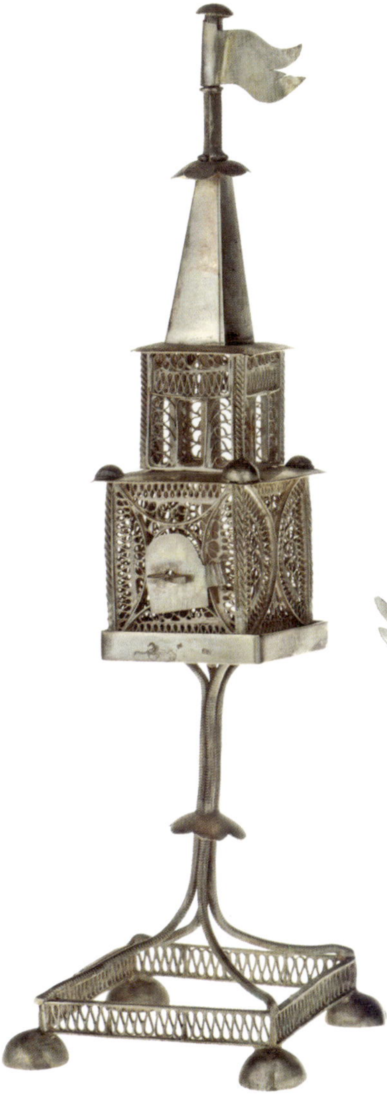

Cat. No. 422

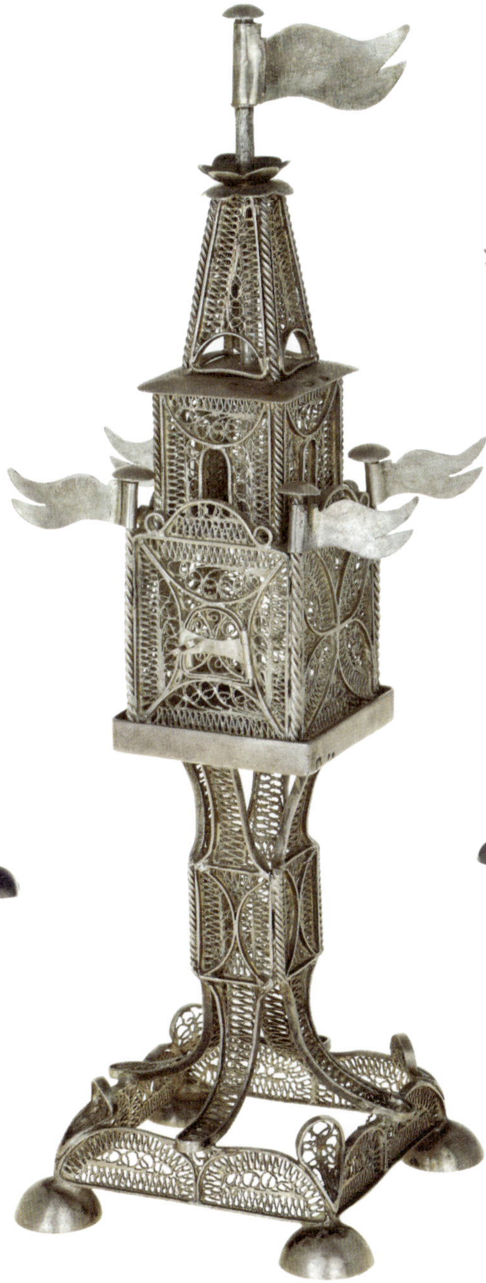

Cat. No. 424

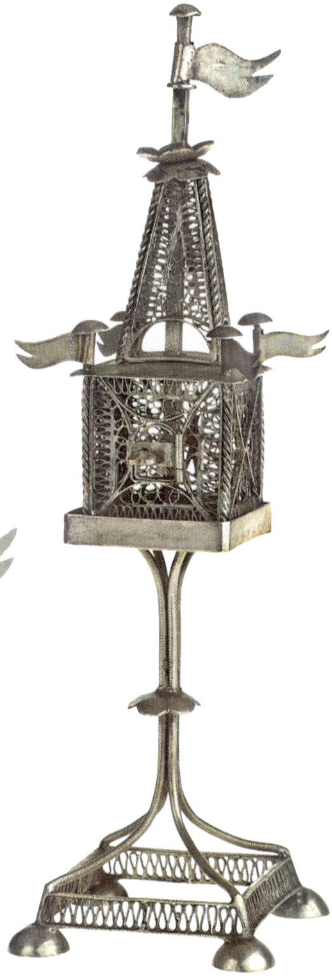

Cat. No. 423

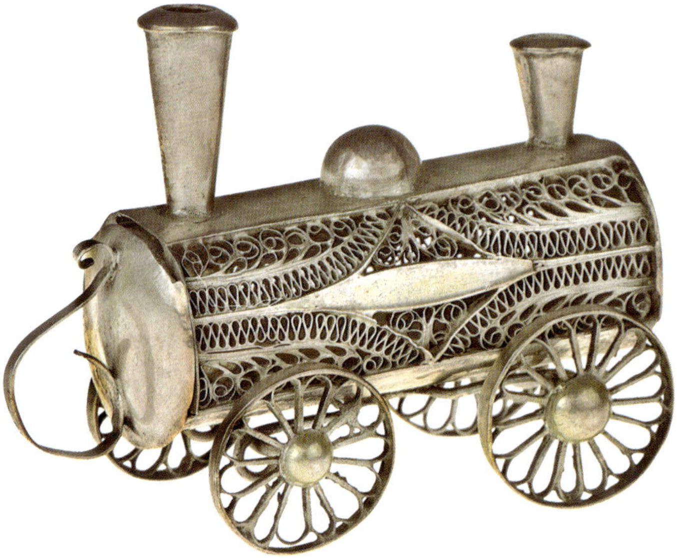

Cat. No. 425

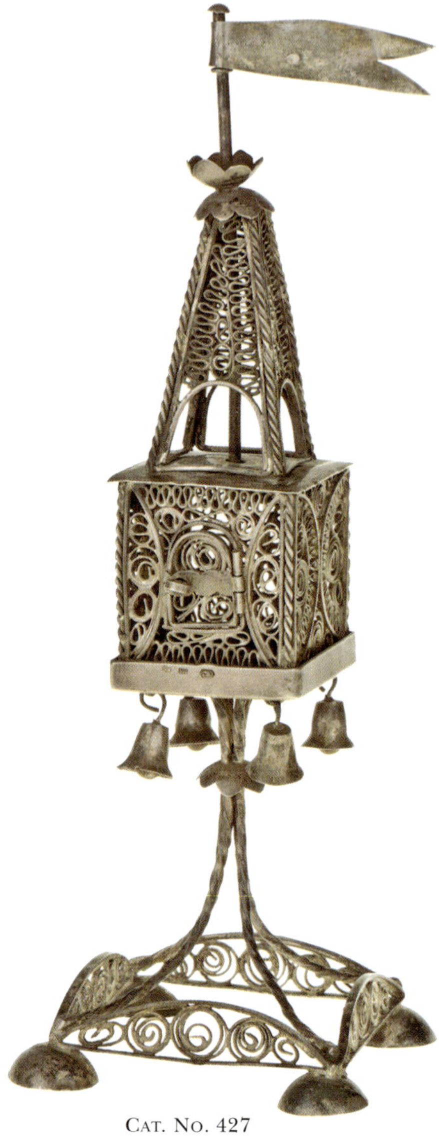

Cat. No. 427

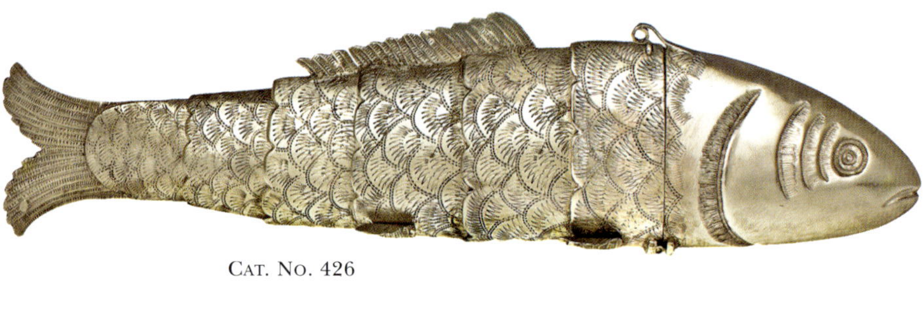

Cat. No. 426

Cat. No. 425
Spice Box
Inv. No. JMP 003.964
Silver, filigree
No maker's mark, Central Europe,
2nd half of 19th century
Height: 55 mm, length: 67 mm
Hallmarks: unmarked
Without inscriptions.
Collection point: Central Jewish Museum for Moravia and Silesia, 1936–1938 in Nikolsburg

Cat. No. 426
Spice Box
Inv. No. JMP 012.736
Silver, repoussé, engraving
Maker SH [?], Krakow, after 1919
Length: 218 mm, height: 57 mm
Hallmarks: 1. SH [?] in oval,
2. hallmark Poland [Krakow] 1920–46
Without inscriptions.
Collection point: Jewish Museum in Prague, 1906–1940

Cat. No. 427
Spice Box
Inv. No. JMP 177.237
Silver, filigree
Maker GB, Vienna, after 1922
Height: 181 mm, width: 63 mm
Hallmarks: 1. GB in rectangle, 2. hallmark Austria [Vienna] after 1922, 3. purity number 800
Without inscriptions.
Purchased by the Jewish Museum in Prague.

Cat. No. 428
Spice Box
Inv. No. JMP 004.281
Silver, filigree
Maker BS, Czechoslovakia, 1921–28
Height: 222 mm, width: 62 mm
Hallmarks: 1. BS in rectangle,
2. hallmark Czechoslovakia 1921–28
Donation inscription written in Latin script, Hebrew dating 691 a. s. c. [= 1931]:
J. L. Wodak.
Collection point: Uherské Hradiště

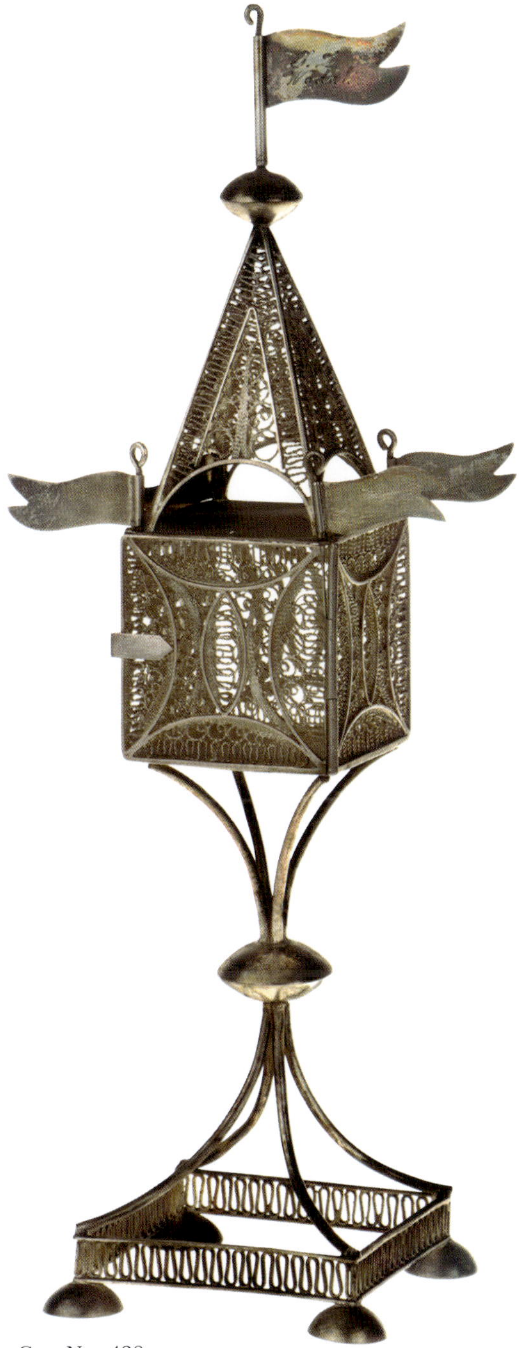

Cat. No. 428

Cat. No. 429
Spice Box
Inv. No. JMP 091.854
Silver, repoussé, cut-out
Maker's mark illegible [MV?],
Czechoslovakia, after 1928
Height: 186 mm, diameter: 54 mm
Hallmarks: 1. illegible maker's mark (MV?),
2. hallmark Czechoslovakia 1929–41,
3. purity number 800
Without inscriptions.
Collection point: Prague

Cat. No. 430
Spice Box
Inv. No. JMP 010.205
Silver, repoussé, cut-out
Maker SM, Krakow, 1936 [inscription]
Height: 210 mm, diameter: 64 mm
Hallmarks: 1. SM in oval,
2. hallmark Poland [Krakow] 1920–46
Donation inscription in Hebrew.
Translation:
A gift of David Anger / Unger and his wife in the year 696 [a. s. c.] [= 1936].
Collection point: Brno

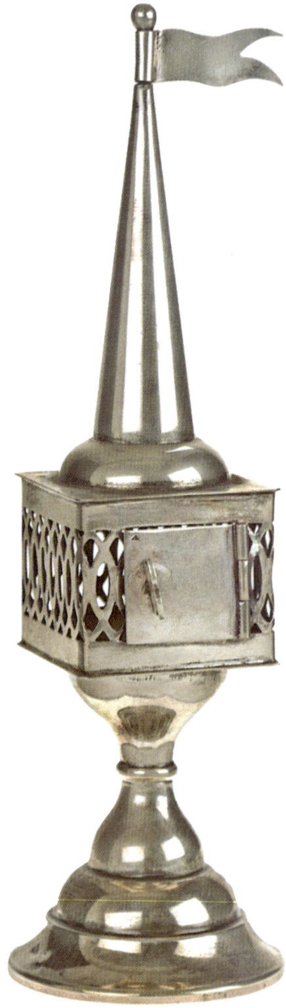

Cat. No. 429

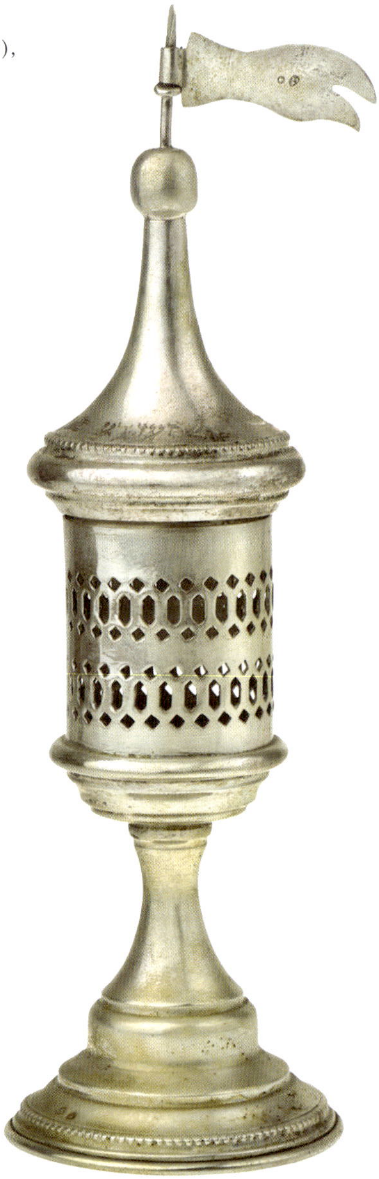

Cat. No. 430

XIII. Mixed

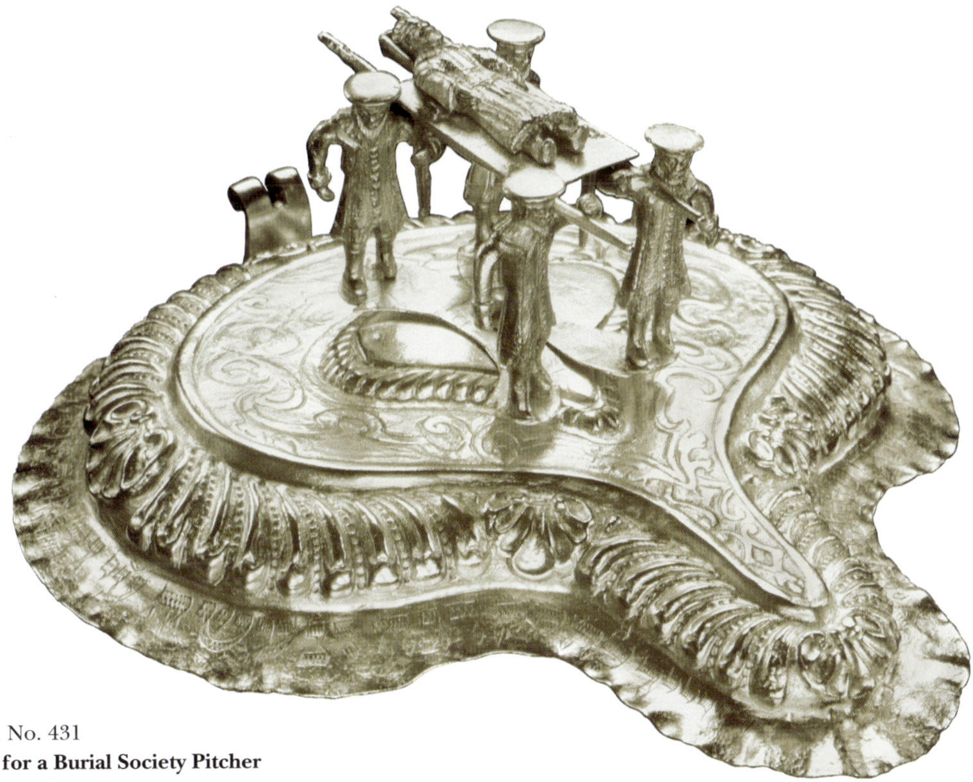

Cat. No. 431
Lid for a Burial Society Pitcher
Inv. No. JMP 003.941
Silver, repoussé, cast, engraving
No maker's mark, Mikulov [?], 1725 [inscription]
Length: 190 mm, width: 195 mm
Hallmarks: 1. recharge mark Brno 1806–7,
2. release mark 1809–10
Inscription in Hebrew.
Translation:
Belonging to the Holy Benevolent Society [Burial Society] *and* [it] *was made through the agency of the custodians R Moses Deutsch, R Meir Bloch, Leib PL, R Hirsch Pisek, in the year 485 a. s. c.* [= 1725].
Collection point: Central Jewish Museum for Moravia and Silesia, 1936–1938 in Nikolsburg

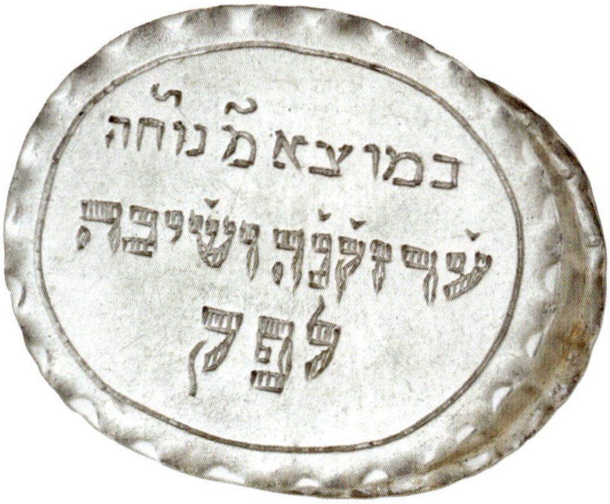

Cat. No. 432 ^
Small Box
Inv. No. JMP 177.371
Silver, repoussé
Maker's mark illegible, Central Europe, 1760 [inscription]
Length: 24 mm, height: 9 mm
Hallmarks: 1. illegible maker's mark
Inscription in Hebrew.
Translation:
On going into retirement [chronogram 54] *until you are old and gray a. s. c.* [dating in the chronogram 520 = 1760].
Donated to the Jewish Museum in Prague

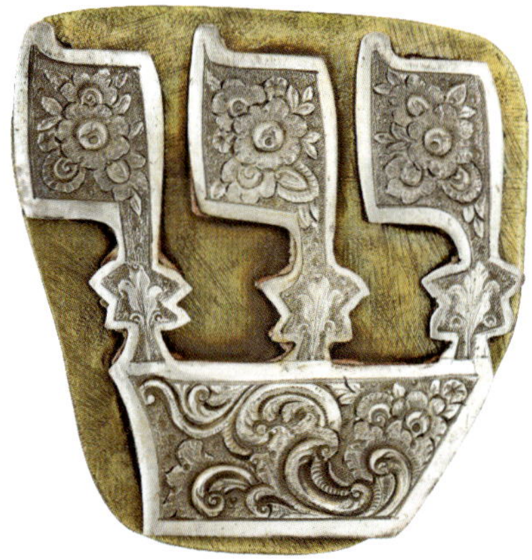

Cat. No. 433
Lettering on Torah Curtain
Inv. No. JMP 063.341/01–08
Silver, brass, engraving
No maker's mark, Bohemia [?], 2nd half of 18th century
Height: 78–18 mm, width: 58–18 mm
Hallmarks: unmarked
Without inscriptions.
Collection point: Prague

Cat. No. 434
Circumcision Shield
Inv. No. JMP 012.784/01
Silver, cut-out
Josef Jakub Raspel, Prague, 1781
Length: 72 mm, width: 42 mm
Hallmarks: 1. IR in irregular shape,
2. hallmark Prague 1781,
3. recharge mark Prague 1806–7
Without inscriptions.
Collection point: Jewish Museum in Prague, 1906–1940

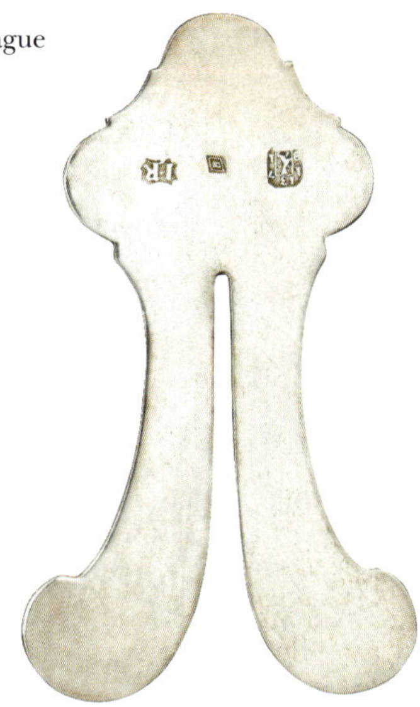

Cat. No. 434

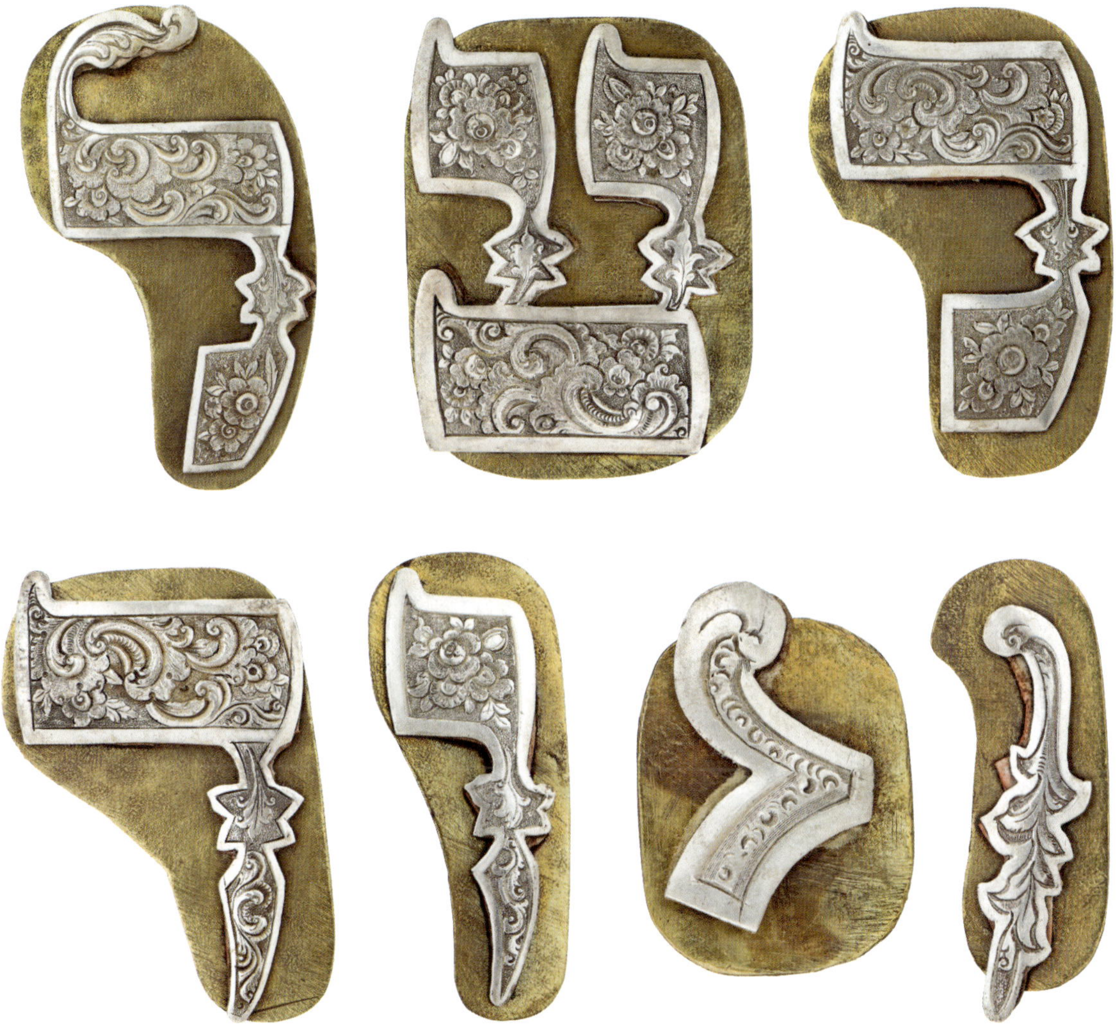

CAT. NO. 433

Cat. No. 435
Curtain Bells
Inv. No. JMP 046.067/01–06
Silver, repoussé, parcel-gilt, engraving
Richard Fleischmann, Prague, 1793
Height: 89 mm, diameter: 63 mm
Hallmarks: 1. RF in rectangle, 2. hallmark Prague 1793, 3. recharge mark Prague 1806–7, 4. release mark 1809–10
Without inscriptions.
Collection point: Prague, Pinkas Synagogue

Cat. No. 436
Circumcision Knife
Inv. No. JMP 012.784/04
Silver, steel, repoussé
Maker AD, Prague, end of 18th century
Length: 160 mm, width: 22 mm
Hallmarks: 1. AD in irregular shape, 2. hallmark Prague [date illegible], 3. purity number 13, 4. recharge mark Prague 1806–7
Without inscriptions.
Collection point: Jewish Museum in Prague, 1906–1940

Cat. No. 437
Seal
Inv. No. JMP 012.792
Silver, cast, engraving
No maker's mark, Bohemia, end of 18th century
Height: 30 mm, width: 18 mm
Hallmarks: 1. recharge mark Prague 1806–7
Inscription in Hebrew.
Translation:
Lipman, son of H Wolf Mestitz of blessed memory, from Turnov.
Collection point: Jewish Museum in Prague, 1906–1940

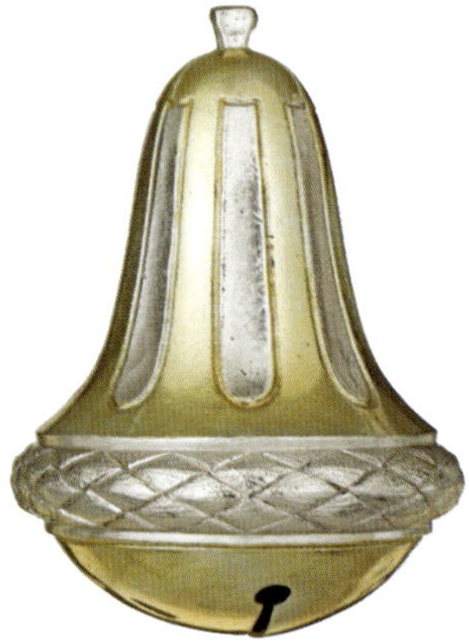

Cat. No. 435

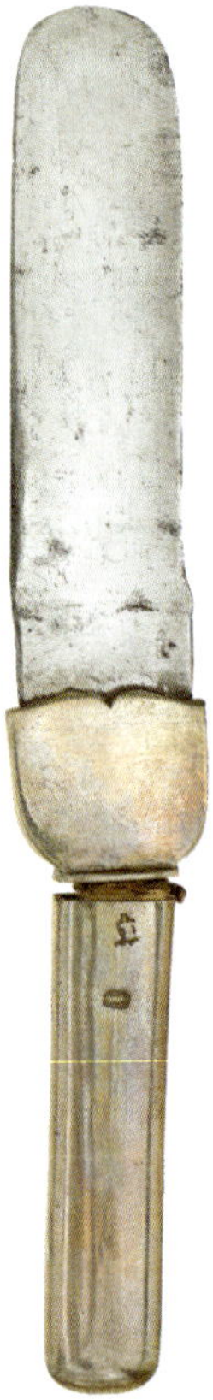

Cat. No. 436

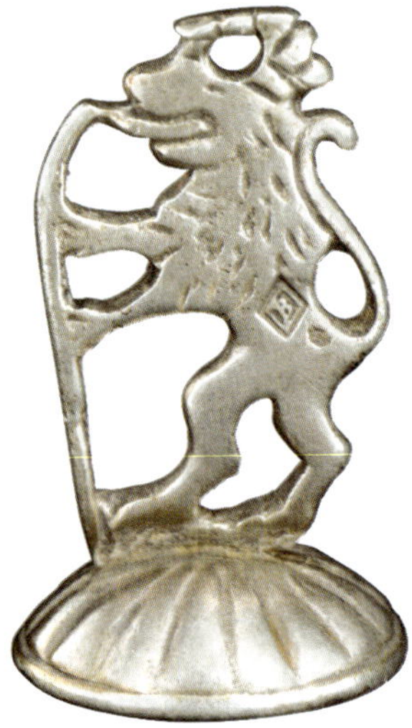

< ^ Cat. No. 437

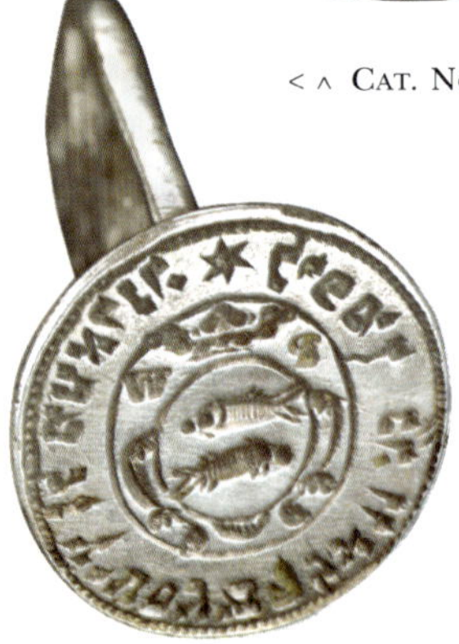

Cat. No. 438
Box
Inv. No. JMP 037.516
Silver, repoussé, engraving, gilded interior
Václav Rummel, Sr. [?], Prague, 1802
Length: 60 mm, height: 17 mm
Hallmarks: 1. WR [?] in oval,
2. hallmark Prague 1802,
3. purity number 13 in oval,
4. tax mark Prague 1810–24
Without inscriptions.
Collection point: Prague

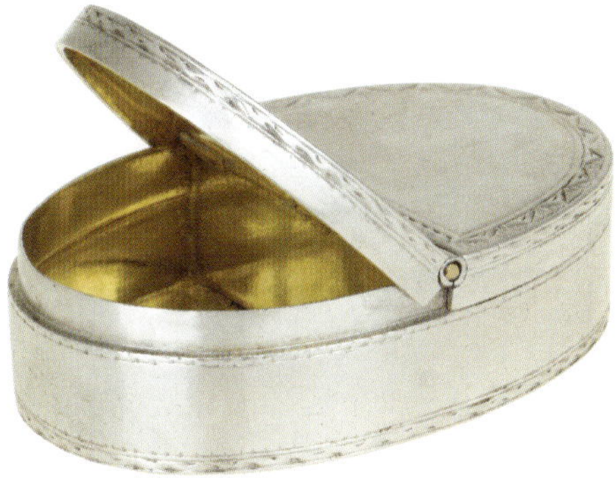

Cat. No. 438

Cat. No. 439
Saltcellar
Inv. No. JMP 173.618
Silver, repoussé, parcel-gilt
Kryštof Wild, Prague, 1802
Length: 123 mm, height: 72 mm
Hallmarks: 1. CW in oval,
2. hallmark Prague 1802,
3. purity number 13,
4. recharge mark Prague 1806–7,
5. release mark 1810–24
Without inscriptions.
Purchased by the Jewish Museum in Prague.

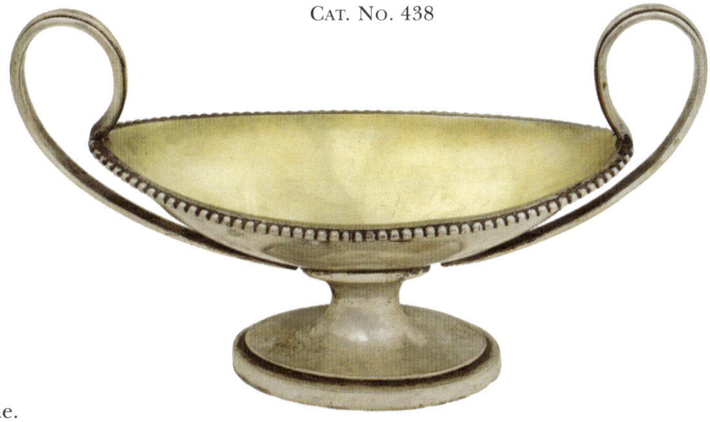

Cat. No. 439

Cat. No. 440
Box
Inv. No. JMP 037.554
Silver, repoussé, gilded interior
Maker FW, Vienna, 1804
Length: 61 mm, height: 30 mm
Hallmarks: 1. FW in rectangle,
2. hallmark Vienna 1804,
3. recharge mark Prague 1806–7,
4. release mark 1809–10
Without inscriptions.
Collection point: Prague

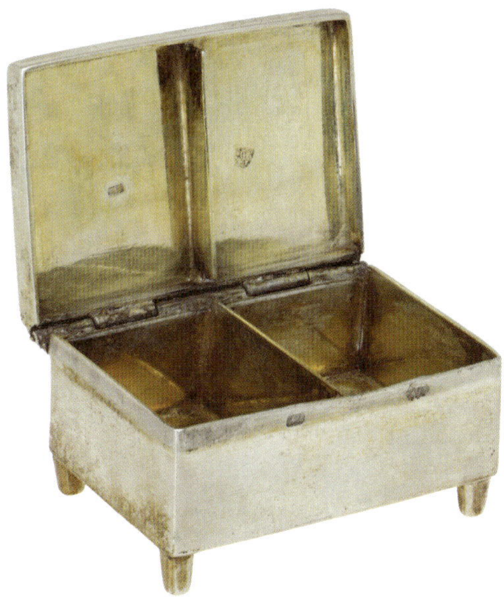

Cat. No. 440

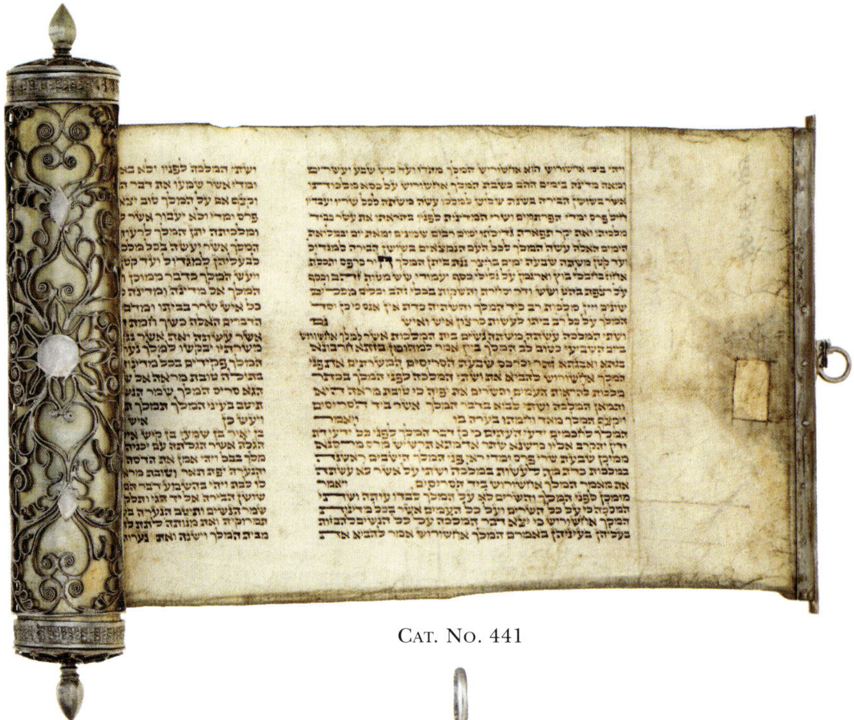

Cat. No. 441

Cat. No. 441
Case with Megillat Esther
Inv. No. JMP 173.099
Silver, filigree
No maker's mark, Poland [?], early 19th century
Length: 204 mm, diameter: 33 mm
Hallmarks: 1. purity number 12 in oval
Without inscriptions.
Purchased by the Jewish Museum in Prague.

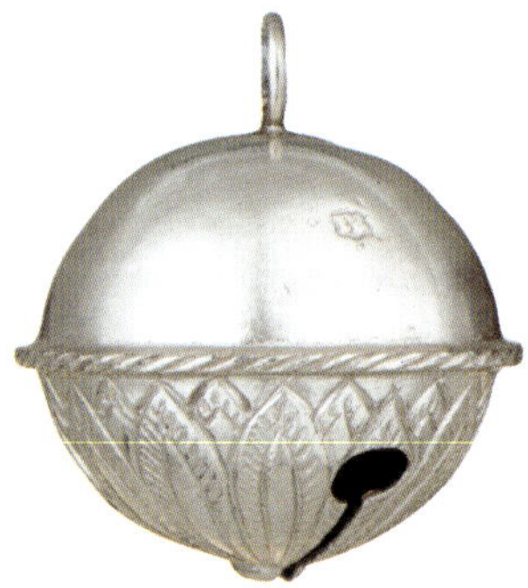

Cat. No. 442

Cat. No. 442
Curtain Bells
Inv. No. JMP 017.524/01, 02
Silver, repoussé, engraving
Maker FZ [?], Central Europe, early 19th century
Height: 44 mm, diameter: 41 mm
Hallmarks: 1. FZ [?] in irregular shape, 2. illegible hallmark
Without inscriptions.
Collection point: Prague, Klausen Synagogue

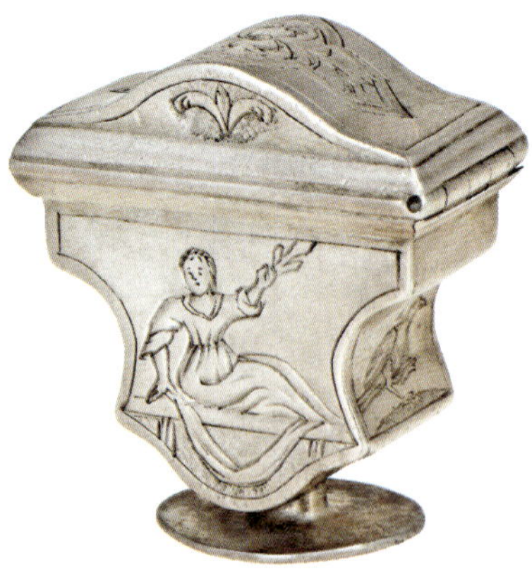

Cat. No. 443

Cat. No. 443
Box with Seal
Inv. No. JMP 012.783
Silver, repoussé, engraving, originally parcel-gilt
No maker's mark, Central Europe, early 19th century
Height: 33 mm, width: 29 mm
Hallmarks: unmarked
Without inscriptions.
Collection point: Jewish Museum in Prague, 1906–1940

Cat. No. 444
Miniature Cart for Charoset
Inv. No. JMP 177.003
Silver, filigree
No maker's mark, Poland [?], early 19th century
Length: 137 mm, height: 51 mm
Hallmarks: 1. purity number 13 in rectangle
Without inscriptions.
Purchased by the Jewish Museum
in Prague.

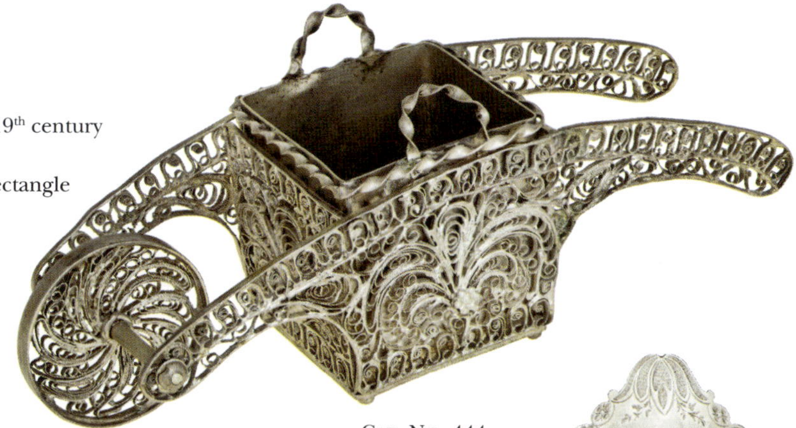

Cat. No. 444

Cat. No. 445
Curtain Bells
Inv. No. JMP 046.065/01–07
Silver, repoussé, engraving
Maker TN, Prague, 1807
Height: 118 mm, diameter: 57 mm
Hallmarks: 1. TN in rectangle,
2. hallmark Prague 1807–9,
3. recharge mark Prague 1806–7,
4. release mark 1809–10
Without inscriptions.
Collection point: Prague, Pinkas Synagogue

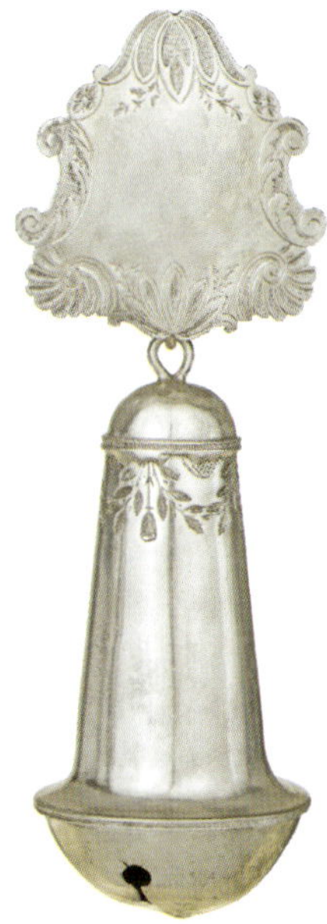

Cat. No. 445

Cat. No. 446
Inv. No. 003.829
Burial Society Jug
Silver, repoussé
No maker's mark, Vienna, 1813
Height: 113 mm, width: 130 mm
Hallmarks: 1. hallmark Vienna 1813,
2. tax mark Vienna 1810–24
Inscription in Hebrew.
Translation:
The Holy Benevolent Society [Burial Society] *the first custodian HH Wolf, second custodian HH Zelig, son of L. third custodian HH Abraham Gershon, son of R Sch., the "great light" sage MHV Solomon SGL* [in the year] *573 a. s. c.* [= 1813].
Collection point: Central Jewish Museum for Moravia and Silesia, 1936–1938 in Nikolsburg

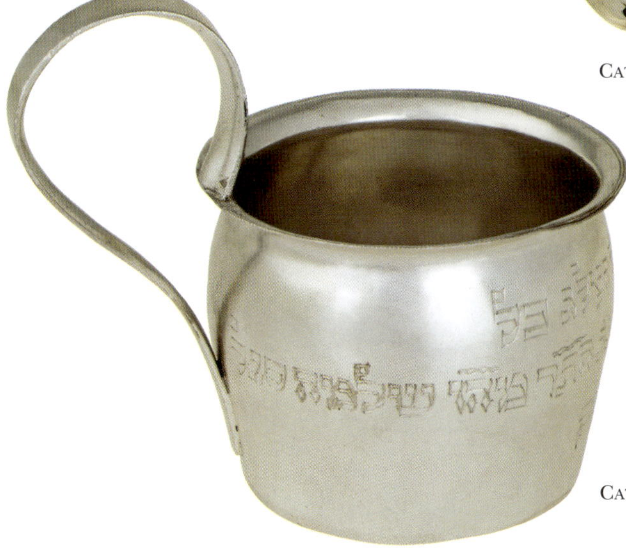

Cat. No. 446

Cat. No. 447
Amulet
Inv. No. JMP 004.000
Silver, repoussé, engraving
No maker's mark, Central Europe,
turn of 18th/19th century
Height: 50 mm, width: 39 mm
Hallmarks: 1. recharge mark Vienna 1806–7
Inscription in Hebrew.
Translation:
L[ord].
Collection point: Central Jewish Museum for Moravia and Silesia, 1936–1938 in Nikolsburg

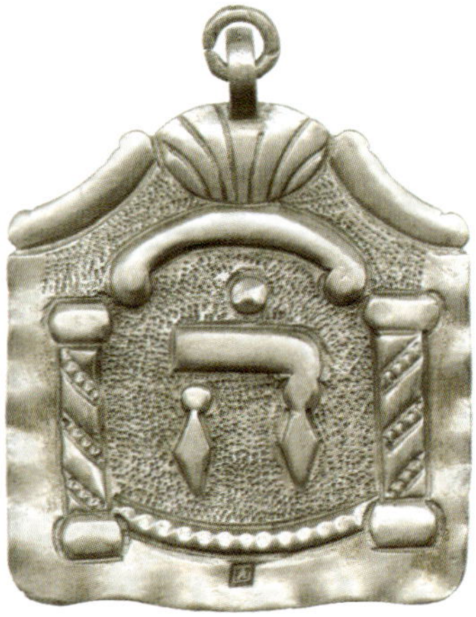

Cat. No. 447

Cat. No. 448
Curtain Bells
Inv. No. JMP 004.032/01, 02
Silver, repoussé, engraving
Antonín Maroušek, Prague, 1816
Height: 93 mm, diameter: 54 mm
Hallmarks: 1. AM in oval, 2. hallmark Prague 1816, 3. tax mark Prague 1810–24
Donation inscription in Hebrew.
Translation:
[beginning of inscription not preserved] [...] *may she live, wife of the generous KH Beer Karpeles, may his Rock and his Redeemer protect him, from Prague.*
Collection point: Kolín

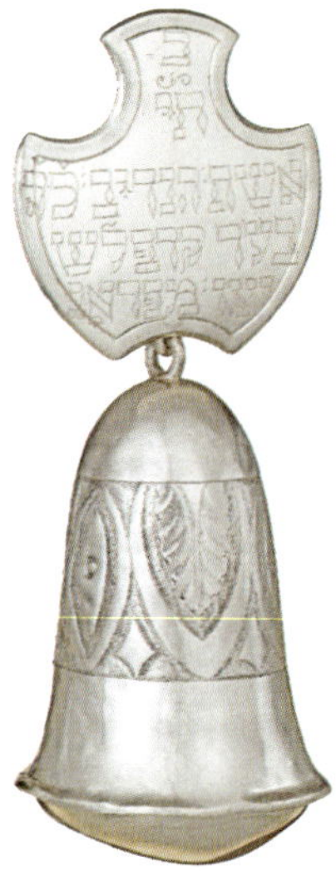

Cat. No. 448

Cat. No. 449
Kittel Clasp
Inv. No. JMP 104.786
Silver, repoussé, engraving
Maker LMM, Lemberg, 1816
Height: 72 mm, width: 125 mm
Hallmarks: 1. LMM in irregular shape,
2. hallmark Lemberg 1816,
3. tax mark Lemberg 1810–24
Without inscriptions.
Purchased by the Jewish Museum in Prague.

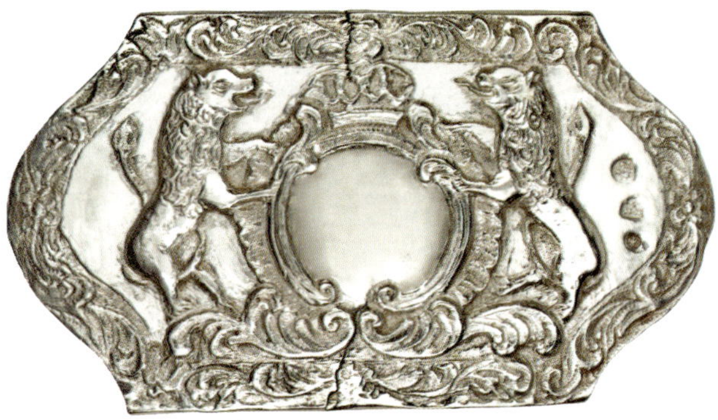

Cat. No. 449

Cat. No. 450
Curtain Bells
Inv. No. JMP 017.519/04–07
Silver, repoussé, engraving
Karel Skřemenec, Prague, 1818
Height: 107 mm, diameter: 59 mm
Hallmarks: 1. CS in rectangle, 2. hallmark Prague 1818, 3. tax mark Prague 1810–24
Without inscriptions.
Collection point: Prague, Klausen Synagogue

Cat. No. 451
Curtain Bells
Inv. No. JMP 002.220/03,06,07
Silver, repoussé, engraving
Antonín Kába, Prague, 1819
Height: 90 mm, diameter: 45 mm
Hallmarks: 1. AK in oval,
2. hallmark Prague 1819,
3. tax mark Prague 1810–24
Inscription in Hebrew.
Translation:
The Holy Society for Visiting the Sick.
Collection point: Mladá Boleslav

Cat. No. 452
Burial Society Cutlery (Eating utensils, Case)
Inv. No. JMP 046.099/01–42
Silver, repoussé, cast
Antonín Kába and maker AN, Prague, 1821
Eating utensils: length: 109–368 mm, width: 20–84 mm
Case: length: 405 mm, height: 128 mm
Hallmarks: 1. AK in oval,
2. AN in oval,
3, hallmark Prague 1821,
4. tax mark Prague 1810–24
Inscription in Hebrew.
Translation:
The Holy Benevolent Society [Burial Society].
Collection point: Prague

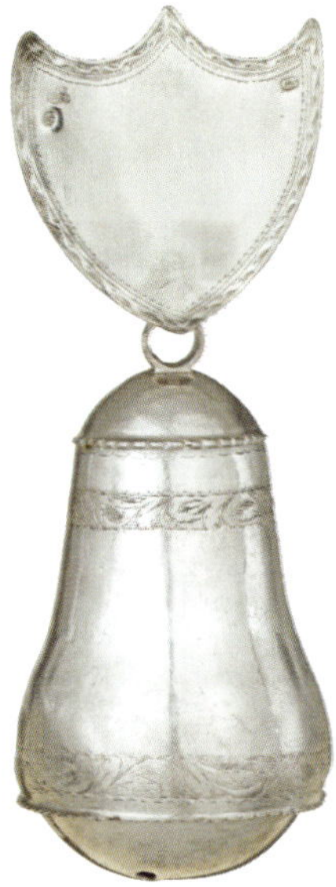
Cat. No. 450

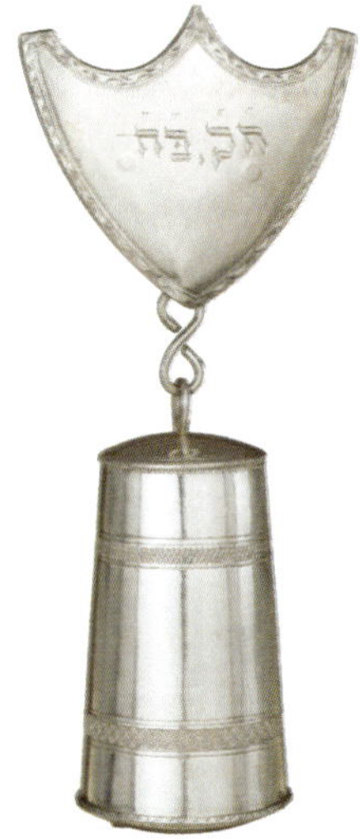
Cat. No. 451

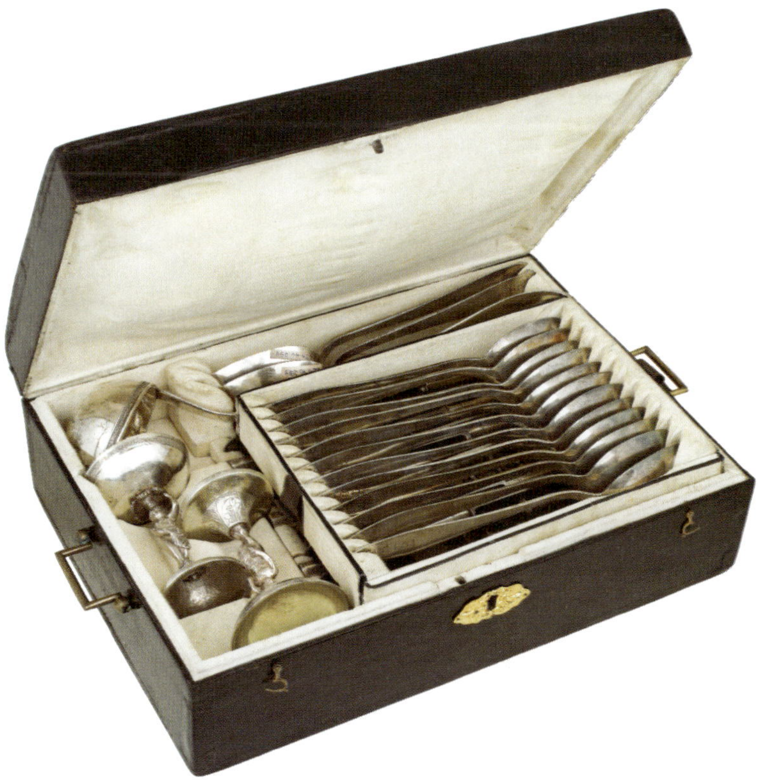
Cat. No. 452

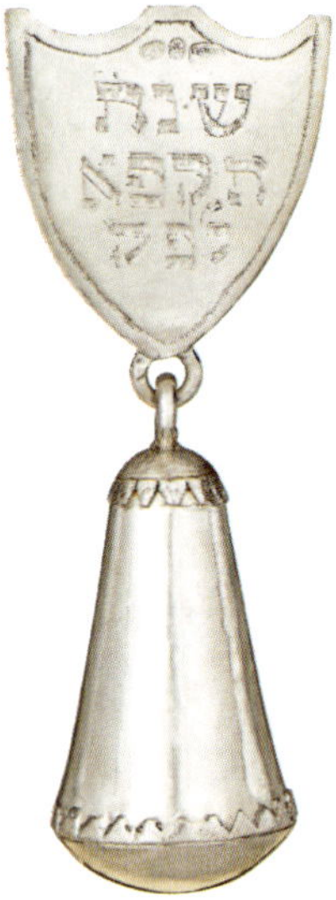

Cat. No. 453

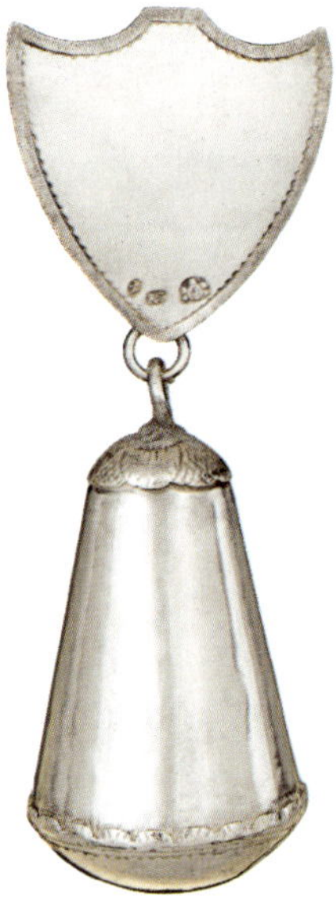

Cat. No. 454

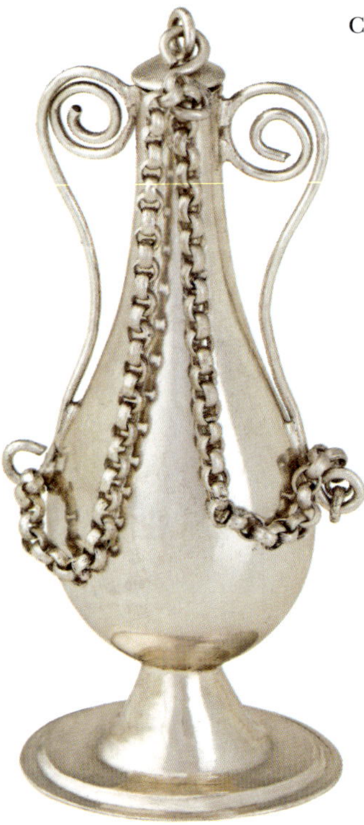

Cat. No. 455

Cat. No. 453
Curtain Bells
Acq. No. JMP 1995/1164–01, 02
Silver, repoussé
Rafael Jonas Goldschmid, Prague, 1821
Height: 71 mm, diameter: 34 mm
Hallmarks: 1. RG in rectangle, 2. hallmark Prague 1821, 3. tax mark Prague 1810–24
Donation inscription in Hebrew.
Translation:
Made from charitable funds through the agency [remainder of inscription missing].
In the year 581 a. s. c. [= 1821].
Catalogued secondarily into the inventory of the Jewish Museum in Prague.

Cat. No. 454
Curtain Bells
Inv. No. JMP 010.717/01–05
Silver, repoussé
Rafael Jonas Goldschmid, Prague, 1821
Height: 85 mm, diameter: 43 mm
Hallmarks: 1. RG in rectangle, 2. hallmark Prague 1821, 3. tax mark Prague 1810–24
Without inscriptions.
Collection point: Libochovice

< Cat. No. 455
Circumcision Vial
Inv. No. JMP 012.787
Silver, repoussé
Maker AN, Prague, 1822 [?]
Height: 91 mm, width: 40 mm
Hallmarks: 1. AN in oval, 2. hallmark Prague 1822 [?], 3. tax mark Prague 1810–24
Without inscriptions.
Collection point: Jewish Museum in Prague, 1906–1940

Cat. No. 456
Tefillin Box
Inv. No. JMP 003.956
Silver, repoussé, filigree
Maker unknown, Poland [?], 1st half of 19th century
Length: 92 mm, height: 58 mm
Hallmarks: 1. unknown maker's mark in rectangle [animal?], 2. purity number 12 in rectangle
Without inscriptions.
Collection point: Central Jewish Museum for Moravia and Silesia, 1936–1938 in Nikolsburg

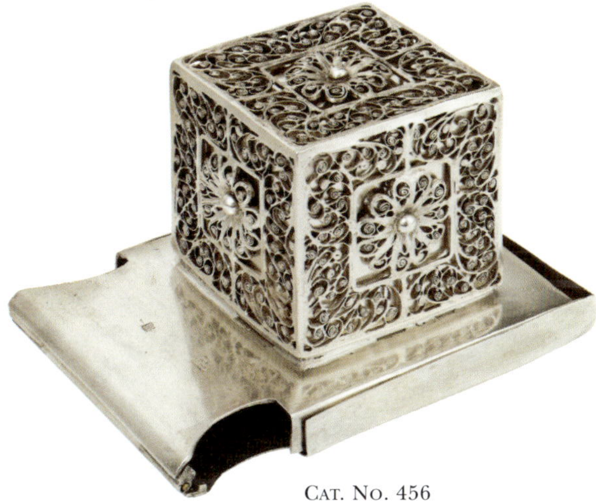

Cat. No. 456

Cat. No. 457
Tefillin Box
Inv. No. JMP 003.976
Silver, repoussé, filigree
Maker unknown, Poland [?], 1st half of 19th century
Length: 90 mm, height: 60 mm
Hallmarks: 1. unknown maker's mark in rectangle [animal?], 2. purity number 12 in rectangle
Without inscriptions.
Collection point: Central Jewish Museum for Moravia and Silesia, 1936–1938 in Nikolsburg

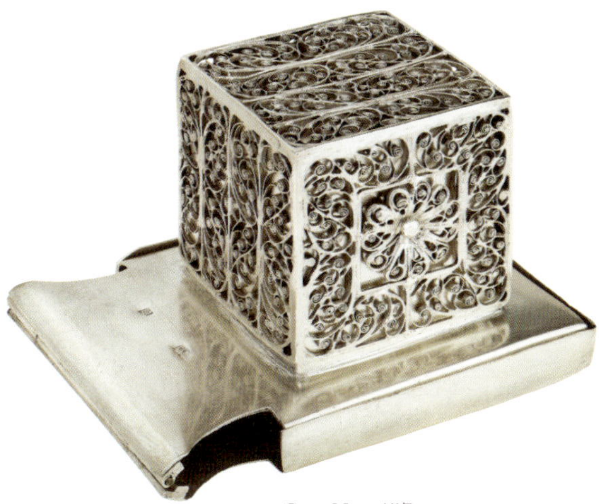

Cat. No. 457

Cat. No. 458
Mezuzah
Inv. No. JMP 003.973
Silver, repoussé, engraving
Maker JVR, Poland [?], mid–19th century
Length: 152 mm, width: 33 mm
Hallmarks: 1. JVR in rectangle, 2. unidentified hallmark [animal]
Without inscriptions.
Collection point: Central Jewish Museum for Moravia and Silesia, 1936–1938 in Nikolsburg

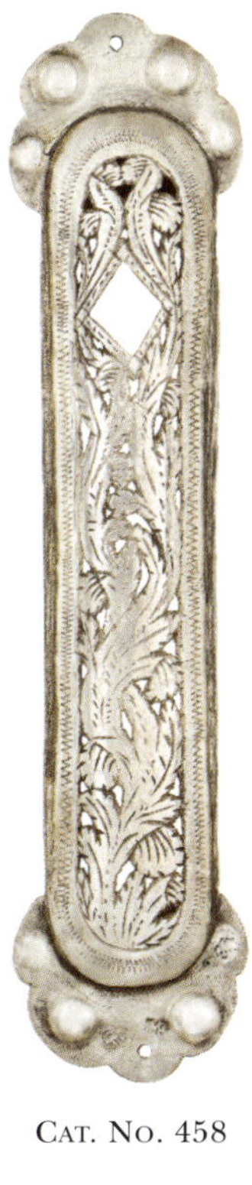

Cat. No. 458

Cat. No. 459 >
Passover Seder Plate
Inv. No. JMP 003.940
Silver, repoussé, engraving, gilt
No maker's mark, Central Europe, mid-19th century
Length: 345 mm, width: 255 mm
Hallmarks: unmarked
Accompanying the individual pictures around the edge of the plate are the names of the months and lunar signs in Hebrew.
Collection point: Central Jewish Museum for Moravia and Silesia, 1936–1938 in Nikolsburg

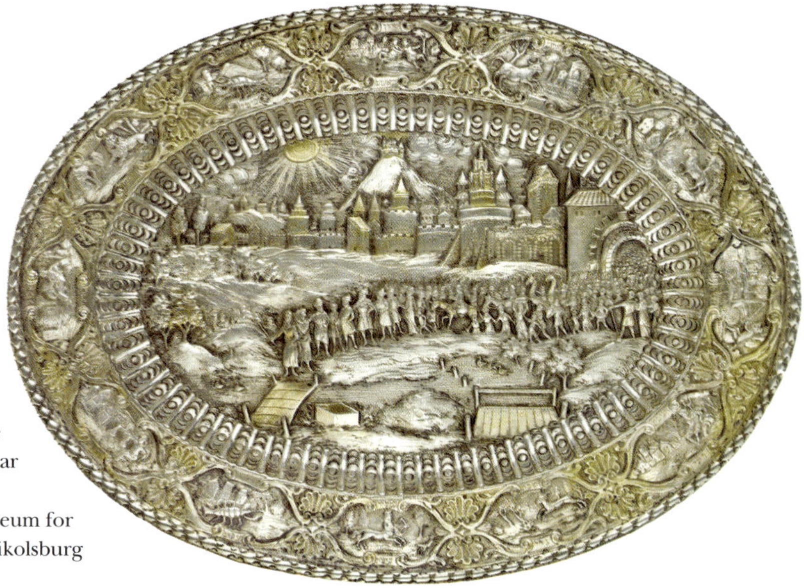

Cat. No. 459

Cat. No. 460
Wedding Ring
Inv. No. JMP 003.993
Silver, repoussé, engraving
No maker's mark, Central Europe, 19th century
Height: 56 mm, width: 27 mm
Hallmarks: unmarked
Inscription in Hebrew.
Translation:
Mazel tov.
Collection point: Central Jewish Museum for Moravia and Silesia, 1936–1938 in Nikolsburg

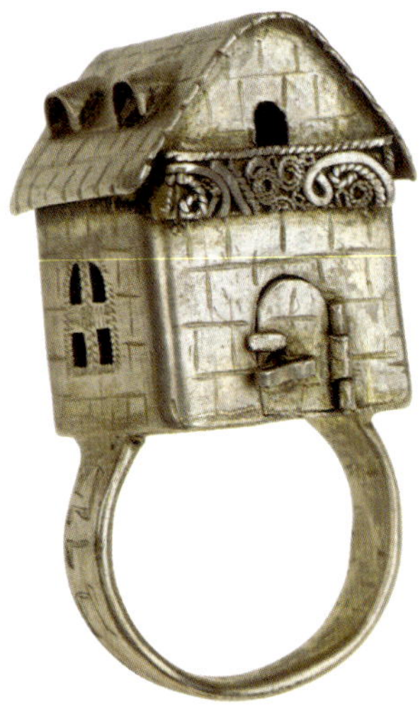

Cat. No. 460

Cat. No. 461
Curtain Bells
Acq. No. JMP 1995/1166–01–07
Silver, repoussé
Václav Kabeš, Prague, 1859
Height: 70 mm, diameter: 42 mm
Hallmarks: 1. WK in oval, 2. hallmark Prague 1859
Donation inscription in Hebrew.
Translation:
The woman elder, lady Belah Fürth from Sušice.
The dear, esteemed Leib Bondi.
Catalogued secondarily into the inventory of the Jewish Museum in Prague.

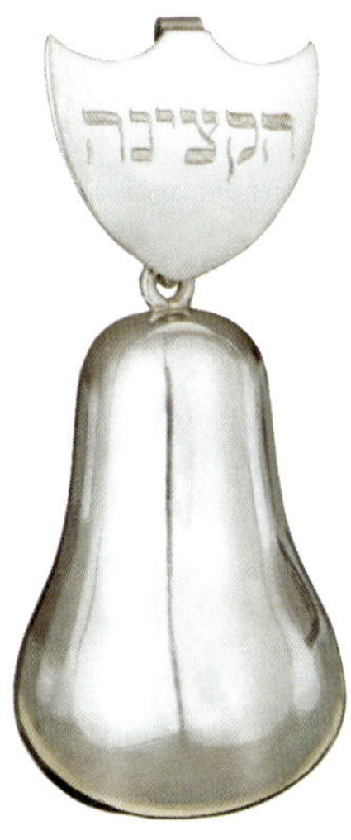

Cat. No. 461

Cat. No. 462
Circumcision Knife
Inv. No. JMP 173.854/01
Silver, steel, repoussé
Jan Novotný, Prague, ca. 1860
Length: 190 mm, width: 19 mm
Hallmarks: 1. JN in rectangle,
2. hallmark Prague [date illegible]
Without inscriptions.
Purchased by the Jewish Museum
in Prague.

Cat. No. 463
Double Saltcellar
Inv. No. JMP 012.610
Silver, repoussé, engraving
Maker HG, Austro-Hungary, 1867–71
Height: 138 mm, width: 136 mm
Hallmarks: 1. HG in rectangle,
2. Austro-Hungary 1867–71
Without inscriptions.
Collection point: Moravská Ostrava

Cat. No. 464
Circumcision Bowl
Inv. No. JMP 012.613/02
Silver, repoussé, engraving
Alexander Muchin (company), Moscow, 1870
Height: 35 mm, diameter: 53 mm
Hallmarks: 1. AM in rectangle,
2. hallmark Moscow,
3. hallmark master's mark 1870,
4. purity number 84 in rectangle
Without inscriptions.
Collection point: Moravská Ostrava

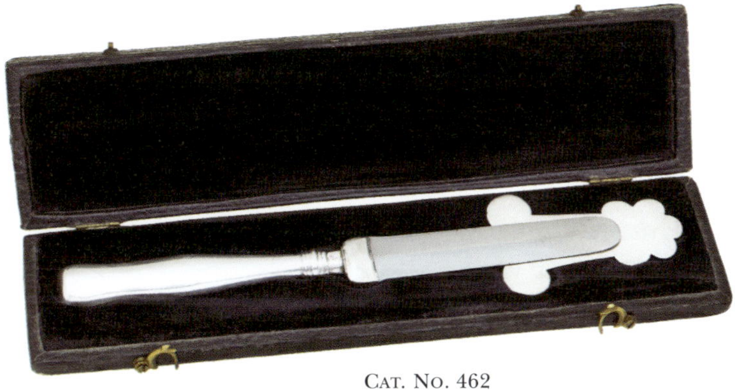

Cat. No. 462

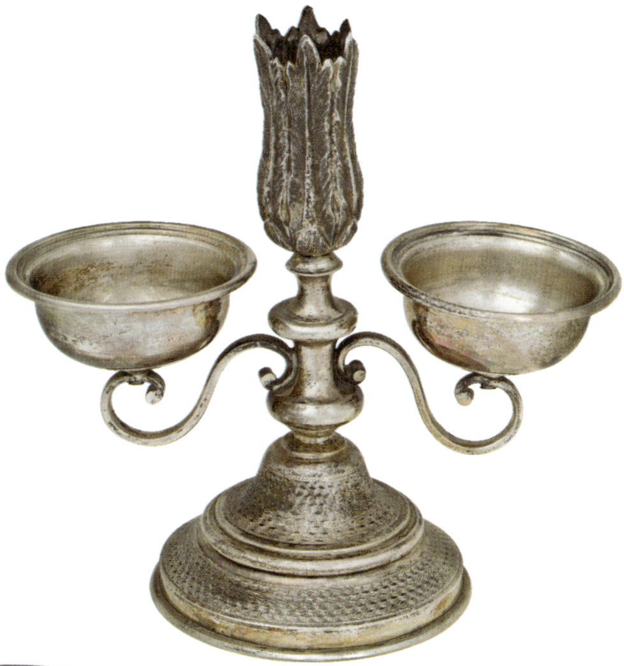

Cat. No. 463

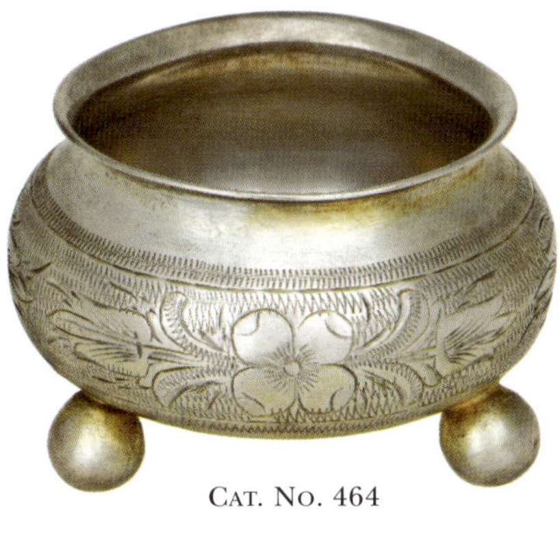

Cat. No. 464

Cat. No. 465
Aliyah Plaques
Inv. No. JMP 037.605/01–12
Silver, engraving
Alfred Pollak (company), Prague, after 1871
Length: 102 mm, width: 50 mm
Hallmarks: 1. AP in rectangle,
2. Austro-Hungary [Prague] after 1871
Inscription in Hebrew.
Translation:
Third Sixth Fourth; Kohain Eighth Fifth; Maftir Tenth Seventh; Levite Ninth Last.
Collection point: Prague

Cat. No. 466
Aliyah Plaques
Inv. No. JMP 001.511/01–11
Silver, engraving
Maker SK, Prague, after 1871
Length: 59 mm, width: 33 mm
Hallmarks: 1. SK in rectangle,
2. Austro-Hungary [Prague] after 1871
Inscription in Hebrew.
Translation:
Fourth Third Sixth;
Maftir Last Ninth;
Seventh Eighth Fifth;
Kohain Levite.
Collection point: Mělník

Cat. No. 467
Aliyah Plaques
Inv. No. JMP 007.069/01–09
Silver, engraving
Maker HS, Vienna, after 1871
Length: 54 mm, width: 33 mm
Hallmarks: 1. HS in rectangle,
2. Austro-Hungary [Vienna] after 1871
Inscription in Hebrew.
Translation:
Kohain Last Levite;
Maftir Third Fourth;
Fifth Sixth Seventh.
Collection point: Třešť

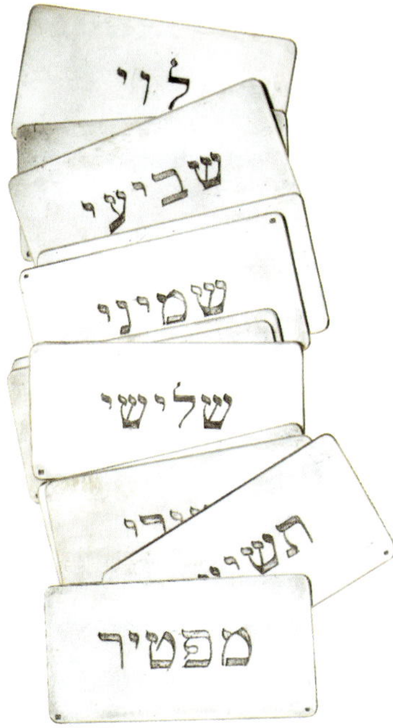

Cat. No. 465

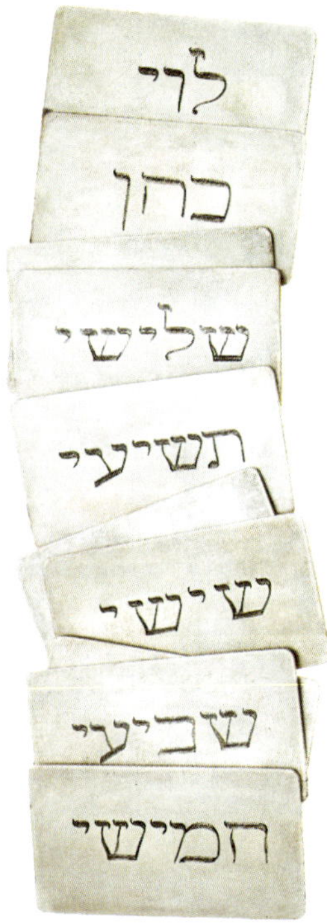

Cat. No. 466

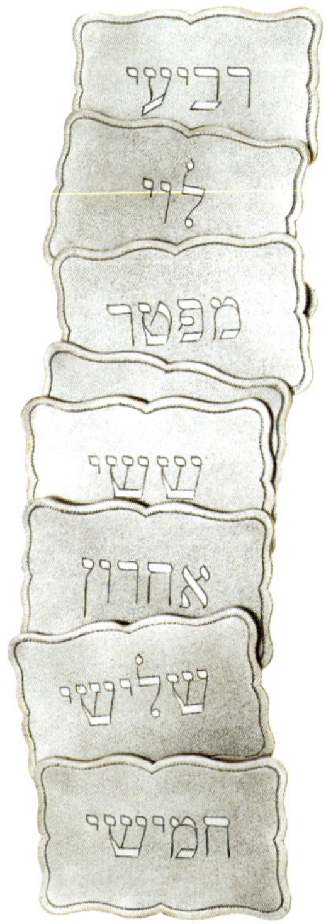

Cat. No. 467

Cat. No. 468
Curtain Bells
Inv. No. JMP 010.617/01–05
Silver, repoussé
Maker EK, Prague, 1872–78
Height: 89 mm, diameter: 51 mm
Hallmarks: 1. EK [unframed],
2. Austro-Hungary [Prague] after 1871
Donation inscription in German
in Latin script.
Translation:
Eduard and Franziska Fanta on the bar mitzvah of their son Alois 23/2 1878.
Collection point: Jičín

Cat. No. 468

Cat. No. 469
Ceremonial Chain
Inv. No. JMP 037.957/01, 02
Silver, engraving
Maker KJ, Prague, 1892 [inscription]
Medallion: diameter: 68 mm
Case: length: 318, width: 322 mm
Hallmarks: 1. KJ in rectangle,
2. Austro-Hungary [Prague] after 1871
Donation inscription in Hebrew,
Czech and German in Latin script.
Translation:
Shammes. The holy community Vinohrady, 652 a. s. c. [= 1892] [in Hebrew on the front side]. *Custos. Israel. The religious community Král. Vinohrady* [in Czech]; *Israel. Cultusgemeinde Kgl.-Weinberge* [in German, on the back side].
Collection point: Prague, Pinkas Synagogue / Vinohrady

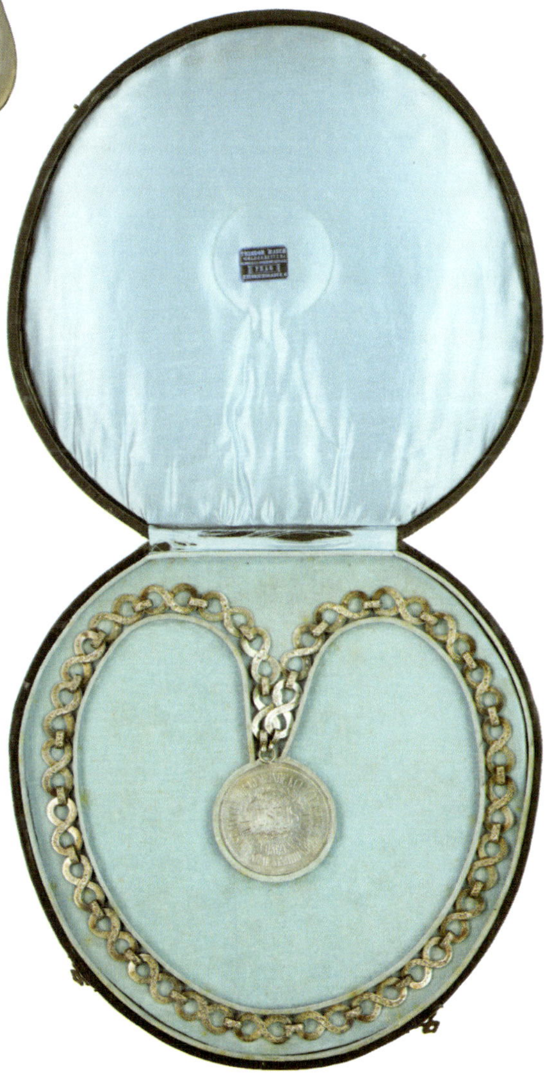

Cat. No. 469

Cat. No. 470
Pidyon HaBen Tray
Inv. No. JMP 032.132
Silver, repoussé, engraving
Maker FV, Austro-Hungary,
turn of 19th/20th century
Length: 338 mm, width: 234 mm
Hallmarks: 1. FV in rectangle,
2. Austro-Hungary after 1866
Without inscriptions.
Collection point: Jewish
Museum in Prague, 1906–1940

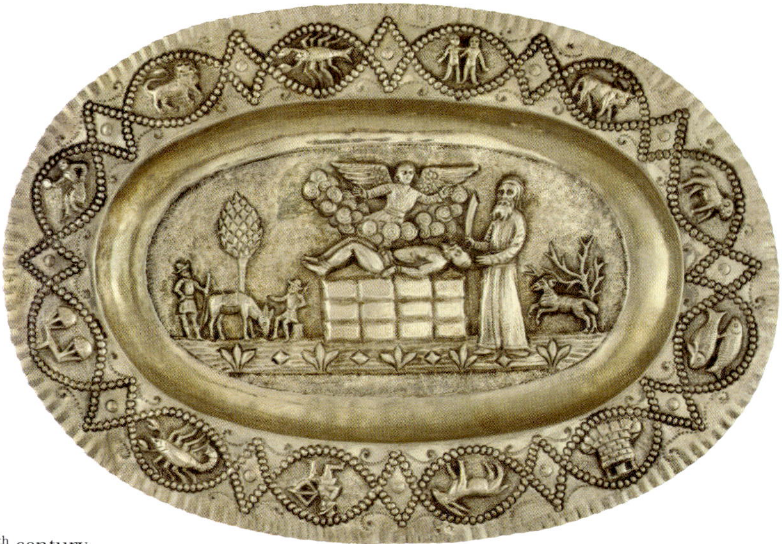

Cat. No. 470

Cat. No. 471
Bottle Label
Inv. No. JMP 046.127
Silver, repoussé
No maker's mark, Germany, early 20th century
Height: 73 mm, width: 62 mm
Hallmarks: 1. German hallmark for silver, 2. purity number 800, 3. import mark Czechoslovakia 1921–28
Inscription in Hebrew.
Translation:
Good Shabbat.
Collection point: Prague

Cat. No. 472
Filigree Spoon
Inv. No. JMP 174.899
Silver, filigree
Bezalel workshops, Palestine, early 20th century
Length: 160 mm, width: 46 mm
Hallmarks: unmarked
Maker's mark in Hebrew: *Bezalel.*
Purchased by the Jewish Museum in Prague.

Cat. No. 473
Clips for a Tallit Atara
Acq. No. JMP 1995/1015
Silver, engraving, cut-out
No maker's mark, Germany [?], early 20th century
Length: 45 mm, width: 30 mm
Hallmarks: 1. purity number 800
Without inscriptions.
Catalogued secondarily into the inventory of the Jewish Museum in Prague.

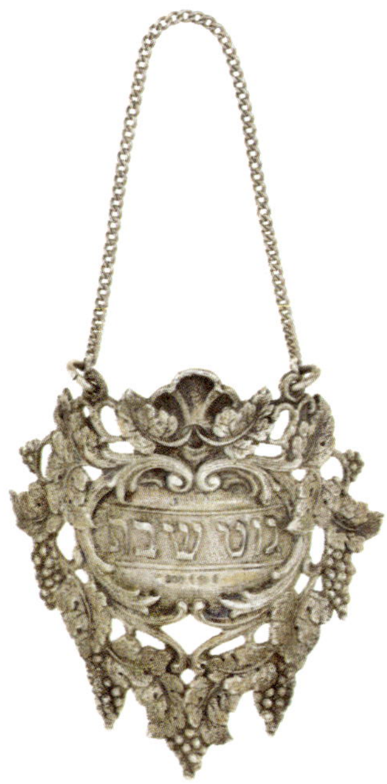

Cat. No. 471

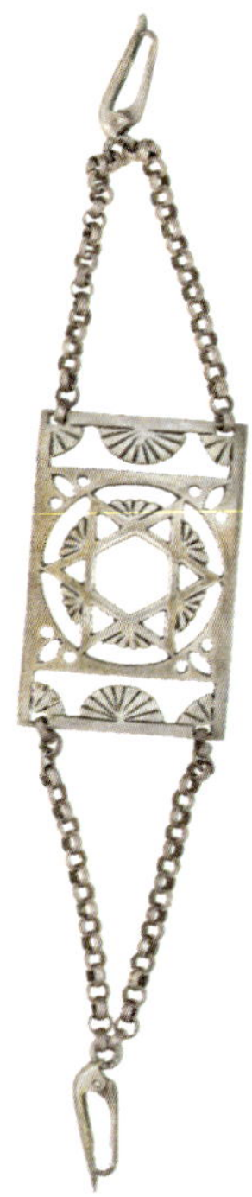

Cat. No. 473

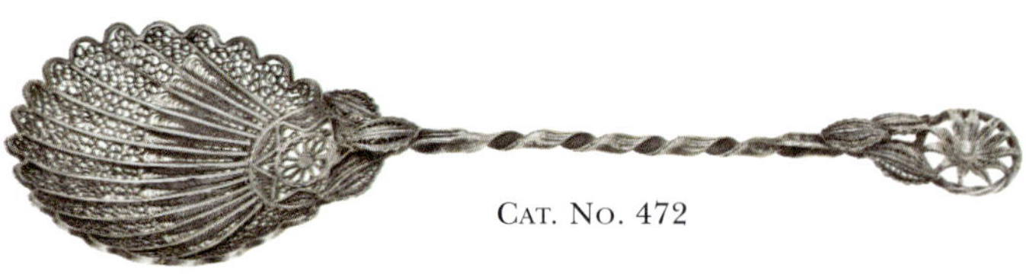

Cat. No. 472

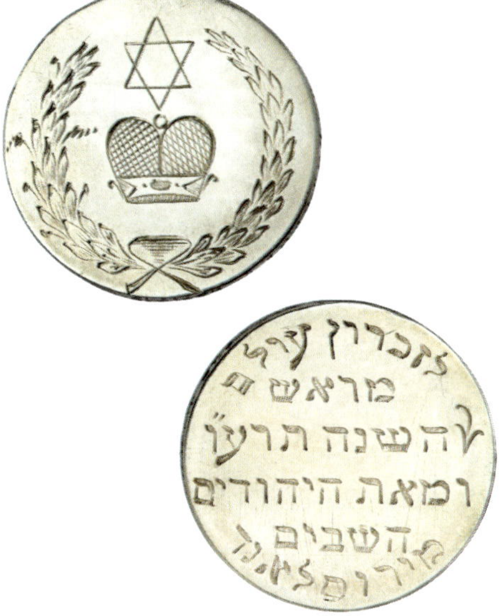

Cat. No. 474

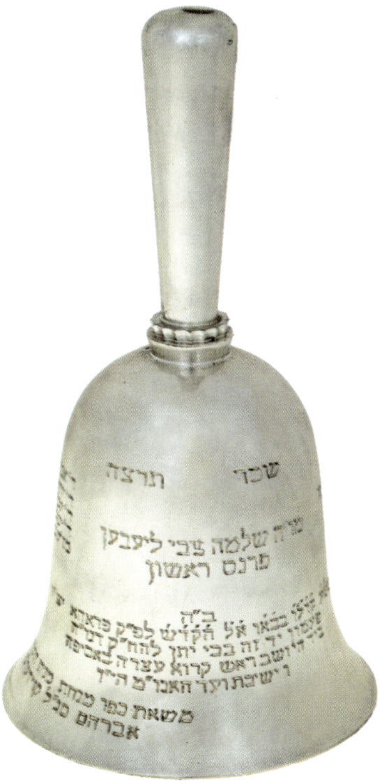

Cat. No. 475

Cat. No. 474
Pendant
Inv. No. JMP 037.719
Silver, engraving
No maker's mark, Bohemia, 1916 [inscription]
Diameter: 34 mm
Hallmarks: unmarked
Donation inscription in Hebrew.
Translation:
To the eternal memory of New Year 676 [a. s. c.] [= 1916] *and from the Jews returning from Russia.*
Collection point: Jewish Museum in Prague, 1906–1940

Cat. No. 475
Bell of the Burial Society
Inv. No. JMP 046.095
Silver, repoussé
František Bibus (company), Czechoslovakia, 1929–35
Height: 175 mm, diameter: 94 mm
Hallmarks: 1. FB in rectangle,
2. hallmark Czechoslovakia 1929–41,
3. purity number 800
Donation inscription in Hebrew.
Translation:
R David Tetzner; R Abraham Winternitz; R Abraham Lederer; R Abraham Synek; R Abraham Kraus [column on right side]. *R Abraham SGL Kauders; R Judah SGL Herman; R Joseph Lampel; R Issachar SGL Lebenhart; MVH Samuel Freiberger* [column on the left side]. *324* [= 1564]. *695* [= 1935]. *MVH Solomon Zevi Lieben. First Parnas* [text centered at top]. *With the help of God. "So that its sound shall be heard when he goes into the Holy Place" a.s.c.* [Exod. 28:35; dating in the chronogram 695 = 1935]. *Prague, let her Rock and Redeemer protect her. This hand bell is a gift to the Holy Benevolent Society* [Burial Society] *for the president to announce breaks during assemblies and board meetings of the prince custodians and leaders, may the Lord watch over and protect them* [text is centered in the middle]. *"Lifting up of my hands as an offering of the Levite portion"* [paraphrase of Ps. 141:2]. *Abraham SGL Kauders* [text centered below].
Collection point: Prague

Index

Page numbers are given first, followed by catalogue numbers in brackets.

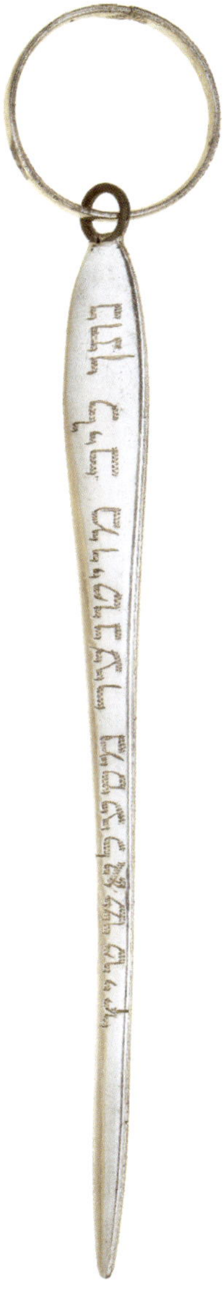

Cat. No. 326

LOCALITIES

MAKERS BY NAME

MAKERS BY INITIALS

FIRST NAMES

SURNAMES

BIBLIOGRAPHY

Altshuler, David, ed. *The Precious Legacy: Judaic Treasures from the Czechoslovak State Collection.* New York: Summit Books, 1983.

Brilling, Bernhard. "Zur Geschichte des jüdischen Goldschmiedegewerbes in Prag: Die ersten Prager Jüdischen Goldschmiede." *Zeitschrift für die Geschichte der Juden,* V., Nummer 1 (Jahrgang 1968): 21-26.

————. "Zur Geschichte des jüdischen Goldschmiedegewerbes in Mähren (1550–1800)." *Zeitschrift für die Geschichte der Juden,* VI., Nummer 3/4 (Jahrgang 1969): 137-146.

Brunner, Moritz. "Geschichte der Juden in Brünn." In *Die Juden und Jugengemeinden Mährens in Vergangenheit und Gegenwart,* edited by Hugo Gold, 137-172. Brno: Jüdischer Buch- und Kunstverlag, 1929.

Flesch, Jindřich. "Umění ve službách synagogy." In *O židovských památkách v Československé republice,* ["Art in the Service of Synagogues," *On Jewish Monuments in the Czechoslovak Republic*], 32-38. Prague: self-published, 1933.

Grafman, Rafi. *Crowning Glory: Silver Torah Ornaments of the Jewish Museum, New York,* edited by Vivian B. Mann. New York: The Jewish Museum, New York, 1996.

Grossová, Anna. "Otec a syn Lackstampferové. Příspěvek k historii stříbrnického řemesla v Brně." In *Brno v minulosti a dnes* ["Father and Son Lackstampfer: Contribution to the History of the Silversmith Trade in Brno," *Brno Past and Present*], 19 (2006): 119-142.

Hráský, Josef. "La corporation juive d'orfevrerie a Prague." In *Judaica Bohemiae,* II/1 (1966): 19-40.

————. *Výrobní značky zlatnických, stříbrnických a ozdobnických mistrů v Čechách v letech 1806–1860.* [Maker's Marks for Goldsmiths, Silversmiths, and Ornament Masters in Bohemia 1806–1860]. Prague: Uměleckoprůmyslové muzeum, 1981.

————. *Zlatníci pražského baroka.* [Goldsmiths of Prague Baroque]. Prague: Uměleckoprůmyslové muzeum, 1987.

Judaica Books, Manuscripts, Works of Art and Pictures, Amsterdam, Wednesday 19 December 1990. Amsterdam: Christies, 1990.

Jiřinec, Martin, ed. *Soupis židovských rodin v Čechách z roku 1793. II., Kouřimský kraj, Bydžovský kraj, Litoměřický kraj.* [Register of Jewish Families in Bohemia from 1793: II., The Regions of Kouřim, Bydžovský, and Litoměřice]. Prague: Státní ústřední archiv v Praze, 2003.

Knies, Karl. *Die Punzierung in Österreich: eine geschichtliche Studie mit mehrens Textabildungen und 10 Lichtdrucktafeln.* Vienna: Manz'sche k k. Hof-Verlags- und Universitätsbuchhandlung, 1896.

Neuwirth, Waltraud. *Lexikon Wiener Gold- und Silberschmiede und ihre Punzen 1867–1922.* I. (1976), II. (1977), Vienna: Selbstverlag Dr. Waltraud Neuwirth.

————. *Wiener Silber: Namens- und Firmenpunzen 1781–1866.* Vienna: Selbstverlag Dr. Waltraud Neuwirth, 2002.

Prokeš, Jaroslav. "Die Prager Judenkonskription vom Jahr 1729." In *Jahrbuch der Gesellschaft für Geschichte der Juden in der Čechoslovakischen Republik 4,* 297-332. Prague: Gesellschaft für Geschichte der Juden in der Čechoslovakischen Republik, 1932.

Ranschburg, *Bezalel ben Joel. She'elot u-Teshuvot ve-Hidushei Rabbenu Betzalel Ranshburg.* Jerusalem: Machon Yerushalayim, 5740 (1980).

Rosenberg, Marc. *Der Goldschmiede Merkzeichen I-IV,* 3d ed. Frankfurt am Main: Frankfurter Verlags-Anstalt A.-G., 1922–1928. (reprint)

Seling, Helmut. *Die Kunst der Augsburger Goldschmiede 1529–1868.* Band I.-III. Munich: Verlag C. H. Beck, 1980.

Shachar, Isaiah. *Jewish Tradition in Art: The Feuchtwanger Collection of Judaica.* Jerusalem: Israel Museum, 1981.

Schirek, Carl. *Die Punzierung in Mähren,* Brno: self-published, 1902.

Stehlíková, Dana. *Encyklopedie českého zlatnictví, stříbrnictví a klenotnictví,* [Encyclopedia of Czech Goldsmiths, Silversmiths, and Jewelers]. Prague: Libri, 2003.

Täubl, Karel ed. *Vývoj českého puncovnictví,* 3d ed. [The Evolution of Czech Hallmarking]. Prague: Assay Office, 2001.

Tebbe, Karin, ed. *Nürnberger Goldschmiedekunst 1541–1868.* Band I: *Meister, Werke, Marken,* Teil 1: *Textband,* Teil 2: *Tafeln.* Band II: *Goldglanz und Silberstrahl.* Nuremberg: Verlag des Germanischen Nationalmuseums, 2007.

Veselská, Magda. *Defying the Beast: The Jewish Museum in Prague, 1906–1940.* Prague: Jewish Museum in Prague, 2006.

Wischnitzer, Mark. *A History of Jewish Crafts and Guilds.* New York: Jonathan David, 1965.

About the Author

Jaroslav Kuntoš was born in 1966 in the former Czechoslovakia. He is currently Curator of Metals and Three-dimensional Objects at the Jewish Museum in Prague.

He began to specialize in arts-and-crafts work of precious and common metals and other materials as a student at the Secondary School of Applied Arts in Turnov, from where he graduated with a degree as a goldsmith-silversmith. The practical education he received here has proven invaluable for his work in determining the provenance and age of an object and evaluating its authenticity.

In 1990, he was accepted to Charles University to study Art History. At the same time he worked part-time in the metal restoration workshop of the former State Jewish Museum in Prague, where he gradually came to understand the problems associated with analyzing the material evidence coming from the Jewish communities of Bohemia and Moravia. Upon completing a research fellowship in Israel, he became a part-time curator of the metals collection at the Jewish Museum in Prague in 1996, and in 1998, after completing his BA and MA degrees, he became the Museum's Curator of Metals and Three-dimensional Objects.

Kuntoš has participated in organizing many regional and international exhibitions, and not only on Jewish themes, and he has contributed catalogue texts to a number of publications, including: *The Glory of the Baroque in Bohemia: Art, Culture, and Society in the 17th and 18th Centuries* (Prague, 2001); *Defying the Beast* (Prague, 2006); *Bayern – Böhmen: 1500 Jahre Nachbarschaft* (Augsburg, 2007); *Path of Life: Rabbi Judah Loew ben Bezalel (ca. 1525–1609)* (Prague, 2009). He is also co-author of *Dictionary of Judaica* (Prague, 2005), a reference work for identifying Ashkenazi Judaica.

In addition to employing the standard methodological approaches common to his field, he often takes an interdisciplinary approach and borrows from other fields, particularly that of natural history, when analyzing the inherent informative value of objects and relating them to other sources.

Silver Judaica
from the Collection of the Jewish Museum in Prague

Text: Jaroslav Kuntoš
Tables and index: Veronika Mědílková
Peer review: PhDr. Alexandr Putík, PhDr. Eva Kosáková, PhDr. Světlana Spiwoková
English translation: Howard Sidenberg
Translation of catalogue entries by Jewish Museum in Prague
Translation of dedicatory inscriptions from Hebrew: Iveta Cermanová, Jana Polišenská
Photography: Dana Cabanová
Photo editing: Dana Cabanová, Karel Bulín
Graphic design: Clara Istlerová
Print: Tiskárna HUGO, s.r.o., Prague
Number of copies: 1000

The Introduction to the catalogue section has incorporated text on collection points authored by Magda Veselská.

Published by the Jewish Museum in Prague
U Staré školy 1-3, 110 00 Prague 1, Czech Republic
Tel: +420-222 749 211 / Fax: +420-222 749 300
www.jewishmuseum.cz / office@jewishmuseum.cz
ISBN: 978-80-87366-12-7

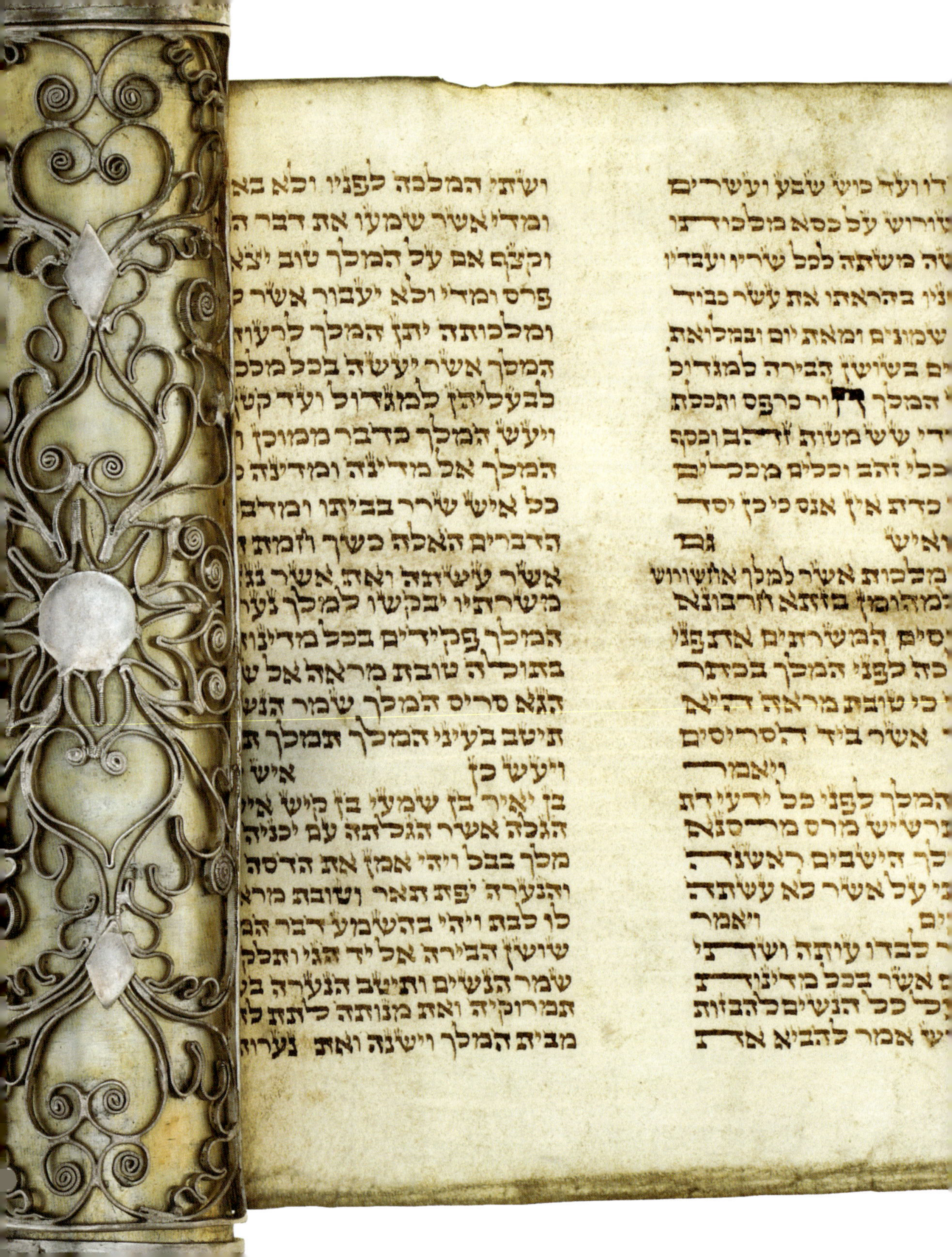

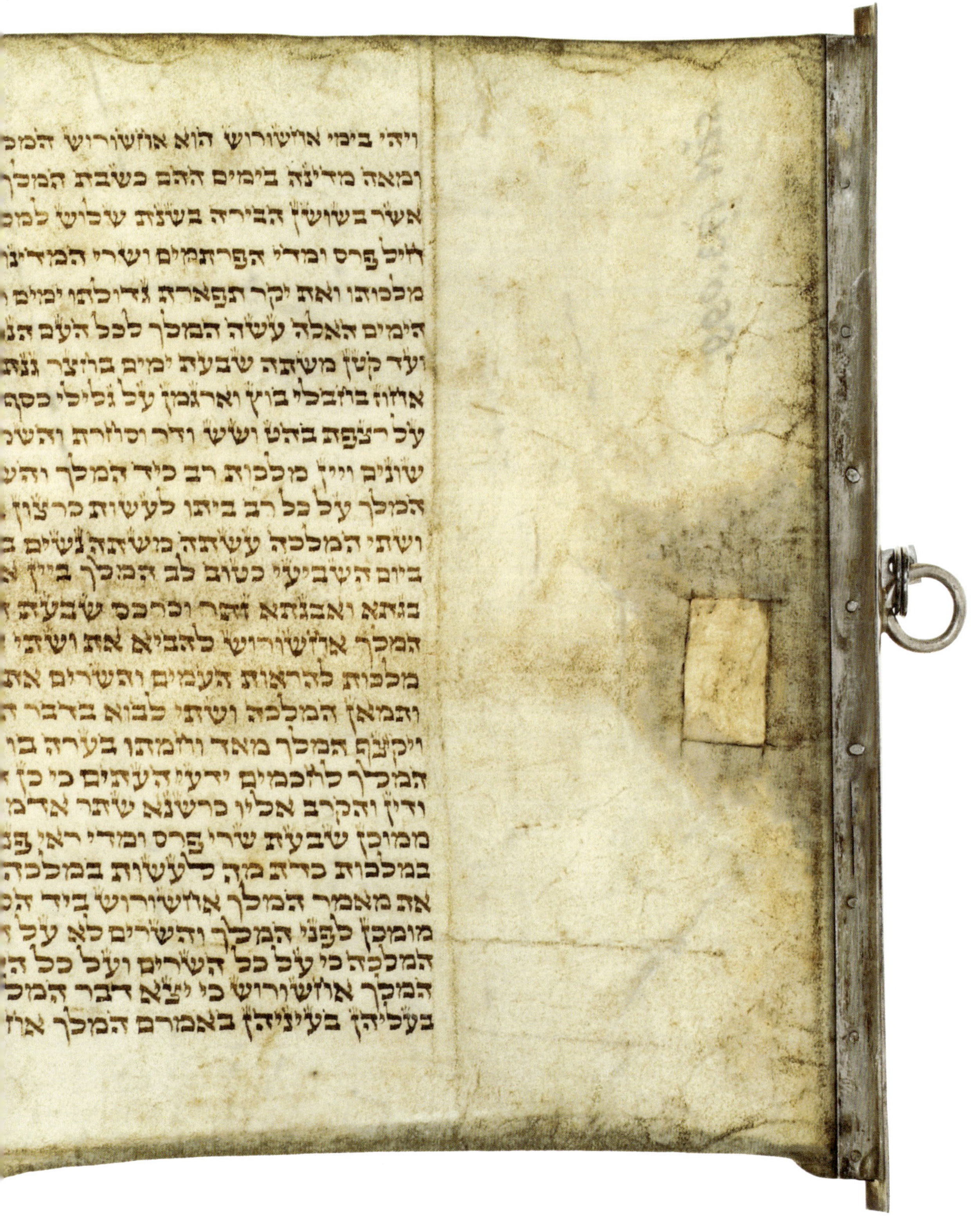
ויהי בימי אחשורוש הוא אחשורוש המ
ומאה מדינה בימים ההם כשבת המלך
אשר בשושן הבירה בשנת שלוש למ
חיל פרס ומדי הפרתמים ושרי המדינו
מלכותו ואת יקר תפארת גדולתו ימים
הימים האלה עשה המלך לכל העם הנ
ועד קטן משתה שבעת ימים בחצר גנת
אחוז בחבלי בוץ וארגמן על גלילי כסף
על רצפת בהט ושש ודר וסחרת והש
שונים ויין מלכות רב כיד המלך והש
המלך על כל רב ביתו לעשות כרצון
ושתי המלכה עשתה משתה נשים ב
ביום השביעי כטוב לב המלך ביין א
בגתא ואבגתא זתר וכרכס שבעת
המלך אחשורוש להביא את ושתי
מלכות להראות העמים והשרים את
ותמאן המלכה ושתי לבוא בדבר ה
ויקצף המלך מאד וחמתו בערה בו
המלך לחכמים ידעי העתים כי כן
ודין והקרב אליו כרשנא שתר אדמ
ממוכן שבעת שרי פרס ומדי ראי פני
במלכות כדת מה לעשות במלכה
את מאמר המלך אחשורוש ביד ה
מומכן לפני המלך והשרים לא על
המלכה כי על כל השרים ועל כל ה
המלך אחשורוש כי יצא דבר המל
בעליהן בעיניהן באמרם המלך א

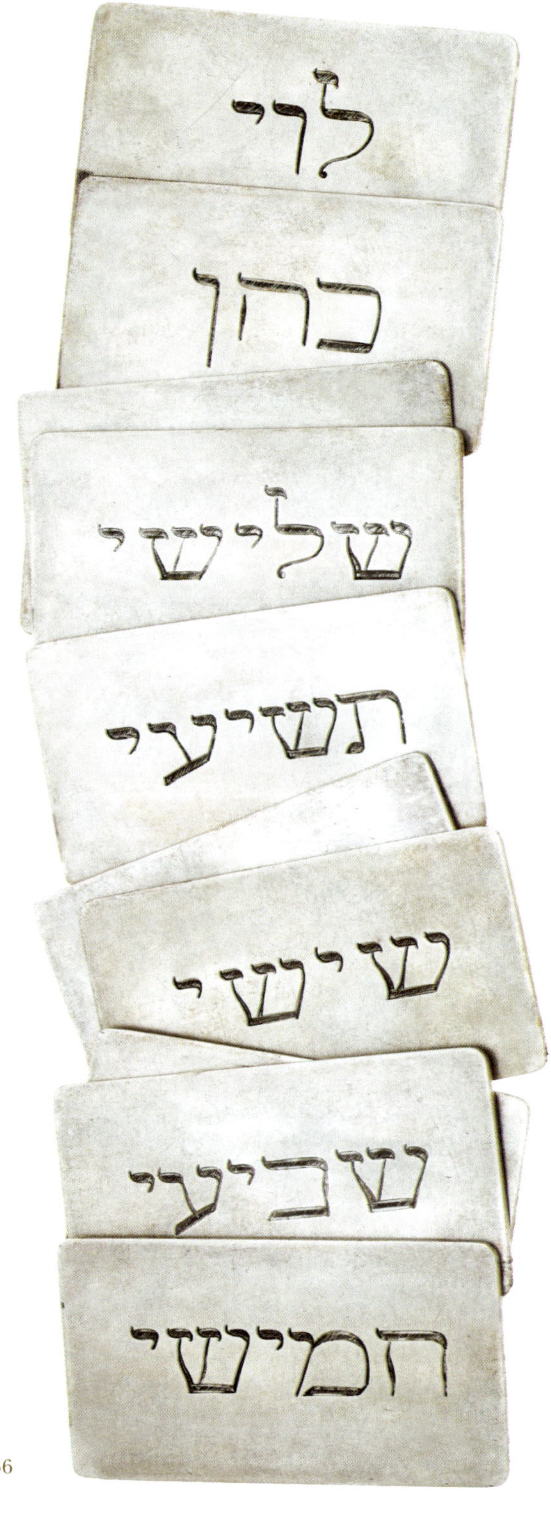

Cat. No. 466

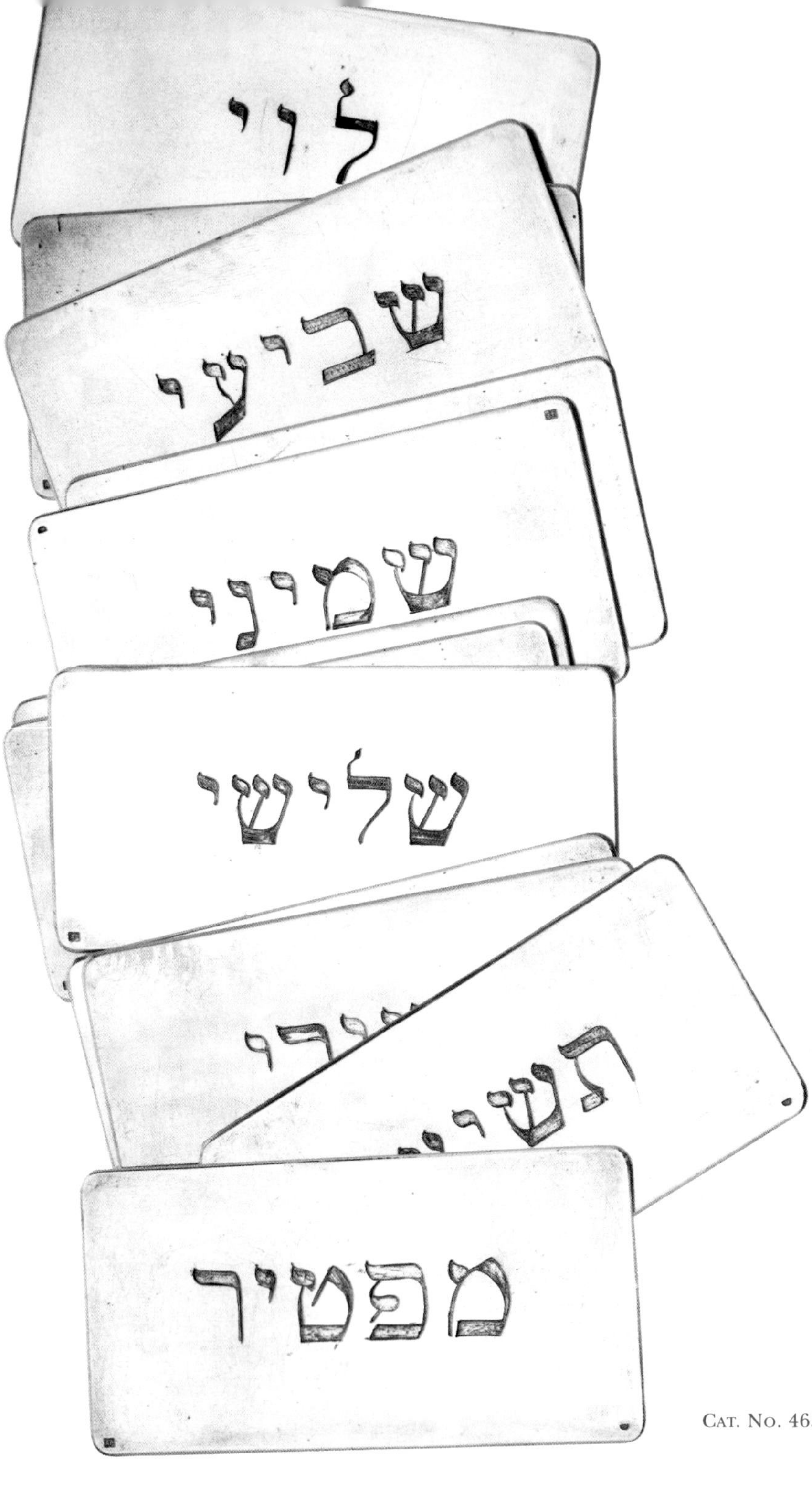

CAT. NO. 465